Citizenship Rights

The International Library of Essays on Rights
Series Editor: Tom Campbell

Titles in the Series:

Sexuality and Rights
Nicholas Bamforth

Rights: Concepts and Contexts
Brian H. Bix and Horacio Spector

Disability Rights
Peter Blanck

Democratic Rights
Corey Brettschneider

The Right to a Fair Trial
Thom Brooks

Global Minority Rights
Joshua Castellino

Indigenous Rights
Anthony J. Connolly

Civil Rights and Security
David Dyzenhaus

Language and Cultural Rights
Leslie Green

Group Rights
Peter Jones

Human Rights and Corporations
David Kinley

Genocide and Human Rights
Mark Lattimer

Animal Rights
Clare Palmer

Gender and Rights
Deborah L. Rhode and Carol Sanger

Health Rights
Michael J. Selgelid and Thomas Pogge

Citizenship Rights
Jo Shaw and Igor Štiks

Economic, Social and Cultural Rights
Manisuli Ssenyonjo

Theories of Rights
C.L. Ten

Bills of Rights
Mark Tushnet

Environmental Rights
Steve Vanderheiden

Citizenship Rights

Edited by

Jo Shaw
University of Edinburgh, UK

Igor Štiks
University of Edinburgh, UK

ASHGATE

© Jo Shaw and Igor Štiks 2013. For copyright of individual articles please refer to the Acknowledgements.

All rights reserved. No part of this publication may be reproduced, stored in a retrieval system or transmitted in any form or by any means, electronic, mechanical, photocopying, recording or otherwise without the prior permission of the publisher.

Wherever possible, these reprints are made from a copy of the original printing, but these can themselves be of very variable quality. Whilst the publisher has made every effort to ensure the quality of the reprint, some variability may inevitably remain.

Published by
Ashgate Publishing Limited
Wey Court East
Union Road
Farnham
Surrey GU9 7PT
England

Ashgate Publishing Company
Suite 3-1
110 Cherry Street
Burlington
VT 05401-3818
USA

www.ashgate.com

British Library Cataloguing in Publication Data
Citizenship rights. – (The international library of essays on rights)
1. Citizenship.
I. Series II. Shaw, Jo, 1961– III. Stiks, Igor, 1977–
342'.083–dc23

Library of Congress Control Number: 2013933846

ISBN 9781409426301

 Printed and bound in Great Britain by the MPG Books Group, UK

Contents

Acknowledgements	vii
Series Preface	ix
Introduction: What Do We Talk About When We Talk About Citizenship Rights?	
by Jo Shaw and Igor Štiks	xi

PART I   WHAT ARE CITIZENSHIP RIGHTS (AND DUTIES)?

1   Etienne Balibar (1988), 'Propositions on Citizenship', *Ethics*, **98**, pp. 723–30.   3
2   Tom Bottomore (1992), 'Citizenship and Social Class, Forty Years On', in
T.H. Marshall and Tom Bottomore, *Citizenship and Social Class*, London:
Pluto Press, pp. 55–96.   11
3   Margaret R. Somers (1994), 'Rights, Relationality, and Membership: Rethinking
the Making and Meaning of Citizenship', *Law and Social Inquiry*, **19**, pp. 63–112.   53
4   Zygmunt Bauman (2005), 'Freedom from, in and through the State: T.H. Marshall's
Trinity of Rights Revisited', *Theoria: A Journal of Social and Political Theory*, **44**,
pp. 13–27.   103
5   James Tully (2008), 'Two Meanings of Global Citizenship: Modern and Diverse',
in Michael A. Peters, Alan Britton and Harry Blee (eds), *Global Citizenship
Education: Philosophy, Theory and Pedagogy*, Rotterdam: Sense Publications,
pp. 15–39.   119

PART II   DIFFERENT STATUS, DIFFERENT RIGHTS

6   Seyla Benhabib (1999), 'Citizens, Residents, and Aliens in a Changing World:
Political Membership in the Global Era', *Social Research*, **66**, pp. 709–44.   147
7   Will Kymlicka (2003), 'Multicultural States and Intercultural Citizens', *Theory
and Research in Education*, **1**, pp. 147–69.   183
8   Rainer Bauböck (2011), 'Temporary Migrants, Partial Citizenship and
Hypermigration', *Critical Review of International Social and Political Philosophy*,
14, pp. 665–93.   207
9   Christian Joppke (2007), 'Transformation of Citizenship: Status, Rights, Identity',
Citizenship Studies, **11**, pp. 37–48.   237

PART III   CITIZENSHIP RIGHTS AND TRANSNATIONAL CHALLENGES

10   Jo Shaw (2007), 'E.U. Citizenship and Political Rights in an Evolving European
Union', *Fordham Law Review*, **75**, pp. 2549–79.   251

vi   *Citizenship Rights*

11 Richard Bellamy (2008), 'Evaluating Union Citizenship: Belonging, Rights and
Participation within the EU', *Citizenship Studies*, **12**, pp. 597–611.   283
12 David Owen (2011), 'Transnational Citizenship and the Democratic State: Modes
of Membership and Voting Rights', *Critical Review of International Social and
Political Philosophy*, **14**, pp. 641–63.   299
13 Yasemin Nuhoğlu Soysal (2000), 'Citizenship and Identity: Living in Diasporas in
Post-War Europe?', *Ethnic and Racial Studies*, **23**, pp. 1–15.   323

PART IV STRUGGLES OVER CITIZENSHIP RIGHTS

14 Engin F. Isin (2009), 'Citizenship in Flux: The Figure of the Activist Citizen',
Subjectivity, **29**, pp. 367–88.   341
15 Aihwa Ong (2006), 'Mutations in Citizenship', *Theory, Culture and Society*, **23**,
pp. 499–505.   363
16 Saskia Sassen (2002), 'The Repositioning of Citizenship: Emergent Subjects and
Spaces for Politics', *Berkeley Journal of Sociology*, **46**, pp. 4–25.   371
17 Nancy Fraser (2009), 'Feminism, Capitalism and the Cunning of History', *New
Left Review*, **56**, pp. 97–117.   393
18 Carole Pateman (2004), 'Democratizing Citizenship: Some Advantages of a Basic
Income', *Politics and Society*, **32**, pp. 89–105.   415
19 Diane Richardson (2000), 'Constructing Sexual Citizenship: Theorizing Sexual
Rights', *Critical Social Policy*, **20**, pp. 105–35.   433
20 David Harvey (2008), 'The Right to the City', *New Left Review*, **53**, pp. 23–40.   465

Name Index   483

Acknowledgements

Ashgate would like to thank our researchers and the contributing authors who provided copies, along with the following for their permission to reprint copyright material:

Berghahn Books for the essay: Zygmunt Bauman (2005), 'Freedom from, in and through the State: T.H. Marshall's Trinity of Rights Revisited', *Theoria: A Journal of Social and Political Theory*, **44**, pp. 13–27.

Berkeley Journal of Sociology for the essay: Saskia Sassen (2002), 'The Repositioning of Citizenship: Emergent Subjects and Spaces for Politics', *Berkeley Journal of Sociology*, **46**, pp. 4–25. Copyright © 2002 Saskia Sassen.

Fordham Law Review for the essay: Jo Shaw (2007), 'E.U. Citizenship and Political Rights in an Evolving European Union', *Fordham Law Review*, **75**, pp. 2549–79.

John Wiley & Sons for the essay: Margaret R. Somers (1994), 'Rights, Relationality, and Membership: Rethinking the Making and Meaning of Citizenship', *Law and Social Inquiry*, **19**, pp. 63–112. Copyright © 1994 American Bar Foundation. Reproduced with permission of Blackwell Publishing. Published by Wiley-Blackwell on behalf of the American Bar Foundation.

New Left Review for the essays: Nancy Fraser (2009), 'Feminism, Capitalism and the Cunning of History', *New Left Review*, **56**, pp. 97–117; David Harvey (2008), 'The Right to the City', *New Left Review*, **53**, pp. 23–40.

Palgrave Macmillan for the essay: Engin F. Isin (2009), 'Citizenship in Flux: The Figure of the Activist Citizen', *Subjectivity*, **29**, pp. 367–88. Copyright © 2009 Palgrave Macmillan.

Pluto Press for the essay: Tom Bottomore (1992), 'Citizenship and Social Class, Forty Years On', in T.H. Marshall and Tom Bottomore, *Citizenship and Social Class*, London: Pluto Press, pp. 55–96.

Sage Publications for the essays: Will Kymlicka (2003), 'Multicultural States and Intercultural Citizens', *Theory and Research in Education*, **1**, pp. 147–69. Copyright © 2003 Sage Publications; Aihwa Ong (2006), 'Mutations in Citizenship', *Theory, Culture and Society*, **23**, pp. 499–505. Copyright © 2006 *Theory, Culture and Society*. Published by Sage on behalf of The TCS Centre, Nottingham Trent University; Carole Pateman (2004), 'Democratizing Citizenship: Some Advantages of a Basic Income', *Politics and Society*, **32**, pp. 89–105. Copyright © 2004 Sage Publications; Diane Richardson (2000), 'Constructing Sexual Citizenship: Theorizing Sexual Rights', *Critical Social Policy*, **20**, pp. 105–35. Copyright © 2000 *Critical Social Policy*.

Sense Publishers for the essay: James Tully (2008), 'Two Meanings of Global Citizenship: Modern and Diverse', in Michael A. Peters, Alan Britton and Harry Blee (eds), *Global Citizenship Education: Philosophy, Theory and Pedagogy*, Rotterdam: Sense Publications, pp. 15–39. Copyright © 2008 Sense Publishers. All rights reserved.

Social Research for the essay: Seyla Benhabib, (1999), 'Citizens, Residents, and Aliens in a Changing World: Political Membership in the Global Era', *Social Research*, **66**, pp. 709–44. Copyright © 1999 New School for Social Research (www.socres.org).

Taylor & Francis for the essays: Rainer Bauböck (2011), 'Temporary Migrants, Partial Citizenship and Hypermigration', *Critical Review of International Social and Political Philosophy*, **14**, pp. 665–93. Copyright © 2011 Taylor & Francis; Christian Joppke (2007), 'Transformation of Citizenship: Status, Rights, Identity', *Citizenship Studies*, **11**, pp. 37–48. Copyright © 2007 Taylor & Francis; Richard Bellamy (2008), 'Evaluating Union Citizenship: Belonging, Rights and Participation within the EU', *Citizenship Studies*, **12**, pp. 597–611. Copyright © 2008 Taylor & Francis; David Owen (2011), 'Transnational Citizenship and the Democratic State: Modes of Membership and Voting Rights', *Critical Review of International Social and Political Philosophy*, **14**, pp. 641–63. Copyright © 2011 Taylor & Francis; Yasemin Nuhoğlu Soysal (2000), 'Citizenship and Identity: Living in Diasporas in Post-War Europe?', *Ethnic and Racial Studies*, **23**, pp. 1–15. Copyright © 2000 Taylor & Francis Ltd (http://www. tandfonline.com).

University of Chicago Press for the essay: Etienne Balibar (1988), 'Propositions on Citizenship', *Ethics*, **98**, pp. 723–30. Copyright © 1988 by The University of Chicago.

Every effort has been made to trace all the copyright holders, but if any have been inadvertently overlooked the publishers will be pleased to make the necessary arrangement at the first opportunity.

Publisher's Note

The material in this volume has been reproduced using the facsimile method. This means we can retain the original pagination to facilitate easy and correct citation of the original essays. It also explains the variety of typefaces, page layouts and numbering.

Series Preface

Much of contemporary moral, political and legal discourse is conducted in terms of rights and increasingly in terms of human rights. Yet there is considerable disagreement about the nature of rights, their foundations and their practical implications and more concrete controversies as to the content, scope and force and particular rights. Consequently the discourse of rights calls for extensive analysis in its general meaning and significance, particularly in relation to the nature, location of content of the duties and responsibilities that correlate with rights. Equally important is the determination of the forms of argument that are appropriate to establish whether or not someone or some group has or has not a particular right, and what that might entail in practice.

This series brings together essays that exhibit careful analysis of the concept of rights and detailed knowledge of specific rights and the variety of systems of rights articulation, interpretation, protection and enforcement. Volumes deal with general philosophical and practical issues about different sorts of rights, taking account of international human rights, regional rights conventions and regimes, and domestic bills of rights, as well as the moral and political literature concerning the articulation and implementation of rights.

The volumes are intended to assist those engaged in scholarly research by making available the most important and enduring essays on particular topics. Essays are reproduced in full with the original pagination for ease of reference and citation.

The editors are selected for their eminence in the study of law, politics and philosophy. Each volume represents the editor's selection of the most seminal recent essays in English on an aspect of rights or on rights in a particular field. An introduction presents an overview of the issues in that particular area of rights together with comments on the background and significance of the selected essays.

TOM CAMPBELL
Series Editor
Professorial Fellow, The Centre for Applied Philosophy and Public Ethics (CAPPE),
Charles Sturt University, Canberra

Introduction

WHAT DO WE TALK ABOUT WHEN WE TALK ABOUT CITIZENSHIP RIGHTS?

In the contemporary world, every claim, be it political, social, economic or private, is almost without exception founded on or justified by 'rights'. We see ourselves by definition as rights-bearing individuals. The rhetoric of rights is thus ubiquitous, to the point where we see a blurring of the very definition of what rights may be, not to mention a blurring of the boundaries between different bundles of rights, their sources and the various institutional practices through which they are 'enjoyed' or asserted. More specifically, 'human rights talk' dominates our discourse to the extent that it seems almost impossible to talk about any types of rights without relating them somehow to human rights, which are in themselves a vast category differently interpreted around the globe. Against that background, it is very tricky to define the concept of *citizenship rights*. Are these to be seen only as the rights *of citizens*, or more broadly as the rights related to *citizenship* as a status? And if so, how do they differ from the universalistic category of *human* rights, or as some might have it, *fundamental* rights?

Citizenship seems to be inextricably associated with rights, although the scope of citizenship rights has evidently varied across time and space, not least as the definition of 'citizen' has ebbed and flowed. Our understanding of citizenship is still under the spell of Arendtian definition; citizenship as 'the right to have rights', expanded by US Supreme Court judge Earl Warren in another famous quote as 'man's basic right', is frequently evoked in citizenship studies and general reflections on citizenship. In other words, citizenship is itself understood as a right, one of the fundamental human rights, that gives us access to other rights. Paradoxically, though, in human rights instruments worldwide this tends to appear more often in the negative sense of protection against statelessness, such as Article 15 of the 1948 Universal Declaration of Human Rights which recognizes the right to *a* nationality (that is, not a specific one) but focuses more on protection against arbitrary withdrawal than on the character of citizenship as a connection to a polity.

Although citizenship encompasses more than rights, rights figure prominently, and without exception, in all attempts to define citizenship and its constitutive components, which are often proposed as a trinity. For example, Christian Joppke (Chapter 9) draws a distinction between citizenship as *status*, as *rights* and as *identity*. Antje Wiener (1994) suggests the use of the categories of *rights*, *access* and *belonging* to express a similar endeavour to invest the notion of citizenship, understood as polity membership, with meaning. Rainer Bauböck's (2001) triadic division consists of *membership, rights* and *practices*. Richard Bellamy (2004) proposes a triad of citizenship as *rights, belonging* and *participation*. Finally, Seyla Benhabib (Chapter 6) offers a slightly different view by segmenting citizenship into collective *identity*, political *membership* and *social rights and claims*.

Noticeable in all these definitions is the absence of duties. Yet the historical citizenship contract involved an exchange: *rights* guaranteed by authorities (city-states, empires, states ...)

were counterbalanced with *duties* and *loyalty*. Citizenship, its political and social function, its meaning in the history of humanity was determined by the dynamic between rights and duties. As if responding to the coming rise of rights-based movements and claims, a popular American president, advised his fellow citizens not to ask 'what your country can do for you' but instead to ask 'what *you* can do for your country'. Historically one of the main services that one could offer to one's state was military duty. As recently as 1974 Raymond Aron (1991 [1974], p. 704), while referring to an anti-militaristic counter-culture, emphasizes that '*le citoyen a la vocation de soldat*', the citizen has the vocation to be soldier. However today in most of the high income countries, and indeed in many others, military service has become an experience remembered only by middle-aged and older people. In the present-day imagination and in theoretical reflections on citizenship, clearly influenced by the progressive withdrawal of conscription, the citizen's main vocation is to be a rights-bearer, and thus capable of claiming rights where such a formal assertion is needed, but certainly not the one primarily subjected to duties. Nevertheless one should not forget that there are still some important duties attached to citizenship status that define a 'good' citizen. They involve above all paying taxes and obeying laws, and in some countries, an additional duty may appear, such as a duty to vote or the duty to participate in jury trial processes. Moreover, despite the widespread disappearance of conscription in western liberal states, those same states still demand elements of loyalty and allegiance on the part of their citizens. This can be particularly pertinent for those who acquire citizenship after birth by naturalization, as migrants. But states such as the UK have in recent years enhanced their largely discretionary powers to strip even birthright citizenship from those deemed disloyal (for example, because of association with terrorist activities), building on the longstanding power to remove citizenship from those who have obtained it fraudulently (for example, by lying in order to obtain asylum status, which in turn led to citizenship status).

In order to understand how the different components of citizenship – including citizenship rights – actually interact with each other within a given social, political, economic and international context, we use the term *citizenship regime*. In our previous works we have defined citizenship regime as a workable analytical tool for understanding citizenship both generally and in certain specific regional circumstances (Shaw and Štiks, 2012). Citizenship regime as an analytical construct captures both the relational and the institutional elements of citizenship, and – as such – can offer a useful framework for understanding of citizenship rights, their expansion and depletion, their formal and substantial existence, as well as their uneven distribution in contemporary societies. Breaking it down further, a 'citizenship regime' comprises the citizenship laws, regulations and administrative practices regarding the citizenship status of individuals, including existing mechanisms of political participation. More precisely, a citizenship regime is based on a given country's citizenship legislation defining the body of citizens (that is, who is entitled to citizenship and all duties and rights attached to that status), on administrative policies in dealing with citizenship matters and the status of individuals (citizens and non-citizens alike), and, finally, on the official or non-official dynamic of political participation, inclusion and exclusion. As we argued in an earlier essay, 'The concept encompasses a range of different legal statuses, viewed in their wider political context, which are central to the exercise of civil rights, political membership and – in many cases – full socio-economic membership in a particular territory' (Shaw and Štiks,

2010, p. 5). Citizenship regime also represents a useful analytical device for combining the two main ways in which the idea of citizenship is 'coded' with different articulations of the membership bond (Habermas, 1998, p. 404): 'citizenship-as-legal-status' and 'citizenship-as-community-bond'.

The 'regime' concept aligns the study of citizenship with a broader literature from international relations which uses the concept of regime in order to capture patterns of behaviour (Krasner, 1982), bringing together principles, rules, norms and decision-making procedures. But within the field of comparative politics, studying citizenship as a 'regime' adapts also an approach drawn from gender studies where scholars use the term 'gender regimes' in order to refer to the range of institutionalized practices relating to how gender issues are regulated in a given society, acknowledging that these differ from state to state (Walby, 2004). Jane Jenson has also applied this term in the context of citizenship studies. She defines a 'citizenship regime' as 'the institutional arrangements, rules and understandings that guide and shape concurrent policy decisions and expenditures of states, problem definitions by states and citizens, and claims-making by citizens' (Jenson, 2007, p. 55).

It is, theoretically and practically, important fully to take into account the link between the citizen and the state. This will include the rules and processes governing the acquisition and loss of membership statuses, external citizenship and various internal 'quasi-citizenship' statuses, as well as the rights and duties which are central to the exercise of full membership of the polity. But that formal set of relationships also needs to be placed within the wider context of political contestation over the question of 'who belongs?' and 'why?', and of concrete struggles over the content and enjoyment of citizenship rights. In other words, the boundaries of polity membership are not just external, but internal as well. Formal possession of citizenship does not guarantee lifelong protection of a defined list of citizens' rights – these may also depend upon territory: that is, upon the place of residence. On the other hand, depending on circumstances, those without formal citizenship might still in practice enjoy certain citizenship rights as a result of their residence status. Thus both expansion and reduction of rights of citizens and non-citizens alike depend on the actual functioning of a citizenship regime, which is always a result of social and political struggles in a given place and in a given time. Finally, it is not just formal rules which define citizenship regimes, but also informal ideologies, narratives, beliefs and practices, which are often just as important.

A citizenship regime could also be said to encompass certain key individual and collective rights protected by national and international human rights law, such as minority rights and non-discrimination rights which profoundly impact upon the exercise of full civic membership within a society and a polity, in particular the right to non-discrimination on grounds of race or ethnic origin, gender and religious affiliation. This is the case even where the exercise of these rights is not strictly limited by reference to citizenship status or where the source of the norm being invoked for protection is not to be found in the national constitution or legislation, but in international law. In other words, no citizenship regime is an island unto itself. It is influenced by other, often neighbouring citizenship regimes, and, conversely, in the age of intensive migrations and the proliferation of dual and multiple citizenship, every national citizenship regime necessarily extends beyond its own borders (and equally is permeated by other regimes).

In short, citizenship regime is constituted, and thus conditioned, by a specific legal set-up that includes not only citizenship laws, and international conventions and norms, but also laws and regulations on public activities. In this respect, citizens, at home or in flux, are determined in their actions by their status and attached rights as well as by legal strait-jackets that condition the practice of citizenship. This influences their social and political struggles, but, on the other hand, it is only through these struggles – as the history of citizenship shows – that citizenship regimes change.

Changing Palette of Citizenship Rights

No discussion of citizenship rights can avoid T.H. Marshall and his ground-breaking 1949 lecture on 'Citizenship and Social Class' in which he divides citizenship according to a typology of three classes of right: *civic*; *political*; and *social*. These rights correspond to three distinct phases in the history of modern citizenship or, to be more precise, in England. In the eighteenth century, citizenship meant the introduction of *civic* rights, entailing individual freedom, the right to own property and the right to justice. *Political* rights, as growing participation in the making or the work of government, would start to expand only a century later and the process would last until the twentieth century. *Social* rights, including economic, educational and social privileges, where the goal was to secure a more egalitarian national society, were acquired in the twentieth century (Marshall, 1992 [1950], pp. 10–14). The process was related to the development of capitalist societies and their expansion. Therefore, civic rights meant mostly economic rights and, at the global level, the rights of commerce or, in reality, the right of Europeans to travel, to engage with others (peacefully or forcefully) and to trade (under their own terms) with the rest of the world (Tully, Chapter 5). The spread of political rights is directly related to emancipatory struggles from bourgeois revolutions to the incorporation of 'dangerous classes' of growing labouring masses into national citizenship in the times of world-wide imperialism of European nations (Balibar, Chapter 1). Finally, growing social-democratic, socialist and communist movements, especially the success of the October revolution in Russia, and the economic depressions and social conflicts in the West, would eventually result in the incorporation of social rights – including reductions in working hours, fair(er) wages, welfare benefits and accessible health care systems – into the bundle of rights guaranteed by citizenship status.

One should not forget that, until the twentieth century, enjoyment of citizenship rights, especially political rights, was reserved for a male minority possessing a certain social-economic status. The twentieth century brought the effective political and social incorporation of vast populations on earth into full citizenship. Besides the incorporation of the working class into the suffrage, through the abolition of property qualifications and similar restrictions, the first half of the twentieth century brought finally, in waves and unevenly, political autonomy to women. The process of decolonization after the Second World War would eventually, by the 1970s, bring into effective citizenship substantial populations who were previously the subjects of colonial rule or simply 'the wretched of the earth'.

The expansion of citizenship and social rights after the Second World War, during a period of unprecedented economic growth in many parts of the world, aimed at annulling or changing citizenship's historic attributes: citizenship status as a privilege with the accompanying social inequality. Formally, with the process of decolonization completed, citizenship status as such for the majority of the world's population ceased to represent a privilege; however, unprecedented migrations soon turned many of those new citizens of freshly minted independent states into non-citizens in host countries of immigration, which more often than not happened also to be the former colonial centres. The struggle against inequality thus turned out to be a much more complex one. Marshall himself accused citizenship of being 'the architect of legitimate social inequality'. Although citizenship is 'a principle in equality', it was not historically 'in conflict … with the inequalities of capitalist society' (Marshall, 1992 [1950], p. 33).

Around the same time, historic struggles against social inequality were also waged in the countries of 'really existing' or state socialism where not only social but properly speaking 'socialist rights' were the most prominent characteristic of citizenship. If social rights came in the context of the drive towards equality proclaimed by modern citizenship against inequality, socialist rights aimed at bridging this gap by annulling the detrimental logic of markets and replacing it with a different economic system that was supposed to ensure the widest social equality. These rights proclaimed in socialist states across the globe went a step further than the welfare state and had finally mixed results (achievements and disappointments). Among other rights, they guaranteed full employment, a publicly funded education and health system, housing rights and, as in Yugoslavia, workers' self-management as social ownership and workplace democracy. Both the West's social and the East's socialist rights would, however, come under renewed scrutiny during the 1970s and dramatically by the end of the 1980s.

At the beginning of the 1990s the state socialist regimes collapsed and with them disappeared almost all socialist rights previously enjoyed by their citizens. Their incorporation into the market economy structure was followed by one more surprise: one could now see the dissipation of the social rights that had been associated with the post-war Western democracies and their welfare states. A set of economic and social policies that became known as 'neo-liberalism' took root from the late 1970s onwards (Harvey, 2005) signalling, historically speaking, the end of a short period of maybe three decades during which social rights were seen as the constitutive part of citizenship rights. Since this period the welfare state has been in a steady decline along with a certain egalitarian vision of modern societies and citizenship. Around the same time we witnessed the rise of cultural or group rights as well as the shift from distribution to recognition (Fraser, 1995). This latter move is crucial for understanding citizenship when it is coupled with rights-based rhetoric and mobilizations. Citizenship policies also changed under the pressure of migration and growing cultural diversity that unleashed different responses. As Joppke (Chapter 9) concludes, liberalized access to citizenship was coupled with the reduction of social rights for all. Recognition of minority rights transformed the identity dimension of citizenship while at the same time triggering the response from the state towards integrationist and restrictive approaches for newcomers.

A rather simplistic belief in the constant enlargement of citizenship rights in liberal democracies made many perceive the cultural and identity rights as yet another historic layer of citizenship rights. What is at stake today, however, is a new dynamic between these different bundles of rights in the face of new realities at a global scale that over the last three decades have deeply transformed contemporary citizenship regimes. In this context, citizenship rights, the practices which engage with them, and the task of understanding these bodies of rights, face, in our view, three general challenges: global markets; transnational and substate phenomena; and human rights.

Transformation of Citizenship Rights: Contemporary Challenges

Policies and practices of citizenship are conditioned by economic and especially financial flows more than ever before. For Somers (2008, p. 1), our age is marked by

> conflicts over the balance of power among the institutions, practices and discourses of states, markets, and civil societies. Whether these conflicts result in regimes of relatively democratic socially inclusive citizenship rights or regimes of social exclusion and statelessness largely depends on the ability of civil society, the public sphere, and the social state to exert countervailing force against the corrosive effects of market-driven governance.

The contemporary landscape therefore reveals deep inequalities, new cosmopolitan elites and new cosmopolitan underdogs:

> [T]he 'ruling class' of modern society, with its internal hierarchies, is multilingual, multicultural, and migratory ... The national passport has changed its meaning (at least for the dominant nationalities); it no longer expresses (except no doubt in the United States) allegiance to an autonomous power, but, rather, a conditional right of access to 'cosmopolis' of communications and modern financial transactions. (Balibar, 1988 [Chapter 1], p. 9)

The trend expressed here by Etienne Balibar at the end of the 1980s only grew in importance with neo-liberal expansion and the globalization of capital transactions and production. 'Mutations in citizenship' are precisely its disarticulation and deterritorialization brought about by markets, new technologies and population shifts (Ong, Chapter 15). The world might be seen not only as divided into states but *zones* of economic growth and decay, often, such as in big cities, coexisting next to each other in dramatic contrasts of wealth and misery. We hear these days many voices, from those of the '*indignados*' and '*occupy*' movements to those of scholars, denouncing the impact of markets on equality and the rights of citizens. For Margaret Somers (2008, p. 2) market fundamentalism has been undermining democratic society, especially in the USA, by creating a vast amount of *de facto* excluded rightless people: 'three decades of what has become market-driven governance are transforming growing numbers of once rights-bearing citizens into socially excluded internally rightless and stateless persons'. Faced with ruthless markets and especially their crash in 2008 and all of the consequences of global economic troubles Somers is not the only one to advocate the right to social inclusion as a basic citizenship right.

The privileged site of modern citizenship (the nation-state) appears too weak to ensure citizenship rights for its citizens, to guarantee effectively protection (including social protection), and thus to require loyalty in return or the full respect of duties. Modern citizenship has been indeed transformed by the process of globalization translated as the unhindered dominance of capital and political power (financial centres, multinational companies and some rising and some declining states). An unprecedented challenge came in a supranational regional market integration in Europe, followed in 1993 by the introduction of a form of European citizenship ('citizenship of the European Union') which essentially only confers rights, even though the texts also refer to duties. However, the extent to which this new legal status adds to citizenship rights conventionally defined remains a contested question. As a (complementary(?) movement to supranational processes of integration, we witness constant fragmentation at subnational level where substate units – through seeking more autonomy or even independence – are trying to assure for themselves (or their elites) better bargaining position (direct control of resources or capital and human flows) vis-à-vis global markets.

All these movements create multiple and often competing sites of sovereignty and destabilize or shatter existing political communities by inducing processes of (sometimes violent) reconfiguration. The rise of cultural rights and recognition politics, and with them the prominence of the right to self-determination and often territorial self-governance, provide a basis for what appear today as legitimate political demands grounded in collectivistic identities, mostly ethnic, linguistic or sectarian/religious ones. Contemporary citizenship regimes are constituted or refigured in relation to internal fragmentations or disintegrations as we can witness in the Balkans, the Middle East, the Caucasus and Africa but equally in the constitutional monarchies of Western Europe such as Spain, Belgium and the UK where political devolution and the drive towards autonomy and independence influence citizenship practices and political visions, stripping bare the essence of compound or union states and putting in question their legitimacy.

The displacement of sovereignty and constant recomposition of political communities are challenging the *territoriality* of citizenship regimes. After all, the question is *where* are the rights granted and protected, and by whom, and *where* are they enjoyed, and by whom? Global migrations have changed the relationship between modern states and their citizens; they cannot count on each other 'from the cradle to the grave', so to speak, because almost nowhere can one find the Rawlsian imaginary closed society to which the entry is 'only by birth and exit from it is only by death'. It is not only that people move (citizens leaving to other places where they become newcomers while at the same time at home someone else is a newcomer), but then even if they remain firmly grounded in their places of birth until the end of their days, a vast majority can expect to live under changing citizenship regimes and authorities.

As a result of migrating populations or identity-based politics, political communities become increasingly overlapping in particular as regards their respective citizenship regimes. This complicates the range of citizenship rights and their beneficiaries; they, or some portion of them, are often enjoyed, apart from resident citizens, by non-citizen residents, non-resident citizens and even (usually in cases of ethnic diasporic solidarity) by non-citizens who are also non-residents. Naturally, migration flows result in a proliferation of partial citizenship for migrants (Bauböck, Chapter 8), dual or even multiple citizenship and diasporic communities. All of this leads to progressive decoupling of membership, belonging, identity and rights (Soysal, Chapter 13) or, rather, to their complex combinations. Blurred borders of citizenship regimes suggest that, irrespective of what is found to be normatively acceptable according to certain conceptions of justice, we will continue to live in a world of multiple statuses, identities and loyalties and vacillating rights, duties and responsibilities.

Human rights and international norms, as well as their use in political and social struggles, are surely yet another specific challenge for modern citizenship rights. To what point are human rights and citizenship rights compatible? What should have precedence? Can human rights replace citizenship rights in such a diverse world as ours? Should we, as suggested by Tom Bottomore (Chapter 2), 'examine civil, political and social rights in the framework of a conception of general human rights, rather than citizenship' (1992, p. 47)? It is difficult to imagine that scenario. The historical and present destiny of the stateless shows that human rights are reduced to their basics in humanitarian interventions or to nothing at all in instances of extreme violence, if one is left without 'man's basic right', namely citizenship of one of the world's internationally recognized political entities. From Auschwitz and recent concentration camps in Bosnia to the challenges currently facing refugees, we can see individuals whose status is questioned because there is no state to which they belong or can prove to belong, because they were stripped of their citizenship, or their states are not recognized internationally or internally as legitimate protecting entities. Universalistic claims of human rights clash with particularities of citizenship or the sovereignty claims of various collectivities and groups for self-determination (Benhabib, 1999, [Chapter 6], p. 148), while at the same time they provide ground for legitimacy of these claims, which are by their nature exclusionary. On the other hand, it is equally difficult for us to imagine – or if we can imagine, we certainly cannot accept – citizenship rights as arbitrarily decided by each sovereign state with no reference to human rights and basic international norms.

Yasemin Soysal (1994, p. 1) argues, over-optimistically it seems, that we are witness to 'a new and more universal concept of citizenship [that] has unfolded in the post-war era, one whose organizing and legitimating principles are based on universal personhood rather than national belonging'. In the post-war period, human rights are a global organizing principle, Soysal maintains, and the existence of a transnational community, international conventions and codes transcend the nation-state and confer rights on individuals regardless of citizenship. Indeed, some citizenship rights, especially for residents, are not conditioned by acquisition of citizenship. Nevertheless, in spite of the rights and privileges enjoyed by legal long-term residents – sometimes termed denizens – only citizenship can secure complete integration into a political community and the enjoyment of the full range of rights and protections, especially political rights and protection against deportation (although those who remain dual citizens are still vulnerable to exclusion, which can come from the unilateral withdrawal of citizenship from those deemed a threat to the public). It is not surprising then that migrants and residents usually aspire to become citizens, even as it becomes harder in many contexts to gain permanent residence or settlement in the host state. This can be explained by the ineffectiveness of rights based on universal personhood, not least because there is no effective authority which can ensure that they are enforced. However, at least within the European political space under the European Union and the European Convention of Human Rights and to a lesser extent under other jurisdictions such as the Inter-American human rights regimes, human rights norms and international conventions do none the less interfere with, exercise some influence upon and offer some prospect of harmonization between citizenship regimes and the rights they offer to their citizens or residents within their jurisdiction. This is despite the fact that the right to be a citizen is not generally recognized in these instruments in those terms. In that context, courts have become central institutions for the protection of these rights, often challenging the legitimacy of national legislative choices to restrict rights for non-citizens. Equally, the legitimacy of such judicial interventions has come under challenge from those arguing in favour of legislative sovereignty in relation to the disposition of citizenship rights. In fact, structures of legal rights whether enshrined in legislation or judicially enforced can and often do protect not only legal non-citizen residents, but also irregular immigrants, or '*sans papiers*', a group who used to receive the benefit of periodic regularizations under national law, but who are increasingly pushed right to the margins of society as immigration regimes incorporate ever harder boundaries and ever stricter conditions of entry.

Citizenship Rights Struggles Today

Struggles for citizenship rights are always struggles for equality. The citizenship dialectic between the promise of equality and its historical record of inequality is where all citizenship struggles, translated mostly as struggles for rights and hardly ever for duties, find their breeding ground. These struggles are based on an understanding of citizenship rather as 'the right to claim rights' than merely 'the right to have rights' (Isin, 2009 [Chapter 14], p. 345). These contemporary struggles can be generally divided into three groups: struggles against depletions of citizenship rights; struggles for access to citizenship rights (by citizens and non-citizens alike); and struggles for the recognition of new citizenship rights.

Before describing concrete demands, we should mention two contemporary depletions related to citizenship rights that form the context for various struggles. One can observe a steady depletion of existing citizenship rights. Reduced access to public services and social provisions – that are not seen, as we observed above, as part of basic citizenship rights any more – is coupled with privatizations and enclosures of public and common space and resources as well as with the increased securitization of public and private life, limits to personal freedoms and freedom of movement. On the other hand, there is a reduction of access to citizenship for residents (longer periods of permanent residence, citizenship and integration tests, strict rules on probity (for example, absolute exclusion of those carrying criminal convictions however minor and however old), probationary citizenship concepts and very high financial costs, etc.) and to temporary or permanent resident status for masses of illegal migrants (criminalization of migrations is a common feature of government policies).

A quick look over a vast array of demands reveals the contestation mostly over the following (non-exhaustive) aspects of citizenship regimes: democratic rights and freedoms; social rights; health; urban conditions; human security; education; economic rights such as decent living and distribution of wealth; the commons, including digital commons; ecological rights; access to natural resources and energy; sexual rights; and gender equality. Depending on claims and demands, these struggles necessarily have different 'scales' – ranging from local, regional, national, continental and global – but due to mutual dependence some of these demands must be put on the agenda across all these levels. We might be able to address locally the use of local natural sources as well as the social and political life of smaller communities. However, a regional approach would be needed for larger communities. Furthermore certain groups in authority – typically residing at the state level – will claim the monopoly on violent and coercive means to enforce and protect certain fundamental rights where this is deemed necessary. It is today still the state level at which we address most of our social, health, educational and economic claims as well as those related to management of resources such as waters, land, minerals or oil. Partly this is to do with the territory of the (receding) welfare state, which is based on state-level segmented tax territories, and partly this is to do with how international law privileges states as actors. However in a globalized world fundamental economic policies can rarely be decided upon solely at the national level; global action – where there is no single final arbiter and where democratic legitimacy may be questionable – is needed when it comes to ecological rights, rights to health protection in the cases of epidemics, sustainability of the earth's natural resources or facing up to climate-related changes. The question is also whether, under current conditions, some rights, traditionally associated with local or state power, such as the rights of urban citizens, can actually be realized solely within the state framework any longer, especially in those cosmopolitan metropolises which also serve as the hubs of global economy.

Common to all these levels are the rights related to gender equality and sexuality that have been traditionally placed on the public/private borderline. The struggle for gender equality and rights remains high on the agenda of emancipatory movements across the globe. In spite of formal political equality (which is not the global rule), many social and economic practices push women outside political and social arenas, especially in the so-called third or developing world. More subtle types of discrimination are at work in the democratic societies where women are still paid less and are at the same time under pressure of both professional and household work. Their formal political and social equality cannot be disconnected from their economic status and general problems related to the impact of the global capitalist economy on gender relations (see Sassen, Chapter 16; Fraser, Chapter 17; Pateman, Chapter 18).

Struggles over citizenship rights bring to the fore new actors who are lending a different meaning to what it is to be a 'global citizen'. Global activism such as for instance the one related to the World Social Forum process or the emergence of the new movements centred on social justice and democratization of both authoritarian and current liberal democratic regimes represent what Tully calls global 'diverse citizenship'. In contradistinction to the idea of modern citizenship as a codified status which successfully conceals the hierarchies with it, the limited extent of democratic rights and global relationships of subordination, the ideas of global active citizenship and civic practices are a counterweight to the domestic and international law limitations on exercising democratic citizenship (Tully, 2008 [Chapter 5], pp. 137–41). The figure of the 'activist citizen', as opposed to the active citizen, is evoked as the one that makes a difference and creates a new space for citizenship (Isin, 2009 [Chapter 14], p. 355). New technologies gave rise to new types of social and political mobilizations whose various demands and claims will inevitably challenge the current status quo of citizenship rights.

One 'space' in particular has been historically related to the origins and history of citizenship. Cities are the main site of citizenship, where the formation of political subjectivities capable of making claims takes place. The 'global city' (Sassen) or 'global assemblages' (Ong) are those nodal points of contemporary citizenship. Although in terms of citizenship and residence rights still governed by the states, these entities, by the virtue of their economic activities, social stratification, cosmopolitan culture, multilingualism and artistic production, represent a huge challenge to a national citizenship and national political communities based on the assumption of a fixed set of shared identity and values. Cities are also places of concentration of wealth and of enormous inequalities, which creates an explosive dynamics between exclusion and inclusions, and outbursts of violence. The relationship between citizens and the urban environment in which they spend most of their lives thus turns out to be crucial for the enjoyment of citizenship rights and entitlements. Should we then include within the body of citizenship rights, or even human rights, 'the right to the city', as suggested by David Harvey (Chapter 20)? The right to decent urban living, equal distribution and participation seems crucial for human and social development and thus cannot be separated from the ways people enact their citizenship, express claims and enjoy rights in the contemporary world.

Outline of the Volume

This volume contains some of the most important reflections and studies on citizenship rights. They offer both description and analysis of citizenship rights but also put the question of rights and citizenship rights into a wider historical, social and political perspective.

What Are Citizenship Rights (and Duties)

The contributions of the first part sketch the historic development of citizenship rights until the present day. In 'Propositions on Citizenship' (Chapter 1) Etienne Balibar traces the history of citizenship through struggles for equality and rights and pays special attention to the formation of modern citizenship as 'national' citizenship in the context of class struggles. Balibar brings us then to contemporary societies and examines national citizenship in the context of immigration and the rise of racism in Western Europe. He sees alarming divisions between the privileged and the underprivileged, especially socially segregated immigrant masses. Written roughly at the same time, Tom Bottomore assesses in 'Citizenship and Social Class, Forty Years On' (Chapter 2) T.H. Marshall's seminal work on citizenship and the social class. He expresses similar concerns about the state of civic, political and particularly social rights in the context of the failure of the state socialist regimes and economies and the rise of neo-liberal global economy. Margaret Somers in 'Rights, Relationality, and Membership: Rethinking the Making and Meaning of Citizenship' (Chapter 3) also examines T.H. Marshall's classic account of the historical development of citizenship rights and offers a slightly different picture of its origins. She traces the institutional roots of modern citizenship before the advent of capitalism. She claims that the rise of citizenship rights is not a direct result of capitalist transformation but stems from medieval legal revolutions in England as well as from local legal and political cultures.

Zygmunt Bauman in 'Freedom from, in and through the State: T.H. Marshall's Trinity of Rights Revisited' (Chapter 4) revisits Marshall's 'trinity of rights' and detects its progressive dismantling as result of the simultaneous processes of deregulation, privatization and individualization. Bauman asserts the crucial importance of receding social rights for the struggle for and the protection of civil and political rights in today's 'globalized' world. James Tully in 'Two Meanings of Global Citizenship: Modern and Diverse' (Chapter 5) analyses the development of modern citizenship rights from civil-economic, democratic, social to multicultural rights. He contrasts two modes of citizenship (modern and diverse): legally and institutionalized status of modern citizenship and the acts of diverse citizenship not bound to status and often operating outside the framework of the legally prescribed field of citizens' participation and activity. He gives a historical overview of how these rights were exercised, especially in the international arena where they favoured the dominant economic and political position of the West, but also of the countercurrent of global diverse citizenship understood as negotiated practices of civic grass-roots engagement in the public sphere.

Different Status, Different Rights

In the second part, we examine the state of citizenship rights in contemporary societies marked by a complex stratification of individuals according to their citizenship-related status: citizens; aliens; residents; (temporary) migrants; asylum seekers; refugees; *sans-papiers*, etc. Seyla Benhabib in 'Citizens, Residents, and Aliens in a Changing World: Political Membership in the Global Era' (Chapter 6) writes about political incorporation in liberal democracies. In her opinion, there is an inherent paradox: no liberal democracy can close its borders to aliens, refugees and asylum seekers but, on the other hand, a liberal democracy should have a right to define immigration and incorporation policies. Benhabib sees the relationship to foreigners and 'others' as a moral and political test of contemporary democracies. One of the most prominent advocates of multicultural citizenship, Will Kymlicka, claims in 'Multicultural States and Intercultural Citizens' (Chapter 7) that liberal societies must remedy the excesses of unicultural nation-building by rejecting the ownership of the state by the dominant group, by recognition and accommodation polices and by acknowledging historic injustices. These states should also move from a unitary model towards federal and consociational arrangements to accommodate multicultural demands. However, he sees tensions between multiculturalism and interculturalism among citizens since multicultural polices at the state level reduce interculturalism at the individual level. Nevertheless, promotion of individual interculturalism should not, in his view, undermine the justice of multicultural state institutions. In the following chapter, 'Temporary Migrants, Partial Citizenship and Hypermigration' (Chapter 8), Rainer Bauböck accounts for a different type of challenge for national communities: a growing phenomenon of temporary migration in its multiple forms results in partial citizenship and, therefore, partial enjoyment of rights for temporary migrants in both the country of origin and in the country of (temporary?) residence. Free movement is to be promoted, argues this author, but pushed to its extremes it might undermine intergenerational and territorial polities. In 'Transformation of Citizenship: Status, Rights, Identity' (Chapter 9) Christian Joppke summarizes recent transformations of citizenship understood as status, rights and identity. He concludes that a liberalized access to citizenship is coupled with reduction of social rights and increase of minority rights. However, contemporary societies reveal a conflict between their actual heterogeneity and official attempts at their integration.

Citizenship Rights and Transnational Challenges

The third part focuses on transnational phenomena as one of the major challenges to citizenship rights. We are witnessing an important increase in citizenship rights in the EU. European citizenship interferes with previously exclusive national sovereign prerogatives but, as legislation and practice show, it has its limits. Jo Shaw in 'E.U. Citizenship and Political Rights in an Evolving European Union' (Chapter 10) examines the emergence of citizenship rights for non-nationals, especially voting rights at the European, national and local level for residents who are at the same time EU citizens. However, the 'mobile' EU citizens are still negligible in numbers and EU citizenship certainly does not replace some fundamental rights provided by national citizenship. Even long-term 'permanent' residents are still excluded from full citizenship rights without acquiring citizenship of their host country. In 'Evaluating Union Citizenship: Belonging, Rights and Participation within the EU' (Chapter 11) Richard Bellamy also assesses the effects of European citizenship on belonging, rights and participation. Bellamy finds the decoupling of these three components as problematic, especially when the exercise of rights and to certain extent participation is not followed by an anchored sense of belonging. The development of political participation at EU level, in his view, should not be an attempt at the creation of European *demos* but a process of negotiation among European *demoi* about their common future.

David Owen in 'Transnational Citizenship and the Democratic State: Modes of Membership and Voting Rights' (Chapter 12) is concerned with transnational migrations and membership. Transnational citizenship deeply changes political membership and blurs the borders between political communities. The problem of political inclusion of resident non-citizens and non-resident citizens, as well as definition of their rights, is a burning issue of our transnational world in which millions of people live in diasporas. In this context, Yasemin Soysal in 'Citizenship and Identity: Living in Diasporas in Post-War Europe?' (Chapter 13) identifies a developing decoupling of rights and identity and a tendency towards particularistic and group claims based on universalistic discourse of personhood. At the same time, she warns that we should move from the traditional notion of diaspora in order to understand the complexity of contemporary membership and belonging and 'new geographies of citizenship' that by their transnational and subnational character increasingly displace national arenas as the primary site of citizenship.

Struggles over Citizenship Rights

Finally, in the fourth part we find contributions debating contemporary struggles over citizenship rights in their global and local context. Engin Isin in 'Citizenship in Flux: The Figure of the Activist Citizen' (Chapter 14) attempts a redefinition and reinvention of a new vocabulary of citizenship for 'new geographies of citizenship'. This novel situation brings new *sites*, new *scales* and new *acts* of citizenship through which these actors transform themselves into 'activist' (as opposed to only 'active') citizens as 'claimants of rights' that constantly challenge the defined spaces of citizenship. Aihwa Ong in 'Mutations in Citizenship' (Chapter 15) and Saskia Sassen in 'The Repositioning of Citizenship: Emergent Subjects and Spaces for Politics' (Chapter 16) see the contemporary global and globalized city as the main *site* of citizenship and the privileged space for struggles over citizenship and rights. Ong sees 'mutations in citizenship' in the disarticulation and deterritorialization of citizenship brought about by markets, technologies and populations. 'Global assemblages' formed around cosmopolitan cities and not nation-states are the place where citizenship rights and claims are increasingly defined. Ong brings to our attention the appearance of specific categories such as entrepreneurial expatriates being privileged and granted citizenship rights, whereas the population of underprivileged, stateless, asylum-seekers, the displaced and the poor struggle for sheer survival. As with Ong, Sassen sees the crucial influence of markets in redefining the role of state and thus of modern citizenship. The 'global city', marked by corporate capital and immigration, is the site of contemporary transformations of citizenship and especially the relationship between citizens and aliens. It is in the cities that membership is both localized and transnational and where the space is open for new political subjectivities. She pays attention to two groups in particular, the 'unauthorized yet recognized' such as undocumented immigrants, and the 'authorized yet unrecognized' who are full citizens but not recognized as political subjects such as many women burdened by household and carework today.

It is precisely the question of the relationship between gender and citizenship that is the focus of Nancy Fraser's 'Feminism, Capitalism and the Cunning of History' (Chapter 17). Fraser examines the results of second-wave feminism and its relationship with specific moments in the recent history of capitalism, particularly the rise of neo-liberalism. She sees feminism's crucial contribution to cultural change that will in itself legitimate structural changes of capitalism but at the same time will be far from feminist ideals of a just society. The crisis of neo-liberalism opens new possibilities for feminism as a social movement that struggles for gender equality and its incorporation into wider struggles for rights, justice and emancipation. Carole Pateman in 'Democratizing Citizenship: Some Advantages of a Basic Income' (Chapter 18) suggests concrete steps to democratize citizenship, including women's freedom, by the introduction of a basic income guaranteed to citizens by their states. In her view, it should be seen as a democratic right, as suffrage or as a political birthright. Basic income thus could change the intimate relationship between marriage, employment and citizenship. She signals that only paid employment is seen as 'work' whereas unpaid work, related to the private sphere and mostly done by women, has been so far 'irrelevant for citizenship'. In the following chapter, 'Constructing Sexual Citizenship: Theorizing Sexual Rights' (Chapter 19), Diane Richardson brings to our attention another marginalized sphere of struggle over citizenship rights. Sexual rights are related to practice or conduct, identity and its expression, and social recognition of sexual relationships. By bringing together sexuality and citizenship, the struggle for sexual rights underlines the previously neglected fact that citizenship rights in their classic civil, political and social forms and membership in a given community are based on institutionalized heterosexuality.

In the final chapter, 'The Right to the City' (Chapter 20), David Harvey brings us to the predicament of most people on earth today, which is their life in an urban environment that as such influences all domains of human existence. Harvey suggests that we have to claim another type of human and citizenship right, *the right to the city*. In a highly urbanized world such as ours this right is crucial for the exercise and enjoyment of all other social, economic and political rights. What shapes the cities actually shapes societies and politics and thus citizenship regimes and rights they offer.

Jo Shaw and Igor Štiks

Bibliography

Aron, Raymond (1991 [1974]), 'Une citoyenneté multinationale est-elle possible?', *Commentaire*, **14**, pp. 595–704.

Bauböck, Rainer (2001), 'Recombinant Citizenship', in Martin Kohli and Alison Woodward (eds), *Inclusions and Exclusions in European Societies*, London: Routledge, pp. 38–58.

Bellamy, Richard (2004), 'Introduction: The Making of Modern Citizenship', in Richard Bellamy, Dario Castiglione and Emilio Santoro (eds), *Lineages of European Citizenship: Rights, Belonging and Participation in Eleven Nation-States*, London: Palgrave, pp. 1–21.

Fraser, Nancy (1995), 'From Redistribution to Recognition? Dilemmas of Justice in a "Post-Socialist" Age', *New Left Review*, **1**, pp. 68–93.

Habermas, Jürgen (1998), 'The European Nation-State: On the Past and Future of Sovereignty and Citizenship', *Public Culture*, **10**, pp. 397–416.

Harvey, David (2005), *A Brief History of Neoliberalism*, Oxford and New York: Oxford University Press.

Jenson, Jane (2007), 'The European Union's Citizenship Regime: Creating Norms and Building Practices', *Comparative European Politics*, **5**, pp. 53–69.

Krasner, Stephen D. (1982), 'Structural Causes and Regime Consequences: Regimes as Intervening Variables', *International Organization*, **36**, pp. 185–205.

Marshall, Thomas H. (1992 [1950]), 'Citizenship and Social Class', in Thomas H. Marshall and Tom Bottomore (eds), *Citizenship and Social Class*, London: Pluto Press, pp. 3–51.

Shaw, Jo and Štiks, Igor (2010), *The Europeanisation of Citizenship in the Successor States of the Former Yugoslavia: An Introduction*, CITSEE Working Paper 2010/01, Edinburgh: University of Edinburgh.

Shaw, Jo and Štiks, Igor (2012), 'Citizenship in the New States of South Eastern Europe', *Citizenship Studies*, **16**, pp. 309–21.

Somers, Margaret R. (2008), *Genealogies of Citizenship: Markets, Statelessness and the Right to Have Rights*, Cambridge: Cambridge University Press.

Soysal, Yasemin N. (1994), *Limits of Citizenship: Migrants and Postnational Membership in Europe*, Chicago, IL and London: The University of Chicago Press.

Walby, Sylvia (2004), 'The European Union and Gender Equality: Emergent Varieties of Gender Regime', *Social Politics*, **11**, pp. 4–29.

Wiener, Antje (1994), 'Citizenship Policy in a Non-State: Implications for Theory', paper presented at the 2nd ECSA world conference on federalism, subsidiarity and democracy in the European Union, Brussels, May.

Part I
What are Citizenship Rights (and Duties)?

[1]

Propositions on Citizenship*

Etienne Balibar

Much has recently been said about "new citizenship," although often in an unclear way. The turn of phrase may be only a gimmick, as was, recently, the "new philosophy" or that kind of *auberge espagnole* where you have to bring your own food, also known as *"la nouvelle cusine."* Most of all, it risks soon passing out of fashion with the ups and downs of French socialism. Yet whatever the future redistribution of political power may be, several of the problems raised by discussions of the "new citizenship" will still have to be faced. These include racism and the status of immigration (or rather of "the communities that have issued from immigration") in France. Nevertheless, the form in which these problems will be faced and the chances of finding a solution to them may be singularly transformed depending on whether dominant parties confront or fail to confront certain fundamental alternatives.

"Citizenship" (in Greek *politeia*) is a concept as old as politics itself and which has always marked two distinctions: it is bound to the existence of a state and therefore to a principle of public sovereignty, and it is bound to the acknowledged exercise of an individual "capacity" to participate in political decisions. This is why the dimension of *equality*—with all the problems of definition which it poses and the mystifications which it may conceal—is always present in the constitution of a concept of citizenship, even when the latter is paradoxically combined with a hierarchical principle and with caste distinctions (as seen in the difference between "active citizens" and "passive citizens" in the nineteenth century). Beyond the conflict between citizenship and allegiance to an actual or transcendentally legitimate state, history still shows that this concept has no definition that is fixed for all time. It has always been at stake in struggles and the object of transformations. Not only because, as Aristotle has already shown, each political regime builds the distribution of powers into a specific defintion of citizenship but also because, in juridically (or quasi-juridically) delimiting a certain type of "human being" and a certain model of rights and duties, this definition crystalizes the constitutive social relations of a society at the level of the individual.

---

* Translated from the French by Simon James Critchley, research student at the University of Essex, England.

724   *Ethics   July 1988*

So it is not surprising—and this has been particularly obvious in France for two centuries—if the conflicts between social groups and the new statuses which are accorded them sooner or later get built into the redefinition of citizenship; although there is nothing automatic, linear, or, as we shall see, irreversible about this process. Citizenship, understood in its strict sense as the full exercise of political rights and in its broad sense as cultural initiative or effective presence in the public space (the capacity to be "listened to" there), has therefore been codified only in order to mark a temporary equilibrium, a relation of forces and interests. Here, of course, there exists a double tendency to elevate a given definition (e.g., the equation of citizenship and nationality) or conversely to consider citizenship a mere "legal fiction" which expresses nothing but the mask of domination. In both cases one loses sight of the differential change and the essential mobility of the "citizen" (or of his relation to the state).

Let us see this more concretely by recalling some large-scale examples. First, that of the status of women. The French Revolution greeted them as "citizens" (*citoyennes*), but they had to wait until 1945 (in France) before their complete political rights were recognized. Previously, the very idea of women voting seemed ridiculous to some and monstrous to others. It has since appeared that this recognition was very far from corresponding immediately to real equality. However, this recognition marks a period of transition and instability marked by a certain dialectic. Indeed, in the nineteenth century, not only were women negatively excluded from the "public" space but also the social roles that were assigned to them, along with the ideologies, the educational practices, and the corresponding symbolic complexes, were an effective condition of the political capacity of men, taken collectively. This is why women's access to citizenship cannot simply present itself as an enlargement in the field of application of a given concept or as the granting of a "right" which is in itself immutable. The "private" relations which have been developed in the framework of the noncitizenship of women must also be at once modified, deconstructed, and, in a certain way, transported into the public space and incorporated into the political domain (e.g., with birth control and child rearing, but also the collusion between the division of labor and the sexual distribution of power). Even in countries such as our own (not to speak of Algeria, Japan, and Iran), the citizenship of women is thus more of a challenge, a source and an object of change, than it is a fait accompli.

It is the same, in a different sense, with the question of the relation between citizenship and labor rights, which was recently (and fugitively) brought to the fore by the slogan "citizenship in enterprise." No doubt the categories of "private" and "public" do not operate in exactly the same way here and yet they are equally crucial. For a long time, under the aegis of *property* and its absolute and unconditional character (one of the "gains" of 1789), the business world had been considered purely private; a veritable "Eden from the rights of man and the citizen," as

Balibar   Propositions on Citizenship   725

Marx noted ironically. This situation went hand in hand, let us not forget, with the fact that only the proprietor, the actual or potential boss (and, by association, his entourage of "executives" and "professionals") enjoyed effective political rights and the title of "active citizen." However, this situation was based on a structural equivocation within capitalism which was, strictly speaking, practically untenable. The fact of the matter is that the "free" worker, the partner in a contractual relation with the proprietor, was all the while treated like a "thing," an honorary "commodity," whether individually in the work process or en masse in the management of his habitat, his reproduction, his migrations, or his "flexible working conditions," as we would say today. From this an acute double contradiction is manifest throughout the nineteenth and twentieth centuries: the contradition between the nonegalitarian constitutional system and the "principles of '89"; the contradiction between the formal autonomy and the actual subjection of the worker-proletarian. We realize that it is the conjunction of these two aspects which gave rise to class struggles, nourished the history of the labor movement, and spread out into reforms or revolutions. A specific result of this has been the constitution of a sociopolitical legal sphere, which is less and less compatible with the classical dichotomy between "private" and "public."

Two things are quite striking here. First, in this matter, the enlargement and transformation of individual rights necessarily passed through a collective action into the constitution of collective power relations and also necessarily through the emergence of more or less "representative" organizations (parties, unions, cooperatives) and more or less administrative institutions (social security, public arbitration, collective conventions). In this way, the growth of individual power and all the progress of equality are "paid" for by development of the state itself, with very ambivalent results. As a result, the very concept of "citizenship" here remains in the balance. De facto, when the objectives of full employment or social insurance are institutionalized and incorporated into the definition of the "common good," which the state guarantees or undertakes to guarantee, it is citizenship which changes and, crucially, it is the collective representation of class or group interests which becomes a constitutive element of "politics"—although in a sense which is fundamentally antithetical to "corporatism." However, "liberal" systems offer formidable resistance (even in countries with long experience of social democracy) to giving legal (and constitutional) expression to this questioning of bourgeois individualism (or rather this questioning of the bourgeois equation of individualism and property). So much so that it is necessary to construct an entire metalegal edifice in order to link social rights to a fictitious "property" of the worker and "economic policy" to national interests, which are construed as transcending individuals. We are therefore led toward a situation of unstable displacement. In practice, citizenship tendentiously embodies the rights (and therefore the values) of man-at-work, which have concrete existence only if the relation of individual to collectivity

726   *Ethics   July 1988*

is redefined. But in theory citizenship is still nothing but equality between individuals independent of their social condition—which clearly allows theory to be used to contain or thwart the tendencies of practice.

However, what has been said is not entirely accurate, and, moreover, in tying the notion of a collective interest or a common good to a national entity, I have already included an element of correction. But how ambiguously! In fact, in the course of the nineteenth and twentieth centuries, citizenship did not remain defined in terms of a pure individuality, the correlate to the *Rechtsstaat*. It was construed in terms of nationality, to the point where, in the present-day world (including, one recognizes, the socialist countries, after an ephemeral phase of at least theoretical reference to a "proletarian" cosmopolitanism), the exercise of citizenship appears inseparable from belonging to a nation, whether through inheritance or naturalization (by descent or by "choice"). Hannah Arendt has clearly shown that in the present-day world the stateless person is not a citizen and consequently, in situations of crisis, not even a human being.[1] Current affairs show her, tragically, to be correct.

If there is not a symmetry between the class problem and that of nationhood (in the sense that one is not rigorously incompatible with the other), then at least nationalism is entirely constituted in its modern form in the context of the class struggle and the "social question" which it has tended to control and, if possible, to supplant. The denial of class identity and the affirmation of national identity go hand in hand, at least as principles of political legitimation. The more that the individuality of the citizen has been replaced by an abstraction in economic relations, the more narrowly it has simply been confused with what is "concrete" and "vital" in national identity, with the help of adequate fictions peddled by literature, civic education, and state symbolism. In this way in the principal European countries (France, Germany, England), the recognition of "universal suffrage" is closely coupled with imperialism, whether colonial or Continental. The "dangerous classes" have been allowed access to citizenship—let alone begun to have their workers' rights acknowledged as one of its necessary components—only on condition that they transform themselves into constituent parts of the "body" of the nation, and therefore into (real or imaginary) masters (*maîtres*) or, more exactly, foremen (*contremaîtres*) of imperialist domination.

Because of this, citizenship has been affected in its very core by a conceptual tension which I have elsewhere attempted to analyze as that between subjects and citizens.[2] Every nationality has had to define itself as the sacred heritage of the ancestors, a power of assimilation and "civilization"—and therefore of domination; a "property" in the double

---

1. See Hannah Arendt, "Imperialism," in *The Burden of Our Time* (London: Secker & Warburg, 1951), pp. 121–298.
2. See E. Balibar, "Sujets ou citoyens? Pour l'égalité," *Les temps modernes*, special edition on North African immigration in France (March/April/May 1984), pp. 1725 ff.

Balibar   Propositions on Citizenship   727

sense of an intimate characteristic of persons (we *are* French) and of the legitimate disposition of things, that guarantees their permanence (we *possess* the soil, the national culture). But at the same time every nationality has had to include in its own space (Commonwealth, *Lebensraum,* French Empire, or American way of life) a mass of individuals from minorities who are at once protected and feared, simultaneously deemed unassimilable and obliged to be educated on the national model. Today in France, after the vicissitudes of a more or less complete decolonization and whatever the contradictions of the civil status may be, the mass of immigrants and of "communities" or "generations" which have issued from immigration perpetuate this central duality (which is not at all as marginal or residual as many, and even well meant, discourses of immigration would like to believe or to make us believe). The mass of immigrants perpetuate this duality much more than the distinction between the French "of good stock" and "immigrants" (which includes many who are no longer immigrants); or again the distinction between legitimate national-citizens and precarious resident subjects (in short, the modern-day "metics").[3] These distinctions largely support those between manual and intellectual labor, urban "centers" and the "problem," "peripheral," or "ghetto" areas, the relatively protected working or employed class and those who are destabilized, if not eliminated, by crisis, and so forth.

By schematically laying out and gathering together all these elements, we see that the legal and paralegal concept of citizenship is inseparable not only from a relatively confined constitutional space (territory, sovereignty) but also from its internal frontiers whose changing position is constantly overdetermined. The limits of the "public" and the "private" as they are fixed by the distribution of masculine and feminine roles, the sensitive area of "social rights" which is at stake in the class struggle, and the use of the distinction between "national" and "foreigner" as a criterion for political citizenship have, theoretically speaking, nothing in common, and it is, in the abstract, possible to conceive that they evolve in complete independence. But in actuality they belong to the same combination of circumstances, or rather they become the stakes of collective becoming in the same combination of circumstances. In reality they cannot be separated and must even be combined.

Therefore, it is impossible to determine a priori whether the economic pressure which would once again wish to "fluidify" the labor force will lead to a new wave in the feminization of "masculine" jobs, where women, of whatever status, would become salaried; or whether, on the contrary, it will be exploited by the tendencies to "return to the home" and to "preserve the family" (for which certain political and religious groups are pushing today). It is imposible to believe that economic pressure will have no effect in this area. Conversely, whatever may be said about the "ebbing of feminism," the level and penetration which it has achieved

---

3. Translator's note.—"Metic" (*métèques*) is a pejorative term for a foreigner or alien.

728 *Ethics July 1988*

will not permit a purely cyclical evolution of the crisis in the system of qualifications and employment, that is, a return to the past order.

Still more clear, at least in France, is the connection between the problem of the citizenship of the worker and that of multinational (or transnational) citizenship. What is there in common, we may ask, between the return to the "free" labor market, the dismantling of trade union "pressure groups" (a fashionable pundit has just baptized these groups, with a straight face, the "syndicracy"), even the privatization of social security, and the citizenship of immigrants?[4] Although formally they have nothing in common, in practice there is much to connect them. For what is at stake is, on the one hand, the clearly understood use of the crisis in the profitability of capital in order to reduce citizenship from that "social" conception of the political domain, which is, by now, partially encoded in law or at least in administrative regulations. On the other hand, there is the pressure not to allow politics to expand officially beyond its "national" definition. A pressure whose force one can gauge from one or another official rhapsody to "French supremacy" and which finds plain expression—although perhaps we should avoid combining these mottos—in the demand for "national preference," that is in the idea that individual rights in France (including cultural, professional, and social rights) must be proportional to the purity, ancestry, and sincerity of "French character." Let us not forget that a political party on the right now has an official program for the (retrospective?) limitation of the possibilities of access to French nationality as well as the exclusion of nonnationals from the benefits of social security and from the right to vote in professional elections, and so forth. Once more there is a strict factual complementarity, beneath the apparent antithesis, between the themes of liberalism and those of nationalism.

So we must ask ourselves—without prejudging the answer—to what extent a defense of social and workers' rights is today connected with progress toward a multinational and multicultural definition of the state, and so toward a regulated extension of the notion of citizenship which breaks with the sacrosanct equation of citizenship and nationality. We must also ask to what extent the latter can, in its turn, remove obstructions and put us back on the road to workers' self-management and allow the participation of workers in economic and social management—citizenship in enterprise.

Seen from this perspective, the movements of the last three years, grouped under the heading of antiracism or of minorities' cultural autonomy and rights to expression, or of the immigrant vote, contain a certain ambiguity. They betray the dynamism of the young generation who, even when reduced to unemployment or designated a "risk population," give shape to a new language and street culture, finding an

---

4. Translator's note.—"Syndicracy" (*syndicratie*) literally means "trade union power" and alludes to the belief that trade unions run the state.

Balibar   Propositions on Citizenship   729

echo in a section of French society. They constitute a pole of resistance and attraction in the face of the rise of nationalistic, "Western," passé ideologies. Yet let us not forget that their emergence, within pretty narrow limits, coincided with the real oppression and isolation of immigrant worker movements (the auto industry, etc.), which, in 1981–82, courageously attempted to insert a proper workers' initiative into the experience of socialism. In other words, antiracism, however intrinsically necessary it may be (which goes without saying), can be labeled a humanistic opposition to the state's decision to practice a selective "modernization" of the productive apparatus and the labor force, and as a very slight compensation for the inability of the labor movement to overcome its national corporatism and to oppose the crisis by better means than through defensive reactions.

Still a further remark must be made here: it is that the financial and even legal internationalization of economies and centers of political decision making is not only a question of structures but also a question of human beings; it is almost a new mode of life and thought. As a matter of fact, the "ruling class" of modern society, with its internal hierarchies, is multilingual, multicultural, and migratory. It studies at Harvard, works in the airplane or with transnational data banks, and spends its vacations between Morocco and the Seychelles. The national passport has changed its meaning (at least for the dominant nationalities); it no longer expresses (except no doubt in the United States) allegiance to an autonomous power but, rather, a conditional right of access to the "cosmopolis" of communications and modern financial transactions. This is why there is such strong resistance to the enlargement of citizenship and to the very exploration of its modalities. For the perpetuation of the traditional cleavages between the dominated represents a keystone in the system of new inequalities. That is why the struggle for citizenship as a struggle for equality must begin again on new ground and with new objectives. It will come about not only through the internationalization of basic culture (in practice, through the education system) but also through the flexibility of the national and "racial" barriers which were set up within the spheres of communication and within the groups (of workers, of residents), who are more or less "metics," whom history has implanted in the soil of old Europe.

There is always a risk in presenting extreme evolutions as unavoidable alternatives. Therefore, while even taking account of the progress of the *Front National* and the increase in racist crimes, let us not hasten to claim that French society has a choice only between giving voting rights to immigrants or the violence and revolt in the ghettos on the English or American model. And yet, the risk is too great to sustain the belief that, in time, the question of the transformations of citizenship could be avoided and that the tensions that it conceals could be "managed" by a mixture of repression and "associated" gimmicks. At the very least, we would be heading toward a truly blocked-up society, split between the corporatism

730   *Ethics   July 1988*

of its diverse economic, cultural, and ethnic minorities and the abstraction of its political language. This is not very modern in the eyes of the surrounding world. It is true that in order to open up other perspectives, we must give a concrete meaning to certain ethical values (and, in the first place, we must at long last accept the consequences of colonization and decolonization, of industrialization and deindustrialization); we must reconstitute a mass political will (which is not a matter of practicing voluntarism) in place of following the trend of the "end of ideology." A vast program indeed.

[2]

Citizenship and Social Class, Forty Years On
Tom Bottomore

1. Citizens, Classes and Equality

T.H. Marshall's lectures, given at Cambridge in 1949 and published in an expanded version the following year (Marshall 1950, reprinted above), made a very original contribution to sociological conceptions and theories of social class, and at the same time to the debates about the emerging post-war welfare state. In both spheres the concept of citizenship had a central place in his argument. Starting out from Alfred Marshall's paper (1873) on 'the future of the working classes'–according to which a certain degree of equality would be attained when, as a consequence of the reduction of heavy and excessive labour, along with greatly improved access to education and to the rights of citizenship, all men became 'gentlemen'–he proposed to substitute for the world 'gentlemen' the word 'civilised' and to interpret the claim to a civilised life as a claim to share in the social heritage, to be fully accepted as a citizen.

The argument was then pursued, initially, through an examination of the relation between citizenship and social class, in which the movement towards greater social equality was seen as the latest phase in the evolution of citizenship over several centuries, from the achievement of civil rights to the acquisition of political rights and finally social rights. This process was elegantly conceptualised in what Marshall himself referred to as a narration of events, but there was relatively little discussion of its causes, giving rise to later criticisms that it had been rather misleadingly represented as a quasi-automatic, harmonious progression to better things which was in some way immanent in the development of capitalism itself. Implicitly though, and to some extent explicitly, Marshall recognised that there were elements of conflict involved, observing that it was reasonable to expect that 'the impact of citizenship on social class should take the form of a conflict between opposing principles'. He did not, however, argue that this conflict was one between classes over the nature and content of citizenship, and he remarked indeed that 'social class occupies a secondary position in my theme'. The impact of citizenship on social classes, rather than the impact of social classes on the extension of citizenship, was clearly his principal concern.

Yet in so far as the development of citizenship in Britain from the latter part of the seventeenth century 'coincides with the rise of capitalism', it is obviously important to consider which social groups were actively engaged in, or on the other hand resisted, efforts to enlarge the rights of citizens, and more generally to bring about greater equality. From this standpoint the growth of civil rights, beginning indeed before the

56   Forty Years On

seventeenth century in medieval cities, can be seen as an achievement of the new bourgeoisie in conflict with dominant feudal groups of the *ancien régime*. Similarly, the extension of political rights in the nineteenth and twentieth centuries, and of social rights in the twentieth, was accomplished largely by the rapidly growing working class movement, aided by middle-class reformers, and in the case of social rights facilitated by the consequences of two world wars. Marshall himself referred to this obliquely when he observed that 'in the twentieth century citizenship and the capitalist class system have been at war', though he thought 'perhaps the phrase is rather too strong' (p. 40) and he did not pursue this aspect of his analysis.

In due course, when considering the changes that have taken place over the past 40 years, we shall need to re-examine Marshall's conception of class and of the relation between the extension of social rights, with their potential for creating a more equal society, and the economic and class system of capitalism. First, however, let us look at the second major theme of his lectures, which is the embodiment of the principle of social rights in the policies of the welfare state. He began by noting 'some of the difficulties that arise when one tries to combine the principles of social equality and the price system', and then observed that the extension of the social services was 'not primarily a means of equalising incomes', which might be tackled in other ways (see p. 61); but that what mattered was that 'there is a general enrichment of the concrete substance of civilised life, a general reduction of risk and insecurity, an equalisation between the more and the less fortunate at all levels' (p. 33). This is very close to the view expressed by R.H. Tawney in his discussion of equality (4th edn, 1952, p. 248):

> There are certain gross and crushing disabilities–conditions of life injurious to health, inferior education, economic insecurity... which place the classes experiencing them at a permanent disadvantage... There are certain services by which these crucial disabilities have been greatly mitigated, and, given time and will, can be altogether removed... The contribution to equality made by these dynamic agencies is obviously out of all proportion greater than that which would result from an annual present to every individual among the forty odd millions concerned of a sum equivalent to his quota of the total cost.

Marshall went on to note the consequences in this sense of the post-war policies in Britain, which created a national system of education and a National Health Service, and initiated a large-scale programme of house-building which included the planning of new towns. But he also pointed out that the more widely available educational opportunities tended to create a new structure of unequal status linked with unequal abilities and that 'through education in its relations with occupational structure, citizenship operates as an instrument of social stratification' (p. 39 above). Nevertheless he concluded that 'status differences can receive the stamp of legitimacy in terms of democratic citizenship provided they do not cut too deep, but occur within a population united in a single civilisation; and provided they are not an expression of hereditary privilege' (p. 44 above). Forty years later however we are still very far away from such a situation–above all in Britain, which increasingly resembles, in the view of many observers, the society of 'two nations' depicted by Disraeli–and from the widespread acceptance of 'socialist measures' in a progressive 'divorce between real and money incomes' (p. 47 above). Later, I shall examine in greater detail the post-war development of class structures and the welfare state, as well as new problems and conceptions of citizenship, drawing in part upon Marshall's own later writings on these subjects, but first it is necessary to consider some more general features of the economic and social framework in which the changes were accomplished or arrested.

2. Capitalism, Socialism and Citizenship

In 1949, in Britain, it was possible to take a fairly optimistic view of the gradual extension of citizens' rights in a democratic society which was becoming more socialist in its structure, through the nationalisation of some major sectors of the economy and the creation of a National Health Service and a system of national education, the latter regarded by many socialists as the first step towards establishing a universal system by the phasing out of private, privileged education (see, for example, the Note of Reservation by Mrs M.C. Jay to the Report of the Royal Commission on Population, June 1949). These policies, together with the priority given to creating and maintaining full employment, and proposals (which were, however, never effectively implemented) for national economic planning, were all intended to achieve equality, to a large extent by the introduction of social rights into new areas, of health, education, employment and the control of productive resources. This movement, as Marshall suggested (p. 47 above), became increasingly identified with socialism '(thus going far beyond Alfred Marshall's conception of 'the amelioration of the working classes') and its main tendency was more strongly characterised by Schumpeter (1949) as a 'march into socialism'.

The drive towards equality, analysed by Schumpeter in a way which had some affinities with Marxist theory, could also be interpreted, as was done at an earlier date by Sidney Webb (1889), as the outcome of 'the

58   Forty Years On

irresistible progress of democracy'; and the latter view has been restated in some more recent writings (for example, Turner 1986) which see the achievement of social rights as following from the gaining of political rights by the working class and other subordinate groups. In 1949 at all events, in Britain and some other European countries, the egalitarian, mainly socialist movement may well have appeared to be an 'irresistible' tendency emerging from the development of capitalism itself, and this 'spirit of the times' no doubt influenced the way in which Marshall presented his analysis.

Just at this time, however, the world situation, and that of Britain, was beginning to change radically. In the context of the emerging cold war the American Marshall Plan for European recovery, implemented from 1948, played a major part in reviving the capitalist economies of Western Europe, notably in West Germany–although it also introduced some degree of national economic planning through the creation of the Organisation of European Economic Cooperation (OEEC, subsequently OECD) to administer the funds made available[1] – and in limiting the possibilities for any further socialist development. The Labour government in Britain, by the beginning of the 1950s, confronted increasing difficulties, due in part to its dependent relationship with the USA and exacerbated by the Korean war, which resulted in a sharp rise in the cost of imported raw materials; and in face of these difficulties it seemed to suffer a loss of vigour and imagination in the formulation and presentation of policies for any further advance towards social equality, though its last memorable achievement, the 1951 Festival of Britain, intimated how, in more favourable circumstances, a genuine renaissance and social renewal might have come about.

On the world scene the prospects for socialism were further dimmed by the imposition of Stalinist regimes in Eastern Europe, from which only Yugoslavia was able to break away. These totalitarian regimes, which remained dictatorial even after the death of Stalin–although in many cases they gradually became somewhat less oppressive–distorted the image of socialism for four decades, despite the fact that they were consistently criticised and opposed by almost all Western socialists. The relative weakness of the democratic socialist movement as a consequence of these two factors–the revival of capitalism in a more planned, or at least 'managed' form, which resulted in exceptionally high rates of economic growth from the 1950s to the mid-1970s, and the deterrent example of self-styled 'real socialism' in Eastern Europe–made any further extension of social rights much more difficult, although there were some phases of renewed activity such as the great expansion of higher education in the 1960s, and in some circumstances, as in Sweden and Austria where socialist governments were in power over fairly long periods,[2] there was a more continuous development of social welfare policies. To a large extent, moreover, the preoccupation with social welfare, after the immediate post-war changes had been effected and welfare states had been created, in more rudimentary or more elaborate forms, was displaced by an overriding concern with economic growth, resulting partly from the experience of achieved growth in the period of reconstruction, and partly from what Postan (1967) called an 'ideology of growth' which he considered had evolved from earlier debates about full employment. Continuous and rapid growth, achieved by technological innovation, rising productivity and full employment, was now seen as the main foundation of social welfare, assuring to a large part of the population steadily improving conditions of life, and providing, through government expenditure financed by taxation and borrowing, those services and benefits which individuals could not effectively procure for themselves, or which were needed by specific disadvantaged groups in the population. Such changes as the expansion of higher education were themselves closely linked with this concentration on economic growth.

In the period 1950–73, which Maddison (1982, Chapter 6) has described as a 'golden age' of exceptionally high growth rates, the economies of the advanced industrial societies in Western Europe (and in a different form in Japan) tended towards a system of 'managed' capitalism, to which the term 'corporatism'[3] was later applied, characterised by a mixed economy with a limited (and varying) degree of public ownership of productive and service enterprises, and in some cases financial institutions, greatly increased government expenditure as a proportion of the gross national product, and much greater involvement of the state in regulating and to some extent planning the economy. In this system, it was argued, economic and social policy is the product of agreements negotiated between the state, the large capitalist corporations and the trade unions, and some kind of 'class compromise' is reached in order to maintain stability (Offe 1980). Marshall (1972) himself referred to 'a social framework that includes representative government, a mixed economy and a welfare state', and in a later afterthought (1981) he analysed more closely what he called the 'hyphenated society' (e.g. welfare-capitalism) rather than corporatism, and went on to consider its relation to democratic socialism, particularly as this had been expounded by an English socialist, E.F.M. Durbin.

For Durbin, Marshall argued (1981, p. 127), 'the crux of the matter... was the relation between socialism and democracy'. A socialist programme must be 'concerned with the transfer of economic control and the redistribution of real income' (Durbin 1940, p. 290), which was the

60 Forty Years On

only road to social justice. 'But the public mind was prone to equate social justice with welfare, which was only part of it, and was likely to press too hard for those purely "ameliorative" measures which affect only the consequences of inequality, not its foundations. The socialist strategy, therefore, must be sure to give a relatively low priority to the social services compared with that given to the more genuinely socialist categories of political action–socialisation of the economy, promotion of prosperity and the redistribution of wealth' (Marshall 1981, pp. 127–8).

This, as Marshall observed, 'goes to the heart of the matter', and he continued (1981, pp. 128–9):

> The wide currency after the war of the term 'welfare state' suggests that there was an urge at that time to find in the concept of 'welfare' a single, unifying axial principle for the new social order. It is not difficult to see why it failed... in this holistic form, it was too vague and nebulous to provide a model for a social system. It expressed a spirit rather than a structure... [and] became quickly associated, or even identified, with that particular, limited sphere of public affairs that we call social policy.

The distinction that Marshall made here was also very clearly formulated by a Hungarian sociologist (Ferge 1979) in the contrast which she drew between 'social policy' and 'societal policy' in her analysis of the changes in Hungarian society, and I shall consider it more fully in relation to the development of citizenship in socialist societies. Marshall, in the passage I have cited, went on to observe that in the system of welfare capitalism and a mixed economy 'the golden calf of democratic socialism had been translated into a troika of sacred cows', and that by the early 1970s the welfare state survived in 'a precarious and somewhat battered condition'. Two decades later it is quite evidently even more battered and precarious, especially in Britain, and numerous studies have been devoted to analysing the 'crisis of the welfare state'.

In the latter part of his essay Marshall (1981, pp. 131–5) considered some of the reasons for what he saw as the declining appeal of the idea of welfare–its 'loss of status'–which he attributed broadly to its loss of identity, emphasising particularly the conflict between the market and welfare as means of satisfying the needs of the population, and especially in dealing with poverty. He summarised his own view as being that democratic freedoms depend to a considerable extent on economic freedom, and that competitive markets make a large contribution to efficiency and economic progress, but on the other hand, that 'the capitalist market economy can be, and generally has been, a cause of much social injustice'; and he concluded that 'the anti-social elements in the capitalist market system which still persist in the mixed economy have to be tackled by action within the economy itself'.

This restates the distinction between socialist and welfare policies, and the dilemma which, as Durbin indicated, is posed for democratic socialist parties, while at the same time it conveys a sense of the direction in which much socialist thought has moved in the post-war period. For it can be said that the European socialist parties (and more recently some communist parties) have in fact become to a large extent 'welfare' parties, whose policies are primarily concerned with, and are seen by a large part of the electorate as being identified with, the promotion of social rights in the narrow sense of providing welfare services in specific areas, rather than with any radical reconstruction of the economic and social system. But this reorientation of thought and policy poses many new problems.

First, the differences between parties in respect of their general policies are attenuated and obscured, and the main issue becomes that of whether there shall be more or less public spending on welfare. This issue is then, however, debated in a context which makes the extension of social rights increasingly difficult, because a sharp distinction is made between the production of wealth, which is conceived as the function of a capitalist market economy, and the distribution of a part of the wealth produced in the form of welfare services. Hence the question can be, and generally is, presented in the form of how much welfare a society can 'afford' in relation to its stock and flow of 'real' wealth provided by mainly private industry. But this is not at all how the issue has been, or should be, formulated in socialist thought, where the fundamental concept is that of the social labour process—that is, productive activity in every sphere, including the provision of welfare services, and involving in advanced economies a massive input of science and technology—and the questions that arise concern the organisation of that process and how its product shall be distributed among various groups in the population. In short, it is not a matter of deducting from some narrowly defined national product that amount which is needed for welfare, but of dividing equitably a national product of which welfare is a major component, and indeed in a broad sense is the sole purpose of the whole labour process. It was clearly in this way that Durbin, like most other socialists, and especially Marxist thinkers, conceived the relation between socialism and welfare, and I shall return to the subject later.

For the present the relation can be illuminated by looking at the experience of the socialist societies in Eastern Europe, especially as it was interpreted by Ferge (1979) in her distinction between 'societal policy' and 'social policy'. Ferge (p. 13) defined these terms in the following way:

62 Forty Years On

> The concept of societal policy... is used in a special sense. It encompasses the sphere of *social policy* (the organisation of social services or the redistribution of incomes), but also includes systematic social intervention at all points of the cycle of the reproduction of social life, with the aim of changing the structure of society.

In the following chapters she then traces this process of social reproduction, first describing 'societal policy dealing with the transformation of basic social relations embedded in the social organisation of work', then analysing 'the relations created or modified through distribution and redistribution', and finally considering 'some aspects of social policy in relation to consumption and ways of life in general'. This provides an admirably clear account of the scope of social policy in a socialist perspective, in terms of which the development of citizenship in these societies can be more closely analysed.

In the Soviet Union and other East European countries during the post-war period it is evident that social policy, directed towards the provision of low-cost housing, public transport, leisure facilities, and health care had a high priority, and was complemented by a societal policy which restructured the economy in ways that were intended to achieve rapid industrialisation and economic growth (as they did in the 1950s and 1960s particularly) together with security of employment and in some cases more active participation by workers in the management of production. The citizens of these countries, therefore, acquired a considerable range of important social rights, the value of which is perhaps more clearly recognised since the changes that took place at the end of 1989, but these gains were qualified by a number of adverse factors. First, the level at which welfare services could be provided depended crucially upon economic growth, and from the early 1970s the socialist economies experienced increasing difficulties, exacerbated by the problems of the world economy, and to some extent by an excessively high rate of investment in industry, financed partly by foreign borrowing and often directed to the wrong kind of industry (Bottomore 1990). Secondly, there emerged in all these societies a privileged group— a 'new class' or 'elite', comprising the upper levels of the party and state bureaucracies—which effectively controlled the social labour process and determined the distribution of the product to its own advantage and to the detriment of workers and consumers.

By far the most important factor, however, which ultimately led to the downfall of these regimes, was that the real enlargement of social rights (even though unequally distributed among different groups in the population) was accompanied by a severe restriction of civil and political rights, at its most savage during Stalin's dictatorship but persisting in somewhat less oppressive forms (and notably less oppressive in Yugoslavia from the early 1950s) in the bureaucratic one-party system which followed. Citizenship in these socialist (but far from democratic socialist) societies had, therefore, quite a different character from that which Marshall was considering in relation to Britain and, by implication, other West European societies. Instead of a progression from civil to political rights, and then to a growth of social rights, as Marshall conceived it, these totalitarian state-socialist societies established some important social rights while virtually extinguishing major civil and political rights; though it should be observed that one factor which facilitated this process was that many of the countries involved had no tradition of securely founded civil and political rights, and little experience of democracy, before their 'socialist' transformation.

The ongoing changes in the Soviet Union and Yugoslavia, and the collapse of the other East European regimes, have created an entirely new situation. Civil and political rights have been restored, or are rapidly being restored, although controversy continues, as in the capitalist countries, about the content and limits of some civil rights, and notably the right to own property where this involves ownership of major productive enterprises. Other civil rights, which Marshall listed as being liberty of the person, freedom of speech, thought and faith, and the right to justice, though complex in their details, are uncontested in principle as essential for individual freedom, and their re-establishment is proceeding rapidly. So too is the restoration of political rights–freedom to organise and participate in social movements, associations, and parties of diverse kinds, without authorisation or interference from the state (except where laws which protect basic rights of other citizens are infringed).

The impact of the recent changes on social rights, however, may be very varied. In those countries which are re-establishing a capitalist economy a number of existing social rights are threatened, among them low-cost housing and public transport, and above all security of employment and some degree of participation in the management of enterprises, while in most of the countries the initial measures introduced by the new regimes, together with a general uncertainty about the economic future, have led to a decline in production, falling standards of living, and growing unemployment. How these societies will develop over the next decade is still unclear, but it is evident already from the emergence of new protest movements that existing social rights will be vigorously defended by a large part of the population, and that a major political division over the extent of welfare spending, similar to that in capitalist countries, will reappear, and has indeed done so in several countries. Whether this division will involve an opposition between capitalism and

64   Forty Years On

socialism—whether, that is to say, the revived socialist parties and re-formed communist parties will connect welfare policy with the maintenance or restoration of public ownership on a significant scale and with some form of planning, in a conception of 'societal policy' which is concerned with the social division of the whole product of the labour process—remains uncertain, just as it is uncertain in the present advanced capitalist countries.

At all events we may say, as Marshall did, that there is some degree of conflict between citizenship and the class system of capitalism, between the satisfaction of needs by welfare services and by the market; and this conflict has been recognised in various ways by later writers. Titmuss (1956), in an early essay on the 'societal division of welfare', raised broad issues concerning welfare and social equality which he pursued in a later work (1962) on income distribution, where he emphasised the 'class distribution of incomes and wealth' (p. 198), and in discussing the meaning of poverty came close to a conception of 'societal policy' that would involve changes in the economic and social structure in order to achieve greater equality. On the other hand, Robson (1976), in his study of the achievements and shortcomings of the welfare state, disputed the view that poverty cannot be abolished in a capitalist society, citing as an example the case of Sweden (though Sweden has pursued more 'socialistic' policies than most European countries and has also experimented recently with means of socialising capital ownership).[4] Robson concluded his study by saying there there were 'few systematic views about the nature and aims of the welfare state', and after rejecting the idea that it is 'just a collection of social services', or 'an instrument whose main purpose is to abolish poverty', or is 'committed to social and economic equality as the supreme good' (p. 171), he went on to say that 'welfare is of unlimited scope. It extends to social and economic circumstances, conditions of work, remuneration, the character and scope of the social services, the quality of the environment, recreational facilities, and the cultivation of the arts' (p. 174). This suggests more radical changes in the social structure, and particularly in the class system, than Robson actually discussed or seemed prepared to consider. His own emphasis was on what he regarded as essential elements in developing the welfare state: a high degree of personal freedom, protection of individual citizens against abuses of power and correlatively, responsible involvement of citizens in the affairs of society, improvement of the environment, continuous improvement of social services, and an evaluation of the standard of living in terms of a considerable range of criteria, taking into account not only money incomes, but also such factors as the quality of the environment, the distribution of wealth, job satisfaction,

Tom Bottomore 65

health education and housing. This again approaches a conception of a societal policy in which social policy is only one element.

The development of citizenship, and its relationship with social class, is evidently more complex, and as a process more variable, than Marshall's lectures conveyed. In capitalist societies the growth of social rights in the welfare state has not fundamentally transformed the class system, nor have welfare services eliminated poverty in most cases, although the more socialistic countries such as Sweden and Austria have advanced farthest in this respect. In the self-styled 'countries of real socialism' in Eastern Europe some important social rights were established, but equally important civil and political rights were diminished or extinguished, while at the same time new forms of hierarchy and inequality emerged. In capitalist societies too, within the existing class system, new types of stratification developed out of welfare policies, as Marshall, and subsequently other writers, observed. Furthermore, increased state intervention in the economy and in the expansion of welfare services tended to create new hierarchies and a greater centralisation of power, which Robson (1976, pp. 176–7), and from a different perspective, many conservative critics of government bureaucracy, particularly noted.

These are not the only issues, however, which need further consideration. Over the past 40 years problems of citizenship have appeared, and have been widely discussed, in quite new contexts, where the connections with social class are less clear; and in the same period not only have significant changes taken place in the class structure of capitalist societies, but the political conflicts in Eastern Europe have culminated in a rapid transformation of the social structure in the state socialist countries. It is with the new questions posed by these changes that the following two sections of this essay will be concerned.

3. New Questions about Citizenship

Marshall's study of the development of citizenship was made in a particular context. It was concerned with Britain (or indeed more narrowly with England) as a more or less homogeneous society, in the immediate post-war period, although its general conceptions could be more widely applied. Today, however, this context seems no longer adequate. A host of new questions about citizenship have emerged which need to be examined in a broader framework, ideally on a world scale, but at all events with reference to the various types of industrially developed countries, and to the problems of citizenship in societies whose populations are far from being homogeneous.

A useful starting point for such a reconsideration is to be found in the

66   Forty Years On

studies by Brubaker (1989, 1992), which examine the problems created by the massive post-war migrations in Europe and North America, against the background of an analysis of the meaning of citizenship in the twentieth century. First, we should note the important distinction made between *formal* and *substantive* citizenship. The former can be defined as 'membership of a nation-state' (Brubaker 1989, p. 3); the latter, in terms of Marshall's conception, as an array of civil, political, and especially social rights, involving also some kind of participation in the business of government. Brubaker (1992, pp. 36–8) then goes on to observe:

> That which constitutes citizenship–the array of rights or the pattern of participation–is not necessarily tied to formal state-membership. Formal citizenship is neither a sufficient nor a necessary condition for substantive citizenship... That it is not a sufficient condition is clear: one can possess formal state-membership yet be excluded (in law or in fact) from certain political, civil, or social rights or from effective participation in the business of rule in a variety of settings... That formal citizenship is not a necessary condition of substantive citizenship is perhaps less evident. Yet while formal citizenship may be required for certain components of substantive citizenship (e.g. voting in national elections), other components... are independent of formal state-membership. Social rights, for example, are accessible to citizens and legally resident non-citizens on virtually identical terms, as is participation in the self-governance of associations, political parties, unions, factory councils, and other institutions...

He then argues that:

> the 'sociologization' of the concept of citizenship in the work of Marshall and Bendix and theorists of participation has indeed been fruitful [but] it has introduced an *endogenous* bias into the study of citizenship. Formal membership of the state has been taken for granted... But the massive immigration of the last quarter-century to Western Europe and North America, leaving in its wake a large population whose formal citizenship is in question, has engendered a new politics of citizenship, centered precisely on the question of membership in the nation-state.

The forms of this new politics of citizenship vary from one country to another, influenced by different conceptions of 'nationhood', and Brubaker (1989, Introduction), in the volume of essays which he edited on immigration and citizenship, makes interesting comparisons between six industrial countries in Europe and North America. First, there is 'a basic difference between nations constituted by immigration and countries in which occasional immigration has been incidental to nation-building. Canada and the United States have a continuous tradition of immigration... and immigration figures prominently in their national myths' (p. 7). But there are also important differences among European

Tom Bottomore 67

countries. In France,

> conceptions of nationhood and citizenship bear the stamp of their revolutionary origin. The nation, in this tradition, has been conceived mainly in relation to the institutional and territorial frame of the state: political unity, not shared culture, has been understood to be its basis (p. 7).

By contrast with this 'universalist, assimilationist, and state-centered' conception, the German conception has been

> particularist, organic, and *Volk*-centered. Because national feeling developed before the nation-state... this German nation... was conceived not as the bearer of universal political values, but as an organic cultural, linguistic, or racial community–as a *Volksgemeinschaft* (p. 8).[5]

Sweden resembles France in that national feeling was attached to political and institutional traditions, and the absence of ethnic or cultural nationalism 'may help explain why Sweden has been able to make citizens of its post-war immigrants with so little fuss or friction' (p. 10). Britain, however, is an exceptional case, where there was (until 1981) no clear conception of citizenship, and 'legal and political status were conceived instead in terms of allegiance', between individual subjects and the monarch; ties of allegiance which 'knit together the British Empire, not the British nation'. This absence of a strong identity as a nation–state and of an established national citizenship contributed, Brubaker suggests, 'to the confused and bitter politics of immigration and citizenship during the last quarter-century'. On the other hand, because Britain had not traditionally defined itself as a nation–state, the post-war immigrants have not, for the most part, been considered aliens, and generally have more economic, social, and political rights than elsewhere (pp. 10–11).

Against this background other essays in Brubaker's volume raise broader questions about citizenship, concerning the criteria for access to citizenship, the status of resident non-citizens, and dual citizenship, which I shall examine later in this essay. First, however, it is necessary to consider more fully those new issues that have arisen in respect of the substantive rights of citizens with which Marshall was primarily concerned. Such rights are distinct from the formal rights of citizenship, which are not a sufficient condition for them (see above), although the two sets of rights are plainly interrelated in many respects. The first question to be discussed here is that of gender. Like almost all social scientists at that time Marshall largely ignored gender differences, as even the initial formulation of his theme in terms of whether every man could become a 'gentleman' makes evident. Yet it is obvious that the

68   Forty Years On

array of civil, political and social rights whose development Marshall traced was extended to women very much more slowly than to men, in Britain as elsewhere, and that some of these rights are still quite unequally distributed. Civil rights, such as the right to own property, were acquired much later by women, and in Britain, for example, it is only since 1990 that married women have gained the right to independent taxation of their incomes instead of having these regarded as an extension of their husband's earnings. Political rights for women also came much later, during the twentieth century in most countries–in some cases only after 1945–and women still form a small minority in legislative assemblies and in the higher reaches of state administration, though on the other hand they have been increasingly active and prominent in social movements. In the domain of social rights women have usually experienced discrimination, and still do so in most countries, in respect of access to better paid and more prestigious occupations, and prospects for promotion, while social provision in areas which are of particular concern to women, such as day-care nurseries, maternity leave and family planning, has generally been extended less rapidly than have other services.

It should be noted here that particular efforts were made in the socialist countries of Eastern Europe to diminish gender inequality in the sphere of employment, and policies adopted in Hungary (especially those concerning maternity leave and child-care) are discussed in detail by Ferge (1979, pp. 98–112), who also considers some broader aspects of family policy (pp. 211–22). But as Ferge observes, traditionally ingrained attitudes and ideas perpetuate gender inequality, notably in the family, where domestic labour is disproportionately performed by women even though both spouses are working, in socialist as well as capitalist countries;[6] and such attitudes can only be influenced very gradually by policies aimed at extending and equalising social rights. Hence the new feminist movements which developed after the war, and especially rapidly in the 1960s, have been concerned not only with civil, political, and social rights as generally understood, but also with the gender stereotypes which profoundly affect the personal and family life of women.[7] Any discussion of citizenship today is obliged, therefore, to consider specifically the social position of women–whether they are still, in many countries, and in certain respects (if decreasingly), 'second-class citizens'–and this poses new questions about the scope and content of social rights.

A second issue that raises similar questions is that of ethnic or ethno-cultural diversity, which has increased in many countries as a result of large-scale post-war immigration. This has created problems

Tom Bottomore   69

both of formal and substantive citizenship, and policies with regard to the former have varied considerably between countries–for example, between Germany, France, and Britain–although there has been a general tendency in the past decade to restrict immigration and access to citizenship. Even where formal citizenship exists, however, the substantive rights of citizenship may not be acquired in practice, or only in an unequal degree, by particular ethnic groups. The civil rights movement of black (Afro-)Americans in the 1960s was a dramatic instance of protest against the effective denial of civil, political, and social rights to a major ethnic group in American society; and other ethnic groups have likewise campaigned, and continue to campaign, against discrimination, particularly in the sphere of social rights, in the USA and other countries. If social rights are interpreted broadly to include access to education, health care, employment, and adequate housing (as is certainly implied in many conceptions of the post-war welfare state), and in addition provision for the special needs of particular groups (for example, working mothers), then it is evident that some of these rights are still very unequally distributed, not only between men and women, but also between groups defined by ethnic and/or cultural characteristics, in many of the countries of welfare capitalism.

Ethnic and cultural differences within nation-states have also posed other problems of citizenship where particular groups–for example in the province of Quebec in Canada, in the Basque country in Spain, in Northern Ireland, and increasingly in Eastern Europe following the collapse of the state-socialist regimes–have initiated movements to achieve a more distinct separate nationhood, in the form of complete independence, or at the least of much greater regional autonomy, or in some cases by adhesion to, or incorporation into, another nation-state. Some of these movements in effect raise the question of a kind of dual citizenship, which is also raised in a different way by such developments towards supra-national political systems as the European Community, where a 'European' citizenship seems to be evolving, already expressed in an embryonic body of rights upheld by the European Court and the Commission on Human Rights, and in the proposals by the European Parliament for a new 'social charter'.

These complexities of modern citizenship, and their implications for conceptions of nationhood and the nation-state, will be considered more fully later. Meanwhile, there are other aspects of the substantive rights of citizens within existing nation-states to be discussed, and in particular the consequences of poverty for such rights. Tawney (1952) wrote of 'gross and crushing disabilities' which placed those experiencing them 'at a permanent disadvantage' (see above, p. 56), and Marshall (p. 33

70 Forty Years On

above) conceived the development of citizenship as 'a general enrichment of the concrete substance of civilised life', to be achieved by reducing risk and insecurity, and equalising the conditions of the more and the less fortunate. Undoubtedly, in the 1940s and 1950s, one of the principal aims of the welfare state was seen as the eradication of poverty, especially by eliminating the large-scale and long-term unemployment which was one of its major causes, but in any case countering the effects of such unemployment as did occur by social security payments on as generous a scale as possible. Initially these policies were fairly effective and social conditions improved considerably compared with the 1930s, but over the past two decades, and particularly in the 1980s, poverty has increased again in most West European countries, although Sweden and Austria are notable exceptions to the general trend. Above all, poverty has increased in Britain, where economic decline, changes in fiscal policy, large-scale unemployment, and diminishing social expenditure have combined to re-create massive inequalities of wealth and income, and a large category of very poor, predominantly working-class citizens.

In the USA and Britain the term 'underclass' has come to be widely used to describe this category, but as Lister (1990, pp. 24–6) points out, there is an ideological element involved in applying this stigmatising label, which tends to define the poor in moral rather than economic terms, and indeed to revive nineteenth-century conceptions of the poor as being responsible for their own poverty. There is also much disagreement about how large this so-called 'underclass' is in Britain, with estimates ranging from 5 per cent to 30 per cent of the population, but there can be no doubt at any rate that the extent of poverty has greatly increased during the past decade, and that poverty has substantial effects on the quality of citizenship for those afflicted by it.

Lister begins her study by quoting Marshall's definition of citizenship as 'a status bestowed on those who are full members of a community. All who possess the status are equal with respect to the rights and duties with which the status is endowed' (p. 18 above), and goes on to consider the debate about citizenship during the past decade, in which the ideas of the New Right have been directed against what is called the 'dependency culture'–that is to say, the body of social rights established by the community as a whole–and in favour of an 'enterprise culture' in which private individuals secure their own welfare by their own efforts, and the role of the state (or of private charity) is limited to providing help to those who, for one reason or another, are unable to help themselves. The dominance of this ideology, now embodied in social policies, has gradually undermined social rights as an attribute of citizenship, placing all the emphasis on privatised activities (private health care and education, privatised municipal services, the introduction of commercial activities into public services of all kinds), and treating the poor generally as recipients of charity who are effectively regarded as second-class citizens. It is not only the social rights of the poor which are affected however, and Lister (pp. 32–40) points to the limitation of civil rights as a result of the inability of many poor citizens to assert their rights through the legal process, and in particular the deficiencies of the legal aid and advice system, as compared with its initial promise which Marshall (pp. 29–31 above) saw as an important step towards equalising civil rights. Lister (pp. 41–6) also notes the various ways in which the poor tend to lose political rights and to become politically 'marginalised', and she rightly draws attention to the influence of economic and social factors in this process.

But the deterioration of the substantive rights of citizenship–civil, political and social–in Britain is due primarily to recent government policies, facilitated by the peculiarities of the British political and electoral system, and it is somewhat exceptional in Western Europe as a whole. In several European countries, to be sure, there have been constraints on the development of the welfare state and the growth of public expenditure that it entails, largely in response to the slowing down of economic growth, but nowhere else has the conception of social rights in particular been rejected in such a thoroughgoing way. In Britain, as Marshall (1981) observed, the welfare state survived at the end of the 1970s in a 'precarious and somewhat battered condition', and by the beginning of the 1990s this was evidently still more the case. In most of Western Europe, however, the welfare system has weathered the economic recession and the doctrines of the New Right rather more successfully, and the countries of the European Community (with the exception of Britain) have indeed signalled their desire to extend social rights through the proposals for a 'social charter'. To a surprising degree already, some of the rights of British citizens are now sustained by European institutions such as the European Court and the Commission on Human Rights; and political rights may well be extended through the influence of the other member countries of the European Community that have systems of proportional representation, now introduced into the voting procedure for the European Parliament. In this sphere, membership of the EC has stimulated a growing movement in Britain (Charter 88) for radical democratic reform of the political system, and it seems that the British may before long finally become citizens in a modern sense rather than subjects of the Crown'.

In the light of the discussion so far we can now consider the ways in which citizenship has developed over the past four decades, and the

72 Forty Years On

problems that have emerged for the kind of continuous enlargement of citizens' rights that Marshall envisaged. As I have noted, questions of formal citizenship (that is, membership of a nation-state) have assumed greater importance, for several reasons: (i) the large post-war immigration into some countries of foreign workers, who may be denied citizenship even though long resident (as is the case with the so-called 'guest-workers' in Germany); (ii) a growing 'internationalisation' of employment, especially in the European Community, which results from the internationalisation of economic activities and creates significant groups of legally resident aliens; and (iii) arising out of these processes more general issues concerning the relation between residence and citizenship, and the extent to which the nation-state should still be regarded as the sole, or principal, locus of citizenship in its substantive sense. Here, the important question arises of whether the rights of citizens should be conceived rather as the human rights of all individuals who are settled members of a community, regardless of their formal membership of a nation-state, and I shall discuss this larger issue at the end of this essay.

The development of substantive citizenship itself has followed a more uneven and variable course than was expected, and hoped for, by Marshall and other writers 40 years ago. The post-war welfare state then seemed to hold out the promise of more equal civil and political rights, and a substantial expansion of social rights which would gradually establish greater economic and social equality. In this sense the idea of citizenship did express a 'principle of equality', but this conflicted with the inequality embodied in the capitalist economic system and the class structure; and the outcome of the contest between the two depended not only on the extension of welfare in the narrower sense of the social services, health care, education, or even full employment, but on changes in property ownership, economic control and the distribution of real income, as Marshall (1981) recognised in his discussion of Durbin's exposition of democratic socialism (see above, pp. 59–61). In the 1950s and 1960s, in most of the West European countries, there was some progress towards greater equality in both these spheres; changes in the distribution of wealth and income, and in economic control through various forms of 'mixed economy', as well as expansion and improvement in the provision of welfare, facilitated by exceptionally high rates of economic growth.

But from the mid-1970s, as economic growth rates declined, the expansion of welfare and social rights was checked. Rising unemployment and ageing populations (and in some countries increased military expenditure) made greater demands on the state budget, while at the same time the mixed economy appeared to be functioning less successfully. Out of these conditions grew the new political doctrines and movements, most prominent in Britain and the USA, which advocated (and in those two countries particularly, implemented as far as possible) policies of retrenchment in government expenditure and a return to *laissez-faire* capitalism. As a result, in Britain notably, and to some extent elsewhere, inequality has increased again, and the capitalist market economy has become dominant over the welfare state. We need, therefore, to reconsider, in the light of post-war experience, what is the relationship between citizenship and social class, and how, in varying circumstances and in different countries, it may fluctuate.

4. Changing Classes, Changing Doctrines

The development of substantive citizenship as a growing body of civil, political, and social rights needs to be explained as well as described, and it is not enough to conceive this process in abstract, teleological terms as one that is somehow immanent in the rise of modern capitalism. Specific social groups were involved in the struggles to extend or restrict such rights, and in these conflicts social classes have played a major part. Marshall recognised that an element of conflict existed, but he expressed it as a clash between opposing principles rather than between classes, and his discussion of class was primarily concerned, as he said, with the impact of citizenship on social class, not with the ways in which the historical development of classes had itself generated new conceptions of citizenship and movements to expand the rights of citizens.

But the impact of class on citizenship is unmistakable. Civil rights, and to some extent political rights, were gained by the burgesses of medieval towns in opposition to the feudal aristocracy, and subsequently on a more extensive, national scale by the bourgeoisie in the early stages of development of industrial capitalism. In the nineteenth century the struggle to extend political rights was carried on mainly by the working class movement, in the revolutions of 1848, the Chartist movement, and the later campaigns for universal suffrage which had a prominent place in the activities of the rapidly growing socialist parties in Europe. These struggles continued into' the twentieth century and broadened into campaigns for social rights, instigated primarily by trade unions and socialist parties, and forming part of a more general movement towards socialism. The post-war welfare state in Western Europe was largely the outcome of these class-based actions, and in the period from the late 1940s to the early 1970s a kind of equilibrium seemed to have been attained, in the form of 'welfare capitalism' and a 'mixed economy',

74 Forty Years On

which Schumpeter (1949) characterised as a possible 'halfway house' on the march into socialism, and later social scientists described as neo-capitalism, organised capitalism or corporatism (Panitch 1977). In this system the interventionist state had a crucial role in negotiating agreements with large capital and organised labour, whereby a 'class compromise' could be reached (Offe 1980).

This compromise, and a degree of underlying consensus about the role of the state in the welfare-capitalist society, depended on the relative strength and the political orientations of different classes, and also to a large extent on the exceptionally high rates of economic growth in the period from the end of the war to the early 1970s. Economic growth and the enlargement of social rights in turn had an important effect on the class structure, as Marshall envisaged in his discussion of the impact of citizenship on social class. In the first place, the antecedent extension of political rights in the course of the twentieth century–itself, as I have argued, the outcome of class actions–had made possible the rapid growth of working-class parties in Western Europe (particularly marked after 1945) in terms of both membership and electoral support in most countries; and this was the crucial factor in the post-war development of social rights within what remained predominantly capitalist economies. At the same time working-class parties (mainly socialist or social democratic) had a conception of citizenship and social rights going considerably beyond what is ordinarily seen as the provision of welfare services. This embodied ideas of radical educational reform, the elimination of poverty, full employment as a major objective, economic democracy, which would involve the socialisation of basic, large-scale industrial, financial and service enterprises, and a general enhancement of the economic role of the state, including national planning in various forms. All this clearly pointed beyond a welfare state towards a more socialist form of society, as was recognised from different points of view in such writings as those of Schumpeter and Durbin, and expressed in the policies of the first post-war Labour government in Britain.

The policies and actions of socialist parties, in some cases as the government, in other cases an an influential partner in coalitions or as a powerful opposition, did in fact result in an extension of public ownership and economic planning in Western Europe, though in different degrees in individual countries; and the introduction of macro-economic planning in particular, it may be argued (Bottomore 1990, Chapter 3), was an important factor in the sustained economic growth of what Maddison (1982, p. 96) called the 'golden age' from 1950 to 1973. These changes, however, produced significant changes in the class structure and in the social and political outlook of different classes. First, post-war economic development, in which rapid technological innovation was a prominent feature, and the expansion of welfare rights (and hence the range of activities of government) steadily diminished the numbers of the manual working class and increased the numbers of those employed in white-collar, service occupations which ranged from clerical work to professional and technical activities in both private and public enterprises and in the extensive social services.[8] In the advanced industrial countries the manual working class now constitutes only half or less of the occupied population.

At the same time the economic situation of the working class changed substantially as a result of economic growth, full employment (until the early 1970s), the expansion of welfare services, and increased opportunities for social mobility determined mainly by the changing occupational structure, but also by somewhat improved access to education. Its social situation, compared with the nineteenth century and the earlier part of the twentieth century, also changed through the acquisition of important civil, political and social rights; that is to say, as a result of the growth of citizenship in Marshall's sense, which produced a condition very far removed from Marx's depiction of it in the 1840s as that of 'a class *in* civil society which is not a class *of* civil society', a class which experienced a '*total loss* of humanity' (Marx 1844). This transformation of the economic and social position of workers in the second half of the twentieth century gave rise, from the late 1950s, to much study and discussion of such phenomena as the 'affluent worker', the 'embourgeoisement' of the working class, and the emergence of a new type of 'middle-class society'. Some of the claims made about the degree to which such fundamental changes had occurred, or were occurring, were undoubtedly exaggerated, as were the conclusions drawn from them. They were critically examined, in the case of Britain, in a series of studies summarised in Goldthorpe et al. (1969), where the authors concluded that when three major aspects of the everyday lives of affluent workers – work, patterns of sociability, aspirations and social perspectives – are examined, the findings show that 'there remain important areas of common social experience which are still fairly distinctively working class', and that the evidence 'is sufficient to show how the thesis [of embourgeoisement] can in fact break down fairly decisively at any one of several points' (p. 157). Other criticisms of the thesis were made by those who pointed to the emergence of a 'new working class' of more affluent, skilled and technically qualified workers who still gave their allegiance to the traditional working class parties (Mallet 1975), and on the other side by those who drew attention to a process of 'proletarianisation' of some sections of the middle class (Renner 1953, Braverman 1974).[9]

76 Forty Years On

At all events it is evident at the present time that the distinction between working class and middle class persists in the capitalist industrial countries (and is now reappearing in the former state socialist societies of Eastern Europe), expressed in the divergent conceptions of social welfare and of the rights of citizenship that are expressed in the programmes and policies of rival, largely class-based parties. These societies can only be regarded as 'middle class' in the limited sense that the middle class, broadly defined, now forms a much larger part of the population; and even then such a conception requires that we should ignore the existence of a wealthy upper class, comprising the owners of large capital, which continues to dominate the economy and many other areas of social life, as well as the very great differentiation within the middle class itself in terms of property ownership, level of income, education and style of life. Nevertheless, the expansion of the middle class as a whole, in conjunction with economic growth and the extension of welfare services, did bring about significant changes in social and political attitudes. By the early 1970s, as I noted earlier, it was widely held that some kind of equilibrium and a broad consensus of opinion had been established in the West European societies on the basis of a welfare state or welfare society, a mixed economy, and a democratic political system. This view was reflected in the programmes of most political parties, and especially the socialist parties, which concentrated their attention increasingly on welfare policies rather than on such longer-term, traditional socialist aims as the extension of public ownership and the achievement of a more fundamental equality in the economic and social condition of all citizens, which used to be described as a 'classless' society.

How far this reorientation of party politics (which was more pronounced in some countries than in others) corresponded with a distinct change in social attitudes within particular classes is a matter of contention. The radical upheavals of the late 1960s indicated the limits of the consensus and the existence of widespread dissatisfaction in some parts of society (though not very prominently in the working class) with the existing hierarchical system; and while the immediate outcome of these events was a strengthening of conservative forces, their effects in the longer term–manifested, for example, in the growth of the women's movement, of green parties, and of the democratic opposition in Eastern Europe–have been more radical. Most attention has been given, however, to the question of changes in working-class attitudes. In some countries during the 1970s and 1980s, and most clearly in Britain, an increasing number of workers, particularly those who were in more highly paid skilled occupations, did transfer their allegiance from socialist parties to liberal or conservative parties, and this undoubtedly reflected in some way a change in the character of their principal economic and social concerns. Full employment, economic growth and an extensive welfare system had brought greater prosperity for a majority of the population, and along with this a preoccupation with individual or family standards of living and an emphasis on private consumption, aided by a rapid expansion of consumer credit. Hence the more prosperous workers, as well as a considerable part of the middle class, became as much or more concerned about inflation, interest rates and levels of personal taxation as about the expansion of the welfare state or the extension of public ownership, which seemed to have less significance for individual well-being. The general nature of this change might be depicted, as by Goldthorpe and Lockwood (1963)–although they were subsequently more critical of the idea of 'embourgeoisement' (see above, p. 75)–as the emergence of 'a distinctive view of society which diverges both from the radical individualism of the old middle class and from the comprehensive collectivism of the old working class'. In this view collectivism is accepted as a means ('instrumental collectivism'), but not as an end, the latter being conceived in more individualistic or family-centred terms, as involving the family's standard of living, the prospects for occupational advancement and the educational and career opportunities for children.

A change of this kind from a more collectivist to a more individualistic social outlook, did probably begin to manifest itself in the late 1950s and through the 1960s,[10] but we should not exaggerate either its novelty, its extent, its universality across countries or its durability. With the development of capitalism, and especially the growth of large corporations, the desire for individual advancement in the occupational hierarchy had already become very powerful early in this century, as Hilferding (1910, p. 347), among others, had noted, but such individualistic aspirations were greatly strengthened by the exceptional economic growth after the Second World War. Yet the extent to which individual and family-centred aims came to prevail was restrained in all the West European countries by a continuing strong attachment of working-class organisations (trade unions and political parties) to the collectivist, and in varying degrees egalitarian, aims that were symbolised above all by the welfare state, and to a lesser degree by public ownership. Furthermore, in those countries where socialist parties were particularly strong–in the Scandinavian countries and especially Sweden, in Austria and West Germany, and in France after 1981–there was little diminution in the support for collectivist ends, and in continental Western Europe as a whole there has been no very marked movement away from the established pattern

78 Forty Years On

of welfare provision and public ownership.[11] The virulent attack on the 'dependency culture' and the massive privatisation of public assets which characterised the outlook and policies of the government in Britain during the 1980s, were therefore quite exceptional.

Nevertheless, it may reasonably be argued that in most countries, by the late 1960s, there was no very strong or widespread desire among large sections of the working class, or in those sections of the middle class which had supported and benefited from the welfare state, to extend significantly either the scope of welfare provision or more particularly public ownership. The existing level of public services, including health and education, though capable of steady improvement, seemed to many people adequate, and the growing prosperity of a large part of the population had diverted attention, as I have noted, from collective provision to the concerns of individuals as consumers.

Since the mid-1970s, however, several factors have brought about a radical change in this situation. Ageing populations entailed higher levels of public spending on pensions and on health services, and this financial pressure on the welfare state was increased by economic recession and a general slackening of economic growth, accompanied by rising unemployment which made fresh demands on public expenditure. At the same time, expectations concerning the quality of public services continued to rise. In Britain, which had experienced since the 1950s growth rates lower than those of many other West European countries (or of Japan and the USA), a decline in manufacturing, and recurrent economic crises, the problems were more acute than elsewhere, and it is hardly surprising that by the end of the 1970s, the British welfare state should have been in a particularly debilitated condition, while the general economic situation provoked sharp fluctuations in political attitudes. By the end of the 1980s, however, the 'new economic policy' pursued for a decade had left the British economy in a still more parlous condition and the welfare state facing a still more uncertain future, in stark contrast with most other West European countries, including other member states of the European Community, which had coped more successfully with the economic recession–to some extent by means of effective economic planning–while retaining a 'mixed' economy of private and public ownership (and in some cases extending the latter), and in several countries even expanding welfare services.

Britain, during the past decade, has pursued idiosyncratic economic and social policies which contrast strongly with those of other European countries and have a greater affinity (also in respect of the problems they have engendered) with the policies of the USA in the same period. Of course, all the industrial societies had to face the difficulties created by

Tom Bottomore 79

recession and more sluggish economic growth from the mid-1970s, but most of the West European countries responded in a different way, maintaining more successfully their welfare systems, their various forms of mixed economy, and an important element of central planning. Hence, in considering the recent development of social rights it is essential to look beyond the case of Britain to the wider, especially European, context. Rydén and Bergström (1982), for example, note that in spite of the harsher economic conditions of the 1970s Sweden continued its policies of democratisation of working life and expansion of the public sector, emphasising the improvement of the environment, increased leisure, and greater scope for making the decisions that affect one's life;[12] and they conclude that 'Swedish society and the Swedish economy–the welfare state–have proved enormously strong against the instability and crises of the 1970s' (p. 8). Similarly, in Austria, the predominantly socialist governments since 1970 have not only maintained the welfare system but have extended social welfare programmes and progressively increased the participation of workers in the management of industry.

The experience of both countries shows how it is possible, even in more difficult conditions, to sustain a high level of material prosperity, low unemployment and low inflation, and at the same time to promote policies which extend the social rights of citizens. Their example has also had a significant influence elsewhere; for example, French governments since 1981, except for a short interlude of bi-partisan compromise, embarked on policies of extending public ownership, as well as increasing public expenditure on welfare services and on the social infrastructure (notably railways). Other European countries, while they have not been so strongly committed to extending social welfare, have for the most part maintained the existing levels of welfare expenditure, and unlike Britain they have not given an overriding priority to reducing public expenditure, privatising public assets, and encouraging the development of an unfettered market economy. The social and political orientation of most of the West European countries can be inferred to some extent from the policies of the European Community. In the European Parliament socialist parties and allied groups now form a majority, and their influence will be a significant factor in shaping the new European 'social charter', which envisages not only a progressive improvement of welfare rights but also an extension of industrial democracy through increased representation of workers in the management of industry. That, together with the influence of countries such as Sweden and Austria which are not at present members of the EC–though likely to join in the course of the 1990s–will probably bring about an enlarge-

80   Forty Years On

ment of social rights throughout Europe, which will also affect conditions in Eastern Europe, and in the longer term raise questions about social rights in the Third World. At the same time these developments are bound to provoke a reconsideration of what social rights *are*, and how far they can be defined in terms of citizenship, and I shall discuss this issue more fully in the following section of this essay.

What is clear at this point is that conceptions of rights, welfare and citizenship vary significantly across the political spectrum. The compromise or consensus of the 1950s and 1960s has largely broken down, and in Britain no longer exists at all, so that there is now more evidently a sharp division between left and right, between the contending principles of equality and inequality which Marshall regarded as being implicit in the relation between citizenship and capitalism. Conservative governments, especially where they have been influenced by the doctrines of the New Right,[13] are primarily concerned to limit, or reduce, public spending (except, in some cases, in the military sphere), and to enhance the role of private enterprise and markets. Socialist governments, on the other hand, are more inclined to maintain, and so far as possible increase, public spending (especially on education, health, and other welfare services); to regulate market relations by various means, including some degree of economic planning; to maintain a substantial element of public ownership (or to increase it) in a mixed economy, and more generally to encourage greater participation by workers in management. In addition, they aim to promote greater economic equality by fiscal and other measures.[14] Some part of these socialist policies (for example, welfare expenditure in some areas, and a mixed economy so long as the public sector is not too large) may also be supported by liberal and centre parties, which have sometimes been influential in coalition governments.

It remains the case, however, that governments of all political complexions have faced during the past two decades some general problems, such as I mentioned earlier, arising from ageing populations, slower economic growth, and the accompanying rise in unemployment, in maintaining or improving the level of welfare services. Here it should also be noted that lower rates of economic growth are not to be regarded simply as a temporary effect of various external shocks, but need to be considered in a much broader context which takes account of the environmental consequences of high growth rates. The 'growth-addiction' of the post-war period in the industrial and industrialising countries now seems more questionable,[15] and comparisons of aggregate growth rates, without regard to what is growing or what the ecological effects may be, no longer seem at all satisfactory as a measure of the level of welfare, in its broadest sense, in different countries.

Looked at more closely indeed these general problems also intimate the existence of other important differences between conservative and socialist parties in their approach to welfare policies. Thus, the changing age structure of the population in the industrial societies, as well as the extension of the period of formal education, call for new reflection on the way in which the social product is divided between different age categories, not simply for palliative measures to deal with hardship among young people or the elderly; and such new conceptions of the division of social welfare are more likely to come from socialist parties. Similarly, low growth rates, which may indeed be desirable in some areas as I have suggested, raise questions particularly about where, and to what extent, growth should be stimulated—for example, in the provision of low-cost housing and improved health care—and this involves a degree of economic planning going beyond what is generally acceptable to conservative parties. The unemployment which is an outcome of economic recession in the traditional areas of capitalist growth does not only add considerably, and wastefully, to public expenditure, but also has a generally demoralising effect on the substantial part of the population which is exposed to it, as well as effectively diminishing their rights as citizens (see above, p. 71). Here the contrast between very right-wing conservative governments, as in Britain, and such socialist governments as those in Sweden and Austria, in the nature and effectiveness of their policies to combat unemployment, is striking.

We have still to consider, however, a further aspect of the development of social rights, which is alluded to by Rydén and Bergström (1982; see above p. 79) when they refer to the sense of alienation experienced by the individual confronting large bureaucracies. This, as they make clear, does not arise only from the existence of public bureaucracies, but as Schumpeter also argued (1942, p. 206), from the general bureaucratisation of life in modern industrial societies, which are increasingly dominated, in almost every sphere, by very large, bureaucratically managed organisations. Nevertheless, it is probably in relation to public bureaucracies that individuals have felt most frustrated, as was most evident in the state socialist countries of Eastern Europe, though here the major resentment was directed specifically against the political dictatorship of communist parties and rule by party officials. In Western Europe the frustrations were experienced more diffusely, and in different ways by particular groups in the population, as limitations on personal freedom, or as problems of the inadequacy or inefficiency of public services; and in Britain especially such sentiments no doubt had some effect in bringing about a change towards a more individualistic attitude,

82 Forty Years On

although dissatisfaction with the poor performance of the economy was a more potent factor, and in the last few years there has been a resurgence of support for increased spending on social welfare.

In any advanced welfare system, however, there are bound to be problems in attaining a balance between efficient administration and concern for the individual as a consumer of public services, between the restrictions necessarily imposed by welfare policies and the liberty of the individual. The achievement of such a balance, which is never likely to reach a state of perfection, may be helped by a greater involvement of consumer groups, and of charitable organisations and mutual aid groups, in the operation of the welfare services, as is discussed in the most recent edition of Marshall's *Social Policy* (completed by A.M. Rees, 1985, Chapter 13). Here, as elsewhere, some mixture of public and private endeavour (the latter, in the form of voluntary associations, being itself an expression of citizenship) may be valuable, even though the foundation and main structure of the welfare system is constituted essentially by publicly provided services.

At work, in the process of production, the individual is faced with either private or public bureaucracies, and individual welfare in this sphere depends very clearly upon the extent of social rights. Health and safety regulations, a statutory minimum wage, the protection given by independent trade unions, are necessary elements in this body of rights, but they need to be complemented by other rights which would give workers more control over the labour process itself, through greater participation in the management of enterprises. This kind of extension of social rights has been undertaken in various forms–in the system of self-management in Yugoslavia, and in other ways, which may be more or less comprehensive, in countries such as Austria, Germany and Sweden–and it is envisaged on a wider scale in the European Community's proposals for a social charter.

It may well be, therefore, that after 1992, with the creation of a single market in the European Community, the eventual accession of new members, and a continuing process of unification, there will be a substantial extension of social rights, and to some extent of civil and political rights, in a direction which has been advocated particularly by socialist parties. But any such extension will need to pay more attention to eradicating those specific inequalities which arise from differences of gender or ethno-cultural origins, and will also confront larger issues concerning the definition and scope of social rights, their implications for the economic structure and the class system, and the relation between social rights in the advanced industrial countries and the rights of individuals elsewhere in the world, especially in the poorest countries.

Tom Bottomore 83

It is to those broader questions that I shall now turn.

5. A Kind of Conclusion

In this essay I have moved some way beyond the themes which Marshall discussed in 1949. The new questions that are raised here concern the relation between formal and substantive citizenship; the connection between rights and citizenship; the diverse and conflicting conceptions of the nature and extent of social rights; the role of classes, and other social groups, in the development of such rights; the tensions between a capitalist market economy and a welfare state, arising from their different aims and outcomes; and the variations of citizenship, in principle and practice, between nations. These questions now need to be more closely considered.

The growing interest in formal citizenship–that is, membership of a nation-state–has been provoked to a large extent by the scale of post-war migration, actual and potential, to the advanced industrial countries. Citizenship, in its formal, legal sense, is clearly a major factor affecting the attribution of rights, even though it is neither a necessary nor a sufficient condition for the effective possession or exercise of various rights (see above p. 66); and the post-war migrations, especially of workers from poorer countries during the period of rapid economic growth up to the early 1970s, led in due course to more stringent definitions of eligibility for citizenship in some industrial countries, and to stricter immigration controls in most of them. From these conditions there has emerged a new debate about formal citizenship, as well as organisations campaigning for more liberal policies in the conferment of citizenship on long-term residents (and on the other side nationalist, not to say xenophobic, movements which aim to exclude or expel foreign workers); and the debate has raised important issues concerning the nature of citizenship in the modern world, and the relationship between residence and citizenship.

Several contributors to Brubaker's (1989) volume discuss various aspects of these questions. Thus Carens (p. 31) argues that 'those allowed to reside and work in a nation should be granted the right to become citizens following a moderate passage of time and some reasonable formalities', basing his argument on 'principles that are implicit in the institutions and practices of liberal democratic societies'. Schuck, however, writing from a similar standpoint, suggests that in the USA changes in recent decades 'have reduced almost to the vanishing point the marginal value of citizenship as compared to resident alien status' (p. 52), and he notes that 'a large number of aliens who are eligible to

84 *Forty Years On*

naturalise fail to do so', one reason for this probably being 'many aliens' continuing hope to return to their native lands to live' (p. 57). In this context Hammar raises the question of dual citizenship, pointing out that in spite of international efforts to limit it 'the number of persons holding more than one citizenship has increased substantially in recent decades and will probably continue to increase' (p. 81). He also observes that there is a large and growing group of 'privileged non citizens', especially in continental Europe, for whom he suggests using the term 'denizens', who have the right to settle in the country, work there, receive social benefits, and even in some circumstances to vote (pp. 83–4).

Dual citizenship raises important political issues in relation to the nation-state and nationality, especially concerning 'dual loyalties', and Hamman goes on to examine some of the problems that emerge, both for states and for individuals, from the reality that 'the formally simple notion of citizenship is in fact a very complex one' (p. 86). The question of dual citizenship is likely to become still more important in Europe, in another sense, as the European Community moves towards closer economic and political union. In effect, citizens of the EC countries will increasingly have a kind of dual citizenship, already existing to some extent, in the EC and their own nation. But this also raises questions about the situation of 'denizens' in the future Community. The creation, from 1992, of a 'Europe without frontiers' will establish freedom of movement within the EC for those who are formally citizens of a member country, not for 'denizens' who are outside this category, and some observers fear that the outcome may be a 'Fortress Europe' with more severe restrictions on entry and immigration for non-citizens.

More generally, the discussions of dual citizenship raise major questions about the connection between citizenship, residence, and the rights of the individual. These rights are already to a considerable extent dissociated from formal citizenship, as Schuck has noted in the case of the USA, and as will be the case (with the qualifications I have indicated) in the EC. Increasingly, civil and social rights, and with some limitations political rights, are granted to all those who live and work, or are retired, in a particular country, regardless of their national citizenship. On the other side, the significance of formal citizenship is to be found mainly in the desire of at any rate a substantial proportion of the population in nation-states to maintain a distinct and separate identity which is the product of a historical tradition, long-established institutions, and a national culture; and the importance of such formal citizenship can be seen not only in the case of existing nation-states, but also in the various movements of 'nations within nation-states' for greater autonomy or complete independence. Nevertheless, this kind of attachment to a

Tom Bottomore   85

particular nation is somewhat diminished by the growth of dual citizenship, and in Europe it may be further reduced by the process of integration in the EC, even though in Eastern Europe at the present time there is an upsurge of nationalist and separatist movements.[16]

From this discussion it will be apparent that formal citizenship and substantive citizenship raise issues of very different kinds; in one case concerning national identity and the historical role of nation-states as the pre-eminent modern form of organisation of a political community, in the other concerning the rights, and particularly the social rights, of individuals living in a community. We should therefore go on to consider whether the idea of citizenship now provides the most useful conceptual framework within which to examine the development of individual rights. The alternative would be to conceive a body of human rights which each individual should possess in any community in which he or she lives and/or works, regardless of national origins and formal citizenship. This body of rights will necessarily vary between different groups of countries, depending to a considerable extent, especially in the case of social rights, upon the level of economic and social development, and I shall confine my discussion largely to the advanced industrial societies.

In these countries themselves, however, rights are still developing, and while it is illuminating in many respects to conceive, as Marshall did, of a progression from civil to political and then to social rights, this tends to obscure the fact that civil and political rights have not been established once and for all, in some near-perfect form, as the basis from which social rights can develop, but are also capable of further extension. Civil rights, including personal liberty, freedom of thought and speech, the right to own property, and access to justice through the courts, are more or less well established, in various forms, in the industrial countries, but many questions concerning them are still hotly debated: such as whether they should be embodied in a bill of rights, and in legislation concerning freedom of information; to what extent the ownership and use of property (especially productive property) should be regulated; what measures are needed to ensure that access to justice is not only in principle, but effectively, equal for all members of the community, whatever their economic and social circumstances.

The industrial countries are, in different ways, political democracies, but here too many controversial issues arise concerning how democratic they are; how far their political institutions and electoral systems allow the effective expression of diverse social and political attitudes, whether government should be more 'open' and less elitist, and whether democracy should be extended more widely, especially in the economic sphere, in order to encourage and facilitate more active participation in

86   Forty Years On

decision-making at all levels of social life.[17] It should also be taken into account in considering the idea of a general progression of rights that in the state-socialist societies of Eastern Europe, until the recent changes, important social rights were established while civil and political rights were severely curtailed. Following the collapse of the communist regimes at the end of 1989, and the cumulative reforms in the Soviet Union, basic civil rights, and political democracy in the form of multi-party systems and free elections, have been restored or created for the first time; but this achievement brings these societies to the point where wider issues of the effective exercise of civil and political rights become matters of controversy. Already in some countries social movements which played a leading role in bringing about the changes have been marginalised, while new nationalist, as well as class movements and parties have emerged. At the same time important social rights, as they were conceived in the social policies of the previous regimes (full employment, low-cost housing and public transport, maternity leave and child care facilities) are either under threat or already being whittled away.

In all the industrial countries indeed, social rights are those which are most fiercely debated, not only with regard to the existing provision for education, health care, pensions, unemployment benefits and other kinds of social assistance in welfare states that differ in their level of development, but in respect of the scope of social rights in principle, and the place they should occupy in the social and societal[18] policies of an advanced industrial country. Do social rights include such things as adequate housing, provided if necessary by public authorities, employment, some degree of participation by employees in the management of enterprises, and protection against discrimination on grounds of ethnic origin or gender? These issues clearly divide political parties of the left and right, along lines which I indicated earlier, but they also involve social movements and organisations concerned with the rights of particular groups in the population: women, pensioners, the very poor, the homeless, the unemployed and others. Undoubtedly, these groups experience specific hardships and problems with which social policy has to deal, but their situation also derives in large measure from a more general state of affairs brought about the societal policies of parties and governments.

Such policies, which are a major factor in the constitution, extension, or contraction of a body of social rights, themselves depend upon the conceptions of society and the social philosophies that guide the actions of political parties in their efforts to influence the course of events, either in government or in opposition. They do so in two particularly important respects; first, in relation to the structure and operation of the economy, and secondly, in respect of the degree of equality that should exist among citizens and residents. Right-wing parties tend to regard society as a collection of individuals connected with each other primarily through contractual relationships such as exist in a private enterprise economy, which provides an underlying model for social relations. This conception, however, may be variously expressed; in an extreme form, inspired by a selective reading of Adam Smith, as the proposition uttered by a former British prime minister, that 'there is no such thing as society', or in a more qualified form in the notion of a 'social market economy'. It is always qualified, in another sense, by an insistence on the importance of the nation-state (that is to say, on the obligations of formal citizenship), and a distaste for dual citizenship. The emphasis on the individual and individual enterprise also entails an acceptance of a large degree of economic and social inequality, and again in the extreme case, hostility to what is called a 'dependency culture'; though in the post-war period such inequality has been mitigated, to a greater or lesser extent in different countries, by welfare provisions designed to benefit the very poor.

Left-wing parties, on the other hand, are more inclined to conceive the economy as a process of social production of goods and services of all kinds (both public and private), which should be regulated, and in some degree planned, for the benefit of all the inhabitants of a country, implying also a greater equality among these inhabitants. The welfare state is generally seen as an important equalising agency, but one which needs to be complemented by other, more socialist measures, including progressive taxation of wealth and income and public ownership of some vital areas of the economy. What is distinctive in the doctrines of left-wing parties is this recognition of the social nature of production, and the emphasis on the ways in which the social product should be distributed in order to provide a comfortable and decent life for all those who live in the society.

In the post-war period, however, the doctrines of many, if not all, conservative and socialist parties have undergone a gradual change, and various intermediate views have emerged, expressed in such conceptions as the 'mixed' economy', the 'social market economy', or the 'socialist market economy'. As a result the opposition between right-wing and left-wing parties is now less extreme than it was earlier in the twentieth century, in many European countries, although this has come about largely through the growing post-war influence of socialist parties and their success in establishing the basic framework of the welfare state. Nevertheless, a conflict persists, as Marshall noted, between the ten-

88 Forty Years On

dency of a capitalist market economy to produce greater inequality, and the tendency, and intention, of the welfare state to create greater equality. What has become less clear, in the policies of many socialist parties, as compared with the ideas expounded by Durbin at the end of the 1930s (above, p. 60), is the part that is to be played in achieving greater equality, or in the longer term an egalitarian society, by other measures, and in particular by public ownership and economic planning, both of which have social effects going far beyond those resulting from the extensive provision of welfare services. Socialist parties, during the past few decades, have withdrawn to a considerable extent from their historical commitment to public ownership and planning, partly in reaction against the experience of the state-socialist societies, partly under the influence of new doctrines extolling the virtues of private enterprise and free markets, and condemning the inefficiency of publicly owned enterprises and the irrationality of planning.

These doctrines, which I have referred to elsewhere as a new 'folklore of capitalism', have been influential beyond their deserts if we consider the real achievements of planning and public enterprise in much of Western Europe since the war (Bottomore 1990, Chapter 3), but they have raised important questions about how extensive public ownership should be and what kind of relationship between planning and markets could achieve at the same time optimum economic efficiency and a less unequal distribution of the social product. The situation confronting all political parties and social movements is, however, still more complex if we consider two other major issues which profoundly affect the present and future state of human rights on a world scale. One is the relationship between the industrial countries and the poorer, less-developed countries of the Third World; the other, the impact of economic growth, as it has been conceived and implemented since the war, on the natural environment.

As to the first question it may be argued that the post-war development of the industrial societies has been, to a considerable extent, at the expense of low-income and some middle-income countries, because the economic dominance of the former has enabled them to dictate the terms of trade, investment and aid.[19] It is also true, however, that the policies pursued by dominant groups, for their own enrichment, in poorer countries themselves, have often created a still greater dependence on the industrial countries and on multinational corporations, and have impeded economic development; while in some countries, and notably at present in some parts of Africa, the failure to control population growth has greatly increased the difficulties.[20] Since the early 1980s many studies have been devoted to what has become known as the North–

South divide (though this is geographically somewhat misleading),[21] but there have not yet emerged effective international policies which would reduce significantly the gap between rich and poor countries, or even prevent its widening; and for as long as this gap remains as wide as it now is, there will be gross inequalities in the extent of human rights, especially social rights, between different regions of the world.

The impact of economic development on the environment provokes equally important questions about social rights, affecting industrial, industrialising and non-industrial countries in various ways. The environmental costs of rapid industrialisation have been highlighted recently by the knowledge of its consequences in Eastern Europe which we have acquired since the revolutions of 1989, but the environmental damage inflicted by the capitalist industrial societies has also been very great, especially in the earlier phase of their development, and has been felt throughout large areas of the Third World as well as in the industrialised countries themselves. Only in the past two decades has such damage begun to be checked, through the actions of ecology movements and newly-formed green parties which challenge traditional conceptions of economic growth. But these new movements and parties still have difficulty in drawing support away from the older parties, and their main influence so far has been in modifying the policies of the latter to take more account of environmental issues.

It is evident today that what have been called the rights of citizenship, which I now refer to in a broader context as human rights, are in a continuous process of development which is profoundly affected by changing external conditions (especially in the economy), by the emergence of new problems and the search for new solutions. One major, more or less constant, factor in this process, as I have emphasised, has been the antithesis between the inegalitarian structure and consequences of a capitalist economy and the claims for greater equality made by diverse social movements since the end of the eighteenth century. Within this general opposition of different interests and values the conflict between classes and class-based parties still plays a leading role as a principal source of policies intended to limit or extend the scope of human rights, and in particular the degree of collective provision to meet what are defined as the basic needs of all members of a society at various stages in its development. Yet it is clear that in the late twentieth century other kinds of inequality besides those of class–between rich and poor countries, between the sexes, between ethnic groups–have become more salient than they were, even if in some cases they can be related, in part, to the inequalities engendered by capitalism.

Looking back to 1949 we can see that the discussion of rights at that

90   Forty Years On

time was profoundly affected by a number of specific factors: the vivid recollection of pre-war unemployment, poverty, inadequate health care and education; the change in social attitudes brought about by the war, and in particular the growing influence of the European socialist movement; and in Britain the commitment of the post-war Labour government to overcoming the social evils of the 1930s, partly through the creation of a welfare state, partly by more socialist measures, such as Durbin (1940) had envisaged, in order to accomplish, by degrees, a radical transformation of the economy and the class system. Marshall's essay made a seminal contribution to this discussion by distinguishing between the three areas of civil, political and social rights, exploring the relationship between them, and emphasising the increasing importance of social rights in the twentieth century. In retrospect his study can be seen as formulating some general principles for the welfare state, and as foreshadowing to some extent the mixed economies of welfare capitalism which later emerged, while recognising the tensions that were likely to persist in this form of society between egalitarian and inegalitarian tendencies. These tensions became more acute in the late 1970s, and Marshall, after having contributed substantially to studies of the welfare state and its problems in successive editions of his book *Social Policy* (1965, 5th edn, 1985), returned in an essay of 1981 (see above pp. 59–61) to a consideration of the relation between capitalism, socialism and welfare, in the course of which he asserted forthrightly that the mixed economy was 'not enough', particularly in that sphere of policy which is concerned with the prevention rather than the relief of poverty. Today, Marshall's conception of citizenship is often invoked to stress the importance of civil and political rights, both in themselves and as means for the extension of social rights–more particularly with reference to the collapse of the communist dictatorships in Eastern Europe–but I do not think he would have been at all enthusiastic about any sweeping restoration of *laissez-faire* capitalism as an outcome of this collapse, and he might well have looked with a sympathetic, if critical, eye on the various projects for democratic 'socialism with markets' which aim to create the kind of new social order, combining economic efficiency with social justice, that he advocated.

It is from such a standpoint, at all events, that I have undertaken this new analysis of the development of rights, in the spirit of Marshall's essay, and endeavouring, as he did, to form new conceptions that may help to illuminate the paths along which further progress is possible. But in certain respects, as will be clear, I have diverged from his approach. First, taking account of the very different issues that are raised by formal and substantive citizenship, I have reached the conclusion that we should examine civil, political and social rights in the framework of a conception of general human rights, rather than citizenship. I have also argued that human rights need to be considered on a global scale, above all in the context of the massive inequalities between rich and poor nations. Further, I have given more attention to ethnic and gender inequalities which coexist with those of class, and in some times and places are more prominent; but at the same time I have emphasised more strongly than Marshall did the historical role that classes, and the conflict between them, have played in limiting or extending the range of human rights. In the same context I have also argued that *all* human rights—civil, political and social—are continually developing and should not be regarded at any historical moment as having attained a final, definitive form. The social inventiveness of human beings seems to me as great as their capacity for technological innovation. Finally, I have emphasised perhaps more strongly than Marshall did the economic and class constraints upon the effective exercise of formally established rights, and from that perspective have attributed greater importance to a socialist reconstruction of the economy which would greatly reduce the concentration of wealth and economic power in the hands of a particular class.

The state of human rights in the world today, and their development, show contradictory features. In many countries the social rights embodied in the institutions of the welfare state have become less secure as a consequence of the economic recession, and in some cases, there has been a greater reliance on market forces rather than public expenditure.[22] At the same time the gap between rich and poor countries has steadily widened, and in the world as a whole poverty has been increasing. On the other side, the revolutions in Eastern Europe and the continuing reforms in the Soviet Union have established fundamental civil and political rights, although in the process some valuable social rights are being lost; while in Western Europe the proposed 'social charter' of the European Community is a notable attempt to extend the range of social rights. For Europe as a whole there is now a prospect, in this decade, of extending human rights in ways which encompass many of the new issues that I have discussed, but this will only come about, in my view, to the extent that social and societal policies are informed by a conception of social production as the planned production of welfare, or well-being, which entails also an equitable division of the product among the members of society. Over the longer term, policies are needed to achieve a more equitable distribution of the product of social labour on a world scale, and it is here, without doubt, that the most daunting and intractable problems have to be faced. The alternative to

92   Forty Years On

solving them, however, is the continued existence of a world riven by discord and conflict, in which islands of well-being are surrounded by oceans of misery.

Notes

1. On these different aspects see Tinbergen (1968), Van der Pijl (1989).
2. In Sweden almost continuously throughout the post-war period, and in Austria for much of the time since 1970.
3. See Panitch (1977), Offe (1980).
4. See Bottomore (1990, pp. 112–13, 130).
5. The differences between France and Germany are more extensively analysed in Brubaker (1992).
6. See A. Szalai (1972).
7. The most influential early study to raise these issues was probably Simone de Beauvoir's *The Second Sex* (1949), which was followed by a spate of publications from diverse standpoints, provoking many disagreements and controversies, for example between feminists and Marxists (Barrett 1988, Banks 1981).
8. The general pattern of change is indicated in a study of occupations in Britain by Routh (1980) who shows that between 1951 and 1979 the proportion of the occupied population classified as manual workers (including foremen) fell from 72 per cent to 54 per cent, while the proportion of clerical and professional workers, managers and employers rose from 28 per cent to 46 per cent (pp. 5, 45). By 1990 the proportion of manual workers had declined still further.
9. I have examined these and other aspects of the changing class structure more fully in Bottomore (1991).
10. I have referred elsewhere (Bottomore 1991, Chapter 5) to studies made in some other European countries.
11. For an account of the different attitudes and policies in some of these countries, see Gallie (1978), Scase (1977), Rydén and Bergström (1982). It should be noted too that in France since 1981 public ownership has been extended, while in Sweden the project for employee investment funds outlined a new conception of collective ownership (Bottomore 1990, p. 130).
12. They also point out, however, that these policies involved 'continued centralisation, bureaucratisation, intensified efficiency and a sense of alienation in the individual facing large private and public bureaucracies'; and these are matters to which I shall return later.
13. For a short survey of these doctrines, see Grant (1992), and for a critical analysis of them King (1987).
14. See the exposition of a project for European recovery from a socialist perspective in Holland (1983).
15. On one important aspect of this question, see Hirsch (1977).

Tom Bottomore 93

16. But in Eastern Europe too there are opposing movements to create a broader federation, especially in the regions of central Europe which once formed part of the Habsburg empire, though the difficulties are formidable (Ash 1989). Furthermore, the admission of new member states to the EC, including some from Eastern Europe, which seems possible during the next decade, would extend the area in which federalist rather than nationalist structures prevail.

17. On the question of democracy and participation see Pateman (1970), and for a critical assessment Holden (1988, Chapter 3).

18. I use this term in the sense given to it by Ferge (above, p. 62).

19. Maddison (1989) has shown that between 1950 and 1987 the average GDP per capita in Latin America and Asia declined relative to that in the industrial (OECD) countries (although there was some improvement in Asia after 1973). Furthermore, in the 1980s an increasing number of countries, especially in Africa and Latin America, experienced an absolute decline in GDP per capita (see *Socialist Economic Bulletin*, 3, December 1990).

20. See the discussion by Myrdal (1968, vol. 2, part 6) in his study of poverty in South Asia, and more recently by Tabah (1982).

21. One of the best known is that produced by the Independent Commission on Development Issues, chaired by Willy Brandt, which gave wide currency to the North–South distinction (Brandt Commission 1983). See also the discussion of this and other reports by Holm (1985).

22. Some of the complexities and problems of the welfare state in Britain, which were already apparent in the 1980s, are indicated in Marshall (1985, in the concluding chapter by A.M. Rees).

Bibliography

Ash, Timothy Garton (1989) 'Does Central Europe exist?' in George Schöpflin and Nancy Wood (eds), *In Search of Central Europe* (Oxford: Polity Press/Blackwell).

Banks, Olive (1981) *Faces of Feminism* (Oxford: Martin Robertson).

Barrett, Michèle (1988) *Women's Oppression Today* (2nd edn; London: New Left Books).

Beauvoir, Simone de (1949) *The Second Sex* (Harmondsworth: Penguin Books, 1983).

Bottomore, Tom (1990) *The Socialist Economy: Theory and Practice* (Hemel Hempstead: Harvester-Wheatsheaf).

Bottomore, Tom (1991) *Classes in Modern Society* (2nd edn; London: Unwin Hyman).

Brandt Commission (1983) *Common Crisis, North–South: Cooperation for World Recovery* (London: Pan Books).

Braverman, H. (1974) *Labour and Monopoly Capital* (New York: Monthly Review Press).

Brubaker, W. Rogers (1992, forthcoming) *Citizenship and Nationhood in France and Germany* (Cambridge, Mass. Harvard University Press).

Brubaker, W. Rogers (ed.) (1989) *Immigration and the Politics of Citizenship in Europe and North America* (Lanham, New York, London: University Press of America).

Durbin, E.F.M. (1940) *The Politics of Democratic Socialism* (London: Routledge).

Ferge, Zsuzsa (1979) *A Society in the Making: Hungarian Social and Societal Policy, 1945–75* (Harmondsworth: Penguin Books).

Gallie, Duncan (1978) *In Search of the New Working Class* (Cambridge: Cambridge University Press).

Goldthorpe, John H. and Lockwood, David (1963) 'Affluence and the British class structure', *Sociological Review*, 11 (2), July.

Goldthorpe, John H. et al. (1969) *The Affluent Worker in the Class Structure* (Cambridge: Cambridge University Press).

Grant, R.A.D. (1992, forthcoming) 'The New Right', in William Outhwaite and Tom Bottomore (eds), *Blackwell Dictionary of Twentieth Century Social Thought* (Oxford: Blackwell).

Hilferding, Rudolf (1910) *Finance Capital: A Study of the Latest Phase of Capitalist Development* (London: Routledge & Kegan Paul, 1981).

Hirsch, Fred (1977) *Social Limits to Growth* (London: Routledge & Kegan Paul).

Holden, Barry (1988) *Understanding Liberal Democracy* (Hemel Hempstead: Philip Allan).

Holland, Stuart (ed.) (1983) *Out of Crisis: A Project for European Recovery* (Nottingham: Spokesman Books).

Holm, Hans-Henrik (1985) 'Brandt, Palme and Thorssen: A strategy that does not work?', *IDS Bulletin*, 16 (4), October (Brighton: Institute of Development Studies at the University of Sussex).

King, D. (1987) *The New Right: Politics, Markets and Citizenship* (London: Macmillan).

Lister, Ruth (1990) *The Exclusive Society* (London: Child Poverty Action Group).

Maddison, Angus (1982) *Phases of Capitalist Development* (Oxford: Oxford University Press).

Maddison, Angus (1989) *The World Economy in the Twentieth Century* (Paris: OECD).

Mallet, Serge (1975) *The New Working Class* (Nottingham: Spokesman Books).

Marshall, Alfred (1873) 'The future of the working classes', in A.C. Pigou (ed.), *Memorials of Alfred Marshall* (London: Macmillan, 1925).

Marshall, T.H. (1972) 'Value problems of welfare-capitalism', reprinted in Marshall 1981.

Marshall, T.H. (1981) *The Right to Welfare and Other Essays* (London: Heinemann).

Marshall, T.H. (1985) *Social Policy* (5th edn, completed by A.M. Rees; London: Hutchinson).

Marx, Karl (1844) 'Critique of Hegel's Philosophy of Right. Introduction'.

Myrdal, Gunnar (1968) *Asian Drama* (New York: Pantheon).

Offe, Claus (1980) 'The separation of form and content in liberal democratic politics', *Studies in Political Economy*, 3.

Panitch, Leo (1977) 'The development of corporatism in liberal democracies', *Comparative Political Studies*, 10(1).

Pateman, Carole (1970) *Participation and Democratic Theory* (Cambridge: Cambridge University Press).

Postan, M.M. (1967) *Economic History of Western Europe, 1945–64* (London: Methuen).

96 Bibliography

Renner, Karl (1953) *Wandlungen der modernen Gesellschaft. Zwei Abhandlungen über die Probleme der Nachkriegszeit* (Vienna: Wiener Volksbuchhandlung).

Report of the Royal Commission on Population, June 1949. Cmd. 7695. (London: Stationery Office).

Robson, William A. (1976) *Welfare State and Welfare Society* (London: Allen & Unwin).

Routh, G. (1980) *Occupation and Pay in Great Britain 1906–79* (London: Macmillan)

Rydén, Bengt and Bergström, Villy (eds) (1982) *Sweden: Choices for Economic and Social Policy in the 1980s* (London: Allen & Unwin).

Scase, Richard (1977) *Social Democracy in Capitalist Society: Working Class Politics in Britain and Sweden* (London: Croom Helm).

Schumpeter, J.A. (1942) *Capitalism, Socialism and Democracy* (6th edn; London: Allen & Unwin, 1987).

Schumpeter, J.A. (1949) 'The march into socialism' (an address to the American Economic Association, incorporated in later editions of *Capitalism, Socialism and Democracy*).

Socialist Economic Bulletin, 3, December 1990 (London).

Szalai, A. et al. (eds) (1972) *The Use of Time* (The Hague: Mouton).

Tabah, L. (1982) 'Population growth', in Just Faaland (ed.), *Population and the World Economy in the 21st Century* (Oxford: Blackwell).

Tawney, R.H. (1952) *Equality* (4th edn; London: Allen & Unwin).

Tinbergen, J. (1968) 'Planning, Economic (Western Europe)', in *International Encylopaedia of the Social Sciences*, vol. 12 (New York: Macmillan and The Free Press).

Titmuss, Richard M. (1956) 'The social division of welfare: some reflections on the search for equity', in *Essays on 'The Welfare State'* (London: Allen & Unwin, 1958).

Titmuss, Richard M. (1962) *Income Distribution and Social Change* (London: Allen & Unwin).

Turner, Bryan S. (1986) *Citizenship and Capitalism* (London: Allen & Unwin).

Van der Pijl, Kees (1989) 'The international level', in Tom Bottomore and Robert J. Brym (eds), *The Capitalist Class; An International Study* (Hemel Hempstead: Harvester-Wheatsheaf).

Webb, Sidney (1989) 'Historic', in G. Bernard Shaw (ed.), *Fabian Essays in Socialism* (London: The Fabian Society and Allen & Unwin, 1931).

[3]

Rights, Relationality, and Membership: Rethinking the Making and Meaning of Citizenship

Margaret R. Somers

The republication after 40 years of T. H. Marshall's Citizenship and Social Class signifies a revived interest in sociolegal historical approaches to citizenship rights. For decades students have been guided by Marshall's classic treatise. But can Marshall's argument for the causal power of the "transition from feudalism to capitalism" continue to provide an adequate grounding for sociolegal approaches to citizenship and rights formation? Building on Marshall's path-breaking expansion of the concept of citizenship, I use institutional analysis and causal narrativity to present an alternative explanation. I argue that modern citizenship rights are a contingent outcome of the convergence of England's medieval legal revolutions with its regionally varied local legal and political cultures, not of the emergence of capitalist markets.

Attention to the meaning and making of citizenship rights has been glaringly absent from recent sociolegal research agendas for far too long. Thirty years have passed since Reinhard Bendix's *Nation-Building and Citizenship*, and over 40 since T. H. Marshall first published his masterful series

---

Margaret R. Somers is an assistant professor of sociology at the University of Michigan. Direct all correspondence to Margaret R. Somers, Department of Sociology, University of Michigan, Ann Arbor, MI 48109.

For their involvement in various aspects of the making and meaning of this article, the author thanks Julia Adams, Daniel Bell, Fred Block, Kacey Christiansen, Frank Dobbin, Gloria Gibson, Thomas Green, Richard Lempert, Larry Miller, Jane Rafferty, Bill Sewell, Marc Steinberg, Arthur Stinchcombe, Charles Tilly, Harrison White and the anonymous *Law and Social Inquiry* referees. For generous support during much of the period during which this research was carried out, she thanks the University of Michigan for Rackham Faculty Recognition, Rackham Faculty Support, Rackham Research Partnership, LSA College Faculty Assistance, and Office of the Vice-President for Research Grants.

64 LAW AND SOCIAL INQUIRY

of lectures, *Citizenship and Social Class*.[1] Happily this is beginning to change with the recent contributions of, among others, Jeffrey Alexander, Rogers Brubaker, Anthony Giddens, Michael Mann, Charles Tilly, Bryan Turner, and Alan Wolfe.[2] Now we truly have cause for scholarly celebration with the republication in a new edition of the T. H. Marshall volume (with a lengthy introduction by Tom Bottomore).[3] Hardly could this be more timely. Rarely have Marshall's driving themes—the politics of citizenship, rights, and social change—more dramatically been yoked together than in the revolutions and upheavals of recent years. Across Europe and Asia, societies constructed and reconstructed on a framework of national state control and putative economic redistribution have collapsed or have been fundamentally challenged by the dynamic momentum of an extraordinary source of power—the mobilizing force of popular claims to citizenship rights and identities. The world-historical impact of these events is obvious. The implications for sociological reflection should also be both large and urgent: Just what is this power we call citizenship and how and why is such an identity constructed as a dynamic force in history?

The exigency of this question makes it important to consider why until very recently sociological discussion of citizenship has been so relatively scant. Among Western intellectuals the reasons for this silence are not hard to identify. The persistence (currently the increase) of Western social inequalities in the face of celebrated liberal freedoms seems only to highlight the structural shallowness of that which we most commonly associate with citizenship—formal civil rights and a limited concern for individual liberties. The discourse of citizenship has similarly been suspect by its association with liberalism's apparent focus on individual rather than social rights. It is thus not surprising that sociologists have concentrated on the politics of class, social inequalities, and state power with research into the develop-

---

1. Reinhard Bendix, *Nation-Building and Citizenship* (Berkeley: University of California Press, 1977 [1967]); T. H. Marshall, *Citizenship and Social Class and Other Essays* (Cambridge: Cambridge University Press, 1950).

2. Jeffrey C. Alexander, "Citizen and Enemy as Symbolic Classification: On the Polarizing Discourse of Civil Society" ("Alexander, 'Citizen and Enemy'"), in M. Lamont & M. Fournier, eds., *Cultivating Differences: Symbolic Boundaries and the Making of Inequality* 289 (Chicago: University of Chicago Press, 1992); Rogers Brubaker, *Citizenship and Nationhood* (Cambridge, Mass.: Harvard University Press, 1992) ("Brubaker, *Citizenship and Nationalhood*"); Anthony Giddens, *Profiles and Critiques in Social Theory* (London: Macmillan, 1982); id., *A Contemporary Critique of Historical Materialism*: vol. 2, *Nation-State and Violence* (Berkeley: University of California Press, 1987); Michael Mann, "Ruling Class Strategies and Citizenship," 21 (3) *Sociology* 339 (Aug. 1987); Charles Tilly, *Coercion, Capital, and European States, A.D. 990–1990* (New York: Basil Blackwell, 1990) ("Tilly, *Coercion*"); id., "Where Do Rights Come from?" New School for Social Research Working Paper No. 98 (July 1990) ("Tilly, 'Where Do Rights Come from?'"); Bryan S. Turner, *Citizenship and Capitalism* (London: Allen & Unwin, 1986) ("Turner, *Citizenship and Capitalism*"); id., ed., *Citizenship and Social Theory* (Beverly Hills, Cal.: Sage Publications, 1992); Alan Wolfe, *Whose Keeper?* (Berkeley: University of California Press, 1989) ("Wolfe, *Whose Keeper?*").

3. T. H. Marshall, *Citizenship and Social Class*, with an introduction by Tom Bottomore (Concord, Mass.: Pluto, 1992).

Rights, Relationality, and Membership 65

ment of economic institutions and movements for social and economic change dominating inquiry.

But there is a sociological message in the political charge recently ignited around the world: People are empowered by an "identity politics"; social change has been made by those whose sense of who they *are* has been violated fundamentally; and it increasingly appears that the identity of one's self as a "rights-bearing" person is perhaps the most inviolable, and the most empowering.[4]

And there are other elements of this message. Despite the similarities of the Eastern European movements, for example, the recent mobilizations—from Prague to Latvia—have nonetheless unfolded in the context of local political cultures, that which the activists call "civil society." Indeed, what is most notable about these rights claims is their political specificity: the politics of citizenship discourse requires them to be called "natural," but in practice they have been consistently justified by membership in historically constructed political communities and cultures. People have argued their rights claims to be held by virtue of political membership in public spheres and civil societies that are not comprised of the sovereign individual, the market, or the state. It is a social and political realm foreign to most social science research.[5]

The implications of this seem striking: The politics of citizenship must be rethought. Citizenship is a "contested truth"—its meaning politically and historically constructed. We need to explore the conditions for the making of citizenship claims as well as why it is that the context of participatory claims has been in the pluralities of local civil societies rather than through markets or directed primarily at national state institutions. And, above all, we need to look at the ways that political issues of par-

---

4. On "identity-politics," see Craig Calhoun, "The Problem of Identity in Collective Action," in Joan Huber, ed., *Macro-Micro Linkages in Sociology* 51 (Beverly Hills, Cal.: Sage Publications, 1991); Margaret R. Somers & Gloria Gibson, "Reclaiming the Epistemological 'Other': Narrative and the Social Constitution of Identity," in Craig Calhoun, ed., *From Persons to Nations: The Social Constitution of Identity* (Oxford: Blackwell, forthcoming); Jean Cohen & Andrew Arato, *Civil Society and Political Theory* (Cambridge, Mass.: MIT Press, 1992) ("Cohen & Arato, *Civil Society*"); Jean Cohen, "Strategy or Identity: New Theoretical Paradigms and Contemporary Social Movements," 52 *Soc. Research* 663 (1985); Alain Touraine, "An Introduction to the Study of Social Movements," 52 *Soc. Research* 749 (1985); Stanley Aronowitz, *The Politics of Identity: Class, Culture, Social Movements* (New York: Routledge, Chapman & Hall, 1992).

5. Alan Wolfe in *Whose Keeper?* documents the exclusion of civil society from social science research. See also Cohen & Arato, *Civil Society*; Craig Calhoun, "Introduction: Habermas and the Public Sphere" ("Calhoun, 'Introduction'"), in *id.*, ed., *Habermas and the Public Sphere* 1 (Cambridge, Mass.: MIT Press, 1992) ("Calhoun, *Habermas*"); Craig Calhoun, "Civil and Public Sphere," 5 *Pub. Culture* 267 (1993); Alexander, "Citizen and Enemy" (cited in note 2); Jeffrey Alexander, "Bringing Democracy Back in: Universalistic Solidarity and the Civil Sphere," in C. Lamont, ed., *Intellectuals and Politics: Social Theory in a Changing World* 157 (Newbury Park, Cal.: Sage Publications, 1991); Jeffrey Alexander & P. Smith, "The Discourse of American Civil Society: A New Proposal for Cultural Studies," 22 *Theory & Soc'y* 151 (1993).

66   LAW AND SOCIAL INQUIRY

ticipatory and civil rights have been integral to—rather than exclusive of—those of market and class inequalities. The themes of civil society and the public sphere suggest realms where economic, legal, and political conceptions of justice converge to influence the formation of rights.

T. H. Marshall wrote in a very different time from ours, and it may seem a far stretch to link recent political upheavals to a work that was intended to explain Western European development, and Britain in particular, in the 1950s—then in its glory days of expanding market controls and state welfare institutions. Marshall's focus, however, on the perduring historical and structural tensions between social class inequalities on the one hand, and the formal equalities of citizenship on the other, is no less relevant today. And although it would be tempting to use Marshall's historical study of the West as a foil for a structural comparison with the East, this essay will not attempt to take on such a challenge; rather it will explore Marshall's work on the same ground that he did.

The reasons for this are straightforward: Like virtually all ambitious works of historical sociology based on the English case, Marshall always intended his work to be a general theory of citizenship. And so it has been treated. Yet it is precisely because Marshall's is a general theory of citizenship that recent approaches to the topic still take it to be the standard against which all discussion should be measured.[6] And like most general theories that have become standard discourse, to the extent that it has been challenged, these challenges have accepted Marshall's argument as appropriate for the English case but then go on to suggest revisions for the new case or cases being studied. To the extent that Marshall is once again being appropriated for comparisons with the East, this will happen again. But this approach to classical texts misses the point: True homage to Marshall requires reconsidering his thesis in the context of its original empirical grounds—the formation, course, and consequences of citizenship in English history. Only then can we freshly evaluate his contribution.

The first part of this essay will discuss the most troubling aspects of Marshall's argument and will formulate five thematic counter-points of contention. The second section offers a counter-argument to Marshall's historical analysis by focusing anew on the conditions for the development of early citizenship rights.[7] And the third section will present a more closely

---

6. See, e.g., J. H. Barbalet, *Citizenship* (Minneapolis: University of Minnesota Press, 1989); Turner, *Citizenship and Capitalism*.

7. This is of course not the place to elaborate a full-scale historical sociology of citizenship but rather to raise serious questions about Marshall's causal argument in the context of his "pre-citizenship" epoch. For a broader analytic deconstruction of Marshall focusing more on "modern" citizenship, see Margaret R. Somers, "Citizenship and the Place of the Public Sphere: Law, Community, and Political Culture in the Transition to Democracy," 58 Am. Soc. Rev. 587 (1993).

I. T. H. MARSHALL AND CITIZENSHIP: POINT COUNTERPOINT

grounded example of an alternative view to the making and meaning of citizenship in one type of local political culture.

Marshall's classic *Citizenship and Social Class* is an explanation for the successive growth of citizenship rights in the context of the development, course, and consequences of the capitalist mode of production. Marshall's path-breaking achievement was to expand and redefine citizenship away from solely a narrow concept of formal individual liberties to one that also embraced social and economic rights. His definition is three-dimensional, including civil, political, and social rights.[8] Civil rights are those we associate with formal individual liberties—habeas corpus, the right of association, the right to sell one's labor on a free market, and the right to justice—the courts of law without which no right would be politically meaningful. Political liberties are participatory rights—the right to vote, to elect representatives, and so on. Social rights are what he calls the "consumer" rights of the modern welfare state. This bundle of rights attaches to persons through what Marshall calls the "status" of citizenship.

It is the relationship between the rights endowed by citizenship status premised on equality on the one side and the fundamental inequalities inherent in the social class system on the other that most interests Marshall. The two sides represent, in his words, "warring principles"—those of status equality and right against contract inequality and markets. Developing a theory to account for the origins and consequences of these warring tensions in modern society forms the heart of his work.

In Marshall's explanation the engine of modern citizenship resides in the forces and conflicts of capitalism. A nascent capitalist demand for free individuals available for labor markets along with bourgeois gentry needs for mobile property get the motor going and lead to the achievement of civil rights. Once set in motion, the drive is kept going through successive popular mobilization by the subsequent contradictions between capitalist social forces and the exclusions and inequalities of the class system. Eventually, all three citizenship rights are sequentially instituted through socioeconomic change and class formation. This initial premise leads his historical periodization to coincide with epochs of class formation.

In the first stage of the 18th century the triumph of the gentry in the Glorious Revolution ushered in civil citizenship; political citizenship was a product of the 19th-century ascendancy of the middle class; while social

---

8. Marshall also has an orphan category of "industrial rights," which he defines as an aggregate of civil liberties relevant to the industrial sphere of labor.

68   LAW AND SOCIAL INQUIRY

citizenship came in the 20th century with the power of the working class and the institutionalization of the welfare state. For Marshall each phase of citizenship is not organically contained in the preceding one. He allows for separate developmental stories for each component. He also dismisses a teleology of rights which derive ultimately from individual property rights. But although the rights are not logically derived in this way, he nonetheless insists that the emergence proceeded in necessary stages, each right a product of the developmental logic of capitalism and its processes of class formation. In this context, the *meaning* of the growth of citizenship is fundamentally Marshall's story of the enlargement of individual rights to greater degrees of autonomy and equality.

Marshall's definition of citizenship as embracing three spheres has yet to be surpassed. The strength of his classifications lies in what they reveal about the political nature of social life and the recognition that both social and political rights can only be explained by attention to that. And indeed one must endorse Marshall's inclusive three-dimensional view of citizenship. His emphasis on the institutionalization of rights as a necessary component of their realization is another contribution. But his greatest contribution perhaps is his originality and clarity in posing what has now become a common problematic among political sociologists—the inherent tension between capitalism and democracy or, in his formulation, between market inequality and the principle of equality. Marshall's intellectual inheritance from R. H. Tawney and other social democrats, as well as his own moral impulses, allow him to powerfully articulate the unexpected consequences of the unification within a single society of these contrary tendencies—the inequalities consequent to legal freedoms in law and markets on the one hand and those toward the equalizing goals of social welfare and democratic education on the other.[9]

II.   FIVE POINTS OF CONTENTION

There are, nonetheless, serious problems with Marshall's account of the growth of citizenship, the meaning he ascribes to it, and its relationship to capitalist development. To be sure, his primary interest was in building a theory that could make sense of its paradoxical consequences for 20th-century social and economic relations. But Marshall's theory of contemporary society is not structurally static; its powerful analysis of the tensions between citizenship and society, as well among the different dimensions of

---

9. Marx of course was the first to pose this problem. More recently it was addressed by Alan Wolfe in his *Limits of Legitimacy* (New York: Free Press, 1979), and by James O'Connor in *Fiscal Crisis of the State* (New York: St. Martin's, 1973). Karl Polanyi has still the most compelling but underrecognized elaboration of the problem in *The Great Transformation* (Boston: Beacon Press, 1957 [1944]) ("Polanyi, *Great Transformation*").

Rights, Relationality, and Membership 69

rights, depends entirely on the historicity of their emergence. To fully consider his theory, there is no choice but to seriously address its historical foundations.

An institutional and narrative approach suggests alternative formulations to five of his explanatory themes—the causal dynamic, the historical agency, the timing, the spatial distribution, and the meaning of citizenship. In brief: (1) Where Marshall sees the causal motor of self-propelling capitalist social forces at work in the development of citizenship, a more nuanced analytic perspective would focus on a shifting configuration of political, legal, community, *and* economic institutions at work in the development of a series of national laws and institutions that only contingently could be transformed into specific political cultures of citizenship rights. (2) Where Marshall sees the agents of citizenship to be social classes, it was as *members* of contesting institutions rather than as such social categories as class that cross-cutting social groups became the protagonists in the drama of rights formation.[10] (3) Where Marshall sees modern citizenship rights "proper" emerging only with the demise of traditional feudal society and the rise of modern capitalist society, the explanation and the causal path of our *modern* citizenship cannot be severed from the legal institutional arrangements of the medieval epoch long before the development of a capitalist society. Moreover, there was an uncertain *contingency* in the enlargement and expansion of rights that cannot be reduced to any macro-processes of feudalism's demise, capitalism's rise, or societal modernization in general. (4) Where Marshall sees a national uniform extension of rights as a key indicator of modern citizenship, the rights of citizenship were notably more localized and unevenly spatially distributed; there was, moreover, an uneven capacity for and consequences of exercising those rights. (5) And where Marshall sees citizenship as the gradual enlargement of individual rights to wider spheres of society through the equality of status, my analysis defines citizenship rights as a *hybrid* set of relationships that at once embodies institutional membership and social attachments, as well as the capacity for the autonomous individual exercising of those rights.[11]

Structural Dynamic and Institutional Analysis

Marshall's analysis of political developments is firmly anchored in the ideal-typical social entities of feudalism and capitalism. The motor of his

---

10. The critique of social categories as analytic focus is major part of institutional analysis. The theoretical treatise on this is Harrison White, *Identity and Control* (Princeton, N.J.: Princeton University Press, 1990) ("White, *Identity and Control*").

11. See Margaret Somers, "The People and the Law: Narrative Identity and the Place of the Public Sphere in the Formation of English Working Class Politics—1300–1850, a Comparative Analysis" (Ph.D. diss., Harvard University, 1986) ("Somers, 'The People and the Law'").

70 LAW AND SOCIAL INQUIRY

sequential process of citizenship formation operates in the needs and inevitable social contradictions of the capitalist mode of production. Modern *national* citizenship rights as we know them were nonexistent before capitalism. Any initial impulses toward, or even early expressions of, "pre-modern" rights were thoroughly impeded by the antimarket ascriptiveness of feudal society. Only the equality of contract necessary to and promoted by capitalist markets enabled their initial takeoff. The expansion of citizenship was in turn driven by capitalism's ensuing conflicting principles—legal equality and social inequality. Marshall then gives his evolutionary theory a social democratic twist; rather than moving from status to contract, he moves from status to contract *and* status.

An institutional and narrative approach is distinguished from Marshall's in that the processes of citizenship formation are not seen to be anchored in holistic ideal-typical social categories—such as those of feudalism and capitalism. Institutional and narrative analysis uses a relational, rather than a categorical, approach to analyzing social arrangements. *Society* is the term that usually performs the work of characterizing the "social system" in sociolegal analysis. When we speak of understanding social action, for example, we speak of locating the actors in their *societal* context. But "society" as a concept is rooted in a falsely totalizing and naturalistic way of thinking about the world. For most practicing social science research, a society is a social *entity*. As an entity, it has a core essence—an essential set of social springs at the heart of the mechanism. This essential core is in turn reflected in broader covarying societal institutions that the system comprises. Thus, when sociologists speak of feudalism, for example, we mean at once "feudal society" as a whole, a particular set of "feudal class relations" at the core of this society, a "feudal economy," and a concomitant set of "feudal institutions" such as *feudal* political units and *feudal* peasant communities. Most significantly for social and historical research, each institution within a society must *covary with each other*. Thus in "feudal societies," the state by definition must be a feudal state whose feudal character covaries with all other feudal institutions; feudal workers must all be unfree and extra-economically exploited peasants. And in "industrial society," a "modern industrial/capitalist" state must be detached from civil society and the industrial economy, and industrial workers must be individual and free. To be sure, the synchrony is not always perfect. In periods of transition from one society to another, there is a "lag effect," and remnants of the old order persist against the pressures of the new. But despite these qualifications, the systemic metaphor assumes that the parts of society covary along with the whole as a corporate entity.

For both empirical and epistemological reasons, an institutional/relational/narrative approach rejects categorical—sometimes called ideal-typical—units of analysis. Empirically, there is simply too much contrary

Rights, Relationality, and Membership   71

evidence to allow one any longer to believe in a holistic medieval (ca. 1100–1500) societal entity defined by a governing set of feudal relations. Susan Reynolds, for example, has convincingly shown us that the construction of the feudal societal entity as a unit of analysis was almost entirely an intellectual construct of 17th- and 18th-century legal scholars and Scottish philosophers, rather than the result of contemporary sources.[12] Once this conceptual lens of "feudalism" was consolidated into the heart of 18th- and 19th-century social and economic analysis (e.g. Smith, Fergusson, Ricardo, Marx, Weber), our reading of contemporary sources was filtered through this totalizing naturalistic vision.[13] Epistemologically, the ideal-type category of "feudalism"—while always surrounded by qualifications as to its purposefully "abstract" and "nonempirical" use as a heuristic—all too inevitably slides from "idealized heuristic concept" to *description* to *explanatory* construct. From there, it is a short, but inexorable, distance to that of defining as *anomalous*, irrational, unintelligible, or simply filtering out any structural characteristics or social activities that do not fit the conceptual bundle of "feudalism" now reified into paradigmatic status.[14]

I thus concur with Charles Tilly, Harrison White, and Michael Mann who each agree in their own way that "It may seem an odd position for a sociologist to adopt; but if I could, I would abolish the concept of 'society' altogether."[15] To make variable and contingent forms of social action and political arrangements intelligible and coherent, these systemic categorical typologies must be broken apart and their parts disaggregated and reassembled on the basis of relational institutional clusters. For a social order is neither a naturalistic system nor a plurality of individuals, but rather an indeterminate configuration of cultural and institutional relationships. If we want to be able to capture the contingency and complexity of social life, we

---

12. Susan Reynolds, *Fiefs, Vassals and Feudalism* (Oxford: Oxford University Press, forthcoming) ("Reynolds, *Fiefs*").

13. See Somers, "The People and the Law" ch. 2, for a discussion of the need to disaggregate our conceptual vocabulary for "feudal society."

14. A paradigm is more than a theory; it is an entire "problematic" or "knowledge culture" which defines what questions, concepts, and hypotheses are even admissable for discussion in the first place, and what is even to be a candidate to be considered as empirically true or false. See Thomas Kuhn, *The Structure of Scientific Revolutions* (Chicago: University of Chicago Press, 1962); Ian Hacking, "Language, Truth and Reason" *in* S. Lukes & M. Hollis, eds., *Rationality and Relativism* (Cambridge, Mass.: MIT Press, 1982); Margaret R. Somers, "Where Is Social Theory after the Historic Turn? Knowledge Cultures, Narrativity, and Historical Epistemologies" ("Somers, 'Where Is Social Theory?'"), *in* Terrence J. McDonald, ed., *The Historic Turn in the Human Sciences* (Ann Arbor: University of Michigan Press, forthcoming) ("McDonald, *Historic Turn*"). Reynolds discusses the process of "filtering-out" in both *Fiefs* (cited in note 12) and her earlier *Kingdoms and Communities in Western Europe, 900–1300* (Oxford: Oxford University Press, 1984) ("Reynolds, *Kingdoms and Communities*").

15. Michael Mann, 1 *The Sources of Social Power* 2 (New York: Cambridge Univesity Press, 1986) ("Mann, *Sources of Social Power*"); Charles Tilly, *Big Structures, Large Processes, Huge Comparisons* (New York: Russell Sage Foundation, 1984) ("Tilly, *Big Structures*"); White, *Identity and Control*.

72 LAW AND SOCIAL INQUIRY

need a way of thinking that can substitute relational metaphors for totalizing ones.

Institutional and narrative analysis makes this possible. The approach presupposes that institutional relationships and relational networks consistently "outrun" social categories. Institutions are defined as organizational and symbolic practices that operate within networks of (breakable) rules, (fixed and unfixed) structural ties, (often-contested) public narratives, binding (and unbound) relationships that are embedded in time and space.[16] The approach conceptually disaggregates categorical entities and reconfigures them as institutional clusters through which people, power, and organizations are contingently connected and positioned. Instead of "society," I thus use the term *relational setting*.[17] A relational setting is a patterned matrix of institutional relationships among cultural, economic, social, and political practices. It invokes spatial and geometric network metaphors rather than systemic ones.[18] The most significant aspect of a relational setting is that there is no governing entity according to which the whole setting can be categorized; it can only be characterized by deciphering its spatial and network patterns and temporal processes. As such, it is a relational matrix, similar to a social network.

One of the most important characteristics of a relational setting is that it has a history[19] and thus must be explored over time and space. Temporally, a relational setting is traced over time not by looking for the indicators of social development but by empirically examining if and when the interaction among the institutions of the setting appears to have produced a decisively different outcome from what was indicated in previous examina-

---

16. See Karl Polanyi, "The Economy as an Instituted Process," in Karl Polanyi *et al.*, eds., *Trade and Market in the Early Empires* 243 (New York: Free Press, 1957); J. March & J. Olsen, "The New Institutionalism: Organizational Factors in Political Life," 78 *Am. Pol. Sci. Rev.* 734 (1984); J. Meyer & B. Rowan, "Institutionalized Organizations: Formal Structure as Myth and Ceremony," in W. W. Powell & P. J. DiMaggio, eds., *The New Institutionalism in Organizational Analysis* 41 (Chicago: University of Chicago Press, 1991 [1977]) ("Powell & DiMaggio, *New Institutionalism*"); R. Jepperson, "Institutions, Institutional Effects, and Institutionalism," in Powell & DiMaggio, *New Institutionalism* 143; R. Friedland & R. Alford, "Bringing Society Back in: Symbols, Practices, and Institutional Contradictions," in Powell & DiMaggio, *New Institutionalism* 232. Especially useful is Friedland and Alford's (p. 243) definition of an institution as "simultaneously material and ideal, systems of signs and symbols, rational and transrational . . . supraorganizational patterns of human activity by which individuals and organizations produce and reproduce their material subsistence and organize time and space. . . . They are also symbolic systems, ways of ordering reality, and thereby rendering experience of time and space meaningful."

17. Somers, "The People and the Law" (cited in note 11); Margaret R. Somers, "Narrativity, Narrative Identity, and Social Action: Rethinking English Working-Class Formation," 16 *Soc. Sci. Hist.* 591 (1992).

18. S. F. Moore, *Law as Process* (London: Routledge & Kegan Paul, 1978) ("Moore, *Law as Process*"); Mann, *Sources of Social Power*; M. G. Smith, "A Structural Approach to Comparative Politics," in D. Easton, ed., *Varieties of Political Theory* (Englewood Cliffs, N.J.: Prentice-Hall, 1966).

19. A. MacIntyre, *After Virtue: A Study in Moral Theory* (Notre Dame, Ind.: University of Notre Dame Press, 1981).

Rights, Relationality, and Membership   73

tions. Social change, from this perspective, is viewed not as the evolution or revolution of one societal type to another, but by shifting relationships among the institutional arrangements and cultural practices that comprise one or more social settings.

From this perspective, it becomes plausible to explore the variable ways in which citizenship formation develops within relational settings of contested but patterned relations among people and institutions. It makes it possible to see that citizenship identities and practices developed in analytic autonomy from the bundle of attributes associated a priori with the categories of feudalism and capitalism. From an institutional and relational perspective, rather than in the transition to capitalism or in the "birth of class society," the conditions for the possibility of citizenship rights can be located in the 12th–14th-century legal revolution of medieval England that produced both national and local public (participatory) spheres as well as a national political culture based on the *idealized master narrative* of English legal and constitutional rights.

The English crown in the 12th century created the institutional outlines of a *national public sphere* by conjoining a revolutionary new territorial-wide public law (common law) with the public (nonfeudal) local governing bodies of the realm. It did so by appropriating from below and extending throughout the land the political and legal public conventions of the medieval cities and (to a lesser extent) those of the public villages. Excluded from the incorporation into royal common law were the private manorial courts. As a result, the national public sphere took on qualities and conventions of urban and nonfeudal public civil society "writ large." As in medieval and early modern urban cultures, seemingly opposing institutions converged in England's national public sphere. Remedies of procedural justice (civil citizenship) promising the public liberty of the rule of law coexisted with both substantive national regulatory and redistributive statutes (potential forms of social citizenship) as well as institutions which promised—or demanded—community participation (potential forms of political citizenship) in the administration of law. As in the municipalities, however, the actual impact of these institutions of potential citizenship rights was not uniform. Precisely because they were embedded in public spheres, the practical meaning of these laws on people's lives depended almost wholly on the varying degrees of power that different local bodies were able to exert in the processes of appropriating political benefits or resisting political tribulation.

My use of the term *public sphere* can be both related to and distinguished from the use of the term made famous by Jurgen Habermas.[20] Habermas's most important contribution was to provide a conceptual means of differentiating between state and economy and public participatory are-

---

20. Jurgen Habermas, *The Structural Transformation of the Public Sphere* (Cambridge, Mass.: MIT Press, 1989 [1962]).

74 LAW AND SOCIAL INQUIRY

nas that *mediate*, rather than belong to, either the state or the market. In this respect, the concept of the public sphere provides a means of addressing the way in which England's legal arena and infrastructure depended for its very workings on the compulsory participation of the local and county population. At the same time, we are reminded that this public sphere of participatory law was not *of*—and thus could not be fully controlled by—either the state or the market. Indeed, it is a sphere where the public associates to both influence and defend against otherwise unmediated national states and markets. I do not, however, accept or incorporate the following aspects of Habermas's conceptualization: (1) that public spheres resulted historically in the 18th century from long-term socioeconomic transformation in Western European trade and commerce; (2) that, as a *normative ideal*, the term can refer only to the class-specific arena of *bourgeois* rational discourse; (3) that identities are formed a priori to participation in the public sphere; (4) that the public sphere can be analytically or historically understood while maintaining the exclusionary gender practices built into Habermas's own normative ideal. My use of the public sphere makes it a contested *participatory* site in which actors, in their overlapping identities as legal subjects, national citizens, economic actors, and family and community members, engage as a public body in negotiations and contestations over public matters and national law. In my use, the public sphere is a "structured setting" which may or may not—depending on distributions of power, participatory and associational capacities, and popular political cultures—be transformed into a more democratic arena of popular participation and cultural contestation.[21]

While the struggles over rights were deeply embroiled with the inequalities—indeed the violence—of capitalism, these struggles and their institutional concomitants were consistently mediated through constitutional and juridical channels. Indeed, as an institutional force in the historical landscape, the culture of contingent rights played a constitutive (rather than a dependent) role in shaping the patterns and timing and character of both feudal and capitalist relations as they changed and developed over the centuries. The history of struggles over citizenship becomes less intelligible in the absence of a full picture of these cultural and institutional foundations.

By appropriating and extending throughout the land the political culture of the city, English state building institutionalized a working definition

---

21. My conception shares much with others' critiques of Habermas's term, especially on the inseparability of the family from a constituitive role in the public world, e.g., Nancy Fraser, *Unruly Practices* (Minneapolis: University of Minnesota Press, 1989) and on the centrality of conflict and negotiation among a wider notion of publics than in Habermas's bourgeois ideal, specifically including popular and working-class publics, e.g., Geoff Eley, "Nations, Publics, and Political Cultures: Placing Habermas in the Nineteenth Century," in Calhoun, *Habermas* (cited in note 5); Calhoun, "Introduction" (cited in note 5).

of liberty and rights linked to public law, local participation and, above all, public membership. Beginning in the 17th century these ideas had to compete with a newly developed idea of liberty based solely on individual rights to property produced from autonomous labor. These Lockean ideas of natural rights have dominated the social histories of citizenship and democratization, including Marshall's. But not only did the former public conception and practices of rights prove remarkably robust in their competition with Locke's ideas; arguably, they were more significant in shaping modern popular conceptions of and claims to citizenship.

Agency

The actors in Marshall's account of citizenship are social classes whose categorical attributes and interests in effect thrust them into the historical arena. In his thesis the dynamism behind these struggles, however, lies less in the class actors than in the contradictory *principles* between the inequalities of class under capitalism and the formal equality of status under citizenship.

In contrast, the actors in my account are members of particular communities, groups, and networks of institutional actors in different sectors of the public sphere.[22] At different times and places, and for different reasons, these membership groups formed alliances or antagonisms with other groups. Some of the contending and coalescing groups included peasant families in pastoral regions of England, monarchical state builders, baronial challengers to the crown, merchant middlemen engaged in the rural putting-out industry, small-fry constables engaged in enforcing the law in local villages, and the artisans and journeymen of guilds. Depending on circumstances and resources, national membership rules were successfully converted into rights, blocked, or neglected in the course of these alliances and contestations.

The explicit reasons motivating particular alignments at particular times included economic reasons, as well as religious, familial, political, moral, military, and so on. Usually there was a combination of reasons. But regardless of the particularities of any given coalition or conflict, the issues were fought out over competing conceptions of membership rules. Because labor relations, for example, were embedded in legal policies applicable to all members of the national state, struggles over labor conditions became

---

22. The word *community* is a loaded term. It is used here as an analytic variable and not as a term referring to the notion of *gemeinschaft*. See Craig Calhoun, "Community: Toward a Variable Conceptualization for Comparative Research," 5 *Soc. Hist.* 105 (1990); Partha Chatterjee, "A Response to Taylor's 'Mode of Civil Society,'" 3 *Pub. Culture* 119 (1990); White, *Identity and Control* (cited in note 10).

76 LAW AND SOCIAL INQUIRY

struggles over the appropriation of law and the conversion of these potentially tyrannical labor regulations into positively defined rights.

In these contestations, legal, cultural, and economic institutions and practices were both the resources and the outcomes of these alliances and antagonisms. It would be difficult, if not impossible, to know which came first in any causal sequence. Examples of some of the institutions and cultural resources involved included the legal right to remedy against the "over mighty," guaranteed trial by jury drawn from one's neighborhood, the administration of justice and governance through local juridical bodies, the discourse of the universality of law, the doctrine of the "king's two bodies," and the existence of statutory regulations mandating that minimum and maximum wages be *locally* administered.

Perhaps most important, the outcomes of these struggles were less attached to their agency in class or status groups but in the political and legal dynamics that unfolded in local sites of contestation—local public spheres. Only occasionally were the agents' intentions or interests translated directly into the sought-after results; more commonly, the struggles over rights and their institutional expression led in directions wholly unanticipated. This was especially true in the frequent popular appropriations of the promises of universal justice.

Periodization

Marshall's sequential timing of citizenship—from civil, to political, to social—is a direct outgrowth of his initial anchoring of the process in the capitalism and its class agents. This initial premise leads his historical periodization to coincide with epochs of class formation—since each right is a product of the developmental conflicts of capitalism and its stages of class formation. Indeed, so strongly does he formulate the functionality of stages of rights for capitalist periodization that he understates the obvious lexically ordered tendency for the development of one type of right to provide leverage in the claim for the next.[23] It follows from this that Marshall's is an amended form of political modernization theory: Modern citizenship can only be truly identified with the decline of traditional feudal society (status) and the rise of a modern capitalist one (contract). Although his amendment of modernity (contract plus status) is a major contribution, like all versions of modernization, a fundamental discontinuity must be located in the transition between the two. This is why Marshall acknowledges the presence of "traditional" limited types of feudal rights but argues that a qualitative break occurred between these and the early emergence of modern rights in the

---

23. Rick Lempert suggested this useful point to me.

Rights, Relationality, and Membership 77

18th century. It also forces him to limit the presence of political rights to the 19th century, and social rights to the 20th.

By contrast, there was a contingent and uneven process to the institutionalization of citizenship rights which does not correspond to a periodization of the transition from feudalism to capitalism—despite the obvious historical interactions between economic processes and citizenship practices. Indeed, virtually all English communities claimed, exercised, benefited, and suffered from both the expansion and the contraction of all three types of citizenship rights long before the triumph of their "proper" capitalist cause. In certain settings, all three dimensions of citizenship existed and were exercised in institutional and practical terms *before* anything resembling the capitalist mode of production arrived in the English countryside. At times, one or more of these rights became faint through repeal or desuetude, while at other times, they were central players in the historical drama. Rather than offering a qualitative break from this period, causal explanation for the particular character of modern citizenship rights must begin— although, of course, not end—from these medieval legal institutional beginnings. No longer can pre-capitalist legal rights be dismissed as "pre-history" only to be replaced by the new players on the social stage that emerge in the epochs of capitalist markets. To be sure, new players do emerge, and emerge to be significant causal factors in the development of citizenship. But they neither replace, displace, nullify, nor even reinvent the institutional configuration that preceded them. Rather, the impact of these new forces of modernity is largely influenced by the *outcome of their convergence* with previously existing legal institutions and practices.

Scope and Scale, the Problem of Place

Marshall views modern citizenship rights as society-wide and universal in scope since they develop concomitantly with holistic societal transformations. The scale of citizenship, the classes who carried the changes out, the breadth of the economic changes, and ultimately the institutionalization of the rights themselves were universal rather than local. In taking such a view, Marshall follows his disciplinary training in the social sciences with its neglect of spatial distinctions and cultural differences within single notions of holistic societies.

By contrast, the paradox of England's national public sphere is that a formal territorial-wide body of law produced highly localized and multiple practices of rights and enforcement procedures. The conversion of laws to rights was local and contingent in effect and was always adapted to the particular settings where the laws were implemented. This was a direct result of the peculiar nature of England's national legal infrastructure. Its hybrid conjoining into the structure of rule national, county, and local spheres

78 LAW AND SOCIAL INQUIRY

of power, community, and law created a point of juncture at the sites of local governance. These in turn served as local public spheres. As I will show below, whether these public spheres were to become sites of popular participation varied radically depending on the setting and the local political relationships. Not surprisingly, the struggles for and over rights were also highly local and unevenly distributed over the social and geographical landscape.[24]

Meaning

For Marshall, the essence of a right is precisely that it is possessed by an autonomous individual. In Marshall's tradition of philosophical liberalism, the status of citizenship is by definition a social *category*; the rights it confers can only be carried by individuals abstracted from their actual relational settings.[25] That Marshall identifies serious conflicts between individual freedoms and the distributive measures necessary for greater social equality does not affect this ontological premise of the rights-bearing individual.

A right is a legal claim brought to bear on a state. When viewed through an institutional lens, those laws that became the source of citizenship rights did not fit into either end of the dichotomy between individual and communitarian conceptions of rights, or negative and positive liberties.[26] In the development of English citizenship, rights developed in *relational* terms (an outcome of what I will call "autonomy in membership" and

---

24. The epistemological implications of recent work in historical geography have been little noted by sociologists. Exceptions include Tilly, *Big Structures* (cited in note 2); Mann, *Sources of Social Power* ch. 1 (cited in note 15). On the importance of historical geography and social theory more generally, see Nicholas Entrikin, *The Betweeness of Place: Towards a Geography of Modernity* (Baltimore: Johns Hopkins Press, 1991); and John A. Agnew & James Duncan, *The Power of Place: Bringing Together Geographical and Sociological Imaginations* (Boston: Unwin Hyman, 1989).

25. On the epistemological significance of relationships over categories see White, *Identity and Control*; Harrison C. White, A. Boorman, & R. Breiger, "Social Structure from Multiple Networks I," 81 *Am. J. Soc.* 730 (1976); and *id.*, "Social Structure from Multiple Networks II," 81 *Am. J. Soc.* 1265 (1976). For an application in historical sociology, see Peter Bearman, *Relations into Rhetorics* (forthcoming).

26. Indeed so dichotomous is this false distinction that most communitarians do not even accept the concept of rights as ontologically consistent with their view of the self. For critiques of the view that rights-claims and community membership identities are fundamentally opposed, see especially M. Walzer, *Spheres of Justice* (New York: Basic Books, 1982); William H. Sewell, Jr., "Le citoyen/la citoyenne: Activity, Passivity, and the Revolutionary Concept of Citizenship," in Colin Lucas, ed., *The Political Culture of the French Revolution*: vol. 2, *The French Revolution and the Creation of Modern Political Culture* (Oxford: Pergamon Press, 1987); Martha Minow, "Interpreting Rights: An Essay for Robert Cover," 96 *Yale L. Rev.* 1860 (1987); S. Hall & D. Held, "Left and Rights," *Marxism Today*, June 1989, at 16. For two especially valuable overviews of the rights debate, see Hendrik Hartog, "The Contitution of Aspiration and the 'Rights that Belong to Us All,'" 74 *J. Am. Hist.* 1013 (Dec. 1987), and Mark Tushnet, "Rights: An Essay in Informal Political Theory," 17 *Politics & Soc'y* 403 (1989).

Rights, Relationality, and Membership   79

"liberty in embeddedness"). It was the relationality of rights that provided the means for exercising autonomy and independence.[27] Citizenship rights were indeed rights that supported a high degree of independence; at the same time they were predicated on the attachments and the constraints of membership within a particular group—from family, to village, to trade union, to local civil society, and public sphere. As will be evident in my discussion below, even the achievement of the civil right to liberty presupposed the achievement of a prior right to membership as well as the maintenance of social attachments. Indeed, the history of rights sadly reveals their diminishment with the attenuation of social attachments, while the attenuation of memberships also reveals the concomitant loss of individual empowerment and independence.[28]

This historical view changes the meaning of citizenship. Rather than being a category of social status, the rights of citizenship comprise a bundle of enforceable claims that are *variably and contingently* appropriated by members of small civil societies and differentiated legal cultures—albeit within a territorially defined nation state. But a right, like all forms of moral and legal power, is not logically *attached* to any one social category or persons; rather, rights are free-floating cultural and institutional resources that must be appropriated and in turn given meaning only in the practical context of power and social relations. In this sense, for example, the legal discourse of common law is one of the most powerful of *abstract* rights—who actually benefits from it depends on the distribution of power among those groups seeking to justify their claims according to that discourse. A citizenship right, like all rights, is not a "thing"; it is a social practice.[29]

III. QUESTIONS POSED

The above five points of contention are all elaborated in my alternative account of citizenship formation, an account propelled by a set of questions and observations. The first concerns periodization: For Marshall the three dimensions of citizenship were historically sequential; they may not have been derivative, but their successive phasing was historically necessary and followed a developmental modernizing continuum. But if his schema makes sense, how are we to explain the *loss* in the early 19th century of long-standing social citizenship rights such as apprenticeship regulations?[30]

---

27. See Minow, 96 *Yale L.J.*, for a similar definition of rights to the one I am using here.
28. In *Sources of Social Power*, Mann addresses the ontological implications of these issues in his distinction between a "societal" versus a "social being." See at 14-16.
29. See Hartog, 74 *J. Am. Hist.*, for a similar conception of the contested character of American constitutional rights.
30. Iowerth Prothero, *Artisans and Politics in Early Nineteenth-Century London: John Gast and His Times* (Baton Rouge: Louisiana University Press, 1979) ("Prothero, *Artisans and Politics*"); P. Mantoux, *The Industrial Revolution in the Eighteenth Century* (rev. ed. New York:

80 LAW AND SOCIAL INQUIRY

After all, social citizenship is supposed to emerge only in the 20th century. And why was there a *decrease* in political citizenship after a notable period of democratic expansion in the 17th?[31] Why did England have 500 years of poor laws which incontrovertibly sedimented into 20th-century social rights? And why were *minimum* wage regulations first passed in 1604—three centuries before Marshall's social citizenship—only to be repealed in 1814?[32] We know, of course, that Marshall knew all this historical evidence; indeed, he discusses the poor laws at length. But it is precisely the value of a critical legal social science to take the same empirical data and use it to reconfigure an alternative interpretation—in this case, one that does not a priori bifurcate citizenship between traditional and modern manifestations.

The same sorts of questions of periodization are applicable for reflecting on the agency involved in citizenship formation. Marshall's explanation raises one of the most perplexing of questions when viewed in the context of the following observation: Rather than there being a radical rupture from "traditional society" to "modernity," when viewed over the very long term, a remarkable degree of continuity in rights claims can be identified before and after the transition from "feudalism" to "capitalism." The long-term evidence is striking: From as early as the 14th century, certain groups of peasant and later rural-industrial communities from the pastoral regions of England claimed rights of and expectations of the law in language and in actions remarkably similar to those of their 19th-century progeny in the industrial northern regions of England (where historians have generally identified the beginnings of popular rights claims with the onset of Chartism—the first mass working-class movement for the franchise).[33] From the

---

Harper & Row, 1955 [1928]); E. P. Thompson, "The Moral Economy of the English Crowd," 50 *Past & Present* 77 (1971); J. Rule, *The Labouring Classes in Early Industrial England 1750–1850* (London: Longman, 1986); *id.*, *The Experience of Labour in Eighteenth-Century Industry* (London: Croom Helm, 1981) (Rule, *Experience of Labour*"); Polanyi, *Great Transformation* (cited in note 9).

31. Derek Hirst, *The Representation of the People? Voters and Voting under the Early Stuarts* (Cambridge: Cambridge University Press, 1975); J. Plumb, "The Growth of the Electorate in England from 1600–1715," 45 *Past & Present* 90 (1969); J. G. A. Pocock, "Varieties of Whiggism," in his *Virtue, Commerce, and History* 215 (Cambridge: Cambridge University Press, 1986) ("Pocock, *Virtue*"); F. O'Gorman, "Campaign Ritual and Ceremonies: The Social Meaning of Elections in England, 1780–1860," 135 *Past & Present* 79 (1992).

32. W. E. Minchinton, *Wage Regulation in Pre-industrial England* (New York: Barnes & Noble, 1972) ("Minchinton, *Wage Regulation*"). There are similar problems of periodization in the more elaborate comparative schema of Gaston Rimlinger in his *Welfare Policy and Industralization in Europe, America and Russia* (New York: Wiley, 1971). See also Asa Briggs, "The Welfare State in Historical Perspective," in C. I. Shotland, ed., *The Welfare State* 25 (New York: Harper & Row, 1967).

33. For examples in the 18th century, see Rule, *Experience of Labour*; C. B. Dobson, *Masters and Men* (London: Croom Helm, 1980) ("Dobson, *Masters and Men*"); K. D. M. Snell, *Annals of the Labouring Poor: Social Change in Agrarian England 1660–1900* (Cambridge: Cambridge University Press, 1985); Roy Porter, *English Society in the Eighteenth Century* (Harmondsworth: Penguin, 1982). For the 17th century see K. Wrightson, *English Society, 1580–1680* (London: Hutchinson, 1982); Snell, *Annals of the Labouring Poor*; and David Underdown, *Revel, Riot and Rebellion: Popular Politics and Culture in England 1603–1660* (New

Rights, Relationality, and Membership 81

14th through the 16th to the 19th centuries, these laboring families also linked the independence and cohesion of their communities to the participatory rights and distributive ideals of English citizenship long before the "proper" capitalist cause. Continuity, of course, is a relative concept—not an empirical fact. In this case, my claim for continuity is made *relative* to the universal presupposition among scholars of a radical rupture in popular behavior between a preindustrial or traditional society and industrial modern society (depending, of course, on what point in time that curtain of "modernity" is lifted). It is in this context of an unquestioned notion of transformation consequent to the transformation of societal categories from preindustrial to industrial—and not from the obvious point that continuities were inflected by concomitant transformations—that a certain degree of substantive continuity in popular political culture is especially notable.[34]

The crucial point is that these popular forms of collective action were highly local and regionally specific. No less striking than a notable degree of substantive continuity in popular political culture over the centuries is the evidence of persistent *spatial* and *regional* specificity in popular rights claims and attitudes toward the law.[35] It was only "the people" from the pastoral, later rural-industrial, and eventually (by the 19th century) industrial villages who, from the 14th century on, demonstrated explicitly positive expectations of their public political, social, and civil rights.[36] Rural-industrial

---

York: Oxford University Press, 1985). For the 16th century, see Buchanan Sharp, *In Contempt of All Authority: Rural Artisans and Riot in the West of England, 1586–1660* (Berkeley: University of California Press, 1982) ("Sharp, *Contempt*"). For the 15th and 14th centuries, see R. H. Tawney, "The Assessment of Wages in England by the Justices of the Peace" ("Tawney, 'Assessment of Wages'"), in Minchinton, *Wage Regulation* 37 (cited in note 32); R. Webber, *The Peasants' Revolt* (Lavenham & Suffolk: Terrence Dalton Ltd., 1980); R. Dobson, *The Peasants Revolt* (2d ed. London: Macmillan, 1983); R. H. Hilton, *Bond Men Made Free* (London: Methuen & Co., 1973); T. H. Aston, ed., *Landlords, Peasants and Politics in Medieval England* (Cambridge: Cambridge University Press, 1987); R. H. Hilton, ed., *Peasants, Knights, and Heretics* (Cambridge: Cambridge University Press, 1976).

34. Part of the problem with advocating continuity is that it invokes fears of either Whiggishness or conservative Burkeanism, the latter most recently illustrated in the work of J. D. C. Clark. It should be clear, however, in the course of this essay that stressing continuity over rupture is not a political choice but an analytic one that derives from an institutionalist conceptual framework—hardly one associated with either Whigs or Burkeans.

35. For a sampling of regional differences see Andrew Charlesworth, *An Atlas of Rural Regional Protest* (London: Croom Helm, 1983) ("Charlesworth, *Atlas*"); Derek Gregory, *Regional Transformation and Industrial Revolution* (Minneapolis: University of Minnesota Press, 1982); Sharp, *Contempt* (cited in note 33); Larry Poos, "The Social Context of the Statute of Labourers' Enforcement," 1 *Law & Hist. Rev.* 27 (Spring 1983); John Bohstedt, *Riots and Community Politics* (Cambridge, Mass.: Harvard University Press, 1983) ("Bohstedt, *Riots and Community Politics*").

36. Although the phenomena of wide spread rural industrialization in the 17th and 18th centuries has long been noted among certain economic historians, the new and more theoretically informed notion of proto-industry is a recent development. See Franklin Mendels, "Proto-Industrialization: The First Phase of the Industralization Process," 32 *J. Econ. Hist.* 241 (1972); Charles Tilly, "Flows of Capital and Forms of Industry in Europe, 1500–1900," 12 *Theory & Soc'y* 123 (1983); Peter Kreidte, Hans Medick, & J. Schlumbohm, *Industrialization before Industrialization* (Cambridge: Cambridge University Press, 1982); Rudolf Braun, "Early

82 LAW AND SOCIAL INQUIRY

communities appear almost "guild-like" and artisanal in their political cultures and expectations of citizenship rights.[37] There is less evidence for any such positive expectations toward the law among those laboring peoples located in the arable regions and comprised primarily of large commercial agricultural labor or, at an earlier time, of unfree villeins.[38] While still unfree villeins, these peasants had possessed a degree of customary right that held relatively firmly in their manorial courts. Some peasants were even able to use these rights to gain copyhold status and eventually access to common law.[39] But for the vast majority, it appears that the contrast was notable: Far from believing that they had "rights," the poor among the arable regions experienced the institutions of law and justice as oppressive, indeed tyrannical. Localism and variation rather than universality clearly marked the development of citizenship rights.

Any theory of the historical development of rights claims would have to be able to account for these surprising problems of time and space.[40]

Industralization and Demographic Change in the Canton of Zurich," in Charles Tilly, ed., *Historical Studies of Changing Fertility* 289 (Princeton, N.J.: Princeton University Press, 1978); Rudolf Braun, "The Impact of Cottage Industry on an Agricultural Population," in David Landes, ed., *The Rise of Capitalism* (New York: Macmillan, 1966).

37. On artisanal politics from the 14th to the 19th centuries, see especially R. A. Leeson, *Travelling Brothers* (London: Granada, 1980) ("Leeson, *Travelling Brothers*"); also Dobson, *Masters and Men*; Rule, *Experience of Labour*; Prothero, *Artisans and Politics* (cited in note 30). For comparisons with French artisans, see especially Michael Sonenscher, "Mythical Work: Workshop Production and the Compagnonnages of Eighteenth-Century France," in P. Joyce ed., *The Historical Meanings of Work* 31 (Cambridge: Cambridge University Press, 1987); Sonenscher, "The Sans-culottes of the Year II: Rethinking the Language of Labour in Revolutionary France," 9 *Soc. Hist.* 301 (1984); *id.*, "Journeymen: The Courts and the French Trades, 1781–1791," 114 *Past & Present* 77 (1987); William H. Sewell, Jr., *Work and Revolution in France: The Language of Labor from the Old Regime to 1848, passim* (Cambridge: Cambridge University Press, 1980) ("Sewell, *Work and Revolution*"); Joan W. Scott, "Work Identities for Men and Women: The Politics of Work and Family in the Parisian Garment Trades in 1848," in *Gender and the Politics of History* 93 (New York: Columbia University Press, 1988); Jacques Ranciere, "The Myth of the Artisan," in Steven Kaplan & Cynthia Koepp, eds., *Work in France: Representations, Meaning, Organization, and Practice* 317 (Ithaca, N.Y.: Cornell University Press, 1986). For comparisons of French rural-industrial and artisanal workers in the 18th and 19th centuries, see especially William H. Sewell, Jr., "Artisans, Factory Workers and the Formation of the French Working Class, 1789–1848," in Ira Katznelson & Aristide Zolberg, eds., *Working-Class Formation: A Comparative Study of France, Germany and the United States* 45 (Princeton, N.J.: Princeton University Press, 1986).

38. See Somers, "The People and the Law" ch. 6 (cited in note 11), for full discussion of these differences.

39. See W. O. Ault, *Open-Field Farming in Medieval England: A Study of Village By-Laws* (London: George Allen & Unwin, 1972) ("Ault, *Open-Field Farming*"); Charles M. Gray, *Copyhold, Equity, and the Common Law* (Cambridge, Mass.: Harvard University Press, 1963) ("Gray, *Copyhold*"); Steven Yeazell, *From Medieval Group Litigation to the Modern Class Action* 46, 132 (New Haven, Conn.: Yale University Press, 1987) ("Yeazell, *Medieval Group Litigation*").

40. Rick Lempert has pointed out correctly that these questions can be sensibly posed as a sociology of knowledge question: Why do we ignore certain rights and not others in our theories of modern citizenship? The answer, in part, is that theories of citizenship are embedded within a prevailing sociolegal knowledge culture (similar to Kuhn's paradigm) constituted by a master-narrative about modern law and institutions which largely defines in advance what is to count as a modern right in the first place. The importance of this sociolegal knowl-

IV. CITIZENSHIP FORMATION: AN OUTLINE OF AN ALTERNATIVE ACCOUNT[41]

The first national entity in England to institutionalize the rules that led contingently to citizenship rights and obligations was the medieval public sphere. An alternative account must trace the making of England's public sphere and its differential impact on the locales in which citizenship rights were developed and contested in medieval and early modern England. It is a history of coalitions and contentions, alliances and antagonisms, which played out in a shifting configuration of institutional relationships. The premise of my alternative account is that the development and the precise character of modern citizenship is as much a direct outcome of these medieval institutional and cultural foundations as it is an outcome of the intervening forces of capitalist revolutions and class formation in the 17th and 18th centuries. It was the *nexus* between the sequential institutional path of citizenship formation and the structural overlay of marketization that was decisive.

The Making of a Legal Revolution

The history of the formation of a national public sphere must begin in 11th- and 12th-century England before the presence of a unified territorial-wide state. Decentralization was the hallmark of this so-called feudal society, and it is generally characterized as a single feudal culture of "parcellized sovereignties" comprised of mighty fiefdoms with the crown being one among many feudal landlords. This ideal-typical characterization of medieval society doggedly persists despite its empirical weaknesses, as Susan Reynolds has recently reminded us.[42] More in line with an institutional and relational approach to the medieval world, I will map the landscape roughly into four different political and legal cultures.

The first of these (and the most commonly associated with "feudalism") was made up of the rich arable regions of England dominated by large manors and their lords and administered through manor courts (*hall moots*). These private spheres of power (which varied tremendously in size and re-

---

edge culture is taken up in the conclusion at greater length. See also Somers, "Where is Social Theory?" (cited in note 14).

41. For additional recent reformulations, see Tilly, "Where Do Rights Come from?"; Tilly, *Coercion*; Brubaker, *Citizenship and Nationhood* (all cited in note 2).

42. Reynolds, *Fiefs* (cited in note 12).

84 LAW AND SOCIAL INQUIRY

sources) most closely fit the stereotype of the feudal social order—a hierarchical chain of relationships connecting lords, vassals, and a large population of servile unfree peasant laborers (*villeins*). In this system of vertical ties, each link played a part in the story of citizenship formation. The most powerful of the manorial lords formed the core of the baronial competition to the crown (leading to the Magna Carta in 1215), which both responded to and catalyzed monarchical state building. It was the relationship of the vassals to their lords, however, that is most significant for our story.[43] Although subordinated in a chain of command and obligation, these obligational chains by their nature concomitantly endowed vassals with significant rights (what I call "relational rights") which gave them a great deal of autonomy. As we will see below, these relational rights came to play an exemplary role in the development of concept of rights among broader segments of the population. At the bottom of the chain of relations were the unfree villein peasants.[44]

The second sphere, and probably the least familiar, was made up of scattered areas of pastoral, woodland, and relatively nonarable lands. These pastoral regions were populated primarily by small free-holding peasant villagers who farmed and lived in scattered villages and hamlets. In contrast to our prevailing images of feudal society, these nonopen field regions had few great manors; often there were was no single resident dominating manor. Governance took place through local public courts—some ancient county and "hundred" courts—which were formally under the jurisdiction of royal sheriffs. In comparison with manorial villeins, these free villagers had considerable legal and social freedoms by virtue of their embeddedness in public jurisdictions. Their lands and rights, nonetheless, were under the constant threat of encroachment by powerful manorial lords outside their immediate environs. Before these free peasants were corralled into an "alliance" between "the people and the (public) law," the primary system of defense against such encroachment was the strict system of horizontal rights and obligations embedded in their inheritance practices and community relationships, as well as in their local courts and councils. These legal and cul-

---

43. In *Fiefs*, Susan Reynolds brings a formidable challenge to our traditional use of vassalage to describe a central mechanism of the European medieval world.

44. Somers, "The People and the Law" ch. 2 (cited in note 14); George Homans, *Sentiments and Activities* (Glencoe, Ill.: Free Press, 1962) ("Homans, *Sentiments and Activities*"); F. Pollock & F. Maitland, 1 *The History of the English Law before the Time of Edward 1* (Cambridge: Cambridge University Press, 1968) ("Pollock & Maitland, *History of English Law*"); Paul Vinogradoff, *Villianage in England: Essays in English Medieval History* (New York: Russell & Russell, 1923); id., *English Society in the Eleventh Century: Essays in English Medieval History* (Oxford: Clarendon Press, 1908); Gray, *Copyhold* (cited in note 39); Sidney Webb & Beatrice Webb, *The Manor and the Borough*, 2 vols. (Hamden, Conn.: Archon Books, 1963); Ault, *Open-Field Farming* (cited in note 39); P. Gatrell, "Studies in Medieval English Society in a Russian Context," 96 *Past & Present* 23 (1982); J. W. Burrow, "'The Village Community' and the Uses of History in Late Nineteenth-Century England," in N. McKendrick, ed., *Historical Perspectives: Studies in English Thought and Society* 255 (London: Europa, 1974).

tural practices came to serve the villagers well in their later struggles to appropriate formal membership laws into actual local citizenship rights.[45]

The third sphere—a kind of hybrid—was comprised of towns, municipalities, and urban boroughs. On the one hand, towns and boroughs were usually located in land controlled by manorial lords. In this setting, urban tenants had the same obligations to the lord as did servile peasant labor; they were answerable to the lords in the manor court and forced to labor regularly on their lands. At same time, their mercantile activities required a great degree of social coordination, and to this end numerous self-governing institutions outside the manor courts developed over time. The first of these was the merchant guild. Its members looked with envy at the rights of vassals, noting that the autonomy endowed by these rights was directly contingent on particularly defined relationships with the lords.[46]

Finally, the fourth sphere was that of the monarchy. In comparison with the rest of Europe, the post-Conquest English monarchy was extremely

---

45. Homans, *Sentiments and Activites*; George Homans, "The Explanation of English Regional Differences," 42 *Past & Present* 29 (1969); Joan Thirsk, "The Farming Regions of England," *in* Joan Thirsk, ed., 4 *The Agrarian History of England and Wales* 1 (Cambridge: Cambridge University Press, 1967); Thirsk, "Industries in the Countryside," *in* F. J. Fisher, ed., *Essays in the Economic and Social History of Tudor and Stuart England* 70 (Cambridge: Cambridge University Press, 1961); H. E. Hallam, *Rural England, 1066–1348* (Brighton, Sussex: Harvester Press, 1981); R. Dodgshon, "The Early Middle Ages, 1066-1350," *in* R. A. Dodgshon & R. Butlin, eds., *An Historical Geography of England and Wales* 81 (London: Academic Press, 1978); E. Power, *The Wool Trade in English Medieval History* (Oxford: Oxford University Press, 1942).

46. On guilds and towns, see Sylvia Thrupp, "The Guilds" ("Thrupp, 'The Guilds'"), *in* M. M. Postan, E. E. Rich, & Edward Miller, eds., *The Cambridge Economic History of Europe*: vol. 3, *Economic Organization and Policies in the Middle Ages* 230 (Cambridge: Cambridge University Press, 1963) ("Postan *et al.*, *Cambridge Economic History of Europe*"); Lujo Brentano, "On the History and Development of Guilds and the Origin of Trade-Unions" ("Brentano, 'History and Development of Guilds'"), *in* Toulmin Smith, ed., *English Gilds* xlix (London: Oxford University Press, 1963) ("Smith, *English Gilds*"); Philip Abrams & E. A. Wrigley, eds., *Towns in Societies: Essays in Economic History and Historical Sociology* (Cambridge: Cambridge University Press, 1977); E. A. Wrigley, *People, Cities and Wealth* (Oxford: Basil Blackwell, 1987); Susan Reynolds, *An Introduction to the History of English Medieval Towns* (Oxford: Oxford University Press, 1977) ("Reynolds, *Introduction to Medieval Towns*"); P. Corfield, "Urban Development in England and Wales in the Sixteenth and Seventeenth Centuries," *in* D. C. Coleman & H. H. Johns, eds., *Trade, Government, and Economy in Pre-Industrial England* 214 (London: Weidenfeld, 1976); Anthony Black, *Guilds and Civil Society in European Political Thought from the Twelfth Century to the Present* (London: Methuen & Co. 1984) ("Black, *Guilds and Civil Society*"); Steve Rappaport, *Worlds within Worlds: Structures of Life in Sixteenth-Century London* (Cambridge: Cambridge University Press, 1989) (Rappaport, *Worlds within Worlds*"); id., "The Extent and Foundations of Companies' Powers in Sixteenth-Century London" (presented at Social Science History Association Meetings, Chicago, 1988); Laurie Nussdorfer, "Urban Politics and the Guilds in Early Modern Europe: Guilds and Government in Baroque Rome" (presented at the Social Science History Association, Chicago, 1988); Gail Bossenga, "Regulating the Local Economy: Guilds and the Town Council in Eighteenth-Century Lille" (presented at the Social Science History Association, Chicago, 1988); Pamela Nightengale, "Capitalists, Crafts and Constitutional Change in Late Fourteenth-Century London," 124 *Past & Present* 3 (Aug. 1989); L. Attreed, "Arbitration and the Growth of Urban Liberties in Late Medieval England," 31 *J. Brit. Stud.* 205 (1992).

86 LAW AND SOCIAL INQUIRY

centralized and bureaucratized.[47] Nonetheless, the crown was hemmed in ultimately by its relentless and urgent need to fill the coffers of war and the power of manorial lords and urban merchants to resist providing the financial support for monarchical military ambitions on the other.[48] The antagonisms between the crown and the barons was exacerbated by royal frustration over both its limited access to baronial resources and its difficulty in controlling the violence of the warring countryside and the political demands of rebelling barons. Even merchant wealth was beyond monarchical reach; indeed, there was good reason to believe that mercantile political loyalties and wealth would follow the lead of the barons' revolts.[49]

The crown, the towns, and the pastoral bodies had nothing in common except an overwhelming mutual antagonism to the manorial spheres of private power. Mercantile antagonism reflected the demands of these urban dwellers for the same degree of autonomy from feudal lords as was possessed by manorial vassals. And in this desire for municipal juridical independence, merchants and urban artisans were united. Merchants, moreover, were indeed inspired by baronial revolts; if their wealth was so much in demand, they saw no reason why they should not expect in return a share in wider political power.[50] Finally, pastoral peasant antagonism reflected the constant attempts on the part of manorial lords to "manorialize" their freeholding farms, rob them of their free legal status, and ultimately to subject them to the condition of relative rightlessness characteristic of those peasants ultimately answerable only to the "will of the lord" in the manor courts.

How did the English crown overcome the political and jurisdictional competition from private manorial and baronial power? In the 12th through 14th centuries, the English crown carried out a legal revolution by deploying Norman administrative institutions and centralizing principles of Roman law, ancient juridical customs of the realm, selected parts of the canon law, and a host of other free-floating resources. What made it revolutionary was both the fact of a crown being able to achieve such precocious

---

47. The capacity for its "precociousness" in centralized administrative methods has been made legendary through the remarkable findings of the Domesday Books.

48. No one has done more for us to come to appreciate the centrality of war to state formation than Charles Tilly. See especially his *Coercion* (cited in note 2).

49. Pollock & Maitland, *History of the English Law*; P. Corrigan & D. Sayer, *The Great Arch: English State Formation as Cultural Revolution* (Oxford: Basil Blackwell, 1985); Joseph Strayer, *On the Medieval Origins of the Modern State* (Princeton, N.J.: Princeton University Press, 1970) ("Strayer, *Medieval Origins of Modern State*"); P. Anderson, *Lineages of the Absolutist State* (London: New Left Books, 1974) ("Anderson, *Lineages of Absolutist State*"); Derek Sayer, "A Notable Administration: English State Formation and the Rise of Capitalism," 97 *Am. J. Soc.* 1382 (1992); W. Bagehot, *The English Constitution*, ed, R. Crossman (London: Fontana, 1965).

50. Gabriel Ardant, "Financial Policy and Economic Infrastructure of Modern States and Nations," in Charles Tilly, ed., *The Formation of National States in Western Europe* 164 (Princeton, N.J.: Princeton University Press, 1975) ("Tilly, *Formation*").

Rights, Relationality, and Membership

territorial-wide unification at this time and the method used to accomplish it—a monarchical strategy to forge institutional links with those prefeudal public juridical units and administrative centers that remained intact throughout the period of wide privatization through manorialism. At the same time, through a widely expanded elaboration of royal legal rules and regulations, especially the king's peace, the English crown formally encircled *all* the local governing bodies of the realm—public and private—by creating powerful territorial-wide public legal institutions that functioned over and above private feudal power. These included the Royal Courts and traveling Assizes as well as royal administrative appointees drawn from the local population. The result was an early (relative to the rest of Europe) national state that incorporated a majority of juridical and administrative units into a single entity but *without dismantling the original local bodies*.

This new legal administrative sphere was thus at heart an institutional matrix of complex connections. It can be pictured as a social map that was transformed from a multiplicity of separate (usually warring) entities to a mapping of multiplex linkages among, and encirclement by, a wide network of public institutions. Most crudely put, over many years and many conflicts the monarchy had managed to carve out a structural institutional "alliance" between "the people" and the "law."[51] The alliance took the institutional shape of a configuration of linkages among the crown, urban merchants, and nonmanorial governing bodies—a geometric matrix of networks and linkages in continual relational tension and movement among and between the connecting nodes. Rather than setting up an alternative political apparatus entirely outside its baronial competitors as in the French case, the English crown thus built a national legal sphere by incorporating into a single formal entity the preexisting public legal and governing bodies, their political institutions and practices. These local conventions and rules, and those from the mercantile cities in particular such as guild and mercantile law, were in turn nationalized by the state through new centralized institutions. Local laws *writ large* were then in turn reapplied to the localities through local administrators who were nonetheless ultimately accountable to the national state.

Susan Reynolds's *Kingdoms and Communities in Western Europe, 900–1300* argues that all early medieval European realms defined themselves as communities and that kingdoms constituted themselves out of such overlapping communities.[52] This is certainly true at the level of self-definition as rulers sought to "naturalize" their territorial consolidation through

---

51. For various historical approaches to the concept of "the people," see C. Hill, "Parliament and People in Seventeenth Century England," 142 *Past & Present* 100 (1981); D. T. Rogers, *Contested Truths: Keywords in American Politics Since Independence* (New York: Basic Books, 1987); Raymond Williams, *Keywords: A Vocabulary of Culture and Society* (Oxford: Oxford University Press, 1976); Prothero, *Artisans and Politics* 59 (cited in note 30).

52. Cited in note 14.

88 LAW AND SOCIAL INQUIRY

ideologies of community and population homogeneity.[53] But the mechanisms and impact of structural consolidation can be more precisely analyzed when viewed on a continuum between the making of a national "community" through incorporation and compulsory participation from the preexisting local bodies, as in the English case, and the making of a national "community" through the direct imposition of state administrators onto preexisting competing units. Tilly presents a two-dimensional typology which he uses to differentiate different states' paths of growth. The two axes of the typology are extent of concentration of capital and extent of concentration of coercion. From this schema, Tilly defines three trajectories: the coercion-intensive path, the capitalized coercion path, and the capital-intensive path.[54] England, when compared to France, her main military rival, looks far more like the dualistic structure of worlds within world consolidation. When viewed from either of these continuums, an appropriate question to ask would be whether the more "legitimate" strategy of English state building became a post hoc ideology that internationalized itself.[55]

I have of course presented a hypostatized and abstract picture of a dramatic historical process driven by momentous conflicts and power relations. This is not the place, however, to spell out in a large canvas that drama of struggle and state building and the making of the national legal sphere. Suffice it to say here that this is the institutional foundation of the English national state. It is this configurational institution to which members of previously separate local bodies first came to belong as national members. And it was this legal sphere that first imposed the rules and legal obligations of national membership.

Early English Citizenship and a Political Culture of Rights

England's national legal sphere was thus constructed through the conjoining and interdependence of local bodies, institutions, practices, and doctrines within a central organizing body. This was a public realm built on mandatory *community inclusion, and participatory law and governance*. The consequence of this historical process was the creation of a *hybrid* political culture which was both new and old, national and local, and which embodied all the principles and power relations of the different local cultural spheres.

What was new was membership in a national body to which subjects were both answerable and by which they were endowed with certain rights. These rights were only meaningful in the context of their linkage to mem-

---

53. Tilly in *Coercion* 106, 115 (cited in note 2), deals with the necessities of national homogenization.
54. *Id.* at 130.
55. This interesting question was raised by an anonymous LSI referee.

Rights, Relationality, and Membership 89

bership in the national sphere and access to its legal system over and above that of private power. What was old, however, was just as important. The linkages were not between the crown and individuals but between public national institutions and local village ones—local juries, the constabulary, local assizes, and so on. The possible benefits and likely sanctions of national membership such as "protective labour regulations" were utterly contingent on membership in these local institutions, making individuals and families also answerable and responsive to local and practices and sanctions, to the old duties and rights attached to local membership.

As a mutually constituted realm, neither the national nor the local had power without the other. Alone, local bodies could not protect themselves from manorial power and, eventually, market exploitation; the crown in turn depended on this newly expanded power base. To borrow a term from a scholar of urban life, this hybrid-like configuration was comprised of "worlds within worlds," or what I will call "membership within membership."[56] "Self-governance at the king's command" was the paradoxical contemporary expression of this political culture constructed on relational tensions and mutual interdependencies among groups and institutions. The resulting political culture was also a hybrid embodying all these principles. And the three dimensions of citizenship that emerged were direct outgrowths of this hybrid political culture created of worlds within worlds.

Civil Citizenship

The first dimension (although not necessarily chronologically) was the right and the obligation to public justice—the origins of civil citizenship. With the formal consolidation of a national legal sphere, the spread, accessibility, institutionalization, and the discourse of public law began to compete with private manorial jurisdiction in shaping English political culture. Its explicit promise was first of all adjudication and peace keeping. But its competitive edge came from its promise to *remedy* the local wrongs of mighty feudal lords—a remedy of *right* that could counter through law the unequal position of rightlessness of the weak when confronted with the local power of private justice. Even though we are speaking of a period when king's remedies only went to certain wrongs, and when manorial courts still had broad jurisdiction, the discursive ideal of common law was its claims to *universality*. As a universal discourse, common law created surprisingly universal expectations. These expectations in turn became resources for popular mobilizations to lay claim to the universal ideals of the rule of law. The frequency of struggles for its realization underlines just how uneven was its application in practice.

---

56. Rappaport, *Worlds within Worlds.*

90 LAW AND SOCIAL INQUIRY

Based not on enacted laws or policies but on the principle of law as a set of public rules to resolve conflict and ensure equal protection to all, principles of civil right established the basis of liberty to be "freedom from . . .," that is, freedom from the overbearing power of private feudal power by the protection of the public law. Linked in the 17th century to the theory of natural rights and property rights in labor and the individual, procedural civil justice gave rise to the animating myths of the "free-born Englishman" and England's much touted "rule of law" as it made universality before the law and the right to rebel against a tyrannical monarch (allegedly called into existence solely to protect the individual's rights) central to its organizing principles. Yet in their origins, these principles of right and property were not connected to the formulation of property as individual ownership in the juridical language of civil law and Locke, but to property as political membership—the contrast being between rights invested in things and rights invested in political relationships.[57] The king's writ, for example, did not determine in advance how property disputes should be resolved but rather ordered the dispute to be moved into the public courts, thus giving certain classes of people—to be sure, not all—the right to be heard in courts of public justice, not the a priori determination of the content of that justice. Once in the royal courts, however, it was the Assize of Clarendon which determined the procedure. Enacted by the crown in the 12th century, the Assize worked in such a way that membership rather than property "ownership" determined political and legal rights. The Assize declared that freeholders were no longer subject to absolute political power by private lords in disputes over their land, even when the freeholder did not "own" the land. If the community supported the freeholder's claim, the freeholder was now given the right to public justice in the kings courts. Because they came from a freeholding heritage, rural-industrial families in particular carried a legacy that rooted economic survival in public membership.

One of the more interesting twists on civil citizenship lies in the non–common law practice of *equity*. When in the 14th century the Chancery first began to take up the business of justice, it offered itself as an alternative means of receiving justice to the lengthy and expensive procedures of the common law courts. In the Chancery no pleading was necessary by law-

---

57. J. G. A. Pocock, "Authority and Property: The Question of Liberal Origins" and "The Mobility of Property and the Rise of Eighteenth-Century Sociology" in his *Virtue* 51 (cited in note 31); James Tully, *A Discourse on Property: John Locke and his Adversaries* (Cambridge: Cambridge University Press, 1980); Richard Tuck, *Natural Rights Theories: Their Origin and Development* (Oxford: Oxford University Press, 1979). An extremely interesting recent discussion is Ian Shapiro, "Resources, Capacities and Ownership: The Workmanship Ideal and Distributive Justice," in John Brewer & S. Staves, eds., *Early Modern Conceptions of Property* (Berkeley: University of California Press, forthcoming). See also Susan Reynold's discussion of property in her "Fiefs, Vassals, and Feudalism" (cited in note 12); and Margaret R. Somers, "'Misteries' of Property: Relationality, Families, and Community in the Making of Political Rights," in Brewer & Staves, *Early Modern Conceptions of Property*.

Rights, Relationality, and Membership 91

yers, no jury had to be convened—although expert witnesses were to be brought; and the initiation of the proceeding was a result of a petition from below. The key to this new swifter form of justice by which the "less mighty" could be protected against the "over mighty" was that by reaching directly to the king's courts, equity bypassed powerful county influence. As a procedure, equity was so popular that the conciliar courts were inundated with petitions for its use and it became the basis of procedure and judgment in the Privy Council, the Star Chamber, and the Court of Requests.[58]

The substance of equity, however, was broader than mere procedural simplicity. In essence it was a concept of justice in which particular *circumstances*, considerations of hardship and mercy, and the putatively high-minded conscience of the king—rather than abstract procedural principles—were factored into the passing of judgments. St. Germain was the most notable 16th-century theorist of equity:

> Equity is righteousness that considers all the particular circumstances of the deed, which is also tempered with the sweetness of mercy. . . . And the wise man says: be not overmuch righteous, for the extreme righteousness is extreme wrong. . . . And therefore to follow the words of the law were in some case both against justice and the common-wealth: wherefore in some cases it is good and even necessary to leave words of the law and to follow that reason and justice require. And to that intent equity is ordained.[59]

Used in the "poor man's courts" where the costs of presentment were not prohibitive, equity appealed to the poor because it claimed, in principle at least, to focus on the relationship between circumstances and justice. It was meant to be a law that was appropriate and adaptable to changing circumstances. As such, it directly competed with common law procedures which were so strictly tied to the letter of the law that the "spirit of necessity" was lost. St. Germain stated the purpose of the Court of Chancery:

> And the Court of the Chancery is called of the common people the court of conscience, because the chancellor is not strained by rigour or

---

58. J. H. Baker, *An Introduction to English Legal History* (2d ed. London: Butterworths, 1983); G. R. Elton, *The Tudor Constitution: Documents and Commentary* (2d ed. Cambridge: Cambridge University Press, 1982 [1960]) ("Elton, *Tudor Constitution*"); Frederick Maitland, *The Constitutional History of England* (Cambridge: Cambridge University Press, 1979 [1908]); W. Fischer & P. Lundgreen, "The Recruitment and Training of Administrative and Technical Personnel," *in* Tilly, *Formation* 456 (cited in note 50). All were under the control of the King's Privy Council and served as alternative educational arenas to the common law courts for statesmen and civil servants.

59. Cited in Donald Hansen, *From Kingdom to Commonwealth: The Development of Civic Consciousness in English Political Thought* 157 (Cambridge, Mass.: Harvard University Press, 1970) ("Hansen, *From Kingdom to Commonwealth*").

92 LAW AND SOCIAL INQUIRY

form of words of law to judge but *ex aequo* and *bono* according to conscience.[60]

Rather than the law in its pristine logic, equity ruled as just the principles of "natural justice, common sense, and common fairness"—principles that were applied by the state's conciliar courts to the task of redressing injustices inflicted on the poor by the unequal power of the "over mighty." The discretionary conscience of the king was to be the basis of such redress; and as long as such conscience was frequently mobilized, the centralized power of the crown could increase. By meeting the needs of those who felt lack of justice at the hands of the rigidities of common law procedures, and by providing redress where other forums of law had failed to adapt to changing circumstances,[61] the courts of equity forged direct links between the people and the institutions of the state while simultaneously carrying on the process of monarchical centralization through the law. It was these procedural burdens of common law less than its substantive failures that propelled the growth of equity in the royal courts until the time of the English civil war in the 17th century.[62]

If the king's conscience came to be a boon to the poor, the king's body—that is, his actual corporeal person—was of less importance. In English legal practice there was an English version of the Roman doctrine of the "king's two bodies."[63] The doctrine specified that every person in the realm, including the king, was subject to the law—even if the king was himself the maker of laws. The king in his person, for all the pomp attached to his physical being, was thus in principle subservient to the law even as *the kingship*—his office—was above it. The crown appropriated the principle of the invincibility of *office* to support the entrenchment of centralized administrative techniques and the power of the conciliar courts. By doing so, English monarchs created the conditions for the expectations of moral obligation and justice from the crown *without necessarily attaching an enduring allegiance to the particular person of the king himself.*

A remarkable mythology of the rule of law was the consequence of the Anglicanization of the doctrine of the king's duality. From oppressive legal proceedings to the most heinous impositions of tyranny by the state, the failing of the law itself was not blamed but rather corrupt individuals, ministers, particular events, and even kings who were abusing the rule of law. Only the English were so obsessed by the conviction of universality of law that they claimed it was within the bounds of law to commit revolution and detach a king's head. To Milton are attributed fits of "legal antinomianism"

---

60. *Id.*
61. Elton, *Tudor Constitution* 152.
62. For examples of equity in copyholding, see Gray, *Copyhold* (cited in note 39).
63. E. Kantorowitz, *The King's Two Bodies: A Study in Medieval Political Theology* (Princeton, N.J.: Princeton University Press, 1957); Hansen, *From Kingdom to Commonwealth.*

Rights, Relationality, and Membership 93

in his cries for the utter legality of regicide.[64] The king's two bodies was essential doctrine for both parliamentarians and the conservative agents of the Restoration.[65]

> Nothing more slackens the reins of government, and the stability of peace, which is upheld by the reverent awe and respect which the people and subjects give to the Magistrate, than when by injustice and unworthiness, they bring their persons and authority under contempt and dislike; but that they seem not as Gods but Idols, which have eares but heare not, eyes but see not, mouths but *speak not true judgement. Against such Magistrates, people are prone to think it, not only just, but meritorious to rebel.*[66]

The doctrine was also at the heart of the law's promise of universality. That the king in his person, for all the pomp attached to his physical being, was allegedly a servant of the law created the conditions for popular expectations of moral obligation and justice from the royal law without attaching an enduring allegiance to the particular person of any one monarch. Universality was at the very core of English common law; king and pauper alike were equally subject to the law. There was no ambiguity about this; the term "magistrate" was applied equally to local political authorities so that in public narrative the power, duties, and accountability of Westminster were allegedly analogous to those of local authorities, and expectations of both were one and the same.[67] If no authority was above the law, it followed naturally that if any acted as if they were, they were subject to legal removal by the injured parties. What was the definition of a governor and legislator? Even a Newcastle Whig answered in 1774 by declaring them as but "trustees to the public" so that any such magistrates who abuse the laws by making "laws more favourable to themselves than to him [the public]," or if they "execute the laws more favourable to one than to another, or stretch them to an oppressive purpose to serve their own ends—they *should be displaced, from the prince to the parish officer; and other chosen in their stead.*"[68] The dissociation of the rule of law from the *rulers* of law gave eminent rationality—a thoroughly "modern" concept—to an expectation of justice.[69]

---

64. Alan Harding, *A Social History of English Law* (Gloucester, Mass.: Peter Smith, 1966); Howard Nenner, *By Colour of Law: Legal Culture and Constitutional Politics in England, 1660–1689* (Chicago: University of Chicago Press, 1980) ("Nenner, *Colour of Law*").

65. Nenner, *Colour of Law*.

66. John Ganden, "A Sermon Preached before the Judges at Chemeford," *cited in* John Walter, "The Essex Grain Rioters," in John Brewer & John Styles, *An Ungovernable People?* 47 (New Brunswick, N.J.: Rutgers University Press, 1980) ("Brewer & Styles, *Ungovernable People?*").

67. John Brewer, "The Wilkesites and the Law, 1763-74: A Study of Radical Notions of Governance," in Brewer & Styles, *Ungovernable People?* 133.

68. *Id.*

69. Noticeably absent from my argument is discussion of the king's peace or the criminal law—arguably the dimensions of royal law that most ordinary people were confronted with

94 LAW AND SOCIAL INQUIRY

Political Citizenship[70]

The second aspect of the political culture of rights, and the oldest of all, was compulsory participation in local governance, administration, and law—the origins of political citizenship. As described above, the public sphere integrated into participatory roles of local courts and villagers, and the crown drew new lines of loyalty throughout the territory. It would be easy to dismiss any democratic outcomes in this structure of participation. But for two reasons this would be a mistake. First, English governance was channeled through its legal system. The local courts served as political arenas and institutions. Second, it was precisely in legal institutions that local participation was not limited to county elites but spread deeply into the communities.[71] The vastly smaller number of English salaried officials, in contrast to the Continental system, was made up by the heavy use of laymen.[72] Joseph Strayer points out that by the 13th century England's royal government was "involving almost the entire free population of the country in the work of the law courts."[73] These popular institutions included juries; bodies of "expert witnesses" drawn from the communities requisite to almost all legal and administrative procedures; petitions; proclamations from the central government; village courts; the method of appointment of the constable; the commands to participate in, and the obligation to raise, hue and cry; and to a limited extent, the participatory capacities exercised in the 16th and 17th centuries by a surprisingly large number of small artisans and freeholders, electors and nonelectors alike.[74]

---

daily. There is a wealth of literature and debate on the social history of the criminal law (see, e.g., the vast debate surrounding Douglas Hay's edited volume, *Albion's Fatal Tree: Crime and Society in Eighteenth-Century England* (New York: Pantheon Books, 1975), and E. P. Thompson, *Whigs and Hunters: The Origin of the Black Act* (New York: Pantheon, 1975)) ("Thompson, *Whigs and Hunters*"). Less attention has been paid these other aspects of law that I argue were so central to the formation of citizenship identities.

70. The next few paragraphs draw from Somers, 58 *Am. Soc. Rev.* (cited in note 7).

71. In France, by contrast, the community was excluded. See Bruce Lenman & Geoffrey Parker, "The State, the Community, and the Criminal Law in Early Modern Europe," *in* V. A. C. Gatrell et al., eds., *Crime and the Law* 11 (London: Europa, 1980) ("Lenman & Parker, 'The State' ").

72. Whereas the French state sold and controlled over 12,000 judiciary jobs throughout the land churning out a massive army of central bureaucrats who tried (but failed) to swallow up local community practices, in England in the 16th century there were only 15 Royal judges; see Lenman & Parker, "The State."

73. Strayer, *Medieval Origins of Modern State* 41 (cited in note 49); see also Pollock & Maitland, *History of English Law* 79, 136 (cited in note 44); William S. Holdsworth, 1 A *History of English Law* (2d ed. London: Methuen & Co., 1914); T. Plucknett, A *Concise History of the Common Law* (5th ed. Boston: Little, Brown, 1956).

74. See especially Thomas A. Green, *Verdict according to Conscience* (Chicago: University of Chicago Press, 1955) ("Green, *Verdict*"); Thomas A. Green & J. S. Cockburn, eds., *Twelve Good Men and True: The Criminal Trial Jury in England, 1200–1800* (Princeton, N.J.: Princeton University Press, 1988) ("Green & Cockburn, *Twelve Good Men and True*"); O'Gorman, 135 *Past & Present* (cited in note 31); Cynthia Herrup, "The Counties and the Country: Some Thoughts on Seventeenth-Century Historiography," 8 *Soc. Hist.* 169 (1983);

Rights, Relationality, and Membership

Political citizenship was thus built on an Janus-faced contingency: The power of the centralized machinery—despite its coercive mechanisms, its prerogative courts, its county agents, its threatening letters, and its allures of patronage—had always to contend with the participatory power of local populations.[75] This counter-pressure, moreover, was grounded in and expressed through more than customary practices or social pressures. Popular participation in local and national governance was institutionally incorporated local popular juridical institutions into the heart of the English bureaucratic apparatus.

A number of paradoxical outcomes developed from this. As a system of state-centered participatory rule—or self-governance at the king's command—the structure of rule could be neither fully state controlled nor fully decentralized. The result was a system of reciprocal enhancement of power between the center and the local branches of the state as the strength of each depended on and in turn fostered the strength of the other. This in turn produced a politicized and negotiable chain of command in the English structure of rule; it was forced to operate through a contingent balance of coercion, negotiation, and multiple points of bargaining among all the bodies in its chain of command. The state could not rule unconditionally but rather was forced to bargain with, exhort, and be vulnerable to local politics and popular practices. "Ruling," observes 17th-century historian Cynthia Herrup, "was a repeated exercise in compromise, co-operation, co-optation and resistance."[76] As a consequence of participatory rights and duties, there was no a priori monopoly of power, and the actual implementation of rights hinged on negotiation and political bargaining.

Social Citizenship

The third aspect of citizenship was the regulation of economic life— the origins of Marshall's social citizenship. The most important of these was the body of industrial and welfare policies devoted not to eliminating but to regulating markets—from labor to grain. With the 1349 and 1351 Ordinance and Statute of Laborers, a body of national laws regulating labor relations was first introduced to cover the entire realm. These were continually reintroduced and adjusted through the famous 1563 Elizabethan Statute of Artificers regulating wages and apprenticeship practices, through the ne-

---

id., *The Common Peace* (Cambridge: Cambridge University Press, 1987) ("Herrup, *The Common Peace*").

75. This approach dovetails with the recent scholarship of Green, *Verdict*; Herrup, *The Common Peace*; John Beattie, *Crime and the Courts in England: 1660–1800* (Princeton, N.J.: Princeton University Press, 1986); Brewer & Styles, *Ungovernable People?* (cited in note 66); Cynthia Herrup, "Law and Morality in Seventeenth-Century England," 106 *Past & Present* 102 (1985).

76. Herrup, 8 *Soc. Hist.*

96 LAW AND SOCIAL INQUIRY

glected 1604 statute instituting *minimum* wage regulations in the rural-industrial regions, until their final repeal in 1813 and 1814.[77] Even more well known, of course, are the Poor Laws—versions of which date to the late 13th century—which included "unemployment benefits" and the recognition of structural unemployment. Many other welfare policies could be included, from the assizes of bread to regulation of working hours.

But why should these laws—usually described as modes of social control and class power—fall under the category of citizenship rights? To understand that, it must be noted that the most significant feature of English welfare and industrial policies was that they were implemented through the normal channels and processes of government and law. The public courts doubled as labor tribunals; local justices and constables served as the administrative personnel; and juries, petitions, legal arbitrations, and national courts were all part of the administrative labour process.[78] The consequences were tremendous: Labor relations operated within the structure of public law, and struggles over labor relations were converted into contestations between employers, workers, and political authorities over whether these laws would be tyrannies or rights.

In the context of political citizenship, this in turn had momentous consequences: Labor relations were negotiated through a legal system built on multiple points of participatory access. By forging a direct link into the villages through JPs, constables, juries, and village courts, and by delegating to local authorities the task of administering labor regulations, the crown had in one swoop made vulnerable to local power all the essential aspects of labor relations—labor supply, labor costs, and the cost of provisioning. Politics, not markets, would determine labor relations. Neither municipal guild regulations, nor magnate or gentry landlords, nor merchant capitalist employers would have a legal claim to an *unmediated* administrative or economic relationship to labor as the public sphere subjected all forms of the private labor contract (whether the private party was a commercial landlord or merchant capital), agricultural and industrial labor alike, to public legal jurisdiction. That all forms of the labor contract were now subject to public participatory legal mediation arguably had more impact on the abolition of feudal villeinage (serfdom) and the continued assertion of the right to freedom from private manorial and/or merchant capitalist power than did the "transition from feudalism to capitalism" or other forms of class power and demographic change.

---

77. See Minchinton, *Wage Regulation* (cited in note 32).

78. Tawney, "Assessment of Wages" (cited in note 33); Dobson, *Masters and Men* (cited in note 33); Margaret Davies, *The Enforcement of English Apprenticeship, 1563–1642: A Study in English Mercantilism* (Cambridge, Mass.: Harvard University Press, 1956); Bertha Putnam, "Justices of Labour in the 14th Century," 21 *Eng. Hist. Rev.* (1906); B. Putnam, *The Enforcement of the Statute of Labourers during the First Decade after the Black Death, 1349–1359* (New York: Columbia University Press, 1908).

Two Legal Cultures

What were the consequences of the politicizing of the labor contract within a public structure of rule whose chief features were its malleability, indeterminacy, and participatory accessibility? Because the English state was built on a participatory basis, exactly how labor relations were resolved in practice depended on the nature of the different local bodies and regions in which the law was actually exercised. *A single public body of membership rules generated, in practical terms, intensely local legal and political cultures.* The structure of rule in general and the character of labor relations in particular took different shape depending on who had the power to participate.

In the agrarian regions, the power to participate was eventually monopolized by large landholding gentry who used the civic liberty of the public law to free themselves from private magnates and assert themselves through the new-found power of public judicial institutions. Within their spheres of unfreedom, however, villeins did have certain customary rights in the manor courts.[79] Some of the luckier peasant families were able over the course of a couple of centuries largely to escape from villeinage into the much more advantageous position of copyholders. Once ensconced in copyhold, they managed to win a wider range of rights for themselves by means first of equity jurisdiction and eventually the common law.[80] Their freedom flowed in the same direction as in the nonmanorial regions, and the closer they were able to move toward public law, the better off they were. The majority of lesser peasants remained relatively rightless, however, the burden of their obligations shifting from the manorial lord to the gentry landlord as they were gradually transformed into agrarian landless laborers by the 17th century. Laboring peasants in these regions with little or no autonomous power were unable to take advantage of public participatory rights and, despite the legal freedom granted by public law, were subordinated anew through the legal process.

In pastoral/rural-industrial regions, by contrast, the absence of powerful social and political elites, the longer history of legal freedom, and the presence of more solidaristic popular communities meant that civic liberties and public participatory law promoted more favorable outcomes to the laboring population. As active participants in the processes of governance, they were able on occasion to prevent private sources of power—both gentry and merchant capitalists—from exploiting to complete advantage the public in-

---

79. The classic text on customary rights of peasants in the manorial courts is still George Homans, *English Villagers of the Thirteenth Century* (New York: Norton, 1960 [1940]).

80. See Ault, *Open-Field Farming*; Gray, *Copyhold*; Yeazell, *Medieval Group Litigation* 46, 132 (all cited in note 39).

98   LAW AND SOCIAL INQUIRY

stitutions of law while they were simultaneously able to demand and appropriate the law to strengthen their own independence.[81]

The local contextualizing of legal processes thus generated different patterns of justice and rights in different types of English regions.[82] There were historically persistent patterns of difference in the structure of early labor markets, in the degree of popular participation in political and legal institutions, in the character of corporate village institutions, and in conceptions of justice and rights. Neither class nor status divisions can account for these differences since those in similar class situations maintained different degrees of power across regions. Instead, these cultural patterns were part of the interaction between England's participatory legal institutions and the presence of contrasting regional political cultures. Popular empowerment varied in the degree to which local populations were able to appropriate the law into a "judicial citizenship."

The significance of the political contingency, plasticity, and multiple points of participatory access in the structure of the public sphere was that it made the institutions of citizenship not the a priori domain of any one class or group but rather a "multiple-use" structure—potentially available to be appropriated by those who had the capacity to appropriate public institutions. No one person, authority, institution, or class was simply free a priori to impose and realize its interests; each was rather forced to negotiate and bargain within the structural constraints and, to be sure, with certain positional structural advantages, of the participatory public sphere. The fluency of the law and the administrative chain of command and the centrality of popular institutions and local governmental offices converged to made it possible under different conditions for different parties to grab hold of legal

---

81. Examples of laborers acting upon and expressing their notion of citizenship rights are numerous. One example comes from Essex in 1686 when woolen workers mobilized fellow workers using the forceful notion that a regulated labor market was a right; those who abused that right were not "free traders" but "law breakers"; and the collective freedom of English citizens was tied to these rights. A similar conviction was expressed in a pamphlet published in 1768: "It cannot be said to be the liberty of a citizen, or of one who lives under the protection of any community; it is rather the liberty of a savage" (*quoted in* Thompson, 50 *Past & Present* (cited in note 30)). Early in the 18th century Parliament received many petitions from workers in the wool producing districts demanding enforcement of apprenticeship law since, as one petition summarized the state of affairs, "great numbers of persons of all trades have intruded into the petitioners' trade so that they cannot get a livelihood" (*quoted in* E. Lipson, 3 *An Introduction to the Economic History of England* 288 (London: A. & C. Black, Ltd., 1943)). For additional discussion of communities pressing for and acting upon notions of citizenship rights, see Bohstedt, *Riots and Community Politics*, and Charlesworth, *Atlas* (both cited in note 35); Dale Williams, "Morals, Markets, and the English Crowd in 1766," 104 *Past & Present* 56 (1984).

82. The import of the "law in context" was originally developed in the early 20th-century American school of Legal Realism; see Laura Kalman, *Legal Realism at Yale* (New Haven, Conn.: Yale University Press, 1987). More recently, the contextual focus has been taken up by anthropologists; see Clifford Geertz, "Local Knowledge: Fact and Law in Comparative Perspective," in his *Local Knowledge* 167 (New York: Basic Books, 1983); and Moore, *Law as Process* (cited in note 18).

mechanisms and turn them to their own advantage. A culture of localism and participatory practices made the meaning of citizenship highly contested and variable depending on distribution of power to exercise rights.

I now take a deeper look at one of those legal cultures within the public sphere: the medieval municipalities and their guilds.

V. THE POLITICAL CULTURES OF TOWNS AND GUILDS: THE RELATIONALITY OF RIGHTS

Images of medieval cities and guilds are more constructed and exploited in theories than analyzed in their historical practices. The effort here will be to ignore the "ideology of normative past" that infuses the historiography and social theory of urban life and to instead focus on what has been neglected—a focus on the forms of urban life and analysis of the intersection of cultural and institutional life.[83] One reason for doing this is that medieval urban life provides an exemplary pattern of a political culture of citizenship rights both in formation and in action. It illustrates how struggles among local governing bodies and between spheres of power transformed into varieties of institutional relationships—relationships marked by ongoing tensions. These dynamic patterns become embodied and expressed within a political culture and are themselves sources of historical change.

A second reason for looking closer at the medieval towns concerns their special impact on the development of England's public sphere. Principles of substantive justice and mercantilist policies for regulating economic life were common to all European state-building strategies. But the manner in which England established territorial-wide political control over economic life was unique—both in its relationship to the urban policies and in its impact on the national political culture. By the 14th century English cities and towns can be characterized by their "autonomy in membership" or "liberty in embeddedness." This meant that their legal self-governance and characteristically medieval economic autarky was wholly contingent on institutional ties of political reciprocity with the crown and the public sphere at large. In its struggles for expanded national wealth (again, for the wages of war), the English crown was able to take advantage of this less than absolute autonomy of the medieval cities. On the Continent early absolutist regimes were unable to counter the complete autonomy of the urban burghers and guilds and thus had to "invent" anew their regulative institutions. Only in England was the crown able to appropriate from below and extend throughout the land the political and legal conventions of the medieval cities. From the mid-14th century through the 17th-century Stuart regime, English monarchs and state builders engaged in a steady process of forcing

---

83. The phrase comes from Perez Zagorin.

100 LAW AND SOCIAL INQUIRY

open fiercely insulated town policies and instituting throughout the country at large the same vast system of regulative and redistributive laws that had previously been limited to urban, guild, and even canon law. Continental monarchs, by contrast, were left with only national regulative control over commodity markets and foreign trade.

These statutes and conventions were a key feature in shaping the development of the English political culture of citizenship—especially in the crucial realm of social rights. In contrast to continental Europe where the culture of the guilds was restricted to urban settings, England's public sphere blended the political and legal cultures of town and country labor.[84] Since urban culture and law was thus so central to the public sphere as a whole, we must look more closely to understand the foundations of the national political culture.

Liberty in Embeddedness: The City and the Crown

In popular lore, medieval cities are most renowned for having been a refuge for personal liberty in an age of arbitrary feudal power and insecurity.[85] "A year and a day" was the customary amount of "city-air" an escaped villein needed to gain freedom. But this was not the kind of freedom Pirenne and others identified as the origins of capitalist individualism.[86] Indeed Pirenne and Weber and even Marx to a degree all believed the motor of modern capitalist growth—whether conceived in Pirenne's terms as free-market individualism, or Weber's as the site of rational domination and legitimacy—lay in the mercantile activities of the medieval cities. Pirenne in particular has been hugely influential in locating in the towns the origins of cultural individualism. But capitalist breakthroughs did not originate primarily from the cities; nor was the secret to its success unregulated mercantile activity. Our interest in the freedoms of the city must take us to a rival and relatively unrecognized concept of liberty—both economic and personal.[87]

The "liberty" of the towns had both a corporate and a personal meaning. But it was from the corporate that individual liberty derived.[88] The

---

84. From a vast comparative perspective Weber argues this in Max Weber, *The City*, trans. & ed. D. Martindale & G. Newsmith (New York: Free Press, 1958) ("Weber, *The City*").

85. Alan Harding, "Political Liberty in the Middle Ages," 55 *Speculum* 427, 442 (1980); Smith, *English Gilds* (cited in note 46); M. Bloch, 1 *Feudal Society* (Chicago: University of Chicago Press, 1961); Black, *Guilds and Civil Society* 39, 42 (cited in note 46).

86. Nor was the city the only place; see Somers, "The People and the Law," *passim* (cited in note 11).

87. The liberal versus communitarian polarization can be seen as more of a philosophical prejudice than a historical one.

88. On the process of transition from corporate to individual liberty, see Harding, 55 *Speculum* at 442.

Rights, Relationality, and Membership 101

hallmark of the English town—and London is of course the most outstanding case—was its liberty in membership and its autonomy in embeddedness. I use the terms to characterize the fact that the very triumph of the English urban commune and its strength of self-governance was contingent on its embeddedness within the political framework of the realm. This is in marked contrast to the autonomy of Italian communes (e.g., the Lombards) the autonomy of which was independent from any wider sphere.[89] This wider national power was in turn sustained by what was also unusual in comparative terms—the inclusion, rather than the locking out, of urban groups in the wider political sphere. How did this autonomy in embeddedness develop?

The story of the political culture of urban rights begins with the initial subordination of towns to fiefdoms or royal desmesnes described above. The struggle for municipal independence takes shape in the 12th century. In a case of discursive appropriation, urban dwellers found a cultural and institutional resource in the language of rights in play between feudal lords and their vassals.[90] This was a language that invested rights in the inviolability of relationships, responsibilities, and above all membership. This discourse, however, could not be inexorably attached to the social foundations of vassallage; with political effort, merchants and artisans appropriated and transformed the specificity of these rights to a potentially similar relationship between themselves and the crown.

The language of rights in reciprocity was a considerable cultural resource for a political struggle. In late 12th and early 13th centuries the English crown was in desperate need of merchant wealth, and had numerous occasions to feel the threatening implications of merchants in alliance with baronial political rebellions. English towns thus began the process of wresting juridical and political power from feudal magnates through winning grants of self-governance from the crown. These charters of liberties, as they were called, endowed local autonomy under ultimate Royal law. In return they paid royal taxes and bought royal farms. The first great victory was the establishment in 1191 of the London commune—"subject to the king's pleasure."[91] Londoners founded their commune on a sworn association of *citizens* with its own juridical personality which existed within a reciprocal relationality with the crown.

---

89. On Italian cities, see Lauro Martines, *Power and Imagination: City-States in Renaissance Italy* (New York: Knopf, 1979). See also the work of Larry Miller, "Machiavelli's Politics" (unpublished ms.), who has written on the historical conditions in which Macchiavelli formulated his political theories.

90. I am grateful to Larry Miller for his suggestions on this aspect of feudal "inspiration" for the expansion of rights to the urban sphere.

91. G. A. Williams, *Medieval London: From Commune to Capital* 2 (London: Athlone Press, 1963) ("Williams, *Medieval London*").

102 LAW AND SOCIAL INQUIRY

Corporate membership in the national public sphere was thus the prerequisite for urban liberties. Communal independence was achieved not through city-state status but by reshifting institutional alignments from those of subordination within private spheres of manorial power, to those of partial autonomy within the sphere of public power. The rights that were gained were the rights of citizens—to rule and be ruled. The cultural and institutional foundations of Marshall's civil, political, and social citizenship rights took shape within this pattern of autonomy in membership.

This triumph of quasi-autonomy was nonetheless precarious; continual struggles to maintain juridical and legal independence, now with the crown, characterized the whole 13th century. But by the 14th century, autonomy in membership developed to the point where not only were merchants included in Parliament, an extremely unusual development in comparative terms, but artisan powers and juridical autonomy were locally and nationally enlarged and buttressed. The strength of the reciprocity is revealed in the *granting* of liberties by the English crown. Neither French territorial lords nor urban burghers needed monarchical grants; they simply took their power. Instead of consolidating tensions within a single public sphere, the French monarchy was forced for centuries to coexist in direct competition with these separate spheres of power.

Guild, Citizenship and the Public Sphere

This account must now move from the "macro" relationship of town and crown, to the "micro" level of individual and guild. The process of individual freedom followed a similar course to that of the communal. Just as communal liberty developed through institutional and membership realignments, so the freedoms and the rights of the urban individual were also contingent on membership—both locally and within the multiple ties and relationships of the larger public sphere.

In the 12th and 13th centuries, artisanal labor was proliferating. In the early days of municipal independence, artisans of lesser wealth, primarily crafts people, found themselves defenseless against the new town authorities (often comprised of urban dynasties) who were not interested in giving the commoners the same powers as themselves. The mode by which artisanal rights were gained within the town parallels the struggle of the commune as a whole within the fiefdom: Total autonomy was traded for partial practical autonomy through the formation of crafts guilds based on strict rules and regulations of membership.[92] Before exploring the culture of guild membership, it is important first to understand its struggle for existence.

---

92. The merchant guild preceded the crafts guild, but the latter (composed of masters and journeymen) became far more important.

Rights, Relationality, and Membership 103

Economic regulation is the first thing we associate with the power of guilds.[93] But alone economic regulations were weak. The challenge and the necessity if guilds were indeed to provide a base for artisanal freedom was for them to become legally constituted bodies, not just informal solidaristic groups. Just as only through membership would an individual gain her own power of autonomy and freedom from greater power, only through constitutional inclusion would artisans as a group gain the power of autonomy and self-governance. This didn't come easily.

The essential step by which individuals found their own local freedom in membership in strictly regulated guilds occurred through a direct "alliance" between guild and crown. In a process of struggle lasting almost a half-century, guilds battled local elites of merchants and authorities to win not only official recognition by, but notable power within, both local and national governance. The triumph occurred in 1319 by Royal Charter under King Edward II. Article 7 was crucial: all "inhabitants to be admitted [into the freedom] shall be of some mistery . . ."; anyone seeking to obtain the freedom who did not belong to a guild "shall then only be admitted with full assent of the commonality assembled."[94] In translation, that meant that to become a citizen, one had to enter into or "possess" the "freedom" of the town or city. Yet entry to the freedom and thus to citizenship *could only be achieved through membership in a guild* (a "mistery").

This remarkable feat was institutionalized in the 1319 charter which became popularly known as the Magna Carta of the London commonality. It represented, according to G. A. Williams, the "highest peak of achievement that a popular movement ever attained in medieval London."[95] That achievement forged a mighty bond between guild membership and citizenship—a bond accomplished through what Rappaport calls "a collaboration of crown, city and companies."[96] Although not created by the crown, guilds were nonetheless required to be registered with the state, which in turn endowed charters of local self-governance. The charters confirmed the ancient privileges of citizenship, and during the two centuries after Edward II granted his famous charter, more than one hundred London guilds were incorporated as livery companies, each with similar provisions and ordinances.

Despite the considerable restrictions and obligations of guild membership by the 16th century, the overwhelming majority of Londoners elected to assume them to gain rights of the freedom. From 1531 through the 1550s the average number of artisans admitted each year into 12 companies (two-fifths of all men admitted in 1551-53) rose by 69%. This was more than

---

93. See note 29.
94. Cited in Rappaport, *Worlds within Worlds* 31 (cited in note 46).
95. Williams, *Medieval London* 282.
96. Rappaport, *Worlds within Worlds* 49.

104 LAW AND SOCIAL INQUIRY

three times the increase in the city's population; by the mid-16th century, approximately three-quarters of London's men were free. Remarkably, nine-tenths of all London citizens had entered the freedom through obtaining apprenticeship and guild membership.[97] One half of all men were citizens in Norwich and York, while in Coventry four out of five male householders were free by the early 16th century.[98] Part of the explanation for this may have been that "foreigners" were not expelled from the towns but coopted into the regulations of membership. London apprenticeship fees, moreover, were significantly reduced in the Acts of 1531 and 1536. Nonetheless, that charters combined the right to self-rule and the guarantee that citizenship alone endowed the right to practice one's craft was certainly the overwhelming reason.

State building and local membership were mutual partners in the enlargement of citizenship rights. The strength of guild law, to the extent that it was structurally allied with the muscle of public law, can be underlined with an example of failed autonomy. As guilds became more hierarchicalized in the 15th and 16th centuries, the journeymen engaged in numerous attempts to establish journeymen's and yeomen's guilds that were autonomous from their masters. This act of counter-sovereignty was a threat to the crown and to Parliament of an entirely different order. Through the establishment of what was to be a long chain of "anti-combination" laws, journeymen's guilds were legally forbidden. Outside of membership in the public sphere, the freedom they sought had no chance of survival.

The Property of Membership: The Culture of the Guild

But what exactly did it mean to be in a guild? The answer to that question lies in the institution of apprenticeship.[99] The strictest guild regulation was that more was required for a skilled artisan to ply the trade than mere knowledge of a craft. To practice the "arte and mistery" of a craft required membership. Only members of a guild could legally practice their craft in a town, but only an apprenticeship earned guild membership. Seven years was the standard apprenticeship time required to acquire the adequate skills and hence the right of entry to a guild. At the end of the service, the

---

97. Sources on guild membership and citizenship include Reynolds, *Introduction to Medieval Towns* chs. 5, 6, 8 (cited in note 46); Rappaport, *Worlds within Worlds* 53; Thrupp, "The Guilds" (cited in note 44); Black, *Guilds and Civil Society* (cited in note 46); Harold J. Berman, *Law and Revolution: The Formation of the Western Legal Tradition* 359 (Cambridge, Mass.: Harvard University Press, 1983) ("Berman, *Law and Revolution*").

98. R. B. Dobson, "Admissions to the Freedom of the City of York in the Later Middle Ages," 26 Econ. Hist. Rev. 15 (1973); D. M. Palliser, *The Age of Elizabeth: England under the Later Tudors, 1547–1603*, at 220 (London: Longman, 1983).

99. On apprenticeship, see especially E. Lipson, 1 *Economic History of England*: vol. 1, *The Middle Ages* ch. 8 (London: A. & C. Black, Ltd., 1920).

crafts person (now a journeyman) was taken through a public ceremony in which he or she swore by oath to follow the guild's rules and obligations.[100] With that oath the artisan was entitled to the mutual benefits of membership, which included guaranteed citizenship, livelihood, employment, mutual aid, religious life, social organizations—indeed an entire cradle-to-grave culture.

But the meaning of an apprenticeship was not primarily one of a temporary period of training. Paradoxically, it was not "over" at the end of seven years. Like an academic credential, the apprenticeship now became the artisan's permanent property—*permanent as long as practiced within the regulative confines of the guild.* This last point is the essential one. Even though the property of apprenticeship reflected the journeyman's specific skill and investment of time, this was not mobile property that attached to the individual crafts person.[101] Far more significantly, the achievement of a successful apprenticeship was the achievement of a guaranteed place in a deep culture of attachments—along with all the rights and obligations consequent to those attachments.

The property of skill acquired during an apprenticeship was in fact a social membership. The medieval word for skill is "mistery" (as in the "art and mistery of weaving"), indicating that knowledge of a craft was viewed as a specialized secret.[102] Used in this way, skill could be seen as an individual attribute—a form of "human capital"—that no one could take away from the owner. But mistery had another meaning and use that prevailed over the first—it was also the medieval word for the craft guild itself, the social body, the fellowship, the corporate and instituted group.[103] Unlike the word "skill," which is singular and individual, mistery was simultaneously individual and corporate. To possess the mistery was to simultaneously "possess" knowledge and membership.

---

100. For the surprisingly impressive number of women in guilds, see Lucy Smith, "Introduction," in Smith, *English Gilds*; Leeson, *Travelling Brothers* 27 (cited in note 37). On oaths and obligations, see Prothero, *Artisans and Politics* 37 (cited in note 30); Thrupp, "The Gilds" 184, 232 (cited in note 44); A. B. Hibbert, "The Economic Policies of Towns" ("Hibbert, 'Economic Policies'"), in Postan et al., *Cambridge Economic History of Europe* 157, 210 (cited in note 46); Leeson, *Travelling Brothers, passim* (cited in note 37).

101. Tramping, one of the most important forms of labor migration, was contained within social membership networks; see Leeson, *Travelling Brothers.*

102. 10 *Oxford English Dictionary* 815 (Oxford: Oxford University Press, 1933). In ancient Greece, the craftsmen were, like priests and doctors, believed to possess some secret power; see M. Godelier, "Work and its Representations: A Research Proposal," 10 *Hist. Workshop J.* (1980).

103. *Oxford English Dictionary* 815; Lujo Brentano, "History and Development of Gilds" at cxxxii (cited in note 46). For various references to "mystery," "mistery," "misterium," "misterium artis," or "mestera, misteria, from ministerium," as the collective body of the craft guild (rather than the skill itself) see Hibbert, "Economic Policies" at 210; Berman, *Law and Revolution* 391; Reynolds, *Introduction to Medieval Towns* 165 (cited in note 46); Black, *Guilds and Civil Society* 14 (cited in note 46); Leeson, *Travelling Brothers* 26.

106 LAW AND SOCIAL INQUIRY

But for both aspects of the concept, skill was a social mistery, not a technical one. It was thus a form of cultural capital rather than human capital as we now understand it. An unskilled worker was not unskilled because he or she was untrained. Indeed, through a wide array of illegal practices, many unskilled workers in fact were technically trained. The definition of "unskilled" was to be without an apprenticeship. And without an apprenticeship one was excluded from a mistery, beyond the bounds and the bonds of relationality, and thus excluded from the rights of membership. The attachments of membership, not training or ability alone, conferred legality and the property of skill.[104]

Citizenship Rights in Action

The rubric of citizenship entailed civil, political, and social rights. The chief expression of civil liberty was in the guaranteed access to public law, the right to defend by law, the capacity to sue and to plead in court under an impartial judge, and the security against arbitrary violence that civil law promised. Citizens could only be prosecuted in the courts of the city for city offenses, and no citizen could sue another or be forced to plead in civil courts outside the walls of the city.[105] The promise of the universality of law—of course, more recognized in the breach—served as a form of empowerment against numerous sources of the over mighty ("we cannot be equal with those more powerful").

At times by choice, at others by compulsion, political rights were the most active dimension of citizenship. The right and necessity to local self-rule mediated the relationship between crown and individual artisan. Only citizenship permitted political participation. Since membership in a guild was the prerequisite for admission into the freedom, guilds effectively determined who exercised full political rights. (These included the right to participate in public ceremonial processions and "mistery plays" which affirmed the political identity of membership.[106])

Local governance was institutionalized through the courts. As a public lawmaking body, guild leaders served public legal functions such as council member, alderman, jury members, and constables.[107] Guilds, moreover, had

---

104. On illegal shops as unapprenticed ones, see E. Lipson, 2 An Introduction to the Economic History of England 41 (London: A. & C. Black, 1931).

105. On the legal rights of individuals, see Helen Jewell, English Local Administration in the Middle Ages 53 (New York: Barnes & Noble, 1972); Weber, The City 91 (cited in note 84); Berman, Law and Revolution 360, 381, 386, 396, 401; Carl Stephenson, Borough and Town: A Study of Urban Origins in England 143 (Cambridge, Mass.: Harvard University Press, 1933); Black, Guilds and Civil Society 34, 38, 40; Rappaport, Worlds within Worlds 35 (cited in note 46).

106. C. Adams-Phythian, "Ceremony and the Citizen: The Communal Year at Coventry 1450-1550," in P. Clark, ed., The Early Modern Town 106 (London: Longman, 1976).

107. Berman, Law and Revolution 391 (cited in note 97).

Rights, Relationality, and Membership 107

their own courts. Both town and guild courts were institutions of governance and administration, as well as of formal juridical procedure. In addition, they served as forums for public discussion and resolution of the disputes of public life and labor (economic conflicts, unfair labor, etc.). Participation in the administration of law, and often with more power than municipal governments, made guilds what Rappaport calls the "courts of daily life."[108] Local governance was permanently shaped by the political culture of the guild.

The third set of rights to which all citizens were entitled came under the category of the right to social justice. Social justice, by law and by guild, was defined as the right to livelihood, to a fair wage, to available employment, to poverty benefits, mutual aid, burial rites, tramping privileges, and many more.[109] Possession of the freedom was again the prerequisite for these rights to justice, and by controlling entry to citizenship, the guild's corporate power of membership became the means to social justice. That rights were defined as monopoly and restriction seemed not a contradiction. As I have tried to show, this was a political culture that embedded freedom in regulation and membership; the regulation of livelihood was the job of the freedom.[110] In the 14th century, the "ancient" right of citizenship was reconfirmed: Only citizens could sell in towns, and only freemen could legally practice their crafts. Justice, regulation, and the freedom coexisted in this unfamiliar political culture.

The culture of the guild was thus constructed on attachment and membership. The body of rights and obligations stemmed from the strength and upkeep of those relationships. But guilds neither promised nor offered the traditional world of gemeinschaft. The purpose of the property of membership was precisely to provide the foundations for artisanal independence and personal liberties.[111] The prominent emphasis among artisans on independence and autonomy suggests the importance of distinguishing the moral from the institutional conception of rights. The right to the freedom of practicing one's skill, as well as that of citizenship, achieved the goal of individual empowerment. But this empowerment only had viability when rooted in the institutional foundations of attachments and membership. Only the possession of membership allowed for individual empowerment and the meaningful exercise of rights.

---

108. Rappaport, *Worlds within Worlds* 29.

109. On social justice as mutual aid, economic regulations and monopoly, see A. Unwin, *Industrial Organization in the Sixteenth and Seventeenth Centuries* (Oxford: Oxford University Press, 1904); Black, *Guilds and Civil Society* ch. 2; Berman, *Law and Revolution* 391; Hibbert, "Economic Policies" at 159, 202, 206 (cited in note 100).

110. Rappaport, *Worlds within Worlds* 45.

111. For the strongest evidence on this point, see Black, *Guilds and Civil Society* (cited in note 46); see also the numerous guild documents collected in Smith, *English Gilds* (cited in note 46).

108 LAW AND SOCIAL INQUIRY

The property of skill and relationality thus turned out to be the key to the city. A multiple matrix of linkages had been established: To become a citizen, one had to enter into or possess the freedom. Yet entry to the freedom, and thus to citizenship, could only be achieved through the channel of guild membership and apprenticeship. Making the guild the source of public and private empowerment was no mean accomplishment; according to Unwin, it gave the crafts a major hold on the constitution and provided the basis for virtually all the political achievements that were to follow.[112]

Creating a public sphere as in part the city writ large did not automatically confer these citizenship rights on all people, or to the same effect. But among "the people," inclusions and exclusions (including gender exclusion) were less based on class divisions or land ownership than on the political contingencies of membership—indeed on the possibilities of membership—in the different sorts of social bodies in which English law actually operated.

CONCLUSION

This institutional, narrative, and relational approach to citizenship formation has several general implications. The first concerns the role of the state: The long neglect of the state in sociolegal analyses has finally been corrected.[113] In this process, however, too little attention has been paid to the ways in which the development of institutionalized legal and political power—both in promise and in structure—was a possible source of popular empowerment, a potential resource against both private power and the coercive aspects of the state itself—indeed a central aspect of identity formation.[114] Power under the law was plural, porous, and contingently embedded in local arenas and sites of contestation, rather than unitary, absolute, and wielded only from above. The plasticity of legal and economic power suggests why different patterns of rights claims could develop in different local bodies. Shifting analysis away from the "role of the state" to the character of the public sphere brings attention to the impact of competing private and public spheres of power over and above traditional class divisions. A malleable and contested legal power was at the core of Anglo citizenship formation and the development of a political culture of rights in relationality.

---

112. G. Unwin, *The Gilds and Companies of London* 70 (4th ed. London: Methuen, 1963 [1908]).

113. See, e.g., Peter Evans, Dietrich Rueschemeyer, & Theda Skocpol, eds., *Bringing the State Back in* (Cambridge: Cambridge University Press, 1985).

114. Social historians have been far more attentive to this. See E. P. Thompson, *Whigs and Hunters* (cited in note 69); Brewer & Styles, *Ungovernable People?* (cited in note 66). For discussion on these and other approaches to the law, see Green, *Verdict* (cited in note 74); Stone, "The Law," in his *The Past and the Present* 189 (Boston: Routledge & Kegan Paul, 1981); Green & Cockburn, *Twelve Good Men and True* (cited in note 74).

Rights, Relationality, and Membership 109

A second point addresses the recent sociolegal moves to abandon the determinancy of economic relations and instead to concentrate principally on culture, discourse, and ideology. These revisions have been invaluable. Paradoxically, however, they have often had the unintended consequence of reinforcing *by neglect* the "economism" of social history. Stressing culture or even politics as separate spheres leaves intact the fiction that markets are self-regulating, autonomous systems. It locates labor and property and material life on one side of a binary opposition and cultural and political concerns on the other. But livelihood is too important to leave to the economists. The challenge to what Polanyi called the "economistic fallacy" must be twofold: It must not only reject the notion that the state (or culture or religion) is driven by the logic of the economy.[115] More fundamentally, it must challenge the idea that there exists a "logic" of the economy that is not itself politically and culturally constructed.[116] Indeed, even the conceptual unity of something called "capitalism" must be questioned.[117] Without both revisions, the special status of the economy is often reinforced by the use of such terms as "extra-economic,"[118] "noneconomic," or the "relative autonomy of the state"—all of which underline the economy as the baseline of social processes.

---

115. See especially Karl Polanyi, *The Livelihood of Man* (New York: Academic Press, 1977).

116. See A. Hirschman, *Rival Views of Market Society and Other Recent Essays* (New York: Viking, 1986); *id.*, "Against Parsimony," *American Economic Papers and Proceedings* 89 (1984); Polanyi, *Great Transformation* (cited in note 9); M. Granovetter, "Economic Action and Social Structure: The Problem of Embeddedness," 91 *Am. J. Soc.* 481 (1985); Fred Block, *Post-industrial Possibilities: A Critique of Economic Discourse* (Berkeley: University of California Press, 1989); Richard Swedberg, "Economic Sociology," 35 *Current Soc.* 1 (1987); Margaret R. Somers, "The Political Culture Concept: The Empirical Power of Conceptual Transformation" (presented at the American Sociological Association Meetings, 1991); *id.*, "Karl Polanyi's Intellectual Legacy," in Kari Polanyi-Levitt, ed., *The Life and Work of Karl Polanyi* 152 (Montreal: Black Rose Books, 1991); F. Block & Margaret R. Somers, "Beyond the Economic Fallacy: The Holistic Social Science of Karl Polanyi," *in* T. Skocpol, ed., *Vision and Method in Historical Sociology* 47 (Cambridge: Cambridge University Press, 1984); D. Bell, "Models and Reality in Economic Discourse" *in* D. Bell & I. Kristol, eds., *The Crisis in Economic Theory* 46 (New York: Basic Books, 1981); M. Sahlins, *Culture and Practical Reason* (Chicago: University of Chicago Press, 1976); Donald N. McCloskey, *The Rhetoric of Economics* (Madison: University of Wisconsin Press, 1985); Sewell, *Work and Revolution* 10 (cited in note 37). See Viviana Zelizar, "Beyond the Polemics of the Market: Establishing a Theoretical Agenda," 3 *Soc. F.* 614 (1988).

117. See Margaret R. Somers, "Workers of the World, Compare!" 18 (3) *Contemp. Soc.* (May 1989); *id.* "Where Is Social Theory?" (cited in note 14); *id.*, 16 *Soc. Sci. Hist.* (cited in note 17); C. Sabel, "Protoindustry and the Problem of Capitalism as a Concept: Response to Jean H. Quartaert," 33 *Int'l Labor & Working-Class Hist.* 30 (1988). Although relatively neglected by social theorists, Daniel Bell made a version of this epistemological argument years ago in his formulation of the differentiation of spheres between culture, politics, and economy; see his *Cultural Contradictions of Capitalism* (New York: Basic Books, 1974).

118. Robert Brenner and Perry Anderson use these terms. See R. Brenner, "Capitalism, Aristocracy and the English Revolution," Davis Center Paper (Fall 1989); Anderson, *Lineages of Absolutist State* (cited in note 49).

110 LAW AND SOCIAL INQUIRY

These concerns bear directly on the difficulty of decoupling the study of citizenship from its saturation in the intellectual legacy of 19th-century classical social theory of modernity and turning instead to medieval institutional foundations.[119] A two-fisted criticism usually lies in wait for those who attempt to do so. The first is the accusation of nostalgia; the second is the accusation of teleology. Both criticisms reflect the enduring power of that very same classical social theory's "master narrative" of modernity. Both suggest that for social scientists, medieval history is little known but much appropriated for normative purposes in its "feudalism" garb.

The concern that a focus on medieval institutions is nostalgic rather than analytic clearly reflects two related problems. The first is the extraordinary degree to which the presupposition of the progressive nature of capitalism remains embedded in scholarship across the ideological spectrum. The deep-seated suspicion of "reactionary romanticism" is shared by liberal and Marxist social scientists alike. The second problem is the perseverance of a holistic conception of society.[120] It has proved almost impossible to give up the idea of *society*—a social science concept that depends on the notion of a singular societal core essence with synchronic covariation among the parts. A careful institutional analysis, however, entails rejecting that the notions of either a "traditional" or a "modern" society bear any resemblance to historically grounded concepts that can actually explain anything empirical. This rejection is in turn an attempt to present an analysis of institutional relationships rather than societal types. Medieval guilds, for example, had institutional aspects both seemingly "traditional," and seemingly "modern."[121]

The worry about teleology reflects another overwhelming issue: the tenacity of our paradigmatic sociolegal *knowledge culture* to define a priori what is even to be considered *rational* scholarship in the first place, as well as what sorts of ideas are even admissible to being considered candidates for truth or falsehood.[122] At the heart of our sociolegal knowledge culture is a master narrative about the making of modern society and its legal institutions. Central to this master narrative is the foundational claim for a massive rupture in history that took place at some time known as the "transition from feudalism to capitalism" (or, alternatively, during the "Industrial Revolution"). Since it is this very sociolegal knowledge culture that has melded abstract categories such as "society" with this master narrative of

---

119. On the foundational role of 19th-century social thought, see especially Tilly, *Big Structures* (cited in note 15).

120. Charles Tilly in *Big Structures* addresses the reasons for this perseverance, as does Michael Mann in his *Sources of Social Power* ch. 1 (cited in note 15).

121. Were its ritual practices of solidaristic inclusion and exclusion through the property and rituals of apprenticeship, for example, more or less modern, or more or less traditional, than, say, the rituals, rites, and certificates involved in graduate training toward the Ph.D?

122. For a discussion of knowledge cultures see Somers, "Where Is Social Theory?" (cited in note 14).

Rights, Relationality, and Membership 111

discontinuity and the progressive nature of capitalism, we should hardly be surprised to find ourselves declaring as "teleology"—or "neo-Whiggism"—any argument that purports to find the analytic roots of the modern world not in the break from, but embedded within, the institutional practices of the medieval legal and public sphere. Surprised, no; but we should, nonetheless, be skeptical of our habitual intellectual collusion with the very categories of sociolegal knowledge that have long made so many legal practices incoherent.[123]

The alternative approach to citizenship and rights formation presented here does not by any means suggest that there were not incomparable contrasts between 14th-century and, say, 16th-century England—let alone between 14th- and 19th- and 20th-century England. There were. Nor does it suggest that new powerful and influential institutional players (e.g., markets in land, labor, and capital) did not emerge to contest, collude with, and transform preexisting social and legal practices. There did. But these and many, many other similar arguments are the reigning theoretical protagonists we find in virtually every extant account of the historical development of rights, citizenship, and democracy. Given the unexpected turns of contemporary history, it is worth asking ourselves whether we want to continue to exclude—even from consideration—challenges from *outside* the accepted terms of sociolegal debate about modernity.

My long-term comparative research, however, surely suggests the hubris and recklessness of the historical sociologist. To be sure; but it nonetheless also makes possible a decisive break with axiomatic connections between economic and "societal" transformation on the one side and legal practices and political cultures on the other. Citizenship can no longer be viewed as a product of progressive stages of socioeconomic development or of the transition from feudalism to capitalism. Indeed, the analysis is meant to call into question the master concepts of our sociolegal knowledge culture—classical notions of political and societal modernization, as well as the primacy of socioeconomic categories—highlighting instead the centrality of ambiguous relationships of legal power, contingent institutions of popular empowerment, and contested cultures of rights.

The analysis presented here also builds on recent methodological challenges increasingly being launched by historical sociologists concerning the causal dynamic of the sociolegal master narrative. Prevailing approaches have used the "variables approach" in which time and space are epistemologically absent, and in which each moment in a single process is defined as a *different* case; hence the compatibility of this methodology with the master

---

123. For an especially congenial argument to the one presented here, see Robert W. Gordon, "Critical Legal Histories," 36 *Stan. L. Rev.* 57 (1984) and his "The Past as Authority and as Social Critic: Stabilizing and Destabilizing Functions of History in Legal Argument," *in* McDonald, *Historic Turn* (cited in note 14).

112 LAW AND SOCIAL INQUIRY

narrative of rupture and discontinuity. New approaches to causality, by contrast, insist on a form of *narrative causality* that incorporates ideas about "path dependency," historical sedimentation, *histoire evenementuelle*, and above all, the *constitutive* role in historical explanation of temporality, sequence, and contingency.[124] From this perspective, embedded institutional practices do not simply disappear or become "lag effects" with the onset of different modes of production or capitalist markets. A causal narrativity allows us to view modern citizenship and rights formation as one conjunctural moment in a long historical process of contestation *and* continuity between and among different historical forces. These processes are "gathered up," as it were, indeed "sedimented," into the constitutive core of our modern institutions and practices. We could not sever these institutions from their causal narratives even if we wanted to. To find institutional roots of modern citizenship *before* the birth of capitalism is not to suggest that things either *had* to turn out the way they did (which is the meaning of teleology) or that there were not fundamental structural changes. It is rather to argue that the method of causal narrativity enjoins us to search as far as necessary to find the conditions of possibility of modern citizenship rights. This is narrative causality, as well as institutional and relational analysis—not teleology. If that search for causal contingencies takes me to the 12th through 14th centuries—so be it.

---

124. See especially, William H. Sewell, Jr., "Three Temporalities: Toward a Sociology of the Event," in McDonald, *Historic Turn*; Peter Abell, "Rational Equitarian Democracy, Minimax Class and the Future of Capitalist Society: A Sketch towards a Theory," 21 *Sociology* 567 (1987); Andrew Abbott, "From Causes to Events: Notes on Narrative Positivism," 20 *Soc. Methods & Res.* 428 (1992); Ronald Aminzade, "Historical Sociology and Time," 20 *Soc. Methods & Res.* 456 (1992); Jill Quadagno & S. Knapp, "Have Historical Sociologists Forsaken Theory? Thoughts on the History/Theory Relationship," 20 *Soc. Methods & Res.* 481 (1992); Somers, "Where Is Social Theory?" and "'We're No Angels': History and Science, Networks and Narratives in Sociological Analysis" (unpublished, 1993); David Stark, "Path Dependence and Privatization Strategies in East Central Europe," 6 (1) *East Eur. Politics & Societies* 17 (Winter 1992).

[4]
Freedom From, In and Through the State: T.H. Marshall's Trinity of Rights Revisited

Zygmunt Bauman

Each one of T.H. Marshall's trinity of human rights *rested on the state* as, simultaneously, its birth place, executive manager and guardian. And no wonder. At the time Marshall tied personal, political and social freedoms into a historically determined succession of won/bestowed rights, the boundaries of the sovereign state marked the limits of what humans could contemplate, and what they thought they should jointly do, in order to make their world more user-friendly. The state enclosed territory was the site of private initiatives and public actions, as well as the arena on which private interests and public issues met, clashed and sought reconciliation. In all those respects, the realm of state sovereignty was presumed to be self-contained, self-assertive and self-sufficient.

That world, sliced into sovereign enclaves of nation-states, rejecting and disallowing any outside or internal interference with the sovereign's absolute hold over the population under its power, was the ultimate stage of a long process that took off around the 17th century and (at least in Europe) reached its final form at the time Marshall sketched the three stage history of human rights. In the course of that process, a new regime, based on the presumption of the indivisibility of the sovereign power of territorial states, displaced and replaced the segmental, partial and often territorially discontinuous, web-like powers of premodern Europe. To quote Giovanni Arrighi, during that fateful couple of centuries,

> rights of private property and rights of public governments become absolute and discrete; political jurisdictions become exclusive and are clearly demarcated by boundaries; the mobility of ruling elites across political jurisdictions slows down and eventually ceases: law, religion, and custom become 'national', that is, subject to no political authority other than that of the sovereign. (Arrighi 2002:31)

14   *Zygmunt Bauman*

Arrighi proceeds to quote Etienne Balibar's succinct summary of the results:

> The correspondence between the nation form and all other phenomena toward which it tends has as its prerequisite a complete ('no omissions') and nonoverlapping divisioning of the world's territory and populations (and therefore resources) among the political entities ... To each individual a nation, and to each nation its 'nationals'. (Balibar 1990)

In the world which emerged fresh from the battlefields of the 20th century 30-years war, that presumption was authoritatively elevated to the rank of the least questionable, indeed unassailable principle of the new world order. The United Nations, the organization brought into being with a briefing to police that order, was charged with the protection of sovereign states against aggression and with the guardianship of their indivisible sovereignty. The sanctification of state sovereignty in the UN charter seemed at the time to be simultaneously the best conceivable foundation for a planet-wide arrangement of human affairs as would serve the cause of the world peace; it was also believed to be a destination preordained by the laws of history helped as they were on their unstoppable forward march by the sometimes blundering, but in the end victorious, human reason.

Indeed, for the preceding two centuries during which the marriages were arranged between nations and states, states and sovereignty, and sovereignty and a territory locked in tightly sealed and vigilantly controlled borders, the world was occupied with making the control of human movements the sole prerogative of state powers, with erecting barriers to all the other (that is, uncontrolled) human movements, and manning those barriers with watchful and heavily armed guards. Passports, entry and exit visas, custom and immigration controls were among the most coveted and jealously guarded inventions of the art of modern government. Hannah Arendt recalled the old and genuinely prophetic Edmund Burke's premonition[1] that the abstract nakedness of 'being nothing but human' proclaimed at the dawn of the modern era (and later found to be mostly a ground-clearing operation for the absolute sovereignty of modern states) was humanity's greatest danger. 'Human rights', as Burke noted, were an abstraction, and humans could expect little protection from them unless the abstraction was fleshed up with an Englishman's or Frenchman's rights. 'The world found nothing sacred in the abstract nakedness of being human'—so Arendt summed up the experience of the years that followed Burke's prediction. 'The Rights of Man, supposedly inalienable, proved to be unenforceable ... whenever people appeared who were no longer citizens of any sovereign state' (Arendt 1989: 300, 293). The new modern configuration offered no choice. It had to be here, or nowhere; in this way, but in no other. Any kind of individual freedom could be hoped for, obtained and preserved solely inside the realm of state sovereignty; courtesy, and by behest, of a sovereign state.

And there were such sovereign states, in abundance, filling fast the surface of the globe, each willing to oblige or ready to be persuaded or compelled to oblige. Monopoly of the rights allotment was the coveted prize of the 'national liberation' struggle. Indeed, the grounding of human rights (whatever their contents) in the all-embracing and indivisible yet also exclusive sovereignty of the nation-state supplied arguably a better protection of its territoriality than even the most fortified and closely watched borderlines. Rights were admittedly perishable goods and bore ill foreign travels. Only the highest and the mightiest among the people would take the risk of leaving their native abode on their own will, while the most desperate and downtrodden would follow their example (if at all) only if forced and left with no other choice.

Territoriality could be a nightmare but it was also the promise of a shelter, a warrant of security, and altogether a better deal for every human in a world that had already made of the territoriality of powers, identities and rights the supreme principle of the world order. In such a world, in each and any of its sovereign territorial segments, the inconceivable could be conceived: in such a world, a marriage of freedom with security, a miracle of secure freedom seemed possible and within reach but also, given the power of human reason and the logic of reason-guided politics, inevitable. T.H. Marshall's account of modern history chimed well with the spirit of the time in which it was written. As it became, however, abundantly clear in the half-century that followed, the Owl of Minerva, true as always to its habits, visited Marshall's study at sunset—at the end of the day ...

Neal Lawson's summary of the most recent trends strikes a dissonant chord when read aside the reassuring story above. Speaking, like Marshall did before, in tune with the wisdom of his time (though a different time, that of the early 21st century), Lawson observes that the government 'becomes merely the handmaiden for the global economy' (Lawson 2005). No longer is the state the omnipotent master of its territory—neither real nor putative, neither in its practice nor in its dreams, neither in its current work nor in its boldest ambitions. Lawson agrees with Thomas Frank (2001) in his diagnosis of the rise and rise of 'market populism'—'with the market now viewed as the ultimate tool of democracy' and 'each individual "casting their vote" all day every day for the good and services that matter to them'; 'everywhere collective voice ... is replaced by atomised and competitive individualised choices'.

Handmaiden of the global economic powers or not, the state cannot simply submit its resignation, pack up its belongings and make itself absent. It remains in charge of law and order inside its territory and held responsible for the way this function is performed. Paradoxically, it is precisely its meek and ever more complete submission to other powers, both inside or outside its territory but in each case beyond its control, that makes well nigh inescapable not just the retention, but the extensive as well as intensive expansion, of its order-protecting policing function.

By freeing the market still further and allowing its boundaries to seep into the public sector, the government has to pick up the bills of market failure, of externalities the market refuses to recognise, and act as a safety net for the inevitable losers of market forces.

Such curtailed and transplaced governmental concerns are a far cry from the kind of engagement Marshall recorded. Instead of a great leap towards equity and justice, they are focused on security operations; instead of the promotion of ever fuller citizenship, they aim at the cleaning of debris and social-waste disposal.

Let us note, however, that it is not just the occasional market *failure* that prompts the present shift in governmental priorities. Deregulation of market forces and surrender of the state to the one-sidedly 'negative' globalization (that is, globalization of business, crime or terrorism, but not of political and juridical institutions able to control them) needs to be paid, and daily, in the currency of social devastation, of the unprecedented frailty of human bonds, ephemerality of communal loyalties and the brittleness and revocability of commitments—whose consequences saddle the state governments with no lesser a burden than did the tasks related to the establishment, maintenance and daily servicing of the social state that endorsed the whole trinity of T.H. Marshall's freedoms. It is the day-in, day-out normality, not the occasional failures of deregulated markets and negative globalization, that now prompts the growth, and ever faster growth, of the social bills which governments find themselves obliged to pick up.

As the protective network of social rights weakens and no longer is trusted to last for the duration and so to offer a solid frame for future plans, the bane of insecurity and fear (which the welfare state vision of Lord Beveridge proposed to eliminate once and for all and whose imminent demise Marshall's historically determined model of three pillars of citizenship implied) returns—but it is obliged now to seek other remedies, elsewhere. To quote Lawson once more: 'As there is nothing else to fall back on it is likely that people then give up on the whole notion of collectivism ... and fall back on the market as the arbiter of provision.'

Let me note that the individuals who 'give up on the whole notion of collectivism' surrender their citizenship. Since there is little they may expect from the state except the measures calculated to increase the fearsome flexibility of their life-setting—and particularly little in the way of securing, not to mention guaranteeing, their social standing—the withdrawal of social rights tends to be closely followed by a surrender or disuse by many of their political rights, with personal rights most probably next on the list of the collateral casualties of deregulation. As Jacques Attali recently observed, 'nations have lost influence on the course of affairs and have abandoned to the forces of globalization all means of orientation in the world's destination and of the defence against all varieties of fear ... Individualism is triumphant. No one, or almost no one, believes any longer that changing lives of others has importance for him or her. No one, or almost no one, believes that voting may change significantly his or her condition, and so the condition of the world' (Attali 2004: 9-10). And little wonder: with the economy removed for all practical purposes out of the reach of governments, rational voters would not expect much from reshuffling the incumbents of the ministerial offices. If, in 1954, 53 per cent of Britons thought that the parties vying for power were really different (concluding that their votes mattered, their use of political rights made a difference), the BBC poll carried on the eve of 2001 election showed that 77 per cent of the respondents believed voting wouldn't change anything. (Conclusion: real choice not on the cards and political rights a sham, their use would be a waste of time.)

And so the individual-*citizen* is turning, or is being turned, into the individual-*consumer*, likely to resort most gladly to the 'voting with their feet', a strategy which, according to the memorable Albert O. Hirschman's suggestion, most seasoned and dutiful shoppers are inclined to prefer over its much more time and energy absorbing alternative: the strategy of voice. If the individuality of a citizen breeds solidarity and prompts the amalgamation of private interests into public issues, the individuality of a consumer is essentially divisive and inspires the reverse process: one of dissolving public interests in the multitude of personal and self-centred pursuits resistant to co-ordination and more often than not making solidarity of action irrelevant, counter-productive or just impossible to envisage.

Elsewhere, I suggested the metaphor of hunters as best conveying both the individual consumer's perception of the world as a container full of the potential trophies, and their life strategies wrapped around the search for the 'next big kill' and oblivious or indifferent to the dent which a successful hunt can make in the game population (and so also to the adverse effect their own good luck may have on other hunters' chances). The advent of hunters, who came to replace in the liquid-modern times the premodern gamekeepers concerned mostly with defending the available supplies against abuse and over-exploitation, and the gardeners of the solid-modern era set to make the supplies more profuse, portends the deepening threat to the 'commons', on whose proper management the shared and mutually assured survival depends.

Let's recall that his project of comprehensive and universal collective insurance against individual misfortune Lord Beveridge presented half century ago as essentially a liberal document, indeed the fullest and most consistent manifestation of the ideas of individual freedom originated, elaborated and promoted in the modern era under the sign of liberalism. Only such communally endorsed social insurance would in Beveridge's view make the individual freedoms dear to a liberal heart feasible and available to all. Rephrasing that opinion in Marshall's terms, we may say that according to Beveridge (and to the prevailing public opinion of his time) the combination of personal and political freedoms (freedom *from* the state and freedom *in* the state, or in the alternative, Isaiah Berlin's terminology, 'negative' and 'positive' freedoms) cannot be truly upheld and would remain unattainable to many, unless capped by social rights freedoms *through* the state.

Even leaving aside the question of resources which true individuality calls for but a great number of 'individuals by decree' (people on the receiving side of individualization) may lack, only on the steady rock of *communal* insurance can in our turbulent times rest the individual self-confidence, courage and the sense of purpose required for a genuine individual self-assertion and the exercise of political rights. Many years later Pierre Bourdieu would restate Beveridge's assertion, pointing out that people who have no hold on their present would hardly summon the courage and determination needed to control the future. People haunted by an incurably uncertain future and put off by the hazards of uninsured ventures would hardly be capable of using their nominal entitlements to autonomous decision and free choice. Granting them freedoms of beliefs, of expression, of life choices, will not by itself enable them to put all such gains into practice.

In as far as such assertions met with loud or tacit, but all the same earnest support across the political spectrum of the time, having been neither questioned not challenged by at least the mainstream politicians of all parties, one can confidently describe them as 'beyond left and right'. Looking around, Marshall had sufficient reason to view the 'social rights sequel' to the entrenchment of habeas corpus and the steady extension of suffrage as a verdict of reason as well as historical inevitability.

Indeed, at the height of the 'solid' phase of the modern era, in nation-states constituting its subjects as, in the first place, producers and soldiers and used to measure their well-being and potency by the numbers of people fit and ready for the hardships of industrial work and soldiering, a constant and comprehensive communal care for people temporarily left out of active service must have appeared to thinking people of all classes and political camps as a most profitable as well as indispensable investment. Without such investment, the state in charge of the nation's well-being would not be able to perform its task of continuous 'recommodification' of capital and labour. Their contentious rhetoric notwithstanding, the otherwise hostile camps of the class and political divisions, would have looked at that point and seen it eye to eye.

They don't any longer, and again they have many sound reasons not to. Or perhaps they are again of the same mind, but what they agree on now and so what commands nowadays the well-nigh universal consent and can be viewed for that reason as the issue 'beyond left and right', is the exact opposite to the object of the old consensus.

The provisions offered for the 'redundant' people unable to provide for their own living no longer seem to be a good investment. The poor and indolent, once classified as the 'reserve army of labour', have been recast as *flawed consumers*, likely to draw on communal resources instead of adding, now or in a near future, to communal prosperity. They are likely to remain a drag on the taxpayer's (that is, the proper, fully fledged and capable consumer's) disposable cash for the duration—a luxury which, as the politicians echoing the tabloids hasten to opine, 'we (that is, members of the society of consumers) cannot afford'.

The wellbeing of a country tends to be measured these days by the amount of money changing hands and by the speed with which the changing is done, rather than by the size of factory crews—and full employment is no longer on the agenda. Neither can the 'excessive', the 'economically redundant' population be siphoned off, as of yore, to far away garrisons, colonial offices and trade posts, or 'no-man's lands' yearning for the pioneers. What follows, is that people laid out by the continuing economic and technological developments can be neither re-included nor effectively excluded from the society of consumers over which the present day governments preside. Purely and simply, the country would be better off were such people suddenly to disappear from the streets and state registers; but there is nowhere to which they could move or be moved. It should not therefore come as a surprise that the underlying shift, seldom articulated explicitly and yet easy to spot between the lines of official speeches, is from the right to care determined by inalienable 'social rights', to social rights being a reward for 'those who've deserved it' through their actual and prospective contribution to the economic prosperity of the country, measured primarily by the viability and vigour of the consumer markets.

The most recent round of curbs imposed in Britain on immigration and asylum policies vividly illustrates that shift. As the Home Secretary Charles Clarke spelled it out, 'migration for work, migration to study is a good thing ... What is wrong is when that system isn't properly policed, and people are coming here who are a burden on the society, and it is that which we intend to drive out ... So we will establish a system ... which looks at the skills, talents, abilities of people seeking to come and work in this country, and ensures that when they come here they have a job and can contribute to the economy of the country'.[2] All the other claimants—prospective immigrants with not enough 'brownie points' for professional education and experience in the kind of services in which the country suffers a deficit of home-grown professionals—are to be denied social rights and in due course deported altogether: just how would one, if only one could, proceed with the native 'redundant' population, recently renamed, symptomatically, 'the underclass'? The prime minister, as the press reported, hailed the home secretary's plans, arguing that they would address the public's justifiable concerns about abuse of the immigration and asylum systems. They would, said Tony Blair, ensure that it is 'only people you really need to come in and work that get work permits'.[3]

As always in Blair's public statements, the words must have been rehearsed in focus groups, carefully chosen and weighed, with the view on striking a responsive chord in the mood of the electors.

Ostensibly, they have been aimed only at the aliens knocking on Britain's door, but they would not amount to a convincing case if they did not chime in with the way 'the population at large', that is a decisive majority of the voters, think about the underdogs, or (what after years of cuts in social provisions amounts to much the same) about the 'welfare recipients' (that is, people who do not just possess, but also use, their 'social rights'). Criteria for 'external exclusion', to deploy Christian Joppke's distinction (2005), are after all brewed and tested at home; they are but applications of the principles arising from domestic practices of 'internal exclusion'.

The prime minister's words manifest the divorce of interests and ethics, in whose marriage 'the welfare state' and Marshall's 'social rights', were born. In Marshall's time, calculation of interests and ethical concerns of the nation used to point in the same direction, and the policies they prompted used to overlap—but they no longer do; the rights to the first and the last word have been assigned to the interest. Social rights are now to be offered selectively. They ought to be given if and only if the givers decide that giving them would accord with their interest; not on the strength of humanity of the recipients. And the two sets of people—those who pass the second test and those who would pass the first—do not overlap.

The routinely offered explication of the current prevalence of interest over ethics is that the extant structures of social state would not be able to accommodate a massive influx of the immigrants. To make such explication as 'self-evident' as it is commonly viewed, or simply to allow it to make sense, many tacit assumptions are needed—and most of those assumptions would not stand scrutiny (most conspicuously, the assumption that admitting more work-able people to the country will detract from the resources needed to finance the collective insurance policy, rather than preventing them from shrinking catastrophically in view of the current demographic trends: falling birth-rate combined with the lengthening of life expectation). But critical voices are few and far between. They are seldom heard and even less frequently listened to if voiced.

What the most common though misleading explanations gloss over is that the old consensus supporting the desirability and necessity of the 'welfare state' had collapsed well before the immigration pressures acquired the volume presently ascribed to them. The majority opinion turned away from the previously unquestioned belief in social rights as integral part of humanity, and quite a few years before those pressures had been promoted to the rank of the 'main reason' of the social state's troubles (a promotion that simultaneously manifests and hides, let me repeat, the tendency to retreat from the postulate of the universality of social rights).

Already in 1988, in his Tanner Lectures, Albert O. Hirschman brought to public attention the impending crisis of the social state— although (not unexpectedly) he did not think it necessary to resort to the new world-wide migration as an explanation. A historian of ideas rather than a sociologist, Hirschman focused on the marked shift in thought, rather than on the more subterranean overhaul of the socio-political configuration which undersigned the now rejected consensus. Summarising the debate already under way for more than a decade, he listed three theses widely deployed to condemn the old consensus and promote the new: the 'perversity', the 'futility', and the 'jeopardy' theses. The first censured the impotence of 'welfare bureaucracy', charged with channelling its services to wrong addresses and offering either wrong cures for genuine ailments or medicines for putative ill-nesses. The second thesis charged the welfare provision with endemic and incurable inefficiency and ineffectiveness. And the third accused the whole idea of social state of the sin (or crime) of breeding dependency and cutting the ground under 'negative liberty'. In direct opposition to Marshall, the 'jeopardy' thesis intimated that far from being the logical culmination of personal rights, social rights were in practice, if not yet in theory, their radical and implacable enemies.

As a sociologist rather than a historian of ideas, I am inclined to focus less on the meanders of common mental attitudes than on the causes of their commonality; more exactly, on the transformation of the socio-political configuration from such as could produce an almost universal endorsement of T.H. Marshall's 'logic of rights', into such as has brought such endorsement under fire, multiplied the ranks of its detractors and paved the way to the central stage for the proponents of (to use the language they most commonly deploy) 'cutting social expenditures and taxes'. This, in last account, led to the denial of the principle of collective insurance and—again in practice if not in theory—of the universal entitlement to social rights that include the right not only to biological survival but also to social respect and human dignity. I suggest that the decisive factor among the set of correlated transformations which underlay the rising popular support for, or the absence of, effective resistance to the gradual dismantling of Marshall's trinity of rights, was the consistent weakening of human bonds resulting from the interrelated processes of deregulation, privatization and individualization.

Virtual elimination of collective bargaining from labour markets for all but a few trades and professions, bringing all forms of collective action including strikes and picketing to the verge of illegality, loosening the limitations previously imposed on dismissals and phasing out almost all protections against redundancy, the new uncurbed 'flexibility' and freedom of movement on the side of employers and managers, coupled with the falling control over the employment conditions and continuing immobility on the side of the employees—all cut at the roots of labour solidarity. When suppressed for a long time and stripped of their past institutional scaffoldings, the impulses of 'joining ranks' and 'marching shoulder to shoulder' tend to wilt and fade, further stifled by ever more vigorous individual competition. Flexible employment, plagued as it must be with scarce or nonexistent expectation of its long-term stability, does not favour solidarity. Indeed, 'flexibility' of labour markets renders solidarity unproductive, if not downright inimical to individual short-term and middle-term interests.

Without solidarity and the institutionalized, as it were, legally protected and authoritatively promoted solidarity, social rights have little chance and surely no certainty of survival. Let us recall Arendt's verdict: the 'Rights of Man, supposedly inalienable, proved to be unenforceable ... whenever people appeared who were no longer citizens of any sovereign state'. Arendt spoke here of personal and political rights. Of social rights one could say that they also prove unenforceable whenever people appear who are no longer party to a viable solidarity action. And, as we argued before, unless they are capped by effective social rights, political and personal rights prove to be for a large part of the nation little more than one more yarn for dreams and a stubbornly elusive target, rather than a reality.

The big question, of course, is whether the time has arrived to shelve T.H. Marshall's trinity of human rights in the archives, filled to capacity with 'iron laws of history' and proved by history to be somewhat less iron-like than their proponents thought, or whether such a decision would be grossly premature. Whatever the answer to this question may be, I suggest that trying to deduce it from the arguments and counter-arguments currently floated whenever the future of the collective insurance against individual misfortune (once promised and hoped to be delivered by the nation-state) is pondered and debated, would be blatantly wrong.

Whatever the future of social rights may be, it is utterly unlikely that it will be decided within nation states and rest on state initiatives and management. The most powerful among the factors which militate against social rights today are *global* and operate in a space stretching well *beyond any single state control*. Any undertaking with a chance of withstanding their pressure could be only, as the pressures themselves are, supra-national, indeed, global. In a nutshell, T.H. Marshall's trinity may survive only if raised to the planetary level. A single state or a combination of states, however large its resources might be, cannot by itself secure the future of social rights and so obliquely the future of the other two members of the trinity. The present crisis of Marshall's formula is a global problem, and solutions to global problems can only be global solutions. The carrying capacity of local politics, ably (though sometimes with results we wouldn't be eager to applaud) represented through the era of 'solid' modernity by the institutions of the nation state, is much too small for the task, and is getting smaller by the year.

There is a widespread consensus among the participants of the current debate as to the direction at which the overhaul of the present world order (or disorder, as most observers tend, rightly, to classify it) should aim. Most of them would probably agree with Chantal Mouffe's succinct diagnosis of the root of trouble: 'The lack of political channels for challenging the hegemony of neoliberal globalization is a root cause of the proliferation of discourses and practices of radical negation of the current order' (Mouffe 2004). And so they would have to agree as well that the building of another order, more viable and more hospitable to humanity, needs to proceed through the construction of such 'political channels' that could effectively control, tame and regulate the heretofore purely negative globalization that consists mostly in emancipating business from political supervision and squeezing power out of the state-conducted politics, still as local as two centuries ago. Consensus does not step, however, far beyond recognition of that rather banally obvious necessity. Beyond that point, views diverge.

Inspired in large part by Carl Schmitt's[4] vision of the future arrangement of planetary affairs, Chantal Mouffe envisages 'a new global order based on the existence of several autonomous regional blocs'. She believes that such a division of the planet 'would provide the conditions for an equilibrium of forces among various large spaces, instituting among them a new system of international law' (Mouffe 2004). Understandably though not necessarily forgivably, Mouffe abstains from justifying her expectation of 'equilibrium' and the emergence of 'international law', limiting herself to revoking the 'Jus Publicum' of Europe split into dynastic estates. What she glosses over in silence is just how many times that 'Jus Publicum' was violated in 30-year or 100-year religious wars and an infinite number of dynastic ones; and over the fact that it was precisely such a planet divided into territorial blocs that George Orwell expected to emerge by 1984, although it did nor occur to him that it would provide the conditions for an equilibrium of forces and a rule of law. She also passes by the fact that whatever grip and binding power the weak and feeble 'Jus Publicum' of premodern Europe could now and then command, it owed not to the 'balance of power' between the independent enclaves, but to the limitation of their sovereignty by the dual all-European powers of the Church and the Holy Roman Emperor. Finally, Mouffe does not mention that more often than not the slogan of the 'power balance', whenever used, signalled simmering antagonisms and imminent wars rather than lasting peace; and that 'balanced power' worked, as a rule, as a standing and perpetually seductive invitation to *divide et impera* initiatives of aspiring emperors who would rather have the extant powers somewhat less balanced than they found them.

Mouffe's suggestion has been advanced in opposition to the alternative itinerary hopefully leading towards the establishment of the potent 'political channels' able to regulate the play of global forces: a 'cosmopolitan democracy', working towards the perspective of 'global democratic governance', to use the terms used by David Held and Daniele Archibugi (Archibugi & Held 1995: 7, Held 1999: 125). In the words of Archibugi, the programme of cosmopolitan democracy is based on the assumption that important objectives—control of the use of force, respect for human rights, self-determination—will be obtained only through the extension and development of democracy. This would require international institutions that, in Mouffe's rendition, would allow individuals 'to have an influence on global affairs independently of the situation in their own countries'. And so the choice on offer is, roughly, between a 'multipolar world order' with a number of blocs ('super states' or alliances of states) vying/co-operating with each other in the process of perpetually rehashing and readjusting the balance of forces on one hand, and a network of essentially non-state institutions of global reach, oblivious to territorial sovereignties and bypassing the state governments, on the other.

Let us note that—at least since Karl Jaspers's blunt condemnation of the nightmarish eventuality of 'one planet-one state' scenario—few if any political thinkers consider a worldwide hegemony of one super-power as a viable solution to the quandary of the new world order. A uniform planetary political body shaped after the pattern of the homogenizing state seems to be decidedly out of political science fashion. In elaborating and debating their own anticipations or projects, most thinkers assume, explicitly or implicitly, that variety (whether territory bound or extraterritorial) is here to stay, and that the management of the planetary political body would have to abandon the uniformizing ambitions which guided the era of nation-building. Clifford Geertz unfailingly captured the dominant mood of our time when, in the Ninth Annual Irving Howe Lecture delivered at the City University of New York in November 2004, he noted the worldwide move from the initial intention of the 'fabrication of unities' to the 'navigation of difference' and concluded that 'multiplicity, "the world in pieces", is with us now, late and soon'.

I can't be sure what T.H. Marshall's choice would be, were he to join the debate at its present stage. I suspect, though, that he might point out that unlike most other intentions and institutions historically developed in the era of nation-building and postulated indivisibility of the nation state's sovereignty, the trinity of rights retains fully its topicality at the times when a new, *planetary* political order, transcending the boundaries and the sovereignty of states, is *in statu nascendi*. Its message has lost nothing of its power of persuasion: now as much as before, no personal and political rights are likely to be secure unless supplemented by social rights, and *the struggle for personal and political rights remains unfinished as long as the social rights have not been won.*

The edge of Marshall's precept therefore remains as sharp as ever. Its apparent loss of cutting capacity derives more from the absence of a firm object on which, once pressed, it could leave a lasting impression, than from its bluntness. The volume of nation state sovereignty is too volatile to be certain that the impression will last, let alone be indelible. As to the planetary level, the well-entrenched institutions which could respond to its pressure by reshaping global social realities through political practice are nowhere in sight. The fate of Marshall's trinity is inextricably interwoven with the fate of such institutions—that is, of such institutions as are potent enough to guide human rights and freedoms, through the times of humanity-building, along the itinerary they traversed once in the era of nation-building; in other words, of the institutions of which one could say what in Marshall's time had been said of the state: that from them, in them and through them humans gain the three equally indispensable, since mutually dependent, aspects of their freedom.

NOTES

1. Edmund Burke, *Reflections on the Revolution in France* (1790), quoted by Arendt after Everyman's Library version edited by E.J. Payne.
2. BBC News, 6 February, 2005.
3. BBC Radio 4's *The Westminster Hour* with Andrew Rawnsley, 6 February, 2005.
4. See in particular Carl Schmitt, 'Die Einheit der Welt', *Merkur,* 1/1952.

REFERENCES

Archibugi, Daniele & David Held (eds). 1995. *Cosmopolitan Democracy: An Agenda for a New World Order.* Cambridge: Polity Press.

Arendt, Hannah. 1986. *The Origins of Totalitarianism.* London: Andre Deutsch.

Arrighi, Giovanni. 2002. *The Long Twentieth Century: Money, Power, and the Origins of our Times.* London: Verso.

Attali, Jacques. 2004. *La voie humaine: Pour une nouvelle social-démocratie.* Fayard.

Balibar, Etienne. 1990. 'The Nation Form: History and Ideology', *Review* 3, pp.329-361.

Frank, Thomas. 2001. *One Market Under God.* London: Sacker & Warburg.

Held, David. 1999. 'The transformation of political community: rethinking democracy in the context of globalization', in I. Shapiro & C. Hacker-Cordon (eds), *Democracy Edges.* Cambridge: Cambridge University Press.

Joppke, Christian. 2005. 'Exclusion in the Liberal State: The Case of Immigration and Citizenship Policy', *European Journal of Social Theory,* 1, pp.43-62.

Lawson, Neal. 2005. *Dare more Democracy: from steam-age politics to democratic self-governance.* London: Compass.

Mouffe, Chantal. 2004. 'Cosmopolitan Democracy or Multipolar World Order?' *Soundings,* Winter, pp.62-74.

[5]

TWO MEANINGS OF GLOBAL CITIZENSHIP

Modern and Diverse

JAMES TULLY

I. TWO CONTESTED WAYS OF THINKING ABOUT GLOBAL CITIZENSHIP

'Global citizenship' has emerged as the locus of struggles on the ground and of reflection and contestation in theory. This is scarcely surprising. Many of the central and most enduring struggles in the history of politics have taken place *in* and *over* the language of citizenship and the activities and institutions into which it is woven. One could say that the hopes, dreams, fears and xenophobia of centuries of individual and collective political actors are expressed in the overlapping and conflicting histories of the uses of the language of citizenship and the forms of life in which they have been employed. This motley ensemble of contested languages, activities and institutions constitutes the inherited *field* of citizenship today.

The language of 'global' and 'globalisation' and the activities, institutions and processes to which it refers and in which it is increasingly used, while more recent than citizenship, comprises a similarly central and contested domain. Globalisation has become a shared yet disputed vocabulary in terms of which rival interpretations of the ways humans and their habitats are governed globally are presented and disputed in both practice and theory. It thus constitutes a similarly contested *field* of globalisation.

When 'globalisation' and 'citizenship' are combined they not only bring their contested histories of meanings with them. They bring into being a complex new field that raises new questions and elicits new answers concerning the meaning of, and relationship between, global governance and global citizenship. When we enquire into global citizenship, therefore, we are already thrown into this remarkably complex inherited field of contested languages, activities, institutions, processes and the environs in which they take place. This conjoint field represents the problematisation of global citizenship: the way that formerly disparate activities, institutions and processes have been gathered together under the rubric of 'global citizenship', so becoming a site of contestation in practice and formulated as a problem in research, policy and theory, and to which diverse solutions are presented and debated.[1]

Among the many contested meanings of global citizenship I will focus on two. Many of the most important struggles around the globe today are *over* these two types and the struggles themselves consist in the enactment of these two modes of citizenship in two corresponding practices of global citizenship. They have been

JAMES TULLY 16

interpreted in different ways under different names in a variety of activist and academic literature: for example, global citizenship from above *versus* global citizenship from below, low intensity *versus* high intensity global citizenship, representative *versus* direct, hegemonic *versus* counter-hegemonic, cosmopolitan *versus* place-based. I call these two families 'modern' and 'diverse' citizenship. I call modern citizenship in a modern state 'civil' citizenship and in a global context 'cosmopolitan' citizenship. The corresponding names of diverse citizenship are 'civic' and 'glocal'. 'Glocal' and 'glocalisation' in the diverse citizenship tradition refer to the global networking of local practices of civic citizenship in contrast to the use of 'global' and 'globalisation' in modern/cosmopolitan citizenship. I begin with a preliminary sketch of one aspect of the two meanings and practices of citizenship as a way of introducing them.

The most familiar aspect of modern citizenship is its role as the modular form of citizenship associated with the historical processes of modernisation/colonisation: (1) the modernisation of the West into modern nation states with representative governments, a system of international law, decolonisation of European empires, supranational regime formations and global civil society; and, in tandem, (2) the dependent modernisation and citizenisation of the non-West through colonisation, the Mandate System, post-decolonisation nation-building and global governance. The language of modern citizenship, in its civil and cosmopolitan forms, presents successive idealisations of this type of citizenship as the uniquely *universal* practice of citizenship for all human societies. This allegedly universal mode of citizenship is also presented as the product of *universal* historical processes or stages of development under successive discourses of progress – civilisation, modernisation, constitutionalisation, democratisation and now globalisation – that began in Europe and have been spread around the world by Euro-American expansion and continuing hegemony. These two features of modern citizenship – a universal modular form of citizenship conjoined with a universal set of historical processes that bring it to the non-West under Western tutelage – are articulated and debated in, respectively, modern normative theories of citizenship and social scientific theories of modernisation from the eighteenth-century to today.[2]

In contrast, diverse citizenship is associated with a multiplicity of different practices of citizenship in the West and the non-West. The language of diverse citizenship, both civic and glocal, presents citizenship as a singular or 'local' practice that takes countless *forms* in different locales. It is not described in terms of universal institutions and historical processes but, rather, in terms of the grass roots democratic or civic *activities* of the 'governed' (the people) in the specific relationships of governance in the environs where they act and of the glocal *activities* of networking with other practices. The local languages of description (stories) of particular citizenship practices are accepted initially and then compared and contrasted critically along various axes and purposes with other practices in dialogues of translation, understanding and critique. Whereas modern citizenship focuses on citizenship as a universalisable legal *status* underpinned by institutions and processes of rationalisation that enable and circumscribe the possibility of civil activity (an institutional/universal orientation), diverse citizenship focuses on the

17   TWO MEANINGS OF GLOBAL CITIZENSHIP

singular civic activities and improvisations of the governed in any practice of government and the diverse ways in which these are more or less institutionalised or blocked in different contexts (a civic activity/contextual orientation). Citizenship is not a status given by the institutions of the modern constitutional state and international law, but a set of negotiated practices in which one becomes a citizen through participation.

II. MODERN CIVIL CITIZENSHIP

The tradition of modern citizenship takes as its empirical and normative exemplar the form of citizenship characteristic of the modern nation state.[3] Citizenship (both civil and cosmopolitan) is defined in relation to two clusters of institutional features of modern nation states: the constitutional rule of law (*nomos*) and representative government (*demos*). The constitutional rule of law is the first condition of citizenship. The 'civil' law (a formal legal order) and its enforcement by a coercive authority establishes (literally 'constitutes') the conditions of civilisation, the city (*civitas*), citizenship, civil society, civil liberty and civility (hence 'civil' citizenship). By definition the 'outside' is the realm of the uncivilised: barbarism, savagery, the state of nature or war, or the uncertainty of informal, customary law and unenforceable natural law. A person has the status of citizenship in virtue of being *subject* to civil law in two senses: to an established and enforced system of law and to the 'civilising', 'pacifying' or 'socialising' force of the rule of law on the subjectivity of those who are constrained to obey over time. This is why cosmopolitan citizenship and global civil society depend on some form of legalisation or constitutionalisation of the global order analogous (in various ways) to the modern nation state.

Relative to the constitutional rule of law, modern citizenship is defined as a *status* (state or condition). This civil status is usually explicated and defined in terms of the historical development of *four tiers of rights and duties* (liberties) of formally equal individual subjects of an association of constitutional rule of law and representative government. This association is either the modern nation state, including its subordinate provinces and cities, or its analogous associations for cosmopolitan citizenship (international law, the United Nations, global governance institutions). I will start with the four citizenship rights and duties within modern nation states as these are the basis for modern/cosmopolitan global citizenship.

The first and indispensable tier of rights is the set of 'civil liberties' (the liberties of the moderns or 'private autonomy') of the modern liberal tradition. This set includes the liberty of the person and of speech, thought and faith, the right to own private property and to enter into contracts, and the right to formal equality before the law. In virtue of these civil liberties citizens are 'at liberty' to engage in these activities if they choose (an 'opportunity' status) and are protected by the law from 'interference' in the spheres where these rights can be exercised: of free speech and voluntary association, the market, and the law respectively. They are classic 'negative' liberties, protecting persons or citizens from interference in these spheres.

JAMES TULLY 18

At the centre of these civil liberties is the modern liberty to participate in the private economic sphere and not to be interfered within it – the right to own property and enter into contracts. This is the modern liberty to engage in the capitalist economy (market freedoms and free trade): to sell one's labouring abilities on the market for a wage to a corporation or, for those with the capital, to establish a corporation, hire the labour of others and sell competitively the products of the free market to consumers. Private corporations gained recognition as 'persons' with the corresponding civil liberty of private autonomy (negative liberty) in the late-nineteenth century. Thus, paradoxically from a civic perspective, the first right of modern citizenship is to participate in the private realm and to be protected from interference by the *demos* (the citizenry and its representatives). This form of participation in the economic sphere ('commercial society') *is* primary – the liberty of the moderns.

The modern civil liberty of private property and contracts accordingly *presupposes* the historical dispossession of people from access to land and resources through their local laws and non-capitalist economic organisations; the accumulation of dispossessed workers into a 'free' market of wage labourers and consumers; the concentration of the means of production in private corporations; and the imposition of modern legal systems of property law, contract law, labour law, and trade law that constitute and protect the system of free markets and free trade. Modern citizenship, in its basic commitment to the civil liberty of private property and contracts, is grounded in and dependent on the spread of these institutions of capitalism. It is also the major justification for the spread of these economic institutions – they are the basis of modern liberty. Moreover, it is not only the civil law acting alone that is said to civilise the uncivilised or less-developed peoples. 'Commerce' or 'economic liberalisation' (a synonym for modern globalisation), by rendering every person and society economically interdependent and competitive within an imposed structure of law, pacifies, refines, polishes, makes predictable, and thus – in tandem with representative government – leads humanity to perpetual peace.

The *second* tier of liberties of modern citizenship is defined in relation to the second cluster of modern institutions: representative government. They consist in the rights to participate in these institutions if one chooses. In the language of modern citizenship 'democracy' and 'democratic' are equated with and restricted to 'representative government' and 'democratisation' with and to the historical processes that bring these representative institutions and rights to participate into being. Other forms of democracy, if they are discussed *as* democracies, are described as less-developed forms of the universal and regulative ideal of 'democracy' (as in the case of 'citizenship' above). These rights of the modern democratic tradition are called public autonomy or the liberties of the ancients. They comprise the ways the *demos* – the citizenry of a nation state as a whole – legally exercise their popular sovereignty. The exercise of these 'democratic' rights enables the people to have a say both within and over the laws and constitutions to which they are subject (and from which their citizenship derives) and thereby to balance the constitutional rule of law with the demands of democracy (the rule of

19   TWO MEANINGS OF GLOBAL CITIZENSHIP

the people). These civil rights include such liberties as: the right to vote for representatives in elections, join parties, interest groups, non-governmental organisations and social movements, stand for election, assemble, dissent and demonstrate in the civil or public sphere, freedom of the press, engage in democratic deliberations, litigate in the Courts, exchange public reasons over constitutional amendments or participate in a constituent assembly, and, at their fullest, to engage in some forms of civil disobedience and accept the punishment.

Like civil liberties and their institutional preconditions, these democratic liberties *presuppose* historically the dispossession of people from access to political power through pre-existing local forms of government and citizenship and the channelling of democratic citizenship into participation in the official public sphere of modern representative governments and its global analogue of global civil society. These processes are described as freeing people from pre-modern forms of subjection and bringing democratic citizenship to them. Second, participation is equated with activities of public arguing (deliberating), bargaining (organising, negotiating and protesting) and litigating over changing the laws, since political power is presumed to be exercised through the rule of law. The objective is to ensure that the law is not imposed unilaterally on those subject to it, but, rather, that they have a say, representatively, in making or amending the laws, and thus can see themselves as co-authors or, more accurately, co-articulators, of the laws to which they are subject *en passant*. The activity of participation thus replicates the ground plan of modern citizenship because the people participate *as* legal citizens exercising their democratic rights and within the constraints of modern civil liberties (even when the people act together and exercise the modern right of self-determination they do so within this juridical-representative framework).

The second tier democratic liberties of the modern are also circumscribed by the first tier civil liberties in three main ways. Their exercise is optional. A member of a modern political association is a citizen and the association is democratic whether or not one exercises rights to participate. Second, the primary use and justification of these rights in the modern tradition is to fight for laws that protect the private liberty of the moderns from too much governmental interference. Third, these rights cannot be extended and exercised in the private sphere (as in economic democracy in the workplace) for this would interfere with tier one liberties. When the leaders of the great powers today (the G8) speak of the spread of 'freedom' and 'democracy' in Afghanistan, Iraq and elsewhere, they are referring to the module of tier one (liberties) and tier two (democracy) rights of citizenship and their underlying institutions of the constitutional rule of law, markets, representative government, and the military as the enforcement institution.

The *third* and weakest tier of modern rights of citizenship comprises the social and economic rights of the modern social democratic tradition. These are the citizenship rights won by working class movements struggling within the historically established priority and constraints of tiers one and two liberties over the last two centuries in nation states and international law. They are a response to the horrendous substantive inequalities in wealth, well-being, living conditions and social power that go along with the unrestrained formal equality of tier one civil liberties and the limited democratic rights of tier two. The modern social democratic argument for them is that they are the *minimum conditions* required for the worst off to enable them to exercise their civil and democratic liberties. The argument against them is that they violate the economic liberties of the moderns by interfering in the private sphere and economic competition, and thus always must be subordinated to tier one civil liberty and the limits of tier two. Under the current economic liberalisation policies of states and institutions of global governance these rights are seen, at best, as means of enabling individuals to exercise their tier one and two rights.

The *fourth* tier of citizenship rights consists of modern minority rights of multiculturalism, religious and ethnic groups, non-state nations, and indigenous peoples. These rights appear to some modern theorists to violate one of the premises of modern citizenship, the primacy of the individual legal subject. However, minority rights can be defined as rights that, first, protect the *individual members* of minorities from interference or dominance by the majority (and by the powerful within the minority) and, second, empower members of minorities to exercise their civil and democratic liberties in more effective ways than through the institutions of the dominant society. They thus can be designed to enhance, rather than to challenge, the spread of modern citizenship, and this is the major way that they have been implemented under modern nation states and international law. That is, they too presuppose the dispossession of 'minorities' of their own forms of legal, governmental and economic organisation, and processes of integrating them into modern forms of citizenship.

Within Europe, this modular form of modern citizenship became the paramount practice of citizenship during the centralisation and consolidation of the modern constitutional representative nation state and the capitalist economy. Diverse local and regional forms of laws, governments, democracy and citizenship – of village commons and free city communes – where they were not destroyed completely, were marginalised or transformed and subordinated as they were brought under the rationalisation of the central institutions of the modern nation state. Modern citizenship was nationalised at the same time as local citizenship was subalternised. The people were socialised by education, urbanisation, military duty, industrialisation and modern citizenisation to see themselves first and foremost, not as citizens of their local communities, but as members of an abstract and 'disembedded' imaginary community of nation, *demos* and *nomos* of formally free and equal yet materially unequal citizens, with an equally abstract imaginary of popular sovereignty they mythically embodied and exercised through the individual liberties of modern citizenship attached to the central legal and representative institutions. These dispossessions and transformations, and the countless resistances to them, were described and justified in the social scientific language of modern citizenship as processes and stages of developments of a modernisation that freed individuals from the backwardness of pre-modern customary practices and made him and then her free and equal citizens.

21   TWO MEANINGS OF GLOBAL CITIZENSHIP

Citizens and especially non-citizens – such as the poor, the property less, women, immigrants, excluded 'races', and others – struggled (and continue to struggle) within-and-against these processes in Europe. When they were not struggling for their local ways, they organised to be included in modern citizenship, to extend the use of political rights beyond the official public sphere, and to gain social and economic rights and minority rights that do more than protect individuals from the majority. These are 'civic activities' against the powerful actors who seek to circumscribe citizenship to tier one civil liberties and a limited module of democratic rights. Since these types of struggles are *for* new kinds of citizenship and *by means of* people who are not official citizens or official citizens who often act beyond the official limits of citizenship of their generation, they cannot be called practices of citizenship in the modern tradition. They are acts of 'civil disobedience'. If these illegal struggles are successful and the extensions institutionalised, then the extensions are redefined as a stage in the development of modern citizenship (as in the case of working class struggles giving rise to social and economic rights and suffragette movements giving rise to women's right to vote). Thus, what are seen as two of the fundamental features of citizenship from the civic tradition – the historical struggles for diverse local forms of citizenship and for extensions of national citizenship rights – fall outside of citizenship for the modern tradition with its institutional orientation.

III. THE GLOBALISATION OF MODERN CITIZENSHIP

The chapter now examines how the modular form of modern citizenship has been spread around the globe as 'global citizenship'.[4] It has been and is being globalised in two forms. *First*, the module of a modern nation state and its institutions of modern *civil* citizenship, at some 'stage of development' towards its mature form, has been and continues to be spread around the world as the universal form of political association recognised as the bearer of legitimate political authority (sovereignty) under international law. *Second*, a modular form of modern *cosmopolitan* citizenship, also at some stage of development towards its mature form, has been and continues to be spread around the world as the universal form of global citizenship recognised as legitimate under international law and global institutions.

During the long period when Europeans were building modern nation states with institutions of modernising citizenship they were also, and simultaneously, building these states as competing *imperial* modern nation states. As imperial states they built and defended vast overseas empires that colonised (in various ways) eighty-five percent of the world's population by 1914. The imperial 'great game' of economic and military competition with other European great powers over the control and exploitation of the resources, labour and markets of the non-European world *and* the counter-actions of the non-European peoples *co-created* the modern west and the modern colonised non-west. After decolonisation in the twentieth century, this unequal relationship continues between the former imperial powers (renamed the 'great eight' or 'great twenty') exercising 'hegemony' rather than 'imperium' through the post-WWII institutions of global governance and the renamed 'post-colonial' world of more than 120 nominally free and equal ('sovereign') yet substantively still *dependent* and *unequal* new modernising nation states, constructed on the foundations of the former colonies. The spread of the institutions of modern citizenship beyond Europe can be understood only in the context of this complex contrapuntal ensemble of Western strategies of expansion and non-Western strategies of counteraction (Mignolo, 2000).

The institutional conditions of modern citizenship were spread in the course of European expansion by a deceptively simple strategy that linked a right of global citizenship to imperial power in a circular relationship. Initially formulated and exercised in different ways by the European imperial powers, this right of global citizenship for Europeans is called the right of commerce (*ius commercium*) or 'cosmopolitan' right. From the earliest phase of European expansion to today the great powers have claimed the cosmopolitan right of *their* citizens, trading companies, monopoly companies, and multinational corporations to travel to other countries and attempt to engage in 'commerce' in two senses of this term. The first is to travel the globe freely and converse with the inhabitants of other societies. This covers such activities as the right – and also the *duty* – of Western explorers, missionaries, religious organisations, voluntary associations, and academics to travel to non-Western countries to, first, study and classify their different customs and ways into developmental stages of different societies and races, and, second, to try to free them from their 'inferior' ways and teach them the uniquely civilised ways of the West. This cosmopolitan right is the historical antecedent of the right of modern cosmopolitan citizenship of civil society associations (modern NGOS) and Western academics to modernise and democratise people in the post-colonial world today by bringing them the institutional preconditions and forms of subjectivity of modern citizenship. The second sense of this cosmopolitan right is to travel and try to engage in 'commerce' (trade) with the inhabitants: to enter into contracts and treaties, gain access to resources, buy slaves, hire and discipline labourers, establish trading posts, and so on. At first it was used by the European powers to establish imperial monopolies over the exploitation of the resources and labour of non-European societies, but monopoly imperialism gradually gave way to 'free trade' imperialism in the nineteenth and twentieth century.

This right correlates with the duty of 'hospitality' of the host country to open their doors to free commerce in this dual sense. If they close the door to entry, break the contract or expropriate the property of a foreigner who has engaged in commerce, or if they expel the voluntary societies, then the appropriate recognised legal authority – under the old law of nations, or imperial law of the respective empire, or, later, international law – has a reciprocal right to open the door by diplomacy or military intervention, punish the violation of the cosmopolitan right and demand reparations or compensation (even for damages caused by the intervention). This correlative duty of hospitality – openness to free commerce – holds even if the cosmopolitan right was initially exercised unjustly: that is where a trading company used force and fraud to establish trade relations and contracts in the first place. This early-modern duty of non-European societies to open

TWO MEANINGS OF GLOBAL CITIZENSHIP

themselves to commerce dominated by the West continues to be one of the core duties of transnational trade law agreements today.

As with modern civil liberty within a modern state, this cosmopolitan right *presupposes* a number of institutions. The host country must either have or adopt the legal, economic and cultural institutions that make possible commerce in this broad sense (private property, corporations, contracts, wage labour, markets dominated by the West, openness to cultural conversion, protection of foreigners, and so on). The imperial power must either submit to and modify the local laws and institutions or impose a structure of commercial law that overrides and restructures them, such as Merchant's Law (*lex mercatoria*), a vast system of global trade law that developed in tandem with Western imperialism.

As we can see, this cosmopolitan right is a right of citizens of the civilised states to exercise the first right of modern citizenship (civil liberties) and a version of the second right (to participate) *beyond their nation state*, and to be protected from interference in so doing. The two cosmopolitan rights – of the trading company to trade and the voluntary organisations to converse and convert – also fit together in the same way as within the nation state. The participatory right to converse with and try to convert the natives complements the primary right of commerce since the inhabitants are taught the requisite forms of subjectivity and modes of civil conduct that go along with the commercialisation of their society and its gradual civilisation: from the discipline of slavery and indentured labour at the bottom to the training of dependent elites at the top. From the perspective of the language of modern citizenship, the two rights of cosmopolitan citizenship appear to globalise the civilising institutions of law, commerce and Western civility across an uncivilised or semi-civilised or less-developed world, thereby laying the foundations for an eventual world of modern civil citizenship in modern nation states. From the perspective of the non-Western civilisations and of diverse citizenship, the two cosmopolitan rights appear as the Trojan horse of Western imperialism (Anghie, 2005).

In practice, this strategy was employed to globalise modern citizenship in three main ways. First, settler colonies were established that *replicated* the basic features and legal, political and economic institutions of the imperial country. These 'new Europes' were established in the Americas, Australia, New Zealand and later in Africa by dispossessing indigenous peoples of their diverse civilisations, territories, resources and citizenship practices, exterminating eighty to ninety percent of the population (which was larger than Europe at the time), marginalising those they could not enslave or indenture, importing 12 millions slaves from Africa onto plantations in North and South America and the Caribbean, and imposing the civilising institutions of property and contract law and rudimentary representative government (colonial legislatures).

Second, by 'indirect' imperial rule, non-Western societies were opened to commerce by establishing a small colonial administration, often run by trading companies, to rule indirectly over a much larger indigenous population. A centralised system of Western colonial law was used to protect the commercial rights of their citizens and traders, while also preserving and modifying the local

JAMES TULLY   24

customary laws and governments so resources and labour were privatised and subject to trade, labour discipline and investment dominated by the Western trading companies. Local rulers were recognised as quasi-sovereigns and unequal treaties negotiated. The local elites were made dependent on Western economic and military power, undermining their accountability to their local citizens, and employed to introduce modernising techniques of governance and to train the local armies to protect the system of property, often against the majority of their own population. This was the major way that the institutional preconditions of modern civil citizenship were introduced in India, Ceylon, Africa and the Middle East.

The third and most recent way is through 'informal' or 'free trade' imperialism. Here the imperial powers permit local self-rule, and eventually self-determination, but within a protectorate or sphere of influence over which they exercise informal 'paramountcy' (now called 'hegemony' or 'dominance'). By various informal means they induce the local governments to open their resources, labour and markets to free trade by establishing the appropriate modern local legal, political and economic institutions – the foundations for eventual modern citizenship, with civil liberties preceding and circumscribing the other rights. The means include: economic, military, technological, educational and aid dependency; the modernisation of the population by Western experts and civil society organisations; bribes and threats; and frequent military intervention when local citizens resist. This requires in turn small but effective military bases strategically located around the world and supported by a global navy and (later) air force and satellite surveillance. The informal imperial powers are thus able to intervene whenever the local population tries to take control of their own economy through their own government and citizenship practices and thus violate the duties of openness and free trade. This type of imperialism was introduced by the British in the nineteenth century, but the United States has become the global leader of informal or 'open door' imperialism, first in Latin America and then throughout the former colonial world by the end of the Cold War. The United States now has over 760 small military bases around the world and the Pentagon claims to exercise 'full spectrum dominance' over an informal global system of commerce and freedom.

The cosmopolitan right and its three modes of imposition were gathered together and formalised as the *standard of civilisation* in the creation of modern international law during the nineteenth century. The European imperial nation states (and the United States after 1895) declared themselves to be 'civilised states' in virtue of their institutions of modern statehood and citizenship (modern rule of law,' open to commerce, representative government and modern liberty). As such they were the sole bearers of sovereignty and subject only to the laws they could agree to among themselves: 'international' law. Their modern institutions provided a 'standard of civilisation' in international law by which they judged all other civilisations in the world as 'uncivilised' to varying degrees (depending on their stage of development) and thus not sovereign subjects of international law, but subjects of the sovereign powers through colonies, indirect protectorates, and informal spheres of influence. They asserted a right and duty of civilisation under international law. 'Civilisation' referred to the historical process of modernisation

TWO MEANINGS OF GLOBAL CITIZENSHIP

and to the end-point of a modern state like the European model. The duty to civilise consisted in the consolidation and international legalisation of the imperial processes they began in the earlier period. The opening of non-European societies to European-dominated commerce, exploitation of their resources and labour, and the destruction or marginalisation of 'uncivilised' ways that hindered this 'progress' were seen as the first steps in the civilising mission. The second and equally important duty was to introduce into the colonies and protectorates more systematic and effective forms of colonial governance (or *governmentalité*) that would shape and form the dependent peoples and 'races' into civilised subjects eventually capable of modern self-government.

This global civilising project under international law lacked an enforcement mechanism and the civilising duty was left to the sovereign empires and their voluntary organisations. The destruction, exploitation, despotism, genocide and wars continued apace and increased after the failure of the Berlin Conference (1884) and the 'scramble over Africa', eventually culminating in the barbarism of World War I (the 'great war of civilisation'). In response to these horrors and to control increasing demands for decolonisation, the first concerted attempt to operationalise the civilising duty under international law was the Mandate System under the League of Nations. The League classified the 'subject' peoples into three categories according to their level of 'backwardness' and gave the respective imperial powers the mandate to civilise them as they increased their economic exploitation, especially in the oil-rich Middle East.

This project was interrupted by the decolonisation movements of the mid-century. Although the people fought for freedom from imperial dependency on the West or the Soviet Union and the development of their own forms of self-government and citizenship, the Westernised national elites (subject to economic and military dependency) and the informal means of the great powers ensured the continuation of the civilising and modernising processes. During the Cold War and the phases of post-independence dependency, the nation-building elites were constrained to destroy or subordinate local economies, governments and citizenship practices, entrench or extend the artificial colonial boundaries, centralise and nationalise governments into the armed nation-state module, open their resources to free trade and promise minimal institutions of modern citizenship, or face military intervention. The result tended to be constitutional and institutional structures that concentrated power at the centre, often entrenching the worst features of colonial administration, or replicating the concentration of power in both urban and rural regions characteristic of the divide and conquer model of indirect imperial rule (as in much of Africa).

During the same period, the great powers set up the institutions of global governance through which informal hegemony and post-colonial subalternity could be continued: the concentration of power in the permanent members of the Security Council of the United Nations, the World Bank (WB), International Monetary Fund (IMF), General Agreement on Trade and Tariffs (GATT), the World Trade Organization after 1995 (WTO) and its transnational trade agreements (such as

TRIPS and GATTS), modernising NGOs, North Atlantic Treaty Organization (NATO), and the United States' system of global military dominance.

At the request of the newly independent states, the language of civilisation was removed from international law and the United Nations. However, it was immediately replaced with the language of modernisation, marketisation, democratisation and globalisation with the same grammatical structure, signifying universal processes of development and a single endpoint of modern citizenship and its institutions. These are now to be brought about, not by the 'civilising mission' of the imperial powers, but by the 'global governance' of the informal federations or coalitions of the modern (or post-modern) states imposing 'good governance' through the global institutions (WB and IMF), their multinational corporations (exercising the cosmopolitan right of commerce), and official NGOs (exercising their cosmopolitan citizenship) building civil societies and civil subjects on the ground. As the leaders of the decolonisation movements recognised after independence, they were thus conscripted into a familiar scenario, but now in a vocabulary of a world system of free and equal nation states that erased any reference to the imperial construction of this world and the persistence of imperial relations of inequality and exploitation (Ayers, 2006; Evans & Ayers, 2006).

The difference from the old colonial strategies of spreading the institutional preconditions of modern citizenship is that the formerly colonised peoples are now seen as active, self-governing agents in these processes at home and in the institutions of global governance (the G120) – and thus bearers of modern civil and cosmopolitan citizenship – yet still under the enlightened leadership of the more advanced or developed peoples. International law provides the legal basis for this by promoting a 'right to democracy', and democracy is equated with tier one civil liberties (neo-liberal marketisation) and a short list of democratic rights (elections). However, if, as often happens, the majority of the people become too democratic and seek to exercise their right of self-determination by taking democratic control of their own government and local economy, and thus violate their duty to open their doors to multinational corporations and subordination to a global economy, one of two strategies of modernisation follow. They are either repressed by their own dependent elites, democratic rights are further reduced or eliminated, and the government becomes more authoritarian. Or, if the people manage to gain power, the repertoire of covert and overt informal means available to the great powers are employed to destabilise and undermine the government, bring about regime change, and institute structural adjustment policies that promote tier one civil liberties of individuals and corporations. The coercive imposition of the global market and the market discipline of civil liberty is said to come first and lay the foundation for democratic rights. The result in either case is the suppression or severe restriction of democratic citizenship, the corresponding rise of a militarised authoritarian rule and market freedoms on one side and violent authoritarian resistance movements on the other. The countries that are subject to these horrendous oscillations are said to be 'failed states'; military intervention follows, resistance intensifies, and instability continues.

27 TWO MEANINGS OF GLOBAL CITIZENSHIP

The consequence is that a restricted 'low intensity' form of modern civil citizenship at the national level is promoted by an equally low intensity form of modern cosmopolitan citizenship of NGOs and multinational corporations under global governance and international law. The first wave of international human rights after World War II sought to give protection to the person from the worst effects of these processes (civil liberties) and to elaborate a set of global democratic, social and economic, and minority rights similar to those at the national level. However, these are hostage to implementation by nation states and thus subject to the processes described above. The second wave of international law brought into force a vast array of transnational trade law regimes (under GATT and the WTO) that override and restrict national constitutions and constrain weaker and poorer countries (hosting the majority of the world's population) to open their economies and labour to free trade, unrestrained exploitation and pollution transfer by the dominant multinational corporations in order to gain loans, aid and debt relief. The third wave of international law after 9/11/01 consists of Resolutions of the Security Council of the UN promoting international security. These global securitisation regimes, which are said to protect the security and liberty of modern citizens, often override the first wave international human rights, force national governments to enact security legislation that rolls back hard won democratic rights, thereby circumscribing democratic opposition to the war on terror and neo-liberal globalisation, and they secure the tier one civil and cosmopolitan liberty of individual and corporate citizens in national and transnational law.[5] This new formulation of the old cosmopolitan right to civilise is now the major justification for the continuation of Western informal imperialism, as in Iraq and Afghanistan today. The result is not only the continued popular resistance, instability and escalating militarisation and repression, as above, but also growing global inequalities between the West and the non-West that are worse now than at the height of the ruthless phase of Western imperialism in the late nineteenth century.

840 million people are malnourished. 6,000,000 children under the age of 5 die each year as a consequence of malnutrition. 1.2 billion people live on less than $1 a day and half the world's population lives on less than $2 a day. 91 out of every 1,000 children in the developing world die before 5 years old. 12 million die annually from lack of water. 1.1 billion people have no access to clean water. 2.4 billion people live without proper sanitation. 40 million live with AIDS. 113 million children have no basic education. 1 in 5 does not survive past 40 years of age. There are one billion non-literate adults, two-thirds are women and 98% live in the developing world. In the least developed countries, 45% of the children do not attend school. In countries with literacy rate of less than 55% the annual per capita income is about $600.

In contrast, the wealth of the richest 1% of the world is equal to that of the poorest 57%. The assets of the 200 richest people are worth more than the total income of 41% of the world's people. Three families alone have a combined wealth of $135 billion. This equals the annual income of 600 million people living in the world's poorest countries. The richest 20% of the world's population receive 150 times the wealth of the poorest 20%. In 1960, the share of the global income of the

JAMES TULLY

bottom 20% was 2.3%. By 1991, this had fallen to 1.4%. The richest fifth of the world's people consume 45% of the world's meat and fish; the poorest fifth consume 5%. The richest fifth consume 58% of total energy, the poorest fifth less than 4%. The richest fifth have 75% of all telephones, the poorest fifth 1.5%. The richest fifth own 87% of the world's vehicles, the poorest fifth less than 1%. As a result of the globalisation of modern citizenship and its underlying institutions the majority of the world's population of the dispossessed are thus 'free' to exercise their modern civil liberty in the growing sweatshops and slums of the planet.[6]

In summary, the globalisation of modern citizenship has not tended to democracy, equality and perpetual peace, but to informal imperialism, dependency, inequality and resistance. This tendency is a consequence of its basic universal/imperial orientation. From within the perspective of modern citizenship modern citizens see their modular form of citizenship as universal and superior, and all others as particular and inferior, and see themselves as having the imperial right and duty to enter into other societies, free them from their inferior ways, impose the institutional preconditions of modern citizenship, which conveniently brings unconscionable profits to their corporations and unconscionable inequality to the people they are modernising, and use violence and military rule against those envious 'anti-moderns' who resist. From the alternative perspective of diverse citizenship, this is neither freedom, nor democracy but five hundred years of relentless tyranny against local citizenship and self-reliance, the undemocratic imposition of institutions of low intensity citizenship over which the majority of the people have little or no effective say and in which they are subject to subordination, exploitation, horrendous inequalities and repression when they refuse to submit.[7]

IV. DIVERSE CIVIC CITIZENSHIP

Although modern civil and cosmopolitan citizenship is the predominant form of global citizenship, a multiplicity of other meanings and practices of citizenship co-exist and, consequently, the global field of citizenship is considerably more complex and contested than the view from the modern tradition suggests. I want now to turn and examine this field from the standpoint of diverse citizenship. I will mention six general aspects of diverse civic citizenship and contrast these with modern civil citizenship.[8]

Rather than looking on citizenship as a status within an institutional framework backed up by world-historical processes and universal norms, the diverse tradition looks on citizenship as *negotiated practices* – as civic actors and activities in local contexts. The modern tradition in social science and political theory overlooks these activities because it presupposes that rights, rules, institutions and processes must be primary (the conditions of civilisation) and human actors and activities secondary (what happens within the civil space constituted by the civilising rights, institutions, rules and processes). The diverse tradition reverses this modernist, institutional orientation and takes the perspective of actual citizens in civic activities in the dwelling places they are enacted and carried on. Institutionalisation

TWO MEANINGS OF GLOBAL CITIZENSHIP

of citizenship practices is seen as secondary; coming into being in countless unpredictable and open-ended ways out of, and in interaction with, the *praxis* of citizens – sometimes furthering, strengthening and formalising these activities; other times dispossessing, channelling, cancelling, downsizing, constraining, limiting and repressing (as we have seen).

The second way the diverse tradition avoids the prejudice of mistaking one institutionalised form of citizenship as the universal model for all possible forms is always to take any specific civic activity in context as one local citizenship practice among countless others. They start from the local languages and practices of citizens *in* their forms of citizenship and compare and contrast their similarities and dissimilarities critically with each other from various standpoints, either by engaging in other forms of citizenship or by civic dialogues of mutual edification among diverse citizens. There is thus no universal module of citizenship but, rather, a multiplicity of criss-crossing and overlapping practices of citizenship, of which modern citizenship can be seen to be one singular and imperious form masquerading as universal.

Third, since civic activities of citizens are primary, people do not become citizens by virtue of a status defined by rights and guaranteed by the institutions of the modern state and international law. This status is simply to be a 'subject' of that system of laws and a 'member' of that association. Individual and collective agents *become* citizens only by virtue of actual participation in civic activities. Through apprenticeship in citizenship practices they acquire the linguistic and non-linguistic abilities, modes of conduct and interaction in relationships with others, forms of awareness of self and other, and use of civic equipment that are constitutive of citizenship as a practice. The difference in meaning between 'citizenship' as a status and as a negotiated practice is made in European languages by the distinction between 'civil' and 'civilisation' (law-based) and 'civic' and 'civicising' (activity-based). Whereas civil citizens have the legally guaranteed opportunity to participate in the civil sphere if they chose, civic citizens engage in and experience 'civics' – the activities and practical arts of becoming and being a citizen, referred to as 'civicism'. Civic citizenry are not seen as bearers of civil rights and duties but of the abilities, competences, character and conduct acquired in participation, often referred to as 'civic virtues'. Civil citizens are civilized by the institutional rule of law, commerce and anonymous processes of civilisation, whereas civic citizens criticise and reject this disempowering picture that conceals the real world of histories of civic struggles. They 'civicise' themselves. They transform themselves into citizens and their institutions into civic spaces by civic activities and the arts of citizenship, whether or not these activities are guaranteed by the rule of law or informal customs and ways, or neither. The civic citizen manifests the freedom *of* participation *in* relationships *with* other citizens. The civic citizen is not the juridical citizen of a national or global institution but the 'free citizen' of the 'free city': that is, any kind of civic 'sphere' or 'world' that comes into being and is reciprocally sustained by the civic freedom of its citizens, from the *deme*, village, common, commune, grass roots federation to a global networks of such civic nodes.

JAMES TULLY

Fourth, whereas modern citizenship always exists in institutions, civic citizenship always exists in relationships. There are two major kinds of civic being-with relationships: (1) relationships among roughly equal citizens acting together in relationships of solidarity, civic friendship and mutual aid (citizen relationships) and relationships between governors and citizens (governance/citizen relationships). Civic citizenship is the *vis à vis* of governance. To see the importance of this contrast we have to set aside the institutional language of the civil tradition (constitutions, rights, autonomous rules, jurisdiction, states and sovereignty) and look at what goes on within, beyond and often in tension with these institutions. What we see are individual and collective actors in citizen and governance/citizen relationships.

A relationship of governance is a relation of power, knowledge and mode of subjectification through which one agent or collection of agents (governors or government) tries to govern or conduct the conduct (thoughts and actions) of another agent or agents (the governed or all affected), either directly or indirectly, formally or informally, by innumerable means and strategies. They exist in small groups, families, workplaces, sweatshops, bureaucracies, colonial administrator and colony, in producing and consuming activities, in our relationship to the environment, between multinational corporations and their suppliers and consumers, in the informal global relations of inequality, and so on. As modern states were consolidated, the term 'government' came to be restricted to the official form of 'representative government', 'the governed' to the body of individual citizens with rights, the relationship between them as the 'rule of law', and 'civil democratic citizenship' as the right to participate in the official public sphere in relation to the rule of law and representative government. The diverse citizenship tradition sees this as one important set of representative governance relationships, albeit highly institutionalised and abstracted. However, there are multiple, overlapping and criss-crossing local, national and global governance relationships in the broader sense that either do not pass through the modern national and global legal and political institutions or, if they do, they are often overlooked by the institutional perspective, to which we are subject, yet over which the governed often have little or no democratic say. This is the field of diverse citizenship.

A governance relationship is the site of citizenship from the civic perspective. In any governance relationship there is always a more or less restricted field of possible ways of acting, of conducting oneself in the relationship, even in the most tightly controlled cases (such as prisons and military training). As a result of this irreducible element of freedom and free play in a governance relationship, it is always a negotiated practice between the partners to some extent. Governance is not a unilateral phenomenon of subjection, but a much more complicated and open-ended *interplay* and *interaction* between governors and governed over time. This dimension of negotiation is the ground of civic citizenship. The governed begin to become civic citizens and initiate civic activities when they not only negotiate how to act in accordance with the governance relationship in which they find themselves, but when they negotiate the relationship itself. Hence, from the perspective of civic citizens, a governance relationship is always a governance/

TWO MEANINGS OF GLOBAL CITIZENSHIP

citizen relationship. Classically this activity of civic negotiation (the public world of *negotium*) consists of (but is not restricted to): citizens organising and non-violently calling a governance relationship into question (speaking truth to power), demanding that those who govern enter into negotiations over the acceptability of the relationship, negotiating a modification or transformation of it, implementing the changes, acting in the new relationship, reviewing it over time, and re-opening the negotiations again whenever the new relationship becomes unacceptable. In contrast to the institutional distinction between public and private in modern citizenship, this activity of calling any governance relationship anywhere into question and subjecting it to public examination and negotiation brings it out of the private sphere (of not being questioned) and into the public sphere of civic enquiry.

Opening the relationships we are part of to the ongoing negotiation and experimentation of the partners (governors–citizens) is to 'civicise' them. They are no longer imposed monologically over the governed who are presumed to simply obey as subjects. They are transformed into civic and dialogical relationships under the shared authority of both partners. The partners become mutually subject to and co-authors of the relationship between them. Governors become 'civic servants', accountable to those they serve, and subjects become free citizens rather than unfree subjects or slaves (who have no say in their despotic relationships). To civicise governance/citizen relationships is also to 'democratise' them; for one ordinary, everyday sense of 'democracy' is that the people (*demos*) in their locale (*deme*) rule by exercising an effective say in and over the relationships in which they are both subjects and citizens. Civic citizenship is thus the practice of grass roots democracy. It civicises and democratises the relationships in which the people find themselves *here and now*. Civil citizenship, in contrast, imposes a singular institutionalised process of civilisation and democratisation from above, often coercively and often over local forms of civic citizenship, on the imperial premise that institutions precede civic activity, and it restricts democracy to a small island of representative participation in a sea of non-democratic relationships in the private sphere. This is the initial and continuing unjust and anti-democratic foundation of modern citizenship from the civic standpoint. Democratic citizenship practices exist in everyday relationships long before institutionalisation and they can be extended only by the same democratic means of non-violent civicisation from the ground up.[5]

Fifth, the other general way civic citizenship is manifested is when citizens organise themselves in citizen relationships: that is, relationships among fellow citizens as equals in which there is no governor/citizen distinction. Sometimes this is done in order to enter into negotiations with governors of various kinds (as above), as in cases of collective bargaining, and negotiating within NGOs and social movements that are organised civically and democratically. But, in many other cases, citizens organise an activity entirely on the basis of citizen relationships for its own sake. The classic examples are the celebrated practices of direct democracy.

However, another important example is the cooperative. If the private corporation is both the basis and flagship of modern citizenship – the institution in which moderns exercise their civil liberties in competing, working, shopping and consuming, then the cooperative is the contrastive organisation of the civic tradition. Here citizens ignore the civil division between (non-democratic) private and (representative) public spheres, between civil liberties and democratic rights. They participate as democratic citizens governing themselves directly in the economic sphere (and other spheres), civicising the relations of supplying, hiring, working, managing, and distributing. In contrast to individual and corporate competition in market relations, cooperatives are founded on the ethic of cooperation. In the place of competitive free trade, they practice fair trade: trade relationships based on non-violent democratic negotiations among all affected. In contrast to the goal of profit, coops are 'not for profit' but for living democracy and mutual aid. All the human creativity that is channelled into the world of commerce and profit by corporations is poured into experimentation with forms of democratic cooperation by the cooperative movements. The most astonishing feature of the countless cooperatives on the planet is that they manifest, in concrete and practical forms, actual alternative worlds of citizenship *within* the interstices of the dominant national and global institutions of modern citizenship. They do not organise to overthrow the state or the capitalist mode of production, or to confront and negotiate with governors to change this or that regulation. They simply *enact* alternative worlds of citizen relationships around various activities, refusing to abjure their civicism to privatization or governmentalisation.

Sixth, modern citizenship is 'egocentric'; oriented towards the protection of the liberty of individuals to be free from interference and to be free to exercise their autonomy in the private sphere (tier one rights) or in the official public sphere (tier two rights). In contrast, diverse citizenship in both citizen and governance/citizen relationships is ecocentric and commune centric. Civic activities are oriented towards *caring for* the public or 'civic goods' of the correlative 'city' – the community bound together by citizen and/or governance/citizen relationships in dependency relationships with non-human animals and the environment they bear as inhabitants of the natural habitat. Civic goods are many and they too are subject to negotiation. They include such procedural goods as civicising relationships in many spheres and the character development and conviviality that come from participation, and such substantive goods as caring for the environment, economic self-reliance, mutual aid, fair trade, equality among citizens, and so on. When civic citizens call a particular governance relationship into question they do so under the general critical ideal that it fails to realise civic goods in some specific way or another. These are goods that make possible and enhance civic forms of life (Tully, 2001b).

Accordingly, civic citizens are thus caretakers of dwelling 'places' in this broad sense that dissolves the modernist distinction between culture and nature, and they care for their relations to the natural world (the ground or mother of their civic life) as carefully as the cultural world. They also take their civic responsibility of caring for the goods of communities and members *in* dwelling places and placeways to be prior to protecting the liberty rights of abstract individuals. They translate the latter back into one important civic good among others (negative freedom) that must vie

TWO MEANINGS OF GLOBAL CITIZENSHIP

for attention in our discursive practices. They also reply that, in many cases, what oppressed individuals and minorities say they want is not protection from their own communities by a tier one right, enforced by a distant national or international court, but democratic empowerment in their communities (civic freedom). In theories of modernity, this grounded civic ethic is discredited by caricaturing it as a pre-modern stage of historical and moral development and as a particular ethos of care in contrast to the allegedly higher and universal theory of morality and justice for abstracted and autonomous individuals. And the 'public good' is defined as the spread of modern liberties and their underlying institutions. Notwithstanding this peculiarly modern stance, multilayered civic ethics of care in human and natural relationships have been and continue to be the more widely held political and ethical orientation of the majority of the world's peoples in their diverse cultures and traditions. Under the dawning awareness of the destruction of local communities, environmental devastation and climate change caused by the last 500 years of Western imperialism under the modernising orientation (in which these public 'bads' are 'externalities'), not only ecological scientists but even former modernisers and globalisers have come around to see the value of this alternative way of citizenship.[10]

V. THE 'GLOCALISATION' OF DIVERSE CITIZENSHIP

The author will now examine two main ways diverse citizenship has spread around the globe.[6] The first is the persistence and recent renaissance of local forms of civic citizenship practices despite the globalisation of modern citizenship. The second is by the global civic federation and networkisation of local diverse citizenship practices. The author terms this global networking 'glocalisation' and the networkers 'glocal citizens' because they are grounded in and hyperextend the civic features of local citizenship.

Two ways of glocalising civic citizenship are proposed in relation to the global crisis of citizenship examined previously in Section III. To recollect, the formal and then informal imperial spread of modern citizenship, and the underlying institutions it sends on ahead to clear the way, has led in many cases, at best, to a form of global cosmopolitan citizenship for official NGOs and multinational corporations; low intensity citizenship for dependent elites of the former colonies; the dispossession or marginalisation of local citizenship and governance, the subordination of local economies and polities to global corporations and trade regimes; enormous inequalities; violent cycles of repression and resistance; and increasing environmental destruction. This crisis of modernity/coloniality has coincided with a crisis of democratic deficit in the representative democracies of the hegemonic states. The informal imperial networks of economic, legal, cultural, media, security, and military relationships not only bypass and undermine the diverse citizenship of billions of people who are governed by them. They also manipulate, downsize and disregard the representative and legal institutions of modern citizenship that are supposed to bring them under representative authority. These trends of globalisation constitute a crisis of global citizenship that, viewed in isolation, is experienced as a pervasive sense of disempowerment and disenchantment. They will now be re-interpreted from the standpoint of glocal citizenship.

First, despite these devastating trends, another world of legal, political and even economic diversity has survived and continues to be the *locus* of civic activities for millions of people. The reason for this remarkable survival and renaissance in the post-colonial world, unknown to the dominant debate over global citizenship, is that Western imperialism governs through indirect or informal means and thus depends on the active collaboration of imperialised peoples exercising constrained local self-government. Those who are not part of the Westernised elite have been able to keep their diverse local citizenship practices alive to some extent within the broad parameters of informal dependency relationships. One of the most astonishing examples among many is the survival and resurgence of 300 million indigenous peoples with their traditions of governance and citizenship after 500 years of genocide, dispossession, marginalisation, and relentless assimilation. The lived experience of citizenship in the present age is thus different from and more complex than it is portrayed through the sweeping generalisations – by both defenders and critics alike – of globalisation theories. Many existing diverse practices of governance have been corrupted into exploitative and despotic relationships by their dependency on indirect rule and others were non-civic from the outset. The point is neither to reject them simply because they are non-modern nor to accept them uncritically because they are different or traditional. It is rather to bring them into critical and comparative discussions with other forms of governance and citizenship and to explore ways citizens can civicise them by speaking and acting within them (Mander & Tauli-Corpuz, 2004; Mamdani, 2001). In the modernised West a vast repertoire of local citizenship practices have also survived within the interstices of state-centric modern citizenship, such as traditional working class organisations and countless new and creative forms of coops and networks linking rural and urban citizens in countless ways and around countless civic goods (the environment, non-violent dispute resolution, low-cost housing, anti-racism, organic farming, place-based pedagogy, neighbourhood security, and so on). These old and new citizenship practices and improvisations are multiplying rapidly today in the 'turn to the local' of a new generation disenchanted with the elite manipulation of representative citizenship.

The second example of glocalizing civic citizenship is the array of movements to 'democratise democracy'. The aim of these movements is to democratise the legal, political and bureaucratic institutions of modern representative democracy so that the people who are subject to them are consulted and have an effective negotiated say within them *wherever* power is exercised non-democratically and unaccountably, in ad-hoc processes of speaking out and 'going public' or in more formal modes of negotiation in which those who govern must listen and give account of themselves. These are thus movements to 'civicise' the civil institutions of modern citizenship. Here civic citizens join hands with civil citizens engaged in the same projects from within – such as proportional representation, deliberative democracy, democratic constitutionalism, legal pluralism, civic *versus* civil security, and the various initiatives to democratise the UN and global governance institutions from within (De Sousa Santos, 2007; Loader & Walker, 2007).

Third, since decolonisation and the triumph of informal imperialism, millions of the world's poor have been forced to migrate from the colonised world to the imperial countries to find work in a closely controlled global labour market. Despite the hardships of poverty, slavery, exploitation, racism, xenophobia, and second class or non-citizenship, they refuse to be servile subjects and exercise their civic citizenship in new and untoward ways; instead, they are negotiating their diverse cultural ways into the public and private institutions of modern citizenship. This 'journey back' or 'boomerang effect' of formerly colonised peoples now civicising the imperial countries challenges the dominant imperial, nationalist and racist cultures encoded in modern citizenship institutions and creates new forms of multiculturalism and multi-civilisationalism, both in the urban centres and the diasporic relationships ('transnational civic scapes') they sustain with their former countries. These deeply multicultural communities in 'mongrel cities' generate new kinds of citizen relationships of 'conviviality' among their members and with supportive local civic citizens groups.

These three examples and many others similar to them are existing practices of local civic citizenship. These worldwide local sources and resources of civic citizenship are much stronger and resilient than are commonly realised. They are the bases of glocal citizenship. Networks such as informal federations, NGOs, social movements and similar creative improvisations are the means by which glocal citizens link together and so glocalize these local civic bases. These networks are civic and glocal just insofar as they are (1) grounded in and accountable to the local civic nodes, and (2) hyperextend civic relationships (citizen and governance/citizen) and other civic aspects in their own organisation and their relationships with others. If, in contrast, they see themselves as bringing the gifts of civilisation and modern citizenship to the less-developed, then they are 'modern' (civil and cosmopolitan) networks. In addition to providing mutual learning and aid to their member civic nodes, they also crucially provide the civic means of democratising the persisting global imperial relationships of inequality, exploitation, and dependency that are the major causes of the crisis of global citizenship. Civic networks do this counter-hegemonic work in two mains ways.

First, as we have seen in Section III, the persisting economic, legal, political, exchange, media, educational and military relationships of informal imperialism are so unequal that, although the elites within the former colonies are able to have a say and negotiate (in global governance institutions and elsewhere), they (the G120) are barely able to modify these governance relationships, let alone transform them into governance/citizen relationships, and they are in turn scarcely in civicised relationships with their own people (the majority of the world's population). Similarly, the hegemonic partners in the relationships – the great powers and their multinational corporations – are not held democratically accountable by their own citizens. Accordingly, the first role of a glocal network is to link together glocally enough local citizenship practices of those who are governed by any of these relationships to single it out and contest it: to call its existence and privacy into the space of public questioning and put enough soft power pressure on the responsible powers-that-be to bring them to negotiations in the most effective place or places. It is thus the glocalization of the whole practice of civic negotiation discussed in Section IV. Networked contestation and negotiation can take place anywhere and by anybody in the relationships (for example, in sweat shops and/or consumer boycott of sweatshop products, in the WTO or in protest against the WTO). It should not be the burden of the wretched of the earth to refuse to submit and act otherwise, as in the dominant theories of resistance, but of the most powerful and privileged to refuse to comply with and engage in the work of glocal citizenship. In doing this, citizens in glocal networks are engaged in civicising and democratising these imperial relationships by bringing them under the shared authority of all those subject to them *in* their local places and ways. If the negotiations take hold, the subaltern partner ceases to be 'dependent' but also does *not* become 'independent' (as was imagined in the unsuccessful theories of decolonisation). Rather, the partners gradually become 'interdependent' on the ongoing democratic relationships between them (as in Section IV). These innumerable practices of glocal negotiation comprise one non-violent path of de-imperialisation and democratisation characteristic of the civic tradition (Escobar, 2004).

The second way glocal networks work to transform imperial relationships into democratic ones is through the spread of cooperative relationships between partners in the North and Global South. These cooperative informal federations are not strategies of contestation and negotiation, but (as in Section IV) of directly acting otherwise; of creating non-violent civic relationships between partners in the North and the Global South. The relationships among all the partners in the network, and within each partner's local association, are worked out civically and democratically as they go along. Although there are thousands of examples, perhaps the best known are glocal cooperative 'fair trade' and self-reliance relationships, such as the specific Fair Trade case, in contrast to competitive free trade; glocal networks of non-violent dispute resolution in contrast to war, militarisation and securitisation; and deep ecology networks in contrast to (oxymoronic) sustainable development. Like their local cooperative partners, these glocal cooperative citizens play within the existing global rules in each case, yet they play a completely different game. They create and live 'another world' in their civic and glocal activities.

Third, the World Social Forum (WSF) has emerged as an important place where civic and glocal citizens can meet each year. It is to diverse citizenship as the World Economic Forum is to modern citizenship. The WSF does not take a position, but, rather, provides a civic space in which participants from diverse citizenship practices can enter into dialogues of translation, comparison, criticism, reciprocal learning and further networking. They share the knowledge of their different arts of citizenship with each other without granting modern citizenship the universal and superior status it claims for itself and on the presumption that each mode of citizenship is partial and incomplete, so each can learn its limitations from others. The WSF also hopes to develop closer links of reciprocal learning between

TWO MEANINGS OF GLOBAL CITIZENSHIP

academic research on citizenship and the practices of citizenship we have been discussing, perhaps setting up popular universities of the social movements for this purpose, thereby deepening relationships of mutual aid (De Sousa Santos, 2006; Conway, 2004).

If all the examples of civic and glocal citizenship practices could be envisaged in a single view, in the way that modern citizenship and globalisation presents itself as a matter of inexorable progress, perhaps this would help to dissipate the sense of disempowerment and disenchantment the present crisis induces. But, from the situated standpoint of diverse citizenship, this cannot be done and the attempt would overlook the very diversity that the civic approach aims to disclose and keep in view. Civic empowerment and enchantment come not from grand narratives of universal progress, but from *praxis* – actual participation in civic activities with others where we become the citizens we can be. But this response raises the question of the motive for participation in the first place. The civic answer has always been the motivating force of role models or exemplars of the civic life.

Today there are millions of exemplars from all walks of life in all locales that move potential citizens of all ages to participate in civic/glocal practices that arguably make up the largest decentralized and diverse movement in the world (Hawken, 2007). But perhaps a particularly exemplary exemplar for our dark times of the kind of glocal citizenship I have sketched is Mahatma Gandhi and his lifelong struggle to rid the world of imperialism. His ordinary civic and glocal life continues to move millions of people to begin to act. The reason for this, I believe, is the sheer simplicity of the four citizenship practices his life manifests. The first is active non-cooperation in any imperial (non-civic) relationship and with any corresponding idea of one universal civilization or cosmopolitanism for all. The second is civic organization and uncompromising non-violent confrontation and negotiation with those responsible for imperial relationships with the aim of converting them to non-violent, democratic relationships. Third, for these two activities to be effective they have to be grounded in the local practice of the alternative world you want to bring about. For Gandhi this consisted of 'constructive work' in local, self-reliant, civically organized villages and respectful participation in their ways. Fourth, all this has to be grounded in 'experiments with truth' – a spiritual relationship to oneself in one's relationship with others and the environing world. This is a relationship of working daily and truthfully on oneself and one's attitude in order to improve how one conducts oneself in these trying yet rewarding civic relationships with others: that is, the daily practice of making oneself an exemplary citizen (Weber, 2004).

NOTES

[1] For introductions to this broad field see Amoore (2005); Brodie (2004); Dower (2003); Dower & Williams (2002); Held & McGrew (2002).

[2] I discuss the various theories of modern citizenship from Immanuel Kant to the present in Tully (2001a, 2002, 2007a, in press).

[3] For the background scholarship to Section II see Tilly (2007); Held (2006); Ishay (2004); Skinner & Stråth (2003); McNally (2006); Tully (2007a).

JAMES TULLY

38

[4] For the background scholarship to Section III, see Tully (in press); Tully (2007a); Potter *et al* (1997), Tilly (2007).

[5] Security Council Resolution 1373. See Scheppele (2007).

[6] These are United Nations statistics from 2000. See Seabrook (2003).

[7] For the origin of the widely used term 'low intensity democracy' see Gills *et al* (1993). For the more recent scholarship see references for sections III and V. Also see Grandin (2007).

[8] For the background scholarship to Section IV see Tully (2001a); Tully (2002); Pocock (2003).

[5] For recent critical work in this complex tradition of civic freedom see Norval (2005); Kompridis (2006).

[10] Moran (2006); Borrows (2002). The best known example of this movement is Joseph Stiglitz, the former head of the World Bank (see Stiglitz, 2002). See, more generally, Rahnewa (2006).

[6] For the background scholarship to Section V see Tully (2007b); Tully (2001b); Tully (2006); Tully (in press); Tully (2002); Sahle (2007); Hawken (2007).

ACKNOWLEDGEMENTS

I am most grateful to Eunice Sahle and Michael Byers for helpful discussions and Michael Peters for inviting me to participate in this important project.

REFERENCES

Amoore, L. (Ed.) (2005). *The global resistance reader.* London: Routledge.

Anghie, A. (2005). *Imperialism, sovereignty and the making of international law.* Cambridge: Cambridge University Press.

Ayers, A. (2006). Demystifying democratization: The global constitution of neo-liberal polities in Africa. *Third World Quarterly, 27,* 312–338.

Borrows, J. (2002). *Recovering Canada: The resurgence of indigenous law.* Toronto: University of Toronto Press.

Brodie, J. (2004). Introduction: Globalization and citizenship beyond the nation state. *Citizenship Studies, 8*(4), 323–332.

Conway, J. (2004). Citizenship in a time of empire: The World Social Forum as a new public space. *Citizenship Studies, 8*(4), 367–381.

De Sousa Santos, B. (Ed.) (2007). *Democratizing democracy.* London: Verso.

De Sousa Santos, B. (2006). *The rise of the global left: The World Social Forum and beyond.* London: Zed Books.

Dower, N. (2003). *An introduction to global citizenship.* Edinburgh: Edinburgh University Press.

Dower, N. & Williams, J. (Eds.) (2002). *Global citizenship: A critical reader.* Edinburgh: Edinburgh University Press.

Escobar, A. (2004). Beyond the third world: Imperial globality, global coloniality and anti-globalisation social movements. *Third World Quarterly, 25*(1), 207–230.

Evans, T. & Ayers, A. (2006). In the service of power: The global political economy of citizenship and human rights. *Citizenship Studies, 10*(3), 289–308.

Gills, B., Rocamora, J. & Wilson, R. (Eds.) (1993). *Low intensity democracy: Political power in the new world order.* Ann Arbor, MI: University of Michigan Press.

Hawken, P. (2007). *Blessed unrest: How the largest movement in the world came into being and why no one saw it coming.* New York: Viking.

Held, D. (2006). *Models of democracy.* Cambridge: Polity Press.

Held, D. & McGrew, A. (Eds.) (2002). *The global transformations reader.* Cambridge: Polity Press.

Ishay, M.R. (2004). *The history of human rights.* Berkeley, CA: University of California Press.

Kompridis, N. (2006). *Critique and disclosure: Critical theory between past and future.* Cambridge, MA: MIT Press.

TWO MEANINGS OF GLOBAL CITIZENSHIP

Loader, I. & Walker, N. (2007). *Civilizing security*. Cambridge: Cambridge University Press.

Mamdani, M. (2001) Beyond settler and natives as political identities: Overcoming the legacy of colonialism. *Comparative Studies in Society and History, 43*(4), 651–64.

Mander, J. & Tauli-Corpuz, V. (Eds.) (2004). *Paradigm wars: Indigenous peoples resistance to economic globalization*. San Francisco, CA: Sierra Club Books.

Mignolo, W. (2000). *Local histories/global designs: Coloniality, subaltern knowledges and border thinking*. Princeton: Princeton University Press.

McNally, D. (2006). *Another world is possible: Globalization and anti-capitalism*. Winnipeg: Arbeiter Ring.

Moran, E.F. (2006). *People and nature: An introduction to human ecological relations*. Oxford: Blackwell.

Norval, A. (2007). *Aversive democracy*. Cambridge: Cambridge University Press.

Pocock, J. (2003). *The machiavellian moment: With a new afterword by the author*. Princeton: Princeton University Press.

Potter, D., Goldblatt, D., Kiloh, M. & Lewis, P. (Eds.) (1997). *Democratization*. Cambridge: Polity Press.

Rahnewa, M. (Ed.) (2006). *The post-development reader*. London: Zed Books.

Sahle, E. (2007). *Global citizenship and transnational civil society: Theory and practice*. Manuscript submitted for publication.

Seabrook, J. (2003). *The no nonsense guide to world poverty*. London: Verso.

Scheppele, K.L. (2007). *The international state of emergency: Challenges to constitutionalism after September 11*. Manuscript submitted for publication.

Skinner, Q. & Stråth, B. (2003). *States and citizens: History, theory, prospects*. Cambridge: Cambridge University Press.

Stiglitz, J. (2003). *Globalization and its discontents*. London: Penguin.

Tilly, C. (2007). *Democracy*. Cambridge: Cambridge University Press.

Tully, J. (2001a). Democracy and globalization. In W. Norman & R. Beiner (Eds.), *Canadian political philosophy* (pp. 36–62). Oxford: Oxford University Press.

Tully, J. (2001b). An ecological ethics for the present: Three approaches. In B. Gleeson & N. Low (Eds.), *Governing for the environment: Global problems, ethics and democracy* (pp. 147–165). Hampshire: Palgrave Publishers.

Tully, J. (2002). The unfreedom of the moderns. *Modern Law Review, 65*(2).

Tully, J. (2006, 22 February). Communication and imperialism. *Ctheory: 1000 Days of Theory*, td035. Retrieved 25 September, 2007, from http://www.ctheory.net/articles.aspx?id=508.

Tully, J. (2007a). The imperialism of modern constitutional democracy. In M. Loughlin & N. Walker (Eds.), *The paradox of constitutionalism* (pp. 315–338). Oxford: Oxford University Press.

Tully, J. (2007b). A new kind of Europe?: Democratic integration in the European Union. *CRISPP, 10*(1), 71–87.

Tully, J. (in press). Law, democracy and imperialism. In E. Christodoulidis & S. Tierney (Eds.), *Political theory and public law*. Aldershot: Ashgate.

Zerilli, L. (2005). *Feminism and the abyss of freedom*. Chicago: University of Chicago Press.

Weber, T. *Gandhi as disciple and mentor*. Cambridge: Cambridge University Press.

James Tully
University of Victoria

Part II
Different Status, Different Rights

[6]
Citizens, Residents, and Aliens in a Changing World: Political Membership in the Global Era*

BY SEYLA BENHABIB

Our contemporary condition is marked by the emergence of new forms of identity/difference politics around the globe. As globalization proceeds at a dizzying rate, as a material global civilization encompasses the earth from Hong Kong to Lima, from Pretoria to Helsinki, world-wide integration in economics, technology, communication, information, armament, and tourism is accompanied by the collective and cultural disintegration of older political entities, and in particular of the nation-state (Benhabib, 1997a). India and Turkey, which are among the oldest democracies of the Third World, are in the throes of struggles that call into question the very concept of a secular, representative democracy. Need one mention in this context ethnic wars, cleansings, and massacres in the former Yugoslavia; the Russian

---

*Earlier versions of this paper were read at the American Political Science Association Meetings in Washington in August 1997; as a plenary address to the German Political Science Association Meetings in Bamberg in October 1997, and at "The Dilemmas of European Citizenship" Conference at Harvard University, also held in October 1997.

I would like to thank Jürgen Habermas, Daniel Bell, Richard Tuck, Caroline Emcke, Glyn Morgan, Sanford Levinson, Andrea San Giovanni, Sayres Rudy, and Arash Abizadeh for their comments on earlier drafts.

An earlier version has appeared in: Benhabib, *Demokratische Gleichheit und kulturelle Vielfalt*. The 1997 Horkheimer Lectures (Frankfurt: Fischer Verlag, 1999), ch.3. An expanded English version of these lectures will appear as *Democracy and Identity. Political Membership in the Global Era. The Gauss Lectures Spring 1998* (Princeton University Press, 2000).

710 SOCIAL RESEARCH

destruction of Chechnya; the simmering nationality conflicts between Azerbaijan and Armenia, Macedonia and Greece, and the continuing tribal massacres in central African states like Rwanda, Uganda, and the Congo. Indicative of a social dynamic that we have hardly begun to understand, global integration is proceeding alongside with socio-cultural disintegration, and the resurgence of ethnic, nationalistic, religious, and linguistic separatism (Barber, 1995; Ignatieff, 1994; Friedman, 1996; Mendes and Soares, 1996).

With globalization and fragmentation proceeding apace, human rights and sovereignty claims come into increasing conflict with each other (Heiberg, ed., 1994). On the one hand, a world-wide consciousness about universal principles of human rights is growing; on the other, particularistic identities of nationality, ethnicity, religion, race, and language (by which one is said to belong to a sovereign people) are asserted with increasing ferocity. Globalization, far from creating a "cosmopolitical order," a condition of perpetual peace among peoples governed by the principles of a republican constitution (Kant [1795], 1963), has brought to a head conflicts between human rights and the claim to self-determination of sovereign collectivities. Because sovereignty means the right of a collectivity to define itself by asserting power over a bounded territory, declarations of sovereignty, more often than not, create distinctions between "us" and "them," those who belong to the sovereign people and those who do not.

Historically, there rarely is a convergence between the identity of those over whom power is asserted because they are residents of a bounded territory and the identity of the sovereign people in the name of whom such power is exercised. In this context, Hannah Arendt's astute observations, although formulated *principally with respect* to the difficulties of protecting human rights in the inter-War period in Europe, are more perspicacious than ever:

> From the beginning the paradox involved in the declaration of inalienable human rights was that it reckoned with an "abstract" human being who seemed to exist nowhere...

POLITICAL MEMBERSHIP IN THE GLOBAL ERA 711

> The whole question of human rights, therefore, was quickly and inextricably blended with the question of national emancipation; only the emancipated sovereignty of the people, of one's own people, seemed to be able to insure them (Arendt [1951], 1979, 291).

The citizenship and naturalization claims of foreigners, denizens, and residents within the borders of a polity, as well as the laws, norms and rules governing such procedures are pivotal social practices through which the normative perplexities of human rights and sovereignty can be most acutely observed. Sovereignty entails the right of a people to control its borders as well as defining the procedures for admitting "aliens" into its territory and society; yet in a liberal-democratic polity, such sovereignty claims must always be constrained by human rights, which individuals are entitled to, not in virtue of being citizens or members of a polity, but insofar as they are human beings *simpliciter*. Universal human rights transcend the rights of citizens and extend to all persons considered as moral beings. What kinds of immigration, naturalization, and citizenship practices then would be compatible with the commitments of liberal democracies to human rights? Can claims to sovereign self-determination be reconciled with the just and fair treatment of aliens and others in our midst?

In contemporary debates around these issues two approaches dominate: the radical univeralist argument for open borders and the civic republican perspective of "thick conceptions of citizenship." Radical universalists argue that, from a moral point of view, national borders are arbitrary and that the only morally consistent universalist position would be one of open borders. Joe Carens, for example, uses the devise of the Rawlsian "veil of ignorance" to think through principles of justice from the standpoint of the refugee, the immigrant, the asylum seeker (Carens, 1995, 229). Are the borders within which we happen to be born, and the documents to which we are entitled, any less arbitrary from a moral point of view than other characteristics like skin color, gender, and genetic make-up with which we are endowed? Carens' answer is

SOCIAL RESEARCH

"no." From a moral point of view, the borders that circumscribe our birth and the papers to which we are entitled, are arbitrary because their distribution do not follow any clear criteria of moral desert, achievement, and compensation. Therefore, claims Carens, liberal democracies should practice policies that are as compatible as possible with the vision of a world without borders.

Opposed to Carens' radical universalism are a range of communitarian and civic-republican positions, articulating more or less "thick" conceptions of citizenship, community, and belonging (see Galston, 1991; Sandel, 1996 ; Kessler, 1998). These theories of citizenship, while not precluding or prohibiting immigration, will want to articulate stricter criteria of incorporation and citizenship of foreigners than the universalists. Only those immigrants who come closest to the model of the republican citizen envisaged by these theories will be welcome; others will be spurned (Honig, 1999). Of course, given how contested such thick conceptions of citizenship inevitably are, communitarian theories can easily lend themselves to the justification of illiberal immigration policies and the restricting of the rights of immigrants and aliens.

I would like to defend a position that will steer a middle course between the radical universalism of open border politics on the one hand and sociologically antiquated conceptions of thick republican citizenship on the other. Instead, stressing the constitutive tension between univeralistic human rights claims and democratic sovereignty principles, I will analyze the contemporary practices of political incorporation into liberal democracies. This essay will focus on dilemmas of citizenship and political membership in contemporary Western Europe against the background of these larger theoretical concerns. Current developments in citizenship and incorporation practices within the member states of the European Union in particular are my primary concern. There are a number of compelling historical as well as philosophical reasons for choosing European citizenship and incorporation practices as the focal point for these concerns at the present time.

POLITICAL MEMBERSHIP IN THE GLOBAL ERA 713

Insofar as they are liberal democracies, member states of the European Union cannot form a "fortress Europe." No liberal democracy can close its borders to refugees and asylum seekers, migrants and foreign workers. The porousness of borders is a necessary while not sufficient condition of liberal democracies. By the same token, no sovereign liberal democracy can lose its right to define immigration and incorporation policies.

I will distinguish conditions of entry into a country, like the permission to visit, work, study and buy property, from conditions of temporary residency, and both in turn from permanent residency and civil incorporation, the final stage of which is political membership. These are different stages of political incorporation, very often collapsed into one another in theoretical discussions, but analytically distinguishable. At each stage, the rights and claims of foreigners, residents and aliens will be regulated by sovereign polities; but these regulations can be subject to scrutiny, debate, contestation as well as protest by those to whom they apply, their advocates, and national and international human rights groups.

There is no step of this process that can be shielded from scrutiny by interested parties. Democratic sovereignty in immigration and incorporation policy is not an unlimited right. The right to self-assertion of a particular people must be examined and evaluated in the light of the commitment of this very same people to universal human rights. Developments of citizenship and immigration practices within contemporary Europe reflect some of the deepest perplexities faced by all nation-states in the era of globalization.

Dilemmas of Citizenship in the European Union

Since 1989 and the fall of authoritarian communism, the worldwide trend toward material global integration and ethnic and cultural fragmentation have coincided with another set of epochal developments on the continent: the end of the Cold War, the unification of Germany, and the transformation of the European

714   SOCIAL RESEARCH

Union from a monetary and financial organization—a customs union—into a political entity with a European Parliament, a European Council of Ministers, a European Court of Justice, and since January 1999, a European currency—the Euro. But what is Europe? (Benhabib, 1997b)

For some Europe is not a continent, a mere geographical designator, but an ideal, the birthplace of western philosophy and the Enlightenment, of democratic revolutions, and human rights. For others Europe is a fig leaf behind which big finance capital and in particular the German Bundesbank hide in order to dismantle the social-welfare states of the Union. Since the Maastricht treaty and the requirement that national governments cut their annual budget deficits to 3%, member states have forced their own populations to accept fiscal stability over full employment, and to place the shared confidence that international financial markets show in their national economies over the quality of life of these countries. Europe has ceased to be an ideal, for some it has long become an illusion. Tony Judt gives voice to the Europessimist position with the following words: "...we shall wake up one day to find out that far from solving the problems of our continent, the myth of "Europe" has become an impediment to our recognizing them. We shall discover that it has become little more than the politically correct way to paper over local difficulties, as though the mere invocation of the promise of Europe could substitute for solving problems and crises that really affect the place" (Judt, 1996, 140).

Whether as ideal or as illusion, "Europe" is being invoked today to define a new set of boundaries. During the time of the Cold War, the terms "east" and "west" came to designate a geopolitical division of regimes. Whereas once the term "east," or the "orient" would have been reserved for that border that separated Europe from the Ottoman Empire, after 1945 and the division of Germany, the line separating "east" from "west" ran through the heart of Europe, i.e., the city of Berlin. The communist regimes of Europe became oddly enough part of the orient; "eastern Europe" designated differences in types of political regime by

POLITICAL MEMBERSHIP IN THE GLOBAL ERA 715

making communism appear as part of "them," the east, as opposed to "us," "the free West." This conversion of geopolitics into physical geography was a political subterfuge through which one rendered the unfamiliar familiar. The term "eastern Europe," which conveniently hid the fact that Prague is to the west of Vienna, rendered communism—the unfamiliar—familiar, by marking it as "oriental," or as "eastern." The revolutions of 1989 showed how illusory it was to mark political, cultural, and historical differences through purportedly neutral geographical designators.

Contemporary Europe is facing the danger that its moral and political boundaries will be redefined via geographical borders. Geography once again will be used to cover the tracks of complex processes of political and moral inclusion and exclusion. Where are Europe's borders after 1989? How can these borders be justified as boundaries? Europe, whether as an ideal or illusion, whom does it include and whom does it exclude? After the Cold War who are Europe's "others"?

According to statistics provided by the Council of Europe, between 1950 and 1992/93 the foreign population in the countries of western Europe grew as follows: while foreigners made up 1.1% of the population in Germany in 1950, in 1992-93 this number rose to 8.6%. During the same period the foreign population of France increased from 4.2% to 6.6%; of Belgium from 4.1% to 9.1%; of Holland from 1.0% to 5.1%: and of Luxembourg from 9.8% to 29.1%. On the whole, the foreign population of Europe increased from 1.3% in 1950 to 4.9% in 1992-93.[1]

The year 1993 marks a turning point in immigration trends in European countries. After the increase in immigration flows during the 1980s and the beginning of the 1990s, a reduction in the number of immigrant entries occurred. The decline in the number of asylum claims during this period was offset by the predominance of flows linked to family reunion and the importance of temporary and highly-skilled workers (SOPEMI, 1998, 15).

Despite peaking at 8.5% of the total population in 1993, the foreign population of Germany stood at 8.9% in 1996. During the

716 SOCIAL RESEARCH

same period, the Netherlands have declined from 5.1% in 1993 to 4.4% in 1996; France has remained steady at about 6.3% and Belgium at about 9.1%. The foreign population in Denmark has increased from 3.6% in 1993 to 4.7 in 1996; in Luxembourg as well there has been an increase in this same period from 31.8% to 34.1%. Among the European Union countries, only Austria has percentages of foreigners among its population lower than Luxembourg but close enough to Germany. The percentage of the foreign population increased slightly from 8.6% in 1993 to 9.0 in 1996 (SOPEMI, 1998, 224).

These figures are not broken down according to different geographical regions and countries of origin. Foreigners from former east European countries are included in these figures along with guest workers from Turkey and refugees from the former Yugoslav countries.[2] A more precise breakdown shows that ethnic Turks and ethnic Kurds are the largest group of foreigners, not only in Germany, but in western Europe in general. In 1993, they numbered 2.7 million. Of that number, 2 million live in Germany and make up 2.5% of the population.[3] The second largest group of foreigners are the members of former Yugoslav states: 1.8 million Croats, Serbians, Bosnian Moslems and, after the war in Kosovo, ethnic Albanians who were driven out by Serb forces, and only a fraction of whom have returned to their old homes. Italians working outside the home country are one and a half million in number; they are followed by the Portuguese, of whom about 900, 000 work and live outside Portugal. Spaniards, who are members of the European Union, and Algerians who are not, each number 600,000.

As European unification proceeds, a two-tiered status of foreignness is developing throughout Europe. There are different rights and privileges accorded to each category of foreigner within member states.

The Treaty of Maastricht makes provisions for a "Union citizenship."[4] Nationals of all countries who are members of the European Union are also citizens of the European Community. What does being a citizen of the Union mean? What privileges and responsibilities, what rights and duties does this entitle one

POLITICAL MEMBERSHIP IN THE GLOBAL ERA 717

to? Is citizenship of the union merely a status category, let us say, just as being a member of the Roman Empire was? Does membership in the Union amount to more than possessing a passport that allows one to pass through the right doors at border crossings?[5]

Clearly, Union membership is intended to be more than that. It is not just a passive status but is also intended to designate an active civic identity. Members of the Union states can settle anywhere in the union, take up jobs in their chosen countries, and can vote, as well as stand for office, in local elections and in elections for the Parliament of Europe.

As the process of European monetary and economic integration progresses, whether or not union citizenship should also entail an equivalent package of social rights and benefits, like unemployment compensation, health care and old age pensions, which members of EU states can enjoy wherever they go, is being debated.[6]

The obverse side of membership in the Union is a sharper delineation of the conditions of those who are non-members. The agreements of Schengen and Dublin intend to uniformize practices of granting asylum and refugee status throughout member states (Neuman, 1993).[7] Referred to as "legal harmonization," these agreements have made the granting of refugee and asylum status in the Union increasingly difficult. If an individual seeks refugee and asylum status in a member country, this individual is not permitted to apply in another country of the Union until the first application is resolved. Although this is left unsaid, the presumption is that once such an application has been denied in one member country, it is unlikely to succeed in another. The decision of the European Council of Ministers to erect a Union-wide office to deal with refugee and asylum issues, while creating legal and bureaucratic homogenization and standardization, by the same token, intends to make Europe's borders less porous by disallowing individuals in need multiple venues of aid and rescue.

As union citizenship progresses, as the treatises of Schengen and Dublin convert the borders of Europe into a fortress, in

718 SOCIAL RESEARCH

nearly each member country discrepancies are arising between those who are foreigners and third-country nationals, and those who are foreign nationals but EU members. A two-tiered status of foreignness is thus developing: On the one hand are third-country national foreign residents of European countries, some of whom have been born and raised in these countries and who know of no other homeland; on the other hand are those who may be near to total strangers to the language, customs and history of their host country but who enjoy special status and privilege in virtue of being a national of a state that is an EU member (Klusmeyer, 1993).

Partially in response to the growing pressures created by this situation, Germany on May 7, 1999 reformed its 1913 citizenship law. The German parliament accepted by a two-thirds majority that the principle of *jus sanguinis*, which bases citizenship on inherited birthright, be supplemented by *jus soli*, which bases citizenship on territorial birth, in the acquisition of German citizenship (see Benhabib, 1999b). From January 1, 2000 children born to foreign parents who have resided in the country for eight years acquire the German citizenship without forfeiting other passes they hold. When they reach the age of 23, they must decide for one pass or another. In addition to the *jus soli* regulation, the new law expedites the acquisition of German citizenship by foreigners in that it reduces the transition period from residency to citizenship from fifteen to eight years. The decision of the German parliament is, of course, to be celebrated but we can only understand the significance of this new law when we place it within a larger conceptual and institutional context.

Dilemmas of citizenship in contemporary Europe have implications for recent debates around citizenship in contemporary political philosophy. In recent discussions, particularly under the influence of the liberal-communitarian debate, the concept and practice of citizenship has been analyzed largely from a normative perspective (Galston, 1991; Macedo, 1990; Oldfield, 1990; Kymlicka and Norman, 1995). Usually one aspect—the privileges of political membership—has been in the foreground.[8] This nor-

POLITICAL MEMBERSHIP IN THE GLOBAL ERA 719

mative discussion, mostly about the duties of democratic citizenship and participatory democratic theory, has been carried out in a sociological vacuum. Political philosophers have paid little attention to citizenship as a sociological category, as a social practice that inserts us into a complex network of privileges and duties, entitlements, and obligations. Political philosophy and the political sociology of citizenship have gone their separate ways. Privileges of political membership are only one aspect of citizenship. Collective identity and the entitlement to social rights and benefits are others. We need to disaggregate the theory and practice of citizenship into these various dimensions and broaden our focus to include the conditions of citizenship in sociologically complex, decentered, welfare state democracies. Through the unprecedented movement of peoples and goods, capital and information, microbes and communication across borders, individuals no longer enter their societies at birth and exit them at death (Kleger, 1995). With reference to recent patterns of immigration within and outside Europe Rainer Bauboeck has observed:

> On the one hand, immigrants who settle in a destination country for good may still keep the citizenship of the sending society and travel there regularly so that the sending country rightly regards them as having retained strong ties to their origins... Temporary migrants, on the other hand, often find it difficult to return and to reintegrate. Some migrants become permanent residents in destination countries without being accepted as immigrants and without regarding themselves as such; others develop patterns of frequent movement between different countries in none of which they establish themselves permanently... Contemporary migration research should go beyond these narrow national views and conceive of migration as a genuinely transnational phenomenon, not only at the moment of border crossings but also with regard to the resulting social affiliations. International migration transnationalizes both

SOCIAL RESEARCH

sending and receiving societies by extending relevant forms of membership beyond the boundaries of territories and of citizenship (Bauboeck, 1998, 26; also Cohen, 2000).[9]

Citizenship as Social Practice

Sociologically, the practice and institution of "citizenship" can be disaggregated into three components: collective identity; privileges of political membership, and social rights and claims.

Collective Identity. Citizenship implies being a member of a political entity that has been formed historically, which has certain linguistic, cultural, ethnic, and religious commonalties, and which can be distinguished from other such political entities. The precise form of such an entity, whether it is a multinational empire or a national republic, a Commonwealth or a Federation, varies historically. Viewed analytically though the concepts of "citizenship," in the sense of being a member of a political community, and "nationality," in the sense of being a member of a particular linguistic, ethnic, religious, and cultural group are to be distinguished from each other. Political communities are not composed of nationally and ethnically homogeneous groups. Historically this was just as little the case in the multinational and multiethnic Hapsburg and Ottoman Empires as it is the case today in the USA, Canada, Australia, New Zealand.

Privileges of Membership. The oldest meaning of citizenship is that of the privileges and burdens of self-governance. For the ancient Greeks the "politos" is the member of the "polis," the one who can be called to military service as well as jury duty, who must pay taxes and serve in the Ecclesia in his capacity as member of his Demei at least one month of the year. The link between the city and the citizen is retained in the etymology of "civitas" and "citoyenne" on the one hand and "Buergher" and "Burgh" on the other.

Citizenship confers upon its holders the right of political participation, the right to hold certain offices and perform certain

POLITICAL MEMBERSHIP IN THE GLOBAL ERA 721

tasks, and the right to deliberate and decide upon certain questions. Aristotle writes in the Politics:

> The state is a compound made of citizens; and this compels us to consider who should properly be called a citizen and what a citizen really is. The nature of citizenship, like that of the state, is a question which is often disputed: there is no general agreement on a single definition: the man who is a citizen in a democracy is often not one in an oligarchy" (Aristotle 1941, 1274b-1275a).

In making the identity of the citizen dependent upon the type of political regime, Aristotle is emphasizing the contingent nature of this concept. It is not nature but the city and its conventions, the nomoi, that create the citizen. Yet precisely in Aristotle's work, we see how this insight into the socially constituted aspect of citizenship goes hand in hand with an exclusionary vision of the psycho-sexual attributes of citizenship. Even if it is regime types that determine who a citizen is, in Aristotle's view, only some are "by nature fit" to exercise the virtues of citizenship, others are not. Slaves, women, and non-Greeks are not only excluded from the statutory privileges of citizenship but their exclusion is viewed as rational insofar as these individuals do not possess the virtues of mind, body, and character essential to citizenship. This tension between the social constitution of the citizen and the psychosexual "natural" substance that the citizen ought to possess accompanies struggles over the meaning of citizenship down to our own days. Struggles over whether women should have the vote, whether non-White and colonial peoples are capable of self-rule or whether a gay person can hold certain kinds of public office are illustrations of the tension between the social and the naturalistic dimensions of citizenship.

Social Rights and Benefits. The view that citizenship can be understood as a status that entitles one to the possession of a certain bundle of entitlements, benefits as well as obligations, derives from T. H. Marshall (Marshall, 1950). Marshall's catalog of civil,

SOCIAL RESEARCH

political, and social rights is based upon the cumulative logic of struggles for the expansion of democracy in the 19th and early part of the 20th centuries. "Civil rights" arise with the birth of the absolutist state and in their earliest and most basic form they entail the rights to the protection of life, liberty, and property, the right to freedom of conscience, and certain associational rights, like those of contract and marriage.

"Political rights" in the narrow sense refer to the rights of self-determination, to hold and to run for office, to enjoy freedom of speech and opinion, the rights to establish political and non-political associations, including a free press and free institutions of science and culture. "Social rights" are last in Marshall's catalogue, because they have been achieved historically through the struggles of the worker's, women's and other social movements of the last two centuries. Social rights involve the right to form trade unions as well as other professional and trade associations; health care rights, unemployment compensation, old age pensions, child care, housing and educational subsidies, etc. These social rights vary widely from one country to another and depend thoroughly upon the social class compromises prevalent in any given welfare-state democracy.

Were we to try to apply Marshall's catalogue to the condition of foreigners in the European Union, we would note an interesting reversal. In all European countries, foreigners possess full protection of their civil rights under the law as well as enjoying most social rights. Non-citizens of EU states enjoy the same protection in the eyes of the law as citizens, their earnings and property are equally protected, and they enjoy freedom of conscience and religion. The extent of their associational rights, however, is limited: since establishing political associations belongs among the core political rights, in most countries, they can only be enjoyed by citizens.

Under the provisions of the social-welfare democracies of European states, most foreigners are entitled to health care benefits, unemployment compensation, old age pensions, childcare and certain educational subsidies. These social benefits are not con-

POLITICAL MEMBERSHIP IN THE GLOBAL ERA 723

ferred automatically. They depend upon the length of residence in the host country, the particular kind of wage or service contract. Despite variations among member states, in most EU countries foreigners benefit from some of these social rights while the enjoyment of political membership is either blocked off or made extremely difficult.

In her book, *Limits of Citizenship: Migrants and Postnational Membership in Europe,* Yasemin Soysal introduces the concept of an "incorporation regime" (Soysal, 1994). She thereby suggests that every host country possesses certain legal, economic, and policy regulations according to which the status of being a foreigner in that country is defined. Often, however, the collective status and identity of such groups will simply be seen to be the consequence of cultural traditions and historical developments that these groups presumably have brought with them from their countries of origin. The interaction between the home and the host cultures and traditions is thereby ignored.

For example: the incorporation policy of the former BRD was to integrate guest workers into the juridical system not in virtue of their membership in a particular ethnic group, but rather in the first place through the status as individual persons and in the second place as workers and employees. Claims to civil and social rights would accrue to them as individuals and as workers. It is this status identity that entitled the individual to a particular set of rights and benefits.

By contrast, in the Netherlands the regime of incorporation has proceeded quite differently. The National Advisory Council of Ethnic Minorities which was founded by the Dutch government in 1982, designates Turks, Moroccans, Tunisians, Surinamese, populations of the Antille and Molukken Islands, as well Greeks, Spanish, Portguese and Gypsies as "official minorities" (von Amersfoot, 1982). When an ethnic group attains the status of being an official minority, then the claims of such a group to housing, education, employment, and other forms of social support are also acknowledged. Such official minority groups then acquire the

SOCIAL RESEARCH

rights to establish and carry out education in their own languages and to form organizations and associations.

This sociological analysis of citizenship and incorporation regimes suggests a methodological perspective that allows us to conceptualize the collective identity of foreigners to result from the complex interaction between various factors: those social and cultural attributes of immigrant groups that originate in their home country and the juridical, political, social as well as cultural norms and practices of the host country. This then suggests the question: why are certain rights granted to foreigners and others not? Why are certain identity-marking characteristics privileged in certain contexts and not in others? Note the difference between Germany and Holland in their practices of defining the collective and individual status of foreigners. What is the relationship between the singling out of certain criteria as being constitutive of the foreigners' identity, and the history and self-understanding of a particular country? The treatment of the "others" reveals who we are, because in Julia Kristeva's words, "nous sommes étrangers à nous même." "We are strangers to ourselves" (Kristeva, 1991).

Political Participation Rights in Europe Today

The highest privilege of citizenship is the possession of political rights in the strict sense. It is also through the entitlement to and exercise of these rights that one's status as a "citizen," as member of the body politic, will be established. The lines that divide members from strangers, citizens from foreigners, the "we" from the "they" are drawn most sharply around these privileges.

Political theory on these issues lags far behind actual developments. None of the following host countries of the European Union grant foreigners the right of participation in national elections: Denmark, the Netherlands, Sweden, Belgium, France, Austria, Germany, and England.[10] Yet in Denmark as well as Sweden, foreigners can participate in local and regional elections and be candidates for

POLITICAL MEMBERSHIP IN THE GLOBAL ERA 725

them. In Norway, Finland, and Holland these rights are granted at the local but not regional levels. In Switzerland, which is not a member of the European Union, the cantons of Neufchatel and Jura grant foreigners these rights as well. Similar attempts in Berlin, Hamburg, and Schleswig-Hollstein, to grant to those foreigners who have resided in Germany for more than five years local election rights, have been declared "unconstitutional" by the German Constitutional Court (Weiler, 1995). What is the link between the status of active citizenship and "national membership"?

The acquisition of citizenship rights proceeds in most countries of the world along three categories: the principle of territory, origin, or consent. The principle of territoriality known as *jus soli* means that a political community has sovereign claims over a territory: persons who live in this territory are considered either as falling under the dominion or authority of this sovereign or are themselves viewed as being part of the sovereign. The first case corresponds to pre-democratic understandings of sovereignty, and defines, as was the case with the Absolutist regimes of Europe, citizens as subjects. Historically, the Ottoman Empire as well as the Hapsburg monarchy and the German Kaiser regime followed this pattern. These old regimes always granted certain protected groups special citizenship rights and privileges, as was the case for example for the "Reichsjuden," the Jews of the Empire, during the period of the Hapsburg Double Monarchy.

The territorial principle of citizenship can also have a democratic variant. The principles of citizenship, introduced by the American and the French Revolutions, follow this variant. According to the democratic understanding of the *jus soli*, each child who is born on the territory of a democratic sovereign is potentially a member of this sovereign and therefore has claims to citizenship (Brubacker, 1992, 45).

The second principle according to which citizenship is granted is that of ethnic origin or belonging, *jus sanguinis*. If one considers France and the USA as prime examples of countries in which citizenship is based on the *jus soli*, the acquisition of German citi-

726 SOCIAL RESEARCH

zenship is seen as paradigm example of *jus sanguinis*. The principle of *jus sanguinis* means that citizenship is attained in virtue of belonging to a people or ethnic group. How is "belonging" to a people or ethnic group to be established? Biological lineage is the simplest and clearest criterion for defining this. The German citizenship law of 23rd July 1913—das Reichs und Staatsbuergerschaftgesetz—which formed the basis of today's law of citizenship in Germany until it was recently reformed, states that citizenship will be inherited (Klusmeyer, 1993). This law was formulated with the specific political purpose of making it impossible for the large numbers of Jews and Poles who then resided in the Kaiserreich to acquire German citizenship (Wertheimer, 1987). Only a century ago, however, the Prussian Edict of Emancipation of 1812 had granted Jews in Prussia the status of citizenship without taking into account criteria of ethnic belonging (Huber, 1961). During the Reichstag, the German Social Democrats, much like to day's coalition government, sought to reintroduce *jus soli* into German citizenship legislation.

Citizenship and Political Theory

I have examined dilemmas of citizenship in contemporary Europe from the standpoint of normative political philosophy and suggested why these political developments should lead us to rethink our normative categories to bring them more into contact with the new sociological and institutional realities of citizenship in the contemporary world.

A central thesis of my argument is that theories of citizenship have often relied upon obsolete and misleading premises. The first among them is the fiction of a "closed society." Most western political thought proceeded from the assumption of a "closed society" with non-porous borders. In Rawls' crystal-clear formulation:

> The first is that we have assumed that a democratic society, like any political society, is to be viewed as a complete and

POLITICAL MEMBERSHIP IN THE GLOBAL ERA 727

closed social system. It is complete in that it is self-sufficient and has a place for all the main purposes of human life. It is also closed, in that entry into it is only by birth and exit from it is only by death... For the moment we leave aside entirely relations with other societies and postpone all questions of justice between peoples until a conception of justice for a well-ordered society is on hand. Thus, we are not seen as joining society at the age of reason, as we might join an association, but as being born into a society where we will lead a complete life (Rawls, 1993, 41).

In the light of global developments in industry, finance, communication, tourism, information, and armament, it is implausible today to proceed from the Rawlsian assumption, even if this is a counterfactual one, that "a democratic society can be viewed as a complete and a closed social system." A theory of political justice must necessarily be a theory of international justice.[11] Not only the current level of development of a global civil society but more significantly the fact that in democratic societies the right of exit remains a fundamental right of the citizen makes this fiction obsolete.

Furthermore, to be a foreigner does not mean to be beyond the pale of the law. It means to have a specific kind of legal and political identity that includes certain rights and obligations while precluding others. In many European host countries we see the softening of those legal restriction that have previously made it impossible for foreigners to participate in elections and running for office. The restrictions that till now have precluded foreigners from political membership rest, in the final analysis, upon assumptions of who the citizens themselves are and what the virtues of citizenship consist of.

In this respect, neither the principles of *jus sanguinis* nor those of *jus soli* are consistent and plausible enough to justify the theory and practice of democratic citizenship. There is a hiatus between the self-understanding of democracies and the acquisition of citi-

728 SOCIAL RESEARCH

zenship. While democracy is a form of life that rests upon active consent and participation, citizenship is distributed according to passive criteria of belonging, like birth upon a piece of land and socialization in that country or ethnic belonging to a people.

A further assumption that has been greatly misleading in these debates is that of "state-centeredness." In insisting that consent was expressed through participation in the numerous activities of civil society, Locke was right (see Locke, [1690], 1980). Our contemporary societies are even more complex, fragmented and contradictory social structures than those in Locke's time. In such societies, human conduct and interactions assume many and diverse forms. We are more authentically members of a family, of a neighborhood, of a religious community or of a social movement than we are members of a state. While the modern nation-state remains a possible structural expression of democratic self-determination, the complexity of our social lives integrates us into associations that lie above and below the level of the nation state. These associations mediate the manner in which we relate to the state. If we stop viewing the state as the privileged apex of collective identity, but instead, along with Rawls, view it "as a union of unions," then citizenship should also to be understood as a form of collective identity mediated in and through the institutions of civil society. In the European context this means: foreigners' claims to citizenship in a political entity are established not through some hierarchical decision from above, but because individuals show themselves to be worthy of membership in civil society through the exercise of certain abilities and the fulfillment of certain conditions. Civil citizenship should lead to political citizenship (Janoski, 1998).

What are some reasonable conditions through the fulfillment of which transitions from one status of alienage to another can be carried out?[12] Length and nature of residency in a particular country are undoubtedly top among such criteria. Minimal knowledge of the language of the host country as well as some "civil knowledge" about the laws and governmental forms of that

POLITICAL MEMBERSHIP IN THE GLOBAL ERA 729

country are others. Criteria such as these can be formulated and applied reasonably.

Increasingly, it is what one does and less who one is, in terms of one's origin, which determines membership and citizenship claims. Applied to the case of contemporary Europe, this means very concretely: if an Italian or a Portuguese national can take up residence in Paris, Hamburg or London and run for office as well as vote in local elections in those countries after about six months, what is the justification for denying similar rights to a Turkish or Croatian national, to a Pakistani or to an Algerian who have resided in these countries, who have participated in the economy and civil society of these countries, who have been members of trade unions and religious groups, school boards and neighborhood associations? The liberal-democratic state is a "union of unions"; while the virtues and abilities that make an individual a good neighbor, a reliable coworker, an honest businessperson may not be immediately transferable to the virtues and abilities required by political citizenship, it is just not the case that there is an ontological divide between them. Hannah Arendt and other thinkers in the civic-republican tradition were wrong in their exaggerated attempt to segregate political from civic identities. Rather, as I have discussed elsewhere, we must focus on those social practices through which the transition from civil to political citizenship can be encouraged and the qualities of mind of an "enlarged mentality" can be cultivated. Such an enlarged mentality allows us to exercise civic imagination in taking the standpoint of the other(s) into account in order to woo their agreement on controversial and divisive norms that affect our lives and interactions. Such an enlarged mentality, which I see as a sine qua non for democratic citizenship, presupposes the virtues of membership and association, the ability to negotiate conflicting perspectives and loyalties, and the ability to distance oneself from one's most deeply held commitments in order to consider them from the hypothetical standpoint of a universalistic morality (Benhabib, 1994). The democratic public sphere in which these

SOCIAL RESEARCH

virtues are cultivated is not opposed to global civil society but is an aspect of it.

Immigration and Emigration: Are They Symmetrical?

Let me return to the central philosophical problem concerning the principles of liberal-democratic membership. Are there any justifiable conditions under which a liberal-democratic polity can close its borders to outsiders seeking admission? My short answer is "No, there are none." There are some justifiable restrictions on the quality and quantity of new immigration which nation-states can allow but never a situation when borders would be completely closed. Furthermore, many of these plausibly justifiable restrictions, like limiting the entry of individuals and groups who can be identified as posing a military, security or immunological threat to a country, themselves often permit serious contestation. Think of how the claim that certain individuals pose a "national security threat" can and has been misused throughout history to prevent political dissidents from entering countries and has led to the creation of categories of "unwanted" aliens. The virtues of liberal-democracies do not consist in their capacities to close their borders but in their capacities to hear the claims of those who, for whatever reasons, knock at our doors. Hearing these claims does not mean automatically granting them or recognizing them, but it does mean that the moral claim of the one who is seeking admission imposes a reciprocal duty upon us to examine, individually and singly, each case of those seeking membership in our midst.

There is, in other words, a fundamental human right to exit as well as to seek admission into political community, a right that is grounded in the recognition of the individual as an autonomous person entitled to the exercise of other rights. The fundamental right to human liberty entails the fundamental right to entry and exit. This fundamental right creates a set of reciprocal obligations

POLITICAL MEMBERSHIP IN THE GLOBAL ERA 731

and duties like not preventing the exit of those who want to leave or not to completely block off those who want to enter. Any restrictions to be placed upon the rights of exit and entry must be made compatible with, as well as being limited by, this fundamental human right.

This fundamental right of exit and entry is a moral claim and not a legal right, which can be defended by established authority with legal, coercive powers.[13] This right articulates a moral claim in that the recognition of the fundamental human liberty to express allegiance to the political order knowingly and willingly entails the right to exit when such allegiance is not forthcoming. Citizens are not prisoners of their respective states. Only a polity that violates other fundamental human liberties would also be one that limited the freedom of its citizens to exit.

In one of the few contemporary discussions of these issues, Michael Walzer argues that "The fact that individuals can rightly leave their own country, however, doesn't generate a right to enter another (any other). Immigration and emigration are morally asymmetrical" (Walzer, 1983, 40). This is wrong: the asymmetry of these rights cannot be maintained, and this for two reasons. The first ground is a pragmatic consideration that is also morally relevant. In a world where the surface of the earth is already divided into nation-states, or at least into political units that exercise sovereignty over their territory, the right to exit effectively means that one lands up on someone else's territory. There is literally nowhere to go in today's world ; at every stretch of the passage one would be crossing into the sovereign territory of some or other political entity. If this is so, then to acknowledge a human right to exit means at least to acknowledge a human right to entry. This right to entry, as I will argue below, must be distinguished from the claim to membership, but at this stage only the human right to entry is under consideration.

The second reason why this asymmetry breaks down is that the fundamental human right to exit is only meaningful if one can reverse moral perspectives and consider that for some to be able

SOCIAL RESEARCH

to go means for others that strangers will come but that we are all potentially strangers in other lands. If we want to argue that we have a right to leave then we are also saying that others have to recognize us potentially as strangers who may want to enter their country. But if we want this claim recognized for ourselves then we also must recognize it for others. It is only the mutual recognition of the reciprocal obligations generated by this right which give it meaning as a moral claim. There is a fundamental human right to exit only if there is also a fundamental human right to entry, to admittance, but not necessarily to membership.

What is the distinction between admittance and membership? All organized political communities have the right to control the criteria of membership, and procedures of inclusion and exclusion. Criteria which need to be fulfilled, qualifications which need to be met, and procedures that need to be followed are usually stipulated by all liberal democracies in granting access to membership and eventually citizenship. Admittance does not create an automatic entitlement to membership but it does entail the moral right to know how and why one can or cannot be a member, whether one will or will not be granted refugee status, permanent residency etc. In articulating these conditions as well, a liberal democratic polity must treat the other, the foreigner and the stranger in accordance with internationally recognized norms of human respect and dignity (cf. Walzer, 1983, 60). The claim of democratic sovereigns to define criteria of political inclusion is not an unconditional right. Democratic sovereignty and human rights considerations must mutually limit and control each other.

Liberal democracies are always under a burden of proof when policing their borders, therefore, to prove that the ways in which they do so do not violate fundamental human rights. A democratic state may wish to examine marriage certificates among citizens and non-citizens for their veracity, but a democratic state which subjects women to gynecological exams in order to test whether or not marriage was consummated, as Margaret Thatcher's England did, is violating fundamental human rights of equal treatment and respect of bodily integrity.

POLITICAL MEMBERSHIP IN THE GLOBAL ERA 733

Democratic states that are anxious to maintain certain standards of living among their population are free to regulate their labour markets such as to punish employers employing illegal aliens without proper documentation, at low wages and unjust conditions. But a democratic state cannot push entire categories of peoples away, as Germany since unification has attempted to do, with the argument that immigrants and asylum seekers affect the domestic standards of living negatively. Besides the dubious causal connections established in such assertions, there is also the more fundamental problem of the violation of human rights, be it those of asylum seekers under internationally recognized conventions, or the rights of foreign residents to claim political membership, with which I have dealt in this paper. It is minimally important to acknowledge that economic self-interest grounds can never alone serve as moral trumps, and that liberal democracies must seek to balance economic welfare considerations—if, in fact, it is the case that external immigration is affecting domestic markets as adversely as some argue—with commitment to, and respect for, fundamental human rights.

Sovereignty, Humans Rights and the Nation-State

In his 1923 work, *The Crisis of Parliamentary Democracy*, Carl Schmitt wrote:

> Every actual democracy rests on the principle that not only are equals equal but unequals will not be treated equally. Democracy requires, therefore, first homogeneity and second—if the need arises—elimination or eradication of heterogeneity... Equality is only interesting and valuable politically so long as it has substance, and for that reason the possibility and the risk of inequality.... <that> every adult person, simply as a person, should eo ipso be politically equal to every other person, this is a liberal, not a democratic idea" (Schmitt, [1923], 1985, 9-11).

SOCIAL RESEARCH

Schmitt drives a wedge between liberal and democratic conceptions of equality. While he understands liberalism to advocate universal moral equality, he views democracy as only stipulating the equality of all as members of a sovereign people. This argument neglects the specificity of the modern as opposed to ancient projects of democracy.

For the moderns, the moral equality of individuals qua human beings and their equality as citizens, are imbricated in one another. The modern social contract of the nation-state bases its legitimacy on the principle that the consociates of the nation are entitled to equal treatment as right-bearing persons precisely because they are human beings. Citizenship rights rest on this more fundamental moral equality that individuals enjoy as persons. "The Rights of Man" and "The Rights of the Citizen" are coeval for the moderns.

To be sure there are conflicts as well as tensions in these formulations: every national social contract circumscribes the circle of its citizens, thus creating distinctions among those who are signatories of the social contract and those to whom the contract applies but who have no standing as signatories. Modern liberal democracies, established in the wake of the American and French Revolutions, proclaim at one and the same time that the consociates of the sovereign body are to treat one another as rights-bearing individuals in virtue of being human beings. At the same time, these very proclamations, articulated in the name of universal truths of nature, reason, or God, define and delimit boundaries, create exclusions within the sovereign people as well as without. There are "mere auxiliaries to the Republic" within, as Kant called women, children and propertyless servants within, and foreigners and strangers without. This constitutive tension does not arise, as Schmidt assumes, because liberalism and democracy contradict one another. Rather, there is a constitutive dilemma in the attempt of modern nation states to justify their legitimacy through recourse to universalist moral principles of human rights which then get particularistically circumscribed. The tension

POLITICAL MEMBERSHIP IN THE GLOBAL ERA 735

between the universalistic scope of the principles that legitimize the social contract of the modern nation, and the claim of this nation to define itself as a closed community, plays itself out in the history of the reforms and revolutions of the last two centuries.

When Hannah Arendt wrote that "the right to have rights" was a fundamental claim as well as an insoluble political problem, she did not mean that aliens, foreigners and residents did not possess any rights (Arendt, [1951], 1979, 296). In certain circumstances, as with Jews in Germany, Greek, and Armenian nationals in the period of the founding of the republic of Turkey (1923), with German refugees in Vichy France, to select but few cases, entire groups of peoples were "denaturalized," or "denationalized" and lost the protection of a sovereign legal body. For Arendt, neither the theoretical nor the institutional solutions to this problem were at hand. Theoretically, she needed to have explored the constitutive tension between national sovereignty and human rights claims further. Institutionally, several arrangements have emerged since the end of World War II that express the learning process of the nations of this world in dealing with the horrors of the past century: the limiting and testing of parliamentarian majorities through constitutional courts, particularly in the domain of human rights issues; the 1951 Convention relating to the Status of Refugees, the creation of the UN High Commissioner on Refugees (UNHCR), the institution of the World Court, and most recently of an International Criminal Court through the treaty of Rome (Robinson 1999). While procedures of constitutional review, which are becoming more prevalent in European political practice through the development of the European Court of Justice, can help protect the fundamental human and civil rights of ethnic, religious, linguistic, sexual and other minorities from the tyranny of the majority, the UN conventions remain non-enforceable humanitarian guidelines. To this day the authority of the World Court of Justice in the Hague is contested, while the United States has refused to sign the Treaty of Rome leading to the establishment of the International Court of Justice. Even

736 SOCIAL RESEARCH

this International Court deals first and foremost with "crimes against humanity." There are still no global courts of justice with the jurisdiction to punish sovereign states for the way they treat refugees, foreigners and aliens. Nor is there a global law enforcement agency that would carry out such injunctions. In this domain, voluntarily self-incurred obligations on the part of nation-states through the signing of treaties remain the norm.

Yet the treatment of aliens, foreigners, and others in our midst is a crucial test case for the moral conscience as well as political reflexivity of liberal democracies. Defining the identity of the sovereign nation is itself a process of fluid, open, and contentious public debate: the lines separating "we" and "you," "us" and "them," more often than not, rest on unexamined prejudices, ancient battles, historical injustices, and sheer administrative fiat. The beginnings of every modern nation-state carry the traces of some violence and injustice. So far Carl Schmitt is right. Nonetheless, modern liberal democracies are self-limiting collectivities which at one and the same time constitute the nation as sovereign all the while proclaiming that the sovereignty of this nation derives its legitimacy from its adherence to fundamental human rights principles. "We, the people," is an inherently fraught formula, containing in its very articulation the constitutive dilemmas of universal respect for human rights and particularistic sovereignty claims (Ackerman, 1991). The rights of foreigners and aliens, whether they be refugees or guest workers, asylum seekers or adventurers, indicate that threshold, that boundary, at the site of which the identity of "we, the people" is defined and renegotiated, bounded and unraveled, circumscribed or rendered fluid.

Notes

[1]Cited by Muenz, "Migrants, Aliens, Citizens. European Migrations and its Consequences," Conference Paper presented for the European Forum, 1995-96 Citizenship Project, 14. After the passage of the new "asylum laws," first on June 26, 1992 and then on July 27, 1993, Germany is controlling its borders and the number of foreigners allowed into the

POLITICAL MEMBERSHIP IN THE GLOBAL ERA 737

country much more effectively. See also Council of Europe Publishing, *Recent Demographic Developments* in Europe, 1996: 18, and 31-32.

[2]Next to foreign workers, asylum applicants, and refugees, the third significant category of foreigners in Germany are the "ethnic Germans." They are not native-born Germans, but ethnic Germans who since the thirteenth-century have settled in various central European, Baltic, and formerly Soviet territories. After WWII, millions of this group, referred to as the "Vertriebene" (expellees) and "Aussiedler" (out-settlers), were expelled from the Soviet Union and other central and east European countries. A 1953 statute defines the Aussiedler as "Volkszugeroehige," belonging to the people, and Article 116 (1) of the Basic Law of Germany allows them with the right to resettle in Germany. In the last twenty years some 1,900, 000 expellees from Poland, Romania, and the former Soviet Union have entered Germany. See Kanstroom 1993: 165-167. For an overview of the changing composition of immigrant groups in various European countries, see Messina 1996: 130-154.

[3]The persecution of the Kurdish population in the northern and southeastern regions of Turkey in particular, and the continuing conflict between the Kurdish Communist Party (known in German as the PKK) and the Turkish government, have given rise to a new group of asylum seekers—ethnic Kurds who are officially Turkish citizens but persecuted by a country friendly to Germany and seeking future membership in the European Union. In 1995, 25,000 Turkish citizens are reported to have sought asylum in Germany; they were preceded by thirty-three thousand citizens of the states of former Yugoslavia. The recent capture of the fugitive leader of the PKK (Communist Party of Kurdistan), Abdullah Ocalan, has led to cofrontations in all major European citizens among Kurdish sympathizers and local and international government authorities.

[4]See Article 8 of C. Part Two. "1. Citizenship of the Union is hereby established. Every Person holding the Nationality of a Member State shall be a citizen of the Union." Facsimile reproduction on file with the author.

[5]The institution of citizenship among individuals who do not have a common language, a common public sphere and effective channels of participation is giving rise to a number of very important and compelling contemporary debates in political theory and jurisprudence. Some see European citizenship as a fig leaf to cover the considerable divestment of the democratic powers of sovereign peoples to an anonymous "Eurocracy" sitting in Brussels and Geneva, and still more others warn of the growing "democracy deficit" in the Union. Citizenship without participation looms on the horizon, they argue. Preuss 1995: 267-

738 SOCIAL RESEARCH

281; Balibar 1996 : 355-376, and Lehning and Weale, eds. 1997. See also special section on "Citizenship and Migration," in *Constellations. An International Journal of Critical and Democratic Theory*, 4, No 3 (January 1988).

[6]"Fuer ein Europa der politischen und sozialen Grundrechte." Report of the "Committee of the Wise" under the Directorship of Maria de Lourdes 1996. Other members of this Committee of the "wise" are: Eduardo Garcia de Enterria, Hartmut Kaelble, Louka Katseli, Frederic Pascal, Bengt Westerberg, Shirley Williams. By contrast, Jytte Klausen pleads for a strong differentiation of citizenship rights from redistributive policies in: 1995, 244-67. While in the European Union context the trend is toward the uniformization of such rights and redistributive benefits through the implementation of Union-wide social rights and benefits, for third-country nationals the curtailment of social rights and benefits, which they have hitherto enjoyed, looms in the offing. Klaus sees an inevitable trade-off between the continuance of protective welfare communities on the one hand, globalization and the development of less exclusionary absorption and immigration politics on the other. 1995: 266. The danger in the current context though is that the political voicelessness of third country nationals in the EU will make it all the more likely that their social rights will be curtailed without, however, a corresponding liberalization trade-off in naturalization and immigration policies. See also, Abram de Swaan 1997: 561-575. For a helpful overview of the current state of policy and jurisprudential reasoning in the Union, and Shaw 1997.

[7]The Dublin Convention and the Second Schengen agreement were signed in June 1990. Schengen included initially Belgium, the Netherlands, Luxemburg, France, and Germany. Italy joined the group in December 1990, and Portugal and Spain in June 1991. Both agreements contain rules for determining a "responsible state" which agrees to process an applicant for asylum from a non-EU country. The Schengen Convention attempts to abolish border controls along the common frontiers of the parties and to compensate for the relaxation of borders by more vigilant migration and law enforcement policies at airports. There is also the establishment of a Schengen Information System that will create an electronic database to facilitate controls of criminals and terrorists. See Neuman 1993: 506-07; Kanastroom 1993: 198ff.; Klusmeyer 1993: 98.

[8]Few notable exceptions to this widespread neglect of citizenship issues have been, J. M. Barbalet 1988; Shklar 1991: 386-439. Undoubtedly, conditions of globalization the world over are leading to a renewal of interest in citizenship in political theory as well, see Spinner, 1994.

POLITICAL MEMBERSHIP IN THE GLOBAL ERA 739

[9]Although this paper focuses on Europe in general, and Germany in particular, with the introduction of NAFTA similar developments are taking place in the North American Continent. So far, the fact that USA and Canada define themselves as "countries of immigration" has created a situation that is normatively different from that of most European Union Countries that do not consider themselves immigrant societies. The passage of proposition 187 in California, the ensuing battle against the curtailment of the social benefits of non-legal resident aliens, the shameful treatment of Haitian refugees as well as recent administrative irregularities at the INS about adequate background checks of prospective citizens etc. are all events pointing to the growing salience of these issues for the USA. Normatively, the theory and practice of acceptance into the political commonwealth through incorporation into civil society is most clearly practiced in Canada and the United States. The practices of immigration and naturalization in these countries present a clear alternative to the models prevailing on the European continent at the present time. See the remarkable arguments of Owen Fiss to defend some of welfare rights and benefits of legal and illegal resident aliens of the USA on the basis of constitutional jurisprudence. Fiss 1998:4-6.

[10]The United Kingdom does permit voting rights to those who hold Commonwealth citizenship.

[11]Several of Rawls' students, aware of the magnitude of this gap, have expanded the premises of political liberalism into the field of international justice. Cf. O'Neil 1986; Pogge 1992: 42; John Rawls began to address some of these issues in his "Law of Nations," Steven Shute and Susan Hurley, eds., Oxford Amnesty Lectures 1993.

[12]From the standpoint of political philosophy, we are entering the domain of administrative detail which should be better left to legislators and bureaucrats. As Hegel is reported to have quipped about Fichte's political theory, he did not have to be concerned about passports! Yet today the passport has become the symbolic document which represents all the perplexities and inequities of current citizenship regimes and practices in its pages. It is no less worthy of philosophical reflection than the postcard!

Also, criteria of immigration, from length of residency to language requirements, can impact diverse sectors of the foreign population of a particular country very differently. These issues of "differential impact" can, in turn, enable or hinder the acquisition of citizenship rights by different groups. For example, a language proficiency proof of some sort seems to me an eminently reasonable requirement on the part of a host country in granting residency and citizenship permits to foreigners. On

740 SOCIAL RESEARCH

the other hand, this requirement will most likely disadvantage women, who usually, though not in all cases, enter the host country under family unification clauses and who do not participate in the civil society and economy of the public sphere of the host country or do so to a very limited extent. Under these circumstances, language proficiency requirements, which would not be accompanied by subsidized language instruction could be discriminatory against women and the elderly members of the foreign population.

[13]This distinction was brought to my attention by Professor Jürgen Habermas. However, although no authority exists for coercing nation-states to accept refugees and asylum-seekers into their countries, citizens' groups of the concerned countries may themselves litigate against their own government and agencies on the grounds that these may have violated fundamental human rights, the constitution, administrative procedures, etc. In such cases, concerned citizens act as the advocates of the stranger and the foreigner against their own governmental authority. Of course this legal right to "sue" your own state authorities is not equivalent to a coercive right against them, but as recent battles over the treatment of refugees, asylum seekers and immigrants the world-over show us, there is "communicative power" that derives from such actions and that may attain coercive influence.

References

Ackerman, Bruce, *We, the People* (Cambridge, MA: Belknap Press at Harvard, 1991).

Arendt, Hannah, *The Origins of Totalitarianism* (New York: Harcourt, Brace and Jovanovich, 1979 [1951]).

Aristotle, *Politics*, Jowett, Benjamin, trans., in: *Basic Works of Aristotle*, Richard McKeon, ed. (New York: Random House, 1941).

Auslaenderrecht, Die Gesetzestexte des "Deutschen Bundesrechts." Version of September 12, 1996 (Frankfurt: Suhrkamp, 1997).

Barber, Benjamin, *Jihad vs. McWorld. How Globalism and Tribalism are Reshaping the World* (Times Books: New York, 1995).

Benhabib, Seyla, "Strange Multiplicities. The Politics of Identity and Difference in a Global Context," *The Divided Self: Identity and Globalization*, Macalaster College International Program, (Spring 1997a): 27–59.

Benhabib, Seyla, "Wer Sind Wir? Probleme politischer Identitaeten im ausgehenden 20. Jahrhundert," Working Papers in Political Science, Institut fuer Hoehere Studien. No. 42. Vienna. 1997b.

POLITICAL MEMBERSHIP IN THE GLOBAL ERA 741

Benhabib, Seyla, *Demokratische Gleichheit und Kulturelle Vielfalt. Die Horkheimer Vorlesungen* (Frankfurt: Fischer, 1999a).

Benhabib, Seyla, "Germany Opens Up," *The Nation,* June 21 1999b: 6.

Benhabib, Seyla, *Situating the Self. Gender, Community and Postmodernism in Contemporary Ethics* (New York and London: Routledge and Polity, 1994).

Balibar, Etienne, "Is European Citizenship Possible?" *Public Culture* 8 (1996): 355-376.

Barbalet, J. M., *Citizenship: Rights, Struggle and Class Inequality* (Minneapolis: University of Minnesota Press, 1988).

Bauboeck, Rainer, "The Crossing and Blurring of Boundaries in International Migration. Challenges for Social and Political Theory," in *Blurred Boundaries: Migration, Ethnicity, Citizenship,* Bauboeck, Rainer and Rundell, John, eds. (Vienna: Ashgate Publications, 1998).

Bauboeck, Rainer, *Transnational Citizenship: Membership and Rights in International Migration* (Cornwall: Edward Elgar, 1994).

Beiner, Ronald, ed., *Theorizing Citizenship* (Albany, NY: SUNY Press, 1995).

Brubacker, Rogers, *Citizenship and Nationhood in France and Germany* (Cambridge, MA: Harvard University Press, 1992).

Constellations, *An International Journal of Critical and Democratic Theory* 4, No 3 (January 1998). Special section on Citizenship and Immigration.

Carens, Joe, "Aliens and Citizens: The Case for Open Borders," in: Beiner, Ronald, ed., *Theorizing Citizenship* (Albany, NY: SUNY Press, 1995: 229-255).

Cohen, Jean L., "Changing Paradigms of Citizenship and the Exclusiveness of the Demos," *International Journal of Sociology* Winter 2000. Forthcoming.

Council of Europe Publishing, *Recent Demographic Developments in Europe* (Belgium, 1996).

De Swaan, Abram, "The Receding Prospects for Transnational Social Policy," *Theory and Society. Renewal and Critique in Social Theory* 26:4 (August 1997): 561-575. Special issue on recasting citizenship.

Fiss, Owen, "The Immigrant as Pariah," *Boston Review* 23:5 (October/November 1998): 4-6.

Friedman, Jonathan, *Cultural Identity and Global Process* (London: Sage Publications, 1995).

Galston, William, *Liberal Purposes: Goods, Virtues, and Duties in the Liberal State* (Cambridge, MA: Cambridge University Press, 1991).

Heiberg, Marianne, ed., *Subduing Sovereignty. Sovereignty and the Right to Intervene* (London: Pinter Publishers, 1994).

742   SOCIAL RESEARCH

Honig. Bonnie, *No Place Like Home* (Princeton University Press, Princeton, NJ: forthcoming).

Honig, Bonnie, "Immigrant America? How 'Foreignness' Solves Democracy's Problems," *Social Text* 3 (Fall 1998): 1-27.

Huber, Ernst, R., *Dokumente zur deutschen Verfassungsgeschichte.* Vol. 1. (Stuttgart: Kohlhammer, 1961).

Ignatieff, Michael, *Blood and Belonging. Journeys into the New Nationalism* (New York: Farrar, Strauss and Giroux, 1994).

Janoski, Thomas, *Citizenship and Civil Society* (New York: Cambridge University Press, 1998).

Judt, Tony, *A Grand Illusion? An Essay on Europe* (New York: Hill and Wang, 1996).

Kant, Immanuel, "Perpetual Peace," in: *On History,* Lewis White Beck, trans. (Indianapolis and New York: The Bobbs-Merrill Co., 1963: 85-137).

Kanstroom, Daniel, "Wer Sind Wir Wieder? Laws of Asylum, Immigration, and Citizenship in the Struggle for the Soul of the New Germany," *Yale Journal of International Law* 18: 155 (1993).

Kessler, Charles R., "The Promise of American Citizenship," in: *Immigration and Citizenship in the 21st Century,* Pickus, Noah, M. J., ed. (New York: Rowman and Littlefield Publishers, 1998: 3-41).

Klausen, Jytte, "Social Rights Advocacy and State Building. T. H. Marshall in the Hands of the Reformers," *World Politics* 47 (January 1995): 244-267.

Klusmeyer, Douglas B., "Aliens, Immigrants, and Citizens: The Politics of Inclusion in the Federal Republic of Germany," *Daedalus* 122:3 (1993): 81-114. Summer Issue on "Reconstructing Nations and States."

Kleger, Heinz, "Transnationale Staatsbuergerschaft oder: Laesst sich Staatsbuergerschaft entnationalisieren?" *Archiv fuer Rechts- und Sozialphilosophie* 62 (1995):85-99.

Kristeva, Julia, *Strangers to Ourselves,* Roudiez, Leon S., trans. (New York: Columbia University Press, 1991).

Kymlicka, Will and Norman, Wayne, "Return of the Citizen: A Survey of Recent Work on Citizenship Theory," in: Beiner, Rondal, ed., *Theorizing Citizenship* (Albany, NY: SUNY Press, 1995), pp. 283-323.

Lehning, Percy and Weale, Albert, eds. *Citizenship, Democracy and Justice in the New Europe* (London and New York: Routledge, 1997).

Locke, John, *Second Treatise of Civic Government.* [1690], McPherson, C. B., ed. (Indiana: Hackett, 1980).

Marshall, T. H. *Citizenship and Social Class and Other Essays* (London: Cambridge University Press, 1950).

POLITICAL MEMBERSHIP IN THE GLOBAL ERA 743

Mendes, Candido and Soares, Luis E. *Cultural Pluralism, Identity, and Globalization* (Rio de Janeiro. UNESCO/ISSC/EDUCAM publications, 1996).

Messina, Anthony, "The Not So Silent Revolution. Postwar Migration to Western Europe," *World Politics* 49 (October 1996): 130-154.

Muenz, Rainer, "Migrants, Aliens, Citizens. European Migrations and its Consequences," Conference Paper presented for the European Forum, 1995-96 Citizenship Project, European University Institute, Florence.

Neuman, Gerald. L., "Buffer Zones Against Refugees: Dublin, Schengen and the German Asylum Amendment," *Virginia Journal of International Law.* 33:503 (1993): 503-526.

O'Neil, Onora, *Faces of Hunger: An Essay on Poverty, Justice and Development* (New York: George Allen and Unwin, 1986).

Pintasilgo, Maria de Lourdes, "Fuer ein Europa der politischen und sozialen Grundrechte," Report of the "Committee of the Wise". Brussels. Publications of the European Commission (October 1995-February 1996).

Plotke, David, "Immigration and Political Incorporation in the Contemporary United States," Manuscript. 1996.

Pogge, Thomas, "Cosmopolitanism and Sovereignty," *Ethics* 103 (1992).

Preuss, Ulrich, "Problems of a Concept of European Citizenship," *European Law Journal* 1:3 (November 1995): 267-281.

Rawls, John, *Political Liberalism* (New York: Columbia University Press, 1993).

Robinson, Darryl, "Defining 'Crimes Against Humanity' at the Rome Conference," *The American Journal of International Law* (January 1999): 43-57.

Sandel, Michael, *Democracy's Discontent. America in Search of a Public Philosophy* (Cambridge, MA: Belknap Press at Harvard University, 1996).

Schmitt, Carl, *The Crisis of Parliamentary Democracy*, Kennedy, Ellen, trans. (Cambridge, MA: MIT Press, 1985).

Shaw, Joe, "The Many Pasts and Futures of European Citizenship in the European Union," *European Law Review* 22 (1997).

Shklar, Judith, "American Citizenship. The Quest for Inclusion," in *The Tanner Lectures on Human Values, vol. 10* (Cambridge, MA: Harvard University Press, 1991: 386-439).

Spinner, Jeff, *The Boundaries of Citizenship. Race, Ethnicity, and Nationality in the Liberal State* (Baltimore and London: the Johns Hopkins University Press, 1994).

Soysal, Yasemin, *Limits of Citizenship: Migrants and Postnational Membership in Europe* (Chicago: University of Chicago Press, 1994).

SOCIAL RESEARCH

SOPEMI Publications (The OECD Continuous Reporting System for Migration), Paris, 1998.

Van Amersfoort, Hans, *Immigrants and the Formation of Minority Groups: The Dutch Experience* (Cambridge: Cambridge University Press, 1982).

Weiler, J. H., "Does Europe Need a Constitution? Demos, Telos and the German Maastricht Decision," *European Law Journal* 1:3 (November 1995): 219-258.

Walzer, Michael, *Spheres of Justice. A Defense of Pluralism and Equality* (New York: Basic Books, 1983).

Wertheimer, Jack, *Unwelcome Strangers. East European Jews in Imperial Germany* (New York: Oxford University Press, 1987).

[7]

Multicultural states and intercultural citizens[1]

WILL KYMLICKA
Department of Philosophy, Queen's University, Kingston, Canada

ABSTRACT

Citizenship refers to membership in a political community, and hence designates a relationship between the individual and the state. One way to explore the idea of 'multicultural citizenship', therefore, is to identify its images of the state and of the individual. First, we can ask about multiculturalism at the level of the state: what would it mean for the constitution, institutions and laws of the state to be multicultural? Second, we can ask about interculturalism at the level of the individual citizen: what sorts of knowledge, beliefs, virtues and dispositions would an intercultural citizen possess? Ideally, these two levels should work together: there should be a fit between our model of the multicultural state and the intercultural citizen. This paper identifies three conflicts between promoting desirable forms of multiculturalism within state institutions and promoting desired forms of interculturalism within individual citizens and discusses the challenges they raise for theories of multicultural education.

KEYWORDS *citizenship, cosmopolitanism, multiculturalism, nationalism, tolerance*

INTRODUCTION

THE TERM 'citizenship' typically refers to membership in a political community, and hence designates a relationship between the individual and the state. Any conception of citizenship, therefore, will inevitably make assumptions about both poles of this relationship, i.e. about the individual and the state. Different models of citizenship rest upon different images of the nature of the state, and/or on different images of the nature of the individuals who belong to it.

One way to explore the idea of 'multicultural' or 'intercultural' citizenship,[2] therefore, is to try to identify its underlying images of the state and of the individual. On the one hand, we can ask about multiculturalism at the level of the state: what would it mean for the constitution, institutions and laws of the state to be multicultural? I will call this the question of the nature of the 'multicultural state'. On the other hand, we can ask about interculturalism at the level of the individual citizen: what sorts of knowledge, beliefs, virtues, habits and dispositions would an intercultural citizen possess? I will call this the question of the 'intercultural citizen'.

Ideally, these two levels should work together in any conception of citizenship: there should be a 'fit' between our model of the multicultural state and our model of the intercultural citizen. The sort of multicultural reforms we seek at the level of the state should help nurture and reinforce the desired forms of intercultural skills and knowledge at the level of individual citizens. Conversely, the intercultural dispositions we encourage within individual citizens should help support and reinforce the institutions of a multicultural state.

That is the ideal. My aim in this paper, however, is to suggest that there are some unresolved tensions between these two levels of analysis. Existing models of the multicultural state do not always fit neatly with our models of the intercultural citizen. Some multicultural reforms at the level of the state reduce the need or incentive for desired forms of interculturalism at the level of individual citizens. Indeed, some multicultural state reforms are demanded precisely in order to avoid the need for individuals to acquire greater levels of intercultural skills and knowledge. Conversely, some proposals to promote increased intercultural skills and knowledge within individual citizens are intended precisely to stave off calls for greater institutional changes within the state.

Thus, the connection between multicultural states and intercultural citizens is complex. As I will try to illustrate, there can be conflicts between promoting desirable forms of multiculturalism within state institutions and promoting desired forms of interculturalism within individual citizens. I believe that existing theories of intercultural citizenship have not yet fully recognized or explored these potential tensions, or developed principles for telling us how we should respond to them. My aim, in this paper, is not to resolve these difficult issues, but simply to identify some of the conflicts, and to highlight some of the dilemmas they raise for our broader theories of intercultural citizenship.

The paper begins by exploring what I take to be the main characteristics of the new models of a multicultural state, and how it differs from older models of the homogenous nation-state. It will then consider some of the main

Kymlicka: Multicultural states and intercultural citizens 149

characteristics of the new models of interculturalism at the level of individual citizens. Finally, we will consider some of the possible tensions between them.

MULTICULTURAL STATES

What are the defining characteristics of a multicultural state? There are many definitions and models of multicultural states in the literature, often tied to the specifics of individual countries.[3] However, I perceive that they all reject the earlier models of the unitary, homogenous nation-state. In order to understand the idea of a multicultural state, therefore, we need first to understand the older model of a homogenous nation-state, and why it has been rejected.

Until recently, most states around the world have aspired to be 'nation-states'. In this model, the state was seen as the possession of a dominant national group, which used the state to privilege its identity, language, history, culture, literature, myths, religion and so on, and which defined the state as the expression of its nationhood. (This dominant group was usually the majority group, but sometimes a minority was able to establish dominance – e.g. whites in South Africa under the apartheid regime, or *criollo* elites in some Latin American countries). Anyone who did not belong to this dominant national group was subject to either assimilation or exclusion.[4]

There is nothing 'natural' about such nation-states. Very few countries around the world are mono-national (Iceland, Portugal and the Koreas are the most frequently cited examples). In most countries, this kind of national homogeneity had to be actively constructed by the state through a range of 'nation-building' policies that encouraged the preferred national identity, while suppressing any alternative identities. Public policies were used to promote and consolidate a common national language, national history and mythology, national heroes, national symbols, a national literature, a national education system, a national media, a national military, in some cases a national religion, and so on. Any groups which resisted these sorts of nationalizing policies were subject not only to political disempowerment, but also typically, to economic discrimination, and to various forms of 'demographic engineering' (e.g. pressuring members of the group to disperse, and/or promoting settlement by members of the dominant group into the homeland of indigenous/minority groups). These and other policies were aimed at constructing the ideal of a nation-state.

Virtually every Western democracy has pursued this ideal at some stage. As discussed later, an increasing number of Western democracies have abandoned this goal in favor of a more 'multicultural' model of the state. But at one point or another, virtually every Western democracy has sought to define itself as a mono-national state. The only exception to this pattern in the West that I am familiar with, is Switzerland. Switzerland has never attempted to try to construct a single national language on the territory of the state. It has always accepted that the French- and Italian-speaking minorities would exist as distinct linguistic groups into the indefinite future. But every other Western democracy – including some that are very diverse, and that now pride themselves on their diversity, like Canada – has at some point or other had the goal of inculcating a common national language and culture.

However, this nation-state model has increasingly been challenged and contested by all sorts of groups. There are many groups within the territory of the state which have their own language, their own history, their own culture, their own heroes, their own symbols. Such groups face either exclusion or assimilation by this process of nation-building. As a result, various groups, particularly indigenous peoples and other kinds of national groups, have always contested this attempt to construct states through a form of homogeneous nation-building, and advocated instead for a more 'multicultural' model of the state.[5]

What would a multicultural state look like? The precise details vary from country to country, for reasons discussed later. The sort of state reforms demanded by African-Americans in the USA differs dramatically from the sort of reforms demanded by indigenous Maori in New Zealand, or by Chinese immigrants in Canada. However, there are some general principles, which I think are common to all of these different struggles for a multicultural state. First and foremost, a multicultural state involves the repudiation of the older idea that the state is a possession of a single national group. Instead, the state must be seen as belonging equally to all citizens. Second, as a consequence, a multicultural state repudiates those nation-building policies that assimilate or exclude members of minority or non-dominant groups. Instead, it accepts that individuals should be able to access state institutions, and to act as full and equal citizens in political life, without having to hide or deny their ethnocultural identity. The state accepts an obligation to accord the history, language and culture of non-dominant groups the same recognition and accommodation that is accorded to the dominant group. Third, a multicultural state acknowledges the historic injustice that was done to minority/non-dominant groups by these older policies of assimilation and exclusion, and manifests a willingness to offer some sort of remedy or rectification for them.

These three inter-connected ideas – repudiating the idea of the state as belonging to the dominant group; replacing assimilationist and exclusionary nation-building policies with policies of recognition and accommodation; acknowledging historic injustice and offering amends for it – seem to me to be common to virtually all real-world struggles for 'multiculturalism' at the level of the state.

Kymlicka: Multicultural states and intercultural citizens 151

However, these commonalities are often dwarfed by the differences between various models of a multicultural state. The precise way in which minority groups wish to be recognized and accommodated, or to have their historic injustices amended, varies enormously from country to country, as well as between different minorities within a single country.

The sort of multicultural state desired by various groups depends, in large part, on the capacities and aspirations of each group, which in turn depends on its numbers and territorial concentration, which in turn depends on the forms and levels of mistreatment it has received historically at the hands of the state. At one end of the spectrum, we can think about sizeable groups that are concentrated on a more or less defined historic territory or homeland, that still form a majority within that territory, that have retained their language, and that historically governed themselves. In such cases, it is almost inevitable that the group will seek to establish (or rather re-establish) some form of self-government, typically through some form of federal or quasi-federal territorial autonomy, with public institutions operating in its own language. Examples would include the Québécois in Canada, the Catalans and Basques in Spain, the Flemish in Belgium, the Puerto Ricans in the USA, the French- and Italian-speaking minorities in Switzerland, the German-speaking minority of South Tyrol in Italy, to name a few. In all of these cases, the shift to a more multicultural state takes the form of replacing a unitary state with a federal or consociational state, replacing a unilingual state with a bilingual or multilingual state, and replacing the idea of a nation-state with that of a 'multination' state.[6] These can be said, perhaps, to represent the most extensive sort of multiculturalism at the level of the state, since they involve the most extensive form of sharing power between majority and minority, and they extend the most complete form of official recognition to the language and culture of the historically subordinate group.

At the other end of the spectrum, we can think about small groups of recent immigrants or refugees who have left their country of origin, and have no historic territory or homeland within their new country, and no history of self-government. Given their size and dispersion, territorial autonomy is unlikely to be feasible. Moreover, they may be too small and dispersed to be able to run many of their own public institutions – e.g. there may not be enough members to support their own high schools or hospitals. In these cases, the shift to a more multicultural state is likely to take the form of fighting any stigmas or barriers that prevent members of the group from fully integrating into the dominant society, or from being fully accepted as equal citizens. In many cases, the state historically defined the nation in a racially- or religiously-exclusive way – e.g. as a white/Christian nation. These exclusionary definitions of the nation must be challenged and repudiated if newer immigrant and refugee groups are to be fully accepted and integrated. These historic biases against certain races or religions are often explicit in laws that define who is eligible for admission, or citizenship, or to hold public office. Replacing such exclusionary laws is the first step towards a multicultural state. But these biases are also likely to be implicit in a much wider range of public institutions and policies: from the school curriculum to Sunday-closing legislation to state symbols. The pursuit of a more multicultural state, in this context therefore, is also likely to involve a long-term and systematic attempt to re-examine all areas of public policy and public institutions, to see if they contain hidden biases that continue to stigmatize or disadvantage members of immigrant groups. A 'multicultural' state, in this context, may still be a unitary state – i.e. it may not have any explicit form of territorial or consociational power-sharing between dominant group and newer immigrant groups – and it may still only have one official language. But it will make efforts to ensure that all public institutions, from the schools to the police and courts to media and the hospitals, fight discrimination, accommodate diversity, promote integration, and present a more open and inclusive image of the nation.

In between these two cases of sizeable and powerful national groups governing themselves on their historic territory, and recent immigrant groups seeking fair terms of integration, we can find a range of groups with varying demands for state reform. In some cases, we find historic groups that are quite numerous and who remain primarily concentrated on their historic homeland, but who no longer form a majority on that territory, perhaps as a result of deliberate state attempts to 'swamp' the group with settlers from the dominant group, and the refusal by the state to respect historic land rights. This the case of many indigenous peoples throughout the Americas. Groups, which once controlled large territories, prior to European colonization, have often been reduced to small villages surrounded by European or *mestizo* settlers. These groups have also typically experienced out-migration, as some members of the group move to the cities in search of jobs. The group therefore may be found both within rural villages on their historic homeland, on the one hand, and in an urban diaspora population, on the other, which may have varying levels of ongoing connection back to their home villages.

Here, the quest for a multicultural state is obviously more complex. Different indigenous groups are likely to need and desire different forms of recognition, accommodation and rectification. The needs and aspirations of the urban diaspora in terms of education, political representation, language and land claims will obviously differ from those living in the rural villages. For the rural villages, achieving some level of local self-government is likely to be a major demand. However, local governments have limitations. Village-level governments can control primary schools, but may not have the numbers or resources to run their own high schools or universities. They can run their own health-care clinics, but not their own hospitals. They can regulate land use locally, but cannot control regional economic development policies and natural resource projects. All of these can only be legislated, funded and administered at levels higher than the local village. Throughout the Americas we therefore see increasing attempts to try to create indigenous governance structures above the level of the local village, often by uniting different indigenous clans/tribes/peoples into a single regional governance structure.[7]

This brief sketch therefore, makes it clear that it is quite misleading to talk about a single model of the 'multicultural state'. There are enormous variations in the sorts of state reforms that are demanded, not only between different countries, but also between different types of groups within a single country (e.g. immigrants versus indigenous peoples), or even within the same type of group, due to differing histories of dispersion/relocation/resettlement (e.g. urban versus rural indigenous populations). Charles Taylor calls this 'deep diversity' (Taylor, 1991), and says that it is a defining characteristic of a multicultural politics of recognition. A genuinely multicultural state recognizes not only that citizens are different in their language and culture, but also that citizens are different in different ways, and so will relate to the state in different ways, with different forms of multicultural membership in the larger state. For some, multiculturalism will involve reducing barriers to integration in the mainstream society, so that they can relate directly to the state; for others it will involve enhancing powers of self-government, so that they relate to the state in a more federal or consociational manner, mediated by their participation in their own group's autonomous government. A 'multicultural state' is one which reforms itself to enable these various forms of multicultural membership in the state.

INTERCULTURAL CITIZENS

Let me now shift levels, and focus on the individuals who belong to this multicultural state. I call this the question of the 'intercultural citizen'. What is an intercultural citizen, and how would he/she deal with diversity? What sorts of habits, beliefs and virtues would an intercultural citizen possess and use when dealing with diversity?

As noted earlier, it is important that our conception of the intercultural citizen 'matches' our model of the multicultural state. For example, it is important that intercultural citizens are able and willing to create and sustain these new forms of a multicultural state. A multicultural state will not come into existence unless it has the support of most of its citizens (at least in a democracy, where popular support is required for significant political reforms).

This means, at a minimum, that a sufficient number of citizens must support the three general principles of the multicultural state, outlined earlier: i.e. that the state is not a possession of the dominant national group, but belongs equally to all citizens; that assimilationist and exclusionary nation-building policies should be replaced with policies of recognition and accommodation; and that historic injustice should be acknowledged. If a sufficient number of citizens do not endorse these political principles, multicultural state reforms will not be sustainable.

This is the minimal first step towards developing a conception of the intercultural citizen. But, this first step is already a difficult one to take. Accepting these three principles often requires fighting against decades or centuries of deeply-rooted prejudices and biases against minority and non-dominant groups. Education has an important role to play here – for example, in teaching children about the reality of historic injustice, and in exploring why earlier ideologies of nationhood were illegitimate.

Much has been written about the sort of education that is needed to inculcate support for these political principles of the multicultural state. However, for the purposes of this paper, I want to focus on what else is required or desired in our conception of the intercultural citizen. After all, it is important to notice that individual citizens can fully accept the political commitment to a multicultural state without possessing a very high level of intercultural skills themselves. They may agree that *the state* should be reformed to accommodate diversity (since it belongs to all citizens, not just the dominant group), without believing that they *as individuals* should learn about how to deal better with diversity in their own lives, or that they should learn more about the culture, traditions and identities of the people with whom they share the state. They may support the idea that the state should reform itself from a unitary, unilingual homogenous nation-state to a more federal or consociational bilingual multination state. Yet they may not accept that they as individuals have any obligation to become more 'intercultural' in their own individual lives.

Indeed, in some cases, the result of multicultural reforms at the level of the state may actually be to reduce the need and incentive for intercultural skills or knowledge at the level of the individual. Consider the status of self-governing minorities in federal multination states like the Flemish in Belgium, Quebecois in Canada or French in Switzerland, or in self-governing territories like Puerto Rico or South Tyrol. In these cases, the repudiation of older models of a unitary nation-state has enabled these national minorities to live more completely within their own institutions operating in their own language. In the past, these minorities often faced extensive economic, political and social pressure to participate in institutions run in the dominant language. For example, all of the courts, or universities, or legislatures, were only

Kymlicka: Multicultural states and intercultural citizens 155

conducted in the majority language. Yet today, as a result of adopting the ideal of a multicultural state that belongs to all citizens, these minorities have been able to build up an extensive array of public institutions in their own language, so that they can access the full range of educational, economic, legal and political opportunities without having to learn the dominant language, or without having to participate in institutions that are primarily run by members of the dominant group. In effect, these sorts of 'multination federations' allow minorities to create 'parallel societies', co-existing alongside the dominant society, without necessarily having very much interaction between them.

The interactions between these parallel societies can be very minimal. The French-speaking and English-speaking societies in Canada have often been described as 'two solitudes', which I believe is an accurate description. Francophones and Anglophones in Canada read different newspapers, listen to different radio programs, watch different TV shows, read different literature. Moreover, they are generally quite uninterested in each other's culture. Few English-speaking Canadians have any desire to learn about internal cultural developments within French-speaking Canada, and vice versa. Anglophones are not interested in reading francophone authors (even in translation), or in learning about the hot new media stars or public intellectuals or entertainers within Quebec (and vice versa).

This kind of parallel societies/two solitudes also exists in Belgium between the Flemish- and French-speaking groups and in Switzerland, between the German, French and Italian-speaking groups. Indeed, Switzerland has been described as composed of three groups that 'stand with their backs to each other' (Steiner, 2001: 145). The French–Swiss stand facing towards France; the Italian–Swiss facing towards Italy; and the German–Swiss facing towards Germany, each focused on their own internal cultural life and the culture of the neighboring country whose language they share. Most members of all three groups accept the principle that Switzerland must be a multilingual state that recognizes and shares power among its constituent groups. But few people have much interest in learning about or interacting with the other groups.

This sort of parallel co-existence creates an interesting paradox. In effect, we have multicultural states populated by citizens who have only minimal levels of intercultural interaction or knowledge. This raises an interesting question about how we should evaluate these models of multinational federations. From one point of view, they are clearly a great success. They are among the most peaceful, democratic and prosperous countries in the world. They have learned how to resolve their conflicts between different linguistic and national groups in a completely peaceful and democratic way. The absence of political violence is quite extraordinary when one remembers that nationalist conflicts have broken up colonial empires, torn apart communist systems in

Eastern Europe, and been a source of violence throughout the world. By contrast, these democratic multi-nation states are resolving their conflicts not only in a peaceful and democratic way, but also in a way that fully respects human rights, including individual civil and political rights. In short, in terms of peace, democracy, human rights, individual freedom and economic prosperity, I would argue that these multination federations have been very successful. Indeed, I have argued elsewhere that they provide the most feasible model for accommodating strong forms of minority nationalism in other parts of the world, such as Eastern Europe (Kymlicka and Opalski, 2001).

From another point of view however, it must be acknowledged that these countries can also be seen as failures, or at least as disappointments. In particular, the lived experience of inter-group relations is hardly a model of robust or constructive intercultural exchange. At best, most citizens are ignorant of, and indifferent to, the internal life of other groups. At worst, the relations between different groups are tinged with feelings of resentment and annoyance, which are exacerbated by the seemingly unending process of reforming public institutions. Despite the significant reforms of state institutions, minorities still typically feel that the older ideology of the homogenous nation-state has not been fully renounced, and that members of the dominant group have not fully accepted the principle of a multicultural state (or at least have not fully accepted all of its implications). By contrast, the members of the dominant group typically feel that members of minority group are ungrateful for the changes that have been made, unreasonable in their expectations and are impossible to satisfy. As a result, inter-group relations are often highly politicized, as members of both sides are (over?)-sensitive to perceived slights, indignities and misunderstandings. As a result, many people avoid inter-group contact, where possible, or at least do not go out of their way to increase their contact with members of the other group. When contact does take place, it tends to reduce quickly to rather crude forms of bargaining and negotiation, rather than any deeper level of cultural sharing or common deliberation. This in turn, reinforces the underlying sense of 'solitude' between the groups.

In short, progress at the level of state institutions has not been matched by progress at the level of the lived experience of inter-group relations. The *state* has made itself accessible to all citizens, and affirms the important contribution that each group makes to the larger society. But from the point of view of individuals, the presence of other groups is rarely experienced as enriching. On the contrary, the level of mutual indifference in these countries (and hence the reduction of inter-ethnic relations to mere bargaining) has been described as 'nauseous' by one critic of multiculturalism.[8] The state has become more just, inclusive and accommodating, but inter-group relations remain divided and strained.[9]

Kymlicka: Multicultural states and intercultural citizens   157

This suggests that one can have a robustly multicultural state – one that truly repudiates the old model of a homogenous nation-state – with only minimally intercultural citizens. Of course, as noted earlier, a robustly multicultural state can only survive if citizens accept the three basic principles of multicultural fairness – i.e. that the state belongs equally to all groups; that policies of assimilation and exclusion must be replaced by recognition and accommodation; and that historic injustice must be acknowledged. But individuals can fully accept these principles and support a state that embodies them, without having a high level of intercultural skills or knowledge themselves. Living in such a multinational federation may in fact require fewer intercultural contacts than before, as groups become more self-sufficient and 'institutionally complete'.[10]

Many people find this picture of self-contained parallel societies unsatisfactory as an account of intercultural citizenship. It may eliminate inter-group oppression, and create fairness between groups, but it lacks the sort of intercultural interaction and mutual sharing and learning that many of us desire.[11]

As a result, many theorists have attempted to formulate a more robust picture of what an intercultural individual is. On this view, an intercultural citizen is someone who not only supports the principles of a multicultural state, but also exhibits a range of more positive personal attitudes towards diversity. In particular, it is someone who is curious rather than fearful about other peoples and cultures; someone who is open to learning about other ways of life, and willing to consider how issues look from other people's point of view, rather than assuming that their inherited way of life or perspective is superior; someone who feels comfortable interacting with people from other backgrounds, and so on.

This sort of personal interculturalism is often said to be increasingly necessary due to forces of globalization. There is a much higher level of interdependence today between the members of different groups. No group is truly 'self-sufficient' anymore. No group is truly 'institutionally complete'. Even the most sizeable group, with the most extensive rights of self-government, is not self-contained, but is integrated into larger transnational economic and political structures, and subject to international forces relating to the economy, or the environment, or security. As a result, everyone today needs to be able to deal with people from outside their own group, and hence must learn how to deal with diversity.

Moreover, we also see high levels of mobility and migration around the world today, so that people are increasingly geographically inter-mixed. Groups which possess significant powers of territorial autonomy are likely to confront immigrants from another country, or migrants from another part of the same country, whose diverse backgrounds must be accommodated within the institutions of the self-governing territory. For reasons of both global interdependence and migration, therefore, it is increasingly impossible to interact solely with members of one's own group. Intercultural skills are needed even for the members of 'institutionally complete' parallel societies within multination federations.

Moreover, these intercultural skills should be seen not just as pragmatic necessities given the reality of global interdependence and inter-ethnic mixing, but also as intrinsically valuable. It enriches our lives to be able to have positive interactions with the members of other cultures: it expands our horizons, provides new perspectives, and teaches us to reflect more critically on our own inherited traditions. It is, in short, an important part of self-development. Someone who only feels comfortable with members of his own group, and who is not able or willing to deal with 'others', is leading a stulti-fied life.

An important part of any theory of intercultural citizenship is to instill high levels of intercultural skills and knowledge. We should encourage individuals to have the ability and desire to seek out interactions with the members of other groups, to have curiosity about the larger world, and to learn about the habits and beliefs of other peoples. Indeed, in some accounts of education for intercultural citizenship, this seems to be the main goal: the focus is less on inculcating the political principles which support the multicultural state, and more on inculcating the personal skills that support positive intercultural exchanges.

POSSIBLE TENSIONS

So far, two ideals have been described: (1) the ideal of a multicultural state that fairly accommodates diversity in its laws and public institutions and (2) the ideal of an intercultural citizen who feels comfortable dealing with diversity in his or her individual interactions. Personally, I find both of these ideas very attractive, and would like to think that they reinforce each other and fit together in a seamless whole. We might hope, for example, that emphasizing the necessity/desirability of individual intercultural skills will help to reduce the strained quality of inter-group relations within many existing multination states. Encouraging greater intercultural skills might reduce the feeling of 'solitudes' between different groups, by encouraging greater interaction, and reducing the danger that this interaction will lead to feelings of resentment or misunderstanding. If so, promoting a more robust conception of intercultural skills would be a 'win-win' proposition: it not only promotes individual self-development, but also helps to reduce inter-group strains in multicultural states, and thereby helps to sustain the sorts of state reforms needed to ensure justice.

Kymlicka: Multicultural states and intercultural citizens 159

However, this may be over-optimistic. I believe that there are some possible tensions between promoting greater multiculturalism at the level of the state and promoting greater interculturalism at the level of individual citizens. A few of them are briefly discussed below.

Local interculturalism versus cosmopolitan interculturalism

The first problem here is that the standard arguments for enhancing the intercultural skills and knowledge of individuals do not tell us much about *which* groups we should learn more about. In particular, they do not give us any reason to learn more about local groups living next to us within our own country, than about distant groups living in other countries or even other continents. Both can be sources of enrichment, learning and expanded opportunities. Indeed, if the primary goal of developing intercultural skills is personal self-development, and/or being able to succeed within a globalized economy and transnational political institutions, then perhaps it is more useful to learn about a large distant culture than about a small neighboring culture. For example, learning a world language like English is likely to open up more economic opportunities, and enable access to a wider range of cultural products (e.g. novels, movies, plays), than learning a neighboring language spoken only by a few hundred thousand people. In fact, people may believe deeply in the value of learning about other peoples and cultures, and hence may seek to develop and exercise their intercultural skills, yet nonetheless remain quite ignorant and indifferent to their local/neighboring cultures. They may be genuinely intercultural, and may be genuinely open and curious about others, but they may choose to train their curiosity on more distant or more powerful languages and cultures than on the languages and cultures of their local co-citizens.

This is precisely what we see in many multination states. As mentioned previously, the members of the 'parallel societies' in countries like Canada, Belgium and Switzerland have little interest in each other. But they are not inward-looking. On the contrary, members of all these societies are very interested in the larger world, and are eager to participate in free trade, transnational educational and cultural exchanges and the learning of foreign languages. In many respects, they are truly 'citizens of the world', with cosmopolitan tastes in food, literature, music, religion, art and travel. They are simply not interested in the language and culture of their neighbors.[12]

For example, although Belgium is officially bilingual, with French and Flemish as the official languages, the Francophones would prefer to learn English than Flemish, since they would rather tap into the global culture made available through English than learn more about the internal life of their

Flemish co-citizens. As a result, while French-speaking Belgians have become more cosmopolitan and intercultural, fewer and fewer of them know or care about the internal life of the Flemish society in Belgium (and vice versa).

The same situation exists in Estonia. The ethnic Estonian majority would rather learn English than Russian, which is the language of over 40 percent of the population. Conversely, the Russian minority would prefer to learn English than Estonian. Each group is trying to reach out and connect to the larger world, but are indifferent to the language and culture of their co-citizens.

Many people seem to prefer a form of global interculturalism, focused on learning about distant/world cultures, to local interculturalism, focused on learning about neighboring groups. This preference for global over local forms of interculturalism is quite explicit in many countries. In Germany, for example, educational programs to promote interculturalism are explicitly aimed at enabling Germans to interact with the citizens of other European countries, as part of building the European Union, rather than on enabling Germans to deal with their (sizeable) local minorities, such as the Turkish 'guest-workers' (Luchtenberg, 2003). Similarly, intercultural education in Russia is focused on teaching Russians about larger world cultures, not on learning about the languages and cultures of the many national minorities within Russia itself, such as their Muslim minorities (Froumin, 2003).

This is not really surprising however, as not only are world languages/cultures attractive in the resources and opportunities they provide, but there is also typically less tension involved in learning about them or interacting with them. For most people, learning about a distant culture carries no historical or political baggage: one can simply enjoy and cherish the intercultural interaction. By contrast, interacting with neighboring groups is typically wrapped up with unresolved political demands and long-standing fears and resentments. Local interculturalism almost always creates more anxiety and tension than global interculturalism, particularly in contexts where there is a long history of mistreatment and mistrust between the groups. In such contexts, even well-meaning attempts by members of the dominant group to interact with members of a historically oppressed group are likely to be viewed with suspicion. It is not surprising therefore that many people who are genuinely open and curious about other cultures, and who cherish opportunities for intercultural exchange, nonetheless prefer global interculturalism to local interculturalism.

This suggests that there is a potential divergence between the goals of inculcating intercultural skills in citizens and of supporting the multicultural state. The standard arguments in favor of intercultural skills, based on self-development and the dynamics of globalization, apply equally to learning about local

Kymlicka: Multicultural states and intercultural citizens 161

and distant cultures. Indeed, according to some commentators, the natural or logical outcome of pursuing the ideal of an intercultural citizen is in fact some form of cosmopolitanism that explicitly views the world as a whole, rather than just local groups, as the appropriate focus of intercultural learning and exchange (e.g. Fullinwider, 2001). Standard conceptions of the intercultural citizen, in short, seem to privilege global interculturalism over local interculturalism.

By contrast, the goal of building and sustaining a multicultural state requires citizens to privilege local interculturalism over global interculturalism. The real challenge of intercultural citizenship is learning how to interact in a constructive manner with one's neighboring groups and to try to overcome the legacies of mistrust and oppression that often strain local inter-group relations. The motive for this, I believe, cannot primarily be self-development and personal enrichment. Those motives, by themselves, are likely to push in the direction of global interculturalism. The willingness of citizens to engage in forms of local interculturalism must instead be grounded, at least in part, on considerations of justice. If we want to promote local interculturalism, we need to tie it to arguments of justice. We need to show how local interculturalism plays an important role in sustaining the just institutions of a multicultural state, and hence is something we have a duty to attempt, even if we do not find it personally enriching (and may instead find it painful and tiring). The sort of intercultural exchange that leads to personal enrichment is not necessarily the same sort as leads to support for just institutions. I do not think we have fully thought through this potential tension.

Interculturalism versus isolationism

Thus far, I have assumed that we all agree with the claim that openness to other peoples and cultures is a virtue that citizens should possess, even if we disagree about whether this openness should primarily be directed locally or globally. But, there is a second problem with the idea that citizens should possess robust intercultural skills and knowledge: namely, there are some groups that reject the underlying claim that intercultural exchange leads to personal growth and enrichment. In particular, some conservative religious groups view intercultural interaction (local or global) as a threat to their way of life, which may depend on a degree of self-isolation. They may view the larger society as a corrupting influence that is likely to lead their members astray. This is of particular concern regarding their children, and many such groups strenuously object to the idea that their children should have to interact with children from the larger society. As a result, they seek to establish separate religious schools, and often seek public funding to do so. Where such separate schools are not feasible (e.g. because the group's members are too few or too dispersed), they may instead seek permission to teach their children at home ('home schooling'), or to withdraw their children before the usual age for mandatory schooling.

These groups reject the ideal of an intercultural citizen. Yet it is interesting to note that they may not reject the idea of a multicultural state. On the contrary, many of them demand separate religious schools precisely by appealing to the principles of the multicultural state. In the Canadian context, for example, the public schools in the nineteenth century were historically defined as Protestant. To accommodate Catholic immigrants, particularly from Ireland, a separate publicly-funded Catholic school system was set up in many provinces. Today, the public schools are fully secular, and so many Canadians see no reason to provide public funding for religious schools for newer immigrant groups (e.g. for Muslims and Hindus from South Asia). Unlike Catholics in the nineteenth century, religious minorities today are not excluded or stigmatized within the (secularized) public school system. However, Muslim community leaders argue, not unreasonably, that if Catholics have publicly-funded separate schools, so should they. Indeed, they argue that the principle of multicultural fairness in state institutions requires that they too be given public funds for separate religious schools.

Here again, we have a potential conflict between the ideals of the multicultural state and the intercultural citizen. These conservative religious groups shun intercultural interaction, yet endorse the principles of a multicultural state. They do not seek to impose their religion or culture on outsiders, and do not claim that the state belongs to them. They ask only that the state extend to them the same accommodation that it has historically provided to other groups, including other religious or ethnic minorities. From the perspective of multicultural state fairness, it is difficult to contest their claim. Yet from the point of view of promoting greater intercultural skills amongst citizens, the proliferation of separate religious schools is regrettable, particularly when they will be controlled by conservative religious leaders who preach that their group is the chosen people, that people outside the church are evil and damned, that inter-marriage is a sin, etc. These schools may in fact generate precisely the sort of fear of 'otherness' that our conceptions of intercultural citizenship were intended to overcome. Many of us may worry that they will seriously constrain the opportunities and self-development of the children.

This is a tension I do not believe has been properly addressed. The sort of schooling required by norms of intercultural self-development may not be the same sort of schooling required by norms of multicultural fairness.[13]

Kymlicka: Multicultural states and intercultural citizens 163

Interculturalism versus tokenism

Finally, I will raise one more possible tension. Let us assume that we have solved the first two problems, and that everyone agrees on the importance of promoting intercultural skills/knowledge, and that this should include knowledge about and interaction with local groups, not just distant ones. We face one further problem: namely, what sort of knowledge should we be seeking about other peoples and cultures?

When the idea of multicultural education was first articulated in the Anglo-American world in the late 1970s and 1980s, the focus tended to be on teaching the more exotic and colorful aspects of other cultures, particularly their traditional holidays, costumes, dances and food. This was known in Britain as the 'saris, samosas and steelbands' model of multiculturalism (Alibhai-Brown, 2000: 17). It taught children that immigrants to Britain wear different clothes (saris), eat different foods (samosas) and enjoy different music (steelbands). Needless to say, this was quickly criticized as trivializing and de-politicizing immigrant cultures and identities. Others have called it the 'commodification' or 'Disneyfication' of culture: the reduction of a complex culture to a few 'safe' items that can easily be understood and 'consumed' by non-members, without really understanding the depths of a culture's beliefs, hopes, loyalties, fears, and identities.[14] It avoids the need to confront the reality that the members of different groups may not only eat and dress differently, but also may have fundamentally different and competing visions of God, the family, the state, the land, society, and of our basic moral and political obligations. Yet it is precisely these more fundamental cultural differences that need to be negotiated in a multicultural society.

Proponents of intercultural education today are quite aware of this danger, and so emphasize the need for a deeper understanding, dialogue and appreciation between the members of different groups. But then we quickly encounter the opposite problem. If earlier models of intercultural understanding were tokenist and undemanding, more recent models are utopian and too demanding. To take one example, in the name of promoting multiculturalism in Bosnia, the international community has sponsored many interfaith seminars that are intended to teach Serbs about the Muslim religion, and teach Bosniacs about the Orthodox religion. The hope was that with greater knowledge about their deepest religious beliefs, each group would respect and appreciate each other more.

Preliminary reports suggest that this exercise is not having the desired effect, and this is unsurprising. A few seminars are not enough to provide any real 'understanding' of something as complex as Islam or Christianity. Moreover, 'understanding' is no guarantee of 'appreciation' or 'respect'. On the contrary,

164 *Theory and Research in Education* 1(2)

where people have deeply-held beliefs about true faith, discovering that other people have quite different views may simply reinforce the belief that they are misguided and/or corrupt.

It seems to me that such models of intercultural education often miss the target. What matters is not that we understand or appreciate *the content* of other people's deeply-held beliefs, but rather that we understand and appreciate the fact that they *have* deeply-held views that differ from ours. Where there are such differences, the state cannot be seen as 'belonging' to one particular group, but rather must try to be even-handed among all groups.

This is how I would explain the basis of religious tolerance in the Western democracies. The historic basis for toleration is not any sort of deep understanding or appreciation of the nature of other religions. Protestants do not have a deep understanding of the tenets of Catholicism, let alone Islam or Hinduism (and vice versa). If Protestants did somehow acquire a deeper understanding of the tenets of other religions, I doubt this would increase their appreciation of them. The basis of religious tolerance, I think, is quite different. Protestants recognize that Catholics and Muslims have deeply-held religious beliefs that matter as much to them as Protestant beliefs matter to Protestants. The precise nature of these different beliefs is not well-understood, but what matters is that we recognize we have different deeply-held beliefs, and we agree that the state does not belong to any one religious group. As a result, we need to find ways of living and governing together that do not depend upon everyone accepting the same religious beliefs. In other words, we need a common understanding of the nature of the state as a secular institution that is not the possession of any one religious group. We do not need a common understanding of each other's religious faith.

I think the same applies to the different views about the nature of land between indigenous peoples and European settlers in the Americas. It is unrealistic, I think, to expect that European settlers will come to have a deep understanding of the significance of land within indigenous cultures, any more than indigenous people are likely to understand European views about the natural world. Even when it seems that we have moments of mutual understanding, these often disappear quickly, as apparent points of contact dissolve beneath the weight of deeper cultural differences. For example, many environmentalists in Canada thought that they understood and shared many of the beliefs about the land that Aboriginals have in Canada, and for this reason the two groups worked effectively to block certain hydro-electric developments. Yet this coalition quickly (and bitterly) broke down when Aboriginals subsequently used their self-government powers to promote similar hydro-electric projects. The apparent similarities in views in fact obscured deep differences about ends and means (Feit, 1980). Here again, what matters is not that we

Kymlicka: Multicultural states and intercultural citizens 165

fully understand each other's deeply-held views about the land, but simply that we acknowledge that groups have differing deeply-held views, and that no one group can ask or expect the state to act solely on its views.

The idea that culturally distinct groups can become transparent to each other is a myth, and a dangerous one, insofar as it encourages members of the dominant group to think that they have understood non-dominant groups, and so can speak for them. We should accept instead, that cultures (and individuals) are always at least partially opaque to each other. This indeed is one of the arguments in favor of self-government or other forms of power-sharing. Self-government is needed in part because it is very difficult to gain a full understanding or appreciation of other cultures.

I believe it is a mistake to suppose that mutual understanding is a prerequisite for citizens to support the principles of a multicultural state. It may in fact be the other way around. I think that acknowledgment of the impossibility of achieving full mutual understanding helps to generate support for the principles of the multicultural state, whose institutions operate to reduce the need for such mutual understanding (since they empower indigenous peoples to speak for, and govern, themselves).

Even with self-government rights, indigenous peoples and the larger society must still talk to one another, cooperate in various institutions, and negotiate various forms of collective action. But under conditions of deep diversity, these discussions may often be more a matter of bargaining and negotiation than of genuinely shared deliberation or mutual understanding. This is indeed what we see emerging in various multination states, like Belgium, where relations between the Flemish and Walloons are described as little more than crude forms of bargaining. I would suggest that relations between Aboriginals and the larger society in Canada are similar.

The limited levels of intercultural exchange and understanding that we see in some multi-nation states are perhaps to be expected. If we accept that mutual understanding is difficult to achieve, particularly in a context of deep cultural differences and histories of mistrust, then the aim of intercultural education should not primarily be deep mutual understanding, but rather acknowledgment of the (partial) opaqueness of cultural differences, and hence the necessity for groups to speak for, and govern, themselves, and the necessity to find ways of co-existing that can be accepted by all. This, I would suggest, is a more realistic goal, which lies in-between the tokenist teaching of superficial cultural differences, and the Utopian quest to understand deep cultural differences. Here again, the quest for a particular form of (deep) intercultural knowledge, rooted in a model of the ideal intercultural citizen, may go beyond, and perhaps even conflict with, the sort of intercultural relations required by a just multicultural state.

CONCLUSION

In this paper, I have tried to suggest that our ideal of an intercultural citizen, with robust levels of intercultural skills/knowledge, does not fit neatly or simply into our ideal of a multicultural state that deals justly with ethnocultural diversity. The ideal of personal self-development underlying the former does not always match up well with the principles of political justice underlying the latter.

In particular, three possible areas of tension have been raised between the two: (1) that the intercultural citizen may prefer global interculturalism, while multicultural justice requires focusing on local interculturalism, (2) that the model of intercultural citizen requires a level of intercultural exchange which may unfairly burden some isolationist groups and (3) that the model of the intercultural citizen requires a level of mutual understanding that is either tokenistic (if focused on superficial cultural differences) or Utopian (if focused on deep cultural differences), while justice requires acknowledging the limits of mutual understanding and accepting the partial opaqueness of our differences.

All three of these conflicts raise difficult issues for the theory and practice of intercultural citizenship. This paper does not try to provide a definitive answer to any of these three conflicts, but simply tries to clarify the source of the tension. However, my own inclination is to agree with Rawls that 'justice is the first virtue of social institutions'. However valuable it is for individuals to acquire various forms of intercultural skills and knowledge, we should ensure that the promotion of individual interculturalism does not undermine the justice of multicultural state institutions. At least in some cases, this may require tempering our promotion of individual interculturalism with the recognition of our special obligations to local (rather than distant) groups, with the accommodation of the claims of isolationist groups, and with the acknowledgment of the partial opaqueness of deep cultural differences.

NOTES

1. This paper was originally presented at the 5th Latin American Congress of Intercultural Bilingual Education, in Lima, Peru in August 2002.

2. Some authors draw a sharp distinction between 'multiculturalism' and 'interculturalism', others treat them as synonyms. In the Anglo-American literature, the former term is more common, in the Latin American literature, the latter seems preferred. In this paper, the term 'multicultural' is used in reference to states, and 'intercultural' in reference to individuals, for the reasons explained.

3. See, for example, the interesting discussion on the different national models of multiculturalism in Britain and France in Favell (2001).

Kymlicka: Multicultural states and intercultural citizens 167

4. This exclusion could take the form of exclusion from the halls of power within the state (e.g. through denial of the vote, or other forms of political disempowerment), or it could literally involve exclusion from the territory of the state, through racial restrictions on immigration, or through ethnic cleansing.

5. This struggle has not always been conducted in the name of 'multiculturalism', and some groups may indeed reject the term. For the reasons discussed, the struggle has often instead been conducted in the name of a 'multinational state', or various ideals of 'partnership', 'federalism', 'historic rights', or simply 'democracy'.

6. For a fuller discussion of the nature and structure of such a multination state (see Gagnon and Tully, 2001; Kymlicka 2001: ch. 5; Requejo, 2002). The Flemish now form a majority in Belgium, but were historically subordinate to the French, and so have faced many of the same struggles for recognition and self-government as national groups that are numerically a minority, such as the Québécois or Catalans.

7. See the debate in Mexico between those who conceive of indigenous self-government solely in terms of local self-government, and those who seek some form of regional autonomy (e.g. the Zapatistas). For a similar debate in Canada, see the report of the Royal Commission on Aboriginal Peoples, which recommended consolidating the 700 or so Aboriginal 'bands' (primarily local villages) into 60 or so 'peoples' that would have greater capacities for self-government.

8. 'The endless process of haggling that is Belgian politics is so nauseating to all concerned . . .' (Barry, 2001: 312).

9. I would not say that inter-group relations have become worse in these countries. Rather, the strains have simply become more visible, and more vocal, now that minorities have the power and voice to make their feelings heard.

10. For the importance of 'institutional completeness' (Breton, 1964).

11. It may also seem unsustainable in the long term: what holds such parallel societies together in a single state? If the members of each group are uninterested in learning about or interacting with other groups, why not just split up into two or more states? For some speculation on this question (Kymlicka, 2003).

12. For a similar observation, see Miscevic (1999), who notes that while nationalists are often interested in interacting with distant strangers (and hence are 'cosmopolitan' in that sense), they are generally hostile to interacting with proximate strangers: i.e. with the members of the neighboring national group, with whom they often have a history of conflict, competition and invidious comparison.

13. For various attempts to untie this Gordian knot, see Levinson (1999), Callan (1997), Spinner-Halev (2000), Macedo (2000) and Reich (2002).

14. This charge has been leveled at Canadian multicultural policies by Gwyn (1995), Bissoondath (1994) and more generally by Waldron (1995).

REFERENCES

Alibhai-Brown, Y. (2000) *After Multiculturalism*. London: Foreign Policy Centre.

Barry, B. (2001) *Culture and Equality: An Egalitarian Critique of Multiculturalism*. Cambridge: Polity.

Bissoondath, N. (1994) *Selling Illusions: The Cult of Multiculturalism in Canada*. Toronto: Penguin.

Breton, R. (1964) 'Institutional Completeness of Ethnic Communities', *American Journal of Sociology* 70: 193–205.

Callan, E. (1997) *Creating Citizens: Political Education and Liberal Democracy*. Oxford: Oxford University Press.

Callan, E. (2000) 'Discrimination and Religious Schooling', in W. Kymlicka and W. Norman (eds) *Citizenship in Diverse Societies*, pp. 45–67. Oxford: Oxford University Press.

Favell, A. (2001) *Philosophies of Integration: Integration and the Idea of Citizenship in France and Britain second edition*. London: St. Martin's Press.

Feit, H. (1980) 'Negotiating Recognition of Aboriginal Rights', *Canadian Review of Anthropology* 1(2): 255–78.

Froumin, I. (2003) 'Citizenship Education and Ethnic Issues in Russia', in J.A. Banks (ed.) *Diversity and Citizenship Education: Global Perspectives*, pp. forthcoming. San Francisco, CA: Jossey-Bass.

Fullinwider, R. (2001) 'Multicultural Education and Cosmopolitan Citizenship', *International Journal of Educational Research* 35: 331–43.

Gagnon, A. and J. Tully, eds (2001) *Multinational Democracies*. Cambridge: Cambridge University Press.

Gwyn, R. (1995) *Nationalism without Walls: The Unbearable Lightness of Being Canadian*. Toronto: McClelland and Stewart.

Keating, M. and J. McGarry, eds (2001) *Minority Nationalism and the Changing International Order*. Oxford: Oxford University Press.

Kymlicka, W. (2001) *Politics in the Vernacular: Nationalism, Multiculturalism, Citizenship*. Oxford: Oxford University Press.

Kymlicka, W. (2003) 'Being Canadian', *Government and Opposition*, 38(3): forthcoming.

Kymlicka, W. and M. Opalski (2001) *Can Liberal Pluralism be Exported? Western Political Theory and Ethnic Relations in Eastern Europe*. Oxford: Oxford University Press.

Levinson, M. (1999) *The Demands of Liberal Education*. Oxford: Oxford University Press.

Luchtenberg, S. (2003) 'Citizenship Education and Diversity in Germany', in J.A. Banks (ed.) *Diversity and Citizenship Education: Global Perspectives*, pp. forthcoming. San Francisco, CA: Jossey-Bass.

Macedo, S. (2000) *Diversity and Distrust: Civic Education in a Multicultural Democracy*. Cambridge: Harvard University Press.

Miscevic, N. (1999) 'Close Strangers: Nationalism, Proximity and Cosmopolitanism', *Studies in East European Thought* 51: 109–25.

Reich, R. (2002) *Bridging Liberalism and Multiculturalism in American Education*. Chicago: University of Chicago Press.

Requejo, F. (2002) *Democracia y Pluralismo Nacional*. Barcelona: Ariel.

Kymlicka: Multicultural states and intercultural citizens 169

Spinner-Halev, J. (2000) *Surviving Diversity: Religion and Democratic Citizenship.* Baltimore: John Hopkins University Press.

Steiner, J. (2001) 'Switzerland and the European Union: A Puzzle', in M. Keating and J. McGarry (eds) *Minority Nationalism and the Changing International Order*, pp. 137–54. Oxford: Oxford University Press.

Taylor, C. (1991) 'Shared and Divergent Values', in R. Watts and D. Brown (eds) *Options for a New Canada*, pp. 53–76. Toronto: University of Toronto Press.

Waldron, J. (1995) 'Minority Cultures and the Cosmopolitan Alternative', in W. Kymlicka (ed.) *The Rights of Minority Cultures*, pp. 93–121. Oxford: Oxford University Press.

BIOGRAPHICAL NOTE

WILL KYMLICKA is the author of five books published by Oxford University Press: *Liberalism, Community, and Culture* (1989), *Contemporary Political Philosophy* (1990; 2nd edn, 2002), *Multicultural Citizenship* (1995), *Finding Our Way: Rethinking Ethnocultural Relations in Canada* (1998) and *Politics in the Vernacular: Nationalism, Multiculturalism and Citizenship* (2001). He is also the editor of *Justice in Political Philosophy* (Elgar, 1992), and *The Rights of Minority Cultures* (OUP, 1995), and co-editor of *Ethnicity and Group Rights* (NYU, 1997), *Citizenship in Diverse Societies* (OUP, 2000), *Alternative Conceptions of Civil Society* (PUP, 2001), *Can Liberal Pluralism Be Exported?* (OUP, 2001), and *Language Rights and Political Theory* (OUP, 2003). He is currently a professor of philosophy at Queen's University, and a visiting professor in the Nationalism Studies program at the Central European University in Budapest. His works have been translated into 27 languages. Correspondence to: Will Kymlicka, Department of Philosophy, Watson Hall 313, Queen's University Kingston, Ontario K7L 3N6, Canada. [email: kymlicka@post.queensu.ca]

[8]

Temporary migrants, partial citizenship and hypermigration

Rainer Bauböck

Political and Social Sciences, European University Institute, San Domenico di Fiesole, Italy

Temporary migration raises two different challenges. The first is whether territorial democracies can integrate temporary migrants as equal citizens; the second is whether transnationally mobile societies can be organized democratically as communities of equal citizens. Considering both questions within a single analytical framework will reveal a dilemma: on the one hand, liberals have good reasons to promote the expansion of categories of free-moving citizens as the most effective and normatively attractive response to the problem of partial citizenship for temporary migrants; yet, on the other hand, if free movement rights were actually used by too many, this might fatally undermine the sustainability of intergenerational and territorial democratic polities.

Keywords: temporary migration; partial citizenship; free movement; hypermigration; life-course perspective

Introduction: the temporary migration dilemma

This paper will consider two challenges raised by temporary migration. The first is whether territorial democracies can integrate temporary migrants as equal citizens; the second is whether transnationally mobile societies can be organized democratically as communities of equal citizens. Considering both questions within a single analytical framework will reveal a dilemma: on the one hand, liberals have good reasons to promote the expansion of categories of free-moving citizens as the most effective and normatively attractive response to the problem of partial citizenship for temporary migrants; yet, on the other hand, if free movement rights were actually used by too many, this might fatally undermine the sustainability of inter-generational and territorial democratic polities.

666   R. Bauböck

Political theorists who address the question of what liberal states owe to outsiders have focused on two categories: immigrants who become long-term residents and external populations residing permanently in other countries. The normative salience of distinguishing between non-citizen residents and non-citizen non-residents seems clear enough. On the one hand, states have special duties towards immigrants who settle in their territory, which on many accounts include granting them certain social and cultural rights and eventually offering them full citizenship status. On the other hand, states have general duties of global justice towards human beings outside their border and may also have special duties towards external populations who are particularly affected by their decisions and policies. Temporary migrants, however, sit on the border between these two categories and therefore the duties that states have towards them seem less clear.

The temptation is to avoid this difficulty by assigning temporary migrants to either one or the other group. For example, in a pioneering statement, Michael Walzer condemned European guest worker policies of the 1960s and 1970s as a tyranny of citizens over aliens and demanded that immigrants must be set on the road to citizenship (Walzer 1983, p. 62). This view is broadly shared by liberal theorists, but tacitly assumes that temporary migrants become long-term immigrants, as most of the European guest workers actually did. The alternative view is to assimilate temporary migrants into the broader category of non-citizen non-residents. If temporary migrants are admitted on a contractual basis, then host state duties towards them seem reducible to honouring universal human rights and special contractual rights. In this view, there is nothing special about temporary migrants, since the same rights would also have to be respected for non-citizens residing in other states with which a government concludes a contract. Alternatively, temporary migrants may also be regarded as if they were external populations from a global distributive justice perspectives by considering how admission for temporary employment can provide many more with better opportunities than they enjoy in their countries of origin and may also benefit those who stay behind through remittances migrants send home (Chang 2003, Bell 2005, Ruhs 2006).

Temporary migrants may eventually become immigrants, but this is not inevitable. Most want to return to their countries of origin and many eventually do so However, as long as they stay they are not outsiders or mere transient visitors either. We call them migrants if, unlike tourists, they take up residence, education or employment. These purposes of their stay make their autonomy and well-being in significant ways dependent on the opportunities and rights they are offered in the host society. If this society is committed to domestic standards of social equality and non-discrimination, then it cannot take the situation in the migrants' countries of origin as reference point. Temporary migrants are often willing to accept conditions of work, housing, public education or health care far below the domestic standards the receiving society sets for its citizens. They often even accept conditions that are worse than before departure in their countries of origin as long as this serves their long-term life plan of improving their situation after return (Ottonelli and Torresi 2010).[1] Their apparent consent cannot be a sufficient reason for tolerating exploitative and discriminatory treatment of temporary migrants. They must be clearly included when assessing a system of rights by a criterion of social justice, such as Rawls' difference principle that considers how the system affects the worst off group.

Yet temporary migrants who are foreign nationals are still partial citizens.[2] Some employment benefits and social rights that depend on long-term residence do not apply to them (Carens 2008a). And, most importantly, they cannot and do not claim equal political participation and representation in the making of the laws to which they are subjected in the host country. The reason is that citizenship in independent states is constructed as a life-long membership that is acquired at birth and passed on across generations through descent or birth in the territory. This intergenerational nature of state membership would be severely disrupted if immigrants could acquire citizenship automatically by taking up domestic residence or if emigrants would automatically lose their citizenship by taking up residence abroad. Intergenerational citizenship is thus characterized not only by automatic birthright acquisition but also by the absence of strict *ius domicilii*, i.e. automatic acquisition or loss as a result of a mere change of residence. First generation immigrants have to apply for naturalization and first generation emigrants lose their citizenship only through explicit renunciation or through withdrawal for other reasons than mere residence abroad.

The intergenerational character of state citizenship has been regarded as morally problematic by some political theorists.[3] In contrast, I consider birthright membership as morally defensible and indeed functionally required for the formation of stable political communities with a potential for comprehensive self-government. While, as will be discussed in the penultimate section of this paper, non-state political communities with more fluid memberships are possible and do already exist in the present world, a general demise of intergenerational citizenship would radically change the conditions for building and sustaining liberal democracy.

The intergenerational character of state citizenship explains why foreign national temporary migrants can be only partial citizens in their host country. It also implies that they remain citizens of their country of origin while residing abroad and can even pass on this citizenship to children born there. So the diagnosis of partial citizenship for temporary migrants has to be modified by considering not only the context of reception but also the context of origin. However, even if all states involved provide temporary migrants with those rights to which they are morally entitled, these still would not add up to a status of full and equal citizenship. Countries of

668   R. Bauböck

origin whose nationals these migrants remain have to grant them a right to return, to diplomatic protection and, arguably, also an absentee franchise since temporary absence does not justify a presumption that these migrants have weaker stakes in the democratic process than current residents. Yet external citizenship (Bauböck 2009) still is a merely partial membership when compared with the status of domestic citizens. In polities constituted as territorial jurisdictions, residence inevitably makes a difference both with regard to the extent of subjection to the laws and with regard to the rights attached to citizenship status. Moreover, neither the right to return nor the absentee vote serves to overcome the lack of temporary migrants' representation in the polity where they reside and work. On the contrary, the unconditional duty of countries of origin to readmit their citizens may make these more vulnerable to threats of deportation in the host state, which in turn reinforce their exploitability by employers and landlords. So, from this perspective, temporary migrants seem to be inevitably partial citizens in both countries of origin and destination.

This conclusion is, however, premature. I have so far assumed that in relation to their host country temporary migrants are foreign nationals. Yet many migrants enjoy citizenship rights in a destination country because they were born abroad with an inherited foreign citizenship, because they are citizens of the European Union making use of their free movement rights, or because they have acquired dual citizenship through naturalization and can then also move freely between a country of origin and destination. For these temporary migrants, the partial citizenship they enjoy vis-à-vis their countries of origin is supplemented by full (or, in the case of mobile European Union citizens, nearly full) citizenship status in a destination country and it is exactly the combination of these statuses that provides them with opportunities for unrestricted temporary migration.

While foreign national temporary migrants are partial citizens in the sense of lacking the protection that depends on full citizenship status, free moving migrants may still be seen as partial citizens in the different sense of lacking a sense of belonging that sustains civic virtues. They are unlikely to participate actively in the self-government of a polity in which they reside only temporarily, even if they have all the rights and opportunities to such participation. This leads me to consider the second challenge of temporary migration. If the numbers of free movers became very large, how would this affect active participation and political cohesion in territorially structured democracies?

The two different kinds of partial citizenship for restricted and free temporary migrants are still connected through a common cause – a lack of strong affiliation that could either justify a fuller set of rights or motivate fuller participation. Analysing both categories of temporary migrants within a single analytical framework thus reveals a dilemma. Liberals have good reasons to promote the expansion of categories of free-moving citizens as

Critical Review of International Social and Political Philosophy 669

the most effective and normatively attractive response to the problem of partial citizenship for temporary migrants because, from a liberal perspective, freedom of movement has both instrumental and intrinsic value (Carens 1992), and because access to citizenship status and rights provides temporary migrants with the best possible protection against discrimination and exploitation. However, if expanded free movement rights were actually used by too many this might undermine the cohesion of intergenerational and territorial polities and active forms of civic participation.

I will start with a conceptual clarification of different meanings of temporary migration and will then present in the third section a typology of empirical varieties ranked on a normative scale of freedom. The fourth section discusses the limitations of strategies that promote full citizenship for temporary migrants. The fifth section considers first a hypothetical world where temporary migration is free and most individuals are temporary migrants and examines then whether in the real world urban and supranational polities already provide alternative models of citizenship that are better able to integrate temporary migrants than state-based citizenship regimes. In my conclusions I suggest that if the dilemma cannot be fully resolved, we might do best by switching back and forth between the perspective of preserving intergenerational citizenship in territorial polities and a life-course perspective on migrants' citizenship transitions.

Unpacking temporariness

Nearly all empirical as well as normative literature on temporary migration deals only with one specific type among a broader range of phenomena covered by this concept. These are public policy programmes by destination states that provide migrant workers with temporally limited – and in most cases non-renewable – work permits. The US Bracero programme of the 1940s and 1950s and guest worker programmes in Germany and several other European states in the 1960s and early 1970s are the best known examples. These programmes are today generally seen as failures, mainly because of the incapacity of liberal democracies to prevent permanent settlement and family reunification. Evidence that it is indeed constraints on state power in liberal constitutions which explain this outcome is provided by the contrasting cases of temporary migrant workers in the Arab Gulf states, where the rotation of temporary migrants has been effectively enforced through depriving these of basic liberties and segregating them from mainstream society. Recently, however, the idea that well-managed circulatory migration can produce win–win–win outcomes for destination and sending countries as well as for migrants themselves has been revived in both the United States and Europe (Global Commission on International Migration (GCIM) 2005, Castles 2006, Ruhs 2006, Vertovec 2007a).

670   *R. Bauböck*

Some deeper normative puzzles about temporary migration remain invisible as long as we look only at programmes designed by destination states. A first step towards a broader view is to consider the different meanings of the adjective 'temporary'. It can be understood as referring to an objective social fact, to subjective expectations, or to normative constraints. The first and most obvious interpretation refers to *de facto* temporary residence of migrants in a destination country that ends after a specified time through return or onward migration to other destinations. In this demographic sense, all immigration is initially temporary. Long-term immigration can be distinguished from temporary migration only retrospectively after a specific time period determined by social or legal convention. Those who have left before that time had been temporary, while those who stayed on are not. A different interpretation of what 'temporary' means refers instead to the future and to migrants' intentions to leave the country after a certain time or to the expectations of resident populations that they will do so. Finally, migration may be temporary in the sense that the duration of their stay is limited by legal or moral norms. Legal norms can positively establish the legitimacy of temporary residence or negatively prohibit the continuation of such residence. Moral norms are invoked primarily when disputing the normative validity of such legal permissions and prohibitions and when proposing alternative justifications for temporary admission or permanent residence rights. We arrive thus at altogether five distinct meanings of temporariness: demographically objective, subjectively intended, collectively expected, legally prescribed and morally justified.

These conceptual distinctions draw our attention to several potential mismatches that generate social conflicts, political disputes and moral dilemmas. Subjective intentions of migrants about the length of their stay frequently change over time and can then conflict with non-corresponding expectations in the wider society about their departure. Non-renewable temporary residence permits as a condition for legal admission may conflict with a moral principle of consolidation of residence according to which the right to stay grows stronger with the duration of stay. This conflict between legal and moral norms will turn into a political one, when there is also a growing mismatch between public policy and demographic reality. In most liberal states the phenomenon of the 'guests who stayed' has triggered policy revisions through renewals of limited residence permits and amnesties for those who entered without permission or overstayed. In some cases, however, the original policy goal was reasserted through offering financial incentives for return migration[4] or through expulsions even after long residence periods. Much less discussed is a converse incongruence between normative and objective temporariness. Some migrants enjoy a full right to permanent residence already when they are admitted but many among them do not intend to stay for long and may *de facto* leave after a short period.

Critical Review of International Social and Political Philosophy   671

Both types of mismatches are not simply odd combinations that occur accidentally, but are systematically generated by causal mechanisms that are well-known in migration studies but generally ignored in migration policy-making. The quip that 'there is nothing more permanent than temporary foreign workers' (Martin 2001) is supported by several explanations. The individual migrant who has been admitted only for a limited period but wants to retain access to the job market of the host country will not return if she risks being shut out in the future. The employer who has recruited temporary migrants who perform well will try to retain them rather than change them for new ones whom she does not know. Employers also prefer informal recruitment strategies through the family networks of already employed migrants to formal recruitment procedures monitored by governments, and family reunification will in turn consolidate the settlement process of temporary migrant workers. Finally, the shutting down of guest worker admission programmes in Europe in the mid-1970s further reduced incentives for return migration and triggered pre-emptive family reunification. It is therefore much more likely that more migrants will stay only temporarily where such legal conditions and constraints are largely absent and migrants can freely enter, take up jobs and remain indefinitely. Under these conditions, even subjectively intended long-term stay may result in *de facto* temporary migration if the economic opportunities in the host country decline or those in the country of origin improve. This has been, by and large, the experience with free movement of workers from other member states in the European Union.

My intention here is, however, not to provide a full explanatory account of how the different modes of temporariness are causally linked with each other, but to prepare the ground for a normative argument: Transforming guests who want to stay into citizens who are ready to leave is the best available liberal response to the dilemmas of temporary migration, but this strategy raises itself a new dilemma of how to secure sufficient levels of democratic continuity and participation in transnationally mobile societies.

Five types of temporary migration

From a normative perspective we can now distinguish different empirical types of migration according to the degrees of freedom of movement and the extent of equality that migrants enjoy compared with permanent residents and citizens.

Irregular migrants

The first category is irregular migrants.[5] Their presence is by definition temporary in the negative legal sense since they have no permission for further residence and are under an obligation to leave. Matters are a bit

672   R. Bauböck

more complicated when we start to look closer at the various categories covered by the term irregular migrant. Some enter the country without permission. Their legal freedom of movement is constrained in two senses: they had no legal right to enter and are under a legal duty to exit. Others have entered through regular channels, as tourists, guest workers, foreign students, asylum seekers or family members of residents but have subsequently lost permission to stay. Some among these are overstayers who extend their residence beyond a time limit defined as a condition for admission. Others have been admitted without a specific time limit, but circumstances have changed thereafter: their asylum applications were turned down or they were separated from an 'anchor' spouse by death or divorce.

States respond to the presence of irregular migrants in three alternative ways: through expulsion efforts, *de facto* toleration or regularization. Only the latter response transfers irregular migrants into one of the other categories that will be discussed below. Apart from the strong constraints on their freedom of movement and right to stay, irregular migrants are also in the most precarious position with regard to other rights. In liberal democracies they are of course not without rights, but these will be either reduced to a minimum set of basic human rights (including due process and humane treatment in case of deportation) or, if more extensive, will remain insecure and difficult to claim because of the looming deportation threat (Bosniak 2006).

The question that is relevant for my present concern is whether irregular migration should sometimes be regarded as an acceptable form of temporary migration with the implication that it ought to be tolerated in liberal democracies. My answer to this is negative. Irregular status is unacceptable not just because it undermines the rule of law, but also because of the constraints on basic freedoms and the precariousness of rights to which it exposes migrants. All arguments against second-class status for regular temporary migrant workers apply *a fortiori* to official toleration of irregular migrants. Once we agree that this status is undesirable, we can also use this judgment as a further objection against the global redistribution argument for temporary migrant worker programmes. Assuming a given level of economic demand for immigrant workers, a state that turns a blind eye to irregular immigration provides economic opportunities to more migrants than a state that regulates and thereby constrains access to temporary migration. So why not let market forces determine the demand for temporary workers and maximize the number of migrants by minimizing their rights?[6]

If we reject such a diabolic case for irregular migration, then toleration can only be defended on pragmatic grounds, such as a lack of state enforcement power or a lack of democratic support for either expulsion or regularization. From a liberal perspective, the conditions for choosing between these remaining two alternatives are also fairly clear. Expulsion can be legitimate only as long as migration may still be considered objectively temporary, i.e. before a threshold of long-term residence has been reached. Within this period, states may decide on humanitarian or pragmatic grounds to offer irregular migrants regularization or a chance to apply for immigration after returning to their countries of origin. Beyond the threshold of permanent residence, individuals acquire a moral claim to regularization (Carens 2008b, Carens *et al.* 2009). What is less obvious is whether the irregular period of residence has to count fully towards entitlements to equal treatment with regard to those rights that are generally reserved for permanent residents, or towards residence requirements for naturalization. Considerations of fairness towards regular migrants ought to permit some discounting of periods of irregular status.

Controlled admission with return conditionality

The guest worker programmes discussed above belong to a second type of migration that is also legally temporary, however in the different sense of being attached to a regular residence permit that has a fixed expiry date and is generally non-renewable. There is thus an expectation in the destination country that migrants admitted under such programmes will actually return to their countries of origin at the end of the predetermined period. Generally, this expectation matches also the subjective intentions of the migrants concerned, although these may change over time as they find that their earning targets are harder to reach than imagined – often because of high costs of living.

Freedom of movement is again constrained here both at entry and with regard to the right to stay, but with the important difference that admission is now based on a contract: the authorities of the destination state agree to admit the migrant if she agrees to the conditions of admission and return. The contract itself is rather asymmetrical, since the destination country can dictate conditions and temporary migrants have *de facto* few choices among alternative destinations. In the case of direct recruitment of guest workers in the country of origin, their choice is of the take-it-or-leave-it kind. Nearly all temporary migrant worker programmes exploit this contractual asymmetry to impose further conditions beyond the time limit of the residence and work permits, such as tying the latter to employment in a particular company or in a particular kind of job. As argued extensively by Carens, such conditions always reinforce the economic exploitability and social vulnerability of temporary migrant workers (Carens 2008a).

Yet it would be wrong to conclude that all temporary admission programmes are indefensible. In principle, foreign worker programmes could be designed in a way that removes any conditionality apart from the limited residence permit. Moreover, temporary migration for employment is also not the only temporary admission programme and the picture looks a bit

674   *R. Bauböck*

brighter when we consider these other programmes. International students also get temporary residence permits that usually expire with the completion of their university courses. They may be charged higher tuition fees and be prohibited from seeking employment in the regular labour market, but inside the university their position is in most schemes equal to that of native students. As in the case of migrant workers, their circumstances can change, for example if they marry a citizen of their host country and acquire then a claim to permanent residence. With growing global competition for highly skilled migrants, host country governments now often consider also whether they should enforce return migration or rather offer successful international students a permanent residence option. As with guest worker programmes, temporary admissions therefore often result in long-term settlement. However, this does not imply that international students should generally be admitted on a permanent basis. What makes temporary admission legitimate in their case is that the purpose of their stay is an activity that has a natural end (the completion of their studies), that the activity is carried out within an institution that keeps them in many ways separate from the larger society without enforced segregation, and that they receive a service – often in exchange for high international student fees.

Refugees who are granted temporary protected status (TPS) form a third category of temporarily admitted foreign citizens. A number of states in North America and Europe have introduced TPS in order to address large-scale refugee movements triggered by wars and civil wars and to circumvent individual procedures for determining asylum status according to the 1951 Geneva Refugee Convention (GRC). In this context, TPS becomes then a flexible alternative approach to refugee flows that destination countries feel obliged to take in. The logic of TPS is that it responds to a major violent conflict in a specific country or region of origin and ends as soon as the crisis is over and the host country government deems the situation safe for return. TPS permits may be renewed or extended until this is the case, but the purpose of the programme is to prevent permanent settlement and enforce return migration.

The legitimacy of TPS programmes is more difficult to assess than that of guest worker programmes, which are generally problematic, or international student programmes, which are generally not. First, given increasingly restrictive asylum policies, TPS can certainly respond effectively to some of the most urgent demands for refugee intake. However, the specific demand for TPS is often created by previous government decisions to constrain access to full asylum status. Second, the duration of a refugee-generating crisis is hard to foresee and the evaluation of conditions for safe return should not be left to governments that have a vested interested in enforcing it. Third, after some time temporary refugees, just like guest workers, become permanently settled immigrants, and an initial condition that their admission is only for the purpose of temporary protection becomes then morally irrelevant.

Controlled admission with initial temporary status

The third type of temporary migration that we need to consider is when admission is initially temporary but a transition towards permanent residence is built into the conditions from the very start. European guest worker programmes evolved in this way when destination countries that were hungry for more foreign labour started to issue renewals of permits that had been designed to be non-renewable. Systems of work and residence permits were then gradually adjusted to introduce conditions for renewal, change of employers and family reunification. Among these conditions were adequate income and housing and a continuous employment record. Similar responses have also been developed in traditional countries of immigration. For example, the United States has an Adjustment of Status procedure that allows temporary residents to apply for permanent residence status (also known as Green Card) without leaving the country. Since the 1970s most European states with a longer immigration experience have developed immigration programmes that foresee a regular option of transition from temporary to permanent residence. In 2003 the European Union brought about a harmonization of conditions for the general transition from temporary to permanent residence permits for non-European Union immigrants. There is now a distinct status of European Union long-term residents for which third country nationals can apply after five years and that allows them also to move to other Member States (Council Directive 2003/109/EC). Most recently, the European Union has created a Blue Card (Council Directive 2009/50/EC) that provides highly skilled immigrants with a work permit valid throughout the European Union (except in Britain, Denmark and Ireland where the directive does not apply) for initially up to two years, but renewable thereafter.

Adjustment of status for guest workers and temporary residents implies, on the one hand, an acknowledgement that programmes designed for strictly temporary stay need a correction mechanism that takes *de facto* settlement into account. Programmes like the European Union Blue Card, on the other hand, select immigrants for presumptive long-term residence but force them to pass through a probationary stage during which their right to stay is still temporary. Initially temporary admission is problematic if the rights enjoyed by non-permanent residents are unduly constrained or if the conditions for permanent settlement are onerous. These criteria may lead to a negative assessment of current policies in Europe, which have recently supplemented conditions of sufficient income and housing with 'integration tests'. These tests require knowledge of a dominant language or the country's history, constitution and values not merely for naturalization but already for

676   *R. Bauböck*

access to permanent residence (Guild *et al.* 2009, Kostakopoulou *et al.* 2010).[7] Such problematic hurdles are, however, not an intrinsic feature of programmes that allow for a gradual transition from temporary to permanent residence. If the only requirement were a clean criminal record during a period of residence of no more than five years, then granting labour migrants initially only temporary instead of permanent residence permits would be hardly objectionable. Doing so may also correspond to the subjective intentions of migrants who do not know at the point of admission whether they will stay indefinitely and who can answer this question only after some experience with work and life in their host society.

Under these conditions, the main constraint on migrants' freedom in this category does not concern their right to stay permanently but their right to enter. Migrants who arrive with initially temporary permits under the various European points or quota systems do not exercise free movement, but, similar to guest workers, are selected mainly for the purpose of satisfying economic demand in the country of destination. For those who pass this test, a mutually beneficial immigration contract that includes the promise of easy transition to permanent residence does not give rise to major concerns about unfair treatment. That transition will, however, never be so smooth for the second subcategory discussed here whose initial status had been irregular or who had been admitted on strictly temporary contracts. The recent European trend to test and select immigrants for family reunification, permanent residence and citizenship can be explained, but not justified, by a widespread perception that most long-term immigrants had not initially been invited to stay for good.

Asylum seekers whose claims are examined after they have crossed the border form a third subcategory. During the asylum determination procedure their stay is temporary and will become permanent only once they have been recognized as refugees according to the GRC. In case of a negative decision they lose their residence permit and are liable to be deported. However, enforcing return is difficult in three cases. First, they cannot be sent back if their country of origin cannot be identified or if that country refuses to cooperate through readmission. Second, even if they cannot satisfy a narrow interpretation of the GRC definition of refugees, they may still be protected against deportation to a country of transit or origin by non-refoulement clauses, such as Art. 33 of the GRC or Art. 3 of the European Convention on Human Rights, which has been interpreted by courts as prohibiting extradition to countries where they would face torture or inhuman or degrading treatment or punishment. Finally, if the asylum determination procedure has gone through several instances and has lasted for several years, then the individuals concerned will have acquired a claim to be treated as immigrants, whose right to stay no longer depends on the circumstances of their admission.

Controlled admission for permanent residence

Traditional immigration countries outside Europe have for a long time operated programmes (the United States quota system, the Canadian and Australian point systems) under which immigrants are selected but enjoy immediate permanent residence status when admitted. There is also an expectation that these immigrants will adopt the citizenship of their country of settlement. Such programmes hardly exist for economic migrants in Europe and the number of immigrants who fit this category has been declining also in the United States and Canada, where transition from temporary to permanent status is now more common.

However, admission for immediate permanent residence is still very important for other types of immigrants. In particular, close family members of permanent resident foreigners or of citizens of the host country have a strong claim to reunification in that country without a specific time limit to their residence permits or handicaps in their access to employment opportunities. As with the status of permanent residents, the European Union has also brought about a significant harmonization of family reunification (Council directive EC/86/2003). This directive foresees that family members admitted for purposes of reunification shall obtain residence permits of the same duration as those already held by their sponsors, shall enjoy the same rights of access to employment, and that residence permits for spouses, unmarried partners and minor children become independent of their sponsor's permit after five years.

There is once again a group of refugees that fall within the category discussed here. The United States, Canada and Australia have comparatively large-scale programmes for refugee resettlement. Different from TPS and individual asylum procedures, refugees admitted for resettlement are selected already outside the host country, mostly in refugee camps close to their region of origin, and are then accepted as permanent immigrants. The selection process does not exclusively refer to their refugee condition, as would be ideally the case in asylum determination procedures, but is frequently driven by economic and political interests of the country admitting them.

Why should immigrants selected for permanent residence be considered as a relevant category on a normative scale of temporary migration? The answer is that even those who have a right to stay for good may decide to return or move on. So legal permanence can still be combined with intended and *de facto* temporariness. This is somewhat less likely to be the case among the immigrants discussed here when we compare them with the fifth category of free movers discussed below. Among those selected for permanent residence there is a presumptive fit between their purpose of immigration and the receiving state's willingness to accept them as part of its future resident and citizen population. But circumstances can change. As

678   R. Bauböck

long as they are foreign residents, immigrants remain exposed to the threat of deportation if they come into conflict with the law, including those laws that apply specifically to foreign residents only. Permanent resident foreigners also lose their status if they spend too much time abroad, for example in order to take care of family members in a country of origin. Finally, immigrants may find conditions for settlement and integration harder than they had imagined or opportunities much better somewhere else. We must therefore consider a possibility that seems a converse of the third category discussed above. Just as a stay that is initially temporary may become permanent after some time, so a stay that is initially intended to be permanent may turn out to be temporary after all.

Free admission for long-term residence

The final category on our scale contains the freest migrants. These are individuals whose movement is neither constrained at admission nor with regard to their right to stay. Political theorists usually consider only internal migration as being free in this dual sense and assume that all international migration is exposed to migration control. But this is a myopic view. Surprisingly large and growing flows are exempted from such controls. The first and most obvious subcategory for which this is true are returning citizens. Under international law, every state is obliged to admit unconditionally its own citizens to its territory.[8]

Many citizens who enjoy this right of free admission are in fact not returnees, but immigrants in the proper demographic sense of the term, since they were born abroad and have inherited a citizenship from their parents that provides them with a free admission ticket in a country where they have never resided. Nearly all contemporary states embrace a principle of *ius sanguinis* for 'second generations' born abroad at least until the age of majority. A significant number of states go much further by permitting that citizenship can be passed on across generations without limits (de Groot and Vink 2010). Large emigration flows in the past combined with strong versions of *ius sanguinis* create therefore large extraterritorial populations who can claim a citizenship-based right of free admission for permanent residence. Finally, extraterritorial citizenship can be acquired not only by birth but also by naturalization. The nationality laws of many states offer naturalization to foreign spouses of citizens, to former citizens and their descendants, or to groups considered as belonging to the nation in an ethnocultural sense without any residence requirement.

In certain cases, co-ethnics are also granted admission without having previously acquired citizenship abroad, but with an expectation that they will do so shortly after arrival. The German *Aussiedler* policy and the Israeli Law of Return are the best-known examples of unconditional - admission of co-ethnics towards whom the 'homeland' has a specific duty

Critical Review of International Social and Political Philosophy 679

of protection. These are, however, certainly not the only states with preferential admission of co-ethnics (Joppke 2005). I do not want to discuss here the democratic legitimacy or liberal justifications for such policies (Bauböck 2009), I merely want to point out the empirical relevance of this category.

A second subcategory of migrants enjoys even wider free movement and permanent residence rights than those who can make use of an external citizenship. Dual or multiple citizenship creates a right of free movement back and forth between several states and of unconditional residence in each of these. Growing toleration of dual citizenship is one of the strongest trends in the evolution of nationality laws since the last quarter of the 20th century. All liberal democracies now accept dual citizenship when it is acquired at birth by descent from parents with different nationality or through the combination of *ius soli* and extraterritorial *ius sanguinis*. A shrinking number still require renunciation of a previous citizenship as a condition for naturalization. The trend towards toleration of dual citizenship obtained through naturalization is fed by two quite different policy goals: countries of immigration want to remove renunciation requests as the biggest obstacle for immigrant naturalization, while states that wish to retain economic, cultural and political ties with their 'diasporas' no longer withdraw their citizenship in case of acquisition of a foreign one (Faist and Kivisto 2007; Blatter *et al.* 2009).

While dual citizenship creates personalized zones of free movement between two states that recognize a particular individual as their citizen independently of each other, the third subcategory of free movement emerges from contracts between states that grant each others' citizens free admission for the purpose of long-term residence. The most prominent example is the European Union in which citizens of member states have extensive rights to enter, reside and work in the other member states. These rights are not fully unconditional. On the one hand, governments can decide to impose temporary restrictions on the citizens of new accession states with regard to access to employment.[9] On the other hand, residence rights of European Union citizens remain conditional on comprehensive sickness insurance coverage and on not becoming a burden for the social assistance system of the host state. European Union citizens can also be expelled when they constitute a threat to public order, but every expulsion order must be examined individually and the measure must be proportional, which implies that the duration of previous residence must be taken into account. The same residence rights and conditions are extended to third country national family members of European Union citizens and apply also to international students from other European Union countries (European Parliament and Council Directive 2004/38/EC). The European Union is not the only example of a free movement zone that offers long-term residence rights to the citizens of particular other states. Britain and

680   R. Bauböck

Ireland formed until 1997 a common travel area without passport controls and both states still grant each other's citizens free admission and indefinite leave to remain. Similarly, since 1954, the Nordic Passport Union has allowed citizens of Denmark, Iceland, Norway, Finland and Sweden to enter freely and stay in any of the other countries.

Regional unions of this kind create the strongest potential for normatively unconstrained and subjectively intended temporary migration. Circulatory migration may be even more free for multiple citizens since states cannot impose any conditions on readmission, but the selection criteria used for awarding citizenship refer to presumptively lasting genuine ties, which reduces somewhat the likelihood of temporary migration as a purely opportunity seeking activity. Specifically, a second citizenship acquired through long-term residence will generally enhance the likelihood of future residence. Migrants with genuine ties to several countries whose citizenship they possess may *de facto* move frequently back and forth, but each temporary stay remains embedded in a longer-term biographical trajectory. Instead of perceiving their stay as temporary, they may therefore rather consider their absence as a temporary interruption of long-term residence. By contrast, in the case of regional unions, freedom of movement is not granted as a recognition of multiple ties that connect migrants to several countries. Citizens of the European Union enjoy freedom of movement simply by virtue of being citizens of a country that subscribes to a reciprocal international agreement. Compared with multiple citizenship that results from previous migration, the effect of such regional agreements is that freedom of movement is granted to large populations most of whom are unlikely to make actual use of it. Those who do are also more likely to be purely opportunity seeking migrants who rarely develop lasting ties to their host society and see little point in acquiring its citizenship. Free movement in regional unions of states is therefore the condition under which a right to permanent residence will most often lead to intended, expected and *de facto* temporary migration.

Enhancing citizenship for temporary migrants

Apart from irregular status, the other four types of temporary migration discussed in the previous section can be regarded as normatively acceptable in the sense that it is possible to define conditions under which the states involved would not commit any moral wrong in offering these statuses. This condition of justifiability can be achieved if temporary migrants are granted a set of rights and liberties that protect not only their human and contractual rights but meet the special responsibilities that the states involved have towards them. From this perspective, the normative problem to be resolved falls largely within the domain of non-ideal theory. Knowing that many states fail to respect the rights of temporary migrants adequately,

Critical Review of International Social and Political Philosophy 681

we have to work out strategies that apply under real-world assumptions and that could improve the protection of temporary migrants until it meets the required standards. This problem will be most acute for migrants of type two and will gradually vanish as we move up the scale of freedom towards those enjoying free movement and permanent residence rights. A concern about rights deficits for temporary migrants explains therefore why most theorists have focused on guest worker programmes, virtually ignoring all other types of temporary migration.

If we consider an absence of human rights protection for temporary migrants as the main problem, then the obvious political response is to promote migrants' workers rights through international law. This effort has led to the 1990 International Convention on the Protection of the Rights of All Migrant Workers and Members of Their Families (ICRMW), which contains a comprehensive list of rights of both regular and irregular migrants and came into force in 2003. However, no major receiving country of migrants has so far ratified the ICRMW. The failure of this convention highlights that a human rights response is in several ways insufficient. Highly developed states that host large numbers of migrants do not object to guaranteeing them human rights and claim that these are already protected under their domestic constitutions and other international legal instruments. The general problem is that sending and receiving states of migrants produce partial citizenships for non-resident citizens and non-citizen residents independently of each other. Many more states adhere to international conventions on the rights of refugees and stateless persons because these groups have been deprived of effective citizenship protection by their countries of origin. By contrast, temporary migrants are external citizens of one state and temporary residents of another and each country regards itself as sovereign in regulating these statuses. This does not exclude bilateral agreements between sending and receiving states. When European countries recruited guest workers they concluded many such agreements, but these reflected the interests of the states involved and did not establish new international human rights standards.

The unwillingness of states to provide adequate human rights for temporary migrants and to coordinate their rights provision with each other is a serious problem, but it does not address what we have identified as the basic distinction between the five categories, which is their freedom to enter and remain indefinitely in a country of destination. At least in the present world, these are not universal rights of human beings, but special rights of citizens.[10] Another goal might then be to expand the spaces of citizenship in such a way that many more temporary migrants are included. This could be achieved through broader acceptance of dual citizenship or through further enlargement of the European space of free movement and the creation of similar unions in other parts of the world.

682   *R. Bauböck*

Both strategies have important merits and have had much greater success than attempts to promote international rights of temporary migrants. In Europe, America and Oceania, the number of states that require that naturalization applicants must renounce a citizenship of origin or that withdraw their nationality if their citizens acquire a foreign one, is shrinking rapidly. As a result, many more individuals enjoy today free movement between at least two states that have to admit them unconditionally. However, there are significant normative constraints on pursuing this strategy. Citizenship as membership in a particular state presupposes a genuine link between an individual and that state.[11] Temporary migration itself cannot create a sufficiently strong link that would justify a claim to citizenship. Therefore, temporary migrants must first become long-term residents before they can obtain their host country's citizenship. Where citizenship can be easily acquired without any genuine link, as is the case in states offering their passports to big investors or to third and later generations of emigrant descent, citizenship loses its intrinsic value as membership in a self-governing political community and is reduced to its instrumental value of facilitating free movement. The normative constraint is here on the state's offer of citizenship, not on individual choice. Persons who meet a criterion of genuine links may apply for citizenship for entirely instrumental reasons without citizenship being thereby devalued through over-inclusion, since the benefits of membership will then still be granted only to those who have a prior claim to inclusion.

The second strategy of promoting regional unions has also brought some spectacular results. The last two rounds of European Union accession have not only regularized large numbers of temporary migrants from Central and Eastern Europe but have provided them additionally with free movement and political representation rights. European Union enlargement is, however, again, only a partial solution to the problem of how to make temporary migration free. Just as individuals must qualify for citizenship status through particular links to the country concerned, so countries must qualify for joining an economic and political union of states. Apart from the 1993 Copenhagen criteria of democracy, the rule of law, human rights, protection of minorities, a functioning market economy and acceptance of the aims of political, economic and monetary union, there is an additional implicit condition that only neighbouring states[12] can join the European Union, which is after all a regional union rather than a Kantian world confederation of free republics. One could then still hope for a replication of supranational unions with internal free movement in other continents, which would eventually provide all human beings with a supranational citizenship that complements their national ones and that provides them with opportunities for temporary migration in other states under conditions of free admission and indefinite residence. Even this politically very remote but normatively attractive goal would, however, leave temporary migration across the external borders of such unions in significant ways less free.

Critical Review of International Social and Political Philosophy 683

All the obstacles discussed so far may be considered as problems within non-ideal theory. This is obvious for states' unwillingness to agree on a set of rights for temporary migrants. But also the difficulties of expanding citizenship or regional unions beyond qualifying candidates would no longer arise if free movement could be disconnected from citizenship status altogether. In an ideal world individuals could move freely across international borders but would still have to take up long-term residence before they can apply for a new citizenship. Similarly, regional unions could remain externally bounded and reserve political rights for the citizens of their member states, but would become open for temporary migration from third countries.

Valeria Ottonelli and Tiziana Torresi have recently argued against such attempts of 'liberal inclusivists' to relegate the temporary migration problem to non-ideal theory (Ottonelli and Torresi 2010). They criticize liberal 'rights fetishism' by pointing out that temporary migrants are vulnerable not only because they lack adequate protection of their rights in the host society, but also because temporary migrants whose life plans are oriented towards return are unlikely to claim citizenship rights and make effective use of them in the destination country. In Ottonelli and Torresi's view, offering them inclusion in the host country cannot overcome their lack of protection there if the migrants' own sense of self-respect is oriented towards the country of origin. The reason is that rights do not have the same meaning and importance for those whose social bases of self-respect do not coincide with the political space of the jurisdiction in which they reside only temporarily.

This is an important insight, but it needs to be unpacked. I find Ottonelli and Torresi's argument not so convincing with regard to the protective rights dimension of citizenship, but very pertinent for its active participatory dimension. A liberal inclusivist could respond that Ottonelli and Torresi misconstrue the space of rights by considering only destination countries. If we identify a transnational space of free movement as the most adequate space of rights for temporary migrants and promote multiple citizenships and regional unions within this space, then there is no more mismatch with the social space of self-respect within which temporary migrants attribute meaning to their rights. This latter space may be narrower than the former but it is embedded rather than disconnected. Dual citizens enjoy both internal and external citizenship and European Union free movers are citizens of the Union as well as of their countries of origin. In this respect, there is not much difference between internal temporary migration within a large state and within the European Union. In both cases migrants tend to accept working conditions that are shunned by locals and refrain from claiming their rights if they regard their migration as merely temporary and driven by short-term income goals. Since internal free movement within states is not considered as giving rise to a significant

684   *R. Bauböck*

mismatch between spaces of rights and of self-respect, building supranational spaces of free movement seems an adequate response to concerns about the protection of temporary international migrants. The deeper worry raised by Ottonelli and Torresi's argument is that the perceived intrinsic value of citizenship of the European Union or of what we might call 'dual passport citizenship' will be generally rather low. These migrants are therefore likely to remain passive citizens protected by rights that they do not help to create through active democratic participation. Providing citizenship rights for temporary migrants may indeed not be a satisfactory answer in this respect if temporary migrants care little about citizenship in the first place.

The second limitation of Ottonelli and Torresi's argument is that they focus on individual temporary migration projects that create a disjuncture between a social space of self-respect and a political space of rights without considering the structural implications of large-scale temporary migration for the institution of democratic citizenship itself. I will explore in the next section whether the inclusion of temporary migrants requires a fundamentally different model of citizenship that is no longer territorial and intergenerational and will then conclude by suggesting the need for a complementary individual perspective of life-course citizenship that addresses the concerns raised by Ottonelli and Torresi.

A hypermigration dystopia and alternative citizenship models

The United Nations Population Division estimates that currently less than four per cent of the world population are international migrants, i.e. persons who have lived for more than one year outside their country of birth (United Nations 2006). This statistic does not include seasonal circulatory migration, but twelve months are generally not considered long-term residence, so most temporary migrants who engage in continuous work will be included in the four per cent estimate.

Imagine now a radically different world in which most people are temporary migrants for most of their lives. Assuming for a moment that the current system of territorial jurisdiction of states and intergenerational citizenship remains in place, the effect would be that in most countries a majority of citizens would be non-residents and a majority of residents would be non-citizens at any given point in time. Let us call this hypothetical scenario a hypermigration world.[13] I suspect the impact on democracy would be quite dramatic. When Henry Sidgwick considered the conflict between a cosmopolitan principle of open borders and the need for patriotic sentiments, he suggested that '...the casual aggregates that might result from perfectly unrestrained immigration would lack internal cohesion (Sidgwick 1897, p. 308). As liberal nationalists today, Sidgwick was mostly concerned about the effect of long-term immigration on a shared public culture that is seen to support citizens' social solidarity and democratic deliberation (e.g. Miller 1995). I think that Sidgwick's worries apply more plausibly to an increase of temporary migration precisely because it does *not* lead to intensive interactions and cultural changes that affect both natives and migrants. In liberal societies the transformation of national cultures through immigration is nothing to be regretted. And long-term settlement of immigrants generates an expectation of mutual adaptation between natives and newcomers that will never be free of conflicts but that promotes also a search for shared interpretations of the citizenship which unites them as members of the polity. By contrast, hypermigration would not only undermine civic solidarity among accidental co-residents but the very preconditions of citizenship as an institution.

The primary reason for this conclusion is that intergenerational territorial citizenship acquired at birth and for life would no longer be sustainable. *Ius soli* would no longer make sense, since the fact of birth in the territory could no longer serve as a proxy for an expectation of future residence. With free movement for everyone in the hypermigration world, the right of return, which sustains this expectation for emigrants in the present world, would become meaningless. *Ius sanguinis* would lead to an even stronger disconnection between territorial population and citizens by descent, most of whom would be born abroad and would never take up long-term residence in the territory of the state whose citizens they are. Citizenship acquired by descent would become just a label derived from one's family tree rather than an allocation mechanism for a status that unites citizens across generations. The only plausible rule for determining who is a citizen in such a world is *ius domicilii*. Citizenship would be acquired automatically after a short time of residence and also lost automatically when moving on to a different state.

Replacing intergenerational citizenship with a purely residential one would have profound consequences for the structure of democratic life. Territorial populations would indeed become 'casual aggregates' of migrants who happen to reside currently in any given territorial jurisdiction but each of whom knows that most others around had not been here for a long time and are not likely to be here in a few years. Such aggregates are not a sufficient basis for self-governing democratic polities, whose citizens authorize the making of laws to which they will be subjected and agree to long-term public investments for the sake of future generations' well-being and the general flourishing of the polity. Temporary co-residents will, however, still have interests in the provision of a public infrastructure that enables them to be mobile and in the preservation of security and public order and could therefore agree to be taxed and subjected to laws that pursue this goal. But their interest in representation by elected lawmakers and in holding public authorities accountable would be greatly diminished. A libertarian or semi-authoritarian government that provides a public infrastructure and security

686   R. Bauböck

without interfering too much with the private business and lives of residents would probably emerge as the system of political rule that best responds to popular interests.

On the other hand, the human desire for belonging to and recognition in a self-governing community of equals is too strong to dissipate completely even in a hypermigration world. Civil society could then become the space where forms of pseudo-citizenship are recreated. Non-territorial associations with stable and intergenerational memberships could substitute many of the public goods currently provided by states to residents with club goods provided by associations to members only. A world that produces hypermigration would also have communication and transportation technologies that make it easy to build and maintain strong forms of self-government within such associations. Some associations could be formed on the basis of social class to secure the provision of services such as quality education for one's children or quality health care for one's parents. Others might emerge on the basis of shared ethnic or religious identities. Many of these associations could be internally democratic and some might establish powerful monopolies in the provision of basic goods that reduce exit options for their members and create a form of subjection that closely resembles government in territorial states.

In contrast with Sidgwick's fear, the major difference to the contemporary world would not be a devastating increase of cultural diversity, but a loss of heterogeneity within these non-territorial polities, whose members would be self-selected to be similar to each other in their interests, identities and ideologies. In a hypermigration world there could be little solidarity across these dividing lines, apart from a shared Hobbesian interest in a political power that is able to preserve public order and territorial mobility.

A purely hypothetical scenario like this one does of course not show that temporary migration at its current pace and volume is in any way corrosive for democratic citizenship as we know it. I have pointed out at the end of the third section that the expansion of free movement regimes is likely to lead to less permanent immigration and more intended, expected and *de facto* temporary migration. Yet the corrosive effects of hypermigration depend on the share of temporary migrants in the total population rather than in the migrant population. Spaces for free movement can be more easily expanded when economic and political disparities between countries that provide structural push and pull factors are reduced. Under these conditions it is more plausible to expect a decline in the overall volume of migration together with an increase in the relative share of temporary migration.

I have introduced the hypermigration dystopia for three reasons. First, it highlights the implicit background assumptions that we tend to make when considering the political integration of migrants. We see them as integrating into stable territorial polities with comprehensive powers, intergenerational citizenship and largely sedentary populations. These conditions are, however, historically contingent facts rather than logical necessities and they might change over time. If and when this happens, the transformation of democracy will be as radical as in the transition from direct democracy in small city-republics to representative democracy in large territorial states.

Second, some developments in contemporary civil society point towards a loss of integrative power of state-based democracy and a trend towards alternative provision of public goods, such as education or health care, as club goods for internationally mobile elites. This trend is caused by a neo-liberal dismantling of social citizenship more than by a rise in temporary migration but it is significant that high income migrants develop a demand for the kind of non-territorial provision of club goods that can be expected as a general pattern in the hypermigration scenario.

Third, regimes of purely residential citizenship exist also in present democracies at sub-state levels and they might be considered as alternative real world models of polities that are fully adapted to the integration of temporary migrants as equal citizens. In contrast with the situation in authoritarian states, such as China, or semi-democracies, such as Russia, where internal migration is still heavily regulated, municipalities and provinces in democratic states are generally open for free internal migration within a state territory. The right of free internal movement is not tied to citizenship but constructed as a human right of all legal residents.[14] Sub-state polities are not only open for territorial admission and residence for citizens and non-citizen residents alike, they also lack any separate system of intergenerational determination of citizenship by birthright or naturalization. Since only a few countries explicitly mention provincial or local citizenship in their constitution, it might seem odd to use the concept of citizenship in this context. However, historically, cities were the cradles of citizenship long before the emergence of the modern state. Moreover, conceptually it makes sense to consider sub-state entities as self-governing polities wherever local and regional governments enjoy substantive autonomous powers and are democratically elected by residents (Bauböck 2003). If cities and provinces have citizens, then there must also be a rule to determine who these citizens are. And this rule is clearly automatic *ius domicilii*, or residence-based citizenship. In most current democratic states, this basic rule is constrained with regard to political citizenship by the state-level regime. Voting in local and regional elections presupposes then national citizenship. In Europe, however, 13 of the 27 European Union member states and two non-member states (Norway and Iceland) have introduced a local franchise that is purely residence-based and includes third country nationals.

Steven Vertovec and other scholars studying migration and ethnic diversity have pointed out that 'super-diverse' metropolises provide social, economic and cultural spaces in which migrants are no longer minorities

688   *R. Bauböck*

facing native sedentary majorities (Vertovec 2007b). To a certain extent these cities provide also politically open and integrative spaces for temporary migration. One might therefore ask whether my picture of the hypermigration dystopia was not painted too black. If cities can be governed democratically based on a regime of residential citizenship in spite of large 'floating populations' of temporary migrants, why should this not be possible for states?

The sceptical answer to this question is that global metropolises may have gained considerable autonomy vis-à-vis national governments in economic and cultural matters, but remain politically dependent and embedded in the larger states where they are located. And if super-diverse cities became independent states they would also adopt an intergenerational citizenship regime. Apart from these 'realist' reservations, there is also a normative concern. If my assumption about a universal human desire for intergenerational membership in political communities is correct, then residential citizenship in sub-state polities should be properly seen as complementing state level intergenerational citizenship without replacing it.

The formula 'complementing without replacing' was also adopted in the 1997 European Union Amsterdam Treaty in order to clarify the relation between European Union citizenship and national citizenship of the member states. In contrast with local citizenship, supranational citizenship in the European Union is derivative from member state nationality rather than from residence. While European Union enlargement has widened the space for free temporary migration, third-country nationals and their descendants can acquire supranational citizenship only through birth or naturalization in one of the member states. Some migrant associations, academic scholars and European Union policy-makers have proposed to offer migrants from outside the European Union an independent residence-based access to European Union citizenship. This reform would risk undermining a basic feature of the union. The derivative nature of supranational citizenship is not a defect, but adequately reflects the constitutional architecture of a union constituted by its member states. A generalized form of residential citizenship at the European Union level would, moreover, greatly exacerbate problems that are already manifest now and that the hypermigration scenario has served to highlight. European Union citizenship is quite strong with regard to rights and most of these rights depend explicitly on making use of the free movement privilege by taking up residence in another member state. But European Union citizenship has no specific legal duties attached to it. National governments have repeatedly rejected proposals to introduce even a modest European Union income tax. Finally, citizenship practices are particularly weakly developed, as low and declining voter turnouts in European Parliament elections illustrate. In many ways, European Union citizenship is already now a 'citizenship light' (Joppke 2010). Severing its link with member state nationality would make it much lighter

Critical Review of International Social and Political Philosophy 689

still and would therefore merely serve to speed up the pace of institutional adaptation to hypermigration, which would eventually also make territorial democracy harder to sustain.

Conclusion: stretching the spaces of citizenship and switching between perspectives on migration

I have explored how democratic citizenship may be reformed to include temporary migrants and how temporary migration could transform the institutions of democratic citizenship. My conclusion is that the dilemma I have sketched at the beginning cannot be completely resolved. Fully integrating temporary migrants as equal citizens in territorial polities is difficult since generalized temporary migration is likely to undermine the very structure of territorial citizenship.

Political liberals can hardly stop critical reflection with a diagnosis of this kind. The question raised, but not answered, by Ottonelli and Torresi is how temporary migrants experience the various citizenship statuses they occupy during their itineraries and what could be done to enable them not merely to claim rights, but also to gain self-respect and recognition by others.

If institutional solutions are inevitably imperfect, then what is needed may be a change of perspective that does not only take the political community as reference point and unit of analysis, but also individual migrants themselves. In addition to the strategies of *stretching* the spaces of citizenship that I have discussed in the third and fourth sections, we should promote a *switching* back and forth between two alternative views of migration. From the perspective of states, temporary migrants enter and leave their territories, but from the perspective of temporary migrants states enter and leave their lives (Bauböck 1998).

This *Gestaltswitch* enriches, first, our epistemological horizon. Taking migrants' life-courses as units of analysis implies a shift from a static and spatial view of migration towards a dynamic and temporally structured one. Second, it widens our normative horizon too. Instead of asking what is needed to make temporary migrants equal with the sedentary citizens of their host or home countries, we can then consider what could make temporary migrants full citizens over the course of their lives. This may sound like an excuse for accepting partial citizenship, but some temporary loss of rights, if voluntarily incurred, could indeed be accepted if it leads eventually to multiple citizenship with its entailed rights of free movement.

The main normative implication of the perspectival switch would, however, not be any specific policy recommendations, but rather the search for a public 'fusion of horizons' between sedentary populations whose citizenships and political identities are determined by a stable set of nested (local, provincial, national and supranational) polities and mobile populations

690   R. Bauböck

whose lives and political identities are shaped by multiple citizenship status transitions.

Acknowledgements

Draft versions of this paper were presented at the Association of Legal and Social Philosophy conference at Southampton University, UK, 9 April 2010; at a GRITIM-UNESCO workshop on the Ethics of Migration at Pompeu Fabra University Barcelona, Spain, 26 April 2010; and at the 'Citizenship and Civil Society: Cosmopolitan Challenges' conference at Sun Yat-sen University, Guangzhou, China, 10 December 2010. I am very grateful to Chris Armstrong, Andrew Mason, David Owen, Valeria Ottonelli, Andrei Stavila, and Tiziana Torresi for generous and helpful written comments on a first draft.

Notes

1. For a microeconomic model confirming that migrants may rationally accept a temporary decline of income in order to reduce relative deprivation in contexts of origin, see Stark (1991), pp. 87–166.
2. Citizenship is often thought of as an all or nothing matter, so that individuals can be either citizens or non-citizens, but not partial citizens. One can distinguish three core dimensions of citizenship as a membership status, as a bundle of legal rights and duties, and as a set of ethical virtues and practices. Whereas membership seems conceptually a dichotomous category (you have it or you do not), the strength of citizenship rights or practices is often measured by degrees and these dimensions can also be disconnected from membership status. I use the term 'partial citizenship', however, in relation to all three dimensions. Individuals are partial citizens when they are deprived of certain core rights of citizenship, when they lack incentives and dispositions for civic participation, and when they are considered as partial insiders and partial outsiders (see also note 10 below).
3. Joseph Carens famously claimed that from a perspective of global justice, birthright citizenship is like a feudal status (Carens 1987, 1989). Ruth Rubio-Marín proposed that long-term residents should automatically be turned into citizens because the imperative of democratic inclusion of all subjected to the laws overrides migrants' right to choose between alternative citizenship statuses (Rubio-Marín 2000). Dora Kostakopoulou suggests that a general system of civic registration should replace citizenship by birth or naturalization (Kostakopoulou 2008). Ayelet Shachar calls for a birthright privilege levy that compensates the citizens of poor countries for the undeserved outcome of the birthright lottery (Shachar 2009), and Jackie Stevens regards the principle of birthright membership as the main cause of endemic violence in the international state system (Stevens 2010).
4. See, for example, the largely failed German efforts in the early 1980s to promote return migration of guest workers through financial incentives.
5. Like Carens, I prefer the term 'irregular migrants' because it is less heavily laden (Carens 2008b, p. 164) than alternative terms such as 'illegal migrants' which attributes illegality to persons as such instead of their actions, or 'undocumented migrants' which conceals the fact of law breaking by suggesting that these migrants merely lack documents.
6. On the rights numbers trade-off in migration, see Martin and Ruhs (2008).

Critical Review of International Social and Political Philosophy 691

7. Immigrants' basic knowledge of a dominant language is clearly in their own interest as well as in the interest of citizens whose mother tongue that language is. This may justify language tests both at the threshold to permanent residence and to naturalization, as long as immigrants are offered sufficient opportunities and incentives for learning this language. What is objectionable are tests designed to deter immigrants from applying for improved legal status or to select immigrants according to their educational background.
8. Of course, this right too is not universally honoured, as some regimes practice various forms of banishment of dissidents or ethnic cleansing. Non-cooperation with readmission requests in case of deportation amounts also to non-compliance with this universal duty.
9. The transition period for free access to the labour market for eight of the 2004 accession countries has ended in May 2011; for Bulgaria and Rumania it may last until 2014.
10. Unconditional rights to stay and return are a defining characteristic of citizenship as nationality in the current international state system. This does not rule out that some non-nationals can also enjoy fairly strong rights to admission and permanent residence. The fact that European Union citizens and some categories of co-ethnic immigrants are granted mobility rights that approximate those of national citizens does not illustrate that these rights can be easily disconnected from citizenship status, but rather that citizenship status itself is no longer strictly tied to nationality. Foreign nationals who are granted unconditional rights to stay and return are quasi-citizens rather than privileged non-citizens.
11. See the judgment of the International Court of Justice in the Nottebohm case (1955 I.C.J. 4). I defend a broader stakeholder principle that all those and only those should be recognized as citizens whose life-courses link their interests in autonomy and well-being to the self-government and flourishing of a particular polity (Bauböck 2009).
12. The condition is not one of strict contiguity, since otherwise the UK, Ireland, Greece, Sweden, Finland, Malta and Cyprus could not have joined, but of geographic location within a broader European region, the borders of which are partly renegotiated through the process of European integration itself.
13. The term 'hyper*mobility*' has been introduced by human geographer John Adams (Adams 2005) to refer to the increasing ease and distance of spatial mobility (in spite of constant numbers of people travelling). I am here not interested in spatial mobility as such, but in migration across political borders and specifically in the effect of increasing numbers of people involved in such migration. This is why I introduce the term 'hyper*migration*' here.
14. Universal Declaration of Human Rights, Art. 13(1); International Covenant on Civil and Political Rights, Art. 12(1).

Notes on contributor

Rainer Bauböck holds a Chair in Social and Political Theory at the Department of Political and Social Sciences, European University Institute, Florence. His fields of research are normative political theory and comparative research on citizenship, European integration, migration, nationalism and minority rights. He is Co-director of the EUDO observatory on citizenship (http://eudo-citizenship.eu).

692   *R. Bauböck*

References

Adams, J., 2005. Hypermobility: a challenge to governance. *In*: C. Lyall and J. Tait, eds. *New modes of governance: developing an integrated policy approach to science, technology, risk and the environment*. Aldershot: Ashgate, 123–138.

Bauböck, R., 1998. The crossing and blurring of boundaries in international migration. Challenges for social and political theory. *In*: R. Bauböck and J. Rundell, eds. *Blurred boundaries. Migration, ethnicity, citizenship*. Aldershot: Ashgate, 17–52.

Bauböck, R., 2003. Reinventing urban citizenship. *Citizenship Studies*, 7 (2), 137–158.

Bauböck, R., 2009. The rights and duties of external citizenship. *Citizenship Studies*, 13 (5), 475–499.

Bell, D.A., 2005. Justice for migrant workers? Foreign domestic workers in Hong Kong and Singapore. *In*: S.-H. Tan, ed. *Challenging citizenship: group membership and cultural identity in a global age*. Aldershot: Ashgate, 41–62.

Blatter, J.K., Erdmann, S., and Schwanke, K., 2009. *Acceptance of dual citizenship: empirical data and political contexts*. Working Paper Series 'Glocal Governance and Democracy' 8, 1–50. Lucerne: University of Lucerne.

Bosniak, L., 2006. *The citizen and the alien: dilemmas of contemporary membership*. Princeton, NJ: Princeton University Press.

Carens, J.H., 1987. Aliens and citizens: the case for open borders. *Review of Politics*, 49 (2), 251–273.

Carens, J.H., 1989. Membership and morality. Admission to citizenship in liberal democratic states. *In*: R.W. Brubaker, ed. *Immigration and the politics of citizenship in Europe and North America*. Lanham, MD: University Press of America, 31–49.

Carens, J.H., 1992. Migration and morality. A liberal egalitarian perspective. *In*: B. Barry and R. Goodin, eds. *Free movement. Ethical issues in the transnational migration of people and of money*. Philadelphia, PA: Pennsylvania State University Press, 25–47.

Carens, J.H., 2008a. Live-in domestics, seasonal workers, foreign students, and others hard to locate on the map of democracy. *Journal of Political Philosophy*, 16 (4), 419–445.

Carens, J.H., 2008b. The rights of irregular migrants. *Ethics and International Affairs*, 22 (2), 163–186.

Carens, J.H., 2009. The case for amnesty. Time erodes the state's right to deport. *Boston Review*, May/June. Available from: http://bostonreview.net/BR34.3/ndf_immigration.php/.

Castles, S., 2006. Back to the future? Can Europe meet its labour needs through temporary migration? Working Papers No. 1, International Migration Institute. Oxford: University of Oxford.

Chang, H., 2003. The immigration paradox: poverty, distributive justice, and liberal egalitarianism. *De Paul Law Review*, 52, 759–776.

de Groot, G.-R. and Vink, M., 2010. Loss of citizenship. Trends and regulations in Europe. European UnionDO CITIZENSHIP Comparative Report 4, 1–53. Available from: http://eudo-citizenship.eu/docs/loss_paper_updated_14102010. pdf/.

Faist, T. and Kivisto, P., 2007. *Dual citizenship in global perspective*. Basingstoke: Palgrave Macmillan.

Global Commission on International Migration (GCIM), 2005. *Migration in an interconnected world: new directions for action*. New York: GCIM.

Critical Review of International Social and Political Philosophy   693

Guild, E., Groenendijk, K., and Carrera, S., eds., 2009. *Illiberal liberal states. Immigration, citizenship and integration in the European Union*. Farnham: Ashgate.

Joppke, C., 2005. *Selecting by origin. Ethnic migration in the liberal state*. Cambridge, MA: Harvard University Press.

Joppke, C., 2010. The inevitable lightening of citizenship. *European Journal of Sociology/Archives européennes de sociologie*, 51 (1), 9–32.

Kostakopoulou, D., 2008. *The future governance of citizenship*. Cambridge: Cambridge University Press.

Kostakopoulou, D., Ersboll, E., and van Oers, R., eds., 2010. *A redefinition of belonging? Language and integration tests in Europe*. Leiden: Brill/Martinus Nijhoff.

Martin, P.L. and Ruhs, M., 2008. Numbers vs. rights: trade-offs and guest worker programs. *International Migration Review*, 42 (1), 249–265.

Miller, D., 1995. *On nationality*. Oxford: Oxford University Press.

Ottonelli, V. and Torresi, T., 2010. Inclusivist egalitarian liberalism and temporary migration: a dilemma. *Journal of Political Philosophy* DOI: 10.1111/j.1467-9760.2010.00380.x.

Rubio-Marín, R., 2000. *Immigration as a democratic challenge: citizenship and inclusion in Germany and the United States*. Cambridge: Cambridge University Press.

Ruhs, M., 2006. The potential of temporary migration programmes in future international migration policy. *International Labour Review*, 146 (1–2), 7–36.

Shachar, A., 2009. *The birthright lottery Citizenship and global inequality*. Cambridge, MA: Harvard University Press.

Sidgwick, H., 1897. *The elements of politics*. London: Macmillan.

Stark, O., 1991. *The migration of labour*. Oxford: Blackwell.

Stevens, J., 2010. *States without nations. Citizenship for mortals*. New York, NY: Columbia University Press.

United Nations, 2006. *International Migration Report 2006. A Global Assessment*. New York, NY: Population Division, United Nations.

Vertovec, S., 2007a. *Circular migration: the way forward in global policy?* Working Papers 4. International Migration Institute. Oxford: University of Oxford.

Vertovec, S., 2007b. Super-diversity and its implications. *Ethnic and Racial Studies*, 29 (6), 1024–1054.

Walzer, M., 1983. *Spheres of justice. A defense of pluralism and equality*. New York, NY: Basic Books.

[9]

Transformation of Citizenship: Status, Rights, Identity

CHRISTIAN JOPPKE
American University of Paris, France

ABSTRACT *In a spirit of stocktaking and identifying frontiers of research, this article reviews recent changes of citizenship in three dimensions: status, rights, and identity. With respect to status, it is argued that access to citizenship has been liberalized. On the rights dimension, there has been a weakening of social rights and rise of minority rights. Citizenship identities today are universalistic, which limits states' attempts to counter the centrifugal dynamics of ethnically diversifying societies with unity and integration campaigns.*

After Brubaker's (1992) agenda-setting work on nationhood and citizenship, the fast growing literature on citizenship in sociology and political science became polarized between those who defended citizenship as master status in the modern nation-state (Brubaker, 1992) and "post-national" critics who saw it devalued by the rise of a global human rights regime (Soysal, 1994). The opposition between defenders and critics of citizenship obscured that both sides addressed different dimensions of citizenship: status, as in Brubaker's Weberian theory of citizenship as social closure, versus rights, which is the focus of Soysal's adaptation to the globalizing world of T. H. Marshall's rights-focused citizenship theory that had dominated liberal postwar sociology. The lively debate over the pros and cons of both positions, while not unaware of the different dimensions of citizenship addressed by them (Joppke, 1999a, 1999b), sidestepped the logical problem that statements about citizenship as status cannot be used to criticize or reject statements about citizenship as rights and vice versa—both talk past one another.

What I seek to undertake here, in admittedly broad and speculative brushes, is to draw connections between developments in the different dimensions of citizenship, which either had not been sufficiently distinguished in the past *or* had been treated in insulation. With respect to the latter, the purpose of such enterprise is to redress what, in my view, is a shortcoming in the existing literature, its high degree of segmentation, as a result of which citizenship is many things to many people. In fact, the notion of citizenship studies, which this journal helped establish, suggests the existence of a joint (if naturally contested) frame of reference, which in reality does not exist. Statements about sexual, urban, or ecological citizenship, with respect to the underlying notion of citizenship, are unintelligible to

38   C. Joppke

someone who thinks of citizenship in terms of nationality law. My point is not to question the advance in knowledge that comes with specialization. But there is need for a comprehensive theory of citizenship that is capable of connecting developments in one dimension of citizenship with developments in other dimensions.

Such a comprehensive account must distinguish between at least three aspects of citizenship: citizenship as status, which denotes formal state membership and the rules of access to it; citizenship as rights, which is about the formal capacities and immunities connected with such status; and, in addition, citizenship as identity, which refers to the behavioral aspects of individuals acting and conceiving of themselves as members of a collectivity, classically the nation, *or* the normative conceptions of such behavior imputed by the state. With respect to the latter, citizenship addresses the unity and integration of society, and it is closely connected with the semantics of nation and nationalism.

Conceiving of citizenship in this way, as combination of status, rights, and identity, still leaves it an intrinsically state-related concept. But even heterodox uses of the citizenship concept, which seek to decouple citizenship from the state, perhaps most ardently urban citizenship (Holston & Appadurai, 1999), draw their acumen from linkage with the state, if only in the negative; and the various claims-making citizenships, which have evolved in the ambit of social movements, such as sexual, multicultural, or ecological citizenship, always entail demands on the state to do certain things (recognize gay marriage, grant minority rights, save the environment and so on).

Against the proliferation of hyphenated citizenships, I suggest to fold citizenship back to what it essentially is: membership in a state, and to throw light from here on the rights and identities connected with it. As obvious as it seems, this is a view that was not always available. In the golden age of nationally closed welfare states that antedated the contemporary era of globalization, citizenship was not visible as a nationally and territorially bounded construct. Tellingly, there is no reflection on citizenship's bounded nature in T. H. Marshall's (1992) universalistic story of evolving citizenship rights. Marshall's key dichotomy was citizenship and class. This reveals that the central line of conflict in the golden age was functional, not territorial: how can workers be citizens? Today, in the era of globalization and blurring state boundaries, conflicts surrounding citizenship have taken on a different meaning, closer to the original meaning of citizenship as state membership: how can foreigners be citizens, and who are we, the Danes?

My argument about the development of citizenship in the three dimensions of status, rights, and identity goes as follows:

1. In the *status* dimension, the most significant development in the past half century has been the liberalization of access to citizenship, removing sexual and racial barriers to naturalization and upgrading territory over descent in the birth attribution of citizenship. The inevitable result of this opening of the citizenry is its internal diversification along ethnic, racial, and religious lines.
2. This has important implications for the *rights* dimension of citizenship. The most important citizen right in the era of national welfare states was social rights. In retrospect, external closure appears as fundamental prerequisite for building strong welfare states, because it created or retained the ethnic homogeneity and solidarities that are required for the redistribution of wealth (See Alesina & Glaeser, 2004; critical of this view are Banting & Kymlicka, 2003). With the ethnic diversification of society the basis for social rights becomes brittle while

other types of right move to the fore: rights of anti-discrimination and multicultural recognition.
3. This again has implications for the *identity* dimension of citizenship. To the degree that citizenship becomes available without ethnic, racial, or cultural provisos and that primordial group affiliations are protected or even furthered by anti-discrimination and multicultural rights, membership in the state no longer connotes a specific identity; membership and identity part ways. Closing the status–rights–identity cycle, this in turn spurs worries about the unity and integration of ethnically diverse societies, and states have responded to this with campaigns to symbolically upgrade citizenship, which may even include a re-tightening of access. States have understood that, having lost control on so many fronts in the age of globalization, their last and quintessential function is to be "people containers" (Hirst & Thompson, 1992), and they won't let this one go lightly. However, the space for the re-nationalization of citizenship is limited by norms of equality and non-discrimination, which allow only universalistic answers to the question of identity.

Michael Walzer (1997) once distinguished the ethnic "nation-states" of Europe, which he deemed partisan "machines for national reproduction", and the "immigrant societies" of North America and Australia, where the state is "neutral" and "committed to none of the groups that make it up". This distinction, if it ever held muster, has become obsolete. The ethnic nation-state is in retreat, as the following review of changes of citizenship in the status, rights, and identity dimensions will demonstrate.

Citizenship As Status: Liberalization of Access

Throughout Western states, there has been a trend toward the non-discriminatory opening of access to citizenship. In North America, racial barriers to naturalization were abolished in the 1950s. Especially in Western Europe, the liberalization trend soon extended to women, in the abolishment of patriarchal descent rules and of women's automatic loss of citizenship in bi-national marriages. Since the 1980s, Western European states abolished high hurdles to citizenship acquisition for long-settled "guest workers" and their children. Above all, the principle of conditional *jus soli* gained in importance over the classic nation-state principle of *jus sanguinis*. As a result, practically all European Union states now provide either automatic or optional citizenship for second- and third-generation immigrants (see Hansen & Weil, 2001). With respect to naturalization, the required legal residence time has generally been reduced, and the old principle of absolute state discretion in this domain has been reduced. In a few European states, such as the Netherlands and Germany, naturalization has even become as-of-right under certain conditions. Especially in the German case, there has been a drastic retreat of the old idea of cultural assimilation as prerequisite for naturalization. Finally, there has been a general trend toward tolerating dual citizenship in Europe, at least de facto, as in countries that remain explicitly opposed to dual citizenship, such as the Netherlands or Germany (see Howard, 2005).

Overall, in the past half century the access to citizenship for non-citizens and their descendants has been transformed from discretionary anomaly to rule-based routine. As a result, citizenship has become de-sacralized and less nationalistic. The logic of individual

40 *C. Joppke*

rights has entered a domain that, according to international law, is still at the discretion of the sovereign state. Considering the removal of ethnic, racial, and cultural restrictions, citizenship is no longer exempt from the sociological commonplace that people have multiple identities, which are already forced upon them by the process of functional differentiation. The state has been transformed from ethnic nation-state, owned by "its" people who could reject or accept newcomers as they saw fit, into post-national state, in which the principle of liberal democracy requires congruence between the subjects and objects of rule. This liberal-democratic principle, which is at the same time threatened and activated by the inter- and trans-nationalization of society that is the inevitable result of international migration, has been the true engine of the liberalization of access to citizenship (see Rubio-Marin, 2000).

If there is an inch of truth to this scenario, Brubaker's (1992) well-known argument that citizenship is determined by long-standing traditions of nationhood has to be rejected. Then Germany could have never had its citizenship reform of 1999, and this proverbial ethnic nation could not, as it now does, grant conditional *jus soli* citizenship to second-generation immigrants. It was never clear how, in a functionally differentiated society, something as technically complex as nationality law, which is written and rewritten by jurists observing other jurists, should have been driven by the profanations of nationalist intellectuals, be they statesmen, composers, or fairy-tale collectors. Instead, it is more plausible to assume that legal innovations, such as *jus sanguinis* in the French Civil Code of 1803 (see Weil, 2002), are taken as model to be emulated elsewhere, either by conquest or by imitation (which now tends to be eulogized as "best practice"). Because of the transformation of Europe into immigrant societies and solid democracies after World War II, perceived "best practice" today happens to be conditional *jus soli*, recommended at least indirectly in Articles 6 and 14 of the 1997 European Convention on Nationality. Such a story of "citizenship without identity" (Joppke, 2005a) is still waiting to be written; but its *prima facie* plausibility is difficult to deny.

In a sweeping comparison of 25 countries, Patrick Weil (2001) identified three factors that, in their combination, make for liberalized, non-discriminatory citizenship laws: past immigration, which creates a high number of long-settled non-citizens on the territory; consolidated borders and the absence of unfinished nation-building concerns, which reduces the perceived need for national-origin discriminations; and, last but not least, liberal-democratic norms, which command a congruence of the subjects and objects of state authority. This grid explains a number of seeming anomalies—Germany, with Europe's largest immigrant population after World War II and arguably committed to liberal-democratic norms, only liberalized access to citizenship once the nation-building concerns connected with the German division had subsided; Italy, a liberal democracy with stable borders, tightened its citizenship law in the early 1990s because of the suddenness and massiveness of third world immigration around that time, but now is about to liberalize because this immigration has come to be accepted as permanent;[1] and Israel, notionally a liberal democracy and entirely a result of immigration, is unlikely to ever turn to non-discriminatory immigration and citizenship policies because of its precarious geopolitical position in the Arab world (see Joppke, 2005b).

However compelling and compact, Weil's analysis suffers from being functionalist and teleological. There is a *politics* of citizenship and with it the possibility of other than liberal outcomes. In an earlier paper, I argued that contemporary reforms of citizenship can be de-ethnicizing, easing access for immigrants inside the state, or re-ethnicizing, strengthening ties with emigrants abroad. Which trend prevails often depends on the ideological orientation of the government, liberal-leftists favoring de-ethnicization, conservatives favoring re-ethnicization (Joppke, 2003). In an interesting variation of this argument, Mark Morjé Howard (2006) argued that what matters is not so much the ideological orientation of the government but the existence or absence of a far right party capable of mobilizing an always xenophobic public opinion.

Questioning the liberalization thesis, a review of acquisition and loss of nationality in 15 EU states concluded that there has been a "new trend" towards raising the hurdles for naturalization in countries with sizeable settled immigrant populations (Bauböck et al., 2006, p. 3), examples being Austria, Denmark, France, the Netherlands and Britain. In fact, past liberalization itself, in feeding populist charges against the "cheapening" of citizenship, is creating the impetus for illiberal reactions. This impetus gained momentum in the wake of the post-2001 worries over Muslim terror and failing immigrant integration in Europe, which moved a number of European countries to impose "civic integration" courses and tests on newcomers (see Joppke, 2007). These civic integration requirements, essentially language skills and knowledge of host society political principles and institutions, are now finding entry into citizenship laws, as it is logical to expect of citizenship applicants what is already expected of entering immigrants. However, this illiberal backlash is notably limited to the naturalization of first-generation immigrants; it generally leaves untouched the more fundamental *jus soli* reforms and the trend toward tolerating dual citizenship.

Citizenship as Rights: From Social Rights to Minority Rights

The ethnic diversification of society, which is partially (of course, not exclusively) the result of liberalized access to citizenship, has shifted the accent in the rights dimension of citizenship from redistributive social rights to procedural civil rights, particularly minority rights. This has been crisply articulated by Pierre Rosanvallon (2000, p. 36):

> The central social values (in a multicultural society) are tolerance rather than solidarity, and impartiality rather than equality. The "good society" is the society that allows the peaceful coexistence of differences, not the society that guarantees inclusion. The principle of citizenship no longer implies a demand for redistribution in this framework, but is reduced to a common trust in autonomy.

While more people have access to citizenship, the substantive benefits accruing from citizenship have thinned down—this is the notorious "crisis of the welfare state". David Goodhart (2004) identified the underlying problem as the "progressive dilemma": a choice has to be made between "solidarity" and "diversity". And, to the degree that there ever was a "choice", it has been in favor of "diversity".

Throughout the West, the past 40 years have experienced a "rights revolution" (Ebb, 1998). But it was mostly a procedural, not substantive rights revolution, oriented on the American model of due process and equal protection. And this rights revolution characteristically goes beyond the citizen to protect the person, especially ascriptive features that mark her as minority. Often "nationality" is even included in the catalogue of targeted discriminations. In this respect it is misleading to address this rights revolution in terms of *citizen* rights because one of its thrusts is to precisely transcend this limitation.

42   C. Joppke

Two legal developments have to be distinguished: first, the extension of citizenship rights to non-citizens; and second, the creation or strengthening of minority rights. The former is the subject of Soysal's (1994) classic study of evolving guest worker rights in Europe (see also the important work of Guiraudon, 2000 which accentuates domestic over global-level processes). What this literature fails to capture is the high variability of differently developed alien rights across countries, internal rights stratification according to type of migrant in any one country (see Morris, 2002), and the possibility of regression, as in the mid-1990s US welfare reform. With respect to the extension of social rights to non-citizens, this has mostly occurred in the case of contribution-based benefits, such as unemployment compensation and pensions. "Big deal", one is tempted to say, because of the reciprocal insurance principle that is at work here, and one may even reasonably exclude the benefits connected with it from the very "concept of social citizenship" (as does Baldwin, 1997, p. 109). With respect to non-contributory, general-tax-based benefits, which indisputably constitute the core of social citizenship, there has been a much higher inclination to either retain benefits to citizens only or to make the "immigration authority" the "watchdog of the welfare state" (p. 111). An interesting case in this respect is Germany. Here the entire welfare function (contributory *and* non-contributory) had never been dependent on nationality. However, this internal universalism is neutralized by restrictive immigration laws that may proscribe the termination of residence for non-citizens who make too much use of the welfare function, especially when out of work. Social rights are thus indirectly restricted through immigration laws, which in this respect have become notably more restrictive in recent years (see Davis, 2006, p. 137f). The enactment of and contest surrounding these micro structures and processes, as well as variations across states, are barely studied. With respect to labor market rights also, there are striking variations. In some countries, like Britain and the Netherlands, public sector employment is or has been made accessible for non-citizens without much ado, while in other countries, like France and Germany, such employment keeps to be reserved for citizens, despite pressures for opening up. Again, not much is known about the legal-political dynamics surrounding these variations.

To be distinguished from this is a second legal development, which consists of the expansion of rights of anti-discrimination and recognition. They target immigrants and their descendants *qua* minority and thus bring into light their ethnicity, race, or religion. The role of citizenship as precondition for such rights is ambiguous. The classic international law of minorities, evolving under the aegis of the League of Nations after World War I and targeting national minorities, requires that its beneficiaries hold the citizenship of the rights-granting state. And, complementing this *legal* prerequisite in the case of national minority protection, the *sociological* impetus behind the creation of domestic anti-discrimination laws, as in the cases of US civil rights law and British race relations law, has been discrimination against people who are considered legitimate fellow members of society, essentially "citizens"; by contrast, countries with minorities that largely retained foreign citizen status have been generally unwilling to put forward anti-discrimination laws, the most notorious example being perhaps Germany, which even has long resisted a European Union mandate to pass such a law. However, the universalistic equality norm inherent in the principle of non-discrimination pushes beyond the nationality limitation so that, as in the example of US civil rights law, a measure that intentionally had targeted only black Americans became extended to third world immigrants (see Skrentny, 2002). And in the European Union, the spirit of the Race Directive of 2000 has even been up front the combating of discrimination against non-citizens, "third state nationals" in Euro-jargon.

Transformation of Citizenship 43

Most empirical and normative studies of minority rights (empirical, Kastoryano, 2002; normative, Kymlicka, 1995) have slighted the different logics of anti-discrimination and multicultural recognition. Anti-discrimination aims at *abolishing* ethnicity or race as marker of individual and group differentiation, whereas recognition seeks to *perpetuate* such differentiation. In a nutshell, anti-discrimination is universalistic; recognition is particularistic.

Liberal states have only exceptionally practiced explicit policies of recognizing minority groups, mostly in an attempt to redress historical injustice, such as slavery, colonialism, and the repression of national minorities. Recognition contradicts the neutrality principle of the liberal state, which moves to the fore in the post-national constellation marked by dissociation of state and nation. According to the neutrality principle, the state is agnostic about substantive ways of life; it therefore cannot "recognize" or pay "respect" to ways of life, as is demanded by multiculturalism theorists (see Parekh, 2000). Rather than through the state-led recognition of groups, cultural difference asserts itself in the liberal state through individual rights, such as religious rights or family rights, which enjoy constitutional status in liberal democracies (for instructive examples of court-driven accommodation of Islamic claims, see Albers, 1994).

As envisioned by classic liberalism, cultural difference has mostly remained limited to the private sphere and to associational life; only rarely could it establish itself in the ambit of the state. Next to principal reasons, this also has practical reasons. Recognition is asymmetric, requiring that the state explicitly singles out a group from other potential groups. Only one group at a time can be "recognized". Such action is only possible if the number of groups (or rather: of claimants for preferred group status) in a society is limited. Against the backdrop of an escalating diversification and multiplication of the ethnic and national origins of migrants, recognition of each single origin group becomes a practical impossibility (see Entzinger, 2003 on the experience in the formerly "multicultural" Netherlands).

However, something akin to recognition may still be the unintended consequence of non-discrimination. If indirect discrimination is included in the catalogue of illicit discriminations, as it was from early on in the United States, and as it is in Europe since the 2000 EU Race Directive, a de facto recognition of groups inevitably follows. This is because to identify statistical discrimination and to calibrate effective remedial measures, a "group" has first to be evoked. This has been the experience of affirmative action in the United States, and also of positive action in Britain. Both originated in color-blind anti-discrimination laws. However, for the sake of effective implementation, there soon was a turn to color consciousness, thus de facto approximating the principle of recognition. Conversely, if a state, like recently the Netherlands, abandons its multicultural policy of group recognition, the price for this is less effectiveness in the fight against discrimination, because ethnically sensitive policy instruments no longer exist (see Poppelaars, 2005). France, which sought to counteract its harsh anti-veiling law of 2004 with large-scale *lutte contre la discrimination*, still operates with non-ethnic proxies, such as economic-cum-territorial *zones d'education prioritaires* (ZEP). This is because of her "Republican" aversion against ethnic and racial origin categories. However, there is significant factual pressure to turn toward explicit ethnic categories, and thus to approximate the despised "Anglo-Saxon" politics of group recognition (see De Montvalon & Eeckhout, 2006).

44   C. Joppke

Citizenship as Identity: The Paradox of Universalistic Unity

Citizenship as identity has two possible meanings: the actual views held by ordinary people; and official views propagated by the state. What ordinary people associate with citizenship is one of the biggest lacunae in the literature. In a study of working-class youth in Berlin, Cynthia Miller-Idriss (2006) found that ordinary Germans espouse surprisingly non-primordial, civic views of legitimate citizenship, in which behavioral traits (such as "honesty" and "hard work") counted more than ethnic pedigree. Such on-the-ground views interestingly match with recent changes in German citizenship law (though one cannot, of course, draw a causal connection, in whatever direction, between both developments). A study of "ethnic affinity migrants" from Argentina to Spain found, now in a mismatch between state policy and the views of ordinary people, that local Spaniards perceived Romanian migrants "more like us" than the official co-ethnics from Argentine, because only the former displayed the "ethic of hard work and modest expectations" that is expected of migrants (Cook & Viladrich, forthcoming). These vignettes from Germany and Spain suggest that in these classic ethnic nation-states there are now astoundingly civic-territorial understandings of legitimate citizenship held by ordinary people.

But what are the official citizenship identities propagated by contemporary states? Let us tackle this question in light of the foregoing changes in the status and rights dimensions of citizenship. The liberalized access to citizenship and rise of minority rights pose the problem of the unity and integration of increasingly pluralistic societies with new, perhaps unprecedented urgency. Remember that state membership and identity are now structurally decoupled: states can no longer impose a substantive identity as a precondition for acquiring citizenship, and primordial group identities even enjoy the status of rights.

As antidote to the decoupling of citizenship from nation and identity, states have tried to load citizenship with new meaning. This is the object of contemporary campaigns for unity and integration, which aim predominantly at the incorporation of immigrants and ethnic minorities. These campaigns are litmus tests for what unity and integration still means in post-national societies, irrespective of and beyond the case of migrants and minorities.

There are multiple examples of state campaigns for unity and integration. The United States perhaps started the movement, in the attempt of the mid-1990s Commission on Immigration Reform to re-valorize the old concept of Americanization, which had been tainted by the racist and repressive connotations of its 1920s predecessor. The late 1990s and periodically renewed campaign for a *Leitkultur* in Germany, brought forward by conservative circles, had or has a quite similar thrust, though it fell on much less fertile soil in the post-national political culture of Germany, even after unification. Britain recently introduced public citizenship ceremonies, in which candidates for naturalization solemnly have to swear an oath to Her Majesty the Queen. In addition, the English language requirement as precondition for naturalization has been significantly tightened and certain minority practices, such as arranged marriages, have been branded as incompatible with British norms and values. The Netherlands passed a Law on the Civic Integration of Newcomers in 1998, which marks a radical departure from two decades of multicultural recognition policy in the Netherlands. The Dutch model has quickly expanded across Europe, and variants of it are now in force in Austria, Denmark, France, Portugal and France, among other countries (see Joppke, 2007). Recent anti-veiling laws passed in France and Germany have a similar tilt, as they seek to set a centrist, integrationist counterpoint to diversifying immigrant societies (Joppke, 2006).

Transformation of Citizenship 45

However, the possibilities of liberal states to produce unity and integration by means of symbolic citizenship policies are tightly limited. Too much of it would immediately raise the charge of discrimination and conflict with the diversity creed, which is now well established from multicultural Canada to Republican France. Considering the multitude of different creeds and ways of life in individualized, pluralistic societies, the contemporary liberal state, more than in the past, has to retain a neutrality posture toward all of them. Accordingly, the unity that in such a society is still possible can only be a universalistic one. This is paradoxical, because a unity *qua* unity, short of planetary unity, cannot but be bounded and particularistic, and thus it has to exclude. A typical formula of unity that is still available in post-national settings is, indeed, neutrality, which has incidentally been the key justification in France and Germany to pass laws against wearing the Islamic headscarf in public schools (Joppke, 2006). Though plainly universalistic, neutrality has still fared here as a device that excludes, in terms of a prohibition. Of course, most unity and integration campaigns continue to be couched in terms of nationhood. But one can notice that contemporary definitions of what it means to be American, British, German, or Dutch are at heart replicas of the self-same idiom of liberal democracy: freedom, equality, tolerance, and so on. For example, when pressed to say what German *Leitkultur* is, an advocate had to concede that "the only really German thing" in this is language, the rest being a variant of nationally indistinct "constitutional patriotism" (see Müller, 2006, p. 23).

In a study of the United States, Eric Kaufmann referred the retreat of national particularisms in the official self-descriptions of Western states to the "decline of dominant ethnicity", which he sees caused by "progress of liberal and egalitarian logic into the cultural sphere" (Kaufmann, 2004, p. 284). Kaufmann only follows other revisionist historians, who have demolished the old notion that national identity in the United States was universalistic from the ground up, and thus set apart in kind from the ethnic nation-state identities of Europe. Instead, the dividing line in this is temporal, not geographic; race and ethnicity were everywhere official state idioms until the mid-twentieth century, in Europe *and* North America, whereas thereafter they were set to decline, surviving only in their re-appropriation by minorities (see Lie, 2004).

If the Dutch government today refuses to publish the content of tightened naturalization exams and does not offer any possibilities to prepare for these exams, arguing that "One cannot study to be Dutch, one has to feel Dutch" (quoted in Van Oers et al., 2006, Vol. 2, p. 415), this raises eyebrows for regressing from post-national integration to nationalist assimilation. There *is* an exclusionary dimension to contemporary state discourse on unity and integration. However, instead of being nationalist, as in the Dutch example, the exclusionary impulse is more often couched in the language of liberalism, in terms of the notion that the liberal state is one for liberal people only. A particularly perfidious example for this comes from Germany. In early 2006, the southern Land government of Baden-Württemberg issued a *Gesprächsleitfaden* (interview guideline) that should help state officers determine whether certain applicants for citizenship were espousing liberal-democratic values, as demanded by German law. Meant to be applied only to applicants originating in Muslim states, the interview guideline construed a binary opposition between liberal democracy and a certain idea of Islam, as prescribing or condoning arranged marriage, patriarchy, homophobia, veiling, and terrorism. While it had to be withdrawn in a storm of protest, this proposal shows the repressive possibilities inherent in liberalism itself, the latter figuring as tool for excluding a specific group,

46   C. Joppke

Muslims (presumably after more straightforward possibilities for exclusion, such as plain nationalism or racism, have fallen out of grace).

Liberalism has always had two souls, one that prescribes toleration, and another that prescribes autonomy. The liberalism of toleration had been the backdrop to the flowering of multiculturalism in the past two or three decades, but now it seems to have seen the day. After September 11, 2001, the liberalism of autonomy moved to the fore, which is much less patient and compatible with any one creed. It answers to the need for an integrative creed in a post-national society, but in being closer than toleration liberalism to a "comprehensive doctrine" (Rawls, 1993) it entails a repressive and disciplining potential that allows illiberals of many stripes, such as provincial state elites in southern Germany, to pursue their altogether different agendas.

Conclusion

This story of the transformation of citizenship might be read as a story of successive causation, in which changes in the first dimension of citizenship (as status) caused changes in the second dimension (citizenship as rights), which again caused changes in the third dimension (citizenship as identity). Read this way, the story would go like this:

- *Dimension 1*: The liberalization of access to citizenship brings about an ethnic pluralization of the citizenry ...
- *Dimension 2*: ... that makes social rights harder to maintain, while minority rights (anti-discrimination and recognition) move to the fore ...
- *Dimension 3*: ... and the state in turn answers to this demographic-cum-legal "flight from the center" with centripetal campaigns for unity and integration, which, however, have to be conducted in a universalistic idiom.

The first thing to notice is that, as a story about the transformation of citizenship, this would be a glaringly incomplete story because it cannot account for the all-important opening shot, the liberalization of access. Furthermore, ethnic pluralization occurred already *before* the liberalization of access to citizenship, which in some cases, such as Germany, is a very recent development, and in others, such as Italy, is still waiting to come. The ethnic pluralization that follows from the opening of citizenship only applies to the citizenry; society as totality of all long-term residents on the territory had been ethnically pluralized long before, as result of a temporarily open migration regime. From this follows that already the fact of an ethnically plural *society* (and not only of an ethnically plural *citizenry*) created pressure toward the creation of minority rights— although citizenship may still be the legal or sociological prerequisite for the applicability or creation of minority rights, as suggested earlier.

At conceptual level, a causal interpretation would espouse a naïve functionalism, in which state policy figures as rational problem-solving. Not only would a functionalist interpretation bracket politics, it would also run against elementary insights from organizational sociology, which showed that states, like all organizations, do not just look for efficient solutions to objective problems but screen their environment for legitimate ways of doing things, irrespective of whether there is a need for doing something or not (Meyer & Rowan, 1978). From this angle, there are anti-discrimination policies not because the citizenry is ethnically diverse but because other states practice such policies and "this is how one does things today". Without insinuating that this *is* the origin of anti-discrimination policy in any one case, this gives a glimpse of what a *really* causal analysis of changing citizenship rules would have to look like.

This suggests instead an interpretation in terms of logical complementariness. Accordingly, the changes in all three dimensions of citizenship add up to a logically coherent *Gestalt*, in which developments in one dimension logically complement and match developments in the other dimensions. Logical complementariness does not prejudice the concrete causes and mechanisms that may have brought about these developments in each single dimension; for the latter, one needs local explanations that cannot be decreed from the green table of theory.

The only uncontestable causality in the transformation of citizenship is situated *prior* to all three of its dimensions, consisting of the de-legitimization of racism and extreme nationalism after World War II and the parallel rise of universal human rights norms. This epochal change, which has concrete political origins (the Holocaust) yet came to permeate the entire socio-cultural sphere, quite literally creating a new world that is now "our world", constitutes the *doxa* or *episteme* that no one sanely can put into doubt. Even those who are unhappy about this new world have to phrase their claims in its idiom, which is the idiom of equality and non-discrimination. Accordingly, to quote the example of the French New Right, the *droit à la différence*, once granted to minorities, would have to apply to majorities too (Taguieff, 2001). From entirely different quarters has come an "Occidentalist" denunciation of equality and human rights as a devious and hypocritical Western plot (see Buruma & Margalit, 2004). Whatever the origins of critique may be, short of a collapse of civilization akin to the rise of European Fascism and National Socialism in the 1930s, there is no way back to the world before, that of blood, hierarchy, and impassable boundaries. Restrictive trends in citizenship may touch the fringes, never the core of what has evolved in the past half century.

Note

[1] In early August 2006, the Italian cabinet under R. Prodi approved a new citizenship law which would reduce the residence time required for naturalization from ten to five years and grant conditional *jus soli* citizenship to the children of immigrants (see Sepe, 2006).

References

Albers, H. (1994) Glaubensfreiheit und schulische Integration von Ausländerkindern, *Deutsches Verwaltungsblatt*, 1, pp. 984–990.

Alesina, A. & Glaeser, E. (2004) *Fighting Poverty in the US and Europe* (New York: Oxford University Press).

Baldwin, P. (1997) State and citizenship in the age of globalisation, in: P. Koslowski & A. Føllesdal (Eds) *Restructuring the Welfare State* (Berlin: Springer).

Banting, K. & Kymlicka, W. (2003) Do multiculturalism policies erode the welfare state?. Paper presented at the Colloquium Francqui 2003, Cultural Diversities versus Economic Solidarity, Brussels, 28 February to 1 March.

Bauböck, R. *et al.* (2006) Introduction, in: R. Bauböck, E. Ersboll, K. Groenendijk & H. Waldrauch (Eds) *Acquisition and Loss of Nationality: Policies and Trends in 15 European States*, 2 Vols (Amsterdam: Amsterdam University Press).

Brubaker, R. (1992) *Citizenship and Nationhood in France and Germany* (Cambridge, MA: Harvard University Press).

Buruma, I. & Margalit, A. (2004) *Occidentalism* (New York: Penguin).

Cook, D. & Viladrich, A. (forthcoming) The problem with similarity: ethnic affinity migrants in Spain, *Journal of Ethnic and Migration Studies*.

48   *C. Joppke*

Davis, U. (2006) Integration of immigrants in Germany, *European Journal of Migration and Law*, 7, pp. 123–144.

De Montvalon, J. -B. & van Eeckhout, L. (2006) La France résiste au comptage ethnique, *Le Monde*, 2–3 July, pp. 3.

Ebb, C. (1998) *The Rights Revolution* (Chicago, IL: University of Chicago Press).

Entzinger, H. (2003) The rise and fall of multiculturalism: the case of the Netherlands, in: C. Joppke & E. Morawska (Eds) *Toward Assimilation and Citizenship: Immigrants in Liberal Nation-States* (Basingstoke: Palgrave–Macmillan).

Goodhard, D. (2004) Too diverse? *Prospect*, 22 January.

Guiraudon, V. (2000) *Les politiques d'immigration en Europe* (Paris: L'Harmattan).

Hansen, R. & Weil, P. (Eds) (2001) *Toward a European Nationality* (London: Palgrave–Macmillan).

Hirst, P. & Thompson, G. (1992) The problem of "globalization". *Economy and Society*, 21(4), pp. 357–396.

Holston, J. & Appadurai, A. (Eds) (1999) *Cities and Citizenship* (Durham, NC: Duke University Press).

Howard, M. M. (2005) Variation in dual citizenship policies in the countries of the EU. *International Migration Review*, 39(3), pp. 697–720.

Howard, M. M. (2006) Comparative citizenship: an agenda for cross-national research. *Perspectives on Politics*, 4(3), pp. 443–455.

Joppke, C. (1999a) *Immigration and the Nation-State: The United States, Germany, and Great Britain* (Oxford: Oxford University Press).

Joppke, C. (1999b) How immigration is changing citizenship, *Ethnic and Racial Studies*, 22(4), pp. 629–652.

Joppke, C. (2003) Citizenship between de- and re-ethnicization, *Archives européennes de sociologie*, 44(3), pp. 301–335.

Joppke, C. (2005a) Citizenship without identity, *Canadian Diversity*, 3(2), pp. 85–87.

Joppke, C. (2005b) *Selecting by Origin* (Cambridge, MA: Harvard University Press).

Joppke, C. (2007) Immigrants and civic integration in Western Europe, in: K. Banting, T. Cochrane & L. Seidle (Eds) *Belonging? Diversity, Recognition and Shared Citizenship in Canada* (Montreal: Institute for Research on Public Policy).

Joppke, C. (2006) *State Neutrality and Anti-Veiling Laws in France and Germany*. Manuscript.

Kastoryano, R. (2002) *Negotiating Identities* (Princeton, NJ: Princeton University Press).

Kaufmann, E. P. (2004) *The Rise and Fall of Anglo-America* (Cambridge, MA: Harvard University Press).

Kymlicka, W. (1995) *Multicultural Citizenship* (Oxford: Oxford University Press).

Lie, J. (2004) *Modern Peoplehood* (Cambridge, MA: Harvard University Press).

Marshall, T. H. (1992) *Citizenship and Social Class* (Concord, MA: Pluto Press).

Meyer, J. & Rowan, B. (1978) Institutionalized organizations: formal structures as myth and ceremony, *American Journal of Sociology*, 83(2), pp. 340–363.

Miller-Idriss, C. (2006) *Blood and Culture*. Manuscript.

Morris, L. (2002) *Managing Migration* (London: Routledge).

Müller, J. -W. (2006) The end of denial, *Dissent*, Summer pp. 21–23.

Parekh, B. (2000) *Rethinking Multiculuralism* (Basingstoke: Macmillan Press).

Poppelaars, C. (2005) Incorporating migrants in the Netherlands. Paper presented at the Social Justice Conference, University of Bremen, 10–12 March.

Rawls, J. (1993) *Political Liberalism* (New York: Columbia University Press).

Rosanvallon, P. (2000) *The New Social Question* (Princeton, NJ: Princeton University Press).

Rubio-Marin, R. (2000) *Immigration as a Democratic Challenge* (Cambridge: Cambridge University Press).

Sepe, S. (2006) L'Italia si allinea all'Europa liberale. *Il Sole-24 Ore*, 6 August.

Skrentny, J. (2002) *The Minority Rights Revolution* (Cambridge, MA: Harvard University Press).

Soysal, Y. (1994) *Limits of Citizenship* (Chicago, IL: University of Chicago Press).

Taguieff, P. -A. (2001) *The Force of Prejudice* (Minneapolis: University of Minnesota Press).

Van Oers, R., De Hart, B. & Groenendijk, K. (2006) Netherlands, in: R. Bauböck, E. Ersboll, K. Groenendijk & H. Waldrauch (Eds) *Acquisition and Loss of Nationality: Policies and Trends in 15 European States*, 2 Vols (Amsterdam: Amsterdam University Press).

Walzer, M. (1997) *On Toleration* (New Haven, CT: Yale University Press).

Weil, P. (2001) Access to citizenship, in: T. Aleinikoff & D. Klusmeyer (Eds) *Citizenship Today* (Washington, DC: Carnegie Endowment for International Peace).

Weil, P. (2002) *Qu'est-ce qu'un Français?* (Paris: Grasset).

Part III
Citizenship Rights and Transnational Challenges

[10]

E.U. CITIZENSHIP AND POLITICAL RIGHTS IN AN EVOLVING EUROPEAN UNION

Jo Shaw*

INTRODUCTION

In 1975, responding to an emerging debate led by the Heads of State and Government of the Member States of what was then the European Communities about the development of special rights for "European citizens," the European Commission articulated what at the time seemed a daring proposition for the development of E.U. law: "[C]omplete assimilation with nationals as regards political rights is desirable in the long term from the point of view of *a European Union.*"[1]

By the mid-2000s, the European Communities had evolved into a "European Union" of sorts, but the "complete assimilation" of nationals of other Member States with the nationals of the host state in relation to political rights, as postulated by the Commission, had not been achieved. E.U. citizens continue to have rather limited rights to vote and stand in elections in the Member States where they are resident, if they lack the nationality of that state. In particular, citizens of the E.U. Member States have no rights under E.U. law to vote in national or regional[2] elections in the state in which they are resident. This stands in sharp contrast to the situation in the United States, where the Citizenship Clause of the Fourteenth Amendment grants U.S. citizens the citizenship of the state in which they reside. Through this guarantee flows the right to vote in state-

---

* Salvesen Chair of European Institutions, School of Law, University of Edinburgh. This essay is a development of one section of Chapter Six of Jo Shaw, The Transformation of Citizenship in the European Union (Cambridge Univ. Press, forthcoming 2007).

1. Commission of the European Communities, *Towards European Citizenship*, point 3.1, COM (75) 321 final (July 2, 1975) (emphasis added), *available at* http://aei.pitt.edu/5572/01/002205_2.pdf.

2. The term "regional elections" is used here to denote elections to representative bodies at the substate level. However, it is a problematic term, because the extent of powers held at the "regional" level varies substantially across the Member States. There are several federal or quasi-federal states in the European Union (including Austria, Belgium, Germany, Spain, and the United Kingdom). In all these cases, the regional authorities exercise some sovereign state powers, guaranteed by constitution, or by constitutional convention (United Kingdom). However, there are considerable variations across these five states, and indeed in some cases (Spain and the United Kingdom), within them. Other states have more limited devolution arrangements, especially for distinctive or peripheral regions (e.g., the Azores within Portugal). In other cases, "regional" elections effectively involve another tier of local or municipal government (e.g., counties or similar units of government), and the elected bodies have relatively few autonomous powers.

2550 *FORDHAM LAW REVIEW* [Vol. 75

level elections. Though never stated explicitly in the European Union's founding treaties, E.U. law, like the U.S. Constitution, guarantees the right of "its" citizens to vote in "federal" elections—in this case, European Parliamentary elections held every five years.[3]

This essay examines the emergence of political rights for nonnationals in the context of the development of the European Union, with a particular focus upon the question of E.U. citizens voting in national and regional elections in the Member States in which they reside but of which they do not hold nationality. It reviews first the development of "European Union" and what that means in political and constitutional terms, and then moves on to review the different mechanisms which could be applied to enhance the political rights of E.U. citizens.

I. A EUROPEAN UNION WITHOUT POLITICAL INTEGRATION

The adoption and entry into force of the Treaty of Maastricht in 1993 inaugurated a European Union, based on the three "pillars" of E.U. policy: the European Communities; Common Foreign and Security Policy (CFSP); and Police and Judicial Co-operation in Criminal Matters (PJCC) (formerly Justice and Home Affairs). The original base of the European Communities in the field of economic integration and "market-building" was gradually deepened through innovations such as the Economic and Monetary Union and complemented through the continued development of flanking policies, such as those concerned with social affairs, the labor market, and environmental questions. It has also been extended into a much broader portfolio of activities covering many matters of foreign policy and internal security policy, historically central to the sovereign identity of the Member States as nation states.

The concept of "European citizens" has also become a legal reality since 1975. The Treaty of Maastricht instituted a formal notion of "citizenship of the Union."[4] E.U. citizens are those persons holding the nationality of the Member States.[5] Therefore, through their systems of nationality laws, the Member States serve as gatekeepers of access to E.U. citizenship by nonnationals. The package of "citizenship" rights introduced by the Treaty of Maastricht was largely limited to codifying the existing range of rights for nationals of the Member States, under the free movement rules

---

3. *See* Opinion of First Advocate Gen. Tizzano, Case C-145/04, Spain v. United Kingdom; Case C-300/04, Eman & Sevinger v. College van burgemeester en wethouders van Den Haag, Apr. 6, 2006, ¶¶ 67-68, *available at* http://eur-lex.europa.eu/LexUriServ/LexUriServ.do?uri=CELEX:62004C0145:EN:HTML.

4. Consolidated Version of the Treaty Establishing the European Community art. 17, Dec. 29, 2006, 2006 O.J. (C 321) 37 [hereinafter EC Treaty].

5. *Id.*

[2007]   *E.U. CITIZENSHIP AND POLITICAL RIGHTS*   2551

contained in articles 39, 43, and 49 EC[6] and the right to nondiscrimination on grounds of nationality, enshrined in article 12 EC.[7]

Since 1993, the Court of Justice has pushed the margins of E.U. citizenship gradually outwards, concluding that the right to reside in the Member States guaranteed by article 18 EC[8] is directly effective and is therefore enforceable by individual citizens in the national courts against the public authorities of the Member States. Member States may place only proportionate restrictions upon E.U. citizens' right of residence, even with respect to those persons who are not economically active.[9] The range of coverage provided the nondiscrimination principle—which was historically linked to the applicant carrying out some form of economic activity in another Member State,[10] even if this only involved being a tourist[11]—has been extended so that the applicant need no longer show an economic nexus.[12] Now, this range has been extended so that the applicant need no longer show an economic nexus. The equal treatment rights of students moving within the single market have been substantially increased.[13] Professor Dora Kostakopoulou has argued that European citizenship has not been the purely symbolic institution which many initially expected it to be.[14] Instead, it has evolved, in the hands of the Court of Justice in particular, in very significant ways beyond the confines of a concept of market citizenship to become both a more political and a more institutionalized figure.[15]

One element of the original citizenship package of 1993 already ventured into political territory. Article 19 EC grants electoral rights (the right to vote and the right to stand) to E.U. citizens in relation to local and European Parliamentary elections.[16] E.U. citizens resident in a Member State other than the one in which they hold nationality may vote and stand in local and European Parliamentary elections in their Member State of residence,

---

6. *Id.* arts. 39, 43, 49.

7. *Id.* art. 12.

8. *Id.* art. 18.

9. Case C-200/02, Chen v. Sec'y of State for Home Dep't, 2004 E.C.R. I-9925; Case C-413/99, Baumbast & R v. Sec'y of State for Home Dep't, 2002 E.C.R. I-7091, I-7125-33.

10. Case C-168/91, Konstantinides v. Stadt Altensteig, 1993 E.C.R. I-1191.

11. Case 186/87, Cowan v. Le Trésor public, 1989 E.C.R. 195.

12. Case C-148/02 Garcia Avello v. État Belge, 2003 E.C.R. I-11613; Case C-85/96, Martínez Sala v. Freistaat Bayern, 1998 E.C.R. I-2691.

13. Case C-209/03, R, *ex parte* Bidar v. London Borough of Ealing, 2005 E.C.R. I-2119; Case C-184/99, Grzelczyk v. Centre public d'aide sociale d'Ottignies-Louvain-la-Neuve, 2001 E.C.R. I-6193. For commentary, see Michael Dougan, *Fees, Grants, Loans and Dole Cheques: Who Covers the Costs of Migrant Education Within the EU?*, 42 Common Market L. Rev. 943 (2005).

14. Dora Kostakopoulou, *Ideas, Norms and European Citizenship: Explaining Institutional Change*, 68 Mod. L. Rev. 233 (2005).

15. *Id.*

16. EC Treaty art. 19.

2552   *FORDHAM LAW REVIEW*   [Vol. 75

broadly under the same conditions as nationals.[17]   The equal treatment principle laid down in article 19 EC was elaborated and implemented in two directives adopted by the Council of Ministers in 1993 and 1994.[18]   These electoral rights are somewhat restricted in nature, and also have been rather limited in their impact (e.g., in the rates of participation of voters and the visibility of nonnational candidates).[19]   Nonetheless, they are symbolically important, as they represent an encroachment by the European Union as a political union into traditionally protected areas of national sovereignty, which are concerned with the organization of the political system on a democratic basis.   While the rights were granted on a top down basis, as a result of the collective will of the Member States expressed in amendments to the EC Treaty, they are dependent for their impact upon their implementation and practical application at a national, subnational, and often local level by the authorities of the Member States with responsibility for electoral matters.

These rights benefit the relatively small, but significant, number of citizens of the Member States resident in a state other than that in which they hold nationality.   Prior to the 2004 European Parliament elections, and with an eye already to the impact of the 2004 enlargement,[20] the European Commission estimated that there were around 6.5 million "Community voters" in the European Union.[21]   This term refers to those who are eligible to vote, but are resident outside their Member State of nationality, and who are covered by the equal treatment guarantee in article 19 EC.   The total population of the twenty-five E.U. Member States in 2006 was over 460 million,[22] but this includes persons not eligible to vote for reasons such as age.   A figure of around 1.5 percent of E.U. citizens resident in other Member States is frequently cited,[23] and this figure has been relatively

---

17. *Id.*

18. Council Directive 94/80, 1994 O.J. (L 368) 38 (EC) ("laying down detailed arrangements for the exercise of the right to vote and stand as a candidate in municipal elections by citizens of the Union residing in a Member State of which they are not nationals"); Council Directive 93/109, 1993 O.J. (L 329) 34 (EC) ("laying down detailed arrangements for the exercise of the right to vote and stand as a candidate in elections to the European Parliament for citizens of the Union residing in a Member State of which they are not nationals").

19. Shaw, *supra* note *, chs. 4, 5.

20. Inevitably, the figures do not anticipate the additional mobility which has occurred since May 2004, particularly from some new Member States, such as Poland, Latvia, and Lithuania, to Member States which have maintained an open labor market, such as Ireland and the United Kingdom.

21. Directorate-General Justice and Home Affairs (EC), Working Paper: EP Elections in 2004, Number of Community Voters under Directive 93/109/EC in the 2004 EP Elections, JAI.C.3/SAS/2004-1 (Mar. 23, 2004).

22. Giampaolo Lanzieri, *Population in Europe 2005: First Results, in* Statistics in Focus: Population and Social Conditions 3 tbl.1 (Eurostat, No. 16/2006, Nov. 2006).

23. Obviously some instabilities have arisen as a result of the substantial enlargements of the European Union in 2004 and 2007, especially since these are coupled with many

2007]   *E.U. CITIZENSHIP AND POLITICAL RIGHTS*   2553

stable for a number of years. To put these figures in context, it is worth noting that 6.5 million "Community voters" would outnumber the electorate in more than a third of those small and medium-sized European states which are E.U. Member States.[24] At the same time, the vast majority of those voters are excluded from those forms of democratic participation which are not covered by article 19 or by national law. This is because, with the exception of certain rights granted under national law in Ireland and the United Kingdom, E.U. citizens are not given rights to vote for representatives elected to parliaments or assemblies at the national, substate, or regional level (e.g., the *Länder* in Germany or the autonomous communities in Spain). It is ironic that while the European Union exists in part to encourage mobility between the Member States, it gives rise at the same time to a structural "citizenship deficit," in that those persons who do exercise mobility rights are excluded from full democratic membership of the state of residence unless they take on the national citizenship of the host state. Indeed, the very essence of E.U. law on mobility since the Union's inception has been to create a legal framework which blurs the distinction between intrastate and interstate mobility within the single market for the citizens of the Member States and to remove the need for mobile E.U. citizens to acquire the citizenship of the host state. This is not least because mobile E.U. citizens might well envisage multiple acts of mobility during their lifetime, perhaps moving successively for educational, employment, family, and lifestyle reasons. This "citizenship deficit" persists despite the fact that the European Union has recently instituted a form of *permanent residence* which Member States must guarantee under the 2004 Citizens' Rights Directive to those nationals of other Member States who have been resident for more than five years in the host state.[25] However, this status of permanent residence does not give access to any additional political rights beyond those guaranteed in article 19 EC.

Discussions of E.U. electoral rights need to be nested within a variety of intellectual and political, legal, and constitutional contexts. One such context, which takes on the challenge of the European Commission's bluesky thinking of 1975 in relation to the allocation of political rights across the Member States of the European Union in the context of a *political* union, is provided by the gradual evolution of the European Union's constitutional framework.

This is not the forum to rehearse in full the arguments regarding the European Union's constitutional past, present, and future. Suffice it to say at this stage that there exists a symbiotic relationship between two reference

---

restrictions on the free movement of labor from the new Member States. However, the figure of 1.5 percent has been remarkably enduring over thirty years.

24. Potential "Community voters" outnumber the electorate not only in the three microstates (Luxembourg, Malta, and Cyprus), but also in Estonia, Latvia, Lithuania, Ireland, Denmark, Finland, Slovenia, and Slovakia.

25. Council Directive 2004/38, art. 16, 2004 O.J. (L 158) 77, 106 (EC).

points for constitution building in the European Union.[26] On the one hand, there exists what one may term the European Union's gradually evolving informal constitutional framework, which is a composite structure based on the existing treaties, as interpreted and applied by the Court of Justice and other political and legal actors. This composite constitutional structure enshrines both the rules according to which the European Union operates and the underlying political and ideological values and structures which infuse these rules.[27] On the other hand, the European Union has been engaged actively since 2000—thus far unsuccessfully—in the attempt to sponsor the drafting and adoption of a more encompassing and unitary documentary constitution for the European Union. This began with the Declaration on the Future of the Union appended to the Treaty of Nice, which recognized the unsatisfactory nature of the Intergovernmental Conference (IGC) which concluded in December 2000 and some of the future challenges facing an enlarging European Union. Eventually, after the work of the Convention on the Future of the Union and a further IGC had been concluded in 2004, that phase of the process concluded with the signature by the Member States of the Treaty Establishing a Constitution for the European Union ("Constitutional Treaty") in October 2004.[28] However, signature merely signaled the beginning of the ratification process. It seems extremely unlikely under current conditions that the Constitutional Treaty will ever come into force, given that it was rejected in popular referendums in France and the Netherlands in mid-2005. With the ratification process stalled indefinitely, the Constitutional Treaty itself seems to exist in limbo.

The Constitutional Treaty was very much a hybrid document. It draws very heavily upon the resources offered by the existing informal constitutional framework, while at the same time innovating in a number of important areas, especially in relation to institutional design. Had the Constitutional Treaty come into force as originally scheduled on November 1, 2006, it would have been impossible to understand the future arrangements without frequent and detailed reference back to what had gone before because of the symbiotic relationship that would exist between the "new" and the "old" E.U. constitutionalism.[29]

With the possibility of a documentary constitutional framework for the European Union now blocked for the foreseeable future, it is likely that

---

26. For more detail, see Jo Shaw, *Europe's Constitutional Future*, Pub. L., Spring 2005, at 132.

27. Neil Walker, *The White Paper in Constitutional Context* (N.Y.U. Sch. of Law, Jean Monnet Ctr., Working Paper No. 6/01, 2001), *available at* http://www.jeanmonnetprogram.org/papers/01/011001.html.

28. Consolidated Version of the Treaty Establishing a Constitution for Europe, Dec. 16, 2004, 2004 O.J. (C 310) 1 [hereinafter Constitutional Treaty].

29. Jo Shaw & Jean Monnet, *Legal and Political Sources of the Treaty Establishing a Constitution for Europe*, 55 N.I.L.Q. 214 (2004).

E.U. CITIZENSHIP AND POLITICAL RIGHTS

Member States and the E.U. institutions will pursue other avenues of constitutional development.[30] On the other hand, some observers suggest that the entire constitution-building enterprise has been an unnecessary distraction for what remains in essence a limited exercise in international cooperation between sovereign states guaranteed already by a sufficiently diverse and effective range of legitimation mechanisms.[31] The constitutional promoters can, however, probably muster the larger number of voices speaking in favor of further developments on the constitutional and/or the treaty reform front. Some of that reforming energy has been diverted into consideration of the possibility of concluding a type of "Constitutional-Treaty-lite," or a "Nice Treaty *bis*," which might garner sufficient support at the national level and which would not necessarily need ratification via referendum. The focus in these proposals has been primarily upon minimal institutional reform to smooth the ongoing effects of both the 2004 and 2007 enlargements, and possible future enlargements.[32] A limited number of observers call for the resurrection of the Constitutional Treaty itself,[33] albeit sometimes in a revised form.[34] The European Commission has tended to avoid too many shrill pronouncements on the Constitutional Treaty, for fear of alienating opinion in the national capitals. However, most individual commissioners who have expressed an opinion are supportive of the Constitutional Treaty[35] and concerned about the implications of potentially "watering it down" in order to achieve acceptance. Perhaps the best view is to take a longer-term perspective.[36] Some commentators have pointed out that over a period of years, or even decades, the most enduring and effective ideas put forward in documents such as the Constitutional Treaty or the earlier Draft Treaty of European

---

30. *See, e.g.*, Nicolas Sarkozy, Speech to the Friends of Europe Foundation and the Robert Schuman Foundation (Sept. 8, 2006), *available at* http://www.demyc.org/fruitbasket/index.php?download=658.pdf (putting forth a proposal for a mini-treaty by French Interior Minister and presidential candidate of the right).

31. *See* Andrew Moravcsik, *What Can We Learn from the Collapse of the European Constitutional Project?*, 47 Politische Vierteljahresschrift 219 (2006).

32. *See, e.g.*, Janis A. Emmanouilidis & Almut Metz, *Renewing the European Answer*, EU-Reform 2006/2 (C.A.P., Bertelsmann Stiftung, Oct. 2006), *available at* http://www.cap.lmu.de/download/spotlight/Reformspotlight_02-06_en.pdf.

33. *European Socialists Set to Relaunch Constitution*, EurActiv, Oct. 24, 2006, http://www.euractiv.com/en/constitution/european-socialists-set-relaunch-constitution/article -159040 (last visited Feb. 6, 2007).

34. Andrew Duff, *Plan B: How to Rescue the European Constitution* (Notre Europe, Studies and Research, No. 52, 2006).

35. *See, e.g.*, Marc Beunderman, *Commissioners Reject Sarkozy Mini Treaty Plan*, EUObserver, Nov. 22, 2006, http://euobserver.com/18/22932; Margot Wallström, Vice President of the European Comm'n Responsible for Institutional Affairs and Commc'n Strategy, The Consequences of the Lack of a European Constitution, Presentation to the Constitutional Affairs Committee of the European Parliament (Nov. 22, 2006) (transcript available at http://europa.eu/rapid/pressReleasesAction.do?reference=SPEECH/06/731&type =HTML&aged=0&language=EN&guiLanguage=fr).

36. *See also* Shaw, *supra* note 26, at 150-51.

2556   *FORDHAM LAW REVIEW*   [Vol. 75

Union elaborated by the first directly elected Parliament after 1979, tend to be incorporated into the European Union's legal and constitutional structure.[37] To put it another way, if what is in the Constitutional Treaty would "work" in an E.U. context, then it will be picked up again in future reforms, probably piecemeal, over a period of years.

However, none of these proposals directly addresses the ongoing challenges faced by the Union as a political union of *citizens*, which is what the Commission was referring to back in 1975 with its "complete assimilation" call. Indeed, the Constitutional Treaty itself largely ignored the question of the structural citizenship deficit highlighted in this paper, although it did address some issues related to democracy. Part I of the Constitutional Treaty included a title on democracy, quaintly headed "the democratic life of the Union."[38] This included interesting innovations such as citizens' initiatives, whereby a million citizens from a significant number of Member States may sign a petition and submit it to the Commission to consider making a proposal in a field where citizens think there should be Union action.[39] However, the Constitutional Treaty's provisions were limited to addressing the role of the principles of participatory and representative democracy regarding the functioning of the Union's institutions, and the policy-making endeavors of the Union itself, not the Member States. Moreover, the Constitutional Treaty does not provide for the development of the concept of Union citizenship. Instead, it reproduces, by and large, the existing provisions of the EC Treaty.

The lack of attention to democracy in any respect other than in relation to the Union's own institutions is, at one level, hardly surprising. It is certainly not for the Union to tell the Member States how their democratic systems should be developed, even though being a functioning liberal democracy is undoubtedly a condition for accession to the Union.[40] Moreover, it should be recalled that back in 1993 the Treaty of Maastricht did partially reshape the democratic institutions of the Member States by adding several million "Community voters" to the rosters of the Member States for local elections, and by offering E.U. citizens the possibility of being elected to local councils in their place of residence. However,

---

37. Philippe de Schoutheete, *Scenarios for Escaping the Constitutional Impasse*, Europe's World, Summer 2006, at 74.

38. Constitutional Treaty tit. VI.

39. *Id.* art. I-47(4). In an example of the peremptory application of the Constitutional Treaty, an online petition arguing for the relocation of the European Parliament's seat solely in Brussels, and away from Strasbourg and Luxembourg, garnered more than one million signatures, before it was presented to the E.U. institutions. *See* The European Parliament should be located in Brussels, http://www.oneseat.eu/ (last visited Feb. 6, 2007). Its chances of success are minimal, however, because of the complex politics associated with the location of the E.U. institutions—a veritable Pandora's box which the Member States are reluctant to reopen, whatever the costs of the current complex and unwieldy arrangements.

40. *See, e.g.*, Treaty on European Union, art. 6(1), Dec. 24, 2002, 2002 O.J. (C 325) 5; *id.* art. 49.

2007]   *E.U. CITIZENSHIP AND POLITICAL RIGHTS*   2557

limitations upon those local electoral rights manifested themselves from the very beginning, in order to permit the Member States to resist too much encroachment upon their national sovereignty. Under article 5(3) of the Local Elections Directive, Member States were permitted to lay down that "only their own nationals may hold the office of elected head, deputy or member of the governing college of the executive of a basic local government unit if elected to hold office for the duration of his mandate."[41] Furthermore, article 5(4) provides that "Member States may also stipulate that citizens of the Union elected as members of a representative council shall take part in neither the designation of delegates who can vote in a parliamentary assembly nor the election of the members of that assembly."[42]

However, the fact that the EU, at its present stage of integration, has not been vested with the relevant powers to develop a comprehensive *federal* vision of political citizenship does not completely frustrate other citizenship initiatives. Indeed, there is no reason why there should not be developments in relation to the constitutionalization of rights of E.U. citizens that are derived from *national* sources, rather than from sources within *European Union* law which rely upon the *Union* institutions. The sources of constitutional law necessary to sustain a multilevel polity such as the European Union have never in practice been confined to those rooted directly in the supranational entity itself, but also have stemmed in different ways from national law and national institutions.[43] To operate effectively, the European Union relies upon the administrative systems and procedural laws of the Member States, and there is no reason why constitutional development could not be seen as fostered by measures taken at the national level, whether autonomously or in response to a collective initiative which the Member States choose to take outside the confines of the current integration framework.

The reason for making this argument is that there is no foreseeable possibility that the Member States will change the E.U. treaties to include a provision akin to article 19 EC that covers elections for national and subnational parliaments and assemblies within the Member States, presidential elections (or similar), and referendums. However, there is already in place a patchwork of electoral rights for E.U. citizens, which does extend a little beyond that which is mandated by the treaties as they stand, notably in Ireland and the United Kingdom. Potentially, that patchwork could be developed in the future, and this essay explores some of the pathways that policy makers and legislators at a number of different

---

41. *See* Council Directive 94/80, *supra* note 18, art. 5(3).

42. *Id.* art. 5(4)

43. For a fully elaborated example of how this interplay can work in the context of the mandate given to national courts to act as "European courts" within the EU's multilevel constitutional system, see Monica Claes, The National Courts' Mandate in the European Constitution (2006).

2558   *FORDHAM LAW REVIEW*   [Vol. 75

levels could take to achieve the goal articulated by the Commission back in 1975.

II. ELECTORAL RIGHTS FOR E.U. CITIZENS IN REGIONAL AND NATIONAL ELECTIONS?

There is some popular support for the electoral rights of E.U. citizens to be extended within the Member States. In 2006, a Eurobarometer survey showed considerable support within many Member States for the premise that one of the best ways to strengthen European citizenship could be instituting the right for E.U. citizens to vote in all elections in the Member State in which they are resident.[44] Reflecting these concerns, the question whether E.U. citizens should have voting rights in regional and national elections has been a consistent theme in written questions posed by Members of the European Parliament to European Commissioners. For example, in a reply to a question about U.K. citizens losing voting rights in national elections after fifteen years outside the United Kingdom, without acquiring them in the host state,[45] Commissioner Antonio Vitorino commented,

> The right to vote of own nationals of a Member State in elections of that Member State belongs fully to the competence of the Member States, independent of whether those citizens reside in its territory or outside of its territory. This is explicitly confirmed in the relevant Directives 93/109/EC (1) and Directive 94/80/EC (2), which provide that nothing in those Directives affects each Member State's provisions concerning the right to vote or to stand as a candidate of its nationals who reside outside of its territory.
>
> . . . .
>
> Because of the lack of the competence the Commission does not plan to take any actions relating to the right to vote of nationals of a Member State residing outside of its territory.[46]

Notwithstanding this negative conclusion about the possibility of regulating expatriate voting, the Commission did devote some attention to the question of regulating the rights of mobile E.U. citizens in the host state in its Fourth Report on Citizenship of the Union in 2004, raising the matter

---

44. Special Eurobarometer, No. 251, The Future of Europe 45-46 (May 2006), *available at* http://ec.europa.eu/public_opinion/archives/ebs/ebs_251_en.pdf.

45. Voting by expatriates from the United Kingdom was originally introduced with a limit set at five years by the Representation of the People Act, 1985, c. 50, § 1. This was increased to twenty years in the Representation of the People Act, 1989, c. 28, § 2, and then reduced once more to fifteen years by § 141 of the Political Parties, Elections and Referendums Act, 2000, c. 41.

46. Written Question E-1301/02 by Michael Cashman (PSE) to the Commission Regarding *Voting Rights of EU Citizens*, 2003 O.J. (E 92) 44.

2007]   *E.U. CITIZENSHIP AND POLITICAL RIGHTS*   2559

initially for the Member States' attention. The Commission noted with regret,

> Recurrent petitions, parliamentary questions and public correspondence reveal the concerns of many Union citizens regarding a gap in electoral rights at the present level of Community law: Union citizens may still be deprived of important civic rights as a result of the exercise of the right to free movement, namely the right to participate in national or regional elections. The Member States do not grant electoral rights at national or regional elections to nationals of other Member States residing in their territory.[47]

This comment about recurrent complaints on this matter, it should be noted, is in stark contrast to the Commission's statement in other reports that it has received few complaints over the years about the workings of the right to vote in local elections.[48] The lack of complaints in the latter area could suggest that these work well; it could also provide a message about the comparative salience of local and national elections for voters, and specifically for voters who find themselves resident in a Member State other than the one of which they are a national. What "special rights"—to reapply the terminology of the early citizenship debates from the 1970s in the European Communities—need to be granted for there to be effective integration of mobile E.U. citizens into the host state? "Complete assimilation as regards political rights" was the solution according to the Commission, and it would seem that some of the feedback to the Commission from disgruntled E.U. citizens does indeed echo that point.

In its conclusion to the Fourth Report, the Commission returned to the same topic, commenting however that "decisions concerning possible measures to be adopted under Article 22(2) of the EC Treaty still require careful consideration."[49] Article 22 allows for amendments to be adopted to the EC Treaty's citizenship provisions using a truncated amendment procedure which avoids the need for a full intergovernmental conference, but still requires any amendments to be ratified by all the Member States following a unanimous agreement in the Council of Ministers, as with all amending treaties. The Commission has yet to make use of its power of proposal in article 22, and while it is conceivable that it might make such a proposal, it would be highly unlikely that any such proposal would garner

---

47. *Fourth Report on Citizenship of the Union (1 May 2001–30 April 2004)*, at 8-9, COM (2004) 695 final (Oct. 26, 2004) [hereinafter *Fourth Report on Citizenship*] (emphasis omitted); *see also* EUROPA, European Year of Workers' Mobility 2006, http://ec.europa.eu/employment_social/workersmobility_2006/index.cfm?id_page=140 (last visited Feb. 6, 2007) (listing personal, but wholly anonymous, "testimonies of people who have had first hand experience of living and working in another EU country").

48. *Commission Report on the Application of Directive 94/80/EC on the Right to Vote and Stand as a Candidate in Municipal Elections*, at 7, COM (2002) 260 final (May 30, 2005).

49. *Fourth Report on Citizenship*, *supra* note 47, at 11.

2560   *FORDHAM LAW REVIEW*   [Vol. 75

the necessary unanimous support in the Council of Ministers at the present time, especially if it concerned the sensitive question of political rights. It is notable that since 1993 and the institution of E.U. citizenship, the provisions have already been amended in small ways twice—by the Treaties of Amsterdam and Nice.[50] However, in both cases the provisions adopted formed part of a larger trade-off between the Member States, insofar as they were concluding a broader bargain on a new treaty ranging across a number of topics. In those circumstances, Member States may feel able to trade sensitivities about the concept of E.U. citizenship against success in securing agreement with their partners to amend other provisions of the E.U. Treaty framework. Article 22 provides, by its very nature, a focused amendment procedure which would deprive the Member States of the capacity to make such trade-offs across different political issues of varying degrees of sensitivity.[51] It is therefore rather hard to see the circumstances in which it could ever be used in practice.

The Commission returned again to the question of national voting rights for E.U. citizens in its communication evaluating the effects of the Tampere Programme in the area of Justice and Home Affairs policy.[52] In its communication, the Commission invited the Member States to open up a dialogue in this area. This is an invitation which they failed to take up when formulating the Hague Programme which followed on from the Tampere Programme. Instead, the European Council declared that it "encourages the Union's institutions, within the framework of their competences, to maintain an open, transparent and regular dialogue with representative associations and civil society and to promote and facilitate citizens' participation in public life."[53] This vague statement hardly seems to presage a collective major initiative from the Member States in this area, and there is nothing in the practical program for action which refers to electoral rights for nonnationals, even though article 22 refers to the

---

50. The Treaty of Amsterdam added a phrase to article 17(1): "Citizenship of the Union shall complement and not replace national citizenship." Treaty of Amsterdam Amending the Treaty on European Union, the Treaties Establishing the European Communities and Certain Related Acts, Oct. 2, 1997, 1997 O.J. (C 340) 1, 27. This was part of a set of trade-offs between Denmark and the other Member States. In part it was retrospective in nature, as the phrase is drawn from the 1992 Conclusions of the Edinburgh European Council which followed the first (failed) Danish referendum on the Treaty of Maastricht, and was agreed to as part of a package to persuade the Danish government and political elite to try, once more, to "sell" the Treaty to the electorate. In terms of the Treaty of Amsterdam itself, it was also part of a complex trade-off related to the incorporation of Schengen within the framework of the E.U. Treaties, which included also an "opt-out" for Denmark in relation to the nature of Schengen law within the domestic legal order, and its continued development, in which Denmark has not participated.

51. EC Treaty art. 22.

52. *Commission Communication: Area of Freedom, Security and Justice: Assessment of the Tampere Programme and Future Orientations*, at 8, COM (2004) 401 final (June 2, 2004).

53. Presidency Conclusions, Brussels European Council, Annex 1, at 16 (Nov. 4/5, 2004).

2007]   *E.U. CITIZENSHIP AND POLITICAL RIGHTS*   2561

possibility of adopting an unspecified measure.[54] But, as we noted above, it is not likely that the Member States will demonstrate the collective will at present to adopt a measure under article 22.

Support for the proposal to extend electoral rights to national elections has come from within the European Parliament. In a somewhat confused and controversial report on the Commission's Fourth Report on Citizenship, which was approved by the Committee on Civil Liberties, Justice and Home Affairs,[55] several references were made to this question:

> 16. [The Parliament] [c]alls upon the Member States to discuss forthwith the possibility of granting European citizens the right to vote and to stand for election in municipal, local and regional elections of the Member State in which they are resident, irrespective of nationality;

> 17. [And] [c]alls upon the Member States to discuss forthwith the possibility of granting EU citizens the choice of voting and standing for election in national elections either in the country in which they are resident or in their country of origin (though not in both), irrespective of nationality . . . [.][56]

Picking up a text contained in the earlier opinion given by the Committee on Constitutional Affairs, the report goes on to suggest that

> the conferring on European citizens who are not nationals of their Member State of residence of the right to vote and to stand for election in national and regional elections would make a tangible contribution to the feeling of belonging to the European Union which is indispensable for genuine EU citizenship.[57]

Of course, it is not necessarily obvious why a citizen of one Member State who is given additional rights of political participation in another Member State where she is resident should feel more *European* in these circumstances, as opposed to feeling more attached to the state (generously) conferring these rights upon her. Perhaps the latter is a necessary precondition for the former? In any event, the report as a whole was rejected by the European Parliament in plenary in January 2006, largely because it was opposed by the center-right majority party grouping of the European People's Party—European Democrats, and thus this text should

---

54. *Council and Commission Action Plan Implementing the Hague Programme on Strengthening Freedom, Security and Justice in the European Union*, point 2.1(e), 2005 O.J. (C 198) 1, 4.

55. *Report of the Committee on Civil Liberties, Justice and Home Affairs on the Commission's Fourth Report on Citizenship of the Union (1 May 2001 – 30 April 2004)*, A6-0411/2005   (Dec.   15,   2005),   *available*   *at* http://www.europarl.europa.eu/sides/getDoc.do?pubRef=-//EP//NONSGML+REPORT+A6-2005-0411+0+DOC+PDF+V0//EN (last visited Feb. 6, 2007).

56. *Id.*

57. *Id.*

be treated with caution as expressing at most the view of a particular committee.[58]

A more sophisticated link between European citizenship and electoral rights for nonnationals in national elections is developed by Heather Lardy, who argues for voting rights in national elections in terms of the link between citizenship and self-government and democracy: "If citizens are denied full voting rights, they are deprived of one of the most effective mechanisms available to them for exerting political power."[59] Furthermore, she adds that "[t]he denial of full voting rights to European Union citizens effectively creates within each Member State two sub-groups of European citizens: those who happen to be national citizens of that state, and those who are not. Only the former group is granted the right to vote in national elections."[60] Against those who would argue that ascribing wider electoral rights to E.U. citizens within the Member States would undermine national sovereignty, she argues trenchantly that "[i]t should be remembered also that the primary purpose of democratic principle is not to prescribe the conditions which will protect national sovereignty, but to set out precepts designed to further and sustain democratic government."[61] In other words, she invites us to look more critically at the relationship between the defense of national sovereignty and the development of European citizenship as a political and democratic project. Those seeking to defend national sovereignty as they see it by excluding certain groups of residents from the franchise should also have to justify the damage to democracy done by excluding those residents in terms of limiting the scope and compass of democratic *self*-government. Lardy's argument is that having now breached the boundary, which a traditionally exclusive conception of national citizenship places around suffrage by introducing at least limited electoral rights in the form of article 19 EC, the Member States consequently must base any rejection of the argument for subsequently extending those rights on something more than the defense of national sovereignty.

As noted above, the normative issue here is how to prevent the E.U. free movement space from becoming a space of negative democratic impetus. To put it another way, if the impulse of the E.U. treaties is positively to encourage E.U. citizens to exercise their free movement rights, then how are they to be protected against the negative consequences of moving

---

58. In a vote held in plenary on January 17, 2006, the report was rejected by 276 votes in favor to 347 against with 22 abstentions. European Parliament, Strasbourg Plenary: 16-19 January 2006, http://www.europarl.europa.eu/news/expert/background_page/008-4356-019-01-03-901-20060113BKG04268-19-01-2006-2006-false/default_p001c018_en.htm (last visited Feb. 6, 2007).

59. Heather Lardy, *The Political Rights of Union Citizenship*, 2 Eur. Pub. L. 611, 625 (1996).

60. *Id.* at 626-27.

61. *Id.* at 632.

2007] *E.U. CITIZENSHIP AND POLITICAL RIGHTS* 2563

without acquiring the host state citizenship (such as the loss of the right to vote in regional and national elections unless they are protected by expatriate voting rights from their home state)? Furthermore, how are the European Union and its Member States as a whole to be protected from losing the democratic input of migrants into regional and national elections? While this number is not necessarily huge at the present time, at around 1.5 percent, it is nevertheless the case that if the exercise of free movement rights under E.U. law consistently coincides with the loss of democratic participation rights, then this must have negative consequences for the Member States as democratic polities. It is arguably wholly inconsistent for the European Union and the Member States to preserve those participation rights by means of nondiscrimination rights instituted at the E.U. level under article 19 EC in relation to *local* and *European* electoral rights, while ignoring the impact upon democratic participation in regional and national elections.

III. DEVELOPING MECHANISMS OF DEMOCRATIC PARTICIPATION IN THE
EUROPEAN UNION: THE CASE OF REGIONAL AND NATIONAL ELECTIONS

In sum, it seems plausible to argue not only that this is a live issue—as demonstrated above—but also that so long as the European Union exists in its current form the issue is likely to become an ever more acute challenge both to the European Union as an emergent polity and to the Member States as more established polities. Consequently, it is useful to consider the various mechanisms by which the Member States, separately or together, in conjunction with the E.U. institutions or alone, might address this challenge, even if the political omens regarding decisive action at the present time are poor. The objective here is not to make a plea for one particular outcome, such as a generalized extension of regional and national electoral rights to E.U. citizens, but rather to illustrate the richness of the legal instruments available to the Member States at the present time, and to indicate how they might be developed in the future.

Under E.U. law as it stands, the Member States enjoy full and unlimited discretion as to the groups upon which they confer the franchise in regional and national elections, subject only to the strictures of the European Convention on Human Rights and Fundamental Freedoms such as article 3 of Protocol No. 1. This means an unlimited power to restrict the franchise to national citizens alone, and an unfettered discretion as to whether, and under what conditions, to grant to expatriates the right to vote in regional and national elections and as to how to deal with issues of voter registration and absentee ballots and postal voting. This is the status quo.

Clearly, if each and every mobile E.U. citizen became a citizen of the Member State in which he or she resided, then there would be less difficulty, although this would still not deal with issues raised by differences of rules on expatriate and absentee voting. However, citizenship acquisition is unlikely to be the answer. As things stand, a

2564 *FORDHAM LAW REVIEW* [Vol. 75

resident nonnational E.U. citizen may be unable or unwilling to acquire the nationality of the host Member State for one or more of the following reasons:

- failure to satisfy a qualifying residence period;

- failure to satisfy probity or wealth tests (e.g., having minor criminal offenses on the record which prevent citizenship acquisition);

- failure to satisfy other country-specific citizenship acquisition conditions requiring applicants to pass language or cultural tests;

- unwillingness to state long-term future residence intentions because of a future intention to migrate to a third state or to return to the home state or to relinquish other nationalities (if dual nationality is not tolerated).

There is presently nothing like a system of automatic or ascriptive citizenship acquisition for resident nonnationals (without prejudice to home state citizenship) in the E.U. Member States. Thus each and every national of a Member State resident in another Member State would have to satisfy whatever conditions on nationality acquisition are imposed by the host. Professor Ruth Rubio-Marín argues in favor of a system of automatic or ascriptive citizenship acquisition by resident nonnationals, making the argument precisely in order to find a normatively satisfactory method for promoting democratic inclusion in the context of migration: She sees "immigration as a *democratic* challenge."[62]

In terms of what such a shift in approach might mean for the development of a more intensive multilevel system of federal-type citizenship in the Union, it is useful to make the comparison with the United States. In combination with the gradual development and hardening of a concept of national citizenship over many years, a matter on which the original U.S. Constitution itself was remarkably silent,[63] the United States developed a form of state citizenship which linked to residence alone, rather than any other marker of belonging. However, this was imposed from above through the Fourteenth Amendment's Citizenship Clause, which provides that U.S. citizens are citizens of the state "in which they reside."[64] It did not result from the separate or even collective decision of the states. Such a decision would be required in the European Union at its present stage of development. In the European Union, article 16 of the Citizens' Rights Directive does at least (and—some might say—"finally") create a

---

62. Ruth Rubio-Marín, Immigration as a Democratic Challenge: Citizenship and Inclusion in Germany and the United States (2000).

63. Rogers M. Smith, Civic Ideals: Conflicting Visions of Citizenship in U.S. History 115-28 (1997).

64. Peter H. Schuck, *Citizenship in Federal Systems*, 48 Am. J. Comp. L. 195, 223 (2000).

2007] *E.U. CITIZENSHIP AND POLITICAL RIGHTS* **2565**

status of permanent resident, which removes any further conditions upon the right of residence of the Union citizen, thus potentially smoothing the pathway for a Union citizen who does in fact seek naturalization in the host state by providing a framework for establishing settled residence.[65] It also seeks to ensure that E.U. citizens are granted equal treatment with nationals so far as pertains to any matter falling within the scope of E.U. law. But it does not directly interfere with national citizenship status, or matters such as electoral rights at the regional or national level. However, it is perhaps arguable that the status of permanent residence should be regarded as a form of "citizenship-of-residence-lite" for resident nonnational E.U. citizens. In that case, could it be seen as a sufficient condition for the granting of electoral rights to vote in regional and national elections in the host state, as the next step towards integration?

Alternatively, we could shift the focus from looking at rights within the *host state*, to consider the case for Member States to facilitate *home state voting* for expatriates resident in other Member States. They could do this without changing the rules on the right to vote simply by relaxing registration arrangements to allow the loosest of connections with the home state to suffice as the basis for registration in the former district of residence. Alternatively, Member States could look more closely at expatriate voting arrangements. In the latter case, this could be either with specialist arrangements for direct representation of expatriates in the legislature (as in France and now, most recently and controversially, Italy, where expatriates effectively decided the outcome of the 2006 general election), or with participation of expatriate voters in the normal elections of home-based representatives, as in the case of the United Kingdom (where expatriate votes are reallocated back to the constituency where the expatriate most recently resided). This may be hard to sustain in the longer term, as indeed may the alternative of allowing flexible arrangements for voter registration in their former domicile, as the connections between the expatriate (and even potentially their children and grandchildren) and their state of origin become ever looser. In turn, of course, that very looseness of the connection undermines the case for arguing that expatriate voting is an adequate form of democratic representation, since it can easily be argued that the expatriate voter may always be a relatively disconnected and ill-informed voter, and thus hardly one who adds to the democratic quality of the electoral process.[66]

In any event, wherever there is a possibility that an expatriate E.U. citizen resident in another Member State could have two votes (in the home and the host state), the question arises as to the desirability and acceptability

---

65. *See* Council Directive 2004/38, *supra* note 25.

66. *See generally* Claudio López-Guerra, *Should Expatriates Vote?*, 13 J. Pol. Phil. 216 (2005).

2566 *FORDHAM LAW REVIEW* [Vol. 75

of dual voting. Under the European Parliament Voting Rights Directive,[67] both dual voting and dual candidatures are emphatically ruled out. Article 4(1) provides that "[c]ommunity voters shall exercise their right to vote either in the Member State of residence or in their home Member State. No person may vote more than once at the same election."[68] It is of course clearly wrong that any person should have two votes in a single election (i.e., the European Parliament elections), albeit one that is still conducted along essentially segmented national lines.[69] However, it is not so clearly problematic that a person should have two votes in separate regional or national elections. Obviously, persons with dual nationality may already be able to vote in general elections in two Member States, depending upon the national rules in place. Interestingly, Maarten Vink comments upon a case of trade-off within Dutch parliamentary politics, where the case for extending electoral rights in national elections to nonnationals (building upon the right to vote in local elections introduced in the 1980s) was traded off in Parliament between the two governing parties, the Christian Democrats (who were against) and the Social Democrats (who were in favor) to produce an outcome which supported greater toleration of dual nationality instead.[70] This emphasizes the intimate link between policies on expatriate voting and voting rights for nonnationals and citizenship policies.

Under the current state of E.U. law and with the current state of competences, any formal change to the rights and status of E.U. citizens within the Member States will need to be driven forward by national action. If this is to be the case, it does not necessarily mean that the European Union will have no future role, but it remains to be established precisely what that might be, and how the national action might impact upon the evolution of the E.U. constitutional framework.

It goes without saying, of course, that the Member States could choose to act together by changing the E.U. treaties to institute an equivalent to article 19 EC in the domain of regional and national elections and thus oblige themselves to secure national implementation of the E.U. citizen's right to equal treatment in relation to regional and national elections, just as they did with local and European Parliamentary electoral rights. This would require a formal extension of existing powers and competences either under article 22 EC by way of a freestanding addition to the citizenship provisions under this truncated amendment procedure (and initiating that process would require an initiative from the Commission), or as part of a generalized treaty amendment process. While I have already commented

---

67. Council Directive 93/109, *supra* note 18.

68. *Id.*

69. Case C-145/04, Spain v. United Kingdom, 2006 ECJ CELEX LEXIS 444 (Sept. 12, 2006) (acknowledging this point).

70. Maarten Vink, Limits of European Citizenship: European Integration and Domestic Immigration 5 (2005).

2007]   *E.U. CITIZENSHIP AND POLITICAL RIGHTS*   2567

about the unlikelihood in practice of the Council and the Commission applying article 22, the latter proposal for generalized treaty amendment also seems unlikely. In the wake of the failure of the Constitutional Treaty to achieve ratification across the Member States in 2005 and 2006, questions must be asked about whether any further treaty amendments are conceivable in the short term. Moreover, even under more propitious political circumstances than those prevailing in the mid-2000s, the need to achieve unanimous agreement around a measure which would necessarily involve an intrusion into national sovereign choices on the boundaries of the suffrage would militate against such a major change in the scope of the E.U. treaties.

Marginally more conceivable is a treaty provision which merely encourages the Member States to adopt electoral rights in regional and national elections. This could be along the lines of article 41 EC, which states that "Member States shall, within the framework of a joint programme, encourage the exchange of young workers."[71]   Any such reference to voting in regional or national elections in the Treaty, even if it did not include a dispositive element such as that which can be found in article 19 EC, would already open the way for the Commission to propose various forms of action promoting convergence or benchmarking as between the Member States in relation to electoral rights practices, so long as such action fell short of proposing formal harmonization of national laws. Even without such a reference, in the interests of promoting E.U. citizenship, the Commission could doubtless already encourage forms of soft law action on the part of the Member States such as, for example, a Council Recommendation on electoral rights for E.U. citizens. These types of measures have been much used in recent years in the field of policy making in relation to the integration of immigrants from third country nationals, where such policy action lies at the margins of the EU's formal competences.[72]   There have even been references in some, but not all, documents on integration to encouraging the Member States to institute local electoral rights for all immigrants.[73]   However, such measures categorically do not impose enforceable obligations upon the Member States.

An alternative way forward could be to use a mechanism of international law outside the formal legal framework of the E.U. treaties, which would have the advantage of providing a flexible structure into which the Member States could opt, as politics and circumstances dictated. Using the mechanisms of international law to promote flexible policy making in the

---

71. EC Treaty art. 41.

72. Shaw, *supra* note *, ch. 7.

73. *See, e.g.*, Draft Conclusions of the Council and the Representatives of the Governments of the Member States on the establishment of Common Basic Principles for immigrant integration policy in the European Union, 14776/04 MIGR 105, Principle 9 (Nov. 18, 2004).

2568   *FORDHAM LAW REVIEW*   [Vol. 75

European Union is a form of "old-fashioned" flexibility, not least because this mechanism has always existed and makes use of the external resources of international law, and in particular the principle of reciprocity of obligations.[74]   Thus, instead of just adopting recommendations or guidelines which the Member States take little notice of, and which it cannot formally enforce, the Commission could try to encourage the Member States to follow the line at least some of them took with the Schengen Agreements in the 1980s and 1990s. The Schengen Agreements were intended to lead to the gradual abolition on border checks on persons moving between the Member States, along with the installation of a common approach at the external frontiers (e.g., the Schengen Visa). It was a laboratory of integration, and it led in the longer term to a substantial extension of the scope of the E.U. treaties in 1999, with the incorporation of Schengen into the E.U. system through the Treaty of Amsterdam.

To put it another way, by analogy with the Schengen experiment, some or all of the Member States could explore the possibilities for further integration in the field of political rights for citizens offered by an international agreement developed outside the framework of the European Union, without prejudice to the possibilities of future Union action or Union competences in the field. Such a convention negotiated between the Member States could lay down a consensual framework for reciprocal recognition of voting rights in regional and national elections to nonnationals on a bilateral and possibly multilateral basis. It might also provide a roadmap to achieving mutual recognition in this field, and thus encourage the development of the requisite trust and common action between the Member States needed for developments to occur in this area. The Convention could be developed such that it would come into force as soon as a minimum of two Member States had formally signed and ratified it, thus creating a framework which all of the states, if they so wished, could gradually opt into as they developed bilateral and multilateral arrangements with their partners within the Union. The level of detail in the convention should at the minimum cover the issues relating to registration and mutual recognition covered in the two electoral rights directives of 1993 and 1994.[75]

It may be objected that there already exist many international instruments in the field of political rights, including ones which are much less far-reaching in nature, such as the Council of Europe Convention on the Political Participation of Foreigners in Public Life at Local Level.[76] Yet the majority of the Member States have declined to adopt and ratify such

---

74. Bruno de Witte, *Old-fashioned Flexibility: International Agreements Between Member States of the European Union, in* Constitutional Change in the EU: From Uniformity to Flexibility? 31 (Gráinne de Búrca & Joanne Scott eds., 2000).

75. *See supra* note 18.

76. Convention on the Participation of Foreigners in Public Life at Local Level, *opened for signature* Feb. 5, 1992, Europ. T.S. No. 144 (entered into force May 1, 1997).

2007] *E.U. CITIZENSHIP AND POLITICAL RIGHTS* 2569

modest instruments. Why should they proceed with a more ambitious agreement along the lines suggested? The reply to this objection would presumably point to the incentives of the Member States resulting from an agreement which would be clearly reciprocal in nature, offering the possibility for Member States creating bilateral or possibly multilateral arrangements of reciprocity in the first instance with close neighbors or states with which they had an existing affiliation. It could reasonably be expected that there may be genuine pressure for such developments from their respective citizens (e.g., Portugal/Spain, Germany/France, Sweden/Finland/Denmark, Czech/Slovak Republics, Baltic states, Benelux and so on). Only after trust has been built up in the context of such relationships might Member States move on towards generalizing the ascription of voting rights in regional and national elections to all resident E.U. citizens. The downside of such alliances, of course, could be the increasing fragmentation of E.U. law, and the danger that some European citizens may find themselves excluded from access to what is regarded as the "gold standard" of political rights (i.e., the right to vote in national elections), just because the Member State where they reside and the one of which they hold the national citizenship do not belong to the same alliance.

IV. BUILDING ON THE STATUS QUO: THE NATIONAL *ACQUIS*

One clear advantage of this manner of proceeding, which stresses reciprocity, is that it could build in interesting ways upon the few examples of the ascription of voting rights to nonnationals in regional and national elections within the Member States of the European Union at the present time. The United Kingdom is the most substantial case, giving rights to Irish citizens, and to Cypriot and Maltese citizens as Commonwealth citizens, to vote in all U.K. elections,[77] subject only to satisfactory immigration status.[78] They may also stand for election, but again subject to satisfactory immigration status.[79] The franchise for Irish citizens and

---

77. The Representation of the People Act, 1918, 7 & 8 Geo. 5, c. 64 (U.K.), established the first truly modern franchise for the U.K. Westminster Parliament, abolishing property qualifications for men and introducing the franchise for (some) women for the first time. At the time it posited the franchise for "British subjects," and when Ireland and what are now the countries of the Commonwealth became independent states, the franchise arrangements were preserved and updated, for example, in the Ireland Act, 1949, 12, 13, & 14 Geo. 6, c. 41 (U.K.). The relevant consolidating legislation laying down the general entitlement to vote is the Representation of the People Act, 1983, c. 2 (U.K.), as amended. For a review of the current scope of the franchise, see Chris Sear, *Electoral Franchise: Who Can Vote?* (House of Commons Library Standard Note SN/PC/2208, March 1, 2005).

78. Oonagh Gay, *The Franchise and Immigration Status* (House of Commons Library Standard Note SN/PC/419, Oct. 11, 2005). There is now a requirement that to be registered a person must have leave to enter and remain in the United Kingdom. Representation of the People Act, 1983, §§ 1, 2, 4 (U.K.), *substituted by* Representation of the People Act, 2000, c. 2, § 1 (U.K.). Such a person is a "Qualifying Commonwealth Citizen."

79. The Act of Settlement, 1700, 12 & 13 Will. 3, c. 2, § 3 (Eng.), prescribes the basic contours of the right to stand for election in the United Kingdom, although its requirement

2570 *FORDHAM LAW REVIEW* [Vol. 75

Commonwealth citizens is a legacy of the British Empire and the slow emergence of a concept of "citizenship" as opposed to "subjecthood" (to the Crown) in the United Kingdom.[80] In that sense, neither Irish citizens nor Commonwealth citizens were treated as "aliens," that is as persons whose influence on domestic politics should be prevented as a matter of principle because of the imputation of some potential malign influence.

From time to time the case for extending the suffrage is canvassed in the U.K. Parliament. The views of the various political parties presented in a 1998 Home Affairs Select Committee of the House of Commons Report on Electoral Law and Administration give a flavor of the range of views, and how these map onto the political landscape:

> [I]t has been suggested that the right to vote in parliamentary elections could be extended to all EU citizens or, further still, that the right to vote in all elections could be given to all foreign residents after they had been in this country for a set period of time. The representatives of the political parties were not at one on this point, with Lord Parkinson for the Conservatives reluctant to extend the current exceptions, Mr Gardner for Labour recognising there might be a case—particularly on the basis of reciprocity—for some extension, and Mr Rennard for the Liberal Democrats suggesting that the present distinctions were artificial and that *prima facie* those who were resident here and paying taxes should have some form of right to vote . . . . [W]e do not think the present voting entitlements for non-UK citizens need extension.[81]

From the U.K. perspective, the franchise for E.U. citizens is already wider than in other Member States, since the United Kingdom allows E.U. citizens to vote in the elections for the devolved Parliaments and Assemblies of the component nations of the United Kingdom, and in the elections for the Mayor of London and the London Assembly. Technically this is because such elections are governed within a framework analogous to local elections for the purposes of the franchise and so the right to vote flows naturally from that conclusion.[82] The use of the local electoral

---

that a person be born in England, Scotland, or Ireland or one of the dominions thereto in order to stand for election does not apply to Irish and Commonwealth citizens. *See* Isobel White, Oonagh Gay, Richard Kelly, & Ross Young, *The Electoral Administration Bill 2005-06*, at 74 (House of Commons Library Research Paper No. 05/65, Oct. 2005). However, until the adoption of the Electoral Administration Act, 2006, c. 22, § 18 (U.K.), the immigration status of the candidates had not been dealt with in like manner to the immigration status of nonnational voters.

80. In Case C-145/04, Spain v. United Kingdom, 2006 ECJ CELEX LEXIS 444, ¶ 79 (Sept. 12, 2006), the court recognized this position as one of the constitutional traditions of the United Kingdom, and, as such, as a position which deserved protection within the framework of Community law so far as possible.

81. Home Affairs Select Committee of the House of Commons, Report on Electoral Law and Administration, 1997-8, H.C. 768-I, ¶ 118.

82. Local Government Elections (Changes to the Franchise and Qualification of Members) Regulations, 1995, S.I. 1995/1948, § 3(1) (U.K.), provides the basic amendments to the local electorate to incorporate the requirements of E.U. law. In relation to the

[2007]   *E.U. CITIZENSHIP AND POLITICAL RIGHTS*   2571

register might seem anomalous in some respects since these bodies may have "legislative competence"[83] or the power to make acts of Parliament.[84] But the choice for the local electoral register may reflect both the need to simplify electoral administration by not creating a new register of electors just for these purposes, and/or the need to emphasize the local character of the devolved functions, in a manner which tends to conceal the emerging federal character of the United Kingdom's territorial and governance settlement.

Moreover, E.U. citizens were able to vote in the regionally based referendums in Scotland and Wales held to ascertain whether the people of these "region-nations" wanted new forms of representation or political authority, and they have had the right to vote in every other referendum held since 1997 (e.g., the one held in London to decide whether to have a Mayor of London and a London Assembly) apart from the one held on the establishment of devolved institutions in Northern Ireland.[85] The degree of openness to this question in the United Kingdom is further illustrated by the fact that prior to the publication of the draft E.U. bill, which if passed would have provided for the United Kingdom's referendum on the Constitutional Treaty, there was some speculation in political circles about whether the government would propose extending the franchise to E.U. citizens resident in the United Kingdom.[86] However, in the event the bill proposed that the franchise should be based on that for general elections in the United Kingdom, and thus included only Irish, Cypriot, and Maltese citizens resident in the United Kingdom. Since Irish citizens would not have had an expatriate electoral right in relation to voting in any Irish referendum, they would not have enjoyed double representation.

---

inclusion of E.U. citizens in the "regional" franchise, see Greater London Authority Act, 1999, c. 29, § 17 (U.K.); Scotland Act, 1998, c. 46, § 11 (U.K.); Government of Wales Act, 2006, c. 32, § 12 (U.K.); Northern Ireland (Elections) Act, 1998, c. 12, § 2(2) (U.K.) (repealed Dec. 2, 1999).

83. Government of Wales Act, 2006, § 94.

84. Scotland Act, 1998, § 28.

85. Referendums (Scotland and Wales) Act, 1997, c. 61, §§ 1(2), 2(2) (U.K.). The parliamentary electoral register was used to determine the franchise in the Northern Ireland referendum, doubtless given the sensitivities of the issues attaching to this referendum, which followed on from the Belfast Agreement of Easter 1998. *See generally* Oonagh Gay, *The Franchise for Referendums* (House of Commons Library Standard Note SN/PC/2583, Aug. 18, 2003).

86. Conspiracy theorists suggested that the Labour Government of Prime Minister Tony Blair might try to extend the franchise in this way to increase the chances of a "yes" vote in the referendum, on the (perhaps misplaced) assumption that E.U. citizens from other Member States resident in the United Kingdom might be more likely to vote "yes." The possible options for the franchise (local or national) are canvassed in Oonagh Gay, *Proposals for a Referendum on the New European Constitution* (House of Commons Library Standard Note SN/PC 3064, May 27, 2004).

2572   *FORDHAM LAW REVIEW*   [Vol. 75

Ireland is the only other E.U. Member State which gives rights to vote in national elections to nationals of another E.U. Member State.[87] It gives the right to vote, but not stand, in *Dáil* elections to U.K. citizens alone. It does not give U.K. citizens the right to vote in referendums or presidential elections.

The text of the ninth amendment to the *Bunreacht na hÉireann* (Irish Constitution), which was passed by referendum in 1984, gives a general power to the *Oireachtas* (Irish Parliament) to legislate to extend rights to vote in *Dáil* elections to noncitizens. These provisions were only introduced after a case had been brought before the Irish Supreme Court which contested a 1983 bill which would have originally extended the franchise to U.K. citizens not only to vote in *Dáil* elections, but also in elections for the President and in referendums.[88] This bill was intended to extend the existing legal position which already gave U.K. citizens the right to vote in local elections (along with all other resident nonnationals) and in European Parliament elections (in the latter case, of course, in advance of introduction of article 19 EC). A primary motivation for the 1983 bill was to introduce some element of reciprocity in relation to the electoral rights granted under U.K. law to Irish citizens.

In finding that the 1983 bill violated the constitution as it stood, the supreme court concluded that article 16 of the Irish constitution, in the form in which it then existed, provided a complete code limiting the electorate for the *Dáil* elections to Irish citizens, and Irish citizens alone. There could be no possibility of extending by ordinary legislation the franchise to other groups of electors, as had been contended by the Attorney General,[89] who was tasked with arguing the case for a bill which had been piloted through Parliament by the *Fine Gael*/Labour coalition government before being challenged before the supreme court. The supreme court based its argument on a conception of the national suffrage oriented around a concept of national popular sovereignty. It found that this conception of sovereignty underpins the Irish constitution:

---

87. Ireland also grants electoral rights to all nonnationals in local elections (voting and standing), and has done so since 1972. Electoral Act, 1992, § 10 (Act No. 23/1992) (Ir.) *available at* http://www.irishstatutebook.ie/1992_23.html (last visited Jan. 23, 2007).

88. *In re* Article 26 of the Constitution and in the Matter of The Electoral (Amendment) Bill, 1983 [SC No 373 of 1983] [1984] I.R. 268 (Ir.). U.K. citizens continue to be excluded from voting in presidential elections and referendums. These are powers reserved under the constitution to citizens alone, by interpretation of article 6 of the constitution. Ir. Const., 1937,   art.   6,   *available*   *at* http://www.taoiseach.gov.ie/attached_files/Pdf%20files/Constitution%20of%20IrelandNov2 004.pdf (last visited Feb. 6, 2007).

89. It is interesting to note that the Attorney General of Ireland at the time was Peter Sutherland, later to become a member of the European Commission and, later still, Director General of the WTO. Throughout, Sutherland has been an important proponent of closer European integration.

E.U. CITIZENSHIP AND POLITICAL RIGHTS

Article 6 [of the Constitution] proclaims that all powers of government derive under God from the people and, further, that it is the people's right to designate the rulers of the State and, in final appeal, to decide all questions of national policy. There can be little doubt that "the people" here referred to are the people of Ireland by, and for, whom the Constitution was enacted. In short, this Article proclaims that it is the Irish people who are the rulers of Ireland and that from them, under God, all powers of government derive and that by them the rulers are designated and national policy decided. It is not possible to regard this Article as contemplating the sharing of such powers with persons who do not come within the constitutional concept of the Irish people in Article 6.[90]

The court went on to distinguish between a provision regarding the basic political organization of the state, such as article 16 on the suffrage, and provisions on fundamental rights such as freedom of association and expression, granted ostensibly under the constitution to citizens alone, but which the Irish courts had also interpreted in certain circumstances as protecting the rights of noncitizens. Consequently, article 16 was interpreted as providing an exhaustive definition of the suffrage, which meant that the introduction of electoral rights for U.K. citizens (and any other noncitizens) would require a constitutional amendment.

After the referendum passing the ninth amendment to the constitution, the Electoral (Amendment) Act, 1985, was passed amending the suffrage for *Dáil* elections to cover British citizens, and to create a power for a minister to extend this on the basis of reciprocity in the event that other E.U. Member States confer the right to vote in their parliamentary elections on Irish citizens. Thus,

(1B) Where the Minister is of opinion that—

(a) the law of a Member State relating to the election of members of, or deputies or other representatives in or to, the National Parliament of that Member State enables citizens of Ireland, by reason of their being such citizens and being resident in that Member State, to vote at such an election, and

(b) the provisions of that law enabling citizens of Ireland who are so resident so to vote are the same, or are substantially the same, as those enabling nationals of that Member State so to vote,

the Minister may by order declare that Member State to be a Member State [whose citizens may vote in *Dáil* elections].[91]

---

90. *In re* Article 26, [1984] I.R. at 268.

91. Electoral (Amendment) Act, 1985, § 2(1B) (Act No. 12/1985) (Ir.) (inserting a new § 1B into §5 of the Electoral Act, 1963 (Act No. 19/1963) (Ir.)). These provisions are now encoded at Electoral Act, 1992, §§ 8(2)-(7) (Act No. 23/1992) (Ir.).

2574   *FORDHAM LAW REVIEW*   [Vol. 75

This is an interesting development on two counts. First, because while the political act of extending the suffrage to U.K. citizens can be regarded as recognizing the historical connection between, and the overlapping citizenships of, the two states of the United Kingdom and Ireland, as well as the rights granted by the United Kingdom to Irish citizens,[92] only the condition of reciprocity is applied for the future to other E.U. Member States. The second curiosity is that it requires only a ministerial order to extend the suffrage beyond its current boundaries, the relevant parliamentary consent having already been given.

As it stands, with the reciprocity requirement in what is now section 8(3) of the Electoral Act, 1992, the trigger for action must in principle come from another Member State, or from common action amongst the Member States. As the Minister for the Public Service, Mr. Boland, stated, during debates in the Irish Parliament,

> [I]t seems appropriate to look forward to the day when member states will be prepared to confer on each other's citizens the right to vote at parliamentary elections. [The Irish Government] would welcome this development and, in anticipation of it, this Bill proposes to enable the Minister by order to extend the *Dáil* vote on a reciprocal basis to nationals of other member states.[93]

While the issue of extending electoral rights to E.U. citizens has not recently been actively debated in Irish politics, it is supported within a number of opposition parties, notably *Sinn Féin* and the Labour Party, even as an issue which should be taken up unilaterally by Ireland, in the absence of common action amongst the Member States.[94]

---

92. Introducing the original Electoral (Amendment) Bill 1983 into the *Dáil*, the Minister stated that

> [t]he aim of this Bill is to give a further measure of practical expression to what has been referred to as the unique relationship which exists between this country and our nearest neighbour, and to acknowledge and reciprocate the voting rights enjoyed by Irish citizens in Britain. It is my hope that measures such as this, reflecting close ties between neighbouring peoples, will make their contribution to promoting peace and reconciliation throughout these islands.

345 Dáil Deb. col. 251 (Oct. 19, 1983). The case for excluding British citizens from the right to vote in presidential elections, *Seanad Éireann* (upper house) elections, and referendums was highlighted by the speaker from *Fianna Fáil*, Bobby Molloy TD, precisely because there cannot be reciprocity in the United Kingdom with a nonelected Head of State and Upper House, and (at that time) no tradition of referendums. 345 Dáil Deb. col. 253 (Oct. 19, 1983). As was noted in the text accompanying *supra* note 86, the franchise for the U.K. Referendum on the Constitutional Treaty would have included all those entitled to vote in general elections in the United Kingdom, including Irish citizens.

93. 108 Seanad Deb. col. 1193 (June 27, 1985).

94. Interviews with TDs (Irish MPs) representing *Sinn Féin* and the Labour Party, at the Irish Parliament (Mar. 3, 2005). A TD representing the Green Party was broadly supportive of the suggestion in the light of wider Green Party policy, some of which is highly critical of developments within the European Union notably in the defense field, but a Senator from the Progressive Democrats, the junior coalition partner of the *Fianna Fáil* government was much more skeptical.

What the combined examples of the existing franchises in the United Kingdom and Ireland show is that there are many conceivable routes within political argument towards the extension of the franchise in national elections to resident nonnational E.U. citizens. In Ireland, a mechanism such as an international agreement between the Member States could be a trigger to developing the reciprocity necessary for extending the existing scope of the franchise within the confines of the existing legislation. However, Ireland, like all the Member States, could apply a "pick and choose" approach to its fellow Member States in relation to the electoral rights granted. It could be argued that such a "pick and choose" approach imports too great an element of flexibility into the system of integration which links the Member States. There may be some force in this objection given that the thrust of European integration for the most part has been towards identifying collective goals for the Member States and then finding the means by which these can be achieved, through as much collective action as possible. However, there are already substantial elements of flexibility built into the system of E.U. law as it stands. Opt-outs are available for states from monetary union and from the Schengen system governing the borders, and thus adding one more element to the system of flexible integration packages does not seem wholly problematic. This argument is particularly powerful if—in comparison to the situation as it stands at present—such a system would lead to an incremental accretion of rights accruing to E.U. citizens, albeit through the medium of national law but triggered by the reciprocity mechanisms of international law.

In the United Kingdom, it would represent a very few steps from acknowledging that the degree of integration of and trust in resident nonnational E.U. citizens, which makes them part of the electorate for elections to the devolved authorities of the non-English parts of the United Kingdom, to acknowledging that the same principles of integration and trust should also mandate the possibility that an E.U. citizen, perhaps having served a qualifying residence period, should be able to participate in Westminster elections as well as elections to institutions based in Edinburgh, Cardiff, or Belfast. This argument might particularly be made in respect of E.U. citizens resident in England (with the exception of those in London who can vote for the Mayor of London and the London Assembly), who do not currently enjoy the opportunities for democratic participation given to their E.U. citizen peers in Scotland, Wales, and Northern Ireland to vote for the authorities that hold powers in fields such as education, agriculture, transport, and health, and in the case of the Scottish Parliament, at least, the power to make primary legislation. In any event, the existing anomalies in relation to the United Kingdom's asymmetric federal arrangements are enhanced by the differences in the franchise between these two types of elections, and any attempt to review the United Kingdom's current constitutional settlement should surely take

2576 *FORDHAM LAW REVIEW* [Vol. 75

that question into account.[95] As in Ireland, a convention mechanism could create the institutional structure in which the necessary trust and reciprocity between the Member States could gradually be seeded and develop.

One final note of caution needs to be sounded, however, and this concerns possible constitutional obstacles at the national level which may be faced by this type of innovation in the broad context of European integration. While the United Kingdom clearly sees no constitutional obstacle to including nonnationals within the franchise for the purposes of national elections—since it already allows Irish and Commonwealth citizens to vote and stand in Westminster elections, and since Ireland has already successfully amended its constitution to make it possible in practice to enfranchise nonnational E.U. citizens—it can be assumed that these two states would not encounter a significant difficulty with the type of proposal set out here. However, if Ireland were to go beyond what has already been established in order to enshrine, for example, a right to stand for election, or the right to vote in presidential elections or referendums, it would undoubtedly require a further amendment to the constitution. Equally, it can be assumed that constitutional changes would be required in most if not all of the other Member States. There is no doubt that the right to vote in regional and national elections cuts closer to the heart of national sovereignty than does the right to vote in local elections, and establishing the latter set of electoral rights at the national level already required constitutional adjustments to be made in many Member States consequent upon the Treaty of Maastricht.[96]

There may in some cases be a further problem beyond the feasibility and political possibility of such a sensitive constitutional amendment, and that concerns its very possibility in constitutional terms, given that it would be proposed to include nonnationals within the group of persons tasked with electing the sovereign legislature. Notwithstanding the powerful normative arguments that can be made in favor of a more inclusionary conception of the *demos*,[97] or indeed the instrumental arguments about E.U. citizenship made earlier in this paper, it may simply be legally impossible for the national constitutions of some Member States to be amended to allow for nonnational E.U. citizens to vote in regional and national elections. To do so would violate their fundamental self-conceptions as *nation* states, where power flows from the "people," and the "people" are the national citizens, bound together in a community. In 1990 the German Federal Constitutional Court annulled *Land* level legislation put forward by Hamburg and

---

95. See Shaw, *supra* note *, ch. 8, for a further discussion of voting in regional elections.

96. Síofra O'Leary, The Evolving Concept of Community Citizenship: From the Free Movement of Persons to Union Citizenship 218 (1996); Peter Oliver, *Electoral Rights under Article 8B of the Treaty of Rome*, 33 Common Mkt. L. Rev. 473, 476-78 (1996).

97. William A. Barbieri, Jr., Ethics of Citizenship: Immigration and Group Rights in Germany (1998); Heather Lardy, *Citizenship and the right to vote*, 17 O.J.L.S. 75 (1997); Lardy, *supra* note 59.

2007] E.U. CITIZENSHIP AND POLITICAL RIGHTS 2577

Schleswig-Holstein to introduce electoral rights for nonnationals at the local level for nonnationals.[98] In ruling that the proposed legislative schemes breached the German Basic Law, the court relied upon a concept of popular sovereignty as the basis for political legitimacy, and linked this to a principle of a bounded *Staatsvolk* (or "state people"), limited by reference to the holding of national citizenship. It explicitly rejected the principle of affected interests as the basis for a claim to political equality and access to the franchise. The key phrase reads,

> [The principle of popular sovereignty] in Article 20(2) of the Basic Law does not mean that the decisions engaging state authority must be legitimated by those who are affected by them; rather state authority must be based on a people understood as a group of persons bound together as a unity.[99]

It extended its conclusion about "state" authority also to the level of local democracy, holding that municipalities, like the elected authorities at the state and federal level, wield state power. Not only did this rule out the Hamburg and Schleswig-Holstein initiatives, but it also meant that the implementation of article 19 EC subsequently required an amendment to article 28 of the Basic Law.

Extrapolating from those rulings to the question as to whether a constitutional amendment would be possible to give nonnational E.U. citizens the right to vote in German national or indeed *Länder* elections raises some obvious problems. The Federal Constitutional Court demonstrates a clear constitutional preference for a bounded concept of the *demos* calculated by reference to the limits of formal legal nationality, with some indications in the text that it has a preference for a concept of national legal community that involves strong societal bonds (of language, culture, and so on). This goes to the untouchable core of the German constitutional framework. The *Staat*, which is the basis for calculating the *Staatsvolk* is defined in the Basic Law as a democratic, federal, and social state based on the rule of law. In addition, the court seems to indicate its support for the principle that there can be no democracy without a *demos*, a legally defined group which in turn wields state power.[100] Even in the liberal and

---

98. Bundesverfassungsgericht [BVerfG] [Federal Constitutional Court] Oct. 31, 1990, 83 Entscheidungen des Bundesverfassungsgericht [BVerfGE] 37 (F.R.G.) (Schleswig-Holstein); Bundesverfassungsgericht [BVerfG] [Federal Constitutional Court] Oct. 31, 1990, 83 Entscheidungen des Bundesverfassungsgerichts [BVerfGE] 60 (F.R.G.) (Hamburg). For detailed commentary, see Seyla Benhabib, The Rights of Others: Aliens, Residents, and Citizens 71-128 (2004); Christian Joppke, Immigration and the Nation State: The United States, Germany, and Great Britain 104-19 (1999); Rubio-Marín, *supra* note 62, at 186-234; Shaw, *supra* note *, ch. 9; Olivier Béaud, *Le droit de vote des étrangers: l'apport de la jurisprudence constitutionnelle allemande à une théorie du droit de suffrage*, 8 Revue Française de Droit Administratif 409 (1992); Gerald L. Neuman, *"We are the People": Alien Suffrage in German and American Perspective*, 13 Mich. J. Int'l L. 259 (1992).

99. 83 BVerfGE 37 (50) (my translation).

100. *See* Rubio-Marín, *supra* note 62, at 205.

2578 *FORDHAM LAW REVIEW* [Vol. 75

increasingly pluralistic society which Germany is today, one does not need to deploy an ethno-cultural reading of the concept of *Volk* in the German Basic Law for it to be possible to envisage difficulties with an attempt to amend the text to allow nonnationals to wield state power due to the tight conception of political responsibility which the court gave in the 1990 judgments. In its rulings, the court did explicitly recognize the possibility of E.U. citizens being given the right to vote in the future in local elections, as this was already under discussion at the time, in 1990. But this did require an amendment to article 28 of the Basic Law, which was introduced as part of the package of measures designed to give effect to the Treaty of Maastricht. It remains, however, a moot point in German constitutional law whether the Basic Law could be stretched to accommodate rights for nonnational E.U. citizens to vote in either regional or national elections.

CONCLUSIONS: ELECTORAL RIGHTS AND THE CONSTITUTIONALIZATION OF
THE EUROPEAN UNION

This essay has used the issue of whether mobile E.U. citizens should be granted the right to vote in the regional and national elections of the Member State in which they reside as a case study showing how the constitutionalization processes of the European Union are not (and should not be) necessarily confined to the European Union level alone. The European Union is a complex system of multilevel governance, in which detailed interconnections with the legal and constitutional orders of the European Union and its Member States (and of the Member States inter se) are an integral component of the overall structure and are as important in their own way as the E.U. treaties themselves or the case law of the Court of Justice. These interconnections would have been sustained, and indeed in some ways developed, had the EU's Constitutional Treaty been ratified and entered into force, as scheduled, on November 1, 2006. However, the rejection of the Constitutional Treaty in two decisive referendums held in France and the Netherlands in mid-2005 effectively froze the ratification process, and it seems very unlikely that the Constitutional Treaty will enter into force in its current form. However, in the absence of decisive treaty-based reform, the EU's underlying composite constitutional framework will continue to develop incrementally, including in the sphere of citizenship.

This case study has illustrated both the possibilities for further development of the political dimension of E.U. citizenship through the type of semi-coordinated trust building advocated in Part II in the form of a convention providing a framework for the reciprocal allocation of electoral rights to resident E.U. citizens, and also—in the latter part of Part III— some of the limitations of such an approach. For, at a certain point, in every sphere, including that of the franchise, the constitution-building process of a limited polity such as the European Union will run up against the "rock" of national sovereignty. There may be, as the German case briefly demonstrates, some conceptions of national political sovereignty,

E.U. CITIZENSHIP AND POLITICAL RIGHTS

which place a claim to exclusive ownership of the concept of *demos*, that even the most skilled and subtle constitutional drafting cannot get around. However, even limiting the discussion to that which is legally possible, and arguably politically desirable, there remains considerable space to develop the political dimension of E.U. citizenship further than it has hitherto been taken.

[11]

Evaluating Union citizenship: belonging, rights and participation within the EU

Richard Bellamy

School of Public Policy, University College, London (UCL), UK

(*Received 20 February 2008; final version received 30 July 2008*)

Union citizenship often gets criticized for complementing rather than offering an alternative to citizenship at the member state level. By contrast, this article defends that complementary status as the most sociologically plausible and normatively acceptable role for this status. Citizenship as it developed within the member states combined the values of belonging, rights and participation. EU citizenship has attempted to develop the first from an attachment to the second, and to employ new and more selective forms of the third. However, neither rights nor participation prove sustainable without a fairly strong sense of belonging, such as has already developed within the member states. To seek to unravel the different ways these three values have modified and promoted each other in each of these states, as certain European Court of Justice (ECJ) cases threaten to do, undermines rather than enhances citizenship and its main achievements: the development of inclusive, democratic welfare systems.

Keywords: European citizenship; rights; belonging; participation

Introduction

The normative potential behind Union citizenship tends to be envisioned in one of two contrasting ways. On the one hand, certain proponents conceive it as analogous, and potentially a rival or successor, to that of the member states. This account links Union citizenship to the promotion of a European identity based around common cultural values and political symbols that parallel and could possibly supersede the national identities of citizens. It seeks to develop an affective relationship among Union citizens towards the EU and their fellow EU citizens similar to that felt by co-nationals towards each other and their state, thereby legitimizing the development of greater competences at the EU level. As Shore (2000) has shown, this view frequently lies behind rhetorical statements by the Commission and Parliament about the need to bring Europe closer to citizens. On the other hand, many academics, and increasingly policy makers too, seek to abandon the nation state as a model for the EU and see Union citizenship as an opportunity to go beyond the traditional values of citizenship as found in the member states. In particular, many propose dissociating the rights of citizenship from either a sense of belonging to and identification with a given cultural or ethnic community (e.g. Habermas 1996), or even active participation in that community's political, economic or social life (e.g. Van Parijs 1997). Instead, they contend EU citizenship should form a component of some kind of post-national cosmopolitan citizenship grounded in the moral entitlements we have as human beings and the obligations we owe each other to secure them in an increasingly interconnected world.

598   R. Bellamy

Such views figured prominently in debates surrounding the EU Charter of Fundamental Rights and the proposed Constitutional Treaty (e.g. Habermas 2001).

From both these perspectives, the actual provisions of EU citizenship prove disappointing. These rights remain dependent on citizenship of a member state and in certain key respects are designed to complement rather than to substitute for or undermine it. Instead of signalling the provision of a distinct set of goods by the EU, the rights conferred by EU citizenship are almost all contingent on residence in another member state. Formally, at least, the relevant Treaty articles and residence directives do not confer an unlimited right to reside in that state but are linked to the EU citizen having either independent resources or participating in the economic life of the host state, thereby avoiding becoming a burden on its services. Far from being either tied to and promotive of any sense of Europeanness and a transfer of key functions and rights to the EU level, or transcending the whole language of national belonging and participation, Union citizenship re-affirms the linkage between belonging, rights and participation within the member states. It facilitates cooperation between citizens of the member states and their access to citizenship of another member state, but does very little to create a distinctive attachment to the EU itself. True, the recent case law of the European Court of Justice (ECJ) has produced an incremental extension of the entitlements of EU citizens within host member states that could be said to have partially undermined this picture. However, this article contests such an extension and defends the normative attractiveness of the complementary role hitherto played by EU citizenship. It does so less for the pragmatic reason that this role remains more realistic and workable than any likely alternative, though such considerations play a part, than because citizenship at the member state level has a normative value of its own that EU citizenship is not only unlikely to be able either to replicate or provide an attractive substitute for, but also would be unjustified in attempting to do so.

The following section sketches the ways the three core values of citizenship – belonging, rights and participation – have reinforced each other within nation states. Subsequent sections then explore how each of these values has come to be reconfigured within the member states and the implications of these changes for EU citizenship. The third section argues that although there has been a partial transformation of the politics of belonging, the shift has been below rather than above or across the level of the nation state. Nevertheless, interaction and the need for cooperation between different spheres of belonging have increased. It might be thought that such relations could and should be regulated by principles of rights that are independent of the political communities involved. However, the fourth section contends that such independence proves chimerical. Rights get shaped by the participative and cultural practices of different peoples. The final section concludes that as a consequence we need to develop political participation as an aspect of Union citizenship. However, consistent with the nature of belonging and rights within the EU, such participation should be conceived not as the activity of a non-existent European demos but as the processes whereby the various *demoi* of the EU negotiate the terms of their co-existence.

The values of citizenship

Citizenship at the member state level developed through the linked processes of state-building, the emergence of commercial and industrial society, and nation-making – all three being driven forward by war (Rokkan 1974, Marshall 1950) Differing social and political circumstances – both structural and contingent – meant their historical phasing and configurations varied considerably between states (Bellamy 2004, pp. 15–17). However, in diverse ways these three processes served respectively to create a sovereign authority presiding over a given territory and possessing a monopoly of military, police and legal-administrative power; promote the partial breakdown of traditional social hierarchies and the creation of an equitable system of justice and the public infrastructure associated with the market; and produce linguistic standardization, a workforce educated to basic standards of literacy and numeracy, and the mobilization of affective bonds between citizens themselves and them and their state.

Citizenship came to be associated with three key values: belonging, rights and participation. First, citizenship involved belonging to the national community. National identity shaped a common civic consciousness and allegiance to the state and one's fellow citizens (Miller 1995, Ch. 3). National systems of education created a public political language and inducted citizens into the nation's civic culture. Second, lack of ascribed status led individuals to being treated as equals possessing certain rights by virtue of their humanity – including the right to be treated equally before the law. Their involvement as actors in markets also gave them equal rights to pursue their interests by buying and selling goods, services and labour (Pocock 1995). Meanwhile, citizens looked to the state to provide social and economic rights as part of its regulatory function and demanded political rights to secure equal access and recognition within its decision-making and organizational structures. Finally, citizenship involved the capacity, entitlement and obligation to participate as a full and equal member within the economy and the polity (Barbalet 1988). For example, the right to vote was standardly tied to the payment of taxes, military service, and the undertaking of such public duties as sitting on juries. Similarly, social and economic rights were linked to the duty and ability to work and to contribute to national schemes of social insurance. Those deemed socially irresponsible, a label applied at various times and places to lunatics, children, criminals, women, the propertyless and the indigent, either forfeited or were ineligible for most citizenship rights.

These three values proved mutually reinforcing, creating a condition of civic equality in the conception and upholding of the laws and policies associated with social-democratic, welfare states. The rights enjoyed by citizens of the member states, and the resulting duties they must perform to provide them, extend way beyond the basic rights most people recognize they owe to humanity in general. This expanded and deepened set of entitlements and responsibilities arises from the ways citizens' rights get shaped and strengthened by their sense of belonging and participation. These two qualities form a virtuous circle that together foster the feelings of solidarity and trust between citizens required to generate a commitment to promote on an equitable basis the public goods on which their rights depend (Bellamy 2008, pp. 12–17).

Solidarity leads citizens to feel certain obligations towards their fellows, while trust gives them faith that others will reciprocate in fulfilling them (Offe 2000, pp. 67–68). Without such sentiments, citizens will be tempted to either free ride or defect from collective arrangements out of fear that others are already doing so. This temptation will be especially strong in the case of those goods of a quasi-public nature in the technical sense, such as education or health care. A sense of commonality both facilitates and is buttressed by cooperation, diminishing these tendencies to distrust and disengage. Those who believe they share common values and interests, including a common language and customs, will be more inclined (and find it easier) to interact. Moreover, regular and open-ended interaction between repeat-players reduces the incentives for free-riding and defection and builds confidence in the possibility of collaboration. It helps engender the bonds of reciprocity needed to produce benefits that are diffuse and public rather than direct and purely personal. The resulting history of interactions leads to a certain way of doing things that further supports a shared identity among participants and gives them a sense of ownership and attachment to their collective arrangements.

Political participation within some form of democracy plays a particularly important role in this regard. At one level, the formation of a demos prepared to make collective decisions on equal terms with each other is itself a product of the solidarity and trust arising from a shared history of social cooperation. At another level, democratic decision making shapes that history, giving both belonging and rights their civic character and rendering them more inclusive and egalitarian. Unlike subjects, citizens are equal before the law because they enjoy an equal influence over the making of the laws through being participants in a democratic process. A subject could belong to a given kingdom – even feel a special attachment to Queen and country – and possess the privileges that go with being one of her majesty's loyal servants. However, subjects are always subordinate to their rulers, dependent for their rights on finding favour and influence with those in power. By contrast, citizens are both ruler and ruled. They are entitled to take part in collective decision making on an equal basis to others to define both the terms of their belonging and their rights. Indeed, the struggle to render political citizenship more inclusive and equitable through expanding the franchise and changing the character of the political rules of the game – for example, by extending the vote to workers and women, and introducing elements of proportional representation and regional devolution – has been instrumental in reconfiguring the political culture of a polity and the public goods it supports in a more encompassing and egalitarian manner (Bellamy 2001). Consequently, political participation forms the right of rights (Waldron 1999, Ch. 11). It is not only the most effective means to claim one's rights; but also gives those rights legitimacy through having been determined within a process that aspires to treat all as political equals, entitled to equality of concern and respect for their views and interests from their fellow citizens (Bellamy 2007, Ch. 4).

None of the above means that citizenship at the member state level is perfect. Of particular relevance here is the way global pressures are altering the nature of belonging, especially through immigration, and challenging the capacity of states to secure certain of the public goods on which their citizens rights depend, with both these changes producing calls for new forms of participation to encompass greater cultural and social diversity, on the one hand, and transnational interests and concerns, on the other. The EU is often portrayed as a response to this situation, with Union citizenship a potential means of overcoming the resulting shortcomings of state-centred citizenship. In particular, it is sometimes suggested that citizenship might be disassociated from national forms of belonging and associated with rights alone, with these providing a basis for novel modes of participation – indeed, in some respects negating the need for political participation altogether. What follows explores these and other ways of reconfiguring the three values of citizenship at the EU level. As we shall see, such proposals confront two main problems. The first is the practical, largely sociological, difficulty of establishing similarly thick forms of citizenship to those currently in place within the member states without creating something like the synthesis of belonging, rights and citizenship these have developed, and the unlikelihood of such a synthesis being achieved at the EU level. The second is the normatively questionable nature of any such attempt to either circumvent or diminish in some way member state citizenship. Citizens within the member states have been able to shape their rights to reflect their collective priorities, traditions and culture. For example, although all the member states adhere to the European Convention of Human Rights, they articulate many of these rights in very different ways – criminal and justice policy, welfare and social security all vary considerably between states, reflecting contrasting values and concerns. The resulting diversity not only possesses value in itself, but also legitimacy through having been produced through the reciprocal and democratic cooperation of the citizens involved. If a similarly legitimizing process cannot be established at the EU level, which absent the necessary sociological preconditions or satisfactory alternatives to them is arguably the case, then a risk exists that Union citizenship might undermine pre-existing processes and settlements and thereby weaken their citizens' right to have rights. As a result, viewing Union citizenship as complementing rather than replacing or subverting member state citizenship continues to offer not only the most plausible but also the most normatively attractive role for this new status.

Citizenship as belonging: a European Community?

The policy of European citizenship was initially conceived as a part of a package of symbolic measures to promote identification with the Union. It went along with the introduction of a European passport, anthem and flag (Adonnino 1985, 1988). The hope was that as member states pooled certain sovereign powers, so citizens would also pool their national identities.

This proposal reflected the belief that the pattern of legitimacy within the EU must mirror that of the nation state and stem from a citizenship of belonging based on a certain symmetry between sovereignty and identity (Shore 2000). According to this model, sovereignty operates at both the 'polity' and the 'regime' level (Bellamy and Castiglione 2003). A sovereign 'polity' holds exclusive sway over a defined people (the polity's 'subjects') residing within a particular territory and with regard to particular public goods or functions (the polity's 'sphere'). Power is regulated within this polity according to a given 'regime' that designates the rules whereby sovereign power is recognized and exercised (the regime's 'style' of politics) and the realm of the political (the regime's 'scope'). According to the ideology, if not always the reality, of the nation state, nationality defined the 'subjects' and territorial 'sphere' of the 'polity'. In democratic versions of the argument, a people or nation could only exercise self-government through being sovereign according to the criteria of the prevailing 'regime' within their own 'polity'. Where other political identities and units existed, these were deemed to be embedded within, and so subordinate to, the larger political identity and unit. Thus, Britishness was supposed to accommodate English, Welsh, Scottish and Northern Irish identities. Each region formed a part of the United Kingdom, with their local governments feeding into the Westminster system (Miller 2000, Ch. 8). As this example indicates, however, the hierarchical and unitary organization of sovereignty and identity was never wholly uncontentious and today it clearly is not. Both the polity and the regime aspects of sovereignty have been challenged, with identity being similarly affected.

With regard to the polity aspect, sovereignty and national identity has been weakened by a combination of related internal and external pressures. Internally, multiculturalism, particularly a resurgence of minority nationalism, and an enhanced individualism among the more affluent, have changed in very different ways the capacity of states to draw on or forge a national identity capable of sustaining an allegiance to the public good and the collective institutions and decisions that define and uphold it. On the one hand, the sense of belonging has been strengthened but at levels below that of existing state units. In particular, regionally concentrated national groups, such as the Scots in the UK, have demanded ever more self-governing rights, producing an asymmetrical devolution of sovereign power to accommodate their demands (Gagnon and Tully 2001, Austin and O'Neill 2000). On the other hand, there has been a weakening of belonging among certain sections of the community. Multiculturalism to accommodate immigrant groups has sometimes been credited with weakening the politics of redistribution by concentrating on issues of recognition that highlight difference rather than social solidarity (Fraser 1995). In fact, there is no evidence that the pursuit of multicultural policies and the granting of special rights have lowered welfare spending (Banting and Kymlicka 2006). By and large, immigrant groups have sought to redefine national identity in non-discriminating ways rather than to abandon such notions altogether. By contrast, though, there has been a growing tendency among the wealthier members of the community to abandon public health, education and even security services for private provision. Indeed, this trend has been accompanied by the partial or complete privatization of many hitherto public services and utilities (Hay 2007). Both sets of changes have altered the spheres of the polity and hence the purposes for which citizens are subject to its authority and owe it their allegiance. Increasingly, more local or even largely personal and familial considerations apply.

Many of these internal changes have been fostered in direct and indirect ways by external pressures stemming from the social and economic processes associated with globalization. Coping with these pressures has motivated states to enter into cooperative arrangements to control their interactions in ever more spheres, especially with regard to the economy and security. These arrangements have weakened their sovereignty to some degree, even if formally speaking they are voluntarily entered into and are under the control of the contracting states who remain free to leave them or renegotiate. However, their chief purpose has been to extend the prevention of illegitimate interferences with the integrity and affairs of another state beyond the traditional concern to avert armed intervention. Contemporary agreements include the fair sharing of the costs and benefits arising from the negative (and positive) externalities of domestic activities, as with quotas for the emission of greenhouse gases, and attempts at the equitable regulation of international and transnational activities, such as trade or crime respectively. On the whole, the success of these arrangements has turned on their appearing to offer long-term Pareto-improvements to all parties. Nevertheless, in certain very specific spheres citizens have become subject – usually indirectly – to the ultimate authority of certain international bodies. Yet none of the resulting organizations – as we shall see, not even the EU, which is by far the most developed of them – has attracted much in the way of affective allegiance from citizens. In other words, there has not been a transfer of any sense of belonging beyond the state to parallel the movement below it noted above. Rather, these institutions have been seen predominantly as instruments for protecting existing spheres of belonging and rendering their relations mutually beneficial. At best, they hold out the possibility of making interactions between states more just and mutually respecting.

These internal and external changes to the polity aspect of states have prompted commensurate changes to their regimes. Thus, the styles of politics have altered. For example, multinational states have adopted more consociational arrangements, while within most advanced democracies there has been a gradual move away from the collaborative politics of political parties towards involvement in more targeted single issue and interest groups. Likewise, there has been a shift in the scope of politics from government to governance, with command and control giving way to softer modes of regulation. However, while within states these changes have been partial, these new styles and scopes are virtually the only forms of politics available within the new international regimes. In different ways, they represent a style and scope of politics where an overarching sense of belonging is lacking. Unfortunately, they carry the risk of upholding the status quo and deepening existing social divisions and inequities. For example, consociational arrangements hand the various national groups a veto over collective policies that may protect their interests but also potentially enhances their differences and the power of their ruling elites. Who governs becomes disassociated from how well people are governed (Barry 1975). Similarly, single issue movements can be effective ways of gaining a hearing for interests and concerns that have been excluded from debate by the major parties. But they can also distort the political agenda if there is no attempt to balance these concerns against those of others within a programme of government of the kind parties have to provide. A danger in these circumstances is that they act as mechanisms whereby the privileged seek to preserve their advantages – a feature of NIMBY campaigns, for instance (Pattie *et al.* 2004, pp. 276–278).

The EU exemplifies these trends (Scharpf 1999). Its core business remains economic collaboration within a single market and the sharing of the resulting costs and benefits, along with the regulation of associated transnational activity. Its 'polity-like' features are strongest in those areas where it can offer plausible 'win-win' improvements in the regulation of cross-border activities and the collective goods involved require international cooperation. Where there are rival suppliers, as is the case with security issues with NATO, or the benefits of cooperation are more contentious, as with the euro, then many member states stand aloof. Meanwhile, the EU has minimal competences in welfare areas involving the redistribution of resources.

By and large, the attitudes of citizens towards the EU tell a similar story (figures below from Eurobarometer 60, 62, 67). The areas enjoying high euro-legitimacy are either those tied to market building, such as freedom of movement (including gender equality), competition policy, and structural funds for disadvantaged regions, or policies that have a clearly transnational dimension and where international cooperation secures a genuine public good for all member states, such as environmental protection, the fight against drugs, foreign trade and relations with other states more generally. Issues relating to socio-economic rights, in so far as they involve health, welfare and education, all have a low euro-legitimacy, with 65% or more of European citizens regarding these as exclusively national responsibilities. Meanwhile, a sense of belonging is low. Although a bare majority of European citizens believe their country has benefited from membership, only around 3% of citizens generally view themselves as 'Europeans' pure and simple, with barely 7% saying a European identity is more important than their national one. By contrast, approximately 40% describe themselves as national only and 47% place nationality first and Europeanness second. Indeed, although 91% of these citizens usually declare themselves attached to their country and 86% to their locality, only 53% feel attached to the EU.

The limited sphere of the EU's 'polity' and the partial sense of belonging it arouses are reflected in its 'regime'. EU decision making remains to a considerable extent 'intergovernmental', with Lisbon potentially strengthening certain member state powers. As commentators have remarked, the EU operates in many respects like consociational systems within multinational states (Chryssochoou 1998). True, the directly elected Parliament's role has steadily increased. However, participation in European elections has just as steadily decreased and at a higher rate than in national elections, with turn out – even with compulsory voting in certain states – on average below 50% and in many countries below 30%. Despite EU support, European parties have failed to develop as electoral mechanisms but are rather groupings of national political parties within the parliament, with the elections themselves retaining a significant 'second order' element (Marsh 1998). Recognizing this problem, the EU has turned increasingly to consultation with citizens groups. Yet, these groups are typically funded by the EU, with little or no accountability to their often small or even non-existent membership and no mechanism for ensuring their representativeness of European public opinion (Warleigh 2001, 2006). Thus, the EU demonstrates the classic characteristics of political systems where belonging has become fragmented or attenuated in various ways. Moreover, there seems little realistic prospect of this changing.

In this context, the complimentary character of Union citizenship seems appropriate. It enables cooperation between member states by allowing citizens to move freely between them and enjoy the services each produces, but not in ways that undermine the sense of belonging at the national level. A period of residence and work is necessary to generate access to welfare services, for example. True, though we can see such cooperative arrangements as reciprocal forms of recognition between the member states, they function as a set of EU level rights even if they do not give access *per se* to services generated by the EU itself rather than each of its component parts. Some commentators see these rights as post-national notwithstanding their clear inter- and transnational characteristics. We turn now to investigating how far such rights might offer a distinct source of allegiance to the EU and a means for building EU level democracy.

Citizenship as rights: a European constitutional patriotism?

Rights have long offered the dominant approach to citizenship within the liberal tradition and inform its conception of the constitutional practices of liberal democracies. This liberal model conceives rights, the rule of law and constitutional democracy in largely juridical terms (Bellamy 2007, Part 1). Although British, American and broadly European models of this juridical paradigm differ, all stress the importance of legal mechanisms for controlling the abuse of power and protecting individuals. They aim to secure a just framework of rights within which citizens and the government can legitimately act. The resulting liberal constitution lays out the entitlements and obligations of citizens vis-à-vis both the state and each other. It constrains what individuals may do to or expect of others and what the state may do to or expect of them.

Recently, a number of theorists – prominent among them Jürgen Habermas – have developed this liberal thesis to argue that rights can define the subjects and sphere of the polity as well as the scope and styles of its regime. Habermas sees rights as potentially replacing belonging as a source of social solidarity within the EU. He contends it is the just political culture of a state that binds us to it, rather than nationality or some other social, religious or ethnic cultural force (Habermas 1996). We identify with a polity because of a constitutional patriotism stemming from the justice of its regime. Moreover, what makes such a regime just is its embodying the rights that establish the conditions of private and public autonomy necessary for free and equal participation in democratic decision making. As a result, citizens can identify with the legal system of rights as theirs because it enables a process of democratic deliberation on their collective policies.

Habermas saw the Charter of Fundamental Rights and the Constitutional Treaty as appropriate vehicles for his proposals (Habermas 2001). Moreover, he conceived them as a means whereby member states could employ the EU to overcome the potential threat to social trust and solidarity posed by the undermining of inclusive forms of belonging by migration and cultural diversity, on the one side, and the individualism and consumerist attitudes encouraged by global markets, on the other. Rights supposedly offer a universal discourse that can transcend the particular attachments of the European peoples, with social rights an important part of the package.

There are numerous objections that can be raised to Habermas' optimistic scenario: from the suitability of the actual constitutional proposals to secure his purposes, to the deficiencies of the processes of drafting and ratification as mechanisms for expressing the will of a European people. Indeed, the very size and linguistic diversity of the Union have led many commentators to doubt the possibility of a European public sphere (Dahl 1999, Kymlicka 1999) – doubts arguably confirmed by the finding that 51% of EU citizens have never heard of the Charter and only 8% claim to know what it is (Gallup Organization 2008). Here, though, I wish to focus not on these possible practical difficulties but on two key problems with the rights thesis itself.

First, rights may provide a source of objective legitimation for an organization, but they are at best a necessary rather than a sufficient condition for subjective legitimation. Habermas elides the legitimacy of a regime with that of its polity. However, a regime may be objectively legitimate yet fail to attract the subjective allegiance of all its citizens because they question the legitimacy of the polity within which it operates. By contrast, citizens of an objectively illegitimate regime often offer it tacit support because they subjectively identify with the polity – presumably many Iraqis felt like this under Saddam Hussein. Likewise, a polity may be objectively legitimate, in not being the result of recent conquest or colonization, but still lack subjective polity legitimacy among a cultural minority. Moreover, this absence of subjective polity legitimacy may lead citizens to question the legitimacy of the regime, even if it meets fairly abstract democratic criteria. For example, few, if any, Quebec nationalists deny that Canada is democratic *per se*. Their own view of rights and democracy is similar to Canadian federalists in abstract terms. Yet, they feel Canada's current political regime lacks democratic legitimacy because they believe the French territories cannot deploy these rights in ways that reflect their cultural interests.

The second problem kicks in here. Habermas contends a consensus on rights is both the end point and the presupposition or rationale of democratic deliberation. We discuss with others in order to (and because we can) agree on rights. The difficulty with this thesis is that beyond the most abstract level, and sometimes even here, there is considerable disagreement about the foundations and character of rights, and how they apply to particular issues. Moreover, debates about rights not only provide the substance of many political debates, they also produce different accounts of the nature of the political.

Take the main ideological divide within liberal democracies between libertarians and social democrats. As Table 1 shows, these two positions generate contrasting views of rights. These different conceptions lie behind the main contemporary political divisions, animating debates about the welfare state, the regulation of the market economy and so on. Moreover, there can be no overarching theory of rights that encompasses both positions. For these views conflict in often incompatible ways. Part of the reason for the intractable character of their conflict arises from the fact that, as Table 2 reveals, each offers a different view of all four of the dimensions of politics. Thus, debates between libertarians and social democrats are not within a political framework of rights, they are about that framework.

Both these sources of disagreement about rights characterize the views of citizens about the EU. On the one hand, we saw in the last section how very few citizens regard the EU as having a high degree of 'polity' legitimacy. On the other hand, within their own states they have elaborated contrasting rights cultures. Although all the member states could be said to share roughly the same liberal democratic values, their valuations of them frequently diverge. Civil, political and social rights are configured in different - and occasionally incompatible – ways in all the member states. Consequently, there is no consensus on either the legitimacy of the EU as the arbitrator of rights, or on what a set of putative European rights might be. Both issues divided the convention that drew up the Charter of Fundamental Rights, which was forced to skirt around them through a mixture of vague drafting and compromise (Bellamy and Schönlau 2004). It will be objected that citizens within the member states can differ just as much. However, they can agree to disagree precisely because a consensus on rights does not provide the basis of their civic union. As a result, they have managed to exercise their right to have rights to fashion a distinctive rights culture that has been shaped by their on-going disagreements.

These different rights regimes render a Union citizenship that complements member state citizenship and promotes the reciprocal recognition of their distinct rights policies more appropriate than one that involves imposing an EU level rights regime. Thus, citizens should be able to move and trade freely between member states, but the employment of such rights

Table 1. Contrasting views of rights.

	Libertarian	Social Democrat
Legal rights (liberties and immunities)	Formally equal -ve liberties	Formally equal -ve liberties though certain immunities for reasons of substantive equality and linked to social rights to defend their equal worth
Political rights (powers)	Protective, limited	Protective and informative, limited
Social rights (claims)	Few (mainly insurance and compensatory) or none	Broad range: including enabling and distributive as well as insurance and compensatory
Civic rights (powers)	Few (consumer) or none	Workers and consumer
	Strict divide between state/civil society, public/private	Need for state to regulate and balance civil society
Duties	Of respect, with duties subordinate to rights	Of concern and respect, with duties being corollary of rights

Note: -ve = negative

Table 2. Contrasting views of politics.

	Libertarian	Social Democrat
Subjects	All autonomous agents capable of entering legally recognized contracts, particularly in the economic sphere	All autonomous agents capable of entering legally recognized contracts, including social and political sphere
Spheres	Political a narrowly defined public framework for social interaction. Political discussion and intervention, if not regulation, inappropriate within a broad private sector	Political a more broadly defined public framework for social interaction. Political discussion and intervention, if not regulation, inappropriate within a narrower private sector
Scope	To protect the natural -ve freedom and formal equality of individuals	To foster autonomy by preserving the broader -ve freedom and more substantive equality of individuals and classes
Styles	Constrained maximization to achieve mutual advantage via market trading	Constrained maximization to achieve mutual benefit via pluralist bargaining

Note: -ve = negative

ought to be constrained by the need not to disrupt the rights enjoyed by national citizens – not least with regard to their access to domestic services. Although this appears to be the position in the Treaties and related legislation (Article 7 (1), 17 (2) EC, Directive 2004/38/EC), the ECJ, notwithstanding its apparent endorsement of this reading in *Uecker* (1997) and *Baumbast* (2002), has gradually eroded this constraint in an attempt to realize the alleged 'destiny' of Union citizenship as 'the fundamental status of nationals of the member states' (*Grzelczk* 2001, para. 31, see also *Martinez Sala* 1998 and especially *Bidar* 2005). Yet, the grounds for this belief are minimal. Recent polling evidence found only 18% of Europeans know their rights as citizens – indeed, only 41% felt they knew what the term 'citizen of the EU' meant.

Social rights are especially problematic in this respect. Advocate General Stix-Hackl has claimed that 'shortfalls in tax revenue are [not] to be taken into consideration as matters of overriding general interest' (*Schwarz* not yet reported) when states seek to overrule free movement and residence rights. Yet, such matters go to the heart of the capacity for states to respond to their citizens priorities when setting their budgets (Nic Shuibhne 2008). Not to take them seriously, risks disturbing the reciprocal ties between citizens that make public spending sustainable. Hitherto in areas such as health the ECJ has accepted that states are not providing 'services' in the commercial, industrial or professional sense of Article 49 EC, but fulfilling a broader social duty. They have acknowledged that limited resources and moral and political differences about the importance and effects of different policies and treatments all make the determination of an individual's entitlements in such areas legitimately subject to democratic decisions among those affected about financial priorities and other public interest considerations, producing differing packages of benefits between member states. The decision in *Watts* (2006) to make such services subject to 'free movement' and allow individuals to escape waiting lists and other forms of rationing in their own country by shopping for treatments elsewhere, undercuts the capacity of states to plan and favours mobile and articulate individuals at the expense of the poor. It also places Courts in the difficult position of making substantive decisions about an individual's health needs without any obligation to consider their knock-on effects for health and other policies (Newdick 2006).

To allow EU level rights to impact upon member state rights in this way undermines citizenship. Rights do not constitute citizenship. Rather, citizenship constitutes rights by allowing citizens to determine the public goods on which their rights depend on an equitable basis (Bellamy 2001). The different rights regimes of the member states reflect the ways the various peoples of Europe have exercised their most basic right as citizens – that is as participants in the collective decision-making processes that determine their rights. And as the famous Maastricht decision of the German constitutional court argued (BVerfGE 89, 155–213, 1993), the lack of a European public sphere and demos means that this 'right of rights' – the right that in practice has operated as the 'right to have rights' (Waldron 1999, Ch. 11) – is not as yet operative at the EU level. For EU rights to be rights of citizenship, citizens need to have a say in defining their sphere, subjects, styles and scope and resolving the many differences they have about all of these. It remains to be seen how far this is possible at the European level.

Citizenship as participation: the role of civic engagement

Although concern over the EU's democratic deficit and the lack of citizen participation has grown in recent years, a number of commentators have insisted EU level democracy is not only unlikely to be achieved but also unnecessary and inappropriate (Majone 1998, Moravscik 2002, Scharpf 1999). Most of the EU's functions, notably economic regulation, monetary policy, and the maintenance of the rule of law within its sphere of competence, are undertaken by non-democratic delegated authorities within the member states. These areas are seen either as too complex for effective democratic control, or as liable to be undermined by myopic or prejudiced democratic pressures. So, decisions over interest rates, say, get handed over to central banks because of the supposed temptations they pose to politicians to manipulate them to engineer short-term, election boosting, economic booms that may be to the long-term detriment of the economy. Moreover, the policy goals in many of these sectors are not seen as particularly politically controversial – that is, as subject to ideological differences. People want sound money, to be secure against fraud and so on, regardless of their political affiliations. Just as local government, being largely about the efficient delivery of an agreed set of services, rarely inflames political passions, so much of EU policy is mainly a technocratic matter of efficient, transnational administration. Small wonder that voter turnout at EU elections is even lower than in local ones.

Although this argument contains elements of truth, it raises numerous difficulties (Bellamy 2006a). The analogy with delegated power at the domestic level proves misplaced, because domestic delegated powers operate within functioning democratic societies. As such, they are influenced by public opinion and often come under considerable indirect political pressure. Courts notoriously follow the polls (Dahl 1957), to a degree regulators and banks do so too. The absence of a 'European' public opinion, as opposed to the national publics of the member states – which often pull in different directions – greatly weakens such indirect democratic control and influence. Nor are the regulations as innocuous as is claimed. Considerable ideological debate occurs within member states over the extent and character of much economic and financial regulation. By and large, those favouring business interests wish to simply promote market freedom, while workers and consumers generally hold a more socially orientated view. Even when agreement exists on the need for and type of regulation, disagreement may exist about whether the EU is the most appropriate level to undertake it. A purely instrumental attachment to the EU may also prove highly fickle. Indeed, as belief in the benefits of membership have declined, from a high of 60% in the early 1990s to the current low of 46%, so has support for membership – from a corresponding early 1990s high of 72% to the current low of 48%. Within nation states, governments often lose popularity when the economy falters. At times, this may even generate calls for changes to the 'regime'. But such dips in support rarely call into question the legitimacy of the 'polity'. In the absence of deeper civic bonds, though, the EU runs this danger.

The concepts of 'subsidiarity' and 'proportionality' supposedly overcome some of these problems by ensuring the EU only tackles those tasks best done at the European level. However, these terms are notoriously, and probably inevitably, vague. Making the ECJ the main arbiter of their meaning more or less guarantees they will be read in an expansive manner. Like all federal courts, it has a built in, and often necessary, bias towards favouring the centre. After all, its *raison d'être* is to lock in the member states to the full implications of their agreements. As we saw, it will always tend to favour incremental moves towards greater integration if unchecked by countervailing influences that direct it otherwise. Till now, these checks have been supplied by the constitutional courts of the member states, which, as I noted, are responsive to domestic democratic pressures. However, their position vis-à-vis the ECJ has been progressively eroded. Theoretically, at least, citizens can also exercise a form of contestatory political power in countries requiring referenda to approve treaty changes. Yet, as the initial response to the French and Dutch rejections of the Constitutional Treaty and to Ireland's initial rejection of the Nice Treaty and its recent rejection of the Lisbon Treaty all reveal, the European elite has been unprepared – in all senses – to respond positively to a 'no'. The European Parliament is also largely a contestatory body. Yet its internal dynamics mean that the one issue it fails to contest is whether integration is appropriate or not. The dominant coalition is always going to be a moderately pro-EU centrist block. Moreover, as I observed, electoral turnout is so low, and elections in any case dominated by national rather than European issues, that its democratic mandate is at best residual. Unsurprisingly, while most EU citizens are satisfied with national democracy, most are dissatisfied with democracy in the EU.

It is sometimes suggested that the failures of party and other traditional forms of democracy at the EU level can be remedied through consultation with European civil society groups, deliberative forums and other new modes of democratic involvement. However, I noted earlier how these forms of participation lack both the basic procedural fairness of party systems based on one person one vote, and the incentives to construct a common political programme by combining with others with different concerns from your own. They tend to be partial and focused on a narrower agenda – often single issues – and lack representativeness and accountability (Bellamy forthcoming). As such, they can offer a useful supplement to electorally based party systems but cannot substitute for them (Kroger 2008).

We seem faced with a dilemma. The degree of belonging necessary to create an EU-wide demos is lacking, and rights provide an inadequate basis to fill this gap. That may suggest that there are democratic limits to the EU. However, despite claims that these limits are in practice respected, they appear to have already been breached. How then can democratic participation on EU matters be meaningfully created? The answer, I suggest, lies in grasping the nettle posed by the EU's poly-centric polity and multi-levelled regime. They provide the basis for shifting from *demos*-cracy to what Kalypso Nicolaïdis (2003) has felicitously termed *demoi*-cracy.

For a *demoi*-cracy to work, far more European policies should be debated at the national and, where appropriate, sub-national level and mechanisms created that give these bodies the ability to review the allocation of competences. In other words, we need European politics to be brought down to the levels that make sense for people – to where they belong. After all, as we have noted, European politics currently works in this fashion, with European issues being framed by national political debates rather than becoming the focus of transnational movements. Uptake of the political rights attaching to Union citizenship largely confirms this fact. These give citizens the right to vote and stand in Municipal and European parliament elections across the Union (Article 19 (1) EC). However, these rights are exercised sporadically at best. According to a Commission study of 2002, the proportion of non-national EU citizens registered to vote ranges from just 9% in Greece and Portugal to 54.2% in Austria. A report on the 2004 EP elections noted that while around 343 million EU nationals exercised their right to vote within their own state, only 6.5 million citizens did so in a host state. Indeed, knowledge of this right is low and appears to have decreased (Gallup Organization 2008). Given the low turnout in European elections anyway, it would appear more appropriate to view the political participation of EU citizens as nested within, rather than autonomous from, national citizenship.

Certain proposals of the Constitutional Treaty that have been kept in the Treaty of Lisbon move in this direction. For example, in the provisions on democratic principles (Title II Article 8 A 2) the new Treaty remarks how as well as being represented in the European Parliament citizens are represented in the European Council and Council of Ministers by their national governments and can hold them accountable either directly or indirectly through their representatives in the national parliaments. Meanwhile, Article 8 C affirms how 'national parliaments contribute actively to the good functioning of the Union' – a role potentially strengthened through the protocols requiring that national parliaments receive Commission consultation documents and draft legislative acts, and giving them the right to offer a reasoned opinion on whether these measures comply with the principle of subsidiarity. However, such measures remain comparatively weak and peripheral. To really give national parliaments and their citizens a voice we need them and not just the European Parliament to discuss the Commission's annual programme and to force Ministers to defend their positions with regard to it. In such circumstances, the key role in EU decision-making of the European Council and the Council of Ministers would have greater legitimacy and a clear rationale exist for why they are in effect of far more importance for the democratic credentials of the EU than the European Parliament.

Even such limited measures are sometimes criticized for being largely negative – a way of constraining further integration. That need not be the case. They may also work to give integration greater legitimacy. By highlighting not just national but also ideological divisions over European policy, many of which cut across national borders, they could also help revitalize EU elections as reflecting European and not simply domestic policy concerns (Magnette 2003, pp. 155–156). However, the fact remains that democratic legitimacy is largely lent to the EU through the old forms of democratic citizenship that prevail in the member states. Given that there is no prospect in the foreseeable future of the EU developing adequate comparable mechanisms of its own, European citizenship must continue to be but an adjunct to national citizenship. Bringing the one more firmly under the scrutiny of the other, particularly with regard to decisions by the Court and other unelected bodies, and to some degree limiting the scope for European integration itself, provides the only viable way to enhance democracy within the EU.

Conclusion

This article has explored the ways the key values of citizenship interact within both the member states and the EU. Although there has been a partial pulling apart of belonging from rights and participation at the national level, there has been no transfer of allegiance to the EU. Moreover, the EU would appear to show that a politics where rights and participation are detached from any sense of belonging is likely to be hard to sustain and potentially have perverse effects. Consequently, the formal status of EU citizenship as dependent on and complementary to national citizenship seems more normatively attractive than is often supposed. Indeed, the attempts to turn Union citizenship into a standalone status that might replace national citizenship proves hard to justify – it can only undermine what remains the main sustainable locus for citizens of the EU to exercise their citizenship – namely, their member states.

610 *R. Bellamy*

Acknowledgements

Research for this paper was undertaken as part of the 'Democracy Task Force' FP6 NEWGOV project (FP6506392). I am grateful for the comments of Chris Hilson, Dario Castiglione, Michael Lister, Christine Reh and two anonymous referees on earlier versions of this paper.

References

Adonnino, 1985. First report of the Adonnino Committee, Bull. EC Supp. 7/85.
Adonnino, 1988. Second report *A people's Europe*, Bull. EC Supp. 2/88.
Austin, D. and O'Neill, M., 2000. *Democracy and cultural diversity*. Oxford: Oxford University Press.
Banting, K. and Kymlicka, W., 2006. *Multiculturalism and the welfare state recognition and redistribution in contemporary democracies*. Oxford: Oxford University Press.
Barbalet, J.M., 1988. *Citizenship: rights, struggle and class equality*. Milton Keynes: Open University Press.
Barry, B., 1975. Political accommodation and consociational democracy. *British journal of political science*, 5 (4), 477–505.
Bellamy, R., 2001. The 'right to have rights': citizenship practice and the political constitution of the EU. *In*: R. Bellamy and A. Warleigh, eds. *Citizenship and governance in the European Union*. London and New York: Continuum, 41–70.
Bellamy, R., 2004. Introduction: the making of modern citizenship. *In*: R. Bellamy, D. Castiglione and E. Santoro, eds. *Lineages of European citizenship: rights, belonging and participation in eleven nation states*. Basingstoke: Palgrave, 1–21.
Bellamy, R., 2006a. Still in deficit: rights, regulation and democracy in the EU. *European law journal*, 12 (6), 725–742.
Bellamy, R., 2006b. Between past and future: the democratic limits of EU citizenship. *In*: R. Bellamy, D. Castiglione and J. Shaw, eds. *Making European citizens: civic inclusion in a transnational context*. London: Palgrave, Ch. 12.
Bellamy, R., 2007. *Political constitutionalism: a Republican defence of the constitutionality of democracy*. Cambridge: Cambridge University Press.
Bellamy, R., 2008. *Citizenship: a very short introduction*. Oxford: Oxford University Press.
Bellamy, R., Forthcoming. Democracy without democracy? Can democratic 'outputs' be separated from the democratic 'inputs' provided by parties and political representation? *Journal of European public policy*.
Bellamy, R. and Castiglione, D., 2003. Legitimizing the Euro-'polity' and its 'regime': the normative turn in EU studies. *European journal of political theory*, 2 (1), 7–34.
Bellamy, R. and Schönlau, J., 2004. The normality of constitutional politics: an analysis of the drafting of the EU Charter of Fundamental Rights. *Constellations: an international journal of critical and democratic theory*, 11 (3), 412–433.
BVerfGE 89, 155–213, 1993.
Chryssochoou, D., 1998. *Democracy in the European Union*. London: I.B. Tauris.
Dahl, R., 1957. Decision-making in a democracy: the Supreme Court as national policymaker. *Journal of public law*, 6, 279–295.
Dahl, R., 1999. Can international organisations be democratic? *In*: I. Shapiro and C. Hacker-Cordón. *Democracy's edges*. Cambridge: Cambridge University Press, 19–36.
EC Directive 2004/38/EC Article 7 (1), 17 (2).
Fraser, N., 1995. From redistribution to recognition? Dilemmas of justice in a 'Postsocialist' age. *New Left review*, 212 (July/August), 68–93.
Gagnon, A.-G. and Tully, J., 2001. *Multinational democracies*. Cambridge: Cambridge University Press.
Gallup Organization, 2008. *Flash Eurobarometer 213*. Hungary: The Gallup Organization. Available from: http://ec.europa.eu/public_opinion/flash/fl_213_sum_en.pdf.
Habermas, J., 1996. *Between facts and norms*. Cambridge: Polity Press, Appendix II.
Habermas, J., 2001. Why Europe needs a constitution. *New Left review*, 11 (September/October), 20–21.
Hay, C., 2007. *Why we hate politics*. Oxford: Blackwell.
Kroger, S., 2008. Nothing but consultation: the place of organised civil society in EU policy-making across policies. EUROGOV No. C-08-03. Available from: http://www.connex-network.org/eurogov/pdf/egp-connex-C-08-03.pdf. [Accessed 15 July 2008]
Kymlicka, W., 1999. Citizenship in an era of globalization. *In*: I. Shapiro and C. Hacker-Cordón. *Democracy's edges*. Cambridge: Cambridge University Press, 112–26.

Magnette, P., 2003. European governance and civic participation: beyond elitist citizenship? *Political studies*, 51 (1), 144–160.

Majone, G., 1998. Europe's democratic deficit: the question of standards. *European law journal*, 4 (1), 5–28.

Marsh, M., 1998. Testing the second-order election model after four European elections. *British journal of political science*, 28, 591–607.

Marshall, T.H., 1950. *Citizenship and social class*. Cambridge: Cambridge University Press.

Miller, D., 1995. *On nationality*. Oxford: Oxford University Press.

Miller, D., 2000. *Citizenship and national identity*. Cambridge: Polity.

Moravscik, A., 2002. In defence of the democratic deficit: reassessing legitimacy in the EU. *Journal of common market studies*, 40 (4), 603–624.

Newdick, C., 2006. Citizenship, free movement and healthcare: cementing individual rights by corroding social solidarity. *Common market law review*, 43, 1645–1668.

Nic Shuibhne, N., 2008. Case comment on *Schwarz, Commission v Germany, and Morgan & Bucher*. *Common market law review*, 48, 771–786.

Nicolaïdis, K., 2003. The new constitution as European demoi-cracy? *Critical review of social and political philosophy*, 7 (1), 76–93.

Offe, C., 2000. The democratic welfare state in an integrating Europe. *In*: M. Green and L. Pauly, eds. *Democracy beyond the state? The European dilemma and the emerging global order*. Lanham: Rowman and Littlefield, 63–89.

Pattie, C., Seyd, P. and Whitely, P., 2004. *Citizenship in Britain*. Cambridge: Cambridge University Press.

Pocock, J.G.A., 1995. The ideal of citizenship since classical times. *In*: R. Beiner, ed. *Theorizing citizenship*. New York: SUNY Press, 29–52.

Rawls, J., 1993. *Political liberalism*. New York: Columbia University Press.

Rokkan, S., 1974. Dimensions of state formation and nation building. *In*: C. Tilly, ed. *The formation of national states in western Europe*. Princeton, NJ: Princeton University Press, 562–600.

Scharpf, F., 1999. *Governing in Europe: effective and democratic?* Oxford: Oxford University Press.

Shapiro, I. and Hacker-Cordón, C., 1999. *Democracy's edges*. Cambridge: Cambridge University Press.

Shore, C., 2000. *Building Europe*. London: Routledge.

Van Parijs, Ph., 1997. Basic income and the political economy of the new Europe. *In*: P. Lehning and A. Weale, eds. *Citizenship, democracy and justice in the new Europe*. London: Routledge, 161–174.

Waldron, J., 1999. *Law and disagreement*. Oxford: Clarendon Press.

Warleigh, A., 2001. 'Europeanizing' civil society: NGOs as agents of political socialisation. *Journal of common market studies*, 39 (4), 619–639.

Warleigh, A., 2006. Making citizens from the market? NGOs and the representation of interests. *In*: R. Bellamy, D. Castiglione and J. Shaw, eds. *Making European citizens: civic inclusion in a transnational context*. London: Palgrave, Ch. 6.

Cases

Baumbast and R v Secretary of State for the Home Department C-413/99 [2002] ECR II-315
Bidar v London Borough of Ealing C-209/03 [2005] ECR I-2119
Grzelczyk v Centre public d'aide sociale d'Ottignies-Louvain-a-Neuve C-184/99 [2001] ECR I-6193
Martinez Sala v Freistaat Bayern C-85/96 [1998] ECR I-2691
Schwarz and Gootjes-Schwarz v Finanzamt Bergisch Gladbach, Judgment of the Grand Chamber of 11 September 2007, not yet reported C-76/05
Uecker and Jacquet v Land Nordrhein-Westfalen C-64 and 65/96 [1997] ECR I-3171
Watts v Bedford Primary Care Trust C-372/04 [2006] ECR 1185

[12]

Transnational citizenship and the democratic state: modes of membership and voting rights

David Owen

Politics and International Relations, University of Southampton, Southampton, UK

> This article addresses two central topics in normative debates on transnational citizenship: the inclusion of resident non-citizens and of non-resident citizens within the demos. Through a critical review of the social membership (Carens, Rubio-Marin) and stakeholder (Baubock) principles, it identifies two problems within these debates. The first is the antinomy of incorporation, namely, the point that there are compelling arguments both for the mandatory naturalization of permanent residents and for making naturalization a voluntary process. The second is the arbitrary demos problem and concerns who determines whether expatriate voting rights are granted (and on what terms). The argument developed provides a way of dissolving the first problem (and defending the proposed solution against possible objections) and resolving the second problem. In doing so it provides a defensible normative basis for the political theory of transnational citizenship.
>
> **Keywords:** transnational citizenship; migration; democracy; membership; voting rights

Introduction

The past 30 years have seen dramatic changes to the character of state membership regimes in which practices of easing access to membership for resident non-citizens, extending the franchise to expatriate citizens as well as, albeit in typically more limited ways, to resident non-citizens and an increasing toleration of dual nationality have become widespread.[1] In relation to voting rights, this transformation is marked by the movement from the requirement that voting rights are grounded in both citizenship and residence to the relaxing of the joint character of this requirement such that citizenship or residence on its own now increasingly serves as a basis for, at least partial, enfranchisement (Baubock 2005, 2007, Stoker *et al.* 2011, ch. 6). In the light of these changes, it is unsurprising that empirically

642 *D. Owen*

informed realistic[2] normative engagement with transnational citizenship – conceived in terms of the enjoyment of membership statuses in two (or more) states[3] – has focused on the issues of access to, and maintenance of, national citizenship, on the one hand (Rubio-Marin 2000, Carens 2005, Baubock 1994, 2003, 2005, 2007), and entitlement to voting rights, on the other hand (Beckman 2006, Rubio-Marin 2006, Baubock 2007). Although there are important limitations to this focus,[4] the argument offered here will work largely within the constraints of this existing debate in order to address two central problems that have arisen from it. The first problem is, what I will refer to as, the antinomy of incorporation, namely, the point that there are compelling arguments for both the mandatory naturalization of permanent residents and for making naturalization a voluntary process. The second problem is, what I will call, the arbitrary demos problem and concerns who determines whether expatriate voting rights are to be granted. To contextualize these issues, I will begin by surveying the three main lines of argument within realistic normative political theory with respect to transnational citizenship (the first section), before turning to address the antinomy of incorporation (the second section) and the arbitrary demos problem (the third section).

Normative framings of transnational citizenship

Within discussions of transnational citizenship, the articulation of grounds of entitlement to full political membership (typically construed as national citizenship) have clustered around the principle that all persons who are subject to the coercive authority of the democratic state (or, to accommodate the European Union, the polity) should be entitled, at least after a limited period of residence (e.g. the European Union norm of five years), to membership of the state. It should be noted that this formulation of the all subjected persons principle is ambiguous between two distinct formulations of the principle: a formulation in terms of subjection to the political authority of the state and a formulation of in terms of subjection to the coercive power of the state. The distinction between these formulations rest on the claim that the political authority of the state is not reducible to, or fully co-extensive with, its ability to enforce coercively its collectively binding decisions. The collectively binding decisions of a democratic state, expressed as law, may legitimately be coercively enforced within the jurisdictional ambit of the law in question (either by the state within its own territorial jurisdiction or by international agencies or partners acting on behalf of the state through which the extended jurisdictional reach of a given law is realized) but being subject to a collective binding norm does not require that the norm is coercively enforceable, it requires only the rather weaker notion that breaches of the norm generate duties of justification and are sanctionable in the absence of adequate justification.[5] It is, of course, true that for a large range of cases, the conceptual distinction between the political authority and coercive power formulations of the all subjected persons principle is a distinction without a practical difference – but not for all cases. Thus, for example, expatriate citizens may be subject to the political authority of the state and yet the state may be unable coercively to enforce compliance with the law (e.g. on income tax and military service) on the part of expatriate citizens. This difference will turn out to matter and I will return to it below, but to do so we need to attend to the three leading variants that cluster around the all subjected persons principle. We can distinguish three positions: the all-subjected persons principle itself, the social membership principle and the stakeholder principle. I will address each in turn but it is worthwhile briefly noting why another well-known principle – the all-affected interests principle – is not taken as basic in this discussion.

The all-affected interests principle

There are two reasons why theorists within this debate may reasonably resist the all-affected interests principle. The first concerns the realistic stance in terms of which the debate is conducted and that point that, on the accounts of its current advocates (e.g. Goodin 2007, Shapiro 2003),[6] the all-affected interest principle would involve a radical restructuring of political decision-making in our contemporary global context.

The second reason is more theoretically fundamental in offering a rejection of the principle as a normative basis for the allocation of membership. As a prelude to addressing the substance of the all-affected interests principle also requires, we need to clarify briefly the relevant formulation of the principle. This task is necessary because although typically the all affected principle is expressed in terms of the all actually affected interests principle, namely, the principle that everyone whose interests are actually affected by a decision should have the right to a political voice in the making of that decision, it has recently been proposed by Goodin that this principle is incoherent:

> Notice first that whose interests are 'affected' by any actual decision depends on what the decision actually turns out to be. Notice second that what the decision actually turns out to be depends, in turn, upon who actually makes the decision. Hence the 'all actually affected interests' principle ... is unable to tell us who is entitled to vote on a decision until after that very decision has been decided. (Goodin 2007, p. 52)

There are several responses available to Goodin's argument; the most economical for current purposes is to note that in relation to any decision, there is a decision-space which is constituted by the options on the table at a given time between which the decision-takers are to choose. Thus, for

644   *D. Owen*

example, in a decision context in which there are three mutually exclusive options – A, B and C – those actually affected would include all whose interests would be affected by the choice of A rather than B or C, B rather than A or C and C rather A or B. Although it is the case that how the interests of those who will be affected are actually affected depends on what the decision turns out to be, that their interests will be affected in one way or another can be specified in advance of whatever the actual decision turns out to be. Hence the incoherence identified by Goodin is dissolved and we can focus on the all-affected interests principle in its classical 'actually affected' form.[7]

So why should the fact that one's morally significant interests are affected by a decision of a polity of which one is neither a resident nor a citizen ground a right to inclusion within the demos? On Goodin's own argument, the all-affected interests principle is grounded on the importance of the intermeshed interests of persons, arguing that 'common reciprocal interests in one another's action and choices are what makes these groups [e.g. territorial, historical, national] appropriate units for collective decision-making' (Goodin 2007, p. 48). But what work is done by this appeal to interlinked interests? Ironically, this view entails that having an interest in membership of a polity or structure of governance is not predicated on one's interests being affected by some decision of that polity but, rather, on one's interests being intermeshed with the interests of others such that one has a common interest with these others in being a member of a legal and/or political community that regulates the relations between the members of this community. This appeal to interlinked interests generates a recursive principle in the sense that while persons whose interests are affected by a decision made by a given polity do not thereby have an interest in membership of that polity, in virtue of having an interest affected by a decision of that polity they do have a common interest with all other persons affected by that decision in membership of a legal and/ or political community that has powers to regulate impartially the decisions made by the interest-affecting polity. This does not however provide a normative basis for the all-affected interests principle as a principle of democratic inclusion. As Baubock notes, the all-affected interests principle 'builds on the plausible idea that democratic decisions have to be justified towards all whose who are affected by them, but implausibly derives from such a duty of justification a criterion of participation and representation in the decision-making itself' (Baubock 2009b, p. 15). Thus, while discussions of the all-affected principle are right to highlight the significance of intermeshed interests, the politically indiscriminate nature of the principle cannot do what is necessary for a consideration of the fundamental question of entitlement to political membership, namely, specify the type of interests whose intermeshing generates a claim to membership of a political community. Put another way:

the 'all-affected interests' principle substantiates ethical duties for democratic legislators to take externally affected interests into account, to seek agreements with the representatives of externally affected polities and to transfer some decision on global problems to international institutions, but ... it cannot provide a criterion for determining claims to citizenship and political participation. (Baubock 2009b, p. 18)

This rejection of the all-affected interest principle opens the way to a focus on the all-subjected persons principle which appeals to the normatively salient point that the basic political relation is that of being governed.

The all subjected persons principle

To illustrate this principle, we can attend to the classic argument for the incorporation of habitual residents provided by Robert Dahl's argument for the 'principle of full inclusion': 'The demos must include all adult members of the association except transients and persons proved to be mentally defective' (Dahl 1989, p. 129), where 'adult members of the association' refers to 'all adults subject to the binding collective decisions of the association' (p. 120). As Lopez-Guerra helpfully notes, Dahl's specification of criteria of democracy can be summarized thus:

(1) governments must give equal consideration to the good and interests of every person bound by their laws (principle of intrinsic equality); (2) unless there is compelling evidence to the contrary, every person should be considered to be the best judge of his or her own good and interests (presumption of personal autonomy); therefore (3) all adults [who are not merely transients (1) and are not shown to be mentally defective (2)] should be assumed to be sufficiently well-qualified to participate in the collective decision-making processes of the polity (strong principle of equality). (Lopez-Guerra 2005, p. 219)

In the context of a democratic polity characterized (in part) by authority over a territorial jurisdiction, Dahl's account implies that any competent adult who is habitually resident within the territory of the polity and, hence, subject to the laws and policies of its government is entitled to full inclusion within the demos.[8] Such an argument can be taken to underwrite Walzer's claim that the denial of full political rights to legally admitted habitual residents amounts to 'citizen tyranny' (Walzer 1983, p. 55).[9]

It has been contended by Lopez-Guerra that, given Dahl's formulation of the principle of full inclusion, 'the demos of a democratic polity must exclude all individuals who are not subject to the laws, together with transients and persons proved incapable of taking part in the decision-making process' (Lopez-Guerra 2005, p. 225). Lopez-Guerra's grounds for this claim are based on the view that, given the territorial jurisdiction of the state, being resident on the territory of the state is a necessary (as well as

646   D. Owen

sufficient) condition for being subject to the collectively binding decisions of the state. Consequently, he argues that:

> Debates so far have focused only on the necessity of granting political rights to all residents. They have ignored the implication that this *requires* the exclusion of long-term expatriates. (p. 234; added emphasis)

Unsurprisingly, this required exclusion encourages the view that citizenship should be granted on a *jus domicile* basis.

The fundamental problem with the interpretation of the all subjected principle that Lopez-Guerra offers is that being present on the territory of a state is not a necessary condition for being subject to its collectively binding decisions. To illustrate this, consider the following (real) examples:

- The event that motivates Lopez-Guerra's own article, namely, the Mexican referendum on expatriate voting.
- The current UK Coalition government proposal to introduce a decent flat rate state pension which is payable only to UK citizens who are resident in the UK.

Who is subject to these collectively binding decisions? The answer is obvious: all citizens, irrespective of the residential status. Hence, while habitual residence is a sufficient condition of subjection to the political authority of the state, it is not a necessary condition.[10]

More generally, states are a form of polity which combine authoritative rules that are conceptually dependent on residency, rules that are conceptually dependent on non-residency and rules that are conceptually independent of one's residential status (though they may be residence-sensitive).[11] Thus, for example, the relationship between a state and its national citizens involves some rights and obligations that are necessarily dependent on residence (i.e. those arising from any law that pertains to actions involving the physical presence of the person with the state), some that are necessarily dependent on non-residence (i.e. the right to re-entry and to diplomatic protection) and some that are residence-indifferent (e.g. paying tax on property owned in the state). One of the political choices that a state can make with respect to issues that are not conceptually tied either to presence on, or absence from, the territory of the state is whether or not to treat them as residence-neutral. So the fact that Joe lives in state F rather than in state H of which he is a national citizen, while his brother and co-national Fred resides in state H does not mean that Joe is not, while Fred is, subject to the authoritative decisions of state H regarding the entitlements, privileges, powers and immunities (and their correlatives) that make up the legal character of citizens of state H. On the contrary, Joe and Fred are both subject to the political authority of state H. What differentiates them is, rather, the specific laws, rights and duties that currently apply to them in virtue of their distinct residence statuses. Thus, a significant range (typically the majority) of the laws of state H are practically tied to, and activated by, residential criteria and, hence, apply to Fred but do not come into effect with respect to Joe as long as he is a non-resident, while other laws which are tied to, and activated by, non-residence apply to Joe, but not to Fred so long as he remains a resident. Further laws may be residence-neutral and apply to both Fred and Joe (e.g. income tax laws can be of this kind and UK laws on the sexual abuse of minors have this character) – and some of these laws may be such that they can be effectively enforced, while others cannot easily be enforced. Citizenship, in its quasi-contractual aspect, is thus like being a signatory to a contract that may have some clauses specifying (reasonable) circumstance-invariant rights and obligations and other clauses where the relevant rights and obligations may vary according to which of a range of circumstances apply.

Notice though that this argument only establishes that, as a citizen, you are subject to the political authority of the state whose nationality you hold. It does not itself provide a justification for why expatriates should be entitled to retain national citizenship of this state. A *jus domicile* rule such as Lopez-Guerra favours would equally meet the basic normative requirement that everyone is entitled to equal membership in a self-governing political community. Essentially the same type of objection is made in a different way by Baubock who argues that "all subjected persons' is too conservative in presupposing the legitimacy of given boundaries':

> If a state turns, for example, the grandchildren of emigrants into citizens through automatic and unlimited *ius sanguinis* rules, then these persons would be subject to the authority of the grandparents' state of origin and could claim democratic representation there. The question is, however, whether such persons should be included as citizens in the first place. Questions about legitimate inclusion must therefore refer to some principle that is not fully derived from de facto exercise of political authority. (Baubock 2009a, pp. 480–481)

The limitation of the all-subjected persons principle exposed by these critical remarks is that it addresses the question of who should be entitled to political membership given an existing structure of political authority and allocation of citizenship, not the question of who should be entitled to national citizenship – and while this limitation plays the useful role of drawing our attention to the distinction between 'political membership' and 'national citizenship' (to which I will return later in this section), it is clear that if we are to develop a criterion for entitlement to national citizenship then, at the very least, the all-subjected persons principle needs supplementation. This limitation is, in part, a product of the fact that the all-subjected persons principle represents an exclusive focus on the democratic state as a

648   D. Owen

regime of rule, where it is precisely this one-sidedness that supports the intuition expressed by Lopez-Guerra that citizenship should be a matter of *jus domicile*. In somewhat different ways, the social membership and stakeholder principles may be seen as attempts to overcome the problem posed by this limitation in ways that acknowledge the value of the democratic state as a site of political community. In the case of the stakeholder principle, this is done directly by specifying the idea of stakeholding in terms of a relationship between the autonomy and/or well-being of an individual and the future of the polity. In the case of the social membership principle, with which I begin, it is done indirectly through an appeal to the salience of social membership.

The social membership principle

The social membership argument is perhaps given its earliest articulation (with respect not to national citizenship but resident non-citizen voting rights) in the case of *Spragins v. Houghton* (1840) which allowed the Illinois Supreme Court to make clear

> a general constitutional preference for democratic inclusion where the simple facts of habitation, residence and common social membership establish a political relationship 'between the governed and [the] governing.' According to the court, the Illinois Constitution: '[I]ntended to extend the right of suffrage to those who, having by habitation and residence identified their interests and feelings with the citizen, are upon the just principle of reciprocity between the governed and the governing, entitled to a voice in the choice of the officers of the government, although they may be neither native nor adopted citizens. (Raskin 1993, p. 1405)

In more contemporary terms, it is advanced by Rubio-Marin (2000) and Carens (1989, 2005) as asserting the principle that people have a moral right to be citizens of any society of which they are members' (Carens 1989, p. 32). The basis of this claim is twofold. First, the general social fact that living in a society makes one a member of a society since as one forges connections and attachments, one's interests become interlinked with those of other members of the society (Rubio-Marin 2000, pp. 21, 31–34; Carens 2005, pp. 33, 39). Second, in living in given society, one is subject to the political authority of the state and, consequently, on democratic grounds, should have access to full political rights within the political community of that state (Rubio-Marin 2000, pp. 28–30; Carens 2005, p. 39).

These arguments are, in several respects, compelling. Moreover, they give rise to the claim – implied by Walzer (1983), advanced by Rubio-Marin (2000) and now accepted by Carens (2005) – that neither the conferral (on the part of the state) nor the acquisition (on the part of the immigrant) of such rights should be optional. The former element rules out selective practices such as citizenship tests on the grounds that while a society can legitimately entertain the reasonable expectation that immigrants will acquire its language and knowledge of its political institutions, it is unreasonable to make acquisition of civic rights conditional on meeting what can only be reasonable expectations given, for example, the differential linguistic abilities of persons.[12] The latter element rules out the possibility of choosing not to acquire such rights on the grounds that such a choice represents voluntary subjection to a condition of political servitude and, hence, is incompatible with the autonomy-valuing character of liberal democratic states.

Further, although the social membership argument was developed in relation to resident non-citizens, it can be extended to address the wider issue of membership more broadly and it is in this extension that its acknowledgement of the non-instrumental value of membership come to the fore. Thus, for example, drawing on the social dimension of the argument, Rubio-Marin (2006) has argued that, in respect of states of origin, expatriates should have a right to retain their nationality of origin even when they naturalize in their state of residence on the basis that, generally speaking, membership of the state of origin is a source of non-instrumental value for them as well as having instrumental value in terms of visiting family and supporting the possibility of return migration. We can extend this argument to reasons for the state of residence also to accept a right to retention of the original nationality when naturalizing, namely, that precisely because membership of the state of origin is typically a significant source of non-instrumental and instrumental value for its emigrant population, requiring them to surrender it unfairly imposes a cost on them which native citizens do not have to bear and, consequently, is liable to engender forms of resentment that damage social cohesion and civic integration (cf. Rubio-Marin 2006, p. 138). We can also note that, although she also does not address this issue, the logic of Rubio-Marin's position would support, given the importance of the family as a site of socialization and the generational proximity of the event of emigration, this right of retention of nationality to be extended to second-generation migrants.

The stakeholder principle

The second supplementary alternative to the all-subjected persons principle is the stakeholder principle proposed by Baubock which expresses the claim that 'self-governing political communities should include as citizens those individuals whose circumstances of life link their individual autonomy or well-being to the common good of the political community' (Baubock 2009a, p. 479). This principle of inclusion is based on the following basic thought:

650   D. Owen

in a self-governing polity, each individual member has a stake in the future of that polity in a dual sense. First, each individual's autonomy or well-being depends to a large degree on how well political institutions work in guaranteeing equal liberties and in providing equal opportunities for all subjected to their authority. Second, citizens can collectively shape the future course of the polity through political participation and by holding political authorities accountable. The notoriously vague notion of the common good may serve as a shorthand term for what it is that citizens have a stake in. (Baubock 2009a, p. 479)

In practical terms, Baubock proposes two criteria for whether people meet this stakeholding requirement:

Those persons and only those persons have a claim to citizenship in a particular political community who (a) depend on that community for long-term protection of their basic rights (dependency criterion) or (b) are or have been subjected to that community's political authorities for a significant period over the course of their lives (biographical subjection criterion). (Baubock 2009a, p. 479)

We can notice first that since first generation migrants are generally stakeholders in both their countries of origin and of habitual residence, this principle lends itself to support of dual nationality. Given the role of family in socialization, it is plausible to argue that second generation migrants are also stakeholders but that by the third generation, this claim is harder to sustain independent of actions on the part of the third generation migrant (such as going to live in the state of their grandparent's origin) to sustain the relationship. Thus, in addition to supporting dual nationality, the stakeholder principle would extend the automatic *jus sanguinis* transmission of citizenship to second-generation migrants but not further (Baubock 2007).

It is notable that in contrast to the social membership argument, the stakeholder principle does not appeal to social ties and attachments but to directly political ties. Baubock offers two reasons for rejecting the social membership argument (which he had earlier endorsed) in favour of the stakeholder principle. The first concerns the increasing problems faced by the concept of a bounded state society in contexts of migrant transnationalism and global interactions. Against this background, Baubock comments, it may appear 'somewhat circular if we derive claims to political membership from factual societal membership, but then have to refer to given political boundaries in order to define societies in the first place' (Baubock 2009a, p. 482) The second is that while the social membership argument 'would substantiate immigrants' claim to citizenship, it cannot account for long-term external membership' when conducted in terms of a statist conception of society. On the other hand, opening out the notion of societal membership beyond such a statist outlook through appeals to notions like family ties 'begs the question why other networks across borders, such as

Critical Review of International Social and Political Philosophy 651

business connections, should not also be regarded as forms of societal membership' (Baubock 2009a, p. 482). Even if we accept the first of these criticisms (as we probably should do), it is not clear that the two points suffice to knockdown the social membership argument as opposed to provide reasons for its reformulation. Hints towards such a reformulation can already be seen in Rubio-Marin's reflections on dual nationality but we can develop this further by considering the following restatement of the social membership argument:

> social membership is characterised by non-instrumentally valuable social attachments and ties that arise from one's (past or present) residence within the territory of the state (or by way of socialisation through parents who were residents of the state in question) and which link one's well-being to the well-being of the (typically transnational) society comprised of all persons characterised by non-instrumentally valuable social attachments and ties that arise from their (past or present) residence within the territory of the state (or by way of socialisation through parents who were residents of the state in question).

This reformulation of the social membership argument does not appeal to the problematic concept of a bounded state society but simply to the non-instrumental value and site of genesis of those social relations that comprise a form of social solidarity, yet since the state remains central to the well-being of this society, the social membership argument may still ground claims to political inclusion. Such a reformulation avoids Baubock's criticisms and, hence, we may take both the revised social membership principle and the stakeholder principle to represent live positions in the debate on transnational citizenship.

Citizenship, membership and resident non-citizens

It is notable that both advocates of the social membership and the stakeholder principles align political membership with national citizenship – and this gives rise to the antinomy of incorporation. The issue at stake concerns whether the resident non-citizen who has legally abided in the state for the relevant period should be automatically entitled to take up national citizenship but not required to do so or should be automatically required to adopt national citizenship. On the one hand, Rubio-Marin and Carens stress the problem of citizen tyranny and, hence, the fundamental democratic good of membership in order to argue for mandatory naturalization. On the other hand, Baubock has argued that there are normatively significant sociological reasons for thinking that it is important for social and political integration that immigrants make a public voluntary commitment to naturalize and, thereby, 'visibly link their own future with that of the country of settlement'. Both of these arguments are, I think, compelling. Consequently,

652   D. Owen

rather than attempt to resolve this dispute by demonstrating the rational superiority of one position over the other, I will attempt the tactic of dissolving the dispute by showing that we can endorse both positions. The central pivot for this tactic is the fact that this antinomy of incorporation arises precisely because both social membership and stakeholder arguments identify political membership with national citizenship. Consequently, one way of negotiating this conflict is to drop this identification and note that neither the all-subjected persons principle or its supplemental variants strictly entail naturalization as the route to political membership. They simply entail political membership, that is, the possession of full political rights – and there is a non-trivial distinction between political membership and national citizenship since the latter, but not the former, automatically includes the 'external rights' of diplomatic protection and automatic right of re-entry to the state as well as the automatic entitlement to pass nationality on to their children via the *jus sanguinis* provisions that states have almost universally and justifiably adopted as part of their nationality laws. Thus, we may hold both that there is a compelling argument for the mandated acquisition of full political rights (which ought, in the case of resident non-citizens, to confer an automatic entitlement to the acquisition of the status of national citizenship), but also that the acquisition of national citizenship itself should involve a voluntary act on the part of the immigrant. The additional features of national citizenship fit the rationale for a voluntary act since their value is immanently related to the immigrant's seeing their relationship to the state as not simply instrumental valuable in protecting them against domination but also as non-instrumentally valuable and, hence, as providing reasons for linking one's own future well-being with that of the state.

However, two significant objections have been proposed to this method of dissolving the antinomy of incorporation which I will address in turn.[13] The first objection concerns mandated membership and points out that denizens are not non-citizens but combine a bundle of extensive quasi-citizenship rights in the country of residence with external citizenship rights in a country of origin. Their denizenship rights include a right to optional naturalization. The objection is thus that this bundle should sufficiently secure their political autonomy. Under this condition, not to make use of their right to naturalization can be seen as akin to enjoying voting rights but not making use of them. To put this point the other way round, an argument for mandatory naturalization would have to meet the same objections as arguments for mandatory voting. Paternalistic arguments for mandatory naturalization or voting are not necessarily illiberal, but they should be grounded on contextual evidence that sufficient inclusion cannot be achieved otherwise.

In response to this first objection, it is important to distinguish between conditions of political autonomy and exercises of political autonomy. In the example of mandatory voting, the argument against the practice swings on the fact that in non-mandatory systems, both voting and not voting are expressions of political autonomy and, hence, while argument for mandatory voting may be plausible, their normative force won't be grounded directly on an appeal to political autonomy (though it may be indirectly so grounded). By contrast, on the account I offer, political membership is a condition of political autonomy, the decision whether to acquire or not acquire political membership may both be expressions of individual autonomy but they are not exercises of political autonomy. Hence, on this view, the question is whether people should be entitled as a matter of personal autonomy to place themselves in conditions of political servitude. I see no reason to accept that claim any more than the claim that people should as a matter of personal autonomy be entitled to sell themselves into slavery.

This initial response, however, depends on the claim that full political membership is a necessary condition of political autonomy – and it is not clear that this claim is sustainable. While it is reasonable to take the claim to hold in the case of 'birthright' citizens who hold no other nationality or 'stateless' residents, the condition of the denizen is quite distinct. The objection suggests that the quasi-citizenship enjoyed by denizens combined with their external citizenship rights in their country of origin suffice for political autonomy, that is, they have external rights of diplomatic protection and of return combined with local voting rights and, typically, some general rights of political participation. If this is the case, it would seem perverse to deny that denizens enjoy some degree of political autonomy and to insist that full political membership is a necessary condition of political autonomy as such. But admitting this point does not settle the argument since once we admit that there are degrees of political autonomy, the pressing question becomes what counts as an acceptable threshold.

Here I think it is worthwhile to return to Dahl's argument concerning the strong principle of equality. The relevant point is that Dahl's argument makes no reference to citizenship; the criterion for membership to which it appeals is subjection to the collectively binding decisions of the polity. While it is the case that resident non-citizens are not subject to all the collectively binding decisions of the polity since not all laws are tied to conditions of residency, it is also true that, given the territorial dimension of the state, a large (and consequential) array of residence-based laws are binding on resident non-citizens. In this respect, one way of reflecting on the issue of the threshold of political autonomy is to note that denizens are situated in different contexts of political autonomy – that of the state of origin and the state of residence – and although some very basic features of political autonomy in the state of residence may be protected through the right of diplomatic protection granted by the state of origin (and the spread of human rights norms), this is hardly sufficient to secure a relevant degree of political autonomy in the context of the state of residence. Considering a

654   D. Owen

related issue raised in relation to dual nationals who have voting rights in both states of their nationality may help to clarify this point. Here the question is raised as to whether this practice breaches the principle of equality since these dual nationals have two votes. The appropriate response is that although they have two votes, the votes are cast in distinct electoral contests and, hence, the principle of equality is not breached since, as long as the votes do not both contribute, directly or indirectly, to the selection of representatives from both states to a supra-national level of governance (as in the case of the European Union), the relevant context of application of the principle of equality is a specific polity (cf. Baubock 2007, p. 2428). By the same token, as long as the relevant states are not linked in a supranational union, the appropriate threshold for political autonomy in a state of residence is given by the application of the principle of equality in that polity – and this, at the very least, supports a strong presumption in favour of full political membership for resident non-citizens.

Notice though that even if we admit that there may be forms of political incorporation that are sufficient to secure the relevant conditions of political autonomy but which fall short of full membership, this does not undermine the argument for mandatory inclusion. On the contrary, it simply revises the principle to state that whatever degree of incorporation in the political community is necessary for securing political autonomy can legitimately be a matter of automatic mandatory inclusion. If it is the case that the quasi-citizenship enjoyed by denizens combined with their external citizenship rights in their country of origin suffice for political autonomy, then the relevant membership rights (e.g. local voting rights and, typically, some general rights of political participation) are not optional (and it is notable that the objection assumes that these rights are not optional). If it is the case, as I have suggested, that full membership rights are required, then these are equally not optional.

The second objection applies to the proposed solution, that is, the distinction between mandated political membership and voluntary national citizenship, claiming that it is paradoxical. It advances this claim on the grounds that the proposed solution suggests that migrants ought to express their commitment to the polity through naturalization, yet the incentives for choosing a status of national citizenship are to gain (1) rights that can be exercised from abroad rather than from within and (2) civil rights and liberties in which individuals have clearly instrumental interests rather than political participation rights whose exercise would express a commitment to the polity.[14] This is, I think, slightly point-missing. To see this, note that a migrant may have two quite different relations to the polity in which it is seen as either instrumentally valuable (as a regime of rule) or non-instrumentally valuable (as a political community) from the first person standpoint. On my account, if the migrant's relationship to the polity is instrumental, then the migrant has an interest in, and claim to, adequate conditions of political autonomy but has no interest in binding his future well-being to the fate of the polity which is precisely what is expressed in the additional rights and obligations involved in national citizenship. On the other hand, if from a first person standpoint the migrant's relationship to the polity is such that it is not only instrumentally valuable but also non-instrumentally valuable, then this grounds an interest in, and claim to, national citizenship. It is not here a matter of providing incentives, but rather of allowing for two different modes of membership of the polity, acknowledging the legitimate claims of each, and marking that distinction in a way that respects the difference. (One quick way of distinguishing the two orientations phenomenologically is to note that only the person who stands in a non-instrumental relationship to the state, that is, who is a member of the state as political community, will experience pride or shame with respect to the actions of the state or its representatives. The person who stands in an instrumental relation to the state, that is, who is a member of the state as political association, may see the state's actions as good or bad but won't experience pride or shame themselves in virtue of such perception.)

Reflecting on these objections does not then, in my view, undermine the cogency of the distinction between mandatory political membership and voluntary national citizenship as a way of dissolving the tension raised by the advocates of the social membership and stakeholder principles; at the most the objections point to a need to distinguish different degrees of political membership. Let us turn now then to the second issue, the disjuncture between political membership and national citizenship from the standpoint of a concern not with resident non-citizens but with non-resident citizens.

Citizenship, membership and non-resident citizens

Intriguingly, theorists of transnational citizenship are more willing to entertain the salience of the distinction between political membership and national citizenship in the case of non-resident citizens. This is, I think, essentially because while the case of expatriates has also focused around national voting rights, the debate here has been structured not by the question of whether democratic exclusion of residents can be justified (as in the case of resident non-citizens) but whether democratic inclusion of non-resident citizens can be justified. I have already discussed and rejected Lopez-Guarra's claim that expatriates are not subject to the political authority of their state of origin and, hence, should be automatically excluded from the demos. But the fact that the exclusion of expatriates is not required does not entail that their inclusion – in terms of national voting rights – is required. So what position is defensible? I will critically consider two leading arguments in order to draw out what I have called 'the problem of the arbitrary demos' and offer a way of resolving this problem.

656   D. Owen

The first is offered by Rubio-Marin who argues that:

> Democratic legitimacy and popular sovereignty require that the people subject to the law and state authority be included, as a matter of right, in the process of shaping how that authority will be formed and exercised. The exercise of public authority affects mostly those who live subject to the jurisdiction of such authority. Since states are geographically bounded communities and their borders express the limits of their jurisdictions, democratic states generally have good reasons to restrict participation in the political process to those who reside within their territorial borders. This would then justify the exclusion of expatriates from the political process as they are not directly and comprehensively affected by the decisions and policies that their participation would help to bring about even if they are likely to be affected by some of those decisions, such as those concerning remittances, nationality, and military service laws. (Rubio-Marin 2006, p. 129)

This argument is still likely to strike one as curiously constructed since it moves between appeals to being subjected to law and being affected by law. On the one hand, Rubio-Marin claims that those subject to the political authority of the state should, as a matter of right, be included. On the other hand, she then moves to address the topic purely in terms of affectedness.

To make sense of this movement, it may help to return to the point that expatriates are subject to the political authority of the state of origin. Consider that since expatriates are subject to the collectively binding decisions of the state, Dahl's principle of strong equality would prima facie require their inclusion within the demos. This is because the principle treats subjection in a non-scalar way, that is, it is not a matter of how much you are subject to collectively binding decisions (the extent of the range of laws that apply to you) but, rather, that you are subject to collectively binding decisions. Yet Dahl's principle was formulated against the background assumption that individuals are broadly equally positioned in terms of the range of laws to which they are subject and this assumption is simply not valid in the context of non-resident citizens. If we drop this assumption though, it becomes reasonable to argue that scalar considerations can enter into the argument which address both the extent of the laws to which you are subject and the consequentiality of these laws for your autonomy and well-being. It is, I think, something like this argument which can make coherent and cogent Rubio-Marin's contention that it is the fact that expatriates are not 'directly and comprehensively affected' by the policies of the state of origin that legitimates their exclusion from national voting rights.

However, while Rubio-Marin's argument provides a basis for the claim that expatriates can be legitimately excluded, it does not entail their exclusion. As she remarks:

> a country may democratically decide to allow for absentee voting of the first generation, thereby including expatriates in the political process ... in

Critical Review of International Social and Political Philosophy   657

> recognition of the fact that it is now easier than ever to remain connected to home state politics from abroad, and thus easier to understand the set of concrete policy options that a country may face ... [and also] in recognition of the fact many emigrants live between two countries, as well as the fact that their return is increasingly becoming a real option because being abroad no longer requires the definite severing of ties that it did in the past. (Rubio-Marin 2006, p. 134)

Although it is obscure why this should be restricted to first generation emigrants (given that a reasonable interpretation of her views on dual nationality would allow for second generation emigrants to retain dual nationality), I take it that the most plausible construal of Rubio-Marin's point is that under conditions in which it is possible for expatriates to engage in informed and up-to-date decision-making, for ongoing ties to be maintained and for return to be a real option (and hence it is possible for expatriates to satisfy the conditions of responsibility and consequentiality in relation to voting), democratic inclusion of expatriate citizens is a legitimate way of recognizing the non-instrumental attachment to the society of their home states that she takes to be a widespread and typical feature of (particularly) first-generation emigrants (Rubio-Marin 2006, p. 142). The justification would be that even though expatriates are not 'directly and comprehensively affected' by state policies, they are subject to its authority and since their individual well-being is non-contingently related to the well-being of the society of the home state, its policies are consequential for them. Notice though that this argument leaves unaddressed the question of who is entitled to make the decision concerning who is to be included in the demos (or, more precisely, national franchise) in effect simply assuming that this is a matter for the current demos (however constituted).

The second argument is offered by Baubock who also claims that expatriate voting is neither required nor forbidden by justice. Consider two sets of remarks. In the first remarks, Baubock reiterates the stakeholder principle:

> The notion of stakeholding expresses, first, the idea that citizens have not merely fundamental interests in the outcomes of the political process, but a claim to be represented as participants in that process. Second, stakeholding serves as a criterion for assessing claims to membership and voting rights. Individuals whose circumstances of life link their future well-being to the flourishing of a particular polity should be recognized as stakeholders in that polity with a claim to participate in collective decision-making processes that shape the shared future of this political community. (Baubock 2007, p. 2422)

This passage suggests that stakeholders have a legitimate claim to participate, although this does not rule out either that the reach of this claim (i.e. the extent of participation it legitimates) may vary or that it may be

658   D. Owen

defeated by other legitimate concerns. In the second set of remarks, Baubock comments:

> In a stakeholder conception of democratic community, persons with multiple stakes need multiple votes to control each of the governments whose decisions will affect their future as members of several *demoi*. This applies, on the one hand, to federally nested *demoi* where citizens can cast multiple vertical votes on several levels and, on the other hand, to the *demoi* of independent states with overlapping membership. (Baubock 2007, p. 2428)

This suggests a stronger view, namely, that the stakeholder principle supports a requirement of inclusion in the demos for stakeholders, where we may surmise this requirement would be legitimately subject only to (1) the basic constraint that such inclusion does not threaten the stability of the state (i.e. its capacity to reproduce itself as a self-governing polity over time) and (2) feasibility constraints. This stronger view is more in line with the remarks concerning contexts of political autonomy advanced in the previous section, yet curiously Baubock does not adopt this stance, remaining content with the view that expatriate voting is permissible but not required, although acknowledging the normative salience of existing state practices of expatriate enfranchisement as having constructed reasonable expectations which it would be unjust to frustrate given the normative permissibility of the practice. Overall, the most one can say if that, for Baubock, the stakeholder principle broadly supports a presumption in favour of such rights for first generation migrants but also acknowledges that this presumption can be either supported or defeated by a wide range of factors relating to the specific circumstances of the polity (Baubock 2007). Thus, for example, the presumption would be strongly supported in the Spanish case in which the introduction of expatriate voting sought to acknowledge the interest of Republican exiles in the restoration of democracy following the end of Franco's rule, but would be undermined in cases in which large expatriate communities exhibit entrenched political divisions that would exacerbate conflicts within the state (e.g. Eire).

As with Rubio-Marin, however, a problem arises in relation to Baubock's stance on permissibility in which it is up to the democratic state to determine whether or not to allow expatriate voting, while, in addition, Baubock also argues that democratic states should have the freedom to introduce conditions 'such as length of residence in the country, maximum duration of residence abroad, or an intention to return (however difficult this may be to verify)' (Baubock 2007, pp. 2426–2427). What this would seem to imply, however, is that the current demos, however it contingently happens to be constituted, has the right to determine not only whether non-resident stakeholders are to be granted national voting rights but also, if such rights are granted, which of these stakeholders is entitled to them. But what justifies that view? After all, all national citizens, resident or not, will be bound by the decision.

The basic limitation in the arguments of both Rubio-Marin and of Baubock, then, is that they don't focus on the question of who is entitled to determine whether or not expatriates are included in the national franchise; they both assume that this is, practically speaking, a matter of whatever contingent specifications of the demos currently hold but provide no normative basis for the legitimacy of this view. This is the problem of the arbitrary demos. To resolve it, what is required is a principled (i.e. non-arbitrary) basis on which to determine who is entitled to decide on this question. Here it is worth noting that there is one type of decision by any polity which not only binds all citizens irrespective of residence but also directs concerns their very status as citizens, namely, constitutional laws that specify the entitlements and obligations of citizens – such as, for example, laws on nationality and expatriate voting rights. Moreover, since it concerns the status of citizenship itself, in the case of such decisions concerning the fundamental character of the civil association to deny any (competent) citizen or group of citizens the right to participate as an equal member of the democratic community in the decision-making process is to deny their status as a citizen; it is to subject them to an alien form of rule. The only legitimate basis for determining who should take part in decisions such as those on expatriate voting is, thus, that all citizens are entitled to inclusion irrespective of their residential status (although this does not rule out that considerations of feasibility and cost may legitimately allow the requirement that votes are cast within the territory of the home state). This universality rule provides the principled basis that is lacking from Rubio-Marin's and Baubock's arguments. (It is worth noting that this argument has particular bite in relation to the stakeholder principle since that principle not only take rights of political participation to be the core of citizenship but construes stakeholding in terms that stress a directly political understanding of the relationship of stakeholders and polity.)

Does this rule also apply to Baubock's further reflections concerning discriminations within the class of non-resident citizens? If such discriminations are permissible, the rule will apply. However, whether the discriminations are permissible hangs on whether we conceive them as contextual determinations of the abstract stakeholder principle by distinct democratic communities or as discriminations within the class of emigrant stakeholders. In the former case, they are permissible since the abstract stakeholder principle does require democratically legitimate contextual determination; in the latter case, they may not be permissible since presumptively they breach the principle of equality with respect to the class of emigrant stakeholders. While we may have good reasons for accepting that the principle of equality is compatible with different political entitlements for resident and non-resident stakeholders, it is not obviously the case that

660   D. Owen

we also have reasons to accept that the principle of equality is compatible with different political entitlements for different classes of emigrant stakeholders. This is not to rule out this possibility but merely to note that a compelling argument would need to be made to justify the permissibility of the relevant inequality. Thus, for example, consider Baubock's argument for the restriction (in the absence of other requirements being met) of external voting rights, when permitted, to first-generation emigrants:

> Members of this so-called second immigrant generation still have a plausible interest in their parents' citizenship, and virtually all democratic countries therefore have external *jus sanguinis* provisions in their citizenship laws. Yet a right to acquire citizenship status at birth need not entail a right to vote. Benefits of external citizenship, such as diplomatic protection and the right to return to, and to inherit and own property in, the country of citizenship reflect interests of a slightly different kind than those that ground a right to political participation. The former refer to potential interests that a second generation external citizen may activate over the course of her life, whereas the latter should presuppose that some of these interests are currently active. (Baubock 2007, p. 2426)

This seems a problematic argument on the basis of the stakeholder principle since either we accept Baubock's argument that the second immigrant generation can be presumed, on the basis of the family as a primary site of socialization, to be stakeholders, that is, by the time they reach the age of majority, to have active interests of the relevant sort that 'link their future well-being to the flourishing of a particular polity' or we reject the presumption that they are stakeholders. In the former case, it is unreasonable to impose additional burdens on them as conditions of their acquiring voting rights. In the latter case, they have no entitlement to voting unless they demonstrate, through taking on additional burdens, that they are stakeholders. To my mind, this example supports a general presumption of scepticism towards discrimination within the general class of expatriate stakeholders.

Conclusion

Transnational citizenship represents a fundamental reconfiguration of political membership and realistic normative theoretical accounts of this phenomenon, most prominently in the work of Baubock, Carens and Rubio-Marin, have focused on the most central practical policy areas impacted by this phenomenon, namely, membership and voting rights. My concern in this article has been to provide an overview of the debates generated by these contrasting accounts and to identify two problems that arise within them. The first problem, the antinomy of incorporation, arises out of compelling but incompatible arguments concerning naturalization. I offer a way of dissolving this antinomy by distinguishing between mandated acquisition of political membership and voluntary acquisition of national citizenship,

Critical Review of International Social and Political Philosophy 661

and defend this proposal against two objections. The second problem, the arbitrary demos problem, emerges in both social membership and stakeholder arguments concerning expatriate voting rights. I offer a way of resolving this problem by appeal to the point that constitutional rules not only apply to all citizens, but also are constitutive of their citizenship and, consequently, the appropriate demos for decisions on expatriate voting rights is the demos of all citizens of the state. Notice that the arguments presented are compatible with the basic normative principles that compose the social membership and stakeholder principles, and consequently do not decide between these two candidate principles for allocating transnational citizenship statuses. That task awaits a further occasion.

Notes

1. For recent overviews of these changes and the reasons for them, see Baubock (2005, 2007), Joppke (2010), and Stoker *et al.* (2011), ch. 6 (of which I was lead author).
2. The classic account of realistic and idealistic approaches is Carens (1996). For the purposes of this argument, the contrast is between attention to *possible* worlds (idealistic approaches) and to *plausible* worlds (realistic approaches).
3. The term 'transnational citizenship' is also used in the wider political theory literature to pick out forms of civil liberty and civic activity that are tied to transnational fora and/or cosmopolitan politics (e.g. Benhabib 2004, 2006, Cohen and Sabel 2006, Forst 2011, Fraser 2008). Reconciling these uses requires addressing the limitations of the 'narrow' use drawn from Baubock and adopted in this article. The relevant limitations are specified in note 4 below.
4. The two primary limitations are, first, that the focus on voting occludes consideration of rights of political participation more generally and, second, that the restrictive understanding of membership invoked in this discussion fails adequately to address the issues raised by the standing of non-resident non-citizens whose morally significant interests are adversely affected by the decision of states (or, more generally, polities and regimes of governance).
5. For a supportive argument against a necessary relationship between political authority and coercion, see Sangiovanni's (2007) critique of Blake. On the idea of sanctionability as distinct from coercion, we may note that breaches of customary norms (e.g. norms of etiquette) are sanctionable in the sense that they attract, for example, forms of ostracism but they are not coercively enforced.
6. For an overview that emphasizes this point, see Nasstrom (2010).
7. I provide a considerably fuller critique of Goodin's argument in Owen (n.d.).
8. Although Dahl talks of the principle of all-affected interests, I agree with Lopez-Guerra (2005, pp. 222–225) that since it is being governed that is the normatively relevant issue for Dahl, the relevant principle is that of being *subjected to* rule rather than *affected by* rule.
9. Walzer links this claim to one in which the polity has the right to determine its own entry criteria as an element of its right to self-determination; for an excellent analysis of the difficulties that this conjunction generates, see Bosniak (2006).
10. This case against Lopez-Guerra's argument is spelled out more fully in Owen (2010) and Stoker *et al.* (2011), ch. 6. For a discussion of the contrast between

662   D. Owen

Lopez-Guerra's position and my own earlier position in Owen (2010), see Baubock (2009a), pp. 480–481.

11. A residence-sensitive rule is one that while not conceptually tied to residence is practically related to residence in terms of its application. Thus, for example, in the 19th century the inability of expatriates to stay up to date with the politics of their home states and participate at a distance in its public political discussions would have reasonably grounded the claim that voting rights should be tied to residence, even though it is not conceptually tied to residence. I am grateful to Rainer Baubock for pressing this point on me.
12. For a defence of citizenship tests, see Miller (2008); and for critiques, see Carens (2005), pp. 38–39, and Seglow (2008).
13. I am grateful to Rainer Baubock for raising these objections and I draw on his formulations of them in presenting them here.
14. Notice that this objection can entertain the thought that rights to return and diplomatic protection should not be an exclusive privilege of national citizenship but could be included in denizenship and thus acquired automatically instead of having to be chosen through naturalization. (On Baubock's view, such external denizenship rights would, however, not be for life, so that national citizens would still enjoy a specific recognition as permanent stakeholders.) The objection is also compatible with resisting the claim that national voting rights ought to be granted only to born or voluntarily naturalized citizens, since if the defense of optional naturalization as a choice to be made by first-generation migrants is successful, then the question of which rights remain attached to full citizenship can be answered in different ways.

Notes on contributor

David Owen is Professor of Social and Political Philosophy at the University of Southampton. He has published nine books, including most recently *Recognition and Power* (co-edited with Bert van den Brink; Cambridge University Press, 2007), *Multiculturalism and Political Theory* (co-edited with Tony Laden; Cambridge University Press, 2007) and *Nietzsche's Genealogy of Morality* (Acumen, 2007), as well as numerous articles. He is currently working on the ethics and politics of migration and issues of transnational citizenship.

References

Baubock, R., 1994. *Transnational citizenship*. Cheltenham: Edward Elgar.

Baubock, R., 2003. Towards a political theory of migrant transnationalism. *International Migration Review*, 37 (3), 700–723.

Baubock, R., 2005. Expansive citizenship – voting beyond territory and membership. *Political Science and Politics*, 38 (4), 683–687.

Baubock, R., 2007. Stakeholder citizenship and transnational political participation: a normative evaluation of external voting. *Fordham Law Review*, 75 (5), 2393–2447.

Baubock, R., 2009a. The rights and duties of external citizenship. *Citizenship Studies*, 13 (5), 475–499.

Baubock, R., 2009b. Global justice, freedom of movement and democratic citizenship. *European Journal of Sociology/Archives européennes de sociologie*, 50 (1), 1–31.

Beckman, L., 2006. Citizenship and voting rights: should resident aliens vote? *Citizenship Studies*, 10 (2), 153–165.

Critical Review of International Social and Political Philosophy   663

Benhabib, S., 2004. *The rights of others*. Cambridge: Cambridge University Press.
Benhabib, S., 2006. *Another cosmopolitanism*. New York, NY: Oxford University Press.
Bosniak, L., 2006. *The citizen and the alien*. Princeton, NJ: Princeton University Press.
Carens, J., 1989. Membership and morality: admission to citizenship in liberal democratic states. *In*: W.R. Brubaker, ed. *Immigration and the politics of citizenship in Europe and North America*. New York, NY: University Press of America, 39–61.
Carens, J., 1996. Realistic and idealistic approaches to the ethics of migration. *International Migration Review*, 30 (1), 156–170.
Carens, J., 2005. The integration of immigrants. *Journal of Moral Philosophy*, 2 (1), 29–46.
Cohen, J. and Sabel, C., 2006. Extra rempublicam nulla justitia? *Philosophy and Public Affairs*, 34 (2), 147–175.
Dahl, R., 1989. *Democracy and its critics*. New Haven, CT: Yale University Press.
Forst, R., Forthcoming 2011. Towards a critical theory of transnational justice. In: *The right to justification*. New York, NY: Columbia University Press.
Fraser, N., 2008. *Scales of justice*. Cambridge: Polity.
Goodin, R., 2007. Enfranchising all-affected interests and its alternatives. *Philosophy and Public Affairs*, 39 (1), 40–67.
Joppke, C., 2010. *Citizenship and immigration*. Cambridge: Polity Press.
Lopez-Guerra, C., 2005. Should expatriates vote? *Journal of Political Philosophy*, 13 (2), 216–234.
Miller, D., 2008. Immigrants, nations and citizenship. *Journal of Political Philosophy*, 16 (4), 371–390.
Nasstrom, S., 2010. The challenge of the all affected principle. *Political Studies*, 59 (1), 116–134. DOI: 10.1111/j.1467-9248.2010.00845.x.
Owen, D., 2010. Resident non-citizens, non-resident citizens and voting rights. *In*: G. Calder, P. Cole and J. Seglow, eds. *Citizenship acquisition and national belonging*. Basingstoke: Palgrave, 52–73.
Owen, D., n.d. The duty of justification: on the form and role of the all-affected interests principle. Unpublished draft manuscript. Available from: http://soton.academia.edu/DavidOwen/Papers/178865/The_Duty_of_Justification_on_the_form_and_role_of_the_all_affected_interests_principle/.
Raskin, J., 1993. Legal aliens, local citizens: the historical, constitutional and theoretical meanings of alien suffrage. *University of Pennsylvania Law Preview*, 141, 1391–1470.
Rubio-Marin, R., 2000. *Immigration as a democratic challenge*. Cambridge: Cambridge University Press.
Rubio-Marin, R., 2006. Transnational politics and the democratic national-state: normative challenges of expatriate voting and nationality retention of emigrants. *New York University Law Review*, 81, 117–147.
Sangiovanni, A., 2007. Global justice, reciprocity, and the state. *Philosophy and Public Affairs*, 35 (1), 2–39.
Seglow, J., 2008. Arguments for naturalisation. *Political Studies*, 57 (4), 788–804.
Shapiro, I., 2003. *The moral foundations of politics*. New Haven, CT: Yale University Press.
Stoker, G. *et al.*, 2011. Transpolitical citizenship. *In*: G. Stoker *et al.*, eds. *Prospects of citizenship*. London: Bloomsbury Academic, 110–133.
Walzer, M., 1983. *Spheres of justice*. New York, NY: Basic.

[13]

Citizenship and identity: living in diasporas in post-war Europe?

Yasemin Nuhoğlu Soysal

Abstract

Diaspora, as a venerated concept, has a strong placement in our political and intellectual discourses. My article questions the deployment of diaspora as an analytical category in explaining the contemporary immigration experience. Focusing peculiarly on the ethnic axis of homelands and abroad, theories of diaspora overlook the transgressions of the national and lose sight of the new dynamics and topography of membership. I suggest that a more productive perspective is achieved by focusing our analytical providence on the proliferating sites of making and enacting citizenship. I do this by elaborating two paradoxes underlying the contemporary formations of citizenship: a) the increasing decoupling of rights and identities, the two main components of citizenship; b) the tendency towards particularistic claims in public spheres and their legitimation through universalistic discourses of personhood. These paradoxes warrant that we have new forms of making claims, mobilizing identity and practising citizenship, which lie beyond the limiting dominion of ethnically informed diasporic arrangements, transactions and belongings.

Keywords: Citizenship; diaspora; identity; rights; claims-making; immigrants; Europe.

Like most Palestinians, who experienced dispossession and displacement from their homes and territory, Edward Said, the Jerusalem-born, British-educated, and American-citizen literary critic, ruminates on life

2 Yasemin Nuhoğlu Soysal

in exile as a 'perpetual self-invention and constant restlessness'. In accounting for his life as an émigré, he quotes from Adorno:

> The past life of emigres is . . . annulled . . . [it is a] life that cannot be directly actualized; anything that lives on merely as thought and recollection. For this a special rubric has been invented. It is called "background" and appears on the questionnaire as an appendix, after sex, age and profession (Said 1998, p. 6).[1]

Diaspora is the location where this background finds meaning. Diaspora is a past invented for the present, and perpetually laboured into shapes and meanings consistent with the present. As such, it exists not as a lived reality but as part of a broader scheme to insert continuity and coherence into life stories that are presumably broken under the conditions of migrancy and exile. It is the reification of categorical homelands, traditions, collective memories and formidable longings. It is a category of awareness, in which present-tense practices lack capacity in and of themselves, but attain significance *vis-à-vis* the inventiveness of the past.

Diaspora is not a new concept. In its classical usage, it provides a normative model for Jewish history and experience, lived in a state of 'worldlessness'.[2] Lately, however, it has found much usage as an analytical category in the vast immigration literature on the global dispersion of migrant populations. It captures much of our analytical and popular imagination, and claims explanatory fortitude in narrating the presence and condition of immigrant populations.[3]

This is something I would like to question: the deployment of diaspora as an analytical category in explaining the contemporary immigration experience. The thrust of my questioning is to do with the very assumption that underlies the concept. That is, its insistence on privileging the nation-state model and nationally-defined formations when conversing about a global process such as immigration. My argument is that this axiomatic primacy granted to nations and nation-states as units of analysis is difficult to hold in the face of contemporary changes in the geography and practice of citizenship and belonging. I shall discuss, here, the post-war developments which render diaspora untenable as an analytical and normative category, and direct our discussions to new formations of membership, claims-making and belonging − which either remain invisible to the conventional conceptions of diaspora, or are frequently deemed insignificant in the face of its normative weight.

The dominant conceptualizations of diaspora presumptively accept the formation of tightly bounded communities and solidarities (on the basis of common cultural and ethnic references) between places of origin and arrival (see Cohen 1997; van Hear 1998). Diasporas form when

Citizenship and identity 3

populations disperse from their homeland to foreign lands, engage in movements between the country of origin and destination, and carry out bi-directional transactions – economic, political and cultural. In this formulation, the primary orientation and attachment of diasporic populations is to their homelands and cultures; and their claims and citizenship practices arise from this home-bound, ethnic-based orientation. In other words, diaspora is a way of theorizing formations that are ethno-cultural, and that constitute foreignness within other nations and ethnicities. As such, the category of diaspora is an extension of the nation-state model, in that it assumes a congruence between the territorial state and the national community, and by implication a congruence between territory, culture and identity. And it is this boundedness, or the closure, that necessitates the definition of diasporas – that is, those who naturally bond together on the basis of their ethnic otherness and identity. Diaspora is the extension of the place left behind, the 'home'. Thus, the presumed rootlessness of immigrant populations in the here and now of the diaspora, and their perpetual longing for then and there. This theoretical move, that is, designating immigrant populations as diasporas, ignores the historical contingency of the nation-state, identity and community, and reifies them as natural.

My argument would be that in the post-war era, the boundaries and imperatives within which diasporas are expected to take shape have changed. Particularly in Europe, in response to transformations affecting the contemporary politics, economies and institutions of the nation-state system, new forms of citizenship, belonging and claims have emerged. These new forms undermine the 'national order of things',[4] thus the very premise of diaspora. Diaspora, as an analytical category is too limiting to explicate the contemporary contours of membership and belonging. We have to move beyond the customary and static precepts of diaspora and expand our theoretical and political vocabulary.

A more challenging and productive perspective is achieved by focusing our analytical providence on the proliferating sites of making and enacting citizenship. In a world of incessant migrations, it is in these novel geographies of citizenship that we recognize the dynamics and distribution of rights and identities, and patterns of exclusion and inclusion. My goal is to address the new forms and sites of citizenship and the broader processes that occasion their emergence. I begin by summarizing briefly the developments that contextualize the changes in the institution and practice of citizenship in the post-war Europe. Then, I elaborate the two paradoxes that I see as crucial in understanding the contemporary formations of citizenship, and exclusions and inclusions. The first paradox relates to the rights and identities, the two main components of citizenship, and their increasing decoupling. The second paradox to the ways collective claims are made and mobilized: an increasing tendency towards particularistic

4   *Yasemin Nuhoğlu Soysal*

and group-based claims and their legitimation through universalistic discourses of personhood and strategies. Finally, I suggest that these two paradoxes warrant a reconsideration of our dominant approaches to immigrants and membership, and categories of exclusion and inclusion.

Post-war changes in the European state system

Contrary to the predominant understandings and conceptualizations in sociology, my work suggests that the limits of citizenship is not singularly located in a nation-state but also encompasses the local and the transnational. Contemporary practice of citizenship is increasingly decoupled from belonging in the national collective. Regardless of their historical or cultural ties to the German nation, and even without a formal German nationality, Turkish immigrants in Berlin make claims on Berlin's authority structures and participate in Berlin's public institutions. When they make demands for the teaching of Islam in state schools, the Pakistani immigrants in Britain mobilize around a Muslim identity, but they appeal to a universalistic language of 'human rights' to justify their claims. And, they not only mobilize to affect the local school authorities, but also pressure the national government, and take their case to the European Court of Human Rights. I argue that these examples undermine the predominant models of citizenship, which are normatively predicated upon the integrity of national communities and their boundaries. I suggest that to provide a meaningful understanding of contemporary formations of citizenship, and exclusion and inclusion, we need to incorporate these seeming anomalies into our analytical 'tool-kit'.

The background to the arguments I am now advancing is a series of interlocking legal, institutional, and ideological changes in the European state system in the post-war period. These changes have complicated the national order of citizenship and introduced new dynamics for membership and participation in the public sphere. I elaborated these changes elsewhere (Soysal 1994). Here I briefly cite four developments that have significant implications for the institution of citizenship and the notions of identity and rights:

- First, the transformations in the existing national and ethnic composition of European countries, as a consequence of massive migratory flows not only from the immediate European periphery but also from 'distant lands'.
- Second, the increasing intensification of transnational discourse and legal instruments that codify 'human rights' or personhood as a world level principle. This elaboration of individual rights, in international agreements and institutions but also in scientific and popular discourses, has laid the ground upon which more expansive claims and rights can be advanced, and led to the introduction of new forms of

Citizenship and identity 5

rights – for women, children, minorities, immigrants, and even for animals and plants (see Turner 1986).

- Third, the increasing legitimacy of the right to 'one's own culture' and identity. This right has been furthered by the massive decolonizations in the post-war period, as well as through the works of the international organizations such as the United Nations, UNESCO, and the Council of Europe. Collective identity has been redefined as a category of human rights. Codified as a right, identities have become important organizational and symbolic tools for creating new group solidarities and mobilizing resources (as in the case of women's movements, environmentalists, gays and lesbians, regional identities and interests, indigenous groups and immigrants).
- Lastly, the diffusion of sovereignty and the emergence of multi-level polities, such as we observe with the gradual unfolding of the European Union and the devolution of some European nation-states into culturally and administratively autonomous regions (Schmitter 1992; Marks and McAdam 1996). The diffusion and sharing of sovereignty among local, national and transnational political institutions, enable new actors, open up an array of new organizational strategies, and facilitate competition over resources and definitions.

All these developments, the transformations in the population composition of the European states, the legitimation of rights at the transnational level, the codification of collective identities as rights, and the increasing diffusion of sovereignty, have paradoxical implications for national citizenship. They have paradoxical implications as regards the ways that rights and identities are defined and allocated; and also as regards the ways in which collective claims are made and mobilized. I now turn to the discussion of these paradoxes of citizenship. By doing so, I also aim to clarify my objection to the uncritical reinsertion of the concept of the diaspora into our discussions and analyses.

Paradoxes of citizenship

Decoupling of rights and identity

The first paradox I would like to elaborate is the increasing decoupling of rights and identity. In the nation-state mode of political community, national belonging constitutes the source of rights and duties of individuals; and citizenship is delimited by national collectivity. The post-war era, however, has witnessed an increasing recasting of (national) citizenship rights as human (or personhood) rights (Soysal 1994).[5] Rights that were once associated with belonging in a national community have become increasingly abstract, and legitimated at the transnational level.

The post-war reification of personhood and individual rights expands

6 *Yasemin Nuhoğlu Soysal*

the boundaries of political community, by legitimating individuals' participation and claims beyond their membership status in a particular nation-state. With the breakdown of the link between the national community and rights, we observe multiple forms of citizenship that are no longer anchored in national collectives, and that expand the sets of right-bearing members within and without the nation-state. These forms are exemplified in the membership of the long-term non-citizen immigrants, who hold various rights and privileges without a formal nationality status; in the increasing instances of dual citizenship, which breaches the traditional notions of political membership and loyalty in a single state; in the European Union citizenship, which represents a multi-tiered form of membership; and in subnational citizenships in culturally or administratively autonomous regions of Europe (for example, Basque country, Catalonia and Scotland).

As the source and legitimacy of rights shift to the transnational level, paradoxically, identities remain particularistic, and locally defined and organized. The same global rules and institutional frameworks which celebrate personhood and human rights, at the same time naturalize collective identities around national and ethno-religious particularisms.

This, as I have already stated, has a lot to do with the works of the international organizations such as the United Nations, UNESCO, the Council of Europe and the like, (as well as the discipline of anthropology), through which the universal right to 'one's own culture' has gained increasing legitimacy, and collective identity has been redefined as a category of human rights. What are considered particularistic characteristics of collectivities – culture, language and standard ethnic traits – have become variants of the universal core of humanness or selfhood. This identity represents the 'unchosen', and is naturalized through the language of kinship, homeland, nation and territory. One cannot help but have identity.[6]

The seeming naturalness and inevitability of diaspora formations (and theorizing immigrant communities as diasporas) are part and parcel of this global and hegemonic discourse of identity. Once institutionalized as natural, the discourse about identities creates ever increasing claims about cultural distinctiveness and group rights. Ethnic/national identities are enacted and improvised for mobilizing and making claims in national and world polities, authenticating diaspora as an idiom for the politics of identity. On the other hand, as exercised in individual and collective actors' narratives and strategies, identity also authorizes ethnic nationalisms and sovereignties. Thus, while rights acquire a more universalistic form and are divorced from national belonging, (thus giving rise to more inclusionary forms of membership), at the same time, identities become intentionally particularistic and exclusionary practices (on the basis of identity) prevail. And this we observe in the increasingly restrictive immigration policies of European countries, the vocalization of ethnic

Citizenship and identity 7

minority and religious groups for cultural closure, and the discriminatory citizenship practices of many of the ex-Soviet republics. So more inclusionary forms of rights clash with more exclusionary practices of identity.

Making particularistic claims through universalistic discourses of personhood and strategies

The second paradox to which I would like to draw attention regards collective claims-making and participation in public spheres; in other words, the practice of citizenship by individuals and groups. With the post-war reconfigurations in citizenship that I described in the previous section, the old categories that attach individuals to nationally defined status positions and distributory mechanisms become blurred. This inevitably changes the nature and locus of struggles for social equality and rights. New forms of mobilizing and advancing claims and participation emerge beyond the frame of national citizenship.

If we recall, our classical notions of citizenship assume the existence of actors whose rights and identities are grounded within the bounds of national collectives. And these collectives constitute the 'authentic' sites for the realization of claims-making and civic participation. My research reveals two trends that diverge from this predominant prescription of citizenship. First, we see an increasing tendency to advance particularistic identities and demands, which, at the same time, are located in and legitimated by the universalistic discourses of human or personhood rights. Second, we see that the mobilization of claims takes place independent of nationally delimited collectives and at different levels (local, national and transnational). In other words, the social and political stages for claims-making proliferate.

I would like to elaborate on these two trends by citing empirical evidence from Muslim immigrant communities and their participation and mobilization in European public spheres. I do not wish to imply that we can observe the emerging forms only in the case of Muslim immigrants. These are broader tendencies, but my focus is on Muslim groups, since these communities are visibly at the centre of contention.

a) The first trend concerns the nature of the claims and discourse. Immigrant groups in Europe mobilize around claims for particularistic provisions and emphasize their group identities. Their claims, however, are not simply grounded in the particularities of religious or ethnic narratives. On the contrary, they appeal to the universalistic principles and dominant discourses of equality, emancipation and individual rights. In other words, the claims that immigrants advance and the identities that they mobilize, though particularistic, derive their legitimacy and authority from universalistic discourses of personhood and human rights. Diaspora theories, with their singular focus on ethnic transactions and community formation, bypass these larger scripts, which activate and

8   *Yasemin Nuhoğlu Soysal*

energize the very claims and identities. In turn, they misread immigrant mobilization simply as enactments of ethnicity.

Let me expand on this point. When Muslim immigrant associations advocate the rights and needs of immigrant children in school, they employ a discourse that appropriates the rights of the individuals as its central theme. They invoke the international instruments and conventions on human rights to frame their position. They forward demands about mother-tongue instruction, Islamic *foulard*, or *halal* food by asserting the 'natural' right of individuals to their own cultures, rather than drawing upon religious teachings and traditions.

To give an example. In 1989 the issue of Islamic *foulard* erupted into a national crisis and debate in France, when three North African students were expelled from school for insisting on wearing their scarfs in class. In the ensuing debates, the issue became not only a topical contention over immigrant integration and French laicism but entered into the public arena as a matter of rights of individuals. During the debates, the head of the Great Mosque of Paris declared the rules preventing the wearing of scarfs in school to be discriminatory on the ground of individual rights. His emphasis was on personal rights, rather than religious traditions or duties: 'If a girl asks to have her hair covered, I believe it is her most basic right' (*Washington Post*, 23 October 1989). In this case, Muslim identity, while symbolized by the headscarf, was asserted and authenticated by the very categories and language of the host society; that is, through a discourse that accentuates individual rights.

In another episode (in Germany this time), on 12 November 1995, which corresponded to the birthday of Fatima (the daughter of the prophet Muhammad), the Shi'ite *Ehlibeyt* mosque in Berlin invited 'all Muslim women' to a celebration of the World's Women's Day. Speakers to the meeting included not only the (male) clergy of the mosque but 'Muslim' women of different nationalities, Turks, Arabs and Germans. The focal point of the speeches delivered was to highlight women's emancipation, including demands to end discrimination against Muslim women in work places and schools, especially on the basis of their wearing the Islamic headscarf. The issues raised encapsulated the very terms of the contemporary gender discourse. The keynote speaker, a young *imam*, traced the issue of the rights of women to the Qur'an. Making references to the Beijing Conference on Women, he claimed the assertion of 'women's rights are human rights' as an original teaching of Islam and its culture. He declared indignantly: 'In the Beijing conference, when someone said, "women's rights are human rights", thousands of women cheered and clapped. What were they cheering for? We already said that 1400 years ago! That is our word!' The meeting was an instance of linking Islamic moral realm to the contemporary concerns and discourses about women, speaking to and through them.

Let me insert a caveat here: Muslim groups in European countries,

Citizenship and identity 9

obviously, do not speak in a uniform discursive framework. The examples that I have just given by no means exhaust the range of narratives employed by Muslim groups. Again, speaking for the Islamic veil, a Turkish *imam* in Nantua declared the practice as 'God's law' and put pressure on the Turkish families to withdraw their daughters from school. This led to serious divisions among the Turkish immigrant community and to his eventual deportation from France (Kepel 1997, pp. 222–23). It is also possible to find Islamic positions which base their claims on religiously codified family laws that sanction status disparity between genders. These proclamations obviously point to alternative, and often conflicting, claims and leadership among Muslim communities. This is not something I deny. My point here is to delineate the prevalent universalistic forms of making claims by Muslim groups that are commonly overlooked, and to elucidate their implications for our theoretical vistas.

Yet another caveat is warranted here. Granted, there is significant variation in the accommodation of the types of claims advanced. While some claims face organizational resistance, others are more readily accepted and incorporated into formal state structures. The educational authorities in Britain, for example, are more willing to accommodate the claims for Islamic dress codes, or even the teaching of immigrant languages in schools. On the other hand, religiously codified family laws (or polygamy, female circumcision) which create status disparity between genders are not viewed as legitimate demands. Here, the principle of gender equality contests the principle of religious equality, both of which are clearly embedded in European citizenships and transnational frameworks. In Europe, the treatment of women is codified in secular laws and institutions, thus the attempts to subject it to a religious, private domain generates conflict. In my research, I attempt to untangle the contradictory dynamics among different legitimating discourses and principles, and explain how these dynamics lead to conflicting claims and empowerments in the public sphere.[7]

To reiterate my main point, the Muslim organizations that I study do not justify their demands by simply reaching back to religious teachings or traditions but through a language of rights, thus, citizenship. By using the rights language they exercise civic projects and link themselves to the broader public spheres. The projects of citizenship in which they engage, however, are not necessarily nationally bounded. They are both spatially and symbolically multi-referential.

When Muslim associations make demands about veiling in schools, theirs is not a claim for belonging to an existing 'French collectivity', but to the educational system itself, which they see as their most natural right. This, I argue, is not necessarily disengagement from the collective life but the collective is no longer bounded by a preordained national community. Indeed, they try to redefine the very nature of national community.

10   *Yasemin Nuhoğlu Soysal*

b) The second trend as regards claims-making is that the organizational strategies employed by immigrant groups increasingly acquire a transnational and subnational character. The terms of their participation extend beyond the limits of the national, span multiple localities, transnationally connect public spheres, thus, diversify the 'spaces for and of politics'.[8] For example, we find political parties, mosque organizations, and community associations which operate at local levels but do not confine their claims only to their localities. During the last elections in Berlin, Turkish immigrant organizations pushed for their local voting rights and demands to vote in European elections, while at the same time, they put pressure on the Turkish government to facilitate their rights to vote in Turkish national elections. As such, they envisage their participation in multiple civic spaces, in Berlin, in Europe and in Turkey. This is increasingly a trend among immigrant populations in other parts of the world. Similar claims are being made by Mexican and Central American immigrant groups in the United States. They demand dual citizenship and dual voting rights in their countries of origin and residence. And, indeed, the governments of Mexico, Columbia and the Dominican Republic recently passed legislation allowing dual nationality.

In pursuing their claims, the mobilization of immigrant groups entails multiple states and political agencies, and they target trans- and subnational institutions. Again, for example, the Islamic *foulard* issue was not simply a matter confined to the discretion of a local school board, but has traversed the realms of local, national, transnational jurisdictions – from local educational authorities to the European Court of Human Rights. Similarly, in the early 1990s, when the local authorities refused to permit the opening of another Islamic primary school, the Islamic Foundation in London decided to take the issue to the European Court of Human Rights. Indeed, more and more Muslim associations elevate their operations to the European level, establishing umbrella organizations and forums to coordinate their activities and pursue a Europewide agenda (Kastoryano 1996).

So, while the claims and mobilization of Muslim groups aim to further particularistic identities and solidarities, paradoxically, they make appeals to the universalistic principles of human rights and connect themselves to a diverse set of public spheres. As such, their mobilization is not simply a reinvention of ethnic or religious particularisms. Their civic projects and mobilization are not ethnically self-referential but reflect larger scripts of rights and personhood. Drawing upon universalistic repertoires of claims-making, they, at the same time, participate in and contribute to the reification of host society and global discourses.

All these point to solidarities and participatory forms which cannot be captured by the concept of diaspora. Focusing peculiarly on the ethnic axis of homelands and abroad, the theories of diaspora overlook the transgressions of national boundaries and collectives and forget the new

Citizenship and identity   11

ways by which immigrants experience and enact their membership. In this new topography of membership, what constitutes the grounds for civic projects is no longer the 'horizontal connectedness' among members of an ethnic community (that is, mutual trust and solidarity on the basis of ethnic belonging). Here, the 'ties that bind' manifest themselves through participation in and by 'vertical connection' to common, universalistic discourses that transcend the very ethnic idiom of community.

To complete the picture, let me briefly refer to the second-generation immigrants, who are seen as enigmatic producers of diasporic cultures and identities. Far from being simple extensions of their 'homelands', the second-generation immigrants – Maghrebins, Pakistanis, Turks, Caribbeans, Bengalis living in the immigration capitals of Europe – negotiate and map collective identities which are dissociated from ethno-cultural citizenships (Bauman 1996; Soysal 1999). They appropriate their identity symbols as much from global cultural flows as host or home country cultural practices. As 'youth subcultures', they are increasingly part of the global (Gilroy 1993; Amit-Talai and Wulff 1995; Hannerz 1996), in many ways bypassing the national or traditional. Thus, it should not come as a surprise that Turkish youth in Germany listen to the rap music as much as, if not more than, they listen to Turkish *Şarkı* or German *Lied*. Or that the immigrant 'youth gangs' adopt names in English: Two Nation Force, Turkish Power Boys, Cobras and Bulldogs. Or that they form rap groups cleverly called Cartel, Microphone Mafia, and Islamic Force, and that their graffiti on Berlin walls very much replicate the acclaimed styles of New York.

By highlighting this plethora of immigrant experience in a multitude of arenas, I wish to maintain that public spaces within which immigrants act, mobilize, advance claims and produce cultures are broader than the ethnic dominion of diaspora. Their connections to multi-level discourses and their access to diverse citizenship practices are invisible under the *modus operandi* of diasporic theorizing. Nor can the expanse and multi-referentiality of their mobilizing be contained by bi-directional ethnic transactions and arrangements.

Conclusion

The experience of post-war immigrants in Europe indicates a diversion from the classical forms of participating in the public sphere, mobilizing identities and making claims. Much of the decolonization and civil rights movements of the 1960s and the early women's movements were attempts to redefine individuals as part of the national collectivity. Similarly, labour movements were historically linked to the shaping of a national citizenry. It is no coincidence that the welfare state developed as part of the national project, attaching labour movements to nations (as

12 Yasemin Nuhoğlu Soysal

in Bismarkian Germany). However, as I have tried to delineate with my examples, the emerging formations of collective participation and claims-making in Europe are less and less nationally delimited citizenship projects. Individuals and collective groups set their agenda for realization of rights through particularistic identities, which are embedded in, and driven by, universalistic and homogenizing discourses of personhood and human rights. This shift in focus from national collectivity to particularistic identities does not necessarily implicate disengagement from participating in common public spheres or creation of disintegrated civic arenas. On the contrary, they are evidence of the emerging participatory forms, and multiple arenas and levels whereby individuals enact and practise their citizenship.

As we approach the turn of the century, citizenship has come to the fore as a trying issue, both theoretically and politically. Our theories and policy prescriptions, however, have yet to respond to the changes in the institutions of citizenship, rights and identity. To do so, we need to move beyond the traditional, and revisit our theoretical agendas and analytical frameworks. Drawing upon the arguments I have developed here, I would like to suggest three correctives to our current sociological thinking on citizenship and identity:

First, the much taken-for-granted dichotomy of particular versus universal no longer holds. We have to consider the mechanisms by which the universalistic rights discourse not only reinforce particularistic identities and claims, but also concurrently normalize these same identities. The particularistic identities and claims we encounter today are inevitable outcomes of the universalistic principles to which we firmly adhere. Thus, the question is not a matter of positive or negative recognition (or even accommodation) of these claims and identities. What really matters is the very process of negotiation, contestation and dialogue in which these claims and identities are mobilized. After all, confrontation and dialogue are what constitute the basis of democratic public spheres.

Second, there are no longer absolute and clear-cut patterns of exclusions and inclusions. Neither do these patterns simply coincide with the bounds of the national. Access to a formal nationality status is not the main indicator for inclusion or exclusion in today's Europe. Rights, membership and participation are increasingly matters beyond the vocabulary of national citizenship. Thus, on the one hand, we have to identify contexts and processes which are beyond the nation-state, and lead to simultaneous inclusions and exclusions. On the other, we need to bring back on to our political agenda one of the main premises of sociology: inclusion and exclusion are also issues of distribution. Not that this is a novel idea, but it does require a strong political will to do so. It is therefore worth repeating.

Citizenship and identity 13

Third, we can no longer frame our debates on membership and identities within the dichotomy of national and transnational, and the expected linear transition from one to the other. There is much confusion around this issue and much time and energy is spent in arguing whether we are approaching a transnational stage or not. Rather than treating national and transnational as stages in progress, we need to incorporate them into our theoretical frameworks as variables, and treat them as concurrent levels within which the current practices of citizenship and identity should be understood.

Postscript

Theories are stubborn. Nation and ethnicity, the 'invented traditions' of the nineteenth century, in the words of Eric Hobsbawm, may be with us for some time. They may even be reinvented, and given extensions in life, as in the renewals of old concepts like diaspora. As I have argued, the concept of diaspora effortlessly casts contemporary population movements as perpetual ethnic arrangements, transactions and belongings. In so doing, it suspends immigrant experience between host and home countries, native and foreign lands, home-bound desires and losses – thus, obscuring the new topography and practices of citizenship, which are multi-connected, multi-referential and postnational.

Diaspora finds a strong placement in our political and intellectual discourses through its naturalizing metaphors of roots, soil and kinship. However, lacking analytical rigour, it is destined to be a trope for nostalgia. Diaspora indexes timeless recollection and animates what has come to be known as identity politics. On this, I turn again to Edward Said and conclude with him:

> Identity as such is about as boring a subject as one can imagine. Nothing seems less interesting than the narcissistic self-study that today passes in many places for identity politics, or ethnic studies, or affirmations of roots, cultural pride, drum-beating nationalism and so on. We have to defend peoples and identities threatened with extinction or subordinated because they are considered inferior, but that is very different from aggrandising a past invented for present reasons (1998, p. 7).

Acknowledgement

Ideas presented here have been debated at various times and places, cyber and real, with Miriam Feldblum, Levent Soysal, Mette Hjort, Jane Jenson, Doug McAdam, Deborah Yashar, Gershon Shafir, Maria Baganha, Damian Tambini, and Hans van der Veen. My thanks to them.

14 *Yasemin Nuhoğlu Soysal*

Notes

1. Said quotes from Adorno's *Minima Moralia* (1974).
2. From Ron H. Feldman's introduction to Hannah Arendt's *The Jew As Pariah* (1978: 22).
3. To get a feel of how expansive the diaspora literature has become, one simply needs to check the list of recent conference titles, funded research programmes, and forthcoming books. Only the University of Washington Press promises several volumes on the topic – a diaspora for all major immigrant groups.
4. The phrase is from Liisa H. Malkki (1995).
5. I use the term 'human rights' in its broad, abstract sense, not necessarily referring to specific international conventions or instruments and their categorical contents.
6. See Anderson (1983), Appadurai (1996), Herzfeld (1992), Malkki (1995), Gupta and Ferguson (1992) and Soysal (1996).
7. By emphasizing the universality of discourses and strategies employed by immigrant groups, I am not taking a naive position and assuming that individuals or groups will bond together and arrive at agreeable positions. Here I diverge from the Habermasian project, according to which the discursive process, when rational, serves to bring reason and will together and create consensus without coercion (Habermas 1962). Public sphere necessarily involves conflict, contestation and incoherent outcomes, however rational. In that sense, the role of the discursive participatory process is to focus on agendas of contestation and provide space for strategic action, rather than consensus building (Eder 1995).
8. I borrow the phrase from Jane Jenson (1993: 138).

References

ADORNO, THEODOR W. 1974 *Minima Moralia: Reflections from Damaged Life*, London: Verso

AMIT-TALAI, VERED and WULLF, HELENA (eds) 1995 *Youth Cultures: A Cross-cultural Perspective*, London: Routledge

ANDERSON, BENEDICT 1983 *Imagined Communities*, London: Verso

APPADURAI, ARJUN 1996 *Modernity at Large: Cultural Dimensions of Globalization*, Minneapolis, MN: University of Minnesota Press

ARENDT, HANNAH 1978 *The Jew As Pariah: Jewish Identity and Politics in the Modern Age*, edited and with an introduction by Ron H. Feldman, New York: Grove Press

BAUMANN, GERD 1996 *Contesting Culture: Discourses of Identity in Multi-Ethnic London*, Cambridge: Cambridge University Press

COHEN, ROBIN 1997 *Global Diasporas: An Introduction*, Seattle, WA: University of Washington

EDER, KLAUS 1995 'The Institutionalization of Environmentalism: Ecological Discourse and the Second Transformation of the Public Sphere', unpublished manuscript, European University Institute, Florence

GILROY, PAUL 1993 *The Black Atlantic: Modernity and Double Consciousness*, Cambridge, MA: Harvard University Press

GUPTA, AKIL and FERGUSON, JAMES 1992 'Beyond "Culture": space, identity, and the politics of difference', *Cultural Anthropology*, vol. 7, pp. 6–23

HABERMAS, JÜRGEN 1962 [1989] *The Structural Transformation of the Public Sphere*, Cambridge, MA: MIT Press

HANNERZ, ULF 1996 *Transnational Connections: Culture, People, Places*, New York: Routledge

HERZFELD, MICHAEL 1992 *The Social Production of Indifference: Exploring the Symbolic Roots of Western Bureaucracy*, New York: Berg

JENSON, JANE 1993 'De-constructing dualities: making rights claims in political

Citizenship and identity 15

institutions', in G. Drover and P. Kerans (eds), *New Approaches to Welfare Theory*, Aldershot: Edward Elgar Publishers

KASTORYANO, RIVA 1996 *Négocier l'Identité: La France, l'Allemagne et leurs Immigrés*, Paris: Armand Colin

KEPEL, GILLES 1997 *Allah in the West: Islamic Movements in America and Europe*, Stanford, CA: Stanford University Press

MALKKI, LIISA H. 1995 *Purity and Exile: Violence, Memory, and National Cosmology among Hutu Refugees in Tanzania*, Chicago, IL: University of Chicago Press

MARKS, GARY and McADAM, DOUG 1996 'Social movements and the changing structure of political opportunity in the European Union', *West European Politics*, vol. 19, no. 2, pp. 249–87

SAID, EDWARD 1998 'Between Worlds', *London Review of Books*, vol. 20, no. 9, pp. 3–7

SCHMITTER, PHILIPPE C. 1992 'Interests, Powers, and Functions: Emergent Properties and Unintended Consequences in the European Polity', unpublished manuscript, Department of Political Science, Stanford University

SOYSAL, LEVENT 1999 'Projects of Culture: An Ethnographic Episode in the Life of Migrant Youth in Berlin', PhD thesis, Harvard University

SOYSAL, YASEMIN NUHOĞLU 1994 *Limits of Citizenship: Migrants and Postnational Membership in Europe*, Chicago, IL: University of Chicago Press

—— 1996 'Boundaries and Identity: Immigrants in Europe', European Forum, Working Paper Series, European University Institute, Florence

TURNER, BRYAN S. 1986 'Personhood and Citizenship', *Theory and Society*, vol. 3, pp. 1–16

VAN HEAR, NICHOLAS 1998 *New Diasporas: The Mass Exodus, Dispersal and Regrouping of Migrant Communities*, Oxford: Oxford University Press

YASEMIN NUHOĞLU SOYSAL is Senior Lecturer in Sociology at the University of Essex.
ADDRESS: Department of Sociology, University of Essex, Wivenhoe Park, Colchester, CO4 3SQ, UK.

Part IV
Struggles Over Citizenship Rights

[14]

Citizenship in flux: The figure of the activist citizen

Engin F. Isin
Politics and International Studies (POLIS), The Open University, Walton Hall, Milton Keynes, MK7 6AA, UK.

Abstract   Throughout the twentieth century the figure of citizenship that has been dominant since the eighteenth and nineteenth centuries has begun to change. We have witnessed the emergence of new rights including ecological, sexual and indigenous rights as well as blurring of the boundaries between human and civil, political and social rights and the articulation of rights by (and to) cities, regions and across states. We have witnessed the birth of new 'acts of citizenship': both organized and spontaneous protests to include situationist and carnivalesque forms. We have also witnessed the emergence of 'activist' international courts (and judges), as well as new media and social networking as sites of struggles. *How subjects act to become citizens and claim citizenship has thus substantially changed.* This article interprets these developments as heralding a new figure of citizenship, and begins the important task of developing a new vocabulary by which it can be understood.
Subjectivity (2009) **29**, 367–388. doi:10.1057/sub.2009.25

Keywords: activist citizenship; sites; scales; rights

Introduction: A New Vocabulary of Citizenship

An as yet unnamed figure is making its appearance on the stage of history. It is unnamed not because it is invisible but because we have not yet recognized it. It is inarticulable. Otherwise, it is quite visible. We have categories to describe this figure: foreigner, migrant, irregular migrant, illegal alien, immigrant, wanderer, refugee, émigré, exile, nomad, sojourner and many more that attempt to fix it (Nyers, 2003). But so far this figure resists these categories not because it has an agency as such but because it unsettles the very attempt to fix it. It is often reported that the number of people living outside their country of birth is now the highest in history. We are told that 'the stocks of foreign-born populations' have reached unprecedented levels (OECD, 2009). The terms 'stocks' and 'foreign-born' already indicate the unsettling aspects of the figure. As Ossman says '... this figure challenges prevalent conceptions of the relationship between identity and appearance, belief and representation. An increasingly global economy facilitates mobility and logically works to produce more adaptable, moveable people. Yet, people with multiple national identifications challenge how we think about stability' (Ossman, 2007, p. 1). The unnamed figure is unsettling because it belies the modern figure of the citizen with singular loyalty, identity and belonging. There are many ways in which this figure is becoming increasingly visible and slowly articulable. It is impossible to capture all its appearances in a single word but all challenge citizenship. We still only dimly understand their consequences for the ways in which these unsettling people develop their identifications and subjectivities (Ossman, 2007).

What interests me is how the emergence of this figure is implicated in the emergence of new 'sites', 'scales' and 'acts' through which 'actors' claim to transform themselves (and others) from subjects into citizens as claimants of rights. What we need to understand is how these sites, scales and acts produce new actors who enact political subjectivities and transform themselves and others into citizens by articulating ever-changing and expanding rights (Schattle, 2008). The rights (civil, political, social, sexual, ecological, cultural), sites (bodies, courts, streets, media, networks, borders), scales (urban, regional, national, transnational, international) and acts (voting, volunteering, blogging, protesting, resisting and organizing) through which subjects enact themselves (and others) as citizens need to be interpreted anew.

We need a new vocabulary of citizenship. We have witnessed the emergence of new sites of struggle and new rights as well as the blurring of boundaries between human rights and other rights, the articulation of rights by and to cities, regions and across states, and the emergence of struggles through streets, cities, courts, international non-governmental organizations and regional alliances. In order to make sense of the implications of such developments for citizenship we require new concepts rather than a recycling of old categories. What seems now obvious is that throughout the twentieth century (and accelerating towards its end) rights, sites, scales and acts of citizenship have proliferated to the extent that these have begun to change our dominant figure of citizenship. We have yet to accept this fully let alone understand it. I will call this figure 'activist citizenship' and its actors 'activist citizens' to contrast it sharply with the figure of 'active citizenship' that emerged during the French Revolution and that persisted for two centuries.

What is Called 'Citizenship'?

If we are to develop a fluid and dynamic conception of citizenship that is historically grounded and geographically responsive, we cannot articulate the

Citizenship in flux

question as 'what is citizenship?' Rather, the challenge is to ask 'what is *called* citizenship?' that evokes all the interests and forces that are invested in making and interpreting it in one way or another. That is why current debates about whether citizenship is status or practice and whether it is a controlling or empowering institution have become rather enervated. It has been acknowledged and often stated that the debate over citizenship has focused on two distinct but related aspects: citizenship as status and citizenship as practice. The studies that focus on citizenship as status often start with the observation that citizenship is acquired by three modes: *jus sanguinis* (a child inherits citizenship via a parent), *jus soli* (a child inherits citizenship via birth regardless of parentage) or *jus domicili* (a person acquires citizenship by naturalization in a state other than his or her birth). They focus on issues of residence, naturalization, passport, immigration, alienage and deportation (Jacobson, 1996; Schuck, 1998; Aleinikoff and Klusmeyer, 2000; Hansen and Weil, 2000; Torpey, 2000; Benhabib, 2004). The studies that emphasize practice typically focus on integration, cohesion, multiculturalism, education, nationalism and transnationalism (Body-Gendrot and Martiniello, 2000; García Canclini, 2001; Ferrera, 2003; Penninx, 2004). Although most studies on either status or practice accept that status and practices of citizenship presuppose each other and also call each other into question, many studies still predominantly emphasize status or practice.

Debates have also focused on whether citizenship eases or hinders domination of one social group over another (Isin and Turner, 2002). It was the debate between Mann (1987) and Turner (1990, 1993) that brought into sharp relief the question of whether citizenship involves ruling class strategies via the state or whether it is an expression of social movements. But this discussion too has become enervated. Clearly, citizenship involves both aspects, and detailed empirical investigation is required to reveal the extent to which citizenship institutes domination of one social group over another (Isin, 2002a). Citizenship can be both domination and empowerment separately or simultaneously.

Yet another focus of interest is whether citizenship remains within the modern boundaries of the state and nation or extends beyond those boundaries. Since Soysal's (1994) influential contribution on how post-national citizenship rights were being made available to claimants of citizenship within the authority and boundaries of nations, post-national, transnational, global or cosmopolitan forms of citizenship have generated a considerable literature (Bauböck, 1994; Linklater, 1998; Hutchings and Dannreuther, 1999; Falk, 2000; Yegenoglu, 2005; Archibugi, 2008; Schattle, 2008). These debates have invigorated our understanding of what it means to be a citizen, but nevertheless by and large almost all contributors continue to take 'citizenship' to mean *membership* of a state.

As debates continue over these aspects (status versus practice, domination versus empowerment, formal versus substantive, national versus transnational),

370 **Isin**

new *actors*, *sites* and *scales* of citizenship have emerged that complicate the ways in which citizenship is enacted not as only membership but also as claims (Sassen, 1996; Flores and Benmayor, 1997; Soysal, 1997; Isin and Siemiatycki, 2002; Scholtz, 2006). It is no longer adequate (if it ever was) to think of states as 'containers' of citizens as its members. New actors articulate claims for justice through new sites that involve multiple and overlapping scales of rights and obligations (Bigo, 2002; Huysmans, 2006; Huysmans *et al*, 2006) *The manifold acts through which new actors as claimants emerge in new sites and scales are becoming the new objects of investigation. This changes our conception of the political as well as of citizenship.*

The attempts to interpret these new developments by engaging already established approaches to political theory such as liberalism, republicanism and communitarianism have been inadequate. But equally the assumption that political theory emerges from interpreting phenomena that precede it is as problematic as the assumption that somehow political theory brings about the changes it prescribes (Tully, 2002; Freeden, 2005). The challenge for theorists of citizenship is not to develop a theory of citizenship by fitting it into already existing 'political' theories or revising theory to accommodate changing realities; rather it is to theorize citizenship as an institution in flux embedded in current social and political struggles that constitute it. 'What is called citizenship?' is itself a call to investigate how political thought is embedded in acts as claims for justice. The aim of this article is not to provide such an analysis (Isin, 2002a). Rather, it aims to provide a vocabulary that has arisen out of such an analysis, which may prove useful for others (Isin, 2005).

I have already used the central concepts of this vocabulary rather casually and without introduction: actors, sites, scales and acts. Although the rest of this article is about explaining them I will now briefly define them. The actors of citizenship are not necessarily those who hold the status of citizenship. If we understand citizenship as an instituted subject-position, it can be performed or enacted by various categories of subjects including aliens, migrants, refugees, states, courts and so on (Bassel, 2008). The political is not limited to an already constituted territory or its legal 'subjects': it always exceeds them. Citizenship as subjectivity enacts that conception of the political. Thus, the actors of citizenship cannot be defined in advance of the analysis of a given site and scale, which are its other central categories.

The 'sites' of citizenship are fields of contestation around which certain issues, interests, stakes as well as themes, concepts and objects assemble. The 'scales' are scopes of applicability that are appropriate to these fields of contestation. When we use already existing categories such as states, nations, cities, sexualities and ethnicities, we inevitably deploy them as 'containers' with fixed and given boundaries. By contrast, when we begin with 'sites' and 'scales' we refer to fluid and dynamic entities that are formed through contests and struggles, and their boundaries become a question of empirical determination.

Citizenship in flux 371

Although sites and scales provide two constantly shifting aspects of struggles over rights, I will argue that the binding thread of investigations of these struggles should be the concept of 'acts' and specifically 'acts of citizenship'. To investigate how new actors, scales and sites of citizenship shift and emerge means to investigate acts of citizenship – those deeds by which actors constitute themselves (and others) as subjects of rights.

The concept of 'acts of citizenship' has been introduced elsewhere (Isin, 2008). Four considerations were provided for its development. First, actors need not be conceived of in advance as to their status. They can be individuals, states, NGOs and other legal or quasi-legal entities or persons that come into being through enactment. To recognize certain acts as acts of citizenship requires the demonstration that these acts produce subjects as citizens. Time and again we see that subjects that are not citizens act *as* citizens: they constitute themselves as those with 'the right to claim rights'. (The concept popularized by Arendt 'the right to have rights' sounds too passive and possessive to capture the activist figure of citizenship.) Second, acts through which claims are articulated and claimants are produced create new sites of contestation, belonging, identification and struggle. These sites are different from traditional sites of citizenship contestation such as voting, social security and military obligation though these continue to be important. Bodies, courts, streets, media, networks and borders have also become sites of contestation for citizenship. Third, acts of citizenship stretch across boundaries, frontiers and territories to involve multiple and overlapping scales of contestation, belonging, identification and struggle. Such contestations stretch across nations and towards urban, regional, transnational and international scales. The focus on acts of citizenship that produce new actors, sites and scales of citizenship is therefore vital for understanding how citizenship has changed in an age of migration and movement (Castles and Davidson, 2000). Fourth, by theorizing acts we shift focus from what people *say* (opinion, perception, attitudinal surveys) to what people *do*. This is an important supplement, and under certain circumstances, corrective, to studies that concern themselves with what people say about their citizenship and identification.

Given these preliminary considerations, we can start with the following relational definition of citizenship. Citizenship is a dynamic (political, legal, social and cultural but perhaps also sexual, aesthetic and ethical) institution of domination *and* empowerment that governs *who* citizens (insiders), subjects (strangers, outsiders) and abjects (aliens) are and *how* these actors are to govern themselves and each other in a given body politic. Citizenship is not membership. It is a relation that governs the conduct of (subject) positions that constitute it. The essential difference between citizenship and membership is that while the latter governs conduct *within* social groups, citizenship is about conduct *across* social groups all of which constitute a body politic. Being a citizen almost always means being more than an insider – it also means to be one who has mastered modes and forms of conduct that are appropriate to being an insider. This creates an actor both in the sense of a *person* (law) but also a *persona* (norm). For subjects and abjects becoming a citizen means either adopting modes and forms of being an insider (assimilation, integration, incorporation) or challenging these modes and forms and thereby transforming them (identification, differentiation, recognition). Just what constitutes citizenship and its appropriate modes and forms of conduct are always objects of struggle among citizens, subjects and abjects through claims to citizenship as justice. It is through these claims to citizenship as justice that citizenship becomes a site of rights (and obligations). These claims and the combination of rights and obligations that define citizenship work themselves out very differently in different sites and produce different actors. Thus, *rights* (civil, political, social, sexual, cultural, ecological), *sites* (bodies, courts, borders, networks, media), scales (cities, empires, nations, states, federations, leagues), *actors* (citizens, subjects, abjects) and *acts* (voting, volunteering, blogging, protesting, resisting and organizing) are the elements that constitute a body politic. The sites and scales are not mutually exclusive and discrete but overlapping and connected. So when investigating an act it is appropriate always to consider the overlapping and connected aspects of sites and scales through which various actions actualize acts. Below I sometimes use site-scales together and sometimes sites and scales as separate attributes depending on the specific exemplification.

I will now provide a brief re-reading of the history of citizenship from the point of view of the vocabulary of citizenship developed above.

Sites, Scales and Actors

The dominant reading of citizenship is one that privileges the ancient Greeks as inventing it roughly around the eighth century BCE by producing a new site-scale of politics: *polis* (Manville, 1990). Until then, god-kings, we are told, governed the city. It appears that cities in ancient kingdoms, states and empires did not develop citizenship precisely because they were 'despotic' regimes of government. But the ancient Greeks themselves did not see much conflict between despotic regimes of government and citizenship. The three forms of governing the city as identified by Greek thought – oligarchy, aristocracy, and democracy – already assumed the existence of the citizen. Nonetheless, what happened in that moment? The answer, ironically, has much to do with what we are struggling over right now. At that moment, it seems that a new actor entered onto the stage of history, which was male, warrior and owned property (not the least of which was the means of warfare). That actor became the dominant figure against god-kings. Those who were not male and did not own property such as women, slaves, peasants, merchants, craftsmen, sailors increasingly

Citizenship in flux

found themselves as the others of the citizen – namely, as subjects and abjects. Being a citizen in this context involved the right to govern his city (belonging) and bequeath that right to his son (blood). In governing himself by the laws of his city, he also governed the strangers, outsiders and aliens of the city. We have already drawn attention to sites (masculinity, warriorship, property) that remained key sites of struggle until modernity. But these sites functioned very differently. *Polis* would remain as the originary scale and site through which citizenship was reinvented through centuries. The issues that *polis* articulated such as the relationship between citizenship and forms of government, subjects and abjects, and rights and obligations of citizenship would, time and again, be repeated albeit producing different sites, actors and rights of citizenship. It is now impossible to conceive citizenship without orienting ourselves to that originary site-scale of history, *polis* and the citizen as its historical actor.

Contrast that with the Roman citizen. When it was fully articulated, being a Roman citizen was above all being a member of an empire that was *beyond* the city (Sherwin-White, 1973). Yet, it is clear that while Romans invented a new scale *for* citizenship, it was articulated *through* the city. 'Being Roman' nicely captures that duality: being of Rome and its empire (Gardner, 1993). What that meant is that while being male, warrior and owning property were still the elements that constituted the Roman citizen, dominating its other actors such as strangers (women, plebeians, clients, slaves), outsiders (merchants, foreigners) and aliens (barbarians); he was still essentially Roman precisely because he was *of* Rome. Being Roman was simultaneously an imperial and civic identity, but it eventually became an imperial identity by the 212 CE *Constitutio Antoniniana*, which gave all freemen in the Roman Empire Roman citizenship (Sherwin-White, 1973, pp. 380–386). How the fall of the empire was related to this declaration in 212 CE will continue to be the subject of debate (Heater, 1990). What is noteworthy for the purpose of my argument is that although the scale of citizenship was constituted differently, masculinity, warriorship and property still remained the key sites of struggle.

The moments of the emergence of new sites and scales of citizenship after the disintegration of the Roman Empire are fascinating. Much has been written about the rebirth of the city during the eleventh and twelfth centuries in Europe. The invention of the charter as the founding instrument of the city as a body politic (and corporate) and the emergence of the new actor-citizen, who was not a warrior but a peaceful merchant and artisan of the medieval commune, has given us a new originary moment. This is not disconnected from Athens and Rome yet has a new inflection. Perhaps the new site and scale of citizenship was now best represented by Florence though, of course, there were regional differences throughout Europe (Weber, 1921b). Between the twelfth and fifteenth centuries, thousands of cities were founded as bodies politic and corporate with varied relationships of autonomy and autocephaly (administrative independence) from the 'surrounding' lordship, kingships and incipient states (Reynolds, 1997). For the emerging European citizenship, its dominant site-scale was definitely the city but more through belonging than blood. The well-known residency requirement in medieval Europe of a year and a day before one could become a citizen (a burgher) is one of the telling clauses of the charter that founded the city (Frug, 1980). Just how these scattered and heterogeneous patchwork worlds of contested sovereignties, autonomies and class of burghers (hence the origins of the bourgeoisie) were transformed into the world of states remains debatable (Strayer, 1970; Poggi, 1978, 1990). But the city was undeniably still at the centre of the development of the state rather than the state being the city writ large. The transformation from the fifteenth to eighteenth century was, if you like, from Florence to Paris. If Florence represented that world of contested sovereignties, Paris embodied a new actor, a new *scale* of citizenship: the republic. Although its own self-image aspired to become even wider, behind that aspiration stood a dominant figure: the bourgeois, male and Christian citizen.

Arendt (1951) called the moment when the state was defined as the territory of a people constituted according to not just bourgeois, Christian and male properties but also according to ethno-cultural properties as the 'conquest of the state by the nation'. What Arendt meant by this conquest is that if the state was a body politic (Arendt called it an artefact) that enabled negotiation of differences among various social groups as their claims to citizenship, nationality instituted the domination of a group over others as immutable. It was then that citizenship was reconfigured as nationality (Balibar, 2004, p. 37). While the difference between citizenship and nationality ought to be as profound as that between citizen and subject or abject, it rapidly became and remains still an accepted, if not given, association or identity.

The three sites of citizenship (masculinity, warriorship, property) persisted well into the modern state and nation-state. The medieval commune was perhaps a departure between the twelfth and fifteenth centuries in Europe when being a warrior was not associated with being a citizen, but rather was associated with being of the city (even if a citizen did not dwell in the city). Yet, being a citizen still involved owning property and being male. Perhaps then, the most significant divergence occurred in the late eighteenth and early nineteenth centuries when citizenship became associated with nationality and was understood as belonging to the state rather than the city. The state was seen as the city, and nation as the citizen, writ large (Black, 1984, p. 152). It was then that the principles of *jus sanguinis* (blood), *jus domicili* (residence) and *jus soli* (birth) were rearticulated through the nation-state.

What these considerations illustrate is that citizenship should always be interpreted with a focus on its fluid and dynamic elements that constitute it and its rights, sites, scales and actors. Taking any one of these elements as given or static, and taking any one of these elements in isolation significantly impoverishes our understanding of the ways in which citizenship institutes domination and/or empowerment. Indeed, such a tendency leads us towards an approach in which citizenship becomes contained within already taken-for-granted boundaries. Similarly, if we are not attentive to significant shifts and divergences such as the transformation from ancient to modern institutions of citizenship, we assume (implicitly or explicitly) a static and unchanging view of citizenship as membership.

Yet, if each site and scale articulates a different actor and if the state constitutes a qualitatively different scale of citizenship, what explains the ostensible unity of 'citizenship' in so much as we talk about 'it' rather than different institutions or designations? The answer, in part, lies in the fact that every dominant social group in the occident reinscribed and reinvested itself in the citizen as the foundation of its symbolic and imaginary occidentality (Isin, 2002b). It also lies in the fact that the originary sites of citizenship – masculinity, warriorship and property – remained effective until the twentieth century, thus playing an important role in the on-going differentiation of citizens from subjects and abjects.

It is these foundational sites of citizenship – masculinity, warriorship and property – and its 'occidental' scale that gradually disappeared in the twentieth century. We may well interpret the twentieth century as having recast the foundational elements of citizenship. It was then that property was no longer tied to citizenship, women became at least formal if not substantive claimants upon it, and the nature of war and warriorship were fundamentally altered by being fought by special kinds of mercenaries (for example, 'operatives for security contractors') and technological weaponry. Moreover, it was in that century that the universal citizen was shown to have represented the attributes of a particular occidental social group: Christian, heterosexual, male, white and adult (Young, 1989, 1990). While the figure of the universal citizen was shown as a chimera, a universal declaration heralded the figure of the human as bearer of rights. Does this mean the end of citizenship? This period is seen as consolidating the gradual expansion of civil rights in the eighteenth, political rights in the nineteenth and social rights in the twentieth century (T.H. Marshall, 1949). Could the twenty-first century mark the end of citizenship just as Roman citizenship ended at the moment of its declaration of universality in 212 CE? Judging how some scholars have come to see human rights supplant citizenship rights, we may well reach that conclusion.

Or, we may think differently. In his overview of modern citizenship since the eighteenth century, Andreas Fahrmeir (2007, p. 232) concludes, '... any prophesy about citizenship's impending demise and on what is likely to replace it will probably prove mistaken'. I agree with that assessment. However, he claims that '... citizenship is likely to prove as impermanent as class or race, and discussions of citizenship would probably do well to take more account of that fact than they have tended to do so far' (Fahrmeir, 2007, p. 232). This is too static and too reductionist a view. Citizenship cannot be reduced to class or race since they have been the conditions and not the substance of citizenship. Moreover, citizenship has gone through significant changes but still remains an institution of domination and empowerment. The emergence of ostensibly 'universal' rights called 'human' does not eclipse social, sexual and other rights as substances of political struggles (Rancière, 2004; Žižek, 2005; Isin and Rygiel, 2007), nor should it be seen as such.

Consequently, while we have witnessed the recasting of the historic sites of citizenship (property, warriorship, masculinity), we have also observed the emergence of new actors that are constituted much less by what they possess than by what they ostensibly lack: strangers, outsiders and aliens had become claimants to citizenship (Isin and Wood, 1999). Perhaps those new historical narratives that are now being told about citizenship indicate this transformation (Isin, 2002a). These narratives interpret and institute citizenship less as a bastion of property, warriorship and masculinity, let alone occidentality or nationality, and more as about the struggles of redistribution and recognition by those who had been its strangers, outsiders and aliens (Smith, 1997). This is a transformation that has been brought out by movements mentioned earlier and whose consequences for citizenship we hardly comprehend or recognize. It is this figure of citizenship that we yet dimly perceive and that I want to name. What is then the substance of citizenship?

Rights: The Substance of Citizenship

> The rights of others constitute a concession on the part of our sense of power to the sense of power of those others. If our power appears to be deeply shaken and broken, our rights cease to exist; conversely, if we have grown very much more powerful, the rights of others, as we have previously conceded them, cease to exist for us. (Nietzsche, 1881, p. 67)

The substance of citizenship is 'rights'. But rights are not substances. Rights are, as Nietzsche suggests, relations. Each site and scale of citizenship configures rights appropriate to the relations of forces that constitute it. If the citizen is dominant in a given site (property, warriorship and masculinity) then the corresponding obligations of those who do not have access to these sites will be making claims to citizenship as justice, and redressing injustices to which domination gives rise. Although not a zero-sum game, rights of citizenship are relationships that reflect dominant sites and actors of citizenship. It would have been inconceivable to imagine claiming rights for 'disabled people' or 'irregular migrants' in either Greek polis or Roman civitas. Similarly, it would be inconceivable today to institute a parliament of warriors. The relationships between and among sites, scales and actors of citizenship are not zero-sum games either. These scales articulate through each other rather than eclipsing

Citizenship in flux 377

each other (Isin, 2007). They also stretch and permeate each other. Rather than being nestled and concatenated, the scales of citizenship are tentacular and amorphous and bleed into each other. It is these intersections between different sites (and scales) that produce different actors and different rights of citizenship. The sites and scales are not mutually exclusive and discrete but are overlapping and connected. A legal court, for example, can become a site of struggles over certain rights. But it may also activate a scale by virtue of its jurisdiction, as its scope of applicability becomes the object of struggle. The European Court of Human Rights, for example, can become a site of contestation for women wearing headscarves in university campuses in Turkey, but it also flexes or stretches those struggles taking place within Turkey to a European legal case. So, when investigating an act it is appropriate always to consider the overlapping and connected aspects of sites and scales through which various actions actualize acts.

So far I have attempted to give a fluid and dynamic view of citizenship, which is constantly in flux combining various elements which I called, on the one hand, sites, scales and actors, and on the other, rights of citizenship. While we can focus on a given geographic scope and historical situation to investigate a particular combination of the fluid and dynamic elements of citizenship, this does not necessarily make us understand the conditions of its transformation. To understand how historical actors (citizens, subjects, abjects) enact themselves to claim certain rights, assume obligations and constitute themselves as citizens, we need to investigate enactments of citizenship. The unit of analysis in such enactments is acts or deeds by which and through which subjects become, or constitute themselves as, citizens.

Acts: Enacting Political Subjectivity

What is an act? We need to consider this question before turning to 'acts of citizenship'. As I have discussed this question in more detail elsewhere, a brief summary will suffice (Isin, 2008). Both as a verb and noun, the word act implies and evokes an impressive range of conduct and outcomes that are related but irreducible to action. So the most important conclusion is that acts and action are different and yet related kinds of things. Yet, while 'action' has long been a concern of modern social and political thought (Weber, 1921a; Parsons and Shils, 1959), the concept of 'acts' has never been a consistent (nor persistent) subject except when linked with performativity and speech acts (Searle, 1969; Butler, 1988). Conflation of acts and action seems widespread. When Stout (2005, p. 3), for example, says 'Being an agent is being something that acts, something that does actions', it sounds promising. But he continues 'in the philosophy of action we are dealing with two types of entities: agents and actions', and acts disappear from analysis (Bennett, 1995). Similarly, Butler

(1988) and Searle (1969) assume that acts can be called actions. The fact that acts can refer both to deeds as well as performance, to process as well as outcomes, to conduct as well as enactment, confounds attempts to develop a concept that focuses on the passage between a performance and its outcomes or between an act and its actualization.

In contemporary political thought, Robert Ware (1973) remains, as far as I know, the sole figure to have argued for a distinction between acts and action. Ware argues that while both acts and actions concern doings rather than happenings, acts are different kinds of doings than actions (Ware, 1973, p. 404). This distinction can already be found in our common use of the expressions 'act' and 'action' but Ware thinks it has been curiously neglected. By noting that many things can be called acts or actions, the fact that they cannot be substituted for each other should be taken to illustrate that these are different entities (Ware, 1973, p. 403).

Ware proposes six necessary conditions for something to be called an act. (I will express these in my own words as Ware's specification of acts and their difference from actions is not always consistent.) First, to specify an act is to indicate a doing. Although actions also involve a doing, it is necessary that they involve movement, change, and motion of objects and bodies. 'What is important for actions is that there be action. Actions and motions are rather alike. They both involve action or motion' (Ware, 1973, p. 408). In contrast, the kind of doing that acts indicate does not need to involve objects and bodies. Second, acts are doings of actors. Actions can happen without actors. Thus, acts are either human or humanized (that is, acts of God or acts of nature). There are actions of non-human beings just as there are actions of human beings, but there are acts only of human beings (Ware, 1973, p. 406). Third, acts happen because of a decision to perform the act. Although acts can be either intentional or non-intentional they are always purposive. Thus, acts always involve a decision. Fourth, while acts take time and space for doing, they do not have spatiotemporal coordinates: 'acts do not have a place or position in the world and thus cannot be seen [or observed]' (Ware, 1973, p. 414). Fifth, acts must have completion. They involve accomplishments. 'The accomplishing of something is not an action although it may take action to accomplish something, and doing something will usually involve action' (Ware, 1973, p. 407). That is to say, acts exist as entities whose absence or presence can, in equal measure, specify an accomplishment. 'Doings that go on for a period of time and that can be continued or broken off might be action or activities [routines or practices], but they are not acts' (Ware, 1973, p. 413). Sixth, acts build upon acts. Acts involve accomplishments with start and end moments but they also have continuity within themselves. They accrete over time.

From these considerations one can suggest that an act is neither a practice, nor a habit nor an action and yet it implies all these forms of conduct. Contra Stout, when theorizing acts we are dealing with three types of entities: acts,

Citizenship in flux   379

actions and actors. Theorizing acts is not possible without focusing on acts *themselves* that exist independently of actors but cannot be actualized without them. By this I essentially follow Reinach (1983) and Mikhail Bakhtin (1993). (For an extended discussion see Isin, 2008.) It was Reinach and Bakhtin – albeit in different ways – who argued that acts should be distinguished from action and that they should be accorded an ontological existence that is before both actors and actions.

Reinach interpreted the essence of an act as an expression of the need for being heard. He investigated various acts such as willing, promising, commanding, requesting and contemplating and concluded that for an act to be a social act it must enact (via linguistic or non-linguistic means) a need to be heard by one party to another (Reinach, 1983, p. 19). As he put it, 'the turning to another subject and the need of being heard is absolutely essential for every social act' (Reinach, 1983, p. 20). This made acts for Reinach inescapably dialogical or relational. It is beyond the scope of this article to discuss how he then used his concept of social acts to demonstrate the foundations of law or to show how his conception can be said to have anticipated speech act theories and can perhaps be used to critique them (Crosby, 1990; Smith, 1990; DuBois, 1995). Nevertheless, it is important to emphasize that a relational and dynamic interpretation he provided for acts is crucial for understanding citizenship as a dynamic institution. *Acts thus stand in contrast to habitus and other concepts that emphasize the relatively enduring disposition of men and women and that account for the persistence and stability of an order or the grounds of the emergence of another order.* To maintain a distinction between acts and action and acts and habitus requires recognizing acts as those that 'create a scene', which means both performance and disturbance. Creating a scene means to call into question the script itself. Acts are ruptures or beginnings but are not impulsive and random reactions to a scene. Acts are always purposive though not always intentional. *By theorizing acts, or attempting to constitute acts as an object of analysis, we must focus on rupture rather than order but a rupture that enables the actor (that the act creates) to create a scene rather than follow a script.* If an act is understood against habitus, practice, conduct, discipline and routine (the latter conceived of as ordered and ordering qualities of how humans conduct themselves), we can then perhaps understand why the question of acts would remain minor and fragmented within social and political thought and social sciences.

How do we understand 'acts of citizenship'? The term immediately evokes such acts as voting, taxpaying and enlisting. But these are routinized social actions that are already instituted. By contrast, acts make a difference. We make a difference when we actualize acts with actions. We make a difference when we break routines, understandings and practices. That is why the common term 'making a difference' puts its emphasis on 'difference'. That means the order of things will no longer be the way it was. Making a difference introduces a break,

380   Isin

a rupture. Thus, to make a difference is to act; to act is to make a difference. Arendt saw being political as the capacity to act (Arendt, 1969, p. 179). She was moved by the ancient Greek conception of act, which meant both governing and beginning (Arendt, 1958, p. 177; 2005, p. 321). To act means to begin. It is not just to begin something new, but to enact oneself as that being that makes a beginning (Arendt, 1958, p. 177). We are beings endowed with the capacity to act, or as Sartre would say, 'to be is to act'. To act is to actualize a rupture in the given, to act always means to enact the unexpected and unpredictable (Sartre, 1957, p. 613; Arendt, 1958, p. 178). While voting, taxpaying and enlisting may make a difference under certain conditions, activist citizenship, in the sense of making a break, a rupture, a difference, is not inherent in them. If so, what are acts of citizenship? I break up this question into three questions and address each in turn with the example of the *sans-papiers* – the struggles of undocumented or irregular migrants and refugees.

In the 1990s, a group of undocumented migrants formed a movement to demand the right to stay in France (Dubois, 2000). Although the movement had been organizing through meetings and demonstrations, it was an act that not only symbolized its claims to rights, but also instigated or accelerated various other acts to actually transform it to a movement. 'On 18 March 1996, 324 irregular migrants occupied a church in Paris, calling themselves the Sans-Papiers (literally "without papers"). Some of the Sans-Papiers were asylum seekers and some were long-term working residents of France whose status had been made irregular as a result of legislative changes. The Sans-Papiers demanded the right to stay in France and the right to regularized status' (McNevin, 2006, p. 135). It was this claim to the right to stay that was enacted by occupying a church not with a language of human rights but political rights of subjects who did not possess these rights. So the claim was not only the right to stay but also the right to claim a right. It became increasingly the defining aspect of the movement – symbolized in that originary act in the church – that *sans-papiers* differentiated themselves from those with papers even if they were supporters (Rodríguez, 2003). The three questions that the act of citizenship the *sans-papiers* staged concerned the boundaries between exclusion and inclusion, gaps between intentions and consequences, and tensions between legality and illegality.

Question 1. Are acts of citizenship inherently (or always) exclusive or inclusive, homogenizing or diversifying, positive or negative? Or do these meanings that we attribute to acts only arise after the fact? Following our discussion of acts, we cannot define acts of citizenship as already inherently exclusive or inclusive, homogenizing or diversifying, or positive or negative. These qualities arise after, or, more appropriately, through the act. In fact, we as interpreters ascribe these qualities to those acts. This means that acts produce such qualities only as their effects not as their causes. Moreover, those acts that are explicitly intended for certain effects (inclusion, diversity, tolerance) may well produce their counter

Citizenship in flux   381

effects (exclusion, homogeneity, intolerance). There are many examples, but the struggle of the *sans-papiers* (those without papers) is appropriate here. Reminiscent of the revolutionary *sans-culottes* (Isin, 2002a, pp. 193–202), the *sans-papiers* and their defenders have created series of actions as acts of citizenship that brought some fundamental injustices of republican citizenship to the fore (McNevin, 2006, p. 135). However, the significance of *sans-papiers*, those without papers and thus without ascribed identities, and their defenders, is not that they simply pointed to the injustice of their situation and sought their 'human rights'. Rather, they enacted themselves as citizens by usurping the right to claim rights. As Balibar, 2004 says '… the *sans-papiers* also made their contribution to the development of active citizenship by arousing, through the forms and content of their action, an activist solidarity that has shown a remarkable long-term continuity, beyond the understandable alternations of mobilization and discouragement' (Balibar, 2004, p. 48). But I wonder if Balibar is neglecting an important issue here by continuing to recognize *sans-papiers* as active citizens while they actually herald the emergence of a new figure of citizenship, which I call activist citizenship. It is hard to imagine *sans-papiers* acting out of an already written script. The first principle of understanding acts of citizenship is to interpret them through their grounds and consequences, which includes actors becoming *activist citizens* through scenes created. Thus, an analysis of 'activist citizens' over an analysis of 'active citizens' is critical to the framework developed here. By contrast to active citizens who act out already written scripts such as voting, taxpaying and enlisting, activist citizens engage in writing scripts and creating the scene. Rather than recognizing the radical challenge of *sans-papiers* is Balibar not interpreting their acts as an instance of 'already-scripted' republican citizenship?

Question 2. Can acts of citizenship be enacted without an explicit motive, purpose or reason? Do those actors that act as citizens, strangers, outsiders or aliens necessarily (or always) attribute reasons to their acts? Acts cannot happen without motives, purposes or reasons but those cannot be the only grounds of interpreting acts of citizenship. Although acts of citizenship involve decisions, those decisions cannot be reduced to calculability, intentionality and responsibility. But because they are irreducible to those qualities, they can be enacted without subjects being able to articulate reasons for becoming activist citizens. Acts of citizenship do not need to originate in the name of anything, though we as interpreters will always interpret how acts of citizenship orient themselves towards justice. The second principle of theorizing acts of citizenship is to recognize that acts produce actors that become *answerable* to *justice*. This is again evident in relation to the *sans-papiers*. As Balibar says, they did not merely make claims to rights for their own but '… made a contribution to the progress of the *democratization of borders* and of the freedom of movement, which states tend to treat as passive objects of a discretionary power' (Balibar, 2004, p. 49).

382 Isin

Question 3. Can acts of citizenship happen without being founded in law or responsibility? Do those actors that act as citizens, strangers, outsiders or aliens necessarily (or always) act in the name of the law and responsibility? As the example of *sans-papiers* shows, acts of citizenship are not necessarily founded on law or responsibility. In fact, for acts of citizenship to be acts at all they must call the law into question and they may, sometimes, break it. Similarly, they must call established forms of becoming responsible into question and they may, sometimes, be irresponsible. *Those activist citizens that act are not a priori actors recognized in law, but by enacting themselves through acts they affect the law that misrecognizes them.* The third principle of theorizing acts is to recognize that acts of citizenship do not need to be founded on law or enacted in the name of the law. As Beneduce (2008) illustrates, by so doing *sans-papiers* broadened the boundaries of responsibility towards answerability and articulated questions about colonial history and its injustices. Balibar captures this aspect in speaking about the struggles of the *sans-papiers*: 'Paradoxically the struggles of the *sans-papiers*, perceived by the government as disturbances of the public order, desperate forms of blackmail or products of conspiracy whose manipulators should be sought among "criminal networks", have been and are privileged moments in the development of *active citizenship* (or, if you prefer, direct participation in public affairs) without which there exists no polity *(cité)*, but only a state form cut off from society and petrified in its own abstraction' (Balibar, 2004, p. 48). Yet, while Balibar almost recognizes the originality of *sans-papiers*, does he not recall active citizenship again by emphasizing their claim to participation in public affairs? In my view, it is not the claim to participate in public affairs that constitutes the originality of *sans-papiers* but their claims to justice when they did not have the legal capacity to do so. The claim of *sans-papiers* is not to become French republican citizens (as it is understood) but to transform it. As McNevin (2006) says 'The Sans-Papiers claim a right of membership which exists prior to the formal allocation of citizenship and upon which basis they now insist on legal recognition' (McNevin, 2006, p. 144). What the *sans-papiers* case here allows us to see is that it is through acts that citizenship is enacted, with citizenship otherwise remaining an abstract category of government.

Actors, who claim rights and obligations, enact themselves as activist citizens and, in the process, differentiate and name others as those who are not citizens (strangers, outsiders, aliens). This is another aspect of *sans-papiers*. By naming themselves with a 'lack' (sans), they differentiate and name those 'with' papers. As McNevin (2006) says 'Perhaps the most powerful and distinguishing strategy [*sans-papiers*] employ is the explicit rejection of the language and image of illegality in favour of the language and image of entitlement' (McNevin, 2006, p. 143). By so doing, *sans-papiers* expose the contingency of the categories with which politics is enacted. Acts of citizenship are those acts through which citizens, strangers, outsiders, aliens emerge not as actors already defined but as

Citizenship in flux   383

ways of being with others. We have considered acts of citizenship as political insofar as these acts constitute constituents (actors with claims). But they can also make ethical (for example, answerable and responsible), cultural (for example, carnivalesque), sexual (for example, pleasurable) and social (for example, affiliation, solidarity, hostility) claims. *We can define acts of citizenship as those acts that transform forms (orientations, strategies, technologies) and modes (citizens, strangers, outsiders, aliens) of being political by bringing into being new actors as activist citizens (that is, claimants of rights) through creating or transforming sites and stretching scales.*

Conclusion: Activist Citizenship

Citizenship is enacted through struggles for rights among various groups in their ongoing process of formation and reformation. Actors, scales and sites of citizenship emerge through these struggles. Investigating citizenship involves analysing groups whose struggles constitute it as a contingent and contested institution rather than beginning with an abstract definition. To recognize that citizenship is in flux is not to lament its fluid and dynamic structure but to theorize and to account for its instability. Citizenship understood as political subjectivity shifts our attention from fixed categories by which we have come to understand or inherit citizenship to the struggles through which these categories themselves have become stakes. It also shifts our attention from already defined actors to the acts that constitute them. Rather than asking 'who *is* the citizen?' the question becomes 'what *makes* the citizen?' The distinction I am making between active and activist citizen is very close to the one Balibar (2004) makes. He opposes two conceptions of citizenship: 'One is both authorization and abstract. It can claim to advance objectives of social transformation and equality, but in the final analysis it always limits itself to the statist axiom, "the law is the law", which presumes the omniscience of the administration and the illegitimacy of conflict' (Balibar, 2004, pp. 49–50). In my words, active citizenship has become a script for already existing citizens to follow already existing paths. It is most often used to denote the kinds of behaviour that citizens ostensibly follow. Thus, it is always tied into governmental practices through which conduct is produced. It is the conduct of those who are already considered as citizens and whose conduct is juxtaposed against those who are not. Balibar contrasts this with another conception of citizenship that 'attempts to form a concrete articulation of the rights of man and the rights of the citizen, of responsibility and militant commitment. It knows that the historical advances of citizenship, which have never stopped making its concept more precise, have always passed by way of struggles, that in the past it has not only been necessary to make "a part of those who have no part", but truly to force open the gates of the city, and thus to redefine it in a dialectic of conflicts and solidarities'

(Balibar, 2004, pp. 49–50). In other words, thinking about citizenship through acts means to implicitly accept that to be a citizen *is* to make claims to justice: to break habitus and act in a way that disrupts already defined orders, practices and statuses.

The emerging figure of the activist citizen making claims to justice is the defining figure of contemporary global politics. For centuries citizenship as status and practice has been grounded in masculinity, warriorship, property within territorial boundaries that contained it. I provided a preliminary definition of citizenship as a dynamic institution of domination *and* empowerment that governs *who* citizens (insiders), subjects (strangers, outsiders) and abjects (aliens) are and *how* these actors are to govern themselves and each other in a given body politic. The emerging figure of the activist citizen calls into question the givenness of that body politic and opens its boundaries wide.

Acknowledgement

I thank the audiences at Central European University, Loughborough University, Durham University, Leeds University and Oxford University who provided challenging responses to earlier drafts of this article. The two anonymous reviewers provided insightful and helpful comments. I also thank Rutvica Andrijasevic who was a superb editor and, beyond discovering an early version of this article languishing in my hard disk, she provided a perceptive reading and precise comments. I am also grateful to Bridget Anderson for her close reading of an earlier draft and very useful comments. I am most grateful to Vicki Squire who provided insightful and incisive criticisms of a late draft. Responding to her comments made it undoubtedly a much stronger article.

About the Author

Engin F. Isin holds a Chair in Citizenship and Professor of Politics in *Politics and International Studies* (POLIS) at the Faculty of Social Sciences, the Open University. He is also director of the Centre for Citizenship, Identities, Governance (CCIG) at the Faculty of Social Sciences. He is the author of *Cities Without Citizens: Modernity of the City as a Corporation* (Montreal: Black Rose Books, 1992), *Citizenship and Identity* with Patricia K. Wood (London: Sage, 1999) and *Being Political: Genealogies of Citizenship* (Minneapolis: University of Minnesota Press, 2002). He has written numerous journal articles and book chapters as well as delivering public lectures. He has co-edited with Bryan S. Turner and Peter Nyers, *Citizenship Between Past and Future* (London: Routledge, 2008) and with Greg Nielsen, *Acts of Citizenship* (London: Zed, 2008). His latest edited book *Recasting the Social in Citizenship*

(University of Toronto Press, 2008) is about bridging social and political struggles over citizenship.

References

Aleinikoff, T.A. and Klusmeyer, D.B. (eds.) (2000) *From Migrants to Citizens: Membership in a Changing World*. Washington DC: Carnegie Endowment for International Peace.

Archibugi, D. (2008) *The Global Commonwealth of Citizens: Toward Cosmopolitan Democracy*. Princeton, NJ: Princeton University Press.

Arendt, H. (1951) *The Origins of Totalitarianism*. New York: Harcourt Brace Jovanovich.

Arendt, H. (1958) *The Human Condition*. Chicago, IL: University of Chicago Press.

Arendt, H. (1969) On violence. *Crises of the Republic*. New York: Harcourt Brace Jovanovich, pp. 105–198.

Arendt, H. (2005) Understanding and politics. *Essays in Understanding, 1930–1954: Formation, Exile, and Totalitarianism*. New York: Schocken Books, pp. 307–327.

Bakhtin, M. (1993) *Toward a Philosophy of the Act*. Austin, TX: University of Texas Press.

Balibar, E. (2004) *We, the People of Europe?: Reflections on Transnational Citizenship*. Princeton, NJ: Princeton University Press.

Bassel, L. (2008) Citizenship as interpellation: Refugee women and the state. *Government & Opposition* 43(2): 293–314.

Bauböck, R. (1994) *Transnational Citizenship: Membership and Rights in International Migration*. Aldershot Brookfield, UK: E. Elgar.

Beneduce, R. (2008) Undocumented bodies, burned identities: Refugees, Sans Papiers, Harraga – When things fall apart. *Social Science Information* 47(4): 505–527.

Benhabib, S. (2004) *The Rights of Others: Aliens, Residents and Citizens*. Cambridge: Cambridge University Press.

Bennett, J.F. (1995) *The Act Itself*. Oxford: Clarendon Press.

Bigo, D. (2002) Security and immigration: Toward a critique of the government of unease. *Alternatives*, Special Issue: 63–92.

Black, A. (1984) *Guilds and Civil Society in European Political Thought from the Twelfth Century to the Present*. Ithaca, NY: Cornell University Press.

Body-Gendrot, S. and Martiniello, M. (2000) *Minorities in European Cities: The Dynamics of Social Integration and Social Exclusion at the Neighbourhood Level*. Basingstoke, UK: Macmillan.

Butler, J. (1988) Performative acts and gender constitution: An essay in phenomenology and feminist theory. *Theatre Journal* 40(4): 519–531.

Castles, S. and Davidson, A. (2000) *Citizenship and Migration: Globalization and the Politics of Belonging*. New York: Routledge.

Crosby, J.F. (1990) Speech act theory and phenomenology. In: A. Burkhardt (ed.) *Speech Acts, Meaning, and Intentions: Critical Approaches to the Philosophy of John R. Searle*. Berlin, Germany: W. de Gruyter, pp. 62–88.

DuBois, J.M. (1995) *Judgement and Sachverhalt: An Introduction to Adolf Reinach's Phenomenological Realism*. Dordrecht, The Netherlands: Kluwer Academic Publishers.

Dubois, L. (2000) *La République Métissée*: Citizenship, colonialism, and the borders of French history. *Cultural Studies* 14(1): 15–34.

386   Isin

Fahrmeir, A. (2007) *Citizenship: The Rise and Fall of a Modern Concept*. New Haven, CO: Yale University Press.

Falk, R. (2000) The decline of citizenship in an era of globalization. *Citizenship Studies* 4(1): 5–17.

Ferrera, M. (2003) European integration and national social citizenship changing boundaries, new structuring? *Comparative Political Studies* 36(6): 611–652.

Flores, W.V. and Benmayor, R. (1997) *Latino Cultural Citizenship: Claiming Identity, Space, and Rights*. Boston, MA: Beacon Press.

Freeden, M. (2005) What should the 'Political' in political theory explore? *Journal of Political Philosophy* 13(2): 113–134.

Frug, G.E. (1980) The city as a legal concept. *Harvard Law Review* 93(6): 1057–1154.

García Canclini, N. (2001) *Consumers and Citizens: Globalization and Multicultural Conflicts*. Minneapolis, MN: University of Minnesota Press.

Gardner, J.F. (1993) *Being a Roman Citizen*. London: Routledge.

Hansen, R. and Weil, P. (2000) *Towards a European Nationality: Citizenship, Immigration and Nationality Law in the EU*. Basingstoke, UK: Macmillan.

Heater, D.B. (1990) *Citizenship: The Civic Ideal in World History, Politics, and Education*. London: Longman Group.

Hutchings, K. and Dannreuther, R. (eds.) (1999) *Cosmopolitan Citizenship*. New York: St. Martin's Press.

Huysmans, J. (2006) *The Politics of Insecurity: Fear, Migration, and Asylum in the EU*. London: Routledge.

Huysmans, J., Dobson, A. and Prokhovnik, R. (eds.) (2006) *The Politics of Protection: Sites of Insecurity and Political Agency*. London: Routledge.

Isin, E.F. (2002a) *Being Political: Genealogies of Citizenship*. Minneapolis, MN: University of Minnesota Press.

Isin, E.F. (2002b) Citizenship after orientalism. In: E.F. Isin and B.S. Turner (eds.) *Handbook of Citizenship Studies*. London: Sage, pp. 117–128.

Isin, E.F. (2005) Engaging, being, political. *Political Geography* 24: 373–387.

Isin, E.F. (2007) City.State: Critique of scalar thought. *Citizenship Studies* 11(2): 211–228.

Isin, E.F. (2008) Theorizing acts of citizenship. In: E.F. Isin and G.M. Nielsen (eds.) *Acts of Citizenship*. London: Zed Books.

Isin, E.F. and Rygiel, K. (2007) Abject spaces: Frontiers, zones, camps. In: E. Dauphinee and C. Masters (eds.) *Logics of Biopower and the War on Terror*. Basingstoke, UK: Palgrave, pp. 181–203.

Isin, E.F. and Siemiatycki, M. (2002) Making space for mosques: Claiming urban citizenship. In: S. Razack (ed.) *Race, Space and the Law: The Making of a White Settler Society*. Toronto, Canada: Between the Lines, pp. 185–209.

Isin, E.F. and Turner, B.S. (eds.) (2002) *Handbook of Citizenship Studies*. London: SAGE.

Isin, E.F. and Wood, P.K. (1999) *Citizenship and Identity*. London: Sage.

Jacobson, D. (1996) *Rights Across Borders: Immigration and the Decline of Citizenship*. Baltimore, MD: The Johns Hopkins University Press.

Linklater, A. (1998) Cosmopolitan citizenship. *Citizenship Studies* 2(1): 23–41.

Mann, M. (1987) Ruling class strategies and citizenship. *Sociology* 21(3): 339–354.

Manville, P.B. (1990) *The Origins of Citizenship in Ancient Athens*. Princeton, NJ: Princeton University Press.

Marshall, T.H. (1949) Citizenship and social class. In: G. Shafir (ed.) *The Citizenship Debates: A Reader*. Minneapolis, MN: University of Minnesota Press, pp. 93–111.

McNevin, A. (2006) Political belonging in a neoliberal era: The struggle of the San-Papiers. *Citizenship Studies* 10(2): 135–151.

Nietzsche, F. (1881) *Daybreak: Thoughts on the Prejudices of Morality*, Translated by R.J. Hollingdale. Cambridge: Cambridge University Press, 1982.

Nyers, P. (2003) Abject cosmopolitanism: The politics of protection in the anti-deportation movement. *Third World Quarterly* 24(6): 1069–1093.

OECD. (2009) International migration outlook 2009, Paris, http://www.oecd.org/els/migration/imo, accessed 6 July 2009.

Ossman, S. (2007) Introduction. In: S. Ossman (ed.) *Places We Share: Migration, Subjectivity, and Global Mobility*. Lanham, MD: Lexington, pp. 1–16.

Parsons, T. and Shils, E.A. (eds.) (1959) *Toward a General Theory of Action*. Cambridge, MA: Harvard University Press.

Penninx, R. (2004) *Citizenship in European Cities: Immigrants, Local Politics and Integration Policies*. Aldershot, UK: Ashgate.

Poggi, G. (1978) *The Development of the Modern State: A Sociological Introduction*. Stanford, CA: Stanford University Press.

Poggi, G. (1990) *The State: Its Nature, Development, and Prospects*. Cambridge: Polity Press.

Rancière, J. (2004) Who is the subject of the rights of man? *The South Atlantic Quarterly* 103(2/3): 297–310.

Reinach, A. (1983) The apriori foundations of civil law. *Aletheia* 3: 1–142.

Reynolds, S. (1997) *Kingdoms and Communities in Western Europe, 900–1300*, 2nd edn. Oxford: Oxford University Press.

Rodríguez, E.G. (2003) 'We need your support, but the struggle is primarily ours': On representation, migration and the Sans Papiers movement. *Feminist Review* 77: 152–156.

Sartre, J.-P. (1957) *Being and Nothingness: An Essay on Phenomenological Ontology*, Translated by H.E. Barnes. London: Methuen.

Sassen, S. (1996) Whose city is it? Globalization and the formation of new claims. *Public Culture* 8: 205–223.

Schattle, H. (2008) *The Practices of Global Citizenship*. Lanham, MD: Rowman & Littlefield.

Scholtz, C.S. (2006) *Negotiating Claims: The Emergence of Indigenous Land Claim Negotiation Policies in Australia, Canada, New Zealand, and the United States*. New York; London: Routledge.

Schuck, P.H. (1998) *Citizens, Strangers, and in-Betweens: Essays on Immigration and Citizenship*. Boulder, CO: Westview Press.

Searle, J.R. (1969) *Speech Acts: An Essay in the Philosophy of Language*. Cambridge: Cambridge University Press.

Sherwin-White, A.N. (1973) *The Roman Citizenship*, 2nd edn. Oxford: Oxford University Press.

Smith, B. (1990) Towards a history of speech act theory. In: A. Burkhardt (ed.) *Speech Acts, Meaning, and Intentions: Critical Approaches to the Philosophy of John R. Searle*. Berlin, Germany: W. de Gruyter, pp. 29–61.

Smith, R.M. (1997) *Civic Ideals: Conflicting Visions of Citizenship in US History*. New Haven, CT: Yale University Press.

388   Isin

Soysal, Y. (1994) *Limits of Citizenship: Migrants and Postnational Membership in Europe.* Chicago, IL: University of Chicago Press.

Soysal, Y. (1997) Changing parameters of citizenship and claims-making: Organized Islam in European public spheres. *Theory and Society* 26(4): 509–521.

Stout, R. (2005) *Action.* Montreal, Canada and Kingston, UK: McGill-Queen's University Press.

Strayer, J.R. (1970) *On the Medieval Origins of the Modern State.* Princeton, NJ: Princeton University Press.

Torpey, J.C. (2000) *The Invention of the Passport: Surveillance, Citizenship, and the State.* Cambridge: Cambridge University Press.

Tully, J. (2002) Political philosophy as a critical activity. *Political Theory* 30(4): 533–555.

Turner, B.S. (1990) Outline of a theory of citizenship. *Sociology* 24(2): 189–217.

Turner, B.S. (1993) Contemporary problems in the theory of citizenship. In: B.S. Turner (ed.) *Citizenship and Social Theory.* London: Sage.

Ware, R. (1973) Acts and action. *The Journal of Philosophy* 70(13): 403–418.

Weber, M. (1921a) *Economy and Society: An Outline of Interpretive Sociology,* Translated by G. Roth and C. Wittich. Berkeley, CA: University of California Press, 1978.

Weber, M. (1921b) *The City.* New York: Free Press, 1958.

Yegenoglu, M. (2005) Cosmopolitanism and nationalism in a globalized world. *Ethnic and Racial Studies* 28(1): 103–131.

Young, I.M. (1989) Polity and group difference: A critique of the ideal of universal citizenship. *Ethics* 99(January): 250–274.

Young, I.M. (1990) *Justice and the Politics of Difference.* Princeton, NJ: Princeton University Press.

Žižek, S. (2005) Against human rights. *New Left Review* 34(July – August): 115–131.

[15]

Mutations in Citizenship

Aihwa Ong

Abstract Mutations in citizenship are crystallized in an ever-shifting landscape shaped by the flows of markets, technologies, and populations. We are moving beyond the citizenship-versus-statelessness model. First, the elements of citizenship (rights, entitlements, etc.) are becoming disarticulated from each other, and becoming re-articulated with universalizing criteria of neoliberalism and human rights. Such 'global assemblages' define zones of political entitlements and claims. Second, the space of the 'assemblage', rather than the national terrain, becomes the site for political mobilizations by diverse groups in motion. Three contrasting configurations are presented. In the EU zone, unregulated markets and migrant flows challenge liberal citizenship. In Asian zones, foreigners who display self-enterprising *savoire faire* gain rights and benefits of citizenship. In camps of the disenfranchised or displaced, sheer survival becomes the ground for political claims. Thus, particular constellations shape specific problems and resolutions to questions of contemporary living, further disarticulating and deterritorializing aspects of citizenship.

Keywords contemporary living, global assemblages, mutation in citizenship, political spaces

We can trace mutations in citizenship to global flows and their configuration of new spaces of entangled possibilities. An ever-shifting landscape shaped by the flows of markets, technologies, and populations challenges the notion of citizenship tied to the terrain and imagination of a nation-state (Anderson 1991[1983]). Mobile markets, technologies, and populations interact to shape social spaces in which mutations in citizenship are crystallized. The different elements of citizenship (rights, entitlements, etc.), once assumed to go together, are becoming disarticulated from one another, and re-articulated with universalizing forces and standards. So while in theory political rights depend on membership in a nation-state, in practice, new entitlements are being realized through situated mobilizations and claims in milieus of globalized contingency.

New connections among citizenship elements and mobile forms suggest that we have moved beyond the idea of citizenship as a protected status in a nation-state, and as a condition opposed to the condition of statelessness (Arendt 1998[1958]). Binary oppositions between citizenship and statelessness, and between national territoriality and its absence, are not useful for thinking about emergent spaces and novel combinations of globalizing and situated variables. For instance, market-driven state practices fragment the national terrain into zones of hypergrowth. These spaces are plugged into transnational networks of markets, technology, and expertise.

Meanwhile, strict discriminations between the citizens and foreigners are dropped in favor of the pursuit of human capital. Such modes of governing engender a checkerboard patterning of the national terrain, thus producing an effect of graduated or variegated sovereignty (Ong, 2000). Some sites and zones are invested with more political resources than others. Meanwhile, rights and entitlements once associated with all citizens are becoming linked to

500 *Theory, Culture & Society 23(2–3)*

neoliberal criteria, so that entreprenuerial expatriates come to share in the rights and benefits once exclusively claimed by citizens. The difference between having and not having citizenship is becoming blurred as the territorialization of entitlements is increasingly challenged by deterritorialized claims beyond the state.

Universalizing market interests, technologies, and NGOs become articulated with citizenship orders, creating new sites for the making of new claims for resources from state as well as non-state institutions.

We used to think of different dimensions of citizenship – rights, entitlements, a state, territoriality, etc. – as more or less tied together. Increasingly, some of these components are becoming disarticulated from each other, and articulated with diverse universalizing norms defined by markets, neoliberal values, or human rights. At the same time, diverse mobile populations (expatriates, refugees, migrant workers) can claim rights and benefits associated with citizenship, even as many citizens come to have limited or contingent protections within their own countries. Thus, the (re)combinations of globalizing forces and situated elements produce distinctive environments in which citizens, foreigners, and asylum-seekers make political claims through pre-existing political membership as well as on the grounds of universalizing criteria.

Given this scenario of shifting 'global assemblages' (Ong and Collier, 2005), the sites of citizenship mutations are not defined by conventional geography. The space of the assemblage, rather than the territory of the nation-state, is the site for new political mobilizations and claims. In sites of emergence, a spectrum of mobile and excluded populations articulates rights and claims in universalizing terms of neoliberal criteria or human rights. Specific problematizations and resolutions to diverse regimes of living cannot be predetermined in advance. For instance, in the EU zone, unregulated markets and migrant flows threaten protections associated with liberal traditions. In emerging Asian sites, the embrace of self-enterprising values has made citizenship rights and benefits contingent upon individual market performance. In camps of the disenfranchised or displaced, bare life becomes the ground for political claims, if not for citizenship, then for the right to survive. In short, instead of all citizens enjoying a unified bundle of citizenship rights, we have a shifting political landscape in which heterogeneous populations claim diverse rights and benefits associated with citizenship, as well as universalizing criteria of neoliberal norms or human rights.

Market Bloc and Political Liberalism

In the West, the European Union has been one of the most ambitious attempts to form a market zone by assembling various polities and cultures. With the rapid expansion of the bloc, the articulation of market interests with political rights has crystallized long-standing ambivalence over the erosion of cultural traditions and liberal norms associated with postwar European citizenship. In the region, global market forces and neoliberal criteria have come to articulate entrenched political norms and entitlements. For instance, opening markets to migrant labor – guest workers and illegal aliens – has ignited fierce debates about the integration of diverse foreign communities. On the one hand, there is talk about the need to balance diverse immigrant populations of non-European origins with an imaginary of European civilization. On the other, pro-human rights movements talk about 'disaggregating' citizenship into different bundles of rights and benefits, so that European states can differently incorporate migrants and non-citizens. Such bundles of limited benefits and civil rights thus constitute a form of partial citizenship, or 'postnational' political membership for migrant workers (Soysal, 1994). This political resolution, it is argued, can accommodate cultural diversity without undermining European liberal democracy and the universals of individual civil rights. But ambivalence remains, as a strong groundswell against the possible inclusion of Muslim Turkey in the bloc has fueled resistance to EU expansion.

Another dimension of the articulation between citizenship and deregulated markets is widely viewed as a threat to what Jürgen Habermas has called the 'democratic achievements of European societies' – inclusive systems of social security, social norms regarding class and gender, investment in public social services, rejection of the death penalty, and so on. To

Problematizing Global Knowledge – Citizenship/The Political/Global Sovereignty **501**

counter the market-generated 'democratic deficit' in public life, Habermas calls for the creation of a Europe-wide public sphere and constitution that can give symbolic weight to the shared political culture underpinned by the cluster of European welfare features (Habermas, 2001). The spring 2005 French and Dutch votes against the ratification of the existing European constitution delivered powerful statements about the primacy of national interests over the unity to be wrought through neoliberal policies. The rejection of the constitution by major members reflects popular sentiments against the widespread adoption of market-based criteria, as well as a positive affirmation of national regimes that preserve elements of social citizenship and protection for their people. There is now profound doubt about the feasibility of a Europe-wide solidarity built primarily on principles of market efficiency and competitiveness.

Zones of Entitlement

In contrast to the Euro zone, emergent sites of growth in Asia currently display less ambivalence over the adoption of neoliberal values in policies shaping citizenship. These sites recognize that articulation with transnational networks and global professionals is crucial for their emergence as centers of global capitalism. Transnational itineraries and practices enhance the capacity of professionals and investors to negotiate national spaces, while the desire for talented actors has induced changes in immigration laws. Complex affiliations by elite mobile actors allow for temporary, multiple, and partial ascription, thus creating conditions for expatriate populations to claim citizenship-like entitlements.

The concept of 'flexible citizenship' describes maneuvers of mobile subjects who respond fluidly and opportunistically to dynamic borderless market conditions. Global markets induce such activities, so that 'flexibility, migration, and relocations, instead of being coerced or resisted, have become practices to strive for rather than stability' (Ong, 1999: 19). Furthermore, nation-states seeking wealth-bearing and talented foreigners adjust immigration laws to favor elite migrant subjects. Thus a new synergy between global capitalism and commercialized citizenship creates milieus where market-based norms articulate the norms of citizenship.

This premium on flexible, self-enterprising subjects originated in advanced democracies that had steadily adopted market-driven rationality in politics. Such neoliberal ideas stem from Frederic von Hayek's theory of the *homo economicus* as an instrumentalist figure forged in the effervescent conditions of market competition. The ideas of individual economic agency as the most efficient form for distributing public resources were embraced under the 'neo-conservative' policies of Thatcherism and Reaganomics.

This shift toward a neoliberal technology of governing holds that the security of citizens, their well-being and quality of life, are increasingly dependent on their own capacities as free individuals to confront globalized insecurities by making calculations and investments in their lives.

For instance, in Tony Blair's New Britannica, citizens are generally governed 'through freedom', or an inducement for formally free subjects to make calculative choices on their own behalf. Government is no longer interested in taking care of every citizen, but wants him/her to act as a free subject who self-actualizes and relies on autonomous action to confront globalized insecurities. There is thus a fundamental shift in the ethics of subject formation, or the ethics of citizenship, as governing becomes concerned less with the social management of the population (biopolitics) than with individual self-governing (ethico-politics) (Rose, 1999). Such ethics are framed as an animation of various capacities of individual freedom, expressed both in the citizen's freedom from state protection and guidance, as well as freedom to make choices as a self-maximizing individual. In the USA, administrative practices that govern through the aspirations of subjects especially target the urban poor, immigrants, and refugees who are viewed as less capable of self-improvement. But as neoliberal values of flexibility, mobility, and entrepreneurialism become ideal qualities of citizenship, they also undermine the democratic achievements of American liberalism based on ideals of equal rights (Ong, 2003). Tensions between neoliberal values of citizens as economic agents, and

502 *Theory, Culture & Society 23(2–3)*

liberal ideals of citizens as defenders of political freedom continue to roil American political life.

Neoliberal ideas and practices migrate and are taken up in new zones of hyper-growth. In democratic, socialist, and authoritarian Asian settings, citizens are urged to be self-enterprising, not only to cope with uncertainties and risks, but also to raise the overall 'human quality' of their societies. Thus, in East and South Asian environments, neoliberal ethics of self-responsible citizenship are linked to social obligations to build the nation. In India and Malaysia, discourses about 'knowledge workers' and 'knowledge society' urge citizens to self-improve in order to develop high-tech industries. In Singapore, the accumulation of intellectual capital as an obligation of citizenship is most extreme. Ordinary citizens are expected to develop new mindsets and build digital capabilities, while professionals are urged to achieve norms of 'techno-preneurial citizenship' or lose out to more skilled and entrepreneurial foreigners and be reduced to a second-class citizenry.

In short, neoliberal values of self-management and self-enterprise have different implications for citizenship, depending on interactions with particular political environments. While the tendency in Britain and the USA is to focus on the self-governing and technologically savvy citizen as a participant in civil society, in Asian growth zones, the discourse of the self-improving and entrepreneurial citizen is linked to 'civic society', or the building of national solidarity. The common feature is that across these diverse milieus, the stakes of citizenship are raised for the majority. Especially in hyper-capitalist zones, those who cannot scale the skills ladder or measure up to the norms of self-governing are increasingly marginalized as deviant or subjects who threaten the security of the globalized milieu. Thus, the articulation of neoliberal criteria and situated citizenship regimes undercuts the protection of citizenship entitlements and blurs political distinctions between citizens and talented foreigners.

Arenas of Political Claims

But the mix of market-opportunism and citizenship has also engendered conditions for greater political activism. In non-democratic countries embracing market-driven policies, new arenas are opening up for ordinary people to claim justice, accountability, and democratic freedoms. The confluence of market forces and digital technologies have pried open cracks in the interstices of highly controlled societies, thus creating conditions for exciting outbursts of popular demands for democracy by ordinary people.

In the Streets

In Southeast Asia, the combined forces of the Asian financial crisis and political instability in the 1990s created an opportunity for the flowering of 'pro-reformasi' movements and nongovernmental organizations in shaping a space of civil society.

In Indonesia, a diversity of humanitarian, non-violent, and women's groups came together to protest state brutality and demand an end to corruption, nepotism, and autocratic rule. In particular, the army-instigated rapes of hundreds of ethnic Chinese women in Indonesia, and the prison beatings of the deputy prime minister in Malaysia, focused public attention on state violence against the human body. In street protests, the cries for reforms are couched less in the language of human rights than articulated in the ethics of culture and religion. Human rights discourses have not been directly useful in negotiations with the state because the human rights regime is viewed as originating in the West, and biased towards Asian countries. Women's groups and religious NGOs frame problems of state violence as violations of humanity, as understood in local religious terms of compassion, reciprocity, and forgiveness. In Malaysia, the NGO Sisters-in-Islam has gained international fame for their capacity to articulate women's rights in terms of Muslim precepts. Various NGOs and social movements in Southeast Asia not only enact in the streets and media the rights of free citizens to protest state action, but they also challenge entrenched habits of state authoritarianism through the discourse of situated ethics.

In Latin America and India, social movements in the streets have developed at the

Problematizing Global Knowledge – Citizenship/The Political/Global Sovereignty **503**

confluence of urban development and migrant communities. Street demonstrations by the disenfranchised – poor migrants, shantytown dwellers, refugees – articulate an array of civil, political, and social rights. The streets form an arena for the political mobilization of the poor to claim public resources such as urban housing, water, and electricity as a kind of substantive citizenship (Holston, 1993). There is the perception that citizenship encoded in law is no guarantee of protection for the marginalized. In many cases, market intrusions and displacement have created arenas for the activation of citizenship in demanding state delivery of resources and justice. Democratic values are becoming performed in public spaces to challenge authoritarian rule, corruption, and the lack of access to rights and benefits for excluded populations.

In Cyber Space

Markets and electronic technology have also opened up other venues of political performance and claims. For a socialist market-economy society like China, the internet is emerging as a space of citizenship formation, but also as a space of government surveillance. Online commentaries, criticisms, and mockery of state policies have flourished in the relatively democratic and elusive cyberspace. A cyberpublic made up of millions of online Chinese uses the internet for accessing foreign news, spreading stories of injustice, and promoting alterative cultural forms. A college student called 'the Stainless Steel Mouse' has written articles spoofing the pomposity of the Chinese Communist Party. Other cyber rebels include 'Reporters without Borders' who seek to expose hidden abuses of peasants by local authorities and the new rich, protest against injustices and corruption, and demand accountability from the government. In response, state anti-cyber interventions have closed down certain dissident websites, blocked access to some foreign news websites, and tracked down and punished dissidents where possible. But the surveillance of the cyberpublic space is very chancy, and 'netizens' has become a term to index this new style of democracy in action.

The cyber space is a new site for mapping out a war of positions, and for playing a cat-and-mouse game over the freedom of information essential to democratic citizenship. The Chinese nexus between market reforms, web technology, and dissidents has enabled criticisms more focused on the lack of freedom of political expression under authoritarian rule than on attacking neoliberal values. In contrast to the assemblage of factors in Europe that induce ordinary citizens to resist unregulated market forces, in China, the confluence of markets, technology and activism is a space that enables people to perform the kind of democratic citizenship that is denied in society at large.

The cyber space, however, can also be the site for the articulation of overweening ethnic power that exceeds the nation-state. In diaspora, transnational groups such as overseas Chinese or ethnic Indians have increasingly turned to the internet to construct a web-based 'global citizenship'. One such internet-based group is 'Global Huaren' (Global Chinese), which acts as a cyber-watchdog, condemning government actions anywhere in the world that are construed to be against co-ethnics. There are, however, dangers when such ethnic networks seek to leverage their cyberpower vis-à-vis a specific state. The outcome is a kind of borderless citizenship based on claims of global ethnicity that is not answerable to any overarching authority.

Sheer Survival

Another arena of political mobilization is the space of endangerment and neglect. Here the question is whether political resolutions to the plight of imperiled or abject bodies are framed in terms of the binary opposition between citizenship and statelessness. Giorgio Agamben draws a stark distinction between citizens who enjoy juridical-legal rights and excluded groups who dwell in 'a zone of indistinction'. Only the erasure of the division between People (political body) and people (excluded bodies), he maintains, can restore humanity to the globally excluded who have been denied citizenship (Agamben 1998: 177, 180). Such views are reflected in claims that the human rights regime is capable of transforming millions of people

504 *Theory, Culture & Society 23(2–3)*

enduring a bare existence in Africa, Latin America, and Asia into citizens, thus actualizing their humanity. But the rhetoric of ethical globalization operates at too vast a scale to deal with specific milieus of exclusion and endangerment. Furthermore, the focus on citizenship and human rights gives short shrift to other modes of ethical reflection and argumentation. It is by no means clear that the right to survival will everywhere be translated into citizenship or merely legitimized on the grounds of common humanity, or relevance to labor markets. Let me briefly cite three situations of interventions on behalf of the injured or threatened body, and their different resolutions in relation to citizenship.

In recent decades, health-based claims have become an important part of citizenship rights in the West. In the aftermath of the Chernobyl accident in the Ukraine, sufferers claimed biomedical resources and social equity, thus giving rise to a notion of 'biological citizenship' (Petryna, 2002). In France, migrants have recently made health the ground for claiming asylum. Didier Fassin argues that the suffering body of the HIV-infected migrant reverses public perception of his biopolitical otherness rooted in race and alien status. Increasingly, some form of legal recognition is awarded in the name of humanity, i.e. the right to a healthy body, regardless of the citizenship of the patient (Fassin, 2001).

The explosive growth of NGOs is an index of the humanitarian industry that seeks to represent the varied interests of the politically dispossessed. Increasingly, such voluntary groups are shaped by specific interests, affiliations, and ethics, forming themselves into socio-political groups in order to make particular claims on states and corporations. Thus, the language of universal human rights is often superseded by more specific categories finely tuned to the criteria of state or philanthropic organizations. In the non-state administration of excluded humanity, groups and individuals are sorted into various categories, in relation to particular needs, prioritized interests, and potential affiliations with powers-that-be. These are 'counter-politics of sheer life' – a situated form of political mobilization that involves ethical claims to resources articulated in terms of needs as living beings (Collier and Lakoff, 2005: 29).

The politics of sheer life is emerging in Southeast Asia, where a vast female migrant population – working as maids, factory workers, or prostitutes – is regularly exposed to slave-like conditions. Feminist NGOs invoke not the human rights of female migrants but something more minimal and attainable, i.e. biological survival, or 'biowelfare'. The claims of a healthy and unharmed migrant body are articulated not in terms of a common humanity, but of the dependency of the host society on foreign workers to sustain a high standard of living. NGOs invoke the ethics of reciprocity or at least recognition of economic symbiosis between migrant workers and the affluent employers who feel entitled to their cheap foreign labor. Where citizenship does not provide protection for the migrant worker, the joining of a healthy body and dependency on foreign workers produces a kind of bio-legitimacy that is perhaps a first step toward the recognition of their moral status, but short of human rights.

A simple opposition between territorialized citizenship and deterritorialized human rights is not able to capture the varied assemblages that are the sites of contemporary political claims by a range of residential, expatriate, and migrant actors. The confluence of territorialized and deterritorialized forces forms milieus in which problems of the human are crystallized and problems posed and resolved. Diverse actors invoke not territorialized notions of citizenship, but new claims – postnational, flexible, technological, cyber-based, and biological – as grounds for resources, entitlements, and protection. These various sites and claims attest to the contingent nature of what is at stake in being human today. Such political mobilizations engage but also go beyond human rights in resolution to situated problems of contemporary life. In addition to the nation-state, entities such as corporations and NGOs have become practitioners of humanity, defining and representing varied categories of human beings according to degrees of economic, biopolitical, and moral worthiness. Diverse regimes of living are in play. In short, global assemblages crystallize specific problems and resolutions to questions of contemporary living, thus further disarticulating and deterritorializing aspects of citizenship.

Problematizing Global Knowledge – Citizenship/The Political/Global Sovereignty **505**

References

Agamben, G. (1998) *Homo Sacer: Sovereign Power and Bare Life*, trans. Daniel Heller-Roazen. Stanford, CA: Stanford University Press.

Anderson, B. (1991[1983]) *Imagined Communities*, 2nd edition. London: Verso.

Arendt, H. (1998[1958]) *The Human Condition*, with an Introduction by Margaret Canovaan, 2nd edition. Chicago, IL: University of Chicago Press.

Collier, S.J. and A. Lakoff (2005) 'Regimes of Living', in A. Ong and S.J. Collier (eds) *Global Assemblages: Technology, Politics, and Ethics as Anthropological Problems*. Malden, MA: Blackwell.

Fassin, D. (2001) 'The Biopolitics of Otherness', *Anthropology Today* 17(1): 3–23.

Habermas, J. (2001) 'Why Europe Needs a Constitution', *New Left Review* 11 (Sept–Oct): 5–26.

Holston, J. (1993) 'Introduction', in J. Holston (ed.) *Cities and Citizenship*. Durham, NC: Duke University Press.

Ong, A. (1999) *Flexible Citizenship: The Cultural Logics of Transnationality*. Durham, NC: Duke University Press.

Ong, A. (2000) 'Graduated Sovereignty in Southeast Asia', *Theory, Culture & Society* 17(4): 55–75.

Ong, A. (2003) *Buddha is Hiding: Refugees, Citizenship, the New America*. Berkeley: University of California Press.

Ong, A. and S.J. Collier (eds) (2005) *Global Assemblages: Technology, Politics, and Ethics as Anthropological Problems*. Malden, MA: Blackwell.

Petryna, A. (2002) *Life Exposed: Biological Citizens after Chernobyl*. Princeton, NJ: Princeton University Press.

Rose, N. (1999) *Powers of Freedom: Reframing Political Thought*. Cambridge: Cambridge University Press.

Soysal, Y. (1994) *The Limits of Citizenship: Migrants and Postnational Membership in Europe*. Chicago, IL: University of Chicago Press.

Aihwa Ong is Professor of Anthropology at the University of California, Berkeley. Recent books include *Flexible Citizenship* (1999, Duke University Press), *Buddha is Hiding* (2003, University of California Press), *Global Assemblages* (2005, Blackwell), and *Neoliberalism as Exception* (forthcoming, Duke University Press).

[16]

The Repositioning of Citizenship: Emergent Subjects and Spaces for Politics

Saskia Sassen*[n]

Abstract:

The two foundational subjects for membership in the modern nation-state, the citizen and the alien, are undergoing significant changes in the current moment. This becomes particularly evident in certain types of contexts, foremost among which are cities. These can be seen as productive spaces for informal or not-yet-formalized politics and subjects. In this examination of emergent possibilities, I first outline these changes vis-à-vis nationality and citizenship. Second, I dissect notions of national membership in order to create a set of tools for reconstructing citizenship analytically. In the third section, I delineate two key, incipient kinds of repositioned membership: unauthorized yet recognized subjects, and authorized yet unrecognized subjects. Fourth, I situate these repositionings within contemporary currents of citizenship theory. In the final section, I theorize the landscape of the global city as an especially salient site for the repositioning of citizenship in practice. At the scale of the city, and the particular urban space of the global city, there are dynamics that signal the possibilities for a politics of membership that is simultaneously localized and transnational.

Most of the scholarship on citizenship has claimed a necessary connection to the national state. The transformations afoot today raise questions about this proposition insofar as they significantly alter those conditions which in the past fed that articulation between citizenship and the national state. The context for this possible alteration is defined by two major, partly interconnected conditions. One is the change in the position and institutional features of national states since the 1980s resulting from various forms of globalization. These range from economic privatization and deregulation to the increased prominence of the international human rights regime. The second is the emergence of multiple actors, groups, and communities partly strengthened by these transformations in the state and increasingly unwilling automatically to identify with a nation as represented by the state.

---

* This text is based on my keynote lecture from the March 7, 2002 conference of the *Berkeley Journal of Sociology*, "Race and Ethnicity in a Global Context," at the University of California, Berkeley. I would like to thank Ryan Centner at Berkeley and Emiko Kurotsu at Chicago for their help with the production of this essay.

5   SASSEN: REPOSITIONING OF CITIZENSHIP

Addressing the question of citizenship against these transformations entails a specific stance. It is quite possible to posit that at the most abstract or formal level not much has changed over the last century in the essential features of citizenship. The theoretical ground from which I address the issue is that of the historicity and the embeddedness of both categories, citizenship and the national state, rather than their purely formal features. Each of these has been constructed in elaborate and formal ways. And each has evolved historically as a tightly packaged bundle of what were in fact often rather diverse elements. The dynamics at work today are destabilizing these particular bundlings and bringing to the fore the fact itself of that bundling and its particularity. Through their destabilizing effects, these dynamics are producing operational and rhetorical openings for the emergence of new types of political subjects and new spatialities for politics.

More broadly, the destabilizing of national state-centered hierarchies of legitimate power and allegiance has enabled a multiplication of non-formalized or only partly formalized political dynamics and actors. These signal a deterritorializing of citizenship practices and identities, and of discourses about loyalty and allegiance. Finally, specific transformations inside the national state have directly and indirectly altered particular features of the institution of citizenship. These transformations are not predicated necessarily on deterritorialization or locations for the institution outside the national state as is key to conceptions of postnational citizenship, and hence are usefully distinguished from current notions of postnational citizenship. I will refer to these as denationalized forms of citizenship.

Analytically, I seek to understand how various transformations entail continuities or discontinuities in the basic institutional form. That is to say, where do we see continuities in the formal bundle of rights at the heart of the institution and where do we see movement towards postnational and/or denationalized features of citizenship? And where might as yet informal citizenship practices engender formalizations of new types of rights? Particular attention goes to several specific issues that capture these features. One of these is the relationship between citizenship and nationality and the evolution of the latter towards something akin to "effective" nationality rather than as "allegiance" to one state or exclusively formal nationality. A later section examines the mix of distinct elements that actually make up the category of citizenship in today's highly developed countries. Far from being a unitary category or a mere legal status, these diverse elements can be contradictory. One of my assumptions here is that the destabilizing impact of globalization contributes to accentuate the distinctiveness of each of these elements. A case in point is the growing tension between the legal form and the

BERKELEY JOURNAL OF SOCIOLOGY

normative project towards enhanced inclusion as various minorities and disadvantaged sectors gain visibility for their claim-making. Critical here is the failure in most countries to achieve "equal" citizenship—that is, not just a formal status but an enabling condition.

The remaining sections begin to theorize these issues with a view towards specifying incipient and typically not formalized developments in the institution of citizenship. Informal practices and political subjects not quite fully recognized as such can nonetheless function as part of the political landscape. Undocumented immigrants who are long-term residents engage in practices that are the same as those of formally defined citizens in the routines of daily life; this produces an informal social contract between these undocumented immigrants and the community. Subjects who are by definition categorized as non-political, such as "housewives" may actually have considerable political agency and be emergent political subjects. Insofar as citizenship is at least partly shaped by the conditions within which it is embedded, conditions that have today changed in certain very specific and also general ways, we may well be seeing a corresponding set of changes in the institution itself. These may not yet be formalized and some may never become fully formalized. Further, social constructions that mark individuals, such as race and ethnicity, may well become destabilized by these developments in both the institution of citizenship and the nation-state. Generally, the analysis in this paper suggests that we might see an unbounding of existing types of subjects, particularly dominant ones such as the citizen-subject, the alien, and the racialized subject.

A concluding section argues that many of these transformations in the broader context and in the institution itself become legible in today's large cities. Perhaps the most evolved type of site for these transformations is the global city.[1] In this process, the global city is reconfigured as a partly denationalized space that enables a partial reinvention of citizenship. This reinvention takes the institution away from questions of nationality narrowly defined and towards the enactment of a large array of particular interests, from protests against police brutality and globalization to sexual preference politics and house-squatting by anarchists. I interpret this as a move towards citizenship practices that revolve around claiming rights to the city. These are not exclusively or necessarily urban practices. But it is especially in large cities that we see simultaneously some of the most extreme inequalities as well as conditions enabling these citizenship practices. In global cities, these practices also contain the possibility of directly engaging strategic forms of power, a fact which I interpret as

---

[1] For the fullest treatment of my concept of the global city, see the updated second edition of *The Global City: New York, London, Tokyo* (Sassen 2001).

I. Citizenship and nationality

In its narrowest definition citizenship describes the legal relationship between the individual and the polity. This relation can in principle assume many forms, in good part depending on the definition of the polity. Thus, in Europe this definition of the polity was originally the city, both in ancient and in medieval times. But it is the evolution of polities along the lines of state formation that gave citizenship in the west its full institutionalized and formalized character and that made nationality a key component of citizenship.

Today the terms citizenship and nationality both refer to the national state. In a technical legal sense, while essentially the same concept, each term reflects a different legal framework. Both identify the legal status of an individual in terms of state membership. But citizenship is largely confined to the national dimension, while nationality refers to the international legal dimension in the context of an interstate system. The legal status entails the specifics of whom the state recognizes as a citizen and the formal basis for the rights and responsibilities of the individual in relation to the state. International law affirms that each state may determine who will be considered a citizen of that state (see Hague Convention 1954). Domestic laws about who is a citizen vary significantly across states and so do the definitions of what it entails to be a citizen. Even within Europe, let alone worldwide, there are marked differences in how citizenship is articulated and hence how non-citizens are defined.

The aggressive nationalism and territorial competition among European states in the eighteenth, nineteenth and well into the twentieth centuries made the concept of dual nationality generally undesirable, incompatible with individual loyalties and destabilizing of the international order. Absolute state authority over a territory and its nationals could not easily accommodate dual nationality. Indeed, we see the development of a series of mechanisms aimed at preventing or counteracting the common causes for dual nationality (Marrus 1985). This negative perception of dual nationality continued into the first half of the twentieth century and well into the 1960s. There were no international accords on dual nationality. The main effort by the international system remained rooting out the causes of dual nationality by means of multilateral codification of the law on the subject (Rubenstein and Adler 2000). It is probably the case that this particular form of the institution of citizenship, centered on exclusive allegiance, reached its highpoint in the twentieth century.

BERKELEY JOURNAL OF SOCIOLOGY 8

The major transformations of the 1980s and 1990s have once again brought conditions for a change in the institution of citizenship and its relation to nationality, and they have brought about changes in the legal content of nationality. Mostly minor formal and non-formal changes are beginning to dilute the particular formalization coming out of European history. The long lasting resistance to dual or multiple nationality is shifting towards a selective acceptance. According to some legal scholars (Spiro 1997; Rubenstein and Adler 2000) in the future dual and multiple nationality will become the norm. Today, more people than ever before have dual nationality (Spiro 1997). Insofar as the importance of nationality is a function of the central role of states in the international system, it is quite possible that a decline in the importance of this role and a proliferation of other actors will affect the value of nationality.

These transformations may give citizenship yet another set of features as it continues to respond to the conditions within which it is embedded (Sassen 1996: Chapter 2). The nationalizing of the institution, which took place over the last several centuries, may today give way to a partial denationalizing. A fundamental dynamic in this regard is the growing articulation of national economies with the global economy and the associated pressures on states to be competitive. Crucial to current notions of competitive states is withdrawal from various spheres of citizenship entitlements, with the possibility of a corresponding dilution of loyalty to the state. Citizens' loyalty may in turn be less crucial to the state today than it was at a time of people-intensive and frequent warfare, with its need for loyal citizen-soldiers (Turner 2000). Masses of troops today can be replaced by technologically intensive methods of warfare. Most importantly, in the highly developed world, warfare has become less significant partly due to economic globalization. Global firms and global markets do not want the rich countries to fight wars among themselves. The "international" project of the most powerful actors on the world stage today is radically different from what it was in the nineteenth and first half of the twentieth centuries.

Many of the dynamics that built economies, polities, and societies in the nineteenth and twentieth centuries contained an articulation between the national scale and the growth of entitlements for citizens. During industrialization, class formation, class struggles, and the advantages of both employers and workers tended to scale at the national level and became identified with state-produced legislation and regulations, entitlements and obligations. The state came to be seen as a key to ensuring the well-being of significant portions of both the working class and the bourgeoisie. The development of welfare states in the twentieth century became a crucial institutional domain for granting entitlements to the poor and the disadvantaged. Today, the growing weight given to notions of the "competitiveness" of states puts pressure on states to cut down on these entitlements. This in turn weakens the reciprocal relationship between the poor and the state (e.g., Munger

9   SASSEN: REPOSITIONING OF CITIZENSHIP

2001). Finally, the growth of unemployment and the fact that many of the young are developing weak ties to the labor market, once thought of as a crucial mechanism for the socialization of young adults, will further weaken the loyalty and sense of reciprocity between these future adults and the state (Roulleau-Berger 2002).

As these trends have come together towards the end of the twentieth century they are contributing to destabilize the meaning of citizenship as it was forged in the nineteenth and much of the twentieth centuries. Economic policies and technical developments we associate with economic globalization have strengthened the importance of cross-border dynamics and reduced that of borders. The associated emphasis on markets has brought into question the foundations of the welfare state. T.H. Marshall (1977 [1950]) and many others saw and continue to see the welfare state as an important ingredient of social citizenship. Today the assumptions of the dominant model of Marshallian citizenship have been severely diluted under the impact of globalization and the ascendance of the market as the preferred mechanism for addressing these social issues. For many critics, the reliance on markets to solve political and social problems is a savage attack on the principles of citizenship. Thus Peter Saunders (1993) argues that citizenship inscribed in the institutions of the welfare state is a buffer against the vagaries of the market and the inequalities of the class system.

The nature of citizenship has also been challenged by a proliferation of old issues that have gained new attention. Among the latter are the question of state membership of aboriginal communities, stateless people, and refugees (Sassen 1999; Knop 2002). All of these have important implications for human rights in relation to citizenship. These social changes in the role of the state, the impact of globalization on states, and the relationship between dominant and subordinate groups also have major implications for questions of identity. "Is citizenship a useful concept for exploring the problems of belonging, identity and personality in the modern world?" (Shotter 1993; Ong 1999: Chapters 1 and 4). Can such a radical change in the conditions for citizenship leave the institution itself unchanged?

II. Deconstructing citizenship

Though often talked about as a single concept and experienced as a unitary institution, citizenship actually describes a number of discrete but related aspects in the relation between the individual and the polity. Current developments are bringing to light and accentuating the distinctiveness of these various aspects, from formal rights to practices and psychological dimensions (see Ong 1996; Bosniak 2000). They make legible the tension between citizenship as a formal legal status and as a normative project or an aspiration. The formal equality granted to all citizens rarely rests on the need for substantive equality in social and

BERKELEY JOURNAL OF SOCIOLOGY 10

even political terms. In brief, current conditions have strengthened the emphasis on rights and aspirations that go beyond the formal legal definition of rights and obligations.

This is mirrored most recently in the reinvigoration of theoretical distinctions: communitarian and deliberative, republican and liberal, feminist, postnational and cosmopolitan notions of citizenship. Insofar as citizenship is a status which articulates legal rights and responsibilities, the mechanisms through which this articulation is shaped and implemented can be analytically distinguished from the status itself and so can the content of the rights. In the medieval cities so admired by Max Weber (1958), it was urban residents themselves who set up the structures through which to establish and thicken their rights in the space of the city. Today it is the national state that provides these mechanisms and it does so for national political space. But these mechanisms may well be changing once again given globalization, the associated changes in the national state, and the ascendance of human rights. In each of these major phases, the actual content and shape of the legal rights and obligations also changed.

Some of these issues can be illustrated through the evolution of equal citizenship over the last few decades. Equal citizenship is central to the modern institution of citizenship. The expansion of equality among citizens has shaped a good part of its evolution in the twentieth century. There is debate as to what brought about the expanded inclusions over this period, most notably the granting of the vote to women. For some (e.g., Karst 2000) it is law itself—and national law—that has been crucial in promoting recognition of exclusions and measures for their elimination. For others (Young 1990; Taylor 1992) politics and identity have been essential because they provide the sense of solidarity necessary for the further development of modern citizenship in the nation-state. Either way, insofar as equality is based on membership, citizenship status forms the basis of an exclusive politics and identity (Walzer 1985; Bosniak 1996).

In a country such as the US, the principle of equal citizenship remains unfulfilled, even after the successful struggles and legal advances of the last five decades (Karst 1997).[2] Groups defined by race, ethnicity, religion, sex, sexual orientation and other "identities," still face various exclusions from full participation in public life notwithstanding formal equality as citizens. Second, because full participation as a citizen rests on a material base (Marshall 1977; Handler 1995) poverty excludes large sectors of the population and the gap is widening. Feminist and race-critical scholarship have highlighted the failure of gender- and race-

---

[2] In Kenneth Karst's interpretation of US law, aliens are "constitutionally entitled to most of the guarantees of equal citizenship, and the Supreme Court has accepted this idea to a modest degree" (Karst 2000: 599; see also fn.20 where he cites cases). Karst also notes that the Supreme Court has not carried this development nearly as far as he might wish.

11 SASSEN: REPOSITIONING OF CITIZENSHIP

neutral conceptions of citizenship, such as legal status, to account for the differences of individuals within communities (Benhabib, Butler, Cornell, and Fraser 1995; Crenshaw, Gotanda, Peller, and Thomas 1996; Delgado and Stefancic 1999; Benhabib 2002). In brief, legal citizenship does not always bring full and equal membership rights. Citizenship is affected by the position of different groups within a nation-state.

Yet it is precisely the position of these different groups that has engendered the practices and struggles that forced changes in the institution of citizenship itself. Thus Kenneth Karst (1997) observes that in the U.S. it was national law that "braided the strands of citizenship"—formal legal status, rights, belonging—into the principle of equal citizenship. This took place through a series of Supreme Court decisions and acts of Congress beginning with the Civil Rights Act of 1964. Karst emphasizes how important these constitutional and legislative instruments are, and that we cannot take citizenship for granted or be complacent about it.

There are two aspects here that matter for my argument. This history of interactions between differential positionings and expanded inclusions signals the possibility that the new conditions of inequality and difference evident today and the new types of claim-making they produce may well bring about further transformations in the institution. Citizenship is partly produced by the practices of the excluded. Secondly, by expanding the formal inclusionary aspect of citizenship, the national state contributed to create some of the conditions that eventually would facilitate key aspects of postnational citizenship. At the same time, insofar as the state itself has undergone significant transformation, notably the changes bundled under the notion of the competitive state, it may reduce the chances that state institutions will do the type of legislative and judiciary work that has led to expanded formal inclusions.

The consequence of these two developments may well be the absence of a lineal progression in the evolution of the institution. The expanding inclusions that we have seen in the US since the 1960s may have produced conditions which make possible forms of citizenship that follow a different trajectory. Furthermore, the pressures of globalization on national states may mean that claim-making will increasingly be directed at other institutions as well. This is already evident in a variety of instances. One example is the decision by first-nation people to go directly to the UN and claim direct representation in international fora, rather than going through the national state. It is also evident in the increasingly institutionalized framework of the international human rights regime and the emergent possibilities for bypassing unilateral state sovereignty.

As the importance of equality in citizenship has grown and become more visible, and as the role of national law to giving presence

BERKELEY JOURNAL OF SOCIOLOGY 12

and voice to hitherto silenced minorities has grown, the tension between the formal status and the normative project of citizenship has also grown. For many, citizenship is becoming a normative project whereby social membership becomes increasingly comprehensive and open ended. Globalization and human rights are further enabling this tension and therewith furthering the elements of a new discourse on rights. These developments signal that the analytic terrain within which we need to place the question of rights, authority and obligations is shifting (Sassen 1996: Chapter 2; Sassen 2003). Some of these issues can be illustrated by two contrasting cases described below.

III. Towards effective nationality and informal citizenship

1) Unauthorized yet recognized

Perhaps one of the more extreme instances of a condition akin to effective as opposed to formal nationality is what has been called the informal social contract that binds undocumented immigrants to their communities of residence (Schuck and Smith 1985). Thus, unauthorized immigrants who demonstrate civic involvement, social deservedness, and national loyalty can argue that they merit legal residency. To make this brief examination more specific, I will focus on one case, undocumented immigrants in the US.

Individuals, even when undocumented immigrants, can move between the multiple meanings of citizenship. The daily practices by undocumented immigrants as part of their daily life in the community where they reside—such as raising a family, schooling children, holding a job—earn them citizenship claims in the US even as the formal status and, more narrowly, legalization may continue to evade them. There are dimensions of citizenship, such as strong community ties and participation in civic activities, which are being enacted informally through these practices. These practices produce an at least partial recognition of them as full social beings. In many countries around the world, including the US, long term undocumented residents often can gain legal residence if they can document the fact of this long term residence and "good conduct." US immigration law recognizes such informal participation as grounds for granting legal residency. For instance, prior to the new immigration law passed in 1996, individuals who could prove seven years of continuous presence, good moral character, and that deportation would be an extreme hardship, were eligible for suspension of deportation, and thus, US residency. NACARA extended the eligibility of this suspension of deportation to some 300,000 Salvadorans and Guatemalans who were unauthorized residents in the US.[3]

---

[3] NACARA is The 1997 Nicaraguan Adjustment and Central American Relief Act. It created an amnesty for 300,000 Salvadorans and Guatemalans to apply for suspension of deportation. This is an immigration remedy that had been eliminated by the Illegal

13 SASSEN: REPOSITIONING OF CITIZENSHIP

The case of undocumented immigrants is, in many ways, a very particular and special illustration of a condition akin to "effective" citizenship and nationality. One way of interpreting this dynamic in the light of the discussion in the preceding sections is to emphasize that it is the fact of the multiple dimensions of citizenship which engenders strategies for legitimizing informal or extra-statal forms of membership (Soysal 1994; Coutin 2000). The practices of these undocumented immigrants are a form of citizenship practices and their identities as members of a community of residence assume some of the features of citizenship identities. Supposedly this could hold even in the communitarian model where the community can decide on whom to admit and whom to exclude, but once admitted, proper civic practices earn full membership.

Further, the practices of migrants, even if undocumented, can contribute to recognition of their rights in countries of origin. During the 1981-92 civil war, Salvadoran migrants even though citizens of El Salvador were directly and indirectly excluded from El Salvador through political violence, enormous economic hardship, and direct persecution (Mahler 1996). They could not enjoy their rights as citizens. After fleeing, many continued to provide support to their families and communities. Further, migrants' remittances became a key factor for El Salvador's economy—as they are for several countries around the world. The government of El Salvador actually began to support the emigrants fight to get residency rights in the US, even joining US based activist organizations in this effort. The Salvadoran government was thus supporting Salvadorans who were the formerly excluded citizens—they needed those remittances to keep coming and they needed the emigrants to stay out of the Salvadoran workforce given high unemployment. Thus the participation of these undocumented migrants in cross-border community, family, and political networks has contributed to increasing recognition of their legal and political rights as Salvadoran citizens (Coutin 2000; Mahler 1996).

According to Coutin (2000) and others, movements between membership and exclusion, and between different dimensions of citizenship, legitimacy and illegitimacy, may be as important as redefinitions of citizenship itself. Given scarce resources the possibility of negotiating the different dimensions of citizenship may well represent an important enabling condition. Undocumented immigrants develop informal, covert, often extra-statal strategies and networks connecting them with communities in sending countries. Hometowns rely on their remittances and their information about jobs in the US. Sending remittances illegally by an unauthorized immigrant can be seen as an act of patriotism, and working as an undocumented can be seen as contributing to the host economy. Multiple interdependencies are thereby established and grounds for claims on the receiving and the

Immigration Reform and Immigrant Responsibility Act in 1996 (see Coutin 2000).

BERKELEY JOURNAL OF SOCIOLOGY 14

originating country can be established even when the immigrants are undocumented and laws are broken (Basch, Glick Schiller, and Blanc-Szanton 1995; Cordero-Guzmán, Smith, Grosfoguel 2001).

2) Authorized yet unrecognized

At perhaps the other extreme of the undocumented immigrant whose practices allow her to become accepted as a member of the political community, is the case of those who are full citizens yet not recognized as political subjects. In an enormously insightful study of Japanese housewives, Robin LeBlanc (1999) finds precisely this combination.

Being a housewife is basically a full-time occupation in Japan and restricts Japanese women's public life in many important ways, both practical and symbolical. A "housewife" in Japan is a person whose very identity is customarily that of a particularistic, non-political actor. Yet, paradoxically, it is also a condition providing these women with a unique vehicle for other forms of public participation, ones where being a housewife is an advantage, one denied to those who might have the qualifications of higher level political life. LeBlanc documents how the housewife has an advantage in the world of local politics or the political life of a local area: she can be trusted precisely because she is a housewife, she can build networks with other housewives, hers is the image of desirable public concern and of a powerful—because believable—critic of mainstream politics.

There is something extremely important in this condition which is shared with women in other cultures and vis-à-vis different issues. For instance, and in a very different register, women emerged as a specific type of political actor during the brutal dictatorships of the 1970s and 1980s in several countries of Latin America. It was precisely their condition as mothers and wives that gave them the clarity and the courage to demand justice and to demand bread and to do so confronting armed soldiers and policemen. Mothers in the barrios of Santiago during Pinochet's dictatorship, the mothers of the Plaza de Mayo in Buenos Aires, the mothers regularly demonstrating in front of the major prisons in El Salvador during the civil war—all were driven to political action by their despair at the loss of children and husbands and the struggle to provide food in their homes.

Further, and in a very different type of situation, there is an interesting parallel between LeBlanc's capturing of the political in the condition of the housewife and a set of findings in some of the research on immigrant women in the US. There is growing evidence that immigrant women are more likely than immigrant men to emerge as actors in the public domain precisely because of their responsibilities in the household. Regular wage work and improved access to other public realms has an impact on their culturally specified subordinate role to men in the household. Immigrant women gain greater personal autonomy and independence while immigrant men lose ground compared to what was their condition in cultures of origin. Women gain more control over budgeting and other domestic decisions, and greater leverage in requesting help from men in domestic chores. Their responsibility for securing public services and other public resources for their families gives them a chance to become incorporated in the mainstream society—they are often the ones in the household who mediate in this process (e.g., Chinchilla and Hamilton 2001). It is likely that some women benefit more than others from these circumstances; we need more research to establish the impact of class, education, and income on these gendered outcomes.

Besides the relatively greater empowerment of immigrant women in the household associated with waged employment, what matters here is their greater participation in the public sphere and their possible emergence as public actors. There are two arenas where immigrant women are active: institutions for public and private assistance, and the immigrant or ethnic community. The incorporation of women in the migration process strengthens the settlement likelihood and contributes to greater immigrant participation in their communities and vis-à-vis the state. For instance, Pierrette Hondagneu-Sotelo (1994) found immigrant women come to assume more active public and social roles, which further reinforces their status in the household and the settlement process. These immigrant women are more active in community building and community activism and they are positioned differently from men regarding the broader economy and the state. They are the ones that are likely to have to handle the legal vulnerability of their families in the process of seeking public and social services for their families. This greater participation by women suggests the possibility that they may emerge as more forceful and visible actors and make their role in the labor market more visible as well.[4]

These are dimensions of citizenship and citizenship practices that do not fit the indicators and categories of mainstream frameworks for understanding citizenship and political life. Women in the condition of housewives and mothers do not fit the categories and indicators used to capture participation in political life. Feminist scholarship in all the social sciences has had to deal with a set of similar or equivalent difficulties and tensions in its effort to constitute its subject or to reconfigure a subject that has been flattened. The theoretical and empirical distance that has to be bridged between the recognized world of politics and the as yet unmapped experience of citizenship of the housewife—not of women as such, but of women as housewives—is a distance we encounter in many types of inquiry. Bridging this distance requires specific forms of empirical research and of theorization.

---

[4] For the limits of this process see, e.g., Parreñas 2001.

BERKELEY JOURNAL OF SOCIOLOGY   16

IV. Postnational or denationalized?

From the perspective of nation-based citizenship theory, some of these transformations might be interpreted as a decline or devaluation of citizenship or, more favorably, as a displacement of citizenship in the face of other forms of collective organization and affiliation, as yet unnamed (Bosniak 2000). Insofar as citizenship is theorized as necessarily national (e.g., Himmelfarb 2001), by definition these new developments cannot be captured in the language of citizenship.[5] An alternative interpretation would be to suspend the national, as in postnational conceptions and to posit that the issue of where citizenship is enacted is one to be determined in light of developing social practice (e.g., Soysal 1994; Jacobson 1996; Torres 1998; Torres, Inda, and Miron 1999).

From where I look at these issues, there is a third possibility, beyond these two. It is that citizenship—even if situated in institutional settings that are "national"—is a possibly changed institution if the meaning of the national itself has changed. That is to say, insofar as globalization has changed certain features of the territorial and institutional organization of the political power and authority of the state, the institution of citizenship—its formal rights, its practices, its psychological dimension—has also been transformed even when it remains centered in the national state. I have argued, for instance, that this territorial and institutional transformation of state power and authority has produced operational, conceptual and rhetorical openings for nation-based subjects other than the national state to emerge as legitimate actors in international and global arenas that used to be exclusive to the state (see *Indiana Journal of Global Legal Studies* 1996).

I distinguish what I would narrowly define as denationalized from postnational citizenship, the latter the term most commonly used and the only one used in the broader debate.[6] In my reading we are dealing with two distinct dynamics rather than only the emergence of locations for citizenship outside the frame of the national state. Their difference is a question of scope and institutional embeddedness. The understanding in the scholarship is that postnational citizenship is located partly outside the confines of the national. In considering denationalization, the focus moves on to the transformation of the

---

[5] Thus for Karst "...In the US today, citizenship is inextricable from a complex legal framework that includes a widely accepted body of substantive law, strong law-making institutions, and law-enforcing institutions capable of performing their task." (2000: 600). Not recognizing the centrality of the law is, for Karst, a big mistake. Post-national citizenship lacks an institutional framework that can protect the substantive values of citizenship. Karst does acknowledge the possibility of rabid nationalism and the exclusion of aliens when legal status is made central.

[6] Bosniak (2000) uses the denationalized interchangeably with postnational. I do not.

17   SASSEN: REPOSITIONING OF CITIZENSHIP

national, including the national in its condition as foundational for citizenship. Thus it could be argued that postnationalism and denationalization represent two different trajectories. Both are viable, and they do not exclude each other.

The national, then, remains a referent in my work (e.g., Sassen 2003). But, clearly, it is a referent of a specific sort: it is, after all, its change that becomes the key theoretical feature through which it enters my specification of changes in the institution of citizenship. Whether or not this devalues citizenship (Jacobson 1996) is not immediately evident to me at this point. Citizenship has undergone many transformations in its history precisely because it is to variable extents embedded in the specifics of each of its eras.[7] Significant to my argument here is also the fact discussed earlier about the importance of national law in the process of expanding inclusions, inclusions which today are destabilizing older notions of citizenship. This pluralized meaning of citizenship partly produced by the formal expansions of the legal status of citizenship, is today contributing to explode the boundaries of that legal status even further.

First, and most importantly in my reading is the strengthening, including the constitutionalizing, of civil rights which allow citizens to make claims against their states and allow them to invoke a measure of autonomy in the formal political arena that can be read as a lengthening distance between the formal apparatus of the state and the institution of citizenship. The implications, both political and theoretical of this dimension are complex and in the making: we cannot tell what will be the practices and rhetorics that might be invented.

Secondly, I add to this the granting, by national states, of a whole range of "rights" to foreign actors, largely and especially, economic actors—foreign firms, foreign investors, international markets, foreign business people (see Sassen 1996: Chapter 2). Admittedly, this is not a common way of framing the issue. It comes out of my particular perspective about the impact of globalization and denationalization on the national state, including the impact on the relation between the state and its own citizens, and the state and foreign economic actors. I see this as a significant, though not much recognized, development in the history of claim-making. For me the question as to how citizens should handle these new concentrations of power and "legitimacy" that attach to global firms and markets is a key to the future of democracy. My efforts to detect the extent to which the global is embedded and filtered through the national (e.g., the concept of the global city [Sassen 2001]; see also

---

[7] In this regard, I have emphasized as significant (1996: Chapter 2) the introduction in the new constitutions of South Africa, Brazil, Argentina and the Central European countries, of a provision that qualifies what had been an unqualified right—if democratically elected—of the sovereign to be the exclusive representative of its people in international fora.

BERKELEY JOURNAL OF SOCIOLOGY 18

Sassen 2000) is one way of understanding whether therein lies a possibility for citizens, still largely confined to national institutions, to demand accountability of global economic actors through national institutional channels, rather than having to wait for a "global" state.

V. Citizenship in the global city

The particular transformations in the understanding and theorization of citizenship discussed thus far bring us back to some of the earlier historical formations around questions of citizenship, most prominently the crucial role played by cities and civil society. The large city of today, most especially the global city, emerges as a strategic site for these new types of operations. It is one of the nexi where the formation of new claims materializes and assumes concrete forms. The loss of power at the national level produces the possibility for new forms of power and politics at the subnational level. The national as container of social process and power is cracked. This cracked casing opens up possibilities for a geography of politics that links subnational spaces. Cities are foremost in this new geography. One question this engenders is how and whether we are seeing the formation of new types of politics that localize in these cities.

If we consider that large cities concentrate both the leading sectors of global capital and a growing share of disadvantaged populations—immigrants, many of the disadvantaged women, people of color generally, and, in the megacities of developing countries, masses of shanty dwellers—then we can see that cities have become a strategic terrain for a whole series of conflicts and contradictions . We can then think of cities also as one of the sites for the contradictions of the globalization of capital, even though, heeding Ira Katznelson's (1992) observation, the city cannot be reduced to this dynamic. Recovering cities along these lines means recovering the multiplicity of presences in this landscape. The large city of today has emerged as a strategic site for a whole range of new types of operations—political, economic, cultural, subjective (Isin 2000; Allen, Massey, and Pryke 1999; Bridge and Watson 2000).

While citizenship originated in cities and cities played an important role in its evolution, I do not think we can simply read some of these current developments as a return to that older historical condition. The significance of the city today as a setting for engendering new types of citizenship practices and new types of incompletely formalized political subjects does not derive from that history. Nor does current local city government have much to do with earlier notions of citizenship and democracy described for ancient and medieval cities in Europe (Isin 2000: 7). It is, rather, more connected to what Henri Lefebvre (1991; 1995) was capturing when describing the city as oeuvre and hence the importance of agency. Where Lefebvre found this agency in the working

19   SASSEN: REPOSITIONING OF CITIZENSHIP

class in the Paris of the twentieth century, I find it in two strategic actors—global corporate capital and immigration—in today's global cities. Here I would like to return to the fact of the embeddedness of the institution of citizenship.

What is being engendered today in terms of citizenship practices in the global city is quite different from what it might have been in the medieval city of Weber. In the medieval city we see a set of practices that allowed the burghers to set up systems for owning and protecting property and to implement various immunities against despots of all sorts.[8] Today's citizenship practices have to do with the production of "presence" of those without power and a politics that claims rights to the city. What the two situations share is the notion that through these practices new forms of citizenship are being constituted and that the city is a key site for this type of political work and is, indeed, partly constituted through these dynamics. After the long historical phase that saw the ascendance of the national state and the scaling of key economic dynamics at the national level, the city is once again today a scale for strategic economic and political dynamics.

In his effort to specify the ideal-typical features of what constitutes the city, Weber sought out a certain type of city—most prominently the cities of the late Middle Ages rather than the modern industrial cities of his time. Weber sought a kind of city that combined conditions and dynamics which forced its residents and leaders into creative, innovative responses and adaptations. Further, he posited that these changes produced in the context of the city signaled transformations that went beyond the city, that could have a far reach in instituting often fundamental transformations. In that regard the city offered the possibility of understanding far reaching changes that could—under certain conditions—eventually encompass society at large.

There are two aspects of Weber's *The City* that are of particular importance here. Weber sought to understand under what conditions cities can be positive and creative influences on people's lives. For Weber cities are a set of social structures that encourage social individuality and innovation and hence are an instrument of historical change. There is, in this intellectual project a deep sense of the historicity of these conditions. For Weber, modern urban life did not correspond to this positive and creative power of cities; Weber saw modern cities as dominated by large factories and office bureaucracies. My own reading of the Fordist city corresponds in many ways to Weber's in the sense that the strategic scale under Fordism is the national scale and cities lose significance. It is the large Fordist factory

---

[8] Only in Russia—where the walled city did not evolve as a center of urban immunities and liberties—does the meaning of citizen diverge from concepts of civil society and cities, and belongs to the state, not the city (Weber 1958).

BERKELEY JOURNAL OF SOCIOLOGY 20

and the mines which emerge as key sites for the political work of the disadvantaged and those without power.

For Weber, it is particularly the cities of the late Middle Ages that combine the conditions that pushed urban residents, merchants, artisans and leaders to address them and deal with them. These transformations could make for epochal change beyond the city itself: Weber shows us how in many of these cities these struggles led to the creation of the elements of what we could call governance systems and citizenship. In this regard struggles around political, economic, legal, cultural, issues which are centered in the realities of cities can become the catalysts for new transurban developments in all these institutional domains: markets, participatory governance, rights for members of the urban community regardless of lineage, judicial recourse, cultures of engagement and deliberation.

The particular analytic element I want to extricate from this aspect of Weber's understanding and theorization of the city is the historicity of those conditions that make cities strategic sites for the enactment of important transformations in multiple institutional domains. Elsewhere (2001) I have developed the argument that today a certain type of city—the global city—has emerged as a strategic site precisely for such innovations and transformations in multiple institutional domains. Several of the key components of economic globalization and digitization instantiate in this type of city and produce dislocations and destabilizations of existing institutional orders and legal, regulatory, and normative frames for handling urban conditions. It is the high level of concentration of these new dynamics in these cities that forces creative responses and innovations. There is, most probably, a threshold effect at work here.

The historicity of this process rests in the fact that under Keynesian policies, particularly the Fordist contract, and the dominance of mass manufacturing as the organizing economic dynamic, cities had lost strategic functions and were not the site for creative institutional innovations. The strategic sites were the large factory and the whole process of mass manufacturing and mass consumer markets, and, secondly, the national government where regulatory frameworks were developed and the Fordist contract instituted. The factory and the government were the strategic sites where the crucial dynamics producing the major institutional innovations of the epoch were located. With globalization and digitization—and all the specific elements they entail—global cities emerge as such strategic sites. While the strategic transformations are sharply concentrated in global cities, many of the transformations are also enacted, besides being diffused, in cities at lower orders of national urban hierarchies. Furthermore, in my reading, particular institutions of the state also are such strategic sites even as there is an overall shrinking of state authority through deregulation and privatization.

21   SASSEN: REPOSITIONING OF CITIZENSHIP

A second analytic element I want to extricate from Weber's *The City* is the particular type of embeddedness of the transformations he describes and renders as ideal-typical features. This is not an embeddedness in what we might think of as deep structures because the latter are precisely the ones that are being dislocated or changed and are creating openings for new fundamental arrangements to emerge. The embeddedness is, rather, in very specific conditions, opportunities, constraints, needs, interactions, contestations, interests. The aspect that matters here is the complexity, detail and social thickness of the particular conditions and the dynamics he identifies as enabling change and innovation. This complexity and thickness also produces ambiguities in the meaning of the changes and innovations. It is not always clear whether they are positive—where we might interpret positive as meaning the creation or strengthening of some element, even if very partial or minor, of participatory democracy in the city—and in what timeframe their positiveness would become evident. In those cities of the late Middle Ages he saw as being what the city is about, he finds contradictory and multivalent innovations. He dissects these innovations to understand what they can produce or launch.

The argument I derive from this particular type of embeddedness of change and innovation is that current conditions in global cities are creating not only new structurations of power but also operational and rhetorical openings for new types of political actors which may have been submerged, invisible or without voice. A key element of the argument here is that the localization of strategic components of globalization in these cities means that the disadvantaged can engage the new forms of globalized corporate power, and secondly that the growing numbers and diversity of the disadvantaged in these cities under these conditions assumes a distinctive "presence." This entails a distinction between powerlessness and invisibility or impotence. The disadvantaged in global cities can gain "presence" in their engagement with power but also vis-à-vis each other. This is different from the 1950s-1970s period in the US, for instance, when white flight and the significant departure of major corporate headquarters left cities hollowed out and the disadvantaged in a condition of abandonment. Today, the localization of the global creates a set of objective conditions of engagement. This can be seen, for example, in the struggles against gentrification—which encroaches on minority and disadvantaged neighborhoods and led to growing numbers of homeless beginning in the 1980s—and the struggles for the rights of the homeless, or also in demonstrations against police brutalizing minority people. These struggles are different from the ghetto uprisings of the 1960s, which were short, intense eruptions confined to the ghettos and causing most of the damage in the neighborhoods of the disadvantaged themselves. In these ghetto uprisings there was no engagement with power.

The conditions that today mark the possibility of cities as strategic sites are basically two, and both capture major transformations

BERKELEY JOURNAL OF SOCIOLOGY 22

that are destabilizing older systems organizing territory and politics. One of these is the re-scaling of what are the strategic territories that articulate the new political-economic system. The other is the partial unbundling or at least weakening of the national as container of social process due to the variety of dynamics encompassed by globalization and digitization. The consequences for cities of these two conditions are many: what matters here is that cities emerge as strategic sites for major economic processes and for new types of political actors. Insofar as citizenship is embedded and in turn marked by its embeddedness, these new conditions may well signal the possibility of new forms of citizenship practices and identities.

There is something to be captured here—a distinction between powerlessness and the condition of being an actor even though lacking power. I use the term presence to name this condition. In the context of a strategic space such as the global city, the types of disadvantaged people described here are not simply marginal; they acquire presence in a broader political process that escapes the boundaries of the formal polity. This presence signals the possibility of a politics. What this politics will be will depend on the specific projects and practices of various communities. Insofar as the sense of membership of these communities is not subsumed under the national, it may well signal the possibility of a politics that, while transnational, is actually centered in concrete localities.

References

Allen, John, Doreen Massey and Michael Pryke, eds. *Unsettling Cities*. London: Routledge, 1999.
Basch, Linda, Nina Glick Schiller, Cristina Blanc-Szanton. 1994. *Nations Unbound : Transnational Projects, Postcolonial Predicaments, and Deterritorialized Nation-States*. Langhorne, PA: Gordon and Breach.
Benhabib, Seyla. 2002. *Democractic Equality and Cultural Diversity: Political Identities in the Global Era*. Princeton, NJ: Princeton University Press.
Benhabib, Seyla, Judith Butler, Drucilla Cornell, Nancy Fraser. 1995. *Feminist Contentions: A Philosophical Exchange*. New York, NY: Routledge.
Bosniak, Linda. 1996. "'Nativism' The Concept: Some Reflections." *Immigrants Out!: The New Nativism and the Anti-Immigrant Impulse in the United States*. Juan Perea, ed. New York: NYU Press.
_____. 2000. "Universal Citizenship and the Problem of Alienage." *Northwestern University Law Review* 94(3): 963-984.

23 SASSEN: REPOSITIONING OF CITIZENSHIP

Bridge, Gary and Sophie Watson, eds. 2000. *A Companion to the City.* Oxford, United Kingdon: Blackwell.

Chinchilla, Norma and Nora Hamilton. 2001. *Seeking Community in the Global City: Salvadorans and Guatemalans in Los Angeles.* Philadelphia, PA: Temple University Press.

Cordero-Guzmán, Héctor R., Robert C. Smith and Ramón Grosfoguel, eds. 2001. *Migration, Transnationalization, and Race in a Changing New York.* Philadelphia, PA: Temple University Press.

Coutin, Susan B. 2000. "Denationalization, Inclusion, and Exclusion: Negotiating the Boundaries of Belonging." *Indiana Journal of Global Legal Studies* 7(2): 585-594.

Crenshaw, Kimberlé, Neil Gotanda, Gary Peller, and Kendall Thomas, eds. 1996. *Critical Race Theory: The Key Writings that Formed the Movement.* New York, NY: New Press.

Delgado, Richard, and Jean Stefancic, eds. 2001. *Critical Race Theory: The Cutting Edge.* Philadelphia, PA: Temple University Press.

Hague Convention. 1954. Available online at http://exchanges.state.gov/education/culprop/hague.html

Handler, Joel. 1995. *The Poverty of Welfare Reform.* New Haven, CT: Yale University Press.

Himmelfarb, Gertrude. 2001. *One Nation, Two Cultures: A Searching Examination of American Society in the Aftermath of Our Cultural Revolution.* New York, NY: Vintage Books

Hondagneu-Sotelo, Pierrette. 1994. *Gendered Transitions: Mexican Experiences of Immigration.* Berkeley, CA: University of California Press.

Indiana Journal of Global Legal Studies. 1996. Special Issue: "Feminism and Globalization: The Impact of The Global Economy on Women and Feminist Theory." 4(1).

Isin, Engin. 2000. "Introduction: democracy, citizenship and the city." *Democracy, Citizenship and the Global City*, Engin Isin, ed. New York, NY: Routledge.

Jacobson, David. 1996. *Rights Across Borders: Immigration and the Decline of Citizenship.* Baltimore, MD: Johns Hopkins Press.

Karst, Kenneth. 1997. "The Coming Crisis of Work in Constitutional Perspective." *Cornell Law Review* 82(3): 523-571.

_____. 2000. "Citizenship, Law, and the American Nation." *Indiana Journal of Global Legal Studies* 7(2): 595-601.

Katznelson, Ira. 1992. *Marxism and the City.* Oxford, United Kingdom: Clarendon.

Knop, Karen. 2002. *Diversity and Self-Determination in International Law.* Cambridge, United Kingdom: Cambridge University Press.

LeBlanc, Robin. 1999. *Bicycle Citizens: The Political World of the Japanese Housewife.* Berkeley, CA: University of California Press.

Lefebvre, Henri. 1991. *The Production of Space.* Cambridge, MA: Blackwell.

_____. 1995. *Writing on Cities.* Cambridge, MA: Blackwell.

BERKELEY JOURNAL OF SOCIOLOGY 24

Mahler, Sarah. 1995. *American Dreaming: Immigrant Life on the Margins.* Princeton, NJ: Princeton University Press.

Marrus, Michael R. 1985. *The Unwanted: European Refugees in the Twentieth Century.* New York, NY: Oxford University Press.

Marshall, T.H. 1977 [1950]. "Citizenship and Social Class." *Class, Citizenship, and Social Development.* Chicago, IL: University of Chicago Press.

Munger, Frank, ed. 2002. *Laboring Under the Line.* New York, NY: Russell Sage Foundation.

Ong, Aihwa. 1996. "Strategic Sisterhood or Sisters in Solidarity?: Questions of Communitarianism and Citizenship in Asia." *Indiana Journal of Global Legal Studies* 4(1):107-135.

_____. 1999. *Flexible Citizenship: The Cultural Logics of Transnationality.* Durham, NC: Duke University Press.

Portes, Alejandro. 1996. "Global Villagers: The Rise of Transnational Communities." *American Prospect* 7(25).

Parreñas, Rhacel Salazar. 2001. *Servants of Globalization: Women, Migration and Domestic Work.* Stanford, CA: Stanford University Press.

Roulleau-Berger, Laurence, ed. 2002. *Youth and work in the postindustrial cities of North America and Europe.* Leiden, Netherlands: Brill.

Rubenstein, Kim and Daniel Adler. 2000. "International Citizenship: The Future of Nationality in a Globalized World." *Indiana Journal of Global Legal Studies* 7(2): 519-548.

Sassen, Saskia. 1996. *Losing Control?: Sovereignty in an Age of Globalization.* New York, NY: Columbia University Press.

_____. 1999. *Guests and Aliens.* New York, NY: New Press.

_____. 2000. "Spatialities and Temporalities of the Global: Elements for a Theorization." *Public Culture* 12(1): 215-232.

_____. 2001. *The Global City: New York, London, Tokyo.* Second edition. Princeton, NJ: Princeton University Press.

_____. 2003. *Denationalization: Territory, Authority, and Rights in a Global Digital Age.* Princeton, NJ: Princeton University Press (Under Contract).

Saunders, Peter. 1993. "Citizenship in a Liberal Society." *Citizenship and Social Theory*, Bryan Turner, ed. London: Sage.

Schuck, Peter and Rogers Smith. 1985. *Citizenship Without Consent: Illegal Aliens in the American Polity.* New Haven, CT: Yale University Press.

Shotter, John. 1993. "Psychology and Citizenship: Identity and Belonging." *Citizenship and Social Theory*, Bryan Turner, ed. London: Sage.

Soysal, Yasemin Nuhoğlu. 1994. *Limits of Citizenship: Migrants and Postnational Membership in Europe.* Chicago, IL: University of Chicago Press.

Spiro, Peter. 1997. "Dual Nationality and the Meaning of Citizenship." *Emory Law Review* 46(4): 1412-1485.

25   SASSEN: REPOSITIONING OF CITIZENSHIP

Taylor, Charles. 1992. "The Politics of Recognition." *Multiculturalism: Examining the Politics of Recognition.* Charles Taylor and Amy Gutmann, eds. Princeton, NJ: Princeton University Press.

Torres, Maria de los Ángeles. 1998. "Transnational Political and Cultural Identities: Crossing Theoretical Borders." *Borderless Borders*, Frank Bonilla, Edwin Mélendez, Rebecca Morales, and Maria de los Ángeles Torres, eds. Philadelphia, PA: Temple University Press.

Torres, Rodolfo D., Jonathan Xavier Inda, and Louis F. Miron. 1999. *Race, Identity, and Citizenship.* Oxford, United Kingdom: Blackwell.

Turner, Bryan. 2000. "Cosmopolitan virtue: loyalty and the city." *Democracy, Citizenship and the Global City*, Engin Isin, ed. New York, NY: Routledge.

Walzer, Michael. 1985. *Spheres of Justice: A Defense of Pluralism and Equality.* New York, NY: Basic Books.

Weber, Max. 1958. *The City.* New York, NY: Free Press.

Young, Iris Marion. 1990. *Justice and the Politics of Difference.* Princeton, NJ: Princeton University Press.

[17]

FEMINISM, CAPITALISM

AND THE CUNNING OF HISTORY

NANCY FRASER

I WOULD LIKE HERE to take a broad look at second-wave feminism. Not at this or that activist current, nor this or that strand of feminist theorizing; not this or that geographical slice of the movement, nor this or that sociological stratum of women. I want, rather, to try to see second-wave feminism whole, as an epochal social phenomenon. Looking back at nearly forty years of feminist activism, I want to venture an assessment of the movement's overall trajectory and historical significance. In looking back, however, I hope also to help us look forward. By reconstructing the path we have travelled, I hope to shed light on the challenges we face today—in a time of massive economic crisis, social uncertainty and political realignment.[1]

I am going to tell a story, then, about the broad contours and overall meaning of second-wave feminism. Equal parts historical narrative and social-theoretical analysis, my story is plotted around three points in time, each of which places second-wave feminism in relation to a specific moment in the history of capitalism. The first point refers to the movement's beginnings in the context of what I will call 'state-organized capitalism'. Here I propose to chart the emergence of second-wave feminism from the anti-imperialist New Left, as a radical challenge to the pervasive androcentrism of state-led capitalist societies in the postwar era. Conceptualizing this phase, I shall identify the movement's fundamental emancipatory promise with its expanded sense of injustice and its structural critique of society. The second point refers to the process of feminism's evolution in the dramatically changed social context of rising neoliberalism. Here, I propose to chart not only the movement's extraordinary successes but also the disturbing convergence of some of its ideals with the demands of an emerging new form of capitalism—post-Fordist, 'disorganized', transnational. Conceptualizing this phase, I shall ask whether second-wave feminism has unwittingly supplied a key ingredient of what Luc Boltanski and Ève Chiapello call 'the new spirit of capitalism'. The third point refers to a possible reorientation of feminism in the present context of capitalist crisis and US political realignment, which could mark the beginnings of a shift from neoliberalism to a new form of social organization. Here, I propose to examine the prospects for reactivating feminism's emancipatory promise in a world that has been rocked by the twin crises of finance capital and US hegemony, and that now awaits the unfolding of Barack Obama's presidency.

In general, then, I propose to situate the trajectory of second-wave feminism in relation to the recent history of capitalism. In this way, I hope to help revive the sort of socialist-feminist theorizing that first inspired me decades ago and that still seems to offer our best hope for clarifying the prospects for gender justice in the present period. My aim, however, is not to recycle outmoded dual-systems theories, but rather to integrate the best of recent feminist theorizing with the best of recent critical theorizing about capitalism.

To clarify the rationale behind this approach, let me explain my dissatisfaction with what is perhaps the most widely held view of second-wave feminism. It is often said that the movement's relative success in transforming culture stands in sharp contrast with its relative failure to transform institutions. This assessment is doubled-edged: on the one hand, feminist ideals of gender equality, so contentious in the preceding decades, now sit squarely in the social mainstream; on the other hand, they have yet to be realized in practice. Thus, feminist critiques of, for example, sexual harassment, sexual trafficking and unequal pay, which appeared incendiary not so long ago, are widely espoused today; yet this sea-change at the level of attitudes has by no means eliminated those practices. And so, it is frequently argued: second-wave feminism has

---

[1] This essay originated as a keynote lecture presented at the Cortona Colloquium on 'Gender and Citizenship: New and Old Dilemmas, Between Equality and Difference' in November 2008. For helpful comments, I thank the Cortona participants, especially Bianca Beccalli, Jane Mansbridge, Ruth Milkman and Eli Zaretsky, and the participants in an EHESS seminar at the Groupe de sociologie politique et morale, especially Luc Boltanski, Estelle Ferrarese, Sandra Laugier, Patricia Paperman and Laurent Thévenot.

FRASER: *Feminism* 99

wrought an epochal cultural revolution, but the vast change in *mentalités* has not (yet) translated into structural, institutional change.

There is something to be said for this view, which rightly notes the widespread acceptance today of feminist ideas. But the thesis of cultural success-cum-institutional failure does not go very far in illuminating the historical significance and future prospects of second-wave feminism. Positing that institutions have lagged behind culture, as if one could change while the other did not, it suggests that we need only make the former catch up with the latter in order to realize feminist hopes. The effect is to obscure a more complex, disturbing possibility: that the diffusion of cultural attitudes born out of the second wave has been part and parcel of another social transformation, unanticipated and unintended by feminist activists—a transformation in the social organization of postwar capitalism. This possibility can be formulated more sharply: the cultural changes jump-started by the second wave, salutary in themselves, have served to legitimate a structural transformation of capitalist society that runs directly counter to feminist visions of a just society.

In this essay, I aim to explore this disturbing possibility. My hypothesis can be stated thus: what was truly new about the second wave was the way it wove together, in a critique of androcentric state-organized capitalism, three analytically distinct dimensions of gender injustice: economic, cultural and political. Subjecting state-organized capitalism to wide-ranging, multifaceted scrutiny, in which those three perspectives intermingled freely, feminists generated a critique that was simultaneously ramified and systematic. In the ensuing decades, however, the three dimensions of injustice became separated, both from one another and from the critique of capitalism. With the fragmentation of the feminist critique came the selective incorporation and partial recuperation of some of its strands. Split off from one another and from the societal critique that had integrated them, second-wave hopes were conscripted in the service of a project that was deeply at odds with our larger, holistic vision of a just society. In a fine instance of the cunning of history, utopian desires found a second life as feeling currents that legitimated the transition to a new form of capitalism: post-Fordist, transnational, neoliberal.

In what follows, I propose to elaborate this hypothesis in three steps, which correspond to the three plot points mentioned earlier. In a first step, I shall reconstruct the second-wave feminist critique of androcentric state-organized capitalism as integrating concerns with three perspectives on justice—redistribution, recognition and representation. In a second step, I shall sketch the coming apart of that constellation and the selective enlistment of some of its strands to legitimate neoliberal capitalism. In a third, I shall weigh the prospects for recovering feminism's emancipatory promise in the present moment of economic crisis and political opening.

I. FEMINISM AND STATE-ORGANIZED CAPITALISM

Let me begin by situating the emergence of second-wave feminism in the context of state-organized capitalism. By 'state-organized capitalism', I mean the hegemonic social formation in the postwar era, a social formation in which states played an active role in steering their national economies.[2] We are most familiar with the form taken by state-organized capitalism in the welfare states of what was then called the First World, which used Keynesian tools to soften the boom–bust cycles endemic to capitalism. Drawing on the experiences of the Depression and war-time planning, these states implemented various forms of *dirigisme*, including infrastructural investment, industrial policy, redistributive taxation, social provision, business regulation, nationalization of some key industries and decommodification of public goods. Although it was the most wealthy and powerful OECD states that were able to 'organize' capitalism most successfully in the decades following 1945, a variant of state-organized capitalism could also be found in what was then termed the Third World. In impoverished ex-colonies, newly independent 'developmental states' sought to use their more limited capacities to jump-start national economic growth by means of import-substitution policies, infrastructural investment, nationalization of key industries and public spending on education.[3]

---

[2] For a discussion of this term, see Friedrich Pollock, 'State Capitalism: Its Possibilities and Limitations', in Andrew Arato and Eike Gebhardt, eds, *The Essential Frankfurt School Reader*, London 1982, pp. 71–94.

[3] Then, too, economic life in the Communist bloc was notoriously state-organized, and there are those who would still insist on calling it state-organized capitalism. Although there may be some truth in that view, I will follow the more conventional path of excluding the region from this first moment of my story, in part because it was not until after 1989 that second-wave feminism emerged as a political force in what were by then ex-Communist countries.

FRASER: *Feminism* 101

In general, then, I use this expression to refer to the OECD welfare states and the ex-colonial developmental states of the postwar period. It was in these countries, after all, that second-wave feminism first erupted in the early 1970s. To explain what exactly provoked the eruption, let me note four defining characteristics of the political culture of state-organized capitalism:

▶ *Economism.* By definition, state-organized capitalism involved the use of public political power to regulate (and in some cases, to replace) economic markets. This was largely a matter of crisis management in the interest of capital. Nevertheless, the states in question derived much of their political legitimacy from their claims to promote inclusion, social equality and cross-class solidarity. Yet these ideals were interpreted in an economistic and class-centric way. In the political culture of state-organized capitalism, social questions were framed chiefly in distributive terms, as matters concerning the equitable allocation of divisible goods, especially income and jobs, while social divisions were viewed primarily through the prism of class. Thus, the quintessential social injustice was unfair economic distribution, and its paradigm expression was class inequality. The effect of this class-centric, economistic imaginary was to marginalize, if not wholly to obscure, other dimensions, sites and axes of injustice.

▶ *Androcentrism.* It followed that the political culture of state-organized capitalism envisioned the ideal-typical citizen as an ethnic-majority male worker—a breadwinner and a family man. It was widely assumed, too, that this worker's wage should be the principal, if not the sole, economic support of his family, while any wages earned by his wife should be merely supplemental. Deeply gendered, this 'family wage' construct served both as a social ideal, connoting modernity and upward mobility, and as the basis for state policy in matters of employment, welfare and development. Granted, the ideal eluded most families, as a man's wage was rarely by itself sufficient to support children and a non-employed wife. And granted, too, the Fordist industry to which the ideal was linked was soon to be dwarfed by a burgeoning low-wage service sector. But in the 1950s and 1960s, the family-wage ideal still served to define gender norms and to discipline those who would contravene them, reinforcing men's authority

102 NLR 56

in households and channelling aspirations into privatized domestic consumption. Equally important, by valorizing waged work, the political culture of state-organized capitalism obscured the social importance of unwaged care work and reproductive labour. Institutionalizing androcentric understandings of family and work, it naturalized injustices of gender and removed them from political contestation.

▶ *Étatism.* State-organized capitalism was also étatist, suffused with a technocratic, managerial ethos. Relying on professional experts to design policies, and on bureaucratic organizations to implement them, welfare and developmental states treated those whom they ostensibly served more as clients, consumers and taxpayers than as active citizens. The result was a depoliticized culture, which treated questions of justice as technical matters, to be settled by expert calculation or corporatist bargaining. Far from being empowered to interpret their needs democratically, via political deliberation and contestation, ordinary citizens were positioned (at best) as passive recipients of satisfactions defined and dispensed from on high.

▶ *Westphalianism.* Finally, state-organized capitalism was, by definition, a national formation, aimed at mobilizing the capacities of nation-states to support national economic development in the name—if not always in the interest—of the national citizenry. Made possible by the Bretton Woods regulatory framework, this formation rested on a division of political space into territorially bounded polities. As a result, the political culture of state-organized capitalism institutionalized the 'Westphalian' view that binding obligations of justice apply only among fellow citizens. Subtending the lion's share of social struggle in the post-war era, this view channelled claims for justice into the domestic political arenas of territorial states. The effect, notwithstanding lip-service to international human rights and anti-imperialist solidarity, was to truncate the scope of justice, marginalizing, if not wholly obscuring, cross-border injustices.[4]

---

[4] For a fuller account of the 'Westphalian political imaginary', see Fraser, 'Reframing Justice in a Globalizing World', NLR 36, November–December 2005.

FRASER: *Feminism* 103

In general, then, the political culture of state-organized capitalism was economistic, androcentric, étatist and Westphalian—all characteristics that came under attack in the late 1960s and 1970s. In those years of explosive radicalism, second-wave feminists joined their New Left and anti-imperialist counterparts in challenging the economism, the étatism, and (to a lesser degree) the Westphalianism of state-organized capitalism, while also contesting the latter's androcentrism—and with it, the sexism of their comrades and allies. Let us consider these points one by one.

▶ *Second-wave feminism contra economism.* Rejecting the exclusive identification of injustice with class maldistribution, second-wave feminists joined other emancipatory movements to burst open the restrictive, economistic imaginary of state-organized capitalism. Politicizing 'the personal', they expanded the meaning of justice, reinterpreting as injustices social inequalities that had been overlooked, tolerated or rationalized since time immemorial. Rejecting both Marxism's exclusive focus on political economy and liberalism's exclusive focus on law, they unveiled injustices located elsewhere—in the family and in cultural traditions, in civil society and in everyday life. In addition, second-wave feminists expanded the number of axes that could harbour injustice. Rejecting the primacy of class, socialist-feminists, black feminists and anti-imperialist feminists also opposed radical-feminist efforts to install gender in that same position of categorial privilege. Focusing not only on gender, but also on class, race, sexuality and nationality, they pioneered an 'intersectionist' alternative that is widely accepted today. Finally, second-wave feminists extended the purview of justice to take in such previously private matters as sexuality, housework, reproduction and violence against women. In so doing, they effectively broadened the concept of injustice to encompass not only economic inequalities but also hierarchies of status and asymmetries of political power. With the benefit of hindsight, we can say that they replaced a monistic, economistic view of justice with a broader three-dimensional understanding, encompassing economy, culture and politics.

The result was no mere laundry list of single issues. On the contrary, what connected the plethora of newly discovered injustices was the notion that women's subordination was systemic, grounded in the deep structures of society. Second-wave

104 NLR 56

feminists argued, of course, about how best to characterize the social totality—whether as 'patriarchy', as a 'dual-systems' amalgam of capitalism and patriarchy, as an imperialist world system, or, in my own preferred view, as a historically specific, androcentric form of state-organized capitalist society, structured by three interpenetrating orders of subordination: (mal)distribution, (mis)recognition and (mis)representation. But despite such differences, most second-wave feminists—with the notable exception of liberal-feminists—concurred that overcoming women's subordination required radical transformation of the deep structures of the social totality. This shared commitment to systemic transformation betokened the movement's origins in the broader emancipatory ferment of the times.

▶ *Second-wave feminism contra androcentrism.* If second-wave feminism partook of the general aura of 1960s radicalism, it nevertheless stood in a tense relation with other emancipatory movements. Its chief target, after all, was the *gender* injustice of state-organized capitalism, hardly a priority for non-feminist anti-imperialists and New Leftists. In mounting their critique of state-organized capitalism's androcentrism, moreover, second-wave feminists had also to confront sexism within the Left. For liberal and radical feminists, this posed no special problem; they could simply turn separatist and exit the Left. For socialist-feminists, anti-imperialist feminists and feminists of colour, in contrast, the difficulty was to confront sexism within the Left while remaining part of it.

For a time, at least, socialist-feminists succeeded in maintaining that difficult balance. They located the core of androcentrism in a gender division of labour which systematically devalued activities, both paid and unpaid, that were performed by or associated with women. Applying this analysis to state-organized capitalism, they uncovered the deep-structural connections between women's responsibility for the lion's share of unpaid caregiving, their subordination in marriage and personal life, the gender segmentation of labour markets, men's domination of the political system, and the androcentrism of welfare provision, industrial policy and development schemes. In effect, they exposed the family wage as the point where gender maldistribution, misrecognition and misrepresentation converged. The result was a critique that integrated economy, culture and politics in a systematic account of women's subordination in state-organized capitalism. Far from aiming simply to promote women's full incorporation as wage-earners in capitalist society, second-wave feminists sought to transform the system's deep structures and animating values—in part by decentring wage work and valorizing unwaged activities, especially the socially necessary carework performed by women.

▶ *Second-wave feminism contra étatism.* But feminists' objections to state-organized capitalism were as much concerned with process as with substance. Like their New Left allies, they rejected the bureaucratic-managerial ethos of state-organized capitalism. To the widespread 1960s critique of Fordist organization they added a gender analysis, interpreting the culture of large-scale, top-down institutions as expressing the modernized masculinity of the professional-managerial stratum of state-organized capitalism. Developing a horizontal counter-ethos of sisterly connection, second-wave feminists created the entirely new organizational practice of consciousness-raising. Seeking to bridge the sharp étatist divide between theory and practice, they styled themselves as a countercultural democratizing movement—anti-hierarchical, participatory and demotic. In an era when the acronym 'NGO' did not yet exist, feminist academics, lawyers and social workers identified more with the grass roots than with the reigning professional ethos of depoliticized expertise.

But unlike some of their countercultural comrades, most feminists did not reject state institutions *simpliciter*. Seeking, rather, to infuse the latter with feminist values, they envisioned a participatory-democratic state that empowered its citizens. Effectively re-imagining the relation between state and society, they sought to transform those positioned as passive objects of welfare and development policy into active subjects, empowered to participate in democratic processes of need interpretation. The goal, accordingly, was less to dismantle state institutions than to transform them into agencies that would promote, and indeed express, gender justice.

106   NLR 56

▶ *Second-wave feminism contra and pro Westphalianism.* More ambivalent, perhaps, was feminism's relation to the Westphalian dimension of state-organized capitalism. Given its origins in the global anti-Vietnam War ferment of the time, the movement was clearly disposed to be sensitive to trans-border injustices. This was especially the case for feminists in the developing world, whose gender critique was interwoven with a critique of imperialism. But there, as elsewhere, most feminists viewed their respective states as the principal addressees of their demands. Thus, second-wave feminists tended to reinscribe the Westphalian frame at the level of practice, even when they criticized it at the level of theory. That frame, which divided the world into bounded territorial polities, remained the default option in an era when states still seemed to possess the requisite capacities for social steering and when the technology enabling real-time transnational networking was not yet available. In the context of state-organized capitalism, then, the slogan 'sisterhood is global' (itself already contested as imperializing) functioned more as an abstract gesture than as a post-Westphalian political project that could be practically pursued.

In general, second-wave feminism remained ambivalently Westphalian, even as it rejected the economism, androcentrism and étatism of state-organized capitalism. On all those issues, however, it manifested considerable nuance. In rejecting economism, the feminists of this period never doubted the centrality of distributive justice and the critique of political economy to the project of women's emancipation. Far from wanting to minimize the economic dimension of gender injustice, they sought, rather, to deepen it, by clarifying its relation with the two additional dimensions of culture and politics. Likewise, in rejecting the androcentrism of the family wage, second-wave feminists never sought simply to replace it with the two-earner family. For them, overcoming gender injustice meant ending the systematic devaluation of caregiving and the gender division of labour, both paid and unpaid. Finally, in rejecting the étatism of state-organized capitalism, second-wave feminists never doubted the need for strong political institutions capable of organizing economic life in the service of justice. Far from wanting to free markets from state control, they sought rather to democratize state power, to maximize citizen participation, to strengthen accountability, and to increase communicative flows between state and society.

All told, second-wave feminism espoused a transformative political project, premised on an expanded understanding of injustice and a systemic critique of capitalist society. The movement's most advanced currents saw their struggles as multi-dimensional, aimed simultaneously against economic exploitation, status hierarchy and political subjection. To them, moreover, feminism appeared as part of a broader emancipatory project, in which struggles against gender injustices were necessarily linked to struggles against racism, imperialism, homophobia and class domination, all of which required transformation of the deep structures of capitalist society.

II. FEMINISM AND THE 'NEW SPIRIT OF CAPITALISM'

As it turned out, that project remained largely stillborn, a casualty of deeper historical forces, which were not well understood at the time. With the benefit of hindsight, we can now see that the rise of second-wave feminism coincided with a historical shift in the character of capitalism, from the state-organized variant just discussed to neoliberalism. Reversing the previous formula, which sought to 'use politics to tame markets', proponents of this new form of capitalism proposed to use markets to tame politics. Dismantling key elements of the Bretton Woods framework, they eliminated the capital controls that had enabled Keynesian steering of national economies. In place of *dirigisme*, they promoted privatization and deregulation; in place of public provision and social citizenship, 'trickle-down' and 'personal responsibility'; in place of the welfare and developmental states, the lean, mean 'competition state'. Road-tested in Latin America, this approach served to guide much of the transition to capitalism in East/Central Europe. Although publicly championed by Thatcher and Reagan, it was applied only gradually and unevenly in the First World. In the Third, by contrast, neoliberalization was imposed at the gunpoint of debt, as an enforced programme of 'structural adjustment' which overturned all the central tenets of developmentalism and compelled post-colonial states to divest their assets, open their markets and slash social spending.

Interestingly, second-wave feminism thrived in these new conditions. What had begun as a radical countercultural movement was now *en route* to becoming a broad-based mass social phenomenon. Attracting adherents of every class, ethnicity, nationality and political ideology, feminist

108   NLR 56

ideas found their way into every nook and cranny of social life and transformed the self-understandings of all whom they touched. The effect was not only vastly to expand the ranks of activists but also to reshape commonsense views of family, work and dignity.

Was it mere coincidence that second-wave feminism and neoliberalism prospered in tandem? Or was there some perverse, subterranean elective affinity between them? That second possibility is heretical, to be sure, but we fail to investigate it at our peril. Certainly, the rise of neoliberalism dramatically changed the terrain on which second-wave feminism operated. The effect, I shall argue here, was to resignify feminist ideals.[5] Aspirations that had a clear emancipatory thrust in the context of state-organized capitalism assumed a far more ambiguous meaning in the neoliberal era. With welfare and developmental states under attack from free-marketeers, feminist critiques of economism, androcentrism, étatism and Westphalianism took on a new valence. Let me clarify this dynamic of resignification by revisiting those four foci of feminist critique.

▶ *Feminist anti-economism resignified.* Neoliberalism's rise coincided with a major alteration in the political culture of capitalist societies. In this period, claims for justice were increasingly couched as claims for the recognition of identity and difference.[6] With this shift 'from redistribution to recognition' came powerful pressures to transform second-wave feminism into a variant of identity politics. A progressive variant, to be sure, but one that tended nevertheless to overextend the critique of culture, while downplaying the critique of political economy. In practice, the tendency was to subordinate social-economic struggles to struggles for recognition, while in the academy, feminist cultural theory began to eclipse feminist social theory. What had begun as a needed corrective to economism devolved in time into an equally one-sided culturalism. Thus, instead of arriving at a broader, richer paradigm that could encompass both redistribution and recognition, second-wave feminists effectively traded one truncated paradigm for another.

---

[5] I borrow the term 'resignification' from Judith Butler, 'Contingent Foundations', in Seyla Benhabib, Judith Butler, Drucilla Cornell and Nancy Fraser, *Feminist Contentions: A Philosophical Exchange*, London 1994.
[6] For this change in the grammar of political claims, see Fraser, 'From Redistribution to Recognition?', NLR I/212, July–August 1995.

FRASER: *Feminism* 109

The timing, moreover, could not have been worse. The turn to recognition dovetailed all too neatly with a rising neoliberalism that wanted nothing more than to repress all memory of social egalitarianism. Thus, feminists absolutized the critique of culture at precisely the moment when circumstances required redoubled attention to the critique of political economy. As the critique splintered, moreover, the cultural strand became decoupled not only from the economic strand, but also from the critique of capitalism that had previously integrated them. Unmoored from the critique of capitalism and made available for alternative articulations, these strands could be drawn into what Hester Eisenstein has called 'a dangerous liaison' with neoliberalism.[7]

▶ *Feminist anti-androcentrism resignified.* It was only a matter of time, therefore, before neoliberalism resignified the feminist critique of androcentrism. To explain how, I propose to adapt an argument made by Luc Boltanski and Ève Chiapello. In their important book, *The New Spirit of Capitalism,* they contend that capitalism periodically remakes itself in moments of historical rupture, in part by recuperating strands of critique directed against it.[8] In such moments, elements of anti-capitalist critique are resignified to legitimate an emergent new form of capitalism, which thereby becomes endowed with the higher, moral significance needed to motivate new generations to shoulder the inherently meaningless work of endless accumulation. For Boltanski and Chiapello, the new 'spirit' that has served to legitimate the flexible neoliberal capitalism of our time was fashioned from the New Left's 'artistic' critique of state-organized capitalism, which denounced the grey conformism of corporate culture. It was in the accents of May 68, they claim, that neoliberal management theorists propounded a new 'connexionist', 'project' capitalism, in which rigid organizational hierarchies would give way to horizontal teams and flexible networks, thereby liberating individual creativity. The result was a new romance of capitalism with real-world effects—a

---

[7] Hester Eisenstein, 'A Dangerous Liaison? Feminism and Corporate Globalization', *Science and Society,* vol. 69, no. 3, 2005.

[8] Luc Boltanski and Ève Chiapello, *The New Spirit of Capitalism,* London 2005 [Paris 1999]. For an interpretation of psychoanalysis as the spirit of 'the second industrial revolution', which concludes by positing feminism as the spirit of the 'third', see Eli Zaretsky, 'Psychoanalysis and the Spirit of Capitalism', *Constellations,* vol. 15, no. 3, 2008.

romance that enveloped the tech start-ups of Silicon Valley and that today finds its purest expression in the ethos of Google.

Boltanski and Chiapello's argument is original and profound. Yet, because it is gender-blind, it fails to grasp the full character of the spirit of neoliberal capitalism. To be sure, that spirit includes a masculinist romance of the free, unencumbered, self-fashioning individual, which they aptly describe. But neoliberal capitalism has as much to do with Walmart, *maquiladoras* and microcredit as with Silicon Valley and Google. And its indispensable workers are disproportionately women, not only young single women, but also married women and women with children; not only racialized women, but women of virtually all nationalities and ethnicities. As such, women have poured into labour markets around the globe; the effect has been to undercut once and for all state-organized capitalism's ideal of the family wage. In 'disorganized' neoliberal capitalism, that ideal has been replaced by the norm of the two-earner family. Never mind that the reality which underlies the new ideal is depressed wage levels, decreased job security, declining living standards, a steep rise in the number of hours worked for wages per household, exacerbation of the double shift—now often a triple or quadruple shift—and a rise in female-headed households. Disorganized capitalism turns a sow's ear into a silk purse by elaborating a new romance of female advancement and gender justice.

Disturbing as it may sound, I am suggesting that second-wave feminism has unwittingly provided a key ingredient of the new spirit of neoliberalism. Our critique of the family wage now supplies a good part of the romance that invests flexible capitalism with a higher meaning and a moral point. Endowing their daily struggles with an ethical meaning, the feminist romance attracts women at both ends of the social spectrum: at one end, the female cadres of the professional middle classes, determined to crack the glass ceiling; at the other end, the female temps, part-timers, low-wage service employees, domestics, sex workers, migrants, EPZ workers and microcredit borrowers, seeking not only income and material security, but also dignity, self-betterment and liberation from traditional authority. At both ends, the dream of women's emancipation is harnessed to the engine of capitalist

FRASER: *Feminism* III

accumulation. Thus, second-wave feminism's critique of the family wage has enjoyed a perverse afterlife. Once the centrepiece of a radical analysis of capitalism's androcentrism, it serves today to intensify capitalism's valorization of waged labour.

▸ *Feminist anti-étatism resignified.* Neoliberalism has also resignified the anti-étatism of the previous period, making it grist for schemes aimed at reducing state action *tout court*. In the new climate, it seemed but a short step from second-wave feminism's critique of welfare-state paternalism to Thatcher's critique of the nanny state. That was certainly the experience in the United States, where feminists watched helplessly as Bill Clinton triangulated their nuanced critique of a sexist and stigmatizing system of poor relief into a plan to 'end welfare as we know it', which abolished the Federal entitlement to income support. In the postcolonies, meanwhile, the critique of the developmental state's androcentrism morphed into enthusiasm for NGOs, which emerged everywhere to fill the space vacated by shrinking states. Certainly, the best of these organizations provided urgently needed material aid to populations bereft of public services. Yet the effect was often to depoliticize local groups and to skew their agendas in directions favoured by First-World funders. By its very stop-gap nature, moreover, NGO action did little to challenge the receding tide of public provision or to build political support for responsive state action.[9]

The explosion of microcredit illustrates the dilemma. Counterposing feminist values of empowerment and participation from below to the passivity-inducing red tape of top-down étatism, the architects of these projects have crafted an innovative synthesis of individual self-help and community networking, NGO oversight and market mechanisms—all aimed at combating women's poverty and gender subjection. The results so far include an impressive record of loan repayments and anecdotal evidence of lives transformed. What has been concealed, however, in the feminist hoopla surrounding these projects, is a disturbing coincidence:

---

[9] Sonia Alvarez, 'Advocating Feminism: The Latin American Feminist NGO "Boom"', *International Feminist Journal of Politics*, vol. 1, no. 2, 1999; Carol Barton, 'Global Women's Movements at a Crossroads', *Socialism and Democracy*, vol. 18, no. 1, 2004.

112   NLR 56

microcredit has burgeoned just as states have abandoned macro-structural efforts to fight poverty, efforts that small-scale lending cannot possibly replace.[10] In this case too, the feminist critique of bureaucratic paternalism has been recuperated by neoliberalism. A perspective aimed originally at transforming state power into a vehicle of citizen empowerment and social justice is now used to legitimate marketization and state retrenchment.

▶ *Feminist contra and pro Westphalianism resignified.* Finally, neo-liberalism altered for better and for worse second-wave feminism's ambivalent relation to the Westphalian frame. In the new context of 'globalization', it no longer goes without saying that the bounded territorial state is the sole legitimate container for obligations of, and struggles for, justice. Feminists have joined environmentalists, human-rights activists and critics of the WTO in challenging that view. Mobilizing post-Westphalian intuitions that had remained impracticable in state-organized capitalism, they have targeted trans-border injustices that had been marginalized or neglected in the previous era. Utilizing new communication technologies to establish transnational networks, feminists have pioneered innovative strategies such as the 'boomerang effect', which mobilizes global public opinion to spotlight local abuses and to shame the states that condone them.[11] The result was a promising new form of feminist activism—transnational, multi-scalar, post-Westphalian.

But the transnational turn brought difficulties too. Often stymied at the level of the state, many feminists directed their energies to the 'international' arena, especially to a succession of UN-related conferences, from Nairobi to Vienna to Beijing and beyond. Building a presence in 'global civil society' from which to engage new regimes of global governance, they became entangled in some of the problems I have already noted. For example, campaigns for women's human rights focused overwhelmingly on

[10] Uma Narayan, 'Informal Sector Work, Microcredit and Third World Women's "Empowerment": A Critical Perspective', paper presented at the XXII World Congress of Philosophy of Law and Social Philosophy, May 2005, Granada; Eisenstein, 'A Dangerous Liaison?'.
[11] Margaret Keck and Kathryn Sikkink, *Activists Beyond Borders: Advocacy Networks in International Politics*, Ithaca, NY 1998.

FRASER: *Feminism* 113

issues of violence and reproduction, as opposed, for example, to poverty. Ratifying the Cold War split between civil and political rights, on the one hand, and social and economic rights, on the other, these efforts, too, have privileged recognition over redistribution. In addition, these campaigns intensified the NGO-ification of feminist politics, widening the gap between professionals and local groups, while according disproportionate voice to English-speaking elites. Analogous dynamics have been operating in the feminist engagement with the policy apparatus of the European Union—especially given the absence of genuinely transnational, Europe-wide women's movements. Thus, the feminist critique of Westphalianism has proved ambivalent in the era of neoliberalism. What began as a salutary attempt to expand the scope of justice beyond the nation-state has ended up dovetailing in some respects with the administrative needs of a new form of capitalism.

In general, then, the fate of feminism in the neoliberal era presents a paradox. On the one hand, the relatively small countercultural movement of the previous period has expanded exponentially, successfully disseminating its ideas across the globe. On the other, feminist ideas have undergone a subtle shift in valence in the altered context. Unambiguously emancipatory in the era of state-organized capitalism, critiques of economism, androcentrism, étatism and Westphalianism now appear fraught with ambiguity, susceptible to serving the legitimation needs of a new form of capitalism. After all, this capitalism would much prefer to confront claims for recognition over claims for redistribution, as it builds a new regime of accumulation on the cornerstone of women's waged labour, and seeks to disembed markets from social regulation in order to operate all the more freely on a global scale.

III. AN OPEN FUTURE?

Today, however, this capitalism is itself at a critical crossroads. Certainly, the global financial crisis and the decidedly post-neoliberal response to it by leading states—all Keynesians now—mark the beginning of neoliberalism's end as an economic regime. The election of Barack Obama may signal the decisive repudiation, even in the belly of the beast, of neoliberalism as a political project. We may be seeing the early stirrings of a new wave of mobilization aimed at articulating an

114 NLR 56

alternative. Perhaps, accordingly, we stand poised at the brink of yet another 'great transformation', as massive and profound as the one I have just described.

If so, then the shape of the successor society will be the object of intense contestation in the coming period. And feminism will feature importantly in such contestation—at two different levels: first, as the social movement whose fortunes I have traced here, which will seek to ensure that the successor regime institutionalizes a commitment to gender justice. But also, second, as a general discursive construct which feminists in the first sense no longer own and do not control—an empty signifier of the good (akin, perhaps, to 'democracy'), which can and will be invoked to legitimate a variety of different scenarios, not all of which promote gender justice. An offspring of feminism in the first, social-movement sense, this second, discursive sense of 'feminism' has gone rogue. As the discourse becomes independent of the movement, the latter is increasingly confronted with a strange shadowy version of itself, an uncanny double that it can neither simply embrace nor wholly disavow.[12]

In this essay, I have mapped the disconcerting dance of these two feminisms in the shift from state-organized capitalism to neoliberalism. What should we conclude from it? Certainly not that second-wave feminism has failed *simpliciter*, nor that it is to blame for the triumph of neoliberalism. Surely not that feminist ideals are inherently problematic; nor that they are always already doomed to be resignified for capitalist purposes. I conclude, rather, that we for whom feminism is above all a movement for gender justice need to become more historically self-aware as we operate on a terrain that is also populated by our uncanny double.

To that end, let us return to the question: what, if anything, explains our 'dangerous liaison' with neoliberalism? Are we the victims of an unfortunate coincidence, who happened to be in the wrong place at the wrong time and so fell prey to that most opportunistic of seducers, a capitalism so indiscriminate that it would instrumentalize any perspective whatever, even one inherently foreign to it? Or is there, as I suggested earlier, some subterranean elective affinity between feminism and neoliberalism? If

---

[12] This formula of 'feminism and its doubles' could be elaborated to good effect with respect to the 2008 US Presidential election, where the uncanny doubles included both Hillary Clinton and Sarah Palin.

FRASER: *Feminism* 115

any such affinity does exist, it lies in the critique of traditional authority.[13] Such authority is a longstanding target of feminist activism, which has sought at least since Mary Wollstonecraft to emancipate women from personalized subjection to men, be they fathers, brothers, priests, elders or husbands. But traditional authority also appears in some periods as an obstacle to capitalist expansion, part of the surrounding social substance in which markets have historically been embedded and which has served to confine economic rationality within a limited sphere.[14] In the current moment, these two critiques of traditional authority, the one feminist, the other neoliberal, appear to converge.

Where feminism and neoliberalism diverge, in contrast, is over post-traditional forms of gender subordination—constraints on women's lives that do not take the form of personalized subjection, but arise from structural or systemic processes in which the actions of many people are abstractly or impersonally mediated. A paradigm case is what Susan Okin has characterized as 'a cycle of socially caused and distinctly asymmetric vulnerability by marriage', in which women's traditional responsibility for child-rearing helps shape labour markets that disadvantage women, resulting in unequal power in the economic market-place, which in turn reinforces, and exacerbates, unequal power in the family.[15] Such market-mediated processes of subordination are the very lifeblood of neoliberal capitalism. Today, accordingly, they should become a major focus of feminist critique, as we seek to distinguish ourselves from, and to avoid resignification by, neoliberalism. The point, of course, is not to drop the struggle against traditional male authority, which remains a necessary moment of feminist critique. It is, rather, to disrupt the easy passage from such critique to its neoliberal double—above all by reconnecting struggles against personalized subjection to the critique of a capitalist system which, while promising liberation, actually replaces one mode of domination by another.

In the hope of advancing this agenda, I would like to conclude by revisiting one last time my four foci of feminist critique:

---

[13] I owe this point to Eli Zaretsky (personal communication). Cf. Eisenstein, 'A Dangerous Liaison?'.

[14] In some periods, but not always. In many contexts, capitalism is more apt to adapt to than to challenge traditional authority. For the embedding of markets, see Karl Polanyi, *The Great Transformation*, 2nd edn, Boston 2001.

[15] Susan Okin, *Justice, Gender and the Family*, New York 1989, p. 138.

116 NLR 56

▸ *Post-neoliberal anti-economism.* The possible shift away from neoliberalism offers the opportunity to reactivate the emancipatory promise of second-wave feminism. Adopting a fully three-dimensional account of injustice, we might now integrate in a more balanced way the dimensions of redistribution, recognition and representation that splintered in the previous era. Grounding those indispensable aspects of feminist critique in a robust, updated sense of the social totality, we should reconnect feminist critique to the critique of capitalism—and thereby re-position feminism squarely on the Left.

▸ *Post-neoliberal anti-androcentrism.* Likewise, the possible shift to a post-neoliberal society offers the chance to break the spurious link between our critique of the family wage and flexible capitalism. Reclaiming our critique of androcentrism, feminists might militate for a form of life that decentres waged work and valorizes uncommodified activities, including carework. Now performed largely by women, such activities should become valued components of a good life for everyone.

▸ *Post-neoliberal anti-étatism.* The crisis of neoliberalism also offers the chance to break the link between our critique of étatism and marketization. Reclaiming the mantle of participatory democracy, feminists might militate now for a new organization of political power, one that subordinates bureaucratic managerialism to citizen empowerment. The point, however, is not to dissipate but to strengthen public power. Thus, the participatory democracy we seek today is one that uses politics to tame markets and to steer society in the interest of justice.

▸ *Post-neoliberal anti-Westphalianism.* Finally, the crisis of neoliberalism offers the chance to resolve, in a productive way, our longstanding ambivalence about the Westphalian frame. Given capital's transnational reach, the public capacities needed today cannot be lodged solely in the territorial state. Here, accordingly, the task is to break the exclusive identification of democracy with the bounded political community. Joining other progressive forces, feminists might militate for a new, post-Westphalian political order—a multi-scalar order that is democratic at every level. Combining subsidiarity with participation, the new constellation of democratic powers should be capable of redressing injustices in every dimension, along every axis and on every scale, including trans-border injustices.

I am suggesting, then, that this is a moment in which feminists should think big. Having watched the neoliberal onslaught instrumentalize our best ideas, we have an opening now in which to reclaim them. In seizing this moment, we might just bend the arc of the impending transformation in the direction of justice—and not only with respect to gender.

[18]

Democratizing Citizenship:
Some Advantages of a Basic Income

CAROLE PATEMAN

If the focus of interest is democratization, including women's freedom, a basic income is preferable to stakeholding. Prevailing theoretical approaches and conceptions of individual freedom, free-riding seen as a problem of men's employment, and neglect of feminist insights obscure the democratic potential of a basic income. An argument in terms of individual freedom as self-government, a basic income as a democratic right, and the importance of the opportunity not to be employed shows how a basic income can help break both the link between income and employment and the mutual reinforcement of the institutions of marriage, employment, and citizenship.

Keywords: *basic income; stakeholding; democratization; women; free-riding*

The essays by Philippe Van Parijs on basic income and Bruce Ackerman and Anne Alstott on a stake (or capital grant) contain very valuable insights into both these ideas. They also provide arguments about feasibility and the best way to present stakeholding or a basic income to gain public support. I am going to focus on the reasons for advocating a basic income, and how a theoretical argument for it should be framed. By a "basic income" I am referring to the payment of a regular sum by a government to each individual (citizen) over an adult lifetime, with no conditions attached. "A stake" means a one-time unconditional capital grant from a government to all individuals (citizens) at, say, age twenty-one.[1]

My view is that in the current political climate in the United States and Britain a stake is likely to prove more acceptable to public opinion than a basic income. The Blair government in Britain has already committed itself to a variant of stakeholding, the Baby Bond. Under this proposal the government will open a capital account for each child at birth, to be available with the accrued interest when the child is eighteen. A basic income stands more chance of being introduced in Europe where, as Van Parijs illustrates in his essay, income support policies have already moved in a direction where a basic income, albeit probably of a partial character, could be seen as a logical "next step."

Stakeholding, I agree, would be an advance over current arrangements in the United States and in Britain. But which is to be preferred: a capital grant or a basic income?

The answer to that question depends upon the reasons each of these ideas is being advocated. All ideas and policies are invariably put forward for a variety of different reasons and involve different hopes about what might be achieved. The reasons that eventually become most prominent in public debate then help shape practical outcomes. All human activities have unintended and unforeseen consequences, so we cannot be certain of the results of introducing either a basic income or stakeholding, not least since a great deal hinges on the level of the income or capital grant. But because the direction of change depends, among other things, on the reasons the change is advocated and what it is expected to achieve, the manner in which the theoretical case is made for a basic income or a stake is crucial.

I became interested in the idea of a basic income some years ago for two main reasons. First, because of the part that basic income could play in furthering democratization, that is, the creation of a more democratic society in which individual freedom and citizenship are of equal worth for everyone. The second, and closely related, reason is because of its potential in advancing women's freedom. My argument is that in light of these reasons a basic income is preferable to a stake. A basic income is a crucial part of any strategy for democratic social change because, unlike a capital grant, it could help break the long-standing link between income and employment and end the mutual reinforcement of the institutions of marriage, employment, and citizenship. In the early twentieth century, Bertram Pickard declared that a state bonus (a forerunner of a basic income) "must be deemed the monetary equivalent of the right to land, of the right to life and liberty."[2] My conception of the democratic significance of a basic income is in the spirit of Pickard's statement.

I will begin with some general arguments about why, if democratization is the goal, a basic income should be preferred to stakeholding, and then discuss the institution of employment and some questions about free-riding and the household.

A BASIC INCOME AND SELF-GOVERNMENT

My argument for a basic income shares the view of Van Parijs and Ackerman and Alstott that both a basic income and a stake expand individual freedom. However, our reasons for holding this view and our conceptions of individual freedom are very different. Basic income in Van Parijs's *Real Freedom for All* and stakeholding in Ackerman and Alstott's *The Stakeholder Society* are justified in terms of freedom as individual opportunity. Despite the many other differences between the form and content of their arguments, they agree about the conception of freedom to be promoted. I am concerned with another conception of freedom, individual freedom as self-government or autonomy, which I see as a political form and as central to democracy. In *Real Freedom for All* Van Parijs explicitly rejects any necessary connection between individual freedom and democracy; if there is a connection it is merely contingent.[3]

Individual freedom as autonomy or self-government has been neglected in the academic debates about stakeholding, but it is central to democracy. Modern (universal) democracy rests on the premise that individuals are born, or are naturally, free and are equal to each other. That is to say, they are self-governing or autonomous. If their self-government is to be maintained they must become citizens with rights, and interact within institutions that further autonomy. In this conception, freedom includes not only individual economic (private) opportunities, and the opportunity to participate in collective self-government, but also individual autonomy. The latter tends to be overlooked, in part because "democracy" has become identified with collective (national) self-government, especially through "free and fair elections." Other forms of government that deny or limit individuals' freedom fall out of the picture, such as government in marriage or the workplace. Insofar as self-government in these areas has received attention in political theory it has been directed to the workplace rather than to marriage, despite three centuries of feminist analysis that has highlighted the denial or limitation of wives' self-government and the political significance of the institution of marriage.

Individual self-government depends not only on the opportunities available but also on the form of authority structure within which individuals interact with one another in their daily lives. Self-government requires that individuals both go about their lives within democratic authority structures that enhance their autonomy and that they have the standing, and are able (have the opportunities and means), to enjoy and safeguard their freedom. A basic income—set at the appropriate level—is preferable to a stake because it helps create the circumstances for democracy and individual self-government.

Little attention has been paid in recent academic debates to the democratic significance of a stake or a basic income. Participants have tended to focus on such questions as social justice, relief of poverty, equality of opportunity, or promotion of flexible labor markets, rather than democracy. I do not want to downplay the importance of these questions, or suggest that they are irrelevant to democracy, but they involve different concerns and arguments than explicit attention to democratization. Academic discussion today is too often conducted in a series of separate compartments, each with its own frame of reference. In political theory, for instance, discussion of social justice has usually been undertaken by one set of theorists and democratic theory by others, with the two discussions seldom intersecting. The terms of the debate about stakeholding have tended to be confined within the framework provided by republicanism, libertarianism, utilitarianism, and liberalism. And, rather oddly in ostensibly "political" theory (though in keeping with the times), political argument is being displaced by neo-classical economic concepts and theories.

The narrowness of the debate is exacerbated by the striking absence of the arguments and insights provided by feminist scholars. Some feminists are opposed to a basic income but their arguments are absent too. Many years of scholarship about marriage, employment, and citizenship are virtually ignored in debates about basic income and stakeholding, and women's freedom (self-government) and its implications for a democratic social transformation have hardly been mentioned.

Now that the nostrums of neo-classical economics enshrined in national and international policy making have begun to look a little tattered, the way is being opened for some new ideas. The idea of a basic income is not, strictly speaking, new; advocates usually trace it back to Tom Paine, and I have mentioned one of its earlier incarnations as a state bonus. But it is now being more widely discussed, and current circumstances (as I shall discuss below) offer a much more favorable environment than in years past. A basic income offers not just an alternative to highly bureaucratized public provision, and to the less eligibility doctrines that have been resurrected in recent years, but an opportunity to move out of the very well-worn ruts of current discussions of welfare policy. As Brian Barry has stated, "Basic income is not just another idea for rejigging the existing system." Rather, it has the potential to lead to "a different way of relating individual and society."[4] Or, at least, it has that potential if it is argued for in terms of democratization and women's freedom.

A DEMOCRATIC RIGHT

One reason for the democratic potential of a basic income is that it would provide an important opportunity, namely, *the freedom not to be employed*. Participants in the debates about a basic income tend to skirt round this distinctive implication, but, as I shall argue, it is central to its democratizing possibilities—providing that the income is set at an appropriate level. Neither the idea of a basic income nor a capital grant says anything about the level at which they should be set. The level proposed will depend on the reasons for supporting such proposals. My assumption is that, for a basic income to be relevant for democratization, it should be adequate to provide what I call a modest but decent standard of life. This is a level sufficient to allow individuals to have some control over the course of their lives, and to participate to the extent that they wish in the cultural, economic, social, and political life of their polity.

It might be objected that the level of basic income has more to do with practical feasibility than why the proposal should be supported. The objection always raised when basic income or stakeholding is mentioned is that both schemes would cost far too much, but political imagination is required here.[5] Besides, before turning to problems of implementation and cost we need to know *why* a basic income or stakeholding should be introduced at all, and what level of income or grant is entailed, given those reasons.

If interest in a basic income is, say, as a means to relieve poverty—a goal that I certainly share—then the level of income will differ from the level required when a basic income is advocated as part of a wider strategy for democratization. Van Parijs remarks that the fight for a basic income "is no game for purists." But if we are going to be "tinkerers and opportunists"[6] in attempts to get a basic income squarely on the political agenda, we need to understand what we are being opportunistic about, including wider goals and the level of the income. What is it that we shall be sacrificing if, as no doubt will be the case, compromises are necessary in practice? Perhaps my notion of a level of basic income sufficient for a modest but decent standard of life makes me a "purist," but this is necessary to appreciate the differences between arguing for basic income as an element in a democratic social transformation or advocating it as a means of improving existing systems of income support. The latter is no doubt more politically feasible, but a great deal of democratic value in the idea of a basic income is lost if immediate political feasibility dominates the academic discussion.

The idea of a basic income has much less political and theoretical interest if the payment is assumed to be below subsistence level and seen merely as a way to alleviate poverty. Thus I would take issue with Van Parijs when he states that "the central case" for a basic income is as a "specific way of handling the joint challenge of poverty and unemployment."[7] To be sure, a basic income is a way of handling this challenge, but this is not, I would argue, the central reason to be interested in the idea. On the face of it, Ackerman and Alstott's case for stakeholding seems much closer to my own argument. They focus not on poverty or unemployment but on citizenship: "Stakeholding is not a poverty program. It is a citizenship program."[8] A capital grant, they write, creates a "proud culture of free citizenship."[9] But the citizenship in question is economic citizenship; a stake is an "economic birthright."[10] In *The Stakeholder Society* they state that "just as one person—one vote expresses political citizenship, an equal stake expresses economic citizenship."[11] The comparison between a basic income and universal suffrage is instructive, but I part company with Ackerman and Alstott in their bifurcation of citizenship.

When I first began to think about basic income I was alerted to the comparison between suffrage and a basic income by a little-noticed passage in T. H. Marshall's famous *Citizenship and Social Class:* "To have to bargain for a living wage in a society which accepts the living wage as a social right is as absurd as to have to haggle for a vote in a society which accepts the vote as a political right."[12] There are, however, two problems with Marshall's argument that are pertinent here.

First, as is well known, he separated citizenship into three different components, civil, political, and social rights. But whether the division is into three parts, or Ackerman and Alstott's two-part economic and political citizenship, the result is the same: attention gets diverted into endless wrangles about which category is primary and which category can properly be seen as "rights" (do social rights count?). Second, Marshall linked standard of life to employment, by which he meant male employment, a matter I shall discuss shortly.

Van Parijs also refers to universal suffrage. In making his comment about purism and tinkering, he compares the fight for a basic income to the fight for universal suffrage, and neither, he states, is an "all-or-nothing affair." This is a curious comment. Countries with restricted suffrage—even restricted to the male half of the population—are often called "democracies," but that reveals less about the suffrage than about a more general wariness of the full implications of democratization. The suffrage is either universal, that is, encompassing all adults, or it is not. Partial enfranchisement means that there are qualifying conditions that only some of the adult population can meet (typically, owning property, being male, having a white skin, or belonging to a certain ethnic group). Where such eligibility conditions exist a vote is a privilege, not a right. Universal suffrage is democratic precisely because the vote ceases to be the privilege of a part of the population and becomes a right of all adults. To be universal, qualifying criteria for the suffrage have to be reduced to the bare minimum that everyone can meet with time, such as an age requirement and length of residence for naturalization, or that all can meet barring accidents of nature, such as being of sound mind.

My argument is that a basic income should be seen, like the suffrage, as a democratic right, or a political birthright. By a "democratic" right I have in mind a fundamental right in Henry Shue's sense of a "basic right." Basic rights "specify the line beneath which no one is to be allowed to sink." Rights are basic "if enjoyment of them is essential to the enjoyment of all other rights."[13] Subsistence is one of Shue's basic rights, which he defines as "what is needed for a decent chance at a reasonably healthy and active life of more or less normal length, barring tragic interventions."[14] Building on this line of argument, a basic income, at a level sufficient for a modest but decent standard of life, can be seen as a fundamental or democratic right. Such an income is necessary to enable all citizens to participate as fully as they wish in all aspects of the life of their society.

A basic income as a fundamental right can more reasonably be compared to the suffrage than can a stake. Citizenship and the suffrage are for life, and a basic income is a right that also exists over a citizen's lifetime, whereas a capital grant is a one-off payment at the beginning of adulthood. A stake provides young people with a valuable start, but what of the rest of their life as citizens? A basic income provides the lifelong security that helps safeguard other rights. Universal suffrage is the emblem of equal citizenship and underpins an orderly change of government through free and fair elections, so enhancing citizens' security. A basic income is the emblem of full citizenship and provides the security required to maintain that political standing. Another way of making this point is that a basic income as a democratic right is necessary for individual freedom as self-government, a political freedom.

One of the major disagreements between Ackerman and Alstott and Van Parijs in their essays is over the latter's prohibition on the capitalization of (future) basic income into a single payment. Van Parijs minimizes the difference between basic income and a capital grant and remarks that the difference between the two "would be essentially annulled if the . . . recipients could freely borrow against their future basic income stream."[15] I shall leave aside the issue of whether the future income stream can be used as collateral for a mortgage on a house, for example, and concentrate on prohibition against conversion of a basic income into a single lump-sum. The question is whether this constitutes a significant limitation on individual freedom.

Ackerman and Alstott argue that it does; a basic income stands in the way of individual freedom. Young people are hindered in achieving their goals if they cannot choose to capitalize their basic income as a capital grant. Ackerman and Alstott, therefore, see a basic income as "a fancy name for a restraint on alienation."[16] The restriction on conversion, they argue, makes basic income into the equivalent of a "spendthrift trust," the beneficiary of which has to apply to a trustee, who administers the trust according to a set of conditions, in order to be able to use the money. They see basic income as a "universal spendthrift trust." To treat adults as potential spendthrifts "demeans their standing as autonomous citizens." In contrast a stake would "promote the real freedom of young adults on the threshold of life."

It might, but the most obvious problem is that a lump-sum capital grant could very easily and quickly be squandered or lost. Many responsible individuals could lose their capital even if they avoided Las Vegas or drugs. Small businesses have a high failure rate despite the best efforts of their owners, and stock markets crash. Of course, Ackerman and Alstott are aware of the problem of stakeblowing, and they supplement the individual stake with an old-age pension that is provided, unconditionally, as right of citizenship. But stakeholding plus a retirement pension are insufficient for democratic citizenship. Too long a period of citizens' lives is open to the vagaries of chance and the market.

For individuals to be able to decide in which form to receive their income means that entrepreneurial activities would no doubt be encouraged as well as trips to Las Vegas. Ackerman and Alstott see the risk of individuals losing their lump-sum as part of individual freedom. As they write in *The Stakeholder Society*, they are "interested in opportunities, not outcomes," and they present a basic income as a cushion for failure, whereas a stake "is launching pad for success."[17] But the launch might well end in a crash. Equality of opportunity is a democratic principle, but the freedom involved in young people being able to convert a basic income to a capital stake hardly looms large from the perspective of democratization and individual freedom as self-government.

Ackerman and Alstott also criticize a basic income on the grounds that it "encourages a short-term consumerist perspective."[18] The only sense in which, as far as I can see, a basic income might do this is if it were introduced at a level below that required for a modest but decent standard of life. A payment below subsistence level might be seen, at least by those well above the poverty level, as merely an extra bit of discretionary income available for immediate spending. But even this would be mitigated if the tax system came into play for those at higher income levels. There seems no good reason why a basic income implemented at the level I am suggesting would encourage consumerism. Indeed, one could make the opposite case; by breaking the link between income and the labor market it would allow individuals, if they so wished, to abstain from the race to accumulate ever more material goods and help combat the identification of freedom with consumerism.

EMPLOYMENT

A basic income would have two important consequences for democratization. First, it would allow individuals more easily to refuse to enter or to leave relationships that violate individual self-government or that involve unsafe, unhealthy, or demeaning conditions. It would, as Van Parijs states, endow "the weakest with bargaining power,"[19] but the bargaining power is a by-product of the full standing as citizens that a basic income helps create. Basic income is not (as Marshall saw) about bargaining but self-government, rights, and democratic citizenship. A basic income would also support citizens' participation in collective self-government by opening up opportunities for citizens to develop their political capacities and skills. A guaranteed standard of life would mean that participation in social and political life would not require heroic efforts on the part of any citizens.

The second consequence, and a crucial difference between basic income and stakeholding, is that a basic income would give citizens the freedom not to be employed. Both a basic income, if set at the appropriate level, and a capital grant would provide enlarged opportunities for individuals, but the opportunities provided by a basic income would be far wider than those offered by a stake, since the new opportunities would not be confined to the competitive market. A basic income, like a stake, would make it possible for anyone (at any point in their life, not merely while they are young) to go back to school, to retrain for a new occupation, or to open a business. But a basic income providing a modest but decent standard of living would do much more.

In *The Constitution of Liberty*, Friedrich von Hayek—like G. D. H. Cole from a very different point on the political spectrum—argued that employment fostered an outlook among employees that was an impediment to freedom. The employed, he wrote, are "in many respects . . . alien and often inimical to much that constitutes the driving force of a free society."[20] His solution was that there should be as many gentlemen of private means as possible to counteract the deleterious effect of employment. In effect, such gentlemen have large basic incomes, albeit not provided by a government. At a very much lower level of resources a basic income democratizes the freedom open to a gentlemen of private means to spend time in scholarly pursuits, good works, writing poetry, cultivating friendships, hunting, or being a drone or a wastrel. A basic income would allow individuals at any time to do voluntary or political work, for example, to learn to surf, to write or paint, to devote themselves to family life, or to have a quiet period of self-reassessment or contemplation.

By opening up this range of opportunities and uncoupling income and standard of life from employment, a basic income has the potential both to encourage critical reassessment of the mutually reinforcing structures of marriage, employment, and citizenship and to open the possibility that these institutions could be remade in a new, more democratic form. A capital grant given to young people with the aim of assisting individual economic success lacks the same potential. In *The Stakeholder Society*, Ackerman and Alstott argue that a stake encourages individuals, in a way that a basic income cannot, to reflect upon what they want to do with their lives, and appraise their situation. "Civic reflection" and attention to "the fate of the nation" become possible when economic anxieties are lifted.[21] A "purer form of patriotism" will arise out of the "simple gratitude to the nation" that citizens will feel as they think about their capital grant and the debt that they owe to their country for the economic citizenship that comes with stakeholding.[22]

Patriotism and gratitude, however, have only a tenuous connection to individual freedom. Provision of a one-time capital grant will no doubt encourage individuals to consider what courses of action are open to them, and might even foster reflection on the debt they owe to their country. But it seems implausible that it would help promote reflection on the political implications of the structural connections between marriage, employment, and citizenship. Both the wide variety of opportunities made possible when employment becomes truly voluntary and the fact that women's freedom would be greatly enhanced mean that, unlike a stake, a basic income has the potential to open the door to institutional change— providing that democratization is at the forefront of discussion and that feminist arguments are taken seriously.

The freedom not to be employed runs counter to the direction of much recent public policy and political rhetoric (especially in Anglo-American countries, though the policies are international), and this makes stakeholding more palatable than basic income in the current political climate. The effect of such policies and rhetoric is to draw even tighter the long-standing link between employment and citizenship, at the very time when a reassessment has been made possible by changing circumstances. The institution of employment is a barrier to democratic freedom and citizenship in two ways. First, economic enterprises have an undem-

98   POLITICS & SOCIETY

ocratic structure, a point that I shall not pursue here.[23] Second, as feminist scholars
have demonstrated, the relationship between the institutions of marriage, employment, and citizenship has meant that the standing of wives as citizens has always
been, and remains, problematic.

The Anglo-American social insurance system was constructed on the assumption that wives not only were their husbands' economic dependents but lesser citizens whose entitlement to benefits depended on their private status, not on their
citizenship. Male "breadwinners," who made a contribution from their earnings to
"insure" that they received benefits in the event of unemployment or sickness, and
in their old age, were the primary citizens. Their employment was treated as *the*
contribution that a citizen could make to the well-being of the community.
Ackerman and Alstott acknowledge this in their criticism of "workplace justice,"[24] and their recognition that unconditional retirement pensions would be particularly important for the many older women whose benefits still largely derive
from their husbands' employment record.[25] That is to say, only paid employment
has been seen as "work," as involving the tasks that are the mark of a productive
citizen and contributor to the polity. Other contributions, notably all the work
required to reproduce and maintain a healthy population and care for infants, the
elderly, the sick, and infirm—the caring tasks, most of which are not paid for and
are undertaken by women—have been seen as irrelevant to citizenship.

FREE-RIDING AND THE HOUSEHOLD

The debates about basic income also center on the figure of a man in—or
avoiding—paid employment. This is very clear in one of the major criticisms of,
and apprehensions about, the idea of a basic income; that is, that it would encourage free-riding and idleness. Free-riders breach the principle of reciprocity by
obtaining the fruits of the efforts of others and contributing nothing themselves in
return; a basic income, it is charged, would "inspire a segment of the able population . . . to abjure work for a life of idle fun."[26] But who is being seen as so prone to
idleness and fun? The assumption guiding the discussion of basic income is that
the problem is about men and employment.[27] A much greater problem about male
free-riding to which a basic income is directly relevant, but a problem about the
household, not employment, is therefore ignored.

Van Parijs appears to be an exception to the prevailing view of free-riding.
Unlike most other participants in discussions of basic income he has noticed that
free-riding exists "on a massive scale" in household interactions.[28] But who are
the free-riders in the household? Barry notes that full-time housewives can be
seen as free-riders.[29] But they can only be seen in that way if "work" is taken to
mean paid employment.[30] As feminist scholars have emphasized for a very long
time, housewives are working (unpaid) by undertaking the necessary caring
work. Given the major contribution they already make for no monetary return at

all, wives (women) are hardly likely to be the target of the objection that a basic income would lead to idleness and fun.

The majority of wives are now in some form of paid employment, but their labor force participation is usually different from that of men. This reflects the legacy of a wage-system that enshrined the belief that husbands (men) not wives (women) are "breadwinners."[31] Many more women than men work part-time, and women earn less than men. The private and public sexual division of labor, that is to say, continues to be structured so that men monopolize full-time, higher paying, and more prestigious paid employment, and wives do a disproportionate share of unpaid work in the home. Given the structure of institutions and social beliefs, this appears as a "rational" arrangement. The mutual reinforcement of marriage and employment explains why husbands can take advantage of the unpaid work of wives and avoid doing their fair share of the caring work. That is why there is massive free-riding in the household—by husbands.

Neither free-riding by husbands nor its scale is usually acknowledged in discussions of basic income and stakeholding. This is because marriage and the household rarely enter the argument. The narrow parameters of discussion and the influence of the assumptions of neo-classical economics preclude attention to institutional structures and their interrelationships. Van Parijs is an exception in recognizing that a problem of free-riding exists in households, but his neo-classical theoretical apparatus leaves him unable to acknowledge that the problem is one of men (husbands) and the work of caring for household members. His argument is that free-riding arises merely because of differences in individual tastes or preferences. Free-riding, Van Parijs states, occurs when benefits enjoyed by both partners in a household are produced by only one of them, the partner who happens to care most about the particular benefit. His example is that the partner who most strongly prefers tidiness will make sure that the home is tidy.

"Tidiness" is part of the more general work of housekeeping, and there is abundant empirical evidence that shows that the female partner is most likely to do the housework, including tidying up. The empirical data do not show this pattern just by chance—female partners do not by some quirk happen to prefer tidiness more strongly than their male partners. The institution of marriage and social beliefs about what it means to be a "wife" or "husband" have vanished in Van Parijs's analysis, and there are merely two individuals, indistinguishable except for their different tastes for tidy surroundings. His theoretical approach in *Real Freedom for All* precludes analysis of the structure of relations between the sexes, and a crucial area of debate is, therefore, removed from discussion of basic income.

Indeed, some advocates of a basic income argue that it would make it easier for women to do "their" work in the home. Van Parijs remarks that some women would probably use their basic income to "lighten the 'double shift' at certain periods of their lives."[32] But, he continues, "who can sincerely believe that working subject to the dictates of a boss for forty hours a week is a path to liberation?"

One can have grave doubts on the latter score—but also ask, first, whether working for a husband at home is the right path either and, second, ask why *men* might not use their basic income to take on their fair share of the caring work?

Now is the time to ask the second question. The conditions under which the institution of employment and the Anglo-American social insurance system were constructed have now crumbled. "Old economy" male breadwinner jobs are being swept away in global economic restructuring and "downsizing." New jobs have been created but many are low paid, lacking benefits, and temporary, and economic insecurity is widespread. Views about femininity, masculinity, and marriage are changing too, but since we are still in the midst of all these changes it is hard to know what the eventual outcome will be. Still, times of rapid change provide opportunities to investigate new ideas and look critically at old arrangements—including the moral hazard of institutions that give incentives to men to avoid their fair share of the unpaid work of caring for others. It has now become possible to rethink the connections between income and paid employment; between marriage, employment, and citizenship; between the private and public division of labor; and between caring work and other work—and to reconsider the meaning of "work." But such rethinking requires a different approach from that taken by many participants in the debate about stakeholding and basic income. This is crucial if proper account is to be taken of women's freedom, which has received rather short shrift in discussions of a basic income.

As early as 1792, Mary Wollstonecraft argued in *A Vindication of the Rights of Woman* that rights, citizenship, and full standing for women required economic independence, whether a woman was married or single.[33] As Ackerman and Alstott emphasize, a capital grant would be a step in this direction, but a basic income would for the first time provide all women with lifelong economic independence. Thus feminists might be expected strongly to support the introduction of a basic income.[34]

Yet this is not the case. Some feminists are critical of the idea because they fear a basic income would reinforce the existing sexual division of labor and women's lesser citizenship. They argue that the provision of an income without having to engage in paid employment would, in light of women's position in the labor market combined with lingering beliefs about the proper place and tasks of women and men, give women an even greater incentive to undertake more unpaid caring work in the household, and, conversely, men would have another incentive to free-ride. A basic income, that is, would reinforce existing limitations on women's freedom.[35]

This objection illustrates the importance of the reasons advanced for supporting a basic income. The probability of feminist fears being borne out is higher, for example, when the argument is made that to avoid weakening the "incentive to work" a basic income should be below subsistence level. This "incentive" is promoted with men and paid employment in mind. A basic income at this level provides no incentive for wives to "work" (i.e., enter paid employment); rather, it would encourage them to do more unpaid caring work. Again, to support basic income on the grounds that it would improve the living standards of the poorest sectors of the population does not promote consideration of the structural connections between marriage, employment, and citizenship, and the private and public sexual division of labor. Without the debates about basic income being informed by feminist arguments, and a concern for democratization (and genuine democratization necessarily includes women's freedom and standing as citizens), the discussion will revolve around ways of tinkering with the existing system rather than encouraging thinking about how it might be made more democratic.

Putting democratization at the center requires attention to institutional structures, especially the institutions of marriage and employment. For instance, Ackerman and Alstott remark in *The Stakeholder Society* that the "case for stakeholding does not ultimately rest on its effects on employment, marriage, or crime. It rests on each American's claim to respect as a free and equal citizen."[36] However (leaving crime aside), the respect accorded to women and men as free and equal citizens has a great deal to do with the institutions of marriage and employment. It is not possible to understand women's lesser citizenship, as Ackerman and Alstott show in their discussion of social security, without understanding the relationship between their position as wives and men's position as workers.

Similarly, Van Parijs argues that while "a defensible long-term vision" of an unconditional basic income at the highest sustainable level is vital, nevertheless more limited and politically feasible proposals are also essential. He states that a household-based guaranteed minimum income "would definitely be a major change in the right direction"[37]—but the right direction according to which reasons? Household-based schemes disregard not only all the problems about the sexual division of labor, and the fact that women earn less than men, but also income distribution *within* households. Can it be confidently assumed that income would be distributed equally between husband and wife? A basic income is important for feminism and democratization precisely because it is paid not to households but *individuals as citizens*.

A focus on individuals does not imply resort to the atomistic individualism of neo-classical economics. The problem of women's self-government and full standing as citizens is visible only when individuals are conceptualized within the context of social relations and institutions. A household-based basic income allows the problem of marriage, employment, and citizenship to be avoided since wives (women) disappear into the category of "the family" or "household." To treat a basic income as a payment to households rather than individuals ignores the question of who performs the work of caring for household members. That is, it is tacitly assumed that reciprocity exists and that free-riding is only a problem about men avoiding employment.

This assumption is nicely illustrated by the picture of a male surfer on the cover of *Real Freedom for All*. In academic discussions the surfer is used to represent non-contributors. But in the popular political imagination and the media other symbols of free-riding are present, such as the African American "welfare queen" or, more recently, the "illegal immigrant" or the "asylum seeker."[38] The figure of the surfer not only obscures the problem for democratization of popular attitudes embodied in these other symbols but also obliterates the systematic avoidance of one form of contribution, the vital caring work, by men who are *in employment*.

Nor do the numerous suggestions for conditions to be placed on payment of a basic income as a solution to free-riding—Atkinson's "participation income" is a well-known example[39]—get to grips with free-riding by men in the household. While the notion of a "contribution" may be broadened to include, for example, the work of caring for others, as in Atkinson's proposal, this is insufficient to focus attention on the structural problem of the connections between marriage, employment, and free-riding by husbands. While payment of a basic income to a husband for his "contribution" through employment and to his wife for her "contribution" in the home is to recognize that she does indeed make a socially valuable contribution, this does little to calm the fears of some feminists that a basic income will merely reinforce women's lesser standing and the idleness of husbands in the household.

An adequate discussion of free-riding and reciprocity in debates about basic income is hampered by, on the one hand, the prevalence of an economistic or contractual sense of "reciprocity." In this interpretation of the term the recipient must make a contribution directly in return for every benefit received, a view that magnifies the problem of free-riding. On the other hand, by ignoring the household, participants in the debate tacitly presuppose that "reciprocity" in another sense, that is, mutual aid, characterizes domestic interactions.[40] To refocus the debate about basic income around its significance for democratization would mean replacing the preoccupation with one kind of free-riding with an examination of how to reinforce reciprocity in the sense of mutual aid across the social order. And that, in turn, would require widening the terms of debate, engaging with the large body of feminist analysis, moving away from the assumptions of neo-classical economics, and developing a political argument.

In conclusion I want to make two further points. First, schemes for a conditional basic income raise another problem. In effect, these proposals declare irrelevant the comparison of basic income with universal suffrage as a democratic right. The criteria for eligibility for a conditional income may be very generously interpreted, but there are always likely to be individuals who fail, or refuse, to meet the conditions. What, then, is their status? Are they, like individuals who lack the franchise, to become second-class citizens? All the time that a basic income is conditional, a privilege not a right, the problem of second-class and lesser citizenship cannot be avoided. The use that citizens make of their freedom is open to no guarantees. Democratic self-government entails that they decide for themselves how and when they will contribute, or whether they will contribute at all. If the cost of improving democratic freedom for all citizens is the existence of some drones, then, I submit, it is a cost worth paying.

Second, let me emphasize that a basic income is not a panacea. In itself, a basic income would not, for instance, provide an adequate stock of affordable housing, sufficient good quality education, adequate health care, an end to racism, or violence-free neighborhoods. Yet if a genuinely democratic society in which the freedom of women is as important as that of men remains an aspiration, it is hard to see that there is a substitute for an unconditional basic income.

NOTES

1. I am focusing on adults and citizens here; a more complete account would also discuss non-citizen residents and children.

2. Bertram Pickard, *A Reasonable Revolution: Being a Discussion of the State Bonus Scheme—A Proposal for a National Minimum Income* (London: Allen and Unwin, 1919), 21.

3. Philippe Van Parijs, *Real Freedom for All: What (if Anything) Can Justify Capitalism?* (New York: Oxford University Press, 1995), 8-9, 15-17. Van Parijs's argument is libertarian or, more exactly, a real libertarian argument that departs in some significant respects from typical libertarianism. I comment further on Van Parijs in Carole Pateman, Freedom and Democratization: Why Basic Income Is to Be Preferred to Basic Capital, in *The Ethics of Stakeholding*, edited by Keith Dowding, Jurgen De Wispelaere, and Stuart White (Palgrave, forthcoming).

4. Brian Barry, The Attractions of Basic Income, in *Equality*, edited by Jane Franklin (London: Institute for Public Policy Research, 1997), 161.

5. Others are much more qualified than I to discuss this aspect, but how public monies are allocated—guns or butter—is as much a political as an economic question. Bruce Ackerman and Anne L. Alstott, *The Stakeholder Society* (New Haven, CT: Yale University Press, 1999), provide a detailed discussion of how a capital grant could be financed through a wealth tax. However, neither wealth taxes nor income taxes are popular at present, so I would suggest consideration of an alternative, hypothecated form of taxation, such as a Tobin tax on speculative financial trading, or a tax on polluting and other environmentally destructive activities. Or, even better, I would advocate far fewer guns and much more butter.

6. Van Parijs, Basic Income: A Simple and Powerful Idea for the Twenty-first Century, *Politics & Society* 32, no. 1 (2004): 7-40.

7. Ibid.

8. Ackerman and Alstott, *The Stakeholder Society*, 197.

9. Bruce Ackerman and Anne Alstott, Why Stakeholding? *Politics & Society* 32, no. 1 (2004): 41-60.

10. Claus Offe, The German Welfare State: Principles, Performance and Prospectives after Unification, *Thesis Eleven* 63 (2000): 11-37, also argues in terms of universal economic citizenship in his proposal for sabbatical accounts, which he presents as a gradualist and experimental approach to basic income.

11. Ackerman and Alstott, *The Stakeholder Society*, 33.

12. T. H. Marshall, Citizenship and Social Class, in *Sociology at the Crossroads and Other Essays* (London: Heineman, 1963), 116.

13. Henry Shue, *Basic Rights: Subsistence, Affluence, and U.S. Foreign Policy*, 2nd ed. (Princeton, NJ: Princeton University Press, 1996), 18, 19.

14. Ibid., 23.

15. Van Parijs, Basic Income, 9.

16. Ackerman and Alstott, Why Stakeholding?

17. Ackerman and Alstott, *The Stakeholder Society*, 24, 215.

18. Ackerman and Alstott, Why Stakeholding?

19. Van Parijs, Basic Income.

20. Friedrich von Hayek, *The Constitution of Liberty* (Chicago: University of Chicago Press, 1960), 119.

21. Ackerman and Alstott, *The Stakeholder Society*, 185.

22. Ibid., 186, see also 43-44.

23. See Carole Pateman, *Participation and Democratic Theory* (Cambridge, UK: Cambridge University Press, 1970); Id., Self-Ownership and Property in the Person: Democratization and a Tale of Two Concepts, *Journal of Political Philosophy* 10, no. 1 (2002): 20-53.

24. Ackerman and Alstott, Why Stakeholding?

25. Ackerman and Alstott, *The Stakeholder Society*, 145-46.

26. Elizabeth Anderson, Optional Freedoms, in Symposium: 'Delivering a Basic Income,' *Boston Review* October-November (2000): 16.

27. The consequence for employment rates of a basic income is hard to determine in the abstract. On the one hand, it would act as a disincentive for individuals to be employed, since, ex hypothesis, they could live on the income. On the other hand, precisely because the income is paid whether or not individuals are employed, they could enjoy a better standard of life by taking a low-paid job than living on a basic income alone. It would thus act as an incentive to employment and improve the flexibility of the labor market.

28. Van Parijs, *Real Freedom for All*, 143.

29. Brian Barry, Real Freedom and Basic Income, *Journal of Political Philosophy* 4 (1996): 242-76, 245.

30. McKay and VanEvery remark that critics of the free-rider objection argue in masculinist terms which ignore the implicit relegation of family careers to this category: Ailsa McKay and Jo VanEvery, Gender, Family, and Income Maintenance: A Feminist Case for Citizens Basic Income, *Social Politics: International Studies in Gender, State, and Society* 7, no. 2 (2000): 281.

31. For a discussion of support for the legacy in the Netherlands, see Janneke Plantenga, J. Schippers, and J. Siegers, Towards an Equal Division of Paid and Unpaid Work: The Case of the Netherlands, *Journal of European Social Policy* 9, no. 2 (1999): 99-110.

32. Philippe Van Parijs, A Basic Income for All, in Symposium: 'Delivering a Basic Income,' *Boston Review*, October/November (2000): 4-8, 7.

33. Mary Wollstonecraft, A Vindication of the Rights of Woman, in *Political Writings*, edited by Janet Todd (Toronto: University of Toronto Press, [1792] 1993).

34. For some examples of discussion of the importance of a basic income for women, see Tony Walter, *Basic Income: Freedom from Poverty, Freedom to Work* (London: Marion Boyers, 1989); Hermione Parker, *Citizen's Income and Women*, BIRG discussion paper 2 (London: Citizens Income, 1993); McKay and VanEvery, Gender, Family, and Income Maintenance, 266-84; Ailsa McKay, Arguing for a Citizen's Basic Income: A Feminist Perspective, paper presented at the 2002 annual meeting of the American Political Science

Association, Boston; and on stakeholding, Anne L. Alstott, Good for Women in Symposium: 'Delivering a Basic Income,' *Boston Review*, 2000 October-November.

35. Like Ingrid Robeyns, Will a Basic Income Do Justice to Women? *Analyse and Kritik: Zeitschrift fur Sozialtheorie* 23, no. 1 (2001): 88-105, I have frequently encountered this objection when I have talked about a basic income. It is less often seen in academic discussions.

36. Ackerman and Alstott, *The Stakeholder Society*, 209.

37 Van Parijs, Basic Income, 25.

38. My thanks to Harvey Goldman for his comments about the surfer at a talk I gave at the University of California San Diego in 2001.

39. Anthony Atkinson, The Case for a Participation Income, *Political Quarterly* 67 (1996): 67-70. For a conditional stake see Robert Goodin, Sneaking Up on Stakeholding, in *The Ethics of Stakeholding*, edited by Keith Dowding, Jurgen De Wispelaere, and Stuart White.

40. To apply reciprocity in the first sense to the household would have dire consequences, not least for infants. Political theorists in an earlier era saw reciprocity in my second sense as the primary law of nature. That is, they recognized that a social order is a system of generalized mutual aid and mutual forbearance, or a system of reciprocity. If reciprocity in this sense of the term breaks down, social order begins to disintegrate.

Carole Pateman teaches political theory at the University of California, Los Angeles, where she is a member of the Center for Social Theory and Comparative History and a faculty affiliate of the Center for the Study of Women. She is a fellow of the American Academy of Arts and Sciences. Her publications include Participation and Democratic Theory *and* The Sexual Contract. *In addition to work on the idea of a basic income, her current research includes other questions in democratic theory and an exploration of the intersection between the sexual and racial contracts.*

[19]

Constructing sexual citizenship: theorizing sexual rights

DIANE RICHARDSON

University of Newcastle

Abstract

Recently, a new body of work on sexuality and citizenship has emerged. In this article I analyse sexual citizenship through an examination of the concept of sexual rights. How has rights language been used to articulate demands in relation to sexuality? What do we mean by sexual rights or duties? Although the concept is not new, there are competing claims for what are defined as sexual rights and lack of rights, reflecting not only differences in how sexuality is conceptualized but also the fact that there is no singular agreed definition of sexual citizenship. The combination of sexual rights as a contested concept and the increasing usage of the language of citizenship in 'sexual politics', underlines the need for a critical analysis of its meaning and value as a concept. To this end, I have outlined a framework which tries to make sense of the different ways of interpreting sexual rights in terms of three main sub-streams apparent within sexual rights discourse: conduct-based, identity-based and relationship-based rights claims. This is not to imply an uncritical acceptance of the concept of sexual rights, however this may be defined. On the contrary, it is to attempt to clarify similarities and differences between both individual writers and social groups campaigning for social change in relation to sexuality, in order that we may have a more detailed understanding of the limitations and potential of the notion of sexual citizenship.

Key words: citizenship, gay, lesbian, sexual citizenship, sexual rights, sexuality

Introduction

In recent years citizenship has been an important focus of debate within both political discourse and the social sciences. With this

CRITICAL SOCIAL POLICY 20(1)

renewed interest, reflected within social policy analyses and critiques, there have emerged new frameworks for thinking about citizenship which require us to question its meaning and application. Indeed, a central theme of these developments is that citizenship is a contested concept. This expansion of the idea of citizenship is evidenced in the diversity of arenas in which citizenship is being claimed and contested (Hall and Held, 1989). Interestingly, and despite an almost exclusive focus on the public sphere in previous considerations of citizenship, it would seem that the everyday practices of individuals are increasingly becoming the bases of citizenship. For example, consider the concept of healthier citizenship, currently being promoted by the government as part of its Health Action Zone programme. As 'good citizens', we are enjoined to take care and assume responsibility for our own health and, especially in the case of women, that of any future children we may have, in a context in which we are provided with 'informed choices' that we are expected to exercise. In addition to patterns of eating and drinking, the 'private' and intimate practices of sex are also part of the realms in which healthy citizenship is constituted. Thus, for example, sexual health promotion, whether understood in the context of concerns about the spread of sexually transmitted diseases such as AIDS or the prevalence of unplanned pregnancies in certain sectors of the community, emphasizes the importance of practising safer sex. That is to say, safer sex is one of the responsibilities incumbent upon responsible and self-governing citizens.

Although the question of how ideas of citizenship are gendered (Lister, 1990, 1996, 1997; Phillips, 1991; Walby, 1997; Voet, 1998), as well as racialized (Alexander, 1994; Taylor, 1996), has emerged as an increasingly important area of debate, there is a lack of similar theoretical attention given to sexuality and its connection to citizenship. Recently, however, commentators from a number of disciplines have written about sexuality and citizenship. This includes work in legal theory (e.g. Herman, 1994; Robson, 1992), political theory (e.g. Phelan, 1994, 1995; Wilson, 1995), geography (e.g. Bell, 1995; Binnie, 1995) and sociology (e.g. Giddens, 1992; Plummer, 1995; Richardson, 1998; Weeks, 1998). Within social policy, by contrast, there has been relatively little discussion about sexual citizenship, mirroring a general lack of theorizing about the relationship between sexuality and social policy (Cooper, 1995; Carabine, 1996 a,b). The main purpose of this article, therefore, is to consider this expansion of the idea of citizenship as it relates to sexuality.

107   RICHARDSON—CONSTRUCTING SEXUAL CITIZENSHIP

In surveying the available literature, it would seem that a distinction can be drawn between analyses of sexual citizenship that place greater emphasis on the discussion on rights per se and struggles for rights acquisition, and those that are concerned with the wider social and theoretical implications of access to or exclusion from certain rights on the grounds of sexuality. These two approaches, although not mutually exclusive, reflect somewhat different forms of usage of the term 'sexual citizenship'. First, it may be used to refer specifically to the sexual rights granted or denied to various social groups. In this sense we may, like Evans (1993), conceptualize sexual citizenship in terms of varying degrees of access to a set of rights to sexual expression and consumption. Second, we can conceptualize sexual citizenship in a much broader sense in terms of access to rights more generally. In other words, how are various forms of citizenship status dependent upon a person's sexuality? Elsewhere (see Richardson, 1998) I have outlined how notions of citizenship as a set of civil, political and social rights, as well as common membership of a shared community, are closely associated with the institutionalization of heterosexuality. In this article I would like to analyse sexual citizenship as defined in the former of the two approaches mentioned above, that is through an examination of the concept of sexual rights. How, then, has rights language been used to articulate demands in the field of sexuality?

What do we mean by 'sexual rights'?

Sexual citizenship here refers to a status entailing a number of different rights claims, some of which are recognized as legitimate by the state and are sanctioned. However, if we conceptualize sexual citizenship using a model of rights and duties, then this raises the question of what we define as sexual rights. Although the concept is not new, there are competing claims for what are defined as sexual rights and lack of rights. Sexual rights can be thought about in different ways, reflecting not only differences in how sexuality is conceptualized, but also the fact that there is no singular agreed definition of sexual citizenship.

Within sexual rights discourse can be detected three main substreams: conduct-based rights claims, identity-based rights claims and claims that are relationship based. For the purposes of this article, these aspects will be dealt with under the headings of practice, identity and relationships (see Figure 1). While I recognize that the analytic scheme

CRITICAL SOCIAL POLICY 20(1)

1) **Seeking rights to various forms of sexual practice in personal relationships (e.g. campaigns for sexual freedom and safety)**

2) **Seeking rights through self-definition and the development of individual identities (e.g. the right to be lesbian and gay; female sexual autonomy)**

3) **Seeking rights within social institutions: public validation of various forms of sexual relations (e.g. interracial and same-sex marriages)**

Figure 1 Sexual rights

presented here is merely an intellectual tool to help make sense of the different ways of interpreting sexual rights, I believe it provides a useful framework by which to clarify similarities and differences between both individual writers and social groups campaigning for social change in relation to sexuality. It also highlights, as will be illustrated later, where the boundaries of tolerance or rejection, inclusion or exclusion are sometimes drawn.

Practice

Claims to rights that centre on sexual practice fall into three main categories: those concerned with forms of social regulation which specify what one can and cannot do; those concerned not only with the right to participate in but also the right to enjoy sexual acts, commonly expressed as the right to sexual pleasure; and those concerned with the rights of bodily self-control. I will consider each of these in turn.

The right to participate in sexual activity

At a fundamental level, the concept of sexual rights can be understood as the right to participate in sexual acts. Historically, the concept of rights has been linked to concepts of need and, in this context, such rights claims may be vindicated through definitions of sexuality as a physical need, integral to the status of being human. This is commonly referred to as an essentialist perspective; sexuality conceptualized as an innate sexual drive which seeks gratification through sexual activity (Weeks, 1990). A further assumption within this model is that the

109   RICHARDSON—CONSTRUCTING SEXUAL CITIZENSHIP

natural and normal aim of this sexual drive or instinct is reproduction. It is a heterosexual drive: ultimately sexuality is defined as the desire to engage in certain practices (vaginal intercourse) with particular individuals (partners of the 'opposite' sex). It is also largely constructed as a male drive, which, as will be demonstrated later, has important implications for female sexual citizenship.[1]

This view of sexuality, as a naturally given series of rights that biology/God has created, has implications for understandings of responsibilities as well as rights. In relation to sexuality, the question of responsibility has largely been concerned with establishing what are and what are not acceptable forms of expression of an assumed pregiven human need. That is, how are needs to engage in sexual activity to be met, in terms of both specific sexual practices and objects of desire? Having said this, there are certain social groups where the assumption of sexuality as a universal human 'need' appears to be challenged. Stereotypes of disability, for example, include assumptions of asexuality; of lack of sexual potential. While historically there has been minimal discussion of the sexual politics of disability, both within disability studies and work on sexuality, in recent years attempts have been made to place sexual rights on the political agenda of disability movements (see Shakespeare et al., 1996). A particular focus has been the ways in which people with disabilities have been denied the capacity for sexual feeling and rights to sexual expression. This has been particularly apparent in the case of people with learning difficulties, for whom sex is not a right normally granted, but can only be achieved by 'breaking the rules for their "kind"' (Brown, 1994). It is also the case that for the many disabled people who live in residential care settings, rights to sexual expression are not assured. In a much broader sense, the process of desexualization of disabled people also has implications for identity and relationship-based claims (see later discussion).

The granting of sexual rights, formalized in age of consent legislation as well as other laws and policies relating to sexual activity, should therefore be viewed as a complex process, in which the context and form of expression of sexual behaviour are key factors. Another way of saying this, is that recognition of the right to participate in sex, *where it is recognized*, should not be confused with claims for the right of individuals to exercise personal choice over the kind of behaviours they engage in. Thus, certain sexual acts may be prohibited by law, reflecting views about what people have a right to do with their bodies. For example, sexual intercourse between people of the same sex is still illegal

CRITICAL SOCIAL POLICY 20(1)

in almost half of the states of the USA and in many parts of the world (Moran, 1996; Bamforth, 1997). In Britain, prior to 1967, consensual sexual contact between men, even in private, was illegal. After the 1967 Sexual Offences Act, such practices remained unlawful unless the following conditions were met: both consenting adults were aged 21 and over and the acts should take place in private. The 1967 reform applied to England and Wales, homosexual practice remained illegal in Scotland until 1981 and in Northern Ireland until 1982. At the time of writing, the current legal age of consent for sexual practices between two men stands at 18 years of age. Having been reduced to 18 from 21 in 1994 under the Criminal Justice Act, it was further decreased to 16 years of age in 1998 as part of the Crime and Disorder Act. However, this was overthrown in the same year by the House of Lords.

It is important not to interpret such liberalization of the law as state recognition of the right to be homosexual. (This distinction is discussed in more detail in the following section.) What these changes in the law represent is the granting of the right, under certain specific contexts, for one man to engage in sexual acts with another man: a right that extends to all adult males, not only those who identify as bisexual or gay.

Of particular importance in analysing the issues surrounding this and other examples of sexual rights claims is the public/private binary. Indeed, arguments for conduct-based rights claims have largely been based on respect for privacy. Although, having said this, it is important to recognize that in recent years there has been a shift in this discourse associated with the emergence of new social movements, such as, for example, queer politics which have emphasized the right to public forms of sexual expression (Bell, 1995; Ingram et al., 1997). This conceptual division between the public and the private is, nevertheless, fundamental to a liberal model of sexual citizenship, which has predominated in Britain since the 1960s, based on a politics of tolerance and assimilation. Thus, for example, those who wish to engage in sexual acts (often referred to as 'unnatural practices') with members of their own gender are granted the right to be tolerated as long as they remain in the private sphere and do not seek public recognition. The 'I don't mind what they do in their own homes as long as I don't have to see or hear about it' argument. Similarly, justifications of the right to consume certain forms of pornography are frequently couched both in terms of individual civil liberties and a respect for privacy.

The justification for the right to engage in various forms of sexual

111   RICHARDSON—CONSTRUCTING SEXUAL CITIZENSHIP

conduct in terms of respect for privacy has not, however, gone unchallenged and in some instances may be seen as illegitimate. In the example given above of the right to consume pornography, for instance, both moral right and certain feminist critiques reject the conceptualization of the public and the private as distinct spheres where what happens in the private is assumed to have no wider social effects, specifically in this case on male attitudes and behaviour towards women (Cameron and Frazer, 1993).[2] Similarly, in the case of gay rights, respect for privacy may be found wanting. Thus, for example, in the now famous Bowers versus Hardwick case in the USA, in 1986, the Supreme Court decided that individuals did not have a fundamental right to engage in 'homosexual sodomy' (see Currah, 1995). The plaintiff, Hardwick, challenged the court's decision, claiming that it violated his right to privacy since he was engaging in consensual sex with another adult male in the privacy of his own bedroom. The two men were 'discovered' by a police officer who was delivering an arrest warrant and had been inadvertently directed to Hardwick's bedroom. The Supreme Court's decision upheld the right of the State of Georgia to send individuals convicted of engaging in anal intercourse with someone of the same gender to prison for up to 20 years. At the same time, the court refused to rule on the constitutionality of laws that apply to 'heterosexual sodomy'.

What are the ideas and assumptions behind the denial of the right to perform certain sexual acts, even when conducted in private? Fundamentally important are institutionalized (hetero)sexual norms and practices, whereby heterosexuality is established as 'natural' and 'normal'; an ideal form of sexual relations and behaviour by which all forms of sexuality are judged. Exclusions from the boundaries of sexual citizenship as practice, therefore, may be on the grounds of 'natural' disqualification. For example, the belief that the body should not be used for acts for which nature did not design it. This understanding of bodies within what Butler (1993) refers to as a 'heterosexual matrix', which operates through naturalizing a heterosexual morphology, is itself an important aspect of heterosexual ideology where the penis and the vagina are assumed to be a natural fit, unlike, for example, the penis and the anus or the vagina and the vagina. In addition to such dominant inscriptions of the body, the belief that vaginal intercourse is naturally the chief purpose of sexual behaviour is another 'norm' by which sexual practices have been judged to be more or less acceptable. For example, although the law has traditionally been much less hostile towards sexual conduct between men and women in both public and private settings, fuelled by this view of what people should properly be engaging in sex for, it can prohibit certain heterosexual practices. It is, for instance, illegal for heterosexual couples to engage in oral sex in a number of states in the USA (Kaplan, 1997).

Lack of recognition of rights claims may also be on the grounds of moral inferiority, where again heterosexual ideology conflates a particular form of heterosexuality with propriety and moral worth. That is, if certain acts are categorized as immoral then the restrictions placed on the right to engage in them may be justified in terms of a moral threat posed to society. This is illustrated by the judgement in the 'Operation Spanner' case, in 1990, where eight adult men were convicted for engaging in consensual sadomasochistic acts in private. Following an appeal, the House of Lords upheld the decision that consensual sadomasochism was against the public interest and should therefore be found unlawful under the Offences Against the Persons Act 1861 (for an account of the case see *R. v Brown*, 1992, 1994). This was an interesting judgement in so far as it appeared to mark a reversal of the law's distinction, post-Wolfendon,[3] between legality and morality; a distinction that was to be crucial to the recognition of future rights claims relating to the practice of, amongst other things, abortion and homosexuality. Indeed, echoing this view, those who dissented from the judgement claimed 'that questions of morality should not be presumed to fall within the remit of the criminal law unless explicitly stated by parliament' (Cooper, 1993: 194). The House of Lords decision was subsequently upheld on appeal, in 1997, to the European Court of Human Rights in Strasbourg, who ruled that it was acceptable for the state to interfere in the 'right of privacy' where it is necessary for the protection of health or morals.

Health and welfare considerations in sexual conduct-based rights claims have also been particularly apparent in relation to AIDS. An example of this from the early years of the epidemic, when AIDS was mistakenly portrayed as a 'gay disease', was the calling for the (re)criminalization of homosexuality as a sexual practice by moral rights organizations in the USA (Altman, 1986). In a European context, by contrast, one of the demands of AIDS activists in organizations such as ACT UP has been the right to safer sexual practice through access to effective education about prevention of the sexual transmission of HIV, as well as health and welfare services that encourage safer sex, such as the provision of condoms (Watney, 1991).

113   RICHARDSON—CONSTRUCTING SEXUAL CITIZENSHIP

The right to pleasure

In the second category of rights claims associated with the right to sexual expression, the emphasis is more upon the right to gratification and enjoyment than simply the right to participate in various forms of sexual activity. Examples of this can be identified in claims for sexual liberation, as well as in some feminist demands. In the so-called sexual revolution of the 1960s libertarians, in demanding freedom of sexual expression, emphasized sexual fulfillment as a right. Such views reflected the influence of writers such as Marcuse (1970) and Reich (1962) who, influenced by both Marxism and Freudian psychoanalytical theory, believed that the 'release' of sexual energy was a means of liberation from repressive social forces. Demands for the right to sexual pleasure were also an important aspect of feminist politics earlier this century and, much more centrally, in the early years of 'second wave' feminism during the 1970s. Sexuality was identified as 'male-defined' and organized around male pleasure, with women's sexuality defined in terms of meeting male sexual needs. Feminists encouraged women to 'reclaim' their sexuality; a sexuality that many believed had been suppressed and denied them.[4] They also sought to challenge the sexual double standard that favoured men, granting them greater sexual rights and fewer responsibilities than women had. In a sense, then, such claims were equal rights claims: equal rights to sexual citizenship, although such demands were not at that time couched in such terms. However, if it was equal rights to sexual pleasure and practice that feminists demanded, it was in the context of a different understanding of these. In particular, feminist writers challenged the centrality of sexual intercourse in definitions of sexual practice and sexual pleasure, pointing out that this is not the major or only source of pleasure for many women. Anne Koedt famously referred to it as 'the myth of the vaginal orgasm' (Koedt, 1974/1996).

Once again, how we understand and explain sexuality has important implications for claims for sexual rights. In this case, what is at stake is not just the right to engage in sexual practices, but the right to gratification of sexual desire. While essentialist notions of sexuality as a reproductive drive may aid recognition of the former claim, in a heterosexual context at least, they are not necessarily supportive of the latter where the recognized aim of sex is individual pleasure. Indeed, one might want to claim that there is no clear bounded right to sexual pleasure per se that is sanctioned by the state.

CRITICAL SOCIAL POLICY 20(1)

However, in countries where, for instance, rape in marriage is not considered illegal, this may be interpreted as a state-sanctioned right of a man's access to a woman's body on the grounds of his rights to sexual fulfillment within marriage. In addition, the right to engage in non-reproductive sexual activities for pleasure can be seen to be linked to the extension of citizenship as consumption. Thus, by laying stress on individual liberty and on the citizen as consumer, the state may recognize various rights claims to consume sexual services and goods, for example, prostitution and certain forms of pornography.[5]

For many feminists the demand for the right to sexual pleasure was not only about gaining greater personal authenticity and equal sexual rights with men, it was also about seeking empowerment in a much broader sense. That is, a connection was frequently made between sexual liberation and women's liberation. With hindsight, many feminists have since questioned this view (see, for example, Campbell, 1980; Jeffreys, 1990; Jackson and Scott, 1996). Commenting on this period, Jackson and Scott, for instance, point out that, in practice, sexual liberation had different consequences for women and men. 'In retrospect many women felt that "sexual liberation" meant greater access for men to women's bodies and the removal of their right to say "No" to sex, lest they be damned as "unliberated".' (Jackson and Scott, 1996: 4–5). What this highlights is that for women the right to sexual pleasure is complex and inextricably linked to other rights of citizenship. For example, it is difficult to envision what it would mean to speak of women's rights to sexual pleasure, without at the same time recognizing rights that enable women's control over their sexuality and reproduction.

The right to sexual (and reproductive) self-determination

This leads on to the third set of conduct-based rights claims, which may be analysed in terms of rights claims concerned with bodily autonomy and integrity. Such claims, as I have already suggested, are particularly evident within feminist discourses, which have interpreted sexual rights in terms not only of the right to sexual pleasure and agency, as described above, but also of the right to control and safety.[6] This latter focus, often characterized as the right to say no, is closely although not exclusively associated with radical feminism. The emphasis is on the right to engage in sex without fear, whether this be in terms of unwanted pregnancy, sexually transmitted diseases, or male

115   RICHARDSON—CONSTRUCTING SEXUAL CITIZENSHIP

demands and force against one's wishes, and includes claims to freedom from sexual harassment, violence, abuse and coercion, as well as rights of access to abortion and contraception. Feminist debates over these issues have further demonstrated the gendered nature of sexual citizenship. Thus, for example, feminist campaigns for changes in policy and practice concerning sexual violence have highlighted how men have traditionally been granted greater sexual rights than women, especially in marriage. In many countries the law decrees that rape in marriage is not a crime, a view that was only overturned a few years ago in England with the introduction of the Rape in Marriage Act in 1991. Under such laws, a man's right of sexual access to his wife's body is privileged over her right to consensual sexual practice. He has the right to take by force that which the law defines as rightfully his: sex within marriage or, more specifically, the act of vaginal penetration. An example of what Wilton (1992) refers to as 'rights of penetration', which she claims, citing HIV/AIDS health promotion as evidence, frequently takes precedence over other considerations, including rights to pleasure and safety. Even in those countries and states where rape in marriage is recognized as a crime, 'the prosecution of offenders and the success of these prosecutions is greatly reduced in comparison with stranger rape, because socially it is not fully accepted as a crime' (Hanmer, 1997: 369). Translated into the language of rights, this means that men still have greater social rights in relation to such forms of sexual practice.

In addition to these feminist campaigns, debates over AIDS have also been significant in the framing of sexual rights in terms of the language of rights of safety, as well as for the reproductive rights of HIV-positive women (Doyal et al., 1994). On the one hand, we have witnessed claims for the extension of sexual rights, such as the right to information about HIV and safer sex as part of rights recognized by the state to sex education in schools, as well as health education more generally (Watney, 1991). On the other hand, some responses to AIDS represent demands for the curtailment of rights to sexual expression which are justified in terms not of protection of public morals, but rather the protection of public health and the protection of the rights and freedoms (including the right to life) of others. Earlier I made reference to the example of calls for the (re)criminalization of male homosexual conduct. Another illustrative case would be the suggestion that it should be a criminal offence for a person who is HIV infected to (knowingly) practice unsafe sex with a sexual partner without their informed consent (Seighart, 1989). This is already the case in some countries. For example, in 1997, in Finland an American man

CRITICAL SOCIAL POLICY 20(1)

who was HIV positive was sentenced to imprisonment for having unprotected intercourse with a series of women, some of whom became infected with the HIV virus as a result.

Many of the conduct-based claims to sexual rights involve claims for civil rights; both in terms of the removal of laws which prohibit or try to restrict certain sexual acts, for example, campaigns by gay rights groups over age of consent and other forms of discriminatory legislation, as well as the creation of new laws that penalize certain practices, for example, feminist campaigns to outlaw rape within marriage. However, such rights claims go beyond protective civil rights. As I have argued earlier, they also include access to social rights, as is evidenced in feminist demands for the recognition of women's sexual needs, and the provision of welfare. Thus, for example, claims for the right to express oneself sexually without fear of unwanted pregnancy are informed by the right of access to education and health services in respect both of abortion and contraception.

Identity

In the 1970s and 1980s, a shift in emphasis occurred in the discourse of sexual rights. There was a partial move away from conduct-based claims, towards a concern with sexual identity rather than sexual practice as the basis for inclusion or exclusion from categories of citizenship. Having said this, we need to recognize the relationship between identity and conduct, in particular the ways in which a person's identity may be a mitigating variable in conduct-based claims. Thus, for example, a person may have differential access to the right to engage in certain forms of sexual activity depending upon whether they are defined as heterosexual or homosexual.

Perhaps the most illustrative case of this shift towards an identity-based approach to sexual rights, was the emergence towards the end of the 1960s, beginning of the 1970s, of gay liberation movements in the USA and Europe. Previous campaigns organized by and on behalf of 'homosexuals' such as, for example, the Homosexual Law Reform Society in Britain, had primarily focused on the removal of criminal laws which prohibited or restricted sexual activity between people of the same sex. Gay liberationist sets of demands went much further than this in challenging discrimination against people on the basis of a lesbian or gay 'identity'. These campaigns were not asking for the

117 RICHARDSON—CONSTRUCTING SEXUAL CITIZENSHIP

right to engage in same-sex activity couched in terms of respect for privacy, but were expressing opposition to social exclusion on the basis of sexual status through the language of the right to sexual freedom and liberation. This reflected an emphasis within this period of gay activism on the importance of being open about one's sexuality through 'coming out' and publicly identifying as lesbian or gay. Subsequently, and with varying degrees of success, gay campaigning groups have pressed for 'the repeal of hostile laws and for the creation of new laws offering protection against social hostility' (Bamforth, 1997: 3). However, it was not merely 'gay rights' in the civil rights meaning of the term that gay liberationists were claiming. In demanding the 'right of a person to develop and extend their character and explore their sexuality' (The Gay Liberation Front Demands cited in Jeffery-Poulter, 1991: 100–1), they were also claiming social and political rights. Thus, in the USA, for example, representatives of National Gay Liberation demanded that gays be represented in all governmental and community institutions. This marked a significant change in claims for sexual citizenship and, associated with this, the development of the notion of sexual rights.

More recently, particularly as postmodern and poststructural influences have brought about new understandings of identities as fragmented and fluid, there has been a problematization of claims to rights on the basis of sexual identity or orientation. Thus, for example, while writers such as Ruthann Robson (1992) advocate the need to develop lesbian legal theory which is responsive to lesbian interests, those who offer a deconstructive treatment of lesbian identity claim that it is far from clear what counts as a lesbian issue or interest (Phelan, 1995). Behind such a recommendation as Robson's, it is argued, lies a conception of identity as distinctive and stable, rather than plural and fluid, to which certain common concerns and issues are assumedly attached. From a postmodern perspective, claims to sexual rights are neither qualified nor limited by a specific sexual identity or orientation. There is not space, in the context of the aims of this article, to enter further into these debates. However, it is important to acknowledge that they form a backdrop to the following analysis of identity-based rights claims.

The right to self-definition

At the most basic level, identity-based sexual rights claims include the right to sexual self-definition and the development of individual sexual identities. This is a model of sexual citizenship based upon notions of who the individual is, rather than what their sexual practices might involve. The right to identify with a specific sexual category defined in terms of a class of people, as distinct from the right to engage in specific sexual practices.

These demands are closely linked to notions of the right to self-ownership and self-determination. However, as in the case of conduct-based rights claims, assumptions and beliefs about sexuality are also extremely important. Thus, for example, a common justification of the right to sexual self-definition is that one's sexuality is predetermined and that there is a natural or essential basis for sexual identities, usually explained in terms of genetics or prenatal hormonal influences on the structure of the brain. This is a view that persists, as is evidenced by the considerable attention and debate generated by the research findings of Le Vay (1991, 1996) and Hamer et al. (1993) who both claim to have discovered evidence of a biological basis to sexuality, despite the weight of the social constructionist argument that sexual identities are socially and historically specific 'inventions' (Foucault, 1979; Weeks, 1990). Indeed, the arguments formulated by contemporary lesbian and gay political groups, especially in the USA, frequently draw upon essentialist notions of sexual categories as fixed and discrete, where one's sexuality is understood to be defined not by one's sexual practices but by one's underlying sexual orientation and attendant identity. It is important to acknowledge that this form of political practice does not necessarily mean adherence to essentialist theories, in which case the term 'strategic essentialism' is more appropriate. Whether strategic or otherwise, within this model 'gay rights' claims to citizenship reproduce the discourse of minority civil rights, with lesbians and gays conceptualized as a legitimate minority group 'having a certain quasi-"ethnic" status' (Epstein, 1987: 12).

The assertion that homosexuality is not a chosen but an inborn orientation/identity constitutes an important aspect of the argument for civil and social rights for lesbians and gay men, as well as for many others campaigning for sexual rights. It has been a feature, for example, of the pursuit of rights by transvestites and transsexuals, as well as, if to a lesser extent, some bisexual and transgender activists. Its significance is that within a liberal democracy it should be possible to claim that discrimination on the basis of a personality trait that is believed to be unchangeable and beyond one's control should be regarded as

119 RICHARDSON—CONSTRUCTING SEXUAL CITIZENSHIP

unfair. However, it is important here to distinguish between conduct and identity-based claims. While such arguments may uphold the right to sexual self-definition, they do not necessarily support the right to express ourselves sexually, on the grounds that, unlike identity, it is assumed that a person can exercise a measure of control over their sexual conduct—although less so in the case of men than women. An example of this is the official policy on homosexuality in the Church of England which recognizes the rights of participation of gay clergy, but does so only on the grounds that they abstain from 'homosexual acts'.

The right to self-expression

The idea that being gay is a constructed identity has often been interpreted as less supportive of identity-based rights claims (although this need not necessarily be the case). An illustrative example of this was the debate surrounding the introduction of Section 28 of the 1988 Local Government Act in Britain which, among other things, became a focus for discussion about the right to be lesbian and gay (Stacey, 1991).[7] Indeed, speaking at the 1987 Tory Party Conference, the then British prime minister Margaret Thatcher expressed such concerns when she remarked that: 'Children who need to be taught to respect traditional moral values are being taught that they have an inalienable right to be gay' (quoted in Evans, 1995: 126). Behind such concerns is not merely the issue of children possibly engaging in same-sex sexual activity (though that was still there), but also the issue of the right to 'choose' to identify with a specific category of people. The implication is that, where possible, the state should try to restrict the construction of such forms of sexual identification.

Arguably, the introduction of Section 28 represented a recognition, as well as a restriction, of the social and civil rights of lesbians and gay men in so far as its proponents were motivated by what they perceived as greater public acceptance of homosexuality and, related to this, a desire to keep homosexuals in their proper place, i.e. within their own private spaces and communities. This is instructive in elucidating the legitimacy of identity-based rights claims. Beyond the right to sexual self-definition, claims for sexual citizenship include the right to public/social recognition of specific sexual identities. Thus, for example, although one may have the right to identify as a lesbian, one does not necessarily have the right to 'come out' and inform others of that identity. The 'Don't Ask/Don't Tell' military policy in the USA is an illustration of this. Although a 'homosexual' identity is itself no longer a bar to military service, any public construction of oneself as lesbian or gay, including 'coming out' speech, constitutes grounds for a discharge. In other words, one has the right to think one is gay, but not the right to say so. The effect of this policy, argues Currah (1995: 66), is to reinforce the public/private binary, leaving room 'only for a wholly private construction of a homosexual orientation'.

As I have already outlined, sexuality is commonly understood to belong to the 'private' sphere, but more especially so in the case of lesbian and gay relationships. For lesbians and gay men the private has been institutionalized as the boundary of sexual citizenship and social tolerance. Indeed, in terms of the sociology of rights, lesbian and gay rights claims have been primarily viewed in this way, as private individual rights rather than as human rights. Thus, for example, the right to recognition of lesbian and gay lifestyles and identities as a legitimate and equal part of social and cultural life is commonly understood as seeking 'a better deal' for particular sexual minority groups, rather than an extension of the right of freedom to choose one's sexual partner to all human beings.

The relative exclusion from the public does not only pertain to 'homosexual practices', then, but also to 'homosexuality' as a public identity and lifestyle. This raises important questions about claims to civil, social, political, as well as sexual citizenship. Indeed if claims to rights are negotiated through public fora, then the negotiation of citizenship rights will be seriously restricted if one is disallowed from those fora, either formally or informally, through fear of stigmatization or recrimination if one identifies publicly as a lesbian or gay man. The ability to be 'out' and publicly visible is therefore crucial to the ability to claim rights.

At the same time, the issues raised by the sexual politics of recent years have raised the question of whether, alongside assertions of the right to be 'out' with impunity, people have the right not to be out about their sexuality as well. One way this has manifested itself is in the politics and practices of outing. Outing refers to the political practice of naming certain individuals as lesbian or gay, usually those in positions of power who are closeted and support homophobic practices. It is a strategy closely associated with queer politics. As an example, in Britain activists in the organization OutRage have threatened to 'out' gay members of parliament who have opposed equal age of consent legislation, as well as those gay clergy deemed to be hypocritical for

121 RICHARDSON—CONSTRUCTING SEXUAL CITIZENSHIP

upholding the policy that lesbians and gay men may only be ministers in the Church if they abstain from 'homosexual acts'. Such practices have been extremely controversial, but in the context of the focus of this article I do not have the space to elaborate on this. (For a study of outing see Johansson and Percy, 1994.) Rather, the point I want to make in using this example is that outing sets itself up to challenge what has been a significant argument in the struggle for sexual rights, the right to privacy.

As I have stated earlier, lesbian and gay politics over the last 30 years have been less about the right to privacy than about claims for the right not to have to be private. There is a paradox here, as Weeks (1998) also notes, in that it is through claiming rights to the public sphere that lesbians and gay men have sought to protect the possibilities of having private lives of their own choosing. This is further complicated by the influence of postmodern ideas about identity as fragmented and fluid, rather than fixed attributes which one may publicly declare or not. In this context, the right not to be out can be considered in a rather different sense from that above, as a right not to be defined in terms of a particular sexual identity.

The right to self-realization

Closely related to rights of expression of our identities, is the right to realize specific sexual identities. This may include the right to develop diverse sexual identities in an unhindered, if not state-assisted, manner. It may also include claims to purchase individual sexual selves. The emergent debates on cultural citizenship (see, for example, the collection edited by Nick Stevenson, 1999) and the shift in recent years towards defining citizenship in terms of consumerism (Evans, 1993) are of relevance here. This is recognized by Pakulski (1997: 80), whose analysis of cultural citizenship includes the 'right to propagation of identities and maintenance of lifestyles (versus assimilation)'.[8] Defined in these terms, Pakulski argues that the concept of cultural citizenship involves 'the right to be "different", to re-value stigmatised identities, to embrace openly and legitimately hitherto marginalised lifestyles and to propagate them without hindrance' (Pakulski, 1997: 83). Examples of this include claims concerning indigenous peoples' rights, as well as what might be termed more radical lesbian/feminist and gay rights campaigns that, recognizing the problematic nature of the concept of tolerance, are concerned with

CRITICAL SOCIAL POLICY 20(1)

restructuring the social institutions which support, maintain and reproduce the conditions of hegemonic (hetero)sexuality (see Cooper, 1993; Wilson, 1993). More specifically, resistance to exclusion from popular culture and negative media coverage, and access to cultural citizenship (Richardson, 1999), have been an important focus of political activity.

What is important to emphasize, in the context of a discussion of sexual citizenship, is the distinction to be drawn between claims for tolerance of diverse identities and active cultivation and integration of these identities without 'normalizing distortion'. The former can embrace the right to self-definition and, within the established boundaries of tolerance, a limited right to express one's identity as a tolerated 'minority'. The latter claims for sexual citizenship are, however, of a different order, they represent a demand for rights to enable the realization of sexual diversity; for access to the cultural, social and economic conditions that will enable previously marginalized and stigmatized identities to develop and flourish as a legitimate and equal part of the 'cultural landscape'. There are, however, inherent problems in conceptualizing sexual citizenship in this way. This is perhaps best illustrated by the question of the claims to sexual citizenship made by 'paedophiles' who identify as a socially excluded sexual minority. As Weeks (1998: 41) states: 'the emergence of "the paedophile", especially, indicates the limit case for any claim to sexual citizenship'.[9]

The right to self-realization of 'identity' can be linked with the shift towards defining citizenship in terms of consumerism, where the focus is on the rights of citizens as consumers, with identities and lifestyles that are expressed through purchasing goods, commodities and services in both the public and private sector. This use of citizenship as a concept that refers to access to the consumption of certain lifestyles, or membership of 'consumer communities' supportive of particular identities, has been viewed positively by some campaigning for sexual rights. Thus, for example, Evans (1993) considers questions of consumer citizenship and the commodification of sexuality in relation to formations of sexual identity and community. Although he is critical of such developments, he nonetheless acknowledges the new commercial power of gay men and, to a lesser extent, lesbians as productively linked to access to sexual and other forms of citizenship (Evans, 1993). However, others take a more critical view of the power of the 'pink pound' to promote lesbian and gay rights (Binnie, 1995; Woods, 1995).

123   RICHARDSON—CONSTRUCTING SEXUAL CITIZENSHIP

Relationships

Although the language of rights largely speaks to the freedoms and obligations of the citizen (Lister, 1997), many citizenship rights are grounded in sexual coupledom rather than rights granted to us as individuals (Delphy, 1996). There are some exceptions, but in most cases heterosexual relations in an 'idealized' marital form are the norm by which the rights of coupledom are measured. For example, in the case of social rights the questioning of the welfare rights of lone mothers who have children outside of marriage reflects the way access to and eligibility for benefits is often linked to normative assumptions about sexuality (Carabine, 1996b). This example also highlights how heterosexual relationship norms may penalize those who do not conform to them, both socially and economically.

Claims to sexual rights which might be termed relationship-based cluster around three main strands: those concerned with the right of consent to sexual behaviours in personal relationships; those concerned with forms of regulation that specify who one can have as a consensual sexual partner; and those concerned with seeking public validation of various forms of sexual relations within social institutions.

The right of consent to sexual practice in personal relationships

In deciding to consider the right to consent to sexual behaviours under relationship rather than conduct-based rights claims, I want to make a distinction between the right to engage in forms of sexual practice such as, for example, masturbation, and the right to participate in sexual acts with others. Age of consent legislation defines the age at which individuals are legitimately regarded as sexual citizens with the right to engage in sexual conduct in personal relationships. Thus, even though dominant discourses of sexuality have defined sexuality as a pregiven need in all human beings, certain rights to sexual expression are also dependent upon the assumed capacity of the individual for self-determined sexual relations. In the case of children, cultural assumptions about when a child may be deemed to have reached a sufficient level of cognitive development and sexual maturity to be able to 'consent' to sex are the main considerations.[10] Such judgements vary between countries. In the Netherlands, for example, the government decided in 1990 to allow heterosexual and homosexual intercourse between those over the age of 12. Under British law, as a number of

CRITICAL SOCIAL POLICY 20(1) **124**

writers have detailed (Evans, 1993; Moran, 1996), the right to consent to sexual behaviours is not only set at a higher age, but is also both gendered and sexualized. The sexual status and rights of boys are recognized at an earlier age than girls, who are regarded as insufficiently mature to 'consent' to heterosexual acts under the age of 16. A further sexual 'double standard' exists in so far as the law recognizes the right to consent to heterosexual acts before (male) homosexual relations.[11]

Claims for the right to an equal age of consent have been an important aspect of lesbian and gay rights campaigns, with organizations like Stonewall lobbying for such legal reform. These can be distinguished from campaigns led by various paedophile organizations for legal recognition of 'cross-generational sex' such as, in the recent past in Britain, PIE (Paedophile Information Exchange) and in the USA by NAMBLA (North American Man/Boy Love Association). As with child-liberationist objections to age of consent laws, though for different reasons, such organizations argue for the right of sexual self-determination for children. They are not, in other words, seeking equal rights in law with heterosexuals, but a reduction in the age children are granted sexual rights or the removal of age of consent laws altogether.

The right to freely choose our sexual partners

In discussing the right to freely choose one's partner I am not referring to the right to engage in various forms of consensual activity with another person. Although such rights may be influenced by who one's partner is, I am concerned here with the question of the right to express sexual feelings for members of specific social groups, irrespective of whether sexual activity actually occurs or not. That is to say, a person may have the right to sexual citizenship on reaching an age where s/he is considered old enough to be a sexual subject, but that does not then mean s/he automatically has the freedom to have sex with any consenting partner. In addition to laws governing age of consent, other restrictions exist on who one can legitimately have as a sexual partner. As with other aspects of sexual citizenship that have been considered, claims for the right of individuals to be free to choose who they have sex with has been an important aspect of lesbian and gay demands, as well as feminist politics—albeit with the recognition that 'choice' is a problematic term in this context. A similar set of demands can be observed in a heterosexual context in rights activism centred upon controls on interracial relationships.

125 RICHARDSON—CONSTRUCTING SEXUAL CITIZENSHIP

Although a thorough analysis of restrictions on the rights to select sexual partners from groups defined as racially different from each other is beyond the scope of this article, it is well documented that many of these have been fuelled by a belief in white superiority and concerns about miscegenation. In the USA, for example, the outlawing of marriage between whites and people of colour has a long history. As Ruth Frankenberg comments:

> The first antimiscegenation law (which is to say, law against marriage between white people and people of color) was enacted in Maryland in 1661, prohibiting white intermarriage with Native Americans and African Americans. Ultimately, over the next three hundred years, thirty-eight states adopted antimiscegenation laws. In the nineteenth century, beginning with western states, antimiscegenation statutes were expanded to outlaw marriages and sexual relationships between whites and Chinese, Japanese, and Filipino Americans. Not until 1967 did the U.S. Supreme Court declare antimiscegenation laws to be unconstitutional. (Frankenberg, 1993: 72)

Elsewhere in the world similar campaigns have been fought against restrictions on interracial sexual relationships. Under apartheid in South Africa, for instance, the prohibitions of the Mixed Marriages Act and section 16 of the Immorality Act were designed to prevent miscegenation. These were among the first pieces of apartheid legislation to be introduced after the National Party came to power in 1948 (Weeks, 1986).

There are parallels with fears of miscegenation and eugenic concerns with 'purity of the race' in attempts to restrict the rights of people with disabilities to form sexual relationships. This has been evident in the social policies of various countries, including the United States, Britain and Germany. For example, shortly after gaining power the Nazi Party introduced a number of laws for 'improving racial stock' which included the 1933 'Sterilisation laws'. Under the terms of this legislation, 'Germans suffering from physical malformation, mental retardation, epilepsy, imbecility, deafness or blindness were compulsorily sterilised' (Grunberger, 1987: 305). People who were sterilized were not allowed to marry and if it was found out that they had done so illegally, their marriages were judicially annulled.

One might of course want to argue that despite legal prohibition of certain forms of consensual relationships, centred on the right to marry and have legitimate children, sexual relations still occurred.

CRITICAL SOCIAL POLICY 20(1)

Such insistence on a restricted right to choose one's partner, however, must be understood in terms of the differential access of different social groups to such forms of sexual citizenship. For example, it is also well documented that in the USA, in the context of colonialism and the slave economy, white men often assumed sexual rights over black women slaves who were their 'property'; those who resisted risked being tortured and punished (hooks, 1992). (There are parallels here with the way in which men have historically been granted rights of access to their wives, defined as their property within marriage.) By contrast, however, it was considered unthinkable that black men should have consensual sexual relations with white women. Indeed, black men were likely to be severely punished if they were even suspected of having made a sexual advance to a white woman. As Rennie Simson (1984) points out, many black men were lynched and publicly castrated in the USA earlier this century as a way of 'protecting white womanhood'. In other words, white men had social and economic rights which enabled them to engage in coercive non-consensual sex with non-white partners, at a time when black men were being denied the right to choose a consensual sexual partner across race lines. What examples such as these clearly demonstrate is that sexual citizenship is not only closely associated with hegemonic heterosexual and gendered norms of sexual behaviour, but is also informed by, and informs, constructions of race.

The right to publicly recognized sexual relationships

The final aspect of relational-based rights claims that I wish to consider are those which are concerned with the right to public recognition and validation of sexual relationships. Many groups are seeking to extend social legitimacy and institutional support to the relationships they are free to have, always assuming they have this right. Lesbian and gay rights movements, for example, have increasingly moved in this direction, most obviously in demanding the right to marry and access to the social and legal benefits accruing from being married. This issue is one that is extremely contentious, especially among feminists who have been critical of the marital model of relationships and rights (Delphy and Leonard, 1992). However, as Jenny Rankine (1997) points out in her examination of the current debates on same-sex marriage, feminist views are likely to differ in different countries, 'even if certain fundamental issues of political principle remain constant', reflecting

127 RICHARDSON—CONSTRUCTING SEXUAL CITIZENSHIP

differences in welfare systems. In the USA, for instance, where public health care is extremely limited, the issue of the right to entitlements to medical cover on one's married partner's insurance takes on a particular significance.

Although the right to marry and form family units is recognized in the UN Declaration of Human Rights, in most countries such rights are denied to same-sex relationships which do not have, for example, the same immigration rights, pension rights, inheritance rights, next of kin status and tax benefits as those accorded to married heterosexual couples.[12] At present, lesbian and gay partnerships are not legally recognized in Britain, although in Denmark and the Netherlands the passing of partnership law that recognizes same-sex relationships could have implications in future for citizens of other European Union member states. In the USA same-sex marriages have been permitted in the state of Hawaii. However, the federal authorities, in 1996, passed the Defense of Marriage Act, which defines marriage as a relationship between a woman and a man.

It is important to recognize that even in countries that provide legal recognition of same-sex relationships, there may still be disparities with the rights granted to heterosexuals. Major focuses of such disparities are the rights of parenthood. In Norway, for example, lesbian and gay couples are denied the right to adopt children. In addition, lesbians who have had children through donor insemination 'find that their lifetime companions have no legal rights to the children, although their combined income is counted when the local county authorities calculate how much they should pay for day care' (Lindstad, 1996: 135).

Conclusion

In this article, I have explored the notion of sexual citizenship in terms of the question of sexual rights. As I have illustrated, the idea of rights in relation to sexuality, although not a new concept, is problematic, not least because it can mean many different things. For feminists, claims to rights in relation to sexuality have largely been about safety, bodily control, sexual self-definition, agency and pleasure. Lesbian and gay movements have emphasized the extension of specific sexual rights, including an equal age of consent, as well as more broadly the right to freely choose adult sexual partners and the right to publicly recognized

CRITICAL SOCIAL POLICY 20(1)

lesbian, bisexual or gay identities and lifestyles. Recently, there have also been attempts to place sexual rights on the agenda of the disability movement (Shakespeare, et al., 1996), especially in relation to disabled people's rights to sexual expression. Some writers (e.g. Evans, 1993, 1995; Binnie, 1995) also include in their discussion of sexual citizenship the right to consume 'sexual commodities', which can be defined as services and goods related to sexual practices and identities. Such 'commodities' might include sex education, lesbian and gay magazines, contraceptives, abortion services, prostitution and pornography.

Recognizing that there is no common or universal agreement about what the term 'sexual rights' might mean, I have presented an analytic schema, which I hope will contribute to emergent debates in sexual citizenship and understandings of citizenship more generally. In my analysis, I offer a way of understanding sexual citizenship as a system of rights, which includes a concern with conduct, identity and relationship-based claims. I am aware that there is an artificiality in listing these as if they were separate when, in practice, individuals may experience these as a complex entanglement. However, for the purpose of distinguishing similarities and differences in demands for sexual rights, and elucidating the boundaries of inclusion and exclusion, I would argue that these categories are extremely useful.

Finally, we need to consider the implications of recognizing these different approaches to understanding sexual rights for social policy. As I and others (Wilton, 1995; Carabine, 1996a,b) have pointed out, there has been a general lack of theorizing of social policy in relation to sexuality across a broad range of social policy issues including welfare, health care, education and housing. In parallel with this, consideration of sexual issues has not been high on welfare agendas, reflecting a view of sexuality as 'human needs', which are not within the remit of social policy. At the same time, as I have mentioned, demands are increasingly being made by a variety of political groups including lesbian, bisexual and gay organizations, sections of disability rights movements and certain feminist campaigning groups, which are couched in the language of sexual rights and citizenship. This represents, as I suggested at the beginning of this article, a shift from what was previously an almost exclusive focus on the public towards an inclusion of the 'private' in recent considerations of citizenship. More specifically, however, this also represents a new and complex subject area for both researchers and policy-makers. The schema presented here may, therefore, provide a way forward in an area where the develop-

129   RICHARDSON—CONSTRUCTING SEXUAL CITIZENSHIP

ment of frameworks is crucially needed for both theoretical and practical reasons. It offers a way of beginning to theorize the varying ways in which a social policy structure intended to support a particular version of heterosexuality shapes the context within which debates about sexual rights take place and the meanings of sexual citizenship are constructed. Such a framework may also help to clarify a basis on which to construct future research. What, for example, are the implications for social policy associated with conduct-based rights claims? How, and in what ways, might these differ from identity and relationship-based sexual rights claims? What are the justifications given for social inclusion or exclusion in repect of different forms of sexual citizenship? How do these vary across social groups, as well as the various categories of rights claims that I have outlined?

As a first stage in mapping out this relatively new area of debate, at least within social policy, what I have attempted to do here is address the question: What are recognized as sexual rights or demands? What is also highlighted is the need to consider other related issues if we are to develop a more comprehensive understanding of the concept of 'sexual citizenship'. For example, should these rights be secured and, if so, how? What are the social and welfare provisions needed to meet recognized sexual 'needs'? What might one mean by 'sexuality policies'? These are all important questions for future work.

Notes

1. There has also been a division of sexual attributes based on race and class as well as gender, which has implications for sexual citizenship.
2. In saying this I want also to stress, especially in the context of accusations of collusion, that the arguments of antipornography feminists are different from those of religious and right-wing movements.
3. The Wolfendon Committee reviewed the law and practice relating to homosexuality and prostitution. Its conclusions, published in 1957, were enacted later in the Street Offences Act 1959, relating to prostitution, and formed the basis of the 1967 law reforms relating to homosexual acts (Wolfendon, 1957).
4. This is interesting, given the important role that feminists have played in critiquing essentialist understandings of sexuality over the last 25 years or more, in so far as such claims appear to reaffirm a notion of sexual essence, while challenging the idea of a reproductive purpose to sexuality.

5. In the case of prostitution, it is important to note that the law in many countries observes the protection of citizens' rights to purchase but not to sell sex (Hotling, 1996).

6. Although by the end of the 1970s the focus had shifted from the assertion of women's right to sexual fulfillment and liberation towards issues such as, for example, the right to freedom from sexual violence, it remains a significant theme in the work of some contemporary feminist writers (see, for example, Segal, 1987, 1994).

7. Section 28 sought to ban the 'promotion of homosexuality' and 'pretended' family relationships by local authority schools. Its use as a case example is particularly interesting, as it suggests that in some respects social constructionist arguments were beginning to be recognized. See Stacey (1991) for a useful discussion of this aspect.

8. Pakulski (1997: 80) also analyses cultural citizenship in terms of 'the right to symbolic presence and visibility (vs marginalization)' and 'the right to endignifying representation (vs stigmatization)'.

9. One might want to make a similar point in relation to 'rapists', although there is no organization claiming rights in the way that paedophile groups have in the past. Having said this, we should note that various 'men's movement' groups such as, in Britain, 'Families Need Fathers' have included as part of their campaign the repeal of the recent Rape in Marriage legislation.

10. The term 'consent' is problematic, in particular it suggests a lack of agency on the part of the person 'consenting' to sexual practice with another and assumes that the ability to say 'yes' or 'no' after a certain age is a 'relatively straightforward affair when in fact it is frequently complicated by relationships of power' (Maynard and Winn, 1997: 189).

11. There is no specific age of consent law for sexual acts between women. However, as no female under 16 can give consent to an 'assault', any woman older than 16 having a relationship with someone younger than 16 can be charged with 'assault' (Evans, 1993).

12. It is also the case that immigration legislation in Britain has been shaped by racist as well as patriarchal interests, which has affected the terms of exclusion from citizenship (Bhavnani, 1997).

References

Alexander, M. J. (1994) 'Not Just (Any) Body Can Be A Citizen: The Politics of Law, Sexuality and Postcoloniality in Trinidad and Tobago and the Bahamas', *Feminist Review* 48: 5–23.

Altman, D. (1986) *AIDS in the Mind of America*. New York: Doubleday.

Bamforth, N. (1997) *Sexuality, Morals and Justice: A Theory of Lesbian and Gay Rights Law*. London: Cassell.

131 RICHARDSON—CONSTRUCTING SEXUAL CITIZENSHIP

Bell, D. (1995) 'Perverse Dynamics, Sexual Citizenship and The Transformation of Intimacy', in D. Bell and G. Valentine (eds) *Mapping Desire. Geographies of Sexualities*. London: Routledge.

Bhavnani, K.-K. (1997) 'Women's Studies and its Interconnection with 'Race', Ethnicity and Sexuality', in V. Robinson and D. Richardson (eds) *Introducing Women's Studies: Feminist Theory and Practice*, 2nd edition. Basingstoke: Macmillan.

Binnie, J. (1995) 'Trading Places: Consumption, Sexuality and the Production of Queer Space', in D. Bell and G. Valentine (eds) *Mapping Desire. Geographies of Sexualities*. London: Routledge.

Brown, H. (1994) '"An Ordinary Sexual Life?": a Review of the Normalisation Principle as it Applies to the Sexual Options of People with Learning Disabilities', *Disability and Society* 9(2): 123–44.

Butler, J. (1993) *Bodies that Matter: On the Discursive Limits of 'Sex'*. London: Routledge.

Cameron, D. and Frazer, E. (1993) 'On the Question of Pornography and Sexual Violence: Moving Beyond Cause and Effect', in C. Itzen (ed.) *Pornography: Women, Violence and Civil Liberties*. Oxford: Oxford University Press.

Campbell, B. (1980) 'A Feminist Sexual Politics: Now You See It, Now You Don't', *Feminist Review* 5: 1–18.

Carabine, J. (1996a) 'A Straight Playing Field or Queering the Pitch: Centring Sexuality in Social Policy', *Feminist Review* 54: 31–64.

Carabine, J. (1996b) 'Heterosexuality and Social Policy', in D. Richardson (ed.) *Theorising Heterosexuality: Telling it Straight*. Buckingham: Open University Press.

Cooper, D. (1993) 'An Engaged State: Sexuality, Governance and the Potential for Change', in J. Bristow and A. R. Wilson (eds) *Activating Theory: Lesbian, Gay and Bisexual Politics*. London: Lawrence and Wishart.

Cooper, D. (1995) *Power in Struggle: Feminism, Sexuality and the State*. Buckingham: Open University Press.

Currah, P. (1995) 'Searching for Immutability: Homosexuality, Race and Rights Discourse', in A. R. Wilson (ed.) *A Simple Matter of Justice? Theorizing Lesbian and Gay Politics*. London: Cassell.

Delphy, C. (1996) 'The Private as a Deprivation of Rights For Women and Children', paper given at the International Conference on Violence, Abuse and Women's Citizenship, Brighton, 10–15 November.

Delphy, C. and Leonard, D. (1992) *Familiar Exploitation: A New Analysis of Marriage in Contemporary Western Societies*. Cambridge: Polity.

Doyal, L., Naidoo, J. and Wilton, T. (eds) (1994) *AIDS: Setting a Feminist Agenda*. London: Taylor & Francis.

Epstein, S. (1987) 'Gay Politics, Ethnic Identity: The Limits of Social Constructionism', *Socialist Review* 93/94: 9–54.

Evans, D. (1993) *Sexual Citizenship. The Material Construction of Sexualities*. London: Routledge.

Evans, D. (1995) ' (Homo) sexual Citizenship: A Queer Kind of Justice' in A. R. Wilson (ed.) *A Simple Matter of Justice? Theorizing Lesbian and Gay Politics*. London: Cassell.

Foucault, M. (1979) *The History of Sexuality*, Vol. 1. London: Allen Lane.

Frankenberg, R. (1993) *White Women, Race Matters: The Social Construction of Whiteness*. London: Routledge.

Giddens, A. (1992) *The Transformation of Intimacy: Sexuality, Love and Eroticism in Modern Societies*. Cambridge: Polity Press.

Grunberger, R. (1987) *A Social History of the Third Reich*. London: Penguin.

Hall, S. and Held, D. (1989) 'Citizens and Citizenship', in S. Hall and M. Jacques (eds) *New Times: The Changing Face of Politics in the 1990s*. Buckingham: Open University Press.

Hamer, D. H., Hu, S., Magnuson, V. L., Hu, N., and Pattatucci, A. M. L. (1993) 'A Linkage Between DNA Markers on the X Chromosome and Male Sexual Orientation', *Science* 26: 321–7.

Hanmer, J. (1997) 'Women and Reproduction', in V. Robinson and D. Richardson (eds) *Introducing Women's Studies: Feminist Theory and Practice*, 2nd edition. Basingstoke: Macmillan.

Herman, D. (1994) *Rights of Passage: Struggles for Lesbian and Gay Equality*. Toronto: University of Toronto Press.

hooks, b. (1992) *Black Looks: Race and Representation*. Boston, MA: South End Press.

Hotling, N. (1996) 'Prostitution: Getting Women Out', paper presented at the International Conference on Violence, Abuse and Women's Citizenship, Brighton, 10–15 November.

Ingram, G. B., Bouthillette, A. and Retter, Y. (eds) (1997) *Queers in Space: Communities/Public Places/Sites of Resistance*. Seattle: Bay Press.

Jackson, S. and Scott, S. (1996) 'Sexual Skirmishes and Feminist Factions: Twenty-Five Years of Debate on Women and Sexuality', in S. Jackson and S. Scott (eds) *Feminism and Sexuality: A Reader*. Edinburgh: Edinburgh University Press.

Jeffery-Poulter, S. (1991) *Peers, Queers and Commons: The Struggle for Gay Law Reform from 1950 to the Present*. London: Routledge.

Jeffreys, S. (1990) *Anticlimax: A Feminist Perspective on the Sexual Revolution*. London: The Women's Press.

Johansson, W. and Percy, W. A. (1994) *Outing: Shattering the Conspiracy of Silence*. Binghampton, NY: Harrington Park Press.

Kaplan, M. B. (1997) *Sexual Justice. Democratic Citizenship and the Politics of Desire*. New York: Routledge.

Koedt, A. (1974/1996) 'The Myth of the Vaginal Orgasm', in The Radical Therapist Collective (eds) *The Radical Therapist*. Harmondsworth:

133   RICHARDSON—CONSTRUCTING SEXUAL CITIZENSHIP

Penguin. Reprinted in S. Jackson and S. Scott (eds) *Feminism and Sexuality. A Reader*. Edinburgh: Edinburgh University Press.

Le Vay, S. (1991) 'A Difference in Hypothalamic Structure Between Heterosexual and Homosexual Men', *Science* 253: 1034–7.

Le Vay, S. (1996) *Queer Science: The Use and Abuse of Research into Homosexuality*. Cambridge, MA: MIT Press.

Lindstad, G. (1996) 'Norway', in R. Rosenbloom (ed.) *Unspoken Rules: Sexual Orientation and Women's Human Rights*. International Gay and Lesbian Human Rights Commission. London: Cassell

Lister, R. (1990) 'Women, Economic Dependency and Citizenship', *Journal of Social Policy* 19 (4): 445–68.

Lister, R. (1996) 'Citizenship Engendered' in D. Taylor (ed.) *Critical Social Policy. A Reader*. London: Sage.

Lister, R. (1997) *Citizenship: Feminist Perspectives*. London: Macmillan.

Marcuse, H. (1970) *Eros and Civilisation*. London: Allen Lane.

Maynard, M. and Winn, J. (1997) 'Women, Violence and Male Power', in V. Robinson and D. Richardson (eds) *Introducing Women's Studies: Feminist Theory and Practice*, 2nd edition. Basingstoke: Macmillan.

Moran, L. (1996) *The Homosexual(ity) of Law*. London: Routledge.

Pakulski, J. (1997) 'Cultural Citizenship', *Citizenship Studies* 1(1): 73–86.

Phelan, S. (1994) *Getting Specific: Postmodern Lesbian Politics*. Minneapolis: University of Minnesota Press.

Phelan, S. (1995) 'The Space of Justice: Lesbians and Democratic Politics', in A. R. Wilson (ed.) *A Simple Matter of Justice? Theorizing Lesbian and Gay Politics*. London: Cassell.

Phillips, A. (1991) 'Citizenship and Feminist Theory', in G. Andrews (ed.) *Citizenship*. London: Lawrence and Wishart.

Plummer, K. (1995) *Telling Sexual Stories: Power, Change and Social Worlds*. London: Routledge.

Rankine, J. (1997) 'For Better or For Worse?', *Trouble and Strife* 34: 5–11.

Reich, W. (1962) *The Sexual Revolution*. New York: Farrar, Straus and Giroux.

Richardson, D. (1998) 'Sexuality and Citizenship', *Sociology* 32, 1: 83–100.

Richardson, D. (1999) 'Extending Citizenship: Cultural Citizenship and Sexuality', in N. Stevenson (ed.) *Cultural Citizenship*. London: Sage.

Robson, R. (1992) *Lesbian (Out)Law: Survival Under the Rule of Law*. Ithaca: Firebrand.

R. v. Brown (1992) 1 QB 491.

R. v Brown (1994) AC 212.

Segal, L. (1987) *Is the Future Female? Troubled Thoughts on Contemporary Feminism*. London: Virago.

Segal, L. (1994) *Straight Sex: Rethinking the Politics of Pleasure*. London: Virago.

Shakespeare, T., Gillespie-Sells, K. and Davies, D. (1996) *The Sexual Politics of Disability: Untold Desires*. London: Cassell.

CRITICAL SOCIAL POLICY 20(1)   **134**

Sieghart, P. (1989) *AIDS and Human Rights: A UK Perspective*. London: British Medical Foundation for AIDS.

Simson, R. (1984) 'The Afro-American Female: the Historical Context of the Construction of Sexual Identity', in A. Snitow, C. Stansell and S. Thompson (eds) *Desire: The Politics of Sexuality*. London: Virago.

Stacey, J. (1991) 'Promoting Normality: Section 28 and the Regulation of Sexuality', in S. Franklin, C. Lury and J. Stacey (eds) *Off Centre: Feminism and Cultural Studies*. London: Unwin Hyman.

Stevenson, N. (ed.) (1999) *Cultural Citizenship*. London: Sage.

Taylor, D. (1996) 'Citizenship and Social Power', in D. Taylor (ed.) *Critical Social Policy: A Reader*. London: Sage.

Voet, R. (1998) *Feminism and Citizenship*. London: Sage.

Walby, S. (1997) *Gender Transformations*. London: Routledge.

Watney, S. (1991) 'Citizenship in the Age of AIDS', in G. Andrews (ed.) *Citizenship*. London: Lawrence and Wishart.

Weeks, J. (1986) *Sexuality*. London: Tavistock.

Weeks, J. (1990) *Sex, Politics and Society*, 2nd edition. London: Longman.

Weeks, J. (1998) 'The Sexual Citizen', *Theory, Culture and Society* 15(3–4): 35–52.

Wilson, A. R. (1993) 'Which Equality? Toleration, Difference or Respect', in J. Bristow and A. R. Wilson (eds) *Activating Theory: Lesbian, Gay, Bisexual Politics*. London: Lawrence & Wishart.

Wilson, A. (1995) 'Their Justice: Heterosexism in A Theory of Justice', in A. R. Wilson (ed.) *A Simple Matter of Justice?: Theorizing Lesbian and Gay Politics*. London: Cassell.

Wilton, T. (1992) 'Desire and the Politics of Representation: Issues for Lesbians and Heterosexual Women', in H. Hinds, A. Phoenix and J. Stacey (eds) *Working Out: New Directions for Women's Studies*. London: Falmer Press.

Wilton, T. (1995) *Lesbian Studies: Setting an Agenda*. London: Routledge.

Wolfendon, J. (1957) Report of the Departmental Committee on Homosexual Offences and Prostitution, Cmnd 247. London: HMSO.

Woods, C. (1995) *State of the Queer Nation: A Critique of Gay and Lesbian Politics in 1990s Britain*. London: Cassell.

❑ Diane Richardson is Professor of Sociology and Social Policy in the Department of Social Policy at the University of Newcastle-upon-Tyne, England. She is currently co-editing, with Steven Seidman, an International Collection on Lesbian and Gay Studies. Previous publications include *Women and the AIDS Crisis* (Pandora, 1989), *Safer Sex* (Pandora, 1990), *Women,*

135   RICHARDSON—CONSTRUCTING SEXUAL CITIZENSHIP

Motherhood and Childrearing (Macmillan, 1993), *Theorising Heterosexuality* (Open University Press, 1996) and, as co-editor, *Introducing Women's Studies: Feminist Theory and Practice* (Macmillan, 2nd edn 1997). A forthcoming book on Sexuality, Social Theory and Social Change will be published later this year by Sage. ❑

[20]

THE RIGHT TO THE CITY

DAVID HARVEY

WE LIVE IN an era when ideals of human rights have moved centre stage both politically and ethically. A great deal of energy is expended in promoting their significance for the construction of a better world. But for the most part the concepts circulating do not fundamentally challenge hegemonic liberal and neoliberal market logics, or the dominant modes of legality and state action. We live, after all, in a world in which the rights of private property and the profit rate trump all other notions of rights. I here want to explore another type of human right, that of the right to the city.

Has the astonishing pace and scale of urbanization over the last hundred years contributed to human well-being? The city, in the words of urban sociologist Robert Park, is:

> man's most successful attempt to remake the world he lives in more after his heart's desire. But, if the city is the world which man created, it is the world in which he is henceforth condemned to live. Thus, indirectly, and without any clear sense of the nature of his task, in making the city man has remade himself.[1]

The question of what kind of city we want cannot be divorced from that of what kind of social ties, relationship to nature, lifestyles, technologies and aesthetic values we desire. The right to the city is far more than the individual liberty to access urban resources: it is a right to change ourselves by changing the city. It is, moreover, a common rather than an individual right since this transformation inevitably depends upon the exercise of a collective power to reshape the processes of urbanization. The freedom to make and remake our cities and ourselves is, I want to argue, one of the most precious yet most neglected of our human rights.

24 NLR 53

From their inception, cities have arisen through geographical and social concentrations of a surplus product. Urbanization has always been, therefore, a class phenomenon, since surpluses are extracted from somewhere and from somebody, while the control over their disbursement typically lies in a few hands. This general situation persists under capitalism, of course; but since urbanization depends on the mobilization of a surplus product, an intimate connection emerges between the development of capitalism and urbanization. Capitalists have to produce a surplus product in order to produce surplus value; this in turn must be reinvested in order to generate more surplus value. The result of continued reinvestment is the expansion of surplus production at a compound rate—hence the logistic curves (money, output and population) attached to the history of capital accumulation, paralleled by the growth path of urbanization under capitalism.

The perpetual need to find profitable terrains for capital-surplus production and absorption shapes the politics of capitalism. It also presents the capitalist with a number of barriers to continuous and trouble-free expansion. If labour is scarce and wages are high, either existing labour has to be disciplined—technologically induced unemployment or an assault on organized working-class power are two prime methods—or fresh labour forces must be found by immigration, export of capital or proletarianization of hitherto independent elements of the population. Capitalists must also discover new means of production in general and natural resources in particular, which puts increasing pressure on the natural environment to yield up necessary raw materials and absorb the inevitable waste. They need to open up terrains for raw-material extraction—often the objective of imperialist and neo-colonial endeavours.

The coercive laws of competition also force the continuous implementation of new technologies and organizational forms, since these enable capitalists to out-compete those using inferior methods. Innovations define new wants and needs, reduce the turnover time of capital and lessen the friction of distance, which limits the geographical range within which the capitalist can search for expanded labour supplies, raw materials, and so on. If there is not enough purchasing power in the market, then new markets must be found by expanding foreign trade, promoting novel products and lifestyles, creating new credit instruments, and

---

[1] Robert Park, *On Social Control and Collective Behavior*, Chicago 1967, p. 3.

HARVEY: *Right to the City*   25

debt-financing state and private expenditures. If, finally, the profit rate is too low, then state regulation of 'ruinous competition', monopolization (mergers and acquisitions) and capital exports provide ways out.

If any of the above barriers cannot be circumvented, capitalists are unable profitably to reinvest their surplus product. Capital accumulation is blocked, leaving them facing a crisis, in which their capital can be devalued and in some instances even physically wiped out. Surplus commodities can lose value or be destroyed, while productive capacity and assets can be written down and left unused; money itself can be devalued through inflation, and labour through massive unemployment. How, then, has the need to circumvent these barriers and to expand the terrain of profitable activity driven capitalist urbanization? I argue here that urbanization has played a particularly active role, alongside such phenomena as military expenditures, in absorbing the surplus product that capitalists perpetually produce in their search for profits.

Urban revolutions

Consider, first, the case of Second Empire Paris. The year 1848 brought one of the first clear, and European-wide, crises of both unemployed surplus capital and surplus labour. It struck Paris particularly hard, and issued in an abortive revolution by unemployed workers and those bourgeois utopians who saw a social republic as the antidote to the greed and inequality that had characterized the July Monarchy. The republican bourgeoisie violently repressed the revolutionaries but failed to resolve the crisis. The result was the ascent to power of Louis-Napoleon Bonaparte, who engineered a coup in 1851 and proclaimed himself Emperor the following year. To survive politically, he resorted to widespread repression of alternative political movements. The economic situation he dealt with by means of a vast programme of infrastructural investment both at home and abroad. In the latter case, this meant the construction of railroads throughout Europe and into the Orient, as well as support for grand works such as the Suez Canal. At home, it meant consolidating the railway network, building ports and harbours, and draining marshes. Above all, it entailed the reconfiguration of the urban infrastructure of Paris. Bonaparte brought in Georges-Eugène Haussmann to take charge of the city's public works in 1853.

26 NLR 53

Haussmann clearly understood that his mission was to help solve the surplus-capital and unemployment problem through urbanization. Rebuilding Paris absorbed huge quantities of labour and capital by the standards of the time and, coupled with suppressing the aspirations of the Parisian workforce, was a primary vehicle of social stabilization. He drew upon the utopian plans that Fourierists and Saint-Simonians had debated in the 1840s for reshaping Paris, but with one big difference: he transformed the scale at which the urban process was imagined. When the architect Jacques Ignace Hittorff showed Haussmann his plans for a new boulevard, Haussmann threw them back at him saying: 'not wide enough . . . you have it 40 metres wide and I want it 120.' He annexed the suburbs and redesigned whole neighbourhoods such as Les Halles. To do this Haussmann needed new financial institutions and debt instruments, the Crédit Mobilier and Crédit Immobilier, which were constructed on Saint-Simonian lines. In effect, he helped resolve the capital-surplus disposal problem by setting up a proto-Keynesian system of debt-financed infrastructural urban improvements.

The system worked very well for some fifteen years, and it involved not only a transformation of urban infrastructures but also the construction of a new way of life and urban persona. Paris became 'the city of light', the great centre of consumption, tourism and pleasure; the cafés, department stores, fashion industry and grand expositions all changed urban living so that it could absorb vast surpluses through consumerism. But then the overextended and speculative financial system and credit structures crashed in 1868. Haussmann was dismissed; Napoleon III in desperation went to war against Bismarck's Germany and lost. In the ensuing vacuum arose the Paris Commune, one of the greatest revolutionary episodes in capitalist urban history, wrought in part out of a nostalgia for the world that Haussmann had destroyed and the desire to take back the city on the part of those dispossessed by his works.[2]

Fast forward now to the 1940s in the United States. The huge mobilization for the war effort temporarily resolved the capital-surplus disposal problem that had seemed so intractable in the 1930s, and the unemployment that went with it. But everyone was fearful about what would happen after the war. Politically the situation was dangerous: the federal government was in effect running a nationalized economy, and

---

[2] For a fuller account, see David Harvey, *Paris, Capital of Modernity*, New York 2003.

was in alliance with the Communist Soviet Union, while strong social movements with socialist inclinations had emerged in the 1930s. As in Louis Bonaparte's era, a hefty dose of political repression was evidently called for by the ruling classes of the time; the subsequent history of McCarthyism and Cold War politics, of which there were already abundant signs in the early 40s, is all too familiar. On the economic front, there remained the question of how surplus capital could be absorbed.

In 1942, a lengthy evaluation of Haussmann's efforts appeared in *Architectural Forum*. It documented in detail what he had done, attempted an analysis of his mistakes but sought to recuperate his reputation as one of the greatest urbanists of all time. The article was by none other than Robert Moses, who after the Second World War did to New York what Haussmann had done to Paris.[3] That is, Moses changed the scale of thinking about the urban process. Through a system of highways and infrastructural transformations, suburbanization and the total re-engineering of not just the city but also the whole metropolitan region, he helped resolve the capital-surplus absorption problem. To do this, he tapped into new financial institutions and tax arrangements that liberated the credit to debt-finance urban expansion. When taken nationwide to all the major metropolitan centres of the US—yet another transformation of scale—this process played a crucial role in stabilizing global capitalism after 1945, a period in which the US could afford to power the whole global non-communist economy by running trade deficits.

The suburbanization of the United States was not merely a matter of new infrastructures. As in Second Empire Paris, it entailed a radical transformation in lifestyles, bringing new products from housing to refrigerators and air conditioners, as well as two cars in the driveway and an enormous increase in the consumption of oil. It also altered the political landscape, as subsidized home-ownership for the middle classes changed the focus of community action towards the defence of property values and individualized identities, turning the suburban vote towards conservative republicanism. Debt-encumbered homeowners, it was argued, were less likely to go on strike. This project successfully absorbed the surplus and assured social stability, albeit at the cost of hollowing out the inner cities and generating urban unrest amongst those, chiefly African-Americans, who were denied access to the new prosperity.

---

[3] Robert Moses, 'What Happened to Haussmann?', *Architectural Forum*, vol. 77 (July 1942), pp. 57–66.

28   NLR 53

By the end of the 1960s, a different kind of crisis began to unfold; Moses, like Haussmann, fell from grace, and his solutions came to be seen as inappropriate and unacceptable. Traditionalists rallied around Jane Jacobs and sought to counter the brutal modernism of Moses's projects with a localized neighbourhood aesthetic. But the suburbs had been built, and the radical change in lifestyle that this betokened had many social consequences, leading feminists, for example, to proclaim the suburb as the locus of all their primary discontents. If Haussmannization had a part in the dynamics of the Paris Commune, the soulless qualities of suburban living also played a critical role in the dramatic events of 1968 in the US. Discontented white middle-class students went into a phase of revolt, sought alliances with marginalized groups claiming civil rights and rallied against American imperialism to create a movement to build another kind of world—including a different kind of urban experience.

In Paris, the campaign to stop the Left Bank Expressway and the destruction of traditional neighbourhoods by the invading 'high-rise giants' such as the Place d'Italie and Tour Montparnasse helped animate the larger dynamics of the 68 uprising. It was in this context that Henri Lefebvre wrote *The Urban Revolution*, which predicted not only that urbanization was central to the survival of capitalism and therefore bound to become a crucial focus of political and class struggle, but that it was obliterating step by step the distinctions between town and country through the production of integrated spaces across national territory, if not beyond.[4] The right to the city had to mean the right to command the whole urban process, which was increasingly dominating the countryside through phenomena ranging from agribusiness to second homes and rural tourism.

Along with the 68 revolt came a financial crisis within the credit institutions that, through debt-financing, had powered the property boom in the preceding decades. The crisis gathered momentum at the end of the 1960s until the whole capitalist system crashed, starting with the bursting of the global property-market bubble in 1973, followed by the fiscal bankruptcy of New York City in 1975. As William Tabb argued, the response to the consequences of the latter effectively pioneered the construction of a neoliberal answer to the problems of perpetuating class

---

[4] Henri Lefebvre, *The Urban Revolution*, Minneapolis 2003; and *Writings on Cities*, Oxford 1996.

HARVEY: *Right to the City*   29

power and of reviving the capacity to absorb the surpluses that capitalism must produce to survive.[5]

Girding the globe

Fast forward once again to our current conjuncture. International capitalism has been on a roller-coaster of regional crises and crashes—East and Southeast Asia in 1997–98; Russia in 1998; Argentina in 2001—but had until recently avoided a global crash even in the face of a chronic inability to dispose of capital surplus. What was the role of urbanization in stabilizing this situation? In the United States, it is accepted wisdom that the housing sector was an important stabilizer of the economy, particularly after the high-tech crash of the late 1990s, although it was an active component of expansion in the earlier part of that decade. The property market directly absorbed a great deal of surplus capital through the construction of city-centre and suburban homes and office spaces, while the rapid inflation of housing asset prices—backed by a profligate wave of mortgage refinancing at historically low rates of interest—boosted the US domestic market for consumer goods and services. American urban expansion partially steadied the global economy, as the US ran huge trade deficits with the rest of the world, borrowing around $2 billion a day to fuel its insatiable consumerism and the wars in Afghanistan and Iraq.

But the urban process has undergone another transformation of scale. It has, in short, gone global. Property-market booms in Britain and Spain, as well as in many other countries, have helped power a capitalist dynamic in ways that broadly parallel what has happened in the United States. The urbanization of China over the last twenty years has been of a different character, with its heavy focus on infrastructural development, but it is even more important than that of the US. Its pace picked up enormously after a brief recession in 1997, to the extent that China has taken in nearly half the world's cement supplies since 2000. More than a hundred cities have passed the one-million population mark in this period, and previously small villages, such as Shenzhen, have become huge metropolises of 6 to 10 million people. Vast infrastructural projects, including dams and highways—again, all debt-financed—are transforming the landscape. The consequences for the global economy

---

[5] William Tabb, *The Long Default: New York City and the Urban Fiscal Crisis*, New York 1982.

and the absorption of surplus capital have been significant: Chile booms thanks to the high price of copper, Australia thrives and even Brazil and Argentina have recovered in part because of the strength of Chinese demand for raw materials.

Is the urbanization of China, then, the primary stabilizer of global capitalism today? The answer has to be a qualified yes. For China is only the epicentre of an urbanization process that has now become genuinely global, partly through the astonishing integration of financial markets that have used their flexibility to debt-finance urban development around the world. The Chinese central bank, for example, has been active in the secondary mortgage market in the US while Goldman Sachs was heavily involved in the surging property market in Mumbai, and Hong Kong capital has invested in Baltimore. In the midst of a flood of impoverished migrants, construction boomed in Johannesburg, Taipei, Moscow, as well as the cities in the core capitalist countries, such as London and Los Angeles. Astonishing if not criminally absurd mega-urbanization projects have emerged in the Middle East in places such as Dubai and Abu Dhabi, mopping up the surplus arising from oil wealth in the most conspicuous, socially unjust and environmentally wasteful ways possible.

This global scale makes it hard to grasp that what is happening is in principle similar to the transformations that Haussmann oversaw in Paris. For the global urbanization boom has depended, as did all the others before it, on the construction of new financial institutions and arrangements to organize the credit required to sustain it. Financial innovations set in train in the 1980s—securitizing and packaging local mortgages for sale to investors worldwide, and setting up new vehicles to hold collateralized debt obligations—played a crucial role. Their many benefits included spreading risk and permitting surplus savings pools easier access to surplus housing demand; they also brought aggregate interest rates down, while generating immense fortunes for the financial intermediaries who worked these wonders. But spreading risk does not eliminate it. Furthermore, the fact that it can be distributed so widely encourages even riskier local behaviours, because liability can be transferred elsewhere. Without adequate risk-assessment controls, this wave of financialization has now turned into the so-called sub-prime mortgage and housing asset-value crisis. The fallout was concentrated in the first instance in and around US cities, with particularly serious

HARVEY: *Right to the City* 31

implications for low-income, inner-city African-Americans and households headed by single women. It also has affected those who, unable to afford the skyrocketing house prices in urban centres, especially in the Southwest, were forced into the metropolitan semi-periphery; here they took up speculatively built tract housing at initially easy rates, but now face escalating commuting costs as oil prices rise, and soaring mortgage payments as market rates come into effect.

The current crisis, with vicious local repercussions on urban life and infrastructures, also threatens the whole architecture of the global financial system and may trigger a major recession to boot. The parallels with the 1970s are uncanny—including the immediate easy-money response of the Federal Reserve in 2007–08, which will almost certainly generate strong currents of uncontrollable inflation, if not stagflation, in the not too distant future. However, the situation is far more complex now, and it is an open question whether China can compensate for a serious crash in the United States; even in the PRC the pace of urbanization seems to be slowing down. The financial system is also more tightly coupled than it ever was before.[6] Computer-driven split-second trading always threatens to create a great divergence in the market—it is already producing incredible volatility in stock trading—that will precipitate a massive crisis, requiring a total re-think of how finance capital and money markets work, including their relation to urbanization.

Property and pacification

As in all the preceding phases, this most recent radical expansion of the urban process has brought with it incredible transformations of lifestyle. Quality of urban life has become a commodity, as has the city itself, in a world where consumerism, tourism, cultural and knowledge-based industries have become major aspects of the urban political economy. The postmodernist penchant for encouraging the formation of market niches—in both consumer habits and cultural forms—surrounds the contemporary urban experience with an aura of freedom of choice, provided you have the money. Shopping malls, multiplexes and box stores proliferate, as do fast-food and artisanal market-places. We now have, as urban sociologist Sharon Zukin puts it, 'pacification by

---

[6] Richard Bookstaber, *A Demon of Our Own Design: Markets, Hedge Funds and the Perils of Financial Innovation*, Hoboken, NJ 2007.

32   NLR 53

cappuccino'. Even the incoherent, bland and monotonous suburban tract development that continues to dominate in many areas now gets its anti-dote in a 'new urbanism' movement that touts the sale of community and boutique lifestyles to fulfill urban dreams. This is a world in which the neoliberal ethic of intense possessive individualism, and its cognate of political withdrawal from collective forms of action, becomes the tem-plate for human socialization.[7] The defence of property values becomes of such paramount political interest that, as Mike Davis points out, the home-owner associations in the state of California become bastions of political reaction, if not of fragmented neighbourhood fascisms.[8]

We increasingly live in divided and conflict-prone urban areas. In the past three decades, the neoliberal turn has restored class power to rich elites. Fourteen billionaires have emerged in Mexico since then, and in 2006 that country boasted the richest man on earth, Carlos Slim, at the same time as the incomes of the poor had either stagnated or dimin-ished. The results are indelibly etched on the spatial forms of our cities, which increasingly consist of fortified fragments, gated communities and privatized public spaces kept under constant surveillance. In the developing world in particular, the city

> is splitting into different separated parts, with the apparent formation of many 'microstates'. Wealthy neighbourhoods provided with all kinds of services, such as exclusive schools, golf courses, tennis courts and private police patrolling the area around the clock intertwine with illegal settle-ments where water is available only at public fountains, no sanitation system exists, electricity is pirated by a privileged few, the roads become mud streams whenever it rains, and where house-sharing is the norm. Each fragment appears to live and function autonomously, sticking firmly to what it has been able to grab in the daily fight for survival.[9]

Under these conditions, ideals of urban identity, citizenship and belonging—already threatened by the spreading malaise of a neolib-eral ethic—become much harder to sustain. Privatized redistribution

---

[7] Hilde Nafstad et al., 'Ideology and Power: The Influence of Current Neoliberalism in Society', *Journal of Community and Applied Social Psychology*, vol. 17, no. 4 (July 2007), pp. 313–27.
[8] Mike Davis, *City of Quartz: Excavating the Future in Los Angeles*, London and New York 1990.
[9] Marcello Balbo, 'Urban Planning and the Fragmented City of Developing Countries', *Third World Planning Review*, vol. 15, no. 1 (1993), pp. 23–35.

HARVEY: *Right to the City*

through criminal activity threatens individual security at every turn, prompting popular demands for police suppression. Even the idea that the city might function as a collective body politic, a site within and from which progressive social movements might emanate, appears implausible. There are, however, urban social movements seeking to overcome isolation and reshape the city in a different image from that put forward by the developers, who are backed by finance, corporate capital and an increasingly entrepreneurially minded local state apparatus.

Dispossessions

Surplus absorption through urban transformation has an even darker aspect. It has entailed repeated bouts of urban restructuring through 'creative destruction', which nearly always has a class dimension since it is the poor, the underprivileged and those marginalized from political power that suffer first and foremost from this process. Violence is required to build the new urban world on the wreckage of the old. Haussmann tore through the old Parisian slums, using powers of expropriation in the name of civic improvement and renovation. He deliberately engineered the removal of much of the working class and other unruly elements from the city centre, where they constituted a threat to public order and political power. He created an urban form where it was believed—incorrectly, as it turned out in 1871—that sufficient levels of surveillance and military control could be attained to ensure that revolutionary movements would easily be brought to heel. Nevertheless, as Engels pointed out in 1872:

> In reality, the bourgeoisie has only one method of solving the housing question after its fashion—that is to say, of solving it in such a way that the solution continually reproduces the question anew. This method is called 'Haussmann' . . . No matter how different the reasons may be, the result is always the same; the scandalous alleys and lanes disappear to the accompaniment of lavish self-praise from the bourgeoisie on account of this tremendous success, but they appear again immediately somewhere else . . . The same economic necessity which produced them in the first place, produces them in the next place.[10]

It took more than a hundred years to complete the embourgeoisement of central Paris, with the consequences seen in recent years of uprisings

---

[10] Friedrich Engels, *The Housing Question*, New York 1935, pp. 74–7.

34 NLR 53

and mayhem in those isolated suburbs that trap marginalized immigrants, unemployed workers and youth. The sad point here, of course, is that what Engels described recurs throughout history. Robert Moses 'took a meat axe to the Bronx', in his infamous words, bringing forth long and loud laments from neighbourhood groups and movements. In the cases of Paris and New York, once the power of state expropriations had been successfully resisted and contained, a more insidious and cancerous progression took hold through municipal fiscal discipline, property speculation and the sorting of land-use according to the rate of return for its 'highest and best use'. Engels understood this sequence all too well:

> The growth of the big modern cities gives the land in certain areas, particularly in those areas which are centrally situated, an artificially and colossally increasing value; the buildings erected on these areas depress this value instead of increasing it, because they no longer belong to the changed circumstances. They are pulled down and replaced by others. This takes place above all with workers' houses which are situated centrally and whose rents, even with the greatest overcrowding, can never, or only very slowly, increase above a certain maximum. They are pulled down and in their stead shops, warehouses and public buildings are erected.[11]

Though this description was written in 1872, it applies directly to contemporary urban development in much of Asia—Delhi, Seoul, Mumbai—as well as gentrification in New York. A process of displacement and what I call 'accumulation by dispossession' lie at the core of urbanization under capitalism.[12] It is the mirror-image of capital absorption through urban redevelopment, and is giving rise to numerous conflicts over the capture of valuable land from low-income populations that may have lived there for many years.

Consider the case of Seoul in the 1990s: construction companies and developers hired goon squads of sumo-wrestler types to invade neighbourhoods on the city's hillsides. They sledgehammered down not only housing but also all the possessions of those who had built their own homes in the 1950s on what had become premium land. Highrise towers, which show no trace of the brutality that permitted their construction, now cover most of those hillsides. In Mumbai, meanwhile,

---

[11] Engels, *Housing Question*, p. 23.
[12] Harvey, *The New Imperialism*, Oxford 2003, chapter 4.

HARVEY: *Right to the City* 35

6 million people officially considered as slum dwellers are settled on land without legal title; all maps of the city leave these places blank. With the attempt to turn Mumbai into a global financial centre to rival Shanghai, the property-development boom has gathered pace, and the land that squatters occupy appears increasingly valuable. Dharavi, one of the most prominent slums in Mumbai, is estimated to be worth $2 billion. The pressure to clear it—for environmental and social reasons that mask the land grab—is mounting daily. Financial powers backed by the state push for forcible slum clearance, in some cases violently taking possession of terrain occupied for a whole generation. Capital accumulation through real-estate activity booms, since the land is acquired at almost no cost.

Will the people who are displaced get compensation? The lucky ones get a bit. But while the Indian Constitution specifies that the state has an obligation to protect the lives and well-being of the whole population, irrespective of caste or class, and to guarantee rights to housing and shelter, the Supreme Court has issued judgements that rewrite this constitutional requirement. Since slum dwellers are illegal occupants and many cannot definitively prove their long-term residence, they have no right to compensation. To concede that right, says the Supreme Court, would be tantamount to rewarding pickpockets for their actions. So the squatters either resist and fight, or move with their few belongings to camp out on the sides of highways or wherever they can find a tiny space.[13] Examples of dispossession can also be found in the US, though these tend to be less brutal and more legalistic: the government's right of eminent domain has been abused in order to displace established residents in reasonable housing in favour of higher-order land uses, such as condominiums and box stores. When this was challenged in the US Supreme Court, the justices ruled that it was constitutional for local jurisdictions to behave in this way in order to increase their property-tax base.[14]

In China millions are being dispossessed of the spaces they have long occupied—three million in Beijing alone. Since they lack private-property

---

[13] Usha Ramanathan, 'Illegality and the Urban Poor', *Economic and Political Weekly*, 22 July 2006; Rakesh Shukla, 'Rights of the Poor: An Overview of Supreme Court', *Economic and Political Weekly*, 2 September 2006.
[14] Kelo v. New London, CT, decided on 23 June 2005 in case 545 US 469 (2005).

rights, the state can simply remove them by fiat, offering a minor cash payment to help them on their way before turning the land over to developers at a large profit. In some instances, people move willingly, but there are also reports of widespread resistance, the usual response to which is brutal repression by the Communist party. In the PRC it is often populations on the rural margins who are displaced, illustrating the significance of Lefebvre's argument, presciently laid out in the 1960s, that the clear distinction which once existed between the urban and the rural is gradually fading into a set of porous spaces of uneven geographical development, under the hegemonic command of capital and the state. This is also the case in India, where the central and state governments now favour the establishment of Special Economic Zones—ostensibly for industrial development, though most of the land is designated for urbanization. This policy has led to pitched battles against agricultural producers, the grossest of which was the massacre at Nandigram in West Bengal in March 2007, orchestrated by the state's Marxist government. Intent on opening up terrain for the Salim Group, an Indonesian conglomerate, the ruling CPI(M) sent armed police to disperse protesting villagers; at least 14 were shot dead and dozens wounded. Private property rights in this case provided no protection.

What of the seemingly progressive proposal to award private-property rights to squatter populations, providing them with assets that will permit them to leave poverty behind?[15] Such a scheme is now being mooted for Rio's favelas, for example. The problem is that the poor, beset with income insecurity and frequent financial difficulties, can easily be persuaded to trade in that asset for a relatively low cash payment. The rich typically refuse to give up their valued assets at any price, which is why Moses could take a meat axe to the low-income Bronx but not to affluent Park Avenue. The lasting effect of Margaret Thatcher's privatization of social housing in Britain has been to create a rent and price structure throughout metropolitan London that precludes lower-income and even middle-class people from access to accommodation anywhere near the urban centre. I wager that within fifteen years, if present trends continue, all those hillsides in Rio now occupied by favelas will be covered

---

[15] Much of this thinking follows the work of Hernando de Soto, *The Mystery of Capital: Why Capitalism Triumphs in the West and Fails Everywhere Else*, New York 2000; see the critical examination by Timothy Mitchell, 'The Work of Economics: How a Discipline Makes its World', *Archives Européennes de Sociologie*, vol. 46, no. 2 (August 2005), pp. 297–320.

HARVEY: *Right to the City* 37

by high-rise condominiums with fabulous views over the idyllic bay, while the erstwhile favela dwellers will have been filtered off into some remote periphery.

Formulating demands

Urbanization, we may conclude, has played a crucial role in the absorption of capital surpluses, at ever increasing geographical scales, but at the price of burgeoning processes of creative destruction that have dispossessed the masses of any right to the city whatsoever. The planet as building site collides with the 'planet of slums'.[16] Periodically this ends in revolt, as in Paris in 1871 or the US after the assassination of Martin Luther King in 1968. If, as seems likely, fiscal difficulties mount and the hitherto successful neoliberal, postmodernist and consumerist phase of capitalist surplus-absorption through urbanization is at an end and a broader crisis ensues, then the question arises: where is our 68 or, even more dramatically, our version of the Commune? As with the financial system, the answer is bound to be much more complex precisely because the urban process is now global in scope. Signs of rebellion are everywhere: the unrest in China and India is chronic, civil wars rage in Africa, Latin America is in ferment. Any of these revolts could become contagious. Unlike the fiscal system, however, the urban and peri-urban social movements of opposition, of which there are many around the world, are not tightly coupled; indeed most have no connection to each other. If they somehow did come together, what should they demand?

The answer to the last question is simple enough in principle: greater democratic control over the production and utilization of the surplus. Since the urban process is a major channel of surplus use, establishing democratic management over its urban deployment constitutes the right to the city. Throughout capitalist history, some of the surplus value has been taxed, and in social-democratic phases the proportion at the state's disposal rose significantly. The neoliberal project over the last thirty years has been oriented towards privatizing that control. The data for all OECD countries show, however, that the state's portion of gross output has been roughly constant since the 1970s.[17] The main achievement of

---

[16] Mike Davis, *Planet of Slums*, London and New York 2006.
[17] *OECD Factbook 2008: Economic, Environmental and Social Statistics*, Paris 2008, p. 225.

38 NLR 53

the neoliberal assault, then, has been to prevent the public share from expanding as it did in the 1960s. Neoliberalism has also created new systems of governance that integrate state and corporate interests, and through the application of money power, it has ensured that the disbursement of the surplus through the state apparatus favours corporate capital and the upper classes in shaping the urban process. Raising the proportion of the surplus held by the state will only have a positive impact if the state itself is brought back under democratic control.

Increasingly, we see the right to the city falling into the hands of private or quasi-private interests. In New York City, for example, the billionaire mayor, Michael Bloomberg, is reshaping the city along lines favourable to developers, Wall Street and transnational capitalist-class elements, and promoting the city as an optimal location for high-value businesses and a fantastic destination for tourists. He is, in effect, turning Manhattan into one vast gated community for the rich. In Mexico City, Carlos Slim had the downtown streets re-cobbled to suit the tourist gaze. Not only affluent individuals exercise direct power. In the town of New Haven, strapped for resources for urban reinvestment, it is Yale, one of the wealthiest universities in the world, that is redesigning much of the urban fabric to suit its needs. Johns Hopkins is doing the same for East Baltimore, and Columbia University plans to do so for areas of New York, sparking neighbourhood resistance movements in both cases. The right to the city, as it is now constituted, is too narrowly confined, restricted in most cases to a small political and economic elite who are in a position to shape cities more and more after their own desires.

Every January, the Office of the New York State Comptroller publishes an estimate of the total Wall Street bonuses for the previous twelve months. In 2007, a disastrous year for financial markets by any measure, these added up to $33.2 billion, only 2 per cent less than the year before. In mid-summer of 2007, the Federal Reserve and the European Central Bank poured billions of dollars' worth of short-term credit into the financial system to ensure its stability, and thereafter the Fed dramatically lowered interest rates or pumped in vast amounts of liquidity every time the Dow threatened to fall precipitously. Meanwhile, some two million people have been or are about to be made homeless by foreclosures. Many city neighbourhoods and even whole peri-urban communities in the US have been boarded up and vandalized, wrecked by the predatory lending practices of the financial institutions. This population is due

HARVEY: *Right to the City*   39

no bonuses. Indeed, since foreclosure means debt forgiveness, which is regarded as income in the United States, many of those evicted face a hefty income-tax bill for money they never had in their possession. This asymmetry cannot be construed as anything less than a massive form of class confrontation. A 'Financial Katrina' is unfolding, which conveniently (for the developers) threatens to wipe out low-income neighbourhoods on potentially high-value land in many inner-city areas far more effectively and speedily than could be achieved through eminent domain.

We have yet, however, to see a coherent opposition to these developments in the twenty-first century. There are, of course, already a great many diverse social movements focusing on the urban question—from India and Brazil to China, Spain, Argentina and the United States. In 2001, a City Statute was inserted into the Brazilian Constitution, after pressure from social movements, to recognize the collective right to the city.[18] In the US, there have been calls for much of the $700 billion bailout for financial institutions to be diverted into a Reconstruction Bank, which would help prevent foreclosures and fund efforts at neighbourhood revitalization and infrastructural renewal at municipal level. The urban crisis that is affecting millions would then be prioritized over the needs of big investors and financiers. Unfortunately the social movements are not strong enough or sufficiently mobilized to force through this solution. Nor have these movements yet converged on the singular aim of gaining greater control over the uses of the surplus—let alone over the conditions of its production.

At this point in history, this has to be a global struggle, predominantly with finance capital, for that is the scale at which urbanization processes now work. To be sure, the political task of organizing such a confrontation is difficult if not daunting. However, the opportunities are multiple because, as this brief history shows, crises repeatedly erupt around urbanization both locally and globally, and because the metropolis is now the point of massive collision—dare we call it class struggle?—over the accumulation by dispossession visited upon the least well-off and the developmental drive that seeks to colonize space for the affluent.

---

[18] Edésio Fernandes, 'Constructing the "Right to the City" in Brazil', *Social and Legal Studies*, vol. 16, no. 2 (June 2007), pp. 201–19.

40 NLR 53

One step towards unifying these struggles is to adopt the right to the city as both working slogan and political ideal, precisely because it focuses on the question of who commands the necessary connection between urbanization and surplus production and use. The democratization of that right, and the construction of a broad social movement to enforce its will is imperative if the dispossessed are to take back the control which they have for so long been denied, and if they are to institute new modes of urbanization. Lefebvre was right to insist that the revolution has to be urban, in the broadest sense of that term, or nothing at all.

Name Index

Ackerman, Bruce 174, 415, 416, 419–20, 421–2
    passim, 423, 424, 426–7
Adler, Daniel 374, 375
Adonnino, Pietro 287
Adorno, Theodor W. 324
Agamben, Giorgio 367
Albers, Hartmut 243
Aleinikoff, Thomas Alexander 343
Alesina, Alberto 238
Alexander, Jeffrey 54
Alexander, M. Jacqui 434
Alibhai-Brown, Yasmin 199
Allen, John 385
Alstott, Anne 415, 416–17, 419–20, 421–2
    passim, 423, 424, 426–7
Altman, Dennis 440
Amersfoot, Hans van 161
Amit-Talai, Vered 333
Anderson, Benedict 363
Anghie, Anthony 127
Appadurai, Arjun 238
Archibugi, Daniele 115, 343
Arendt, Hannah 6, 104–5, 113, 148–9, 167, 173,
    345, 348, 354, 363
Aristotle 3, 159
Aron, Raymond xii
Arrighi, Giovanni 103–4
Atkinson, Anthony 428
Attali, Jacques 107
Austin, Dennis 287
Ayers, Alison J. 130

Bakhtin, Mikhail 353
Baldwin, Peter 242
Balibar, Etienne xvi, xxi, 3–10, 104, 348, 355–8
    passim
Bamforth, Nicholas 438, 445
Banting, Keith 238, 287
Barbalet, J.M. 285
Barber, Benjamin 148
Barry, Brian 288, 418, 424

Basch, Linda 381
Bassel, Leah 344
Bauböck, Rainer xi, xvii, xxii, 157–8, 207–35,
    241, 299, 300, 302–3, 305, 307–9
    passim, 312, 315–18 *passim*, 343
Bauman, Gerd 333
Bauman, Zygmunt xxi, 103–117
Beckman, Ludvig 300
Bell, Daniel A. 208, 434, 438
Bellamy, Richard xi, xxiii, 283–97
Bendix, Reinhard 22, 53
Beneduce, Roberto 356
Benhabib, Seyla xi, xviii, xxii, 147–82, 343,
    378
Benmayor, Rina 344
Bennett, Jonathan F. 351
Bergström, Villy 35, 37
Berlin, Isaiah 108
Beveridge, Lord William107, 108
Bidar, Dany 292
Bigo, Didier 344
Binnie, John 434, 450, 456
Bismarck, Otto von 468
Black, Antony 348
Blair, Tony 110, 365
Blanc-Szanton, Cristina 381
Blatter, Joachim J. 221
Bloomberg, Michael 480
Body-Gendrot, Sophie 343
Boland, John 276
Boltanski, Luc 394, 405–6
Bonaparte, Louis-Napoleon 467, 469
Bosniak, Linda 214, 376, 383
Bottomore, Tom xviii, xxi, 11–52, 54
Bourdieu, Pierre 108
Bowers, Michael J. 439
Braverman, Harry 31
Bridge, Gary 385
Brown, Hilary 437
Brubaker, W. Rogers 22–3 *passim*, 39, 54, 163,
    237, 240

Burke, Edmund 104
Buruma, Ian 247
Butler, Judith 351, 378, 439

Cameron, Deborah 439
Carabine, Jean 434, 451, 456
Carens, Joseph H. 39, 149–50 *passim*, 209, 211, 215, 299, 300, 306, 309, 318
Castiglione, Dario 287
Castles, Stephen 211, 345
Chang, Howard F. 208
Chiapello, Eve 394, 405–6
Chinchilla, Norma 382
Chryssochoou, Dimitris 289
Clarke, Charles 110
Clinton, Bill 407
Cohen, Jean L. 158
Cohen, Robin 324
Cole, G.D.H. 422
Collier, Stephen J. 364, 368
Conway, Janet 141
Cook-Martin, David 244
Cooper, Davina 434, 440, 450
Cordero-Guzmán, Héctor R. 381
Cornell, Drucilla 378
Coutin, Susan B. 380
Crenshaw, Kimberlé 378
Crosby, John F. 353
Currah, Paisley 439, 448

Dahl, Robert A. 290, 293, 303, 311, 314
Dannreuther, Roland 343
Davidson, Alistair 345
Davis, Mike 474
Davis, Ulrich 242
De Sousa Santos, Boaventura 139, 141
Delgado, Richard 378
Delphy, Christine 451, 454
Disraeli, Benjamin 13
Doyal, Lesley 443
DuBois, James M. 353
Dubois, Laurent 354
Durbin, E.F.M. 15, 17, 28, 30, 44, 46

Ebb, C. 241
Edward II, King of England 93
Eeckhout, Laetitia van 243
Engels, Friedrich 475–6
Entzinger, Han 243

Epstein, Steven 446
Escobar, Arturo 140
Evans, David 435, 447, 449, 450, 452, 456
Evans, Tony 130

Fahrmeir, Andreas 349
Faist, Thomas 221
Falk, Richard 343
Fassin, Didier 368
Feit, Harvey A. 200
Ferge, Zsuzsa 16, 17, 24
Ferguson, Adam 61
Ferrera, Maurizio 343
Flores, William V. 344
Foucault, Michel 446
Franco, General Francisco 316
Frank, Thomas 106
Frankenberg, Ruth 453
Fraser, Nancy xv, xx, xxiv, 287, 378, 393–413
Frazer, Elizabeth 439
Freeden, Michael 344
Friedman, Jonathan 148
Froumin, Isak 196
Frug, Gerald E. 348
Fullinwider, Robert K. 197

Gagnon, Alain-G. 287
Galston, William 150, 156
Gandhi, Mahatma 141
Garcia Canclini, Néstor 343
Gardner, David 272
Gardner, Jane F. 347
Geertz, Clifford 116
Giddens, Anthony 54, 434
Gilroy, Paul 333
Gleaser, Edward 238
Glick Schiller, Nina 381
Goldthorpe, John H. 31, 33
Goodhart, David 241
Goodin, Robert E. 301–3 *passim*
Gotando, Neil 378
Groot, Gerard–René de 220
Grunberger, Richard 453
Grzelczk, Rudy 292
Guild, Elspeth 218
Guiraudon, Virginie 242

Habermas, Jürgen xiii, 63–4, 283, 284, 290, 364–5

Hall, Stuart 434
Hamer, Dean H. 446
Hamilton, Nora 382
Hammar, Tobias 40
Handler, Joel 377
Hanmer, Jalna 443
Hannerz, Ulf 333
Hansen, Randall 239, 343
Hardwick, Michael 439
Harvey, David xv, xxi, xxiv, 465–82
Haussmann, Georges-Eugène 467–8, 469, 470, 472, 475
Hawken, Paul 141
Hay, Colin 287
Hayek, Friedrich von 365, 422
Hear, Nicholas van 324
Heater, Derek B. 347
Heiberg, Marianne 148
Held, David 115, 434
Herman, Didi 434
Herrup, Cynthia 85
Hilferding, Rudolf 33
Himmelfarb, Gertrude 383
Hirschman, Albert O. 107, 112
Hirst, Paul 239
Hittorff, Jacques Ignace 468
Hobsbawm, Eric 335
Holston, James 238, 367
Hondagneu-Sotelo, Pierrette 382
Honig, Bonnie 150
Hooks, Bell 454
Howard, Marc Morjé 239, 241
Huber, Ernst R. 164
Hussein, Saddam 290
Hutchings, Kimberly 343
Huysmans, Jef 344

Ignatieff, Michael 148
Inda, Jonathan Xavier 383
Ingram, Gordon Brent 438
Isin, Engin F. xix, xx, xxiii, 341–62, 385

Jackson, Stevi 442
Jacobs, Jane 470
Jacobson, David 383. 384
Janoski,Thomas 166
Jaspers, Karl 115
Jay, M.C. 13
Jeffery-Poulter, Stephen 445

Jeffreys, Sheila 442
Jenson, Jane xiii
Johansson, Warren 449
Joppke, Christian xi, xv, xxii, 111, 221, 230, 237–48
Judt, Tony 152

Kant, Immanuel 148, 172
Kaplan, Morris B. 440
Karst, Kenneth 377, 378
Kastoryano, Riva 243, 332
Katznelson, Ira 385
Kaufman, Eric 245
Kepel, Gilles 331
Kessler, Charles R. 150
King, Martin Luther 479
Kivisto, Peter 221
Kleger, Heinz 157
Klusmeyer, Douglas B. 156, 164, 343
Knop, Karen 376
Koedt, Anne 441
Kostakopoulou, Dora 218, 253
Krasner, Stephen D. xii
Kristeva, Julia 162
Kroger, Sandra 294
Kymlicka, Will xxii, 156, 183–205, 238, 243, 287, 290

Lakoff, Andrew 368
Lardy, Heather 264
Lawson, Neal 105–6, 107
Le Vay, Simon 446
LeBlanc, Robin 381
Lefebvre, Henri 385, 470, 478, 482
Leonard, Diana 454
Lie, John 245
Lindstad, G. 455
Linklater, Andrew 343
Lister, Ruth 26–7, 434, 451
Loader, Ian 139
Locke, John 65, 80, 166
Lockwood, David 33
Lopez-Guerra, Claudio 303–5 passim, 306, 313
Luchtenberg, Sigrid 196

Macedo, Stephen 156
Maddison, Angus 15, 30
Magnette, Paul 295
Mahler, Sarah 380

Majone, Giandomenico 293
Mallet, Serge 31
Mamdani, Mahmood 138
Mander, Jerry 138
Mann, Michael 54, 61
Manville, Philip Brook 346
Marcuse, Herbert 441
Margalit, Avishai 247
Marks, Gary 327
Marrus, Michael R. 374
Marsh, Michael 289
Marshall, Alfred 11, 13
Marshall, T.H. xiv, xv, xxi, 11–13 *passim*, 15–16,
    19–22 *passim*, 23, 24, 25, 26–9 *passim*,
    30, 31, 36, 38, 39, 43, 46, 47, 53, 54,
    56–60 *passim*, 65, 66, 67–8, 69–70, 73,
    85, 92, 103, 105, 106, 107, 108, 109, 111,
    112, 113–14, 116, 159–60, 237, 238, 284,
    349, 376, 377, 419–20, 422
Martin, Philip 213
Martiniello, Marco 343
Marx, Karl 5, 31, 61, 90
Massey, Doreen 385
McAdam, Doug 327
McNevin, Anne 354, 355, 356
Mendes, Candido 148
Meyer, John W. 246
Mignolo, Walter D. 126
Miller, David 227, 285, 287
Miller-Idriss, Cynthia 244
Milton, John 82
Miron, Louis F. 383
Montvalon, Jean-Baptiste de 243
Moran, Leslie J. 438, 452
Moravscik, Andrew 293
Morris, Lydia 242
Moses, Robert 469, 470, 476, 478
Mouffe, Chantal 114–15 *passim*
Müller, Jan-Werner 245
Munger, Frank 375

Napoleon III 468
Neuman, Gerald L. 155
Newdick, Christopher 292
Nic Shuibhne, Niamh 292
Nicolaïdis, Kalypso 294
Nietzsche, Friedrich 350
Norman, Wayne 156

Nyers, Peter 341

O'Neill, Michael 287
Obama, Barack 394, 409
Oers, Ricky van 245
Offe, Claus 15, 30, 285
Okin, Susan 411
Ong, Aihwa xvi, xx, xxiii, xxiv, 363–9, 376
Opalski, Magda 192
Orwell, George 115
Ossman, Susan 342
Ottonelli, Valeria 209, 225–6 *passim*, 231
Owen, David xxiii, 299–321

Paine, Tom 418
Pakulski, Jan 449
Parekh, Bhikhu 243
Pareto, Vilfredo 288
Park, Robert 465
Parkinson, Lord Cecil 272
Parsons, Talcott 351
Pateman, Carole xx, xxiv, 415–31
Pattie, Charles 288
Peller, Gary 378
Penninx, Rinus 343
Percy, William A. 449
Petryna, Adriana 368
Phelan, Shane 434, 445
Phillips, Anne 434
Pickard, Bertram 416–17
Pinochet, Augusto 381
Pirenne, Henri 90
Plummer, Ken 434
Pocock, J.G.A. 285
Poggi, Gianfranco 348
Polanyi, Karl 99
Poppelaars, Caelesta 243
Postan, Michael M. 15
Pryke, Michael 385

Rancière, Jacques 350
Rankine, Jenny 454
Rappaport, Steve 93, 97
Raskin, Jamin 306
Rawls, John 164–5, 166, 202, 209, 246
Reagan, Ronald 403
Rees, A.M. 38
Reich, Wilhelm 441

Reinach, Adolf 353
Rennard, Chris 272
Renner, Karl 31
Reynolds, Susan 61, 73, 77, 348
Ricardo, David 61
Richardson, Diane xxiv, 433–63
Robinson, Darryl 173
Robson, Ruthann 434, 445
Robson, William A. 20, 21
Rodríguez, Encarnación Gutiérrez 354
Rokkan, Stein 284
Rosanvallon, Pierre 241
Rose, Nikolas 365
Roulleau-Berger, Laurence 376
Rowan, Brian 246
Rubenstein, Kim 374, 375
Rubio-Marin, Ruth 240, 266, 299, 300, 306–7
    passim, 309, 314–15 *passim*, 316, 317,
    318
Ruhs, Martin 208, 211
Rydén, Bengt 35, 37
Rygiel, Kim 350

Said, Edward 323–4, 335
Sala, Martinez 292
Sandel, Michael 150
Sartre, Jean-Paul 354
Sassen, Saskia xx, xxiii, xxiv, 344, 371–92
Saunders, Peter 376
Scharpf, Fritz W. 293
Schattle, Hans 342, 343
Schmitt, Carl 114, 171–2, 174
Schmitter, Philippe 327
Scholtz, Christa S. 344
Schönlau, Justus 291
Schuck, Peter H. 39, 40, 343, 379
Schumpeter, Joseph A. 13, 30, 37
Schwarz, Herbert 292
Scott, Sue 442
Searle, John R. 351, 352
Seighart, Paul 443
Shakespeare, Tom 437, 456
Shapiro, Ian 301
Shaw, Jo xi–xxvi, 251–81
Sherwin-White, Adrian N. 347
Shils, Edward A. 351
Shore, Cris 283, 287
Shotter, John 376

Shue, Henry 420
Sidgwick, Henry 226–7, 228
Siemiatycki, Myer 344
Simson, Rennie 454
Skrentny, John D. 242
Slim, Carlos 474, 480
Smith, Adam 43, 61
Smith, Barry 353
Smith, Rogers M. 350, 379
Soares, Luis E. 148
Somers, Margaret R. xvi, 53–102
Soysal, Yasemin Nuhoğlu xvii, xviii, xxiii, 161,
    237, 242, 323–37, 343, 344, 364, 380,
    383
Spiro, Peter 375
St. Germain, Christopher 81
Stacey, Jackie 447
Stalin, Joseph 18
Stefancic, Jean 378
Steiner, Jürg 191
Stevenson, Nick 449
Štiks, Igor xi–xxvi
Stix-Hackl, Christine 292
Stoker, Gerry 299
Stout, R. 351, 352
Strayer, Joseph R. 84, 348

Tabb, William 470
Taguieff, Pierre-André 247
Tauli-Corpuz, Victoria 138
Tawney, R.H. 12, 25, 58
Taylor, Charles 189
Taylor, David 434
Thatcher, Margaret 170, 403, 407, 447, 478
Thomas, Kendall 378
Thompson, Grahame 239
Tilly, Charles 54, 61, 78
Titmuss, Richard M. 20
Torpey, John C 343
Torres, Maria de los Ángles 383
Torresi, Tiziana 209, 225–6 *passim*, 231
Tully, James xx, xxi, 119–43, 287, 344
Turner, Bryan S. 14, 54, 327, 343, 375

Unwin, George 98

Van Parijs, Philippe 283, 415, 416, 417, 419–20,
    421, 422, 424–5 *passim*, 427

Vertovec, Steven 211, 229–30
Viladrich, Anahi 244
Vink, Maarten 220, 268
Vitorino, Antonio 260
Voet, Rian 434

Walby, Sylvia xiii, 434
Waldron, Jeremy 286, 293
Walker, Neil 139
Walzer, Michael 169, 170, 208, 239, 303, 306
Ware, Robert 352 *passim*
Warleigh, Alex 289
Warren, Earl xi
Watney, Simon 440
Watson, Sophie 385
Watts, Yvonne 292
Webb, Sidney 13
Weber, Max 61, 90, 347, 351, 377, 386–8 *passim*
Weber, Thomas 141
Weeks, Jeffrey 434,436, 446, 448, 450, 453

Weil, Patrick 239, 240, 343
Weiler, J.H. 163
Wertheimer, Jack 164
White, Harrison 61
Wiener, Antje xi
Williams, G.A. 93
Wilson, Angelia R. 434, 450
Wilton, Tamsin 443, 456
Wolfe, Alan 54
Wolfendon, John 440
Wollstonecraft, Mary 411, 426
Wood, Patricia K. 350
Woods, Chris 450
Wulff, Helena 333

Yegenoglu, Meyda 343
Young, Iris M. 349

Žižek, Slavoj 350
Zukin, Sharon 473